How—and why—does astrology work ?

People get crazy and sexy and even bleed more on the full moon. Sunspot flare-ups shoot the stock market all over the place. Even buildings respond to the movements of planets. Why? Enough evidence is now in to show that astrology *does* work. We know *what* happens, if not why. While we're waiting for scientists to discover what makes the planets influence human behavior, astrologers are working to improve the human condition as affected by those rocks in space.

SECRETS FROM A STARGAZER'S NOTEBOOK

will streamline your life and will tell you when to *go after what you want.*

SECRETS FROM A STARGAZER'S NOTEBOOK:

Making Astrology Work For You

Debbi Kempton–Smith

BANTAM BOOKS
NEW YORK · TORONTO · LONDON · SYDNEY · AUCKLAND

SECRETS FROM A STARGAZER'S NOTEBOOK

A Bantam Book / October 1982
2nd printing . . . March 1983
3rd printing . . . July 1984

Computerized Tables designed and created by Astro-Computing Services

Grateful acknowledgment is made for permission to include the following copyrighted material:

Specified excerpts from THE WAY OF LIFE ACCORDING TO LAOTZU, translated by Witter Bynner. Copyright, 1944 by Witter Bynner. Renewed, 1972 by Dorothy Chauvenet and Paul Horgan. Reprinted by permission of Harper & Row, Publishers, Inc.

From F. Scott Fitzgerald, "Winter Dreams," in All the Sad Young Men. Copyright 1922, 1926 by Charles Scribner's Sons; copyright renewed. Reprinted with the permission of Charles Scribner's Sons.

Line from Somerset Maugham in, The Mixture As Before, Doubleday-Doran 1940. Reprinted by permission.

Specified excerpts from I CHING by J. Blofeld. Reprinted by permission of George Allen & Unwin (Publishers) Ltd.

Horoscopic data from Profiles of Women by Lois Rodden, copyright © 1979 by American Federation of Astrologers, Inc. Reprinted by permission.

Specified excerpts from "The Call Girls," by Arthur Koestler, copyright © 1972 by The Hutchinson Group Ltd.

ISBN 0-553-24687-9

Published simultaneously in the United States and Canada

Bantam Books are published by Bantam Books, Inc. Its trademark, consisting of the words "Bantam Books" and the portrayal of a rooster, is Registered in U.S. Patent and Trademark Office and in other countries. Marca Registrada. Bantam Books, Inc., 666 Fifth Avenue, New York, New York 10103.

PRINTED IN THE UNITED STATES OF AMERICA

O   12 11 10 9 8 7

. . . for Al H. Morrison

friend
astrologer
troublemaker

Before it move, hold it,
Before it go wrong, mould it,
Drain off water in winter before it freeze,
Before weeds grow, sow them to the breeze.
You can deal with what has not happened, can foresee
Harmful events and not allow them to be.
Though—as naturally as a seed becomes a tree of
                                   arm-wide girth—
There can rise a nine-tiered tower from a man's handful
                                   of earth
Or here at your feet a thousand-mile journey have birth,
Quick action bruises,
Quick grasping loses.
Therefore a sane man's care is not to exert
One move that can miss, one move that can hurt.
Most people who miss, after almost winning,
Should have 'known the end from the beginning.'.
                                   —Lao Tzu

Contents

III. ASTROLOGY IN DAILY LIVING From A to X

IV. HOW TO USE THE TABLES IN THIS BOOK

Acknowledgements

The tables and computer charts in this book are provided by:

ASTRO COMPUTING SERVICES, Box 16297, San Diego, California 92116
Tel. 714-297-5648

Horoscope data supplied courtesy of:

ASTRO CARTOGRAPHY, Box 959-KS, El Cerrito, California 94530
C.A.O. TIMES MAGAZINE, Box 75, Old Chelsea Station, NYC 10113
Al H. Morrison
Lois Rodden, *Profiles of Women,* published by American Federation of Astrologers
Bill Sarubbi
Zane Stein, The Association for Studying Chiron, c/o C.A.O. Times
Clients wishing to be famous
Clients wishing to remain anonymous
New asteroids data from C.A.O. Times magazine

Thanks:
Roy Alexander
Eleanor Bach
Michal Bigger
Maureen Burk
Ram Dass
Liz Greene
Karen Haas, a brilliant editor *and* a scholar!
Rob Hand
Betsy Hooper
Charles Jayne
Vivia Jayne
Peter LeGuillou
Dr. Lee Lehman
Brian Lorentz
Dr. Brian Marsden, Smithsonian Astrophysical Observatory

H. Craig Merrell, beyond the call of all
Neil F. Michelsen
Al H. Morrison
Bob Pike
Lois Rodden
Kim Rosston
Bill Sarubbi
Lynn Schaffer
Jane Schreiber
Norman Schreiber
Dr. Dennis Schwartz
Rod Serling
Susan Sewell
Zane Stein
Matthew Taylor
Jill Wood
Tom Wood
Sydny Weinberg
The James Davis Band, The Paddock Lounge, Bourbon Street,
New Orleans

The book was written in the howling night hours in London,
New York, San Diego, Los Angeles, New Orleans, Fort Lauderdale,
Munich, and in the wild woods of Main Line Philadelphia.

Musical aids were provided by Dr. John the Nighttripper,
Jimi Hendrix, The Rolling Stones, The Kinks, and Tubular Bells.

The example horoscopes appearing in Secrets from a Stargazer's
Notebook were triple-checked for accuracy; unfortunately 100%
accuracy regarding birth data is difficult to obtain. Some
inaccuracies may have occurred.

Introduction

Kings and queens of the Age of Aquarius, come *on* now, I know what *you* want. You want everything.

Let me guess. You want a retreat in the country with chickens and goats and a year's supply of food just in case they drop The Big One, right?

And you need a place in town, just a modest brownstone—I *understand!*—and a baby Lear jet with its own landing strip and lots of pots of money *to spend on your friends,* of course! But you want deeper things too. A job that fulfills you. A romantic Significant Other. A code to live by. Awesome spiritual insight. World peace, inner peace, love, truth, beauty, wisdom, and nirvana every now and again. Freedom from anxiety, depression, bills, pills, taxes, loneliness, fear, death, and boredom. A holiday in Fiji. A night at the Ritz. Little lunches at the Russian Tea Room with Bianca and Andy.

What's that? Your needs are more *modest* than that? You want your tomatoes to come up right and the mushroom crop in the cellar to flourish and multiply? You want your kids to stop rotting their precious jelly-brains on television and to grow up kind and amusing, healthy and happy? You want your old job back; you want a new job; you want a raise; you want Robert Redford to tie you up with silken cords? You want the Pope to wink as he goes by? Do you dream of discovering an oil substitute out of *dirt,* ending both the energy problem and world starvation at a single blow? You want your friends to like you and your enemies to screw themselves so royally that you *sincerely* pity the poor bastards? You wish, perhaps, to save the whale?

Try voodoo.

Me, I wouldn't touch it with a barge pole. That gris-gris get over *everything*.

That leaves astrology, and to Get Serious for just a moment here, nobody's asking you to take it on faith.

Some people say that the stars are God's handwriting across the sky, but I call them the Amtrak timetable. You are free to take whatever train you like—that's free will. The trains available to take are what we call Fate.

Life is not all Fate and not all free will (sorry EST). Each one of us is made up of differing proportions of nature and nurture. Germaine Greer is a good example of free will. Others, like the royal family of England, are born to fated roles and lives.

Now nobody likes to think the planets are shoving them around, even if the planets *do* knock us about like pool balls . . . and yes, it is *decidedly undignified* to yank out the astrology book before phoning the bookie.

But the hideous truth is that astrology works, at least a lot of it works; enough of it works so that stockbrokers, money managers, lawyers, doctors, scientists, journalists, politicians, psychiatrists, psychologists, and psychoanalysts sneak in to see me regularly and leave just as furtively as patrons of some low-rent bordello.

Secrecy is a big deal in this business. Astrologers subscribe to a Code of Ethics. The first rule is: "The client is paranoid." Taken as a group, astrologers are as odd and paranoid as anyone else. It is a weird life, and we have to listen to twisted, often horrible stories day in and day out.

Does it worry you that the high-muck-a-mucks of our political, legal, medical, and economic systems use astrology? It shouldn't rattle you as long as we all remember that the price of freedom is eternal vigilance. We'd better be better at it than they are if we want to keep all our options open. Even President Reagan has admitted he believes in astrology, so much so that his birth time is, in reality, different from the ones we see printed in the magazines. *That'll* fool the Ruskies! During World War II, Churchill had several astrologers working for him. He didn't have to believe in astrology, but he wanted to know what *Hitler's* astrologers were telling *him*.

Nobody knows how astrology works. It's a problem, but somebody out there is working on it.

People get crazy and sexy and even bleed more on the full moon. Sunspot flare-ups shoot the stock market all over the place. Even the ooky oysters know when the moon is new, locked away in lonely rooms, miles from the sea. Even *buildings* respond to the movements of the planets, though we don't know why. At least enough evidence is in now to show that astrology works. We know *what* happens, if not why. While we're waiting for scientists to discover what makes the planets influence human behavior, astrologers are working to improve the human condition as affected by those rocks in space.

Stargazing will streamline your life. First we need to know what you are doing and who you are. Once we know that, the planets will tell you *when to go after what you want.* Astrology can help you find a good place to live, get a raise, increase your luck in gambling, find a new romance, and help you psych out your boss or baby or boyfriend. It is more accurate on timing than ESP, palmistry, clairvoyance, or a train in Germany. It is cheaper and as accurate as a battery of psychological tests. It is more fun than swimming in a pool full of root beer.

Astrology is a soft science like psychology. Both are still in the infant stages. Astrology at its best is hard, complicated, and contradictory—like life. It has nothing to do with newspaper columns, nor does it deal with shoving human beings into twelve categories called Sun Signs. You don't have to be psychic to do astrology. You learn it from books and schools and watching people. *The more you do it, the better you get at it.*

We're going to keep it simple. Math masochists can go home now. Nobody needs to do logarithms to make charts anymore. Get your day, month, year, time and place of birth and send it to an astrological computing service. They'll send you back your horoscope. It costs less than a tuna fish sandwich.

If you're reading this on a Greyhound bus, or you're feeling lazy, skip the computer chart and check out the tables in this book. They'll tell you most of what you need to know.

We have tables here so you can check out your honey, make more money, spy on your neighbor, avoid getting clobbered, soothe your buddies. We even have tables that show you how to refine yourself spiritually and get off the Awful Wheel of Karma. If it's important to you, it's important to Mars, Venus, Neptune, and Co. They're here to help.

You can put your thumb on the free-will scale and control your own destiny *if you learn what the timetable is.* Astrology can change your entire life.

Don't take it on faith. Experiment with the tables in this book and see what you can do to increase your success, your luck, your understanding. It will rock you.

Part
I

How to Look
at a Chart

How to Look
at a Chart

Scary looking thing, isn't it? Yet the horoscope is just a big pizza divided into twelve slices. Astrologers like to argue about how to cut up the pizza, which is why we have different house systems: Koch, Placidus, Campanus, Regiomantanus, Porphryry, Topocentric, Meridian, Equal.

HOUSE SYSTEMS

A "house" is just one of the twelve slices of pizza. Each house division system has its rabid adherents, and if you want a sock in the jaw, all you need to say is, "*My* house system works better¦ than *your* house system." The subject is a touchy one because when you try them out, all house systems work if you are a good enough interpreter. Then again, some houses have termites.

Placidus is the darling of the Old Auntie Boring astrology magazines, so you've probably seen charts calculated in it. It is the most popular of all the systems and the majority of astrology fans like it. It became popular because in the past two hundred years it was the only easy-to-get house tables people could buy. It is particularly popular in Britain, accurately reflecting the Victorian consciousness of a nation whose public transportation stops at 11:30 P.M. and where central heating is still optional. The Placidus system still works nicely today, and it shows the deeper, more old-fashioned you, the you before the nukes and computers and The Rolling Stones.

So what makes the smart-brains, top-notch, bee's knees predictive astrologers suddenly spurn the Placidus system and leap straight into the arms of Koch? Here are soothsayers who, like the scientists, don't eat unless their predictions are accurate. The Placidus system does not work when calculated for people born in high latitudes.

The late Dr. Walter Koch, a survivor of the Dachau concentration camp, first presented his new system in 1964. Many astrologers theorized that perhaps the newest system of house division might reflect modern circumstances more accurately than Placidus, and so far this seems to be the case: a Koch chart accurately maps your goals, attitudes, and pressures in the nuclear age.

A third advantage of the Koch system is its accuracy in predicting events. Like so many gizmos invented by German sticklers for precision, those Koch charts *run on time!* When a planet goes over a Koch cusp, something happens in your life. A cusp is the dividing line between one house and the next; Koch cusps are extremely sensitive if your birth time is accurate.

PIZZA PIE CHART
A DEMONSTRATION

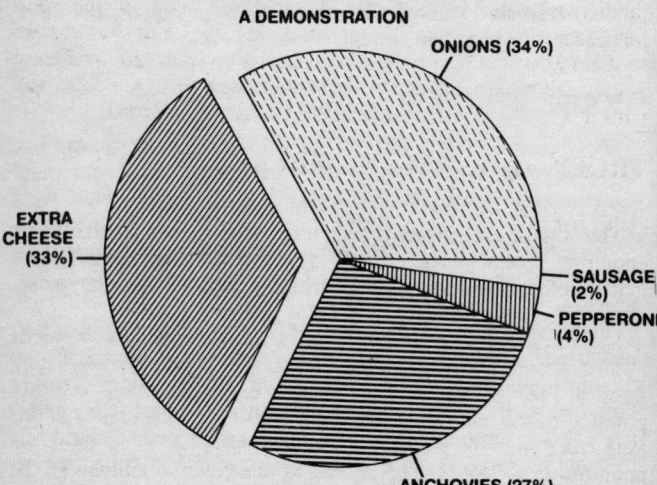

ONIONS (34%)

EXTRA CHEESE (33%)

SAUSAGE (2%)

PEPPERONI (4%)

ANCHOVIES (27%)

This ancient diagram was discovered near the Blarney Stone in Ireland. It dates back to April 1949 B.C., and it was probably stolen from the entrail-readers of Rome. Astrological researchers believe it to have been a primitive attempt at perceiving the Cosmos; it marked the beginning of the Irish zodiac.

When good old Jupiter crosses over the second house line, grab the opportunity and you're going to be one rich astrologer. A midwestern astrologeuse mopped up $17,000 at the racetrack in one summer gambling with the Koch system. When the planets say yes and my bank balance says no, I sometimes hit the roulette table. I scoop up my winnings, and a warm feeling creeps up the back of my neck. Somewhere Up There the venerable Dr. Koch is smiling. It is a pleasant way to pay the telephone bill.

Money is not the only game you can play with the Koch system. Astrology deals with all of life, and with twelve accurate Koch cusps in a chart, it is like having twelve extra secret agents going to work for you.

Most of the charts in this book are done in the Koch system. Remember—things go better with Koch!

Want to play? Try using a couple of different house systems for your chart, and see what the variations are. I like Equal Houses or Placidus for a psychological profile, and Koch for predictive work. Charles and Vivia Jayne, two of the most highly rated astrologers in the world, use the Campanus system to great effect. If you're stuck out in the boonies and your local yogi-savant-soothsayer scrawls out something else on a rock, roll with it. Compare these two charts of London, England.

TROPICAL VERSUS SIDEREAL

"Aw, come *on*, not that old walnut *again*!"

That's what astrologers think, but never say, when some eager enquiring human being, usually at a cocktail party, reminds us that astrology doesn't match up with the constellations anymore, the way it did 2,000 years ago.

It's true. The top of the earth's axis points now towards Polaris, the Pole Star. It's just a tad off true north. The stars look fixed in their positions to us because the earth seems to rotate pointing to the Pole Star. Back in 3000 B.C., Draconis was our Pole Star, and by 7500 A.D. we will have wobbled until we point towards Cephei. This screws up the chain of animals in the sky we call the zodiac, and the chain doesn't match the constellations anymore.

Hipparchus started it 2,000 years ago when he discovered the displacement of the earth's axis. At that time the first day of spring coincided with zero degrees of the constellation Aries. As of January 1, 1980, the zero Aries point differed 24 degrees 27 minutes and 31.5 seconds from its position 2,000 years ago.

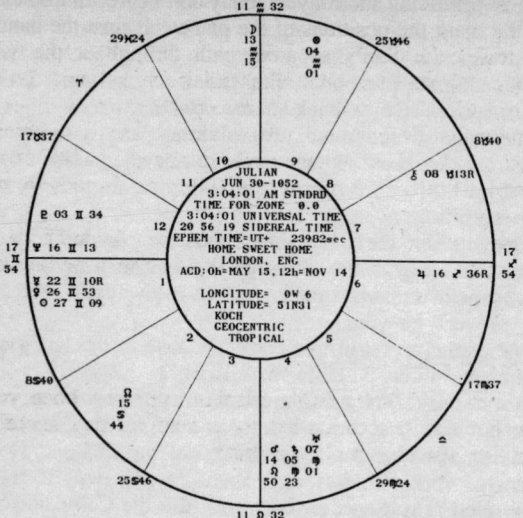

London, England—Koch

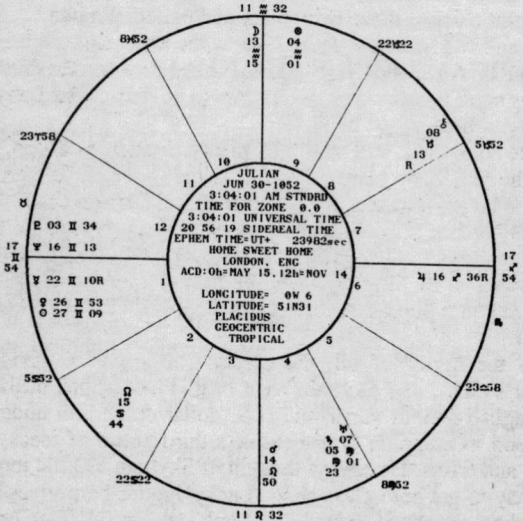

London, England—Placidus

Most practicing soothsayers today don't care. In tropical astrology we mark the positions of the planets against the band of sky that traces the Sun's apparent path throughout the year, the ecliptic. We start this band, the zodiac, at zero Aries on the first day of spring, and to hell with the constellations.

Tropical astrology measures planetary positions against the ecliptic. Sidereal astrologers measure planets against the stars. In sidereal astrology we subtract the 24½-odd degrees from all the planetary positions in the book.

Both systems work. Naturally, most people don't want to do extra math, so tropical astrology is what most people use. It's become a universal language.

THE NATAL CHART

. . . is the diagram of the planets' positions when you were born. For a full, accurate chart you need the day, month, year, exact time, and exact place of birth.

THE SOLAR CHART

. . . is what you're stuck with if you can't get the exact time of birth. Stick the Sun on the Ascendant. Runs good.

Even Freddie Laker doesn't know the exact time he was born. His mother had died just before I asked him for the birth time. It was not a good moment to ask him to go through his baby books in case a time might be in it.

The solar chart still shows us plenty. Freddie is a Leo, and he has the new baby planet, Chiron, in the house of foreign travel. Chiron breaks impasses, showers benefits and brings chaos. Freddie Laker battled, singlehanded, for seven years before he brought the Big Boys to their knees so that everybody could have cheap air travel with Skytrain. Chiron helped him break the rules, and Skytrain *forced* the competing airlines to offer cheap air travel.

To the horror of all, the planet Chiron did a whoopsie in Laker's chart, and Skytrain went bust. Fluctuations in the value of English pounds versus the U.S. dollar drove him under.

Good luck Jupiter is in Freddie's third house of ideas, buses, cars, and trains. He always thought of Skytrain as little more than an easy-to-get-onto choo-choo. Lucky Jupiter here gives him an unending supply of ideas. . . . Look out, world! Our hero will be back.

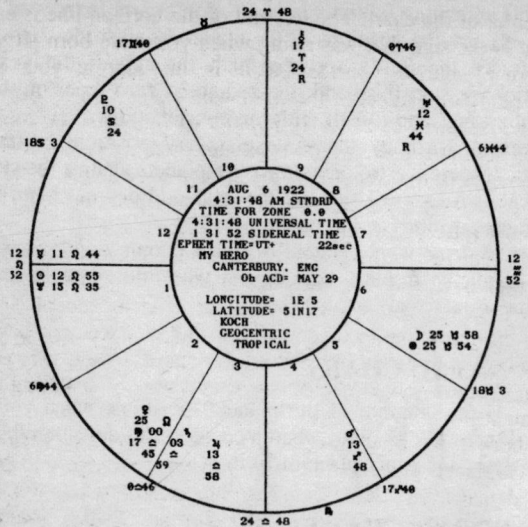

Freddie Laker

Just look at the Moon on Freddie's solar chart. It's in the work box, the sixth house. Since the Moon shows what you need, it's a fair guess that Laker is a bit of a workaholic. See the sign Aries at the very top of the chart? That's what Freddie wants to be: *first, dashing, independent, pioneering.*

Many lesser mortals watch their dream turn to guano. The Sun with Neptune in Freddie's chart gives him bags of faith; he's a visionary. He was knighted by the Queen of England, you know.

"Stop regimenting the human race," says Sir Freddie.

THE PROGRESSED CHART

. . . is the key to all the future stuff, predictions. Save yourself a lot of arithmetic and an ulcer and look up your friendly astrologer.

THE ASCENDANT, ALSO CALLED THE RISING SIGN

Take up your trusty pizza wheel and slice the horoscope from left to right. This represents the horizon, and your birthplace is

n the center of the chart. The left end of the horizon line is east,
nd on it is the sign that was rising when you were born. If you
vere born at sunrise, your ascendant is the same as your Sun
ign, and the Sun symbol in the chart will be right on it. Born at
oon? The Sun will be at the high point of the chart, on top. If
ou were born at sunset, which is less common, the Sun will be
n the far right of the wheel, and those born at midnight will find
he Sun at the bottom of the chart, below the horizon line. This
s how baby astrologers make sure the chart's right.

Mick Jagger is quiet, even reserved when you meet him on a
ne-to-one basis. This first impression has little to do with the
.eo Sun position boiling inside the man. The ascendant is the
ow-dee-doo? first handshake. It is how others see you before
hey know you. In a superficial dress-for-success way, it is your
ome on, your defense mechanism, your way of handling the
nvironment.

Your body type, how you get sick, the clothes you like, the
ind of childhood you had, the way you want strangers to treat
ou all depend on your ascendant. No matter what you are
eeling, it has to come out through this sieve, this strainer,
efore you can express it in the real world. It is The Editor of
our inner 1,008 selves.

You can't look up your rising sign in the tables in this book
ecause it would be a shuck, it wouldn't be accurate. Rising
igns depend on the time and the place you were born. A
omputer service will do the job for you, and cheap.

THE MIDHEAVEN, OR M.C.

And slice again! This time cut the wheel from top to bottom.
This tippy-top point is the Midheaven. Every day at midday the
Sun crosses the Midheaven point except in the British Isles, where
here is no Sun. (It was last seen on a Tuesday afternoon in July
1976 and has not been seen since.) M.C. is Latin for *medium
coeli*, the middle of the sky, and I.C. is the bottom of the
chart, *imum coeli*. The whole vertical line itself is called the
meridian.

The M.C. is just that, the emcee. The sign on the M.C. shows
what you are like as Master of Ceremonies. It is your public
image and is what you seem to be from afar. Mick Jagger's
mocking, wild stage image contradicts his quiet ascendant when
you meet him in person. The Midheaven is what we are reaching
up to be, the way we wish we were, and the way we *are*, if we

do the work on ourselves. It is the side of *you* that shows up i
group of people.

The M.C./I.C. axis spills the beans on how you relate to yo
parents. Shrinks love to work with this one.

THE CHART IS A MAP CREATED BY A MADMAN FROM DIXIE

That's why east is on the left, west is on the right, north
behind you and you are facing south. It's not your usual ma
The twelve signs keep moving up clockwise round the chart;
different sign rises about every two hours.

HOW TO FIND FATE VERSUS FREE WILL IN YOUR CHART

Take a chart, any chart. Find the center line, the meridian. P
your hand on the left half of the chart, covering it up. Look
what's on the right side of the chart. How many planets a
there? More than five? That's more than half of the ten usu
planets. A person with a lot of stuff on the right side of the cha

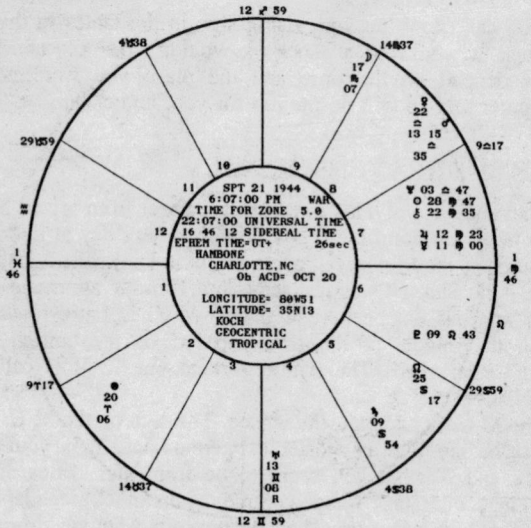

Hamilton Jordan

eels that his fate is in the hands of the gods, other people, the RS. Destiny is in control. You don't believe in destiny? Then why has fate decreed that he feels that fate is in control of his ife? *If you feel that your life is in the hands of destiny, you put your life in the hands of destiny.* The obviously negative side to this reasoning is that here is a person who is all too ready to put the blame on circumstances for his fate. It is an elegant way of refusing to take responsibility for the way your life is . . . just blame your family, your bad breaks, your hair color, and on and on. The positive person with a lot of stuff on the right-hand side of the chart finds his *joie de vivre* in other people. When bad times come, he bends to a will greater than his own—and survives. He needs other people in his life to work with, play with, lean on, give to. He waits to be acted upon.

Now put your hand on the right side of the chart, and cover that up. How many planets are on the left side? More than five? Here is another kind of survival expert. He is the master of his fate, the captain of his soul. He feels that life is in his hands, and it is. He makes it that way. He doesn't believe in destiny, he believes in preparation for opportunity. The positive attributes of a take-charge attitude are obvious. What the left-sider doesn't

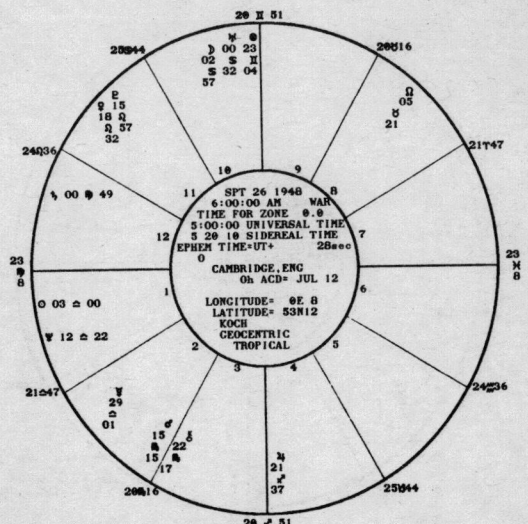

Olivia Newton-John

see is that he is missing out on a lot of understanding. He's no
particularly interested in other people and could live quite hap
pily on a desert island, self-absorbed, and wishing for people h
could prove himself against. If he'd believe in fate a little more
fate wouldn't have to conk him on the head with a sledgehamme
every so often—he'd go with the flow and pick up the signals
The left-sider is scared of signals—he wants to be in control o
his own life. Who can blame him? He needs to feel he can stan
upon his own corny feet.

Most people have a mixture of fate and free-will feelings. An
no matter how hard or how often those hands of destiny squeez
us, applaud us, goose us, or tickle us, some of us will think w
brought it all on ourselves while the rest of us say it's the fault o
the politicians, the stars, the society.

ARE YOU AN "INNIE OR AN OUTIE"?

Not your belly button, dear heart, just find the horizon line
Cover up the top half of the chart with your hand. More than fiv
planets below the horizon makes you a *subjective* type. When th
chips are down, your own feelings and personal integrity ar

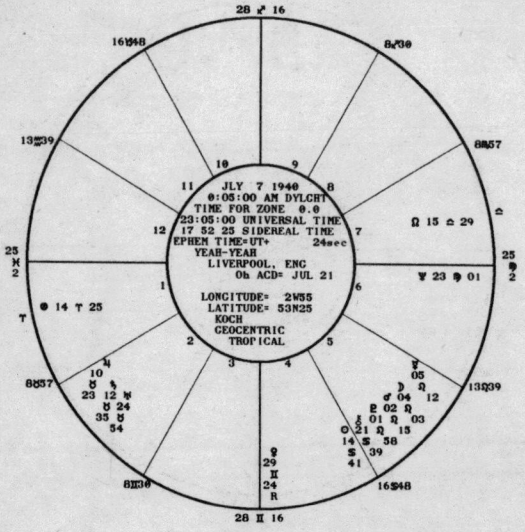

Ringo Starr

more important to you than to be seen in the hots spots every night. You have a whole world of wealth inside yourself and a lot to give other people. Too much stuff below the horizon may mean that you allow your feelings and eccentricities to swamp you, at the expense of what the real world thinks—and *requires*. Learn to play the world game and be thankful that inside you are so rich.

Hide the lower part of the chart with your hand. Five or more squiggles above the horizon means you are a *worldly* type. You need an audience and a wide arena of action or you're not really living. You learn quickly how the world works and generally you will find some way of making it work for you because you have so much to give society. If there are too many planets above the horizon, you may find it hard to be on your own and harder still to separate your beliefs from what is expected in the marketplace. This can make you world-weary, or awfully fashionable, a trend-setter. It will help you to learn about philosophies in other times and other cultures and to develop independent reserves of original thinking.

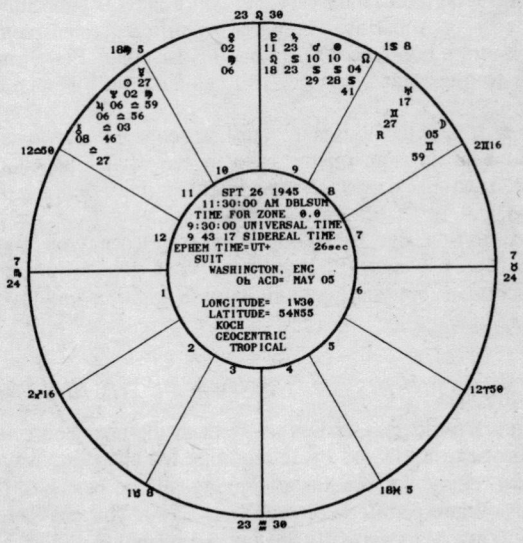

Brian Ferry

DEVELOP A FEEL FOR THE SHAPE OF A CHART

The late Marc Edmund Jones worked out a system of interpret ing charts based on the patterns the planets make as they fall i a chart. There are buckets and bowls, choochoos and kite seesaws and pineapples in his excellent books. Obviously on bunch opposite another bunch is going to show a person wh swings from one extreme to the other, but at least he sees bo viewpoints. If all your planets are globbed together in one sec tion of the chart, you may not be a "well-rounded" person in th conventional sense, but you are one mean specialist in the con centrated areas.

CUSPS

Sloppy astrology is the cause of this cusp business. Is the hea the same as the lungs because they're next to each other? I woul not wish my surgeon to think so, and you shouldn't expect you astrologer to slop around either.

There is no such thing as being born on the cusp. You migh have been born on January 19 and don't know if your Sun sign i Capricorn or Aquarius. There's a big difference between a har rumph and a hoo-hah. You're one or the other. For a couple o bucks to a computer service, you can find out for once and fo all.

The edges of the houses in your horoscope are known as cusps We look at the sign on the cusp to see what kind of a hous you're running. *Cusps are the dividing lines between houses period*.

If your Sun sign turns out to be Capricorn, you may hav some nearby planets in Aquarius. Your goals (Sun) may b Capricornian, but you may talk like a Sagittarius and love like Pisces.

WHEN A PLANET IS ON THE EDGE OF THE NEXT HOUSE

If it's five degrees or less away from the next house, sling i into the next house and try interpreting the chart that way. The you can enjoy the benefits of having all the best bits of bot houses. When people point out your flaws, you can say, "Oh no . . . my Mars is really in the *second* house," just like th real astrologers do.

STELLIUMS

They're called Satellitiums in England, but that's too much of a jawbreaker these days.

Eyeball the chart a little. Are there three or more planets (not including the Sun or the Moon) in one sign *other* than the signs of the Sun and Moon? You've got yourself a stellium. All it means is that at times you act more like the sign of the stellium than your Sun or Moon signs.

TRANSITS

Transits are movements of the planets for any given time. If Jupiter in the sky right now is about to transit your money box, it's time to ask for a raise. If Saturn will be transiting your natal Sun (the place the Sun was in when you were born) soon, prepare to shape up! When the astrologer says to you "let me look up your transits," he means no harm. He wants to compare the stars in the sky to the stars in your chart—unless he offers you a double Dewars on the rocks, then check his license and call the C.A.O. Times.

HARD AND SOFT ASPECTS

This is astrology trying to be more Fritz Perls-Esalen groovy. In the old days these were called "good" and "bad" aspects. A hard angle makes you dynamic and interesting, but twisted. A soft angle makes you charming, lazy, and dull, but lucky.

The Horoscope Houses: Dark Enchantments at the Gazebos Twelve-Unit Motel

"A house is not a home . . ."
—So goes the saying

President and Mrs. Gazebo have invited you to their horoscope home. How can you refuse? You have heard the stories of how the Gazebos turned the Presidential Palace into a sleazy motel-in-the-round. You know about the Test of the Twelve Units, the missing tourists, and the iguana pit in the back where the swimming pool used to be. And still here you are, clammy-palmed, arriving at the estate; one look at the joint is enough to keep your dry-bones manufacturing white blood cells faster than MacDonalds cranks out hamburgers. It is no comfort to know that many frightened tourists have visited here before you, lost in a world rife with squiggles and astrological mumbo-jumbo. You keep your paranoid forebodings to yourself.

We call it a horoscope, and it is round and has twelve rooms, shaped like pizza slices.

"Wanna see the love box?" leers Mrs. Gazebo. President Gazebo just stands there. He sucks on his corncob pipe and looks you over, but he says nothing. Somehow you get the feeling that they have guided many an innocent mark through these rooms before. Astrologers call the twelve rooms houses, but President and Mrs. Gazebo call them boxes. You will not argue with your hosts over petty syntax on this night.

Houses, uh, boxes, are where astrologers plop the planets. Each house represents an *area* of life's experience. Think of the horoscope as a twelve-unit motel, or a theatre with twelve stages.

When you interpret a chart, pay attention to the *sign* on the beginning edge (cusp) of each house. Think of the signs as colored spotlights, with a different color for each house or stage.

"Shall we begin?" says Mrs. Gazebo. Weird and evil forbodings swish about in the ethers. Your will power has vanished; your spine has turned to jelly, and you have no choice but to follow her inside. You drag your shuddering bones to the front entrance and bid adieu to the world as you once knew it. If Fortuna frowns on you this night when the moon is full, you will emerge maybe in days, a slobbering husk of what was once a human being. If Lady Luck is kind, you will most likely come out of the twelve rooms happier, stronger, and wiser.

THE FIRST HOUSE—THE EGO BOX

Your body type
Childhood experiences
Leadership qualities
Your personality
Your view of the world
The impression you make on others at first meeting
Defense mechanisms
The "persona"
This is where you find the rising sign, or Ascendant
Your ego
The way you feel about your face, body, and, to an extent, yourself

THE SECOND HOUSE—THE STUFF BOX

Money
Safety
Security
Possessions
What you have to give in bed
Your attitude toward food, with the sixth house
Questions of self-worth
Your noble or sleazy values
Your personal form of greed and generosity

THE THIRD HOUSE—THE LEARNING AND TEACHING BOX

School up until college
The outside world
Short trips
Cars, buses and trains
Your ability to learn
The way your mind works, positive and negative thinking
Writing and reading and talking and teaching
Letters
Magazines, newspapers, and cheap paperbacks
Brothers and sisters, near relatives
Neighbors and your neighborhood
Radios, televisions, and Walkmans

THE FOURTH HOUSE—THE ROOTS BOX

Conditions in your old age
Your home
Your attitudes toward family
The ability to nurture people emotionally
Integrity in the sense that your opinion of yourself is or is not more important to you than the opinion of the world or marketplace
Real estate, land, agriculture, and gardening
The father (usually)
The country of your birth
Mines, graves, underground places (like subways)
This is the box the psychiatrists use first, along with the tenth house; it shows any kinks or abilities passed on to you by your parents, usually the father
Possibly research may link this house with genetics

THE FIFTH HOUSE—THE FUN BOX

Love affairs
Children
Drama, theaters, show biz, art
Your ability to be creative
Risk taking
How you have fun
Some gambling and some functions of investing

Schools
Resorts
Games and sports
Your ability to receive love and to give it
Your perception of the love you got as a child
Child*like* or child*ish* qualities
The ability to be romantic

THE SIXTH HOUSE—THE EVERYDAY WORK AND DUTY BOX

Little animals and pets
Health and diets
Food
Your attitudes toward cleanliness and order
Old relatives
Obligations
People who work for you or in lesser rank at work
The way you approach work
The ability to be inventive
Your taste in clothes
Servants (Good help is *so* hard to find these days)
Daddy's brothers and sisters
Community needs
The weather as it affects your health

THE SEVENTH HOUSE—THE PARTNER BOX

Marriage
Business partners and clients
Best friends and peers
Mentors
Live-in or steady relationships
Bitter enemies in the open
Dealings with the public
Contracts
Art
Diplomacy
Social urges
Opponents in games or debate
Grandparents
What you think you lack, so you look for it in other people;

if you don't care for what specimens you have around you, be a little bit more like them. This is what you *think* you lack, not *what* you lack.

THE EIGHTH HOUSE—THE DEEP MERGING BOX

Secrets
Psychology, therapy, and psychiatry
The deep one-to-one emotional relationship; soul mates
The occult—everything from astrology and yoga to nasty
    little Ouija boards
Detective work
Psychic powers
Sex
Great changes brought about by crisis
Death and taxes
Your partner's money
Legacies and wills
Your response to crisis
Emotional truth
Hidden talents
The ability to be reborn and the ability to be alone
What you think of other people's values
Tycoonery

THE NINTH HOUSE—THE MIND EXPANSION BOX

Gurus
Religions
Your philosophy
Foreign countries
Import-Export businesses
Publishing
Fancy hard-cover books and mass-circulation magazines
International anything
Travel
Large enterprises
College and beyond
Spiritual occurances
In-laws

Lawyers, judges, lawsuits, The Law
Your ability to perceive right and wrong
Faith
Fame for the sake of mind expansion

THE TENTH HOUSE—THE PUBLIC IMAGE BOX

This is where the M.C. or Midheaven is
Your reputation
Your mother, usually
Your profession
Honor, rank, and credit, or lack thereof
What you are striving to be like
People with power over you—bosses, the government, etc.
Your attitude toward authority figures
Your sense of responsibility
Fame for the sake of power
Zee public eye
A gold mine of hang-ups for psychiatrists to dig through
Homosexuality
Promotions

THE ELEVENTH HOUSE—THE IDEALISM BOX

Friends
Associates
Your income from your main profession
Peer group pressure
The advice you get—for good or ill
Advisers
The social circles you move in
The boss's money
Your hopes
Your wildest dreams
How you do or don't make the world a better place
Groups and how you relate to being in them
Clubs
Other people's children

THE TWELFTH HOUSE—THE GOD BOX

Everything that makes you alone, having to work out your
relationship with That Which is Eternal belongs here

Prison, bondage, confinement, hospitals
Large institutions
Secret enemies
Everyday saints
Hidden ways you screw yourself up, hence psychiatry and
  psychology
Large animals
Your Mummy's relatives
Escapist tendencies—imaginative and banal
The Unconscious
Your response when your back is to the wall
Psychic gifts, especially healing
Emotional service to others
That which you give with no strings attached
Karma and past lives
The old soybean "serve or suffer" is the best way to
  approach matters of the twelfth house
Hidden power, behind the throne
The past

Welcome to the Zodiac Zone

Zodiac signs. You know them. I know them. We're all sick of the platitudinous little suckers by now. It is hard not to hate the signs of the zodiac.

You know the kind of stuff: Virgos make good nurses, they are hardworking, dedicated, kind and trivial—this kind of rhubarb. Sometimes that's even true, although most of the Virgos I know would rather chop a leg off than hold down a steady job, at least the nine to five variety gig.

Before they drag you screaming from the paperback section of Woolworth's—"Another Sun-sign overdose, Sam!"—please understand something: this is no Sun-sign tome, and if you yearn to be an astrologeuse, you've got to grab these twelve signs by the throat and *feel* them.

Signs are styles in which we express ourselves. Most of the world's personality problems boil down to differences in *style*, not inner values. Conflict occurs because the other guy is shy, sarcastic, conservative, timid, radical, sexy, stodgy, sneaky, stubborn, aggressive, ambitious, nit-picking, dramatic, subtle, grabby, greedy, understated, superficial, or else he smells funny.

Too often we judge people by their styles and not by their *intentions*.

An example. Traditional astrology books tell us that Virgos do not get along with Sagittarians. Virgos are workers. They roll up their trousers and wade into the muck and clean it up from bottom to the top. Most of them are quiet. *All* of them are idealistic. They want to make things better, right here and now, in the real world. Hand me that bedpan!

Sagittarians are here to learn and compare and see. Then they want to tell us what they've absorbed so far. Why not have a grand old time while doing it? Sagittarians love nothing better than to sit around over a sherry and *talk* about how the world could be a better place. You see, they're idealistic too. No wonder they find Virgos grim, dull, and petty; hardly surprising that Virgos wish Sagittarians would stop shooting off their big mouths and *do something*. They're *both* idealistic—and that's the conflict.

You can get along with any sign if you give them the freedom to be what they are anyway. You do not try to persuade Aries to do things the sneaky way, to be Number Two, or to put up with shabby moral codes. You do not ask the Scorpio to forgive and forget. Let them be *as they are* and hope that they may want to refine their more obnoxious traits in order to get along with *you*.

Stare at your computer chart, if you have one. See the signs of the zodiac scattered, in order, round the outside of the wheel?

You have all the signs in your chart. You may be like a Pisces when it comes to money and like a Leo in bed. Human beings are subtle, complicated animals. Forget the Sun sign columns in the newspaper if you want the real astrology.

Poke around the pizza, study it slice by slice, and you will build up a complete profile of what you are like in every area of your life. We call these slices houses, and there is a sign on the cusp, or edge, of every house.

Say you find the sign Scorpio on the fifth house cusp, which is the house of love affairs. You're intense, deep, jealous about your lover. If Scorpio is on the money box instead (the second house) you're intense and secretive about your money, but easy-come-easy-go about love affairs with Aquarius on the love-affair box.

Where is Scorpio in *your* chart?

Next, look up in this book or on your computer chart each one of your planets.

If Mars is the planet of anger and it is in the sign Libra, you get angry in Libra style. Richard Burton expresses his anger sweetly, as in flirting.

If the Sun is in Pisces, you express your soul and self in a style that is subtle, mystical, tolerant, sensitive, sympathetic, ambivalent, slippery, gooshy, and complicated.

If Mercury is in Sagittarius, the way you talk comes out sounding optimistic, pompous, Pollyanna-ish, sell-'em-the-goods, and not always as if you take into account other people's sore spots!

Signs are styles. All styles are in you, somewhere. Let's have a look at them then.

ARIES's symbol is a ram's horns or the fountain of youth. It is a pushy fire sign, ruled by Mars, planet of zip and zap. Aries are like commandos. They charge right in and wipe out the opposition. Their lives are open books; why do anything you wouldn't want the world to see? They're self-centered and selfish, but they're willing to reveal themselves, warts and all. They are the bravest of all the signs, take ludicrous chances, and scare people to death, but they don't know that. At its best Aries is nothing if not noble. They have heros and villians. One old textbook says Aries is "the lamb that is shorn that the world may be warm." Like most knights in shining armor, the Aries hasn't been born who wouldn't give his time, money, even life for those he loves. Aries and Leo are the best signs for self-expression, for they assert themselves openly.

What's disgusting about Aries? They really think they're more interesting than you are. They talk about themselves all the time. They like head butting with opponents. They like to fight. Fortunately their skulls are hard as rocks, capable of withstanding numerous bops. I guess the most horrifying side of Aries is that *they will not see or take responsibility for their effect on other people.* If they did that, they'd have to grow up.

Look around your chart. Note any planets in Aries. Find the house or houses with Aries on the cusp. These are areas where you think, "Me first!" You won't share; you have to be boss. Think of Aries on the home box (fourth house): tyrant at home! Think of Aries on the death box (eighth house): no nurse is going to tell you how to die when you're eleventy-hundred and nine! These are also the areas where you do things in new ways. You're an original here, and fiercely competitive. Apply the Aries principles where you find Aries in a chart. You're brave, here, too!

Aries is an impulsive sign, and they're not good judges of character. They'll naïvely associate with con artists and dismiss a person of worth if he doesn't sparkle in the first five minutes of meeting. It's a pity people are afraid of their I-can-do-it-myself strength, because Aries folks need to be told when they're screwing up; few people have the guts to tell them. Aries people just ignore things they don't find palatable until disaster strikes. They want to believe the best in everybody. Their secret deep dark fear is that *you won't like them.* Yes, really.

Being First is what turns them on. They don't like old, used stuff; if you're old and used, they'll find a way to make you special and new. Have you ever had a pomegranate? Have you been to Bognor Regis? Tell them the things you've never done, let Aries do it with you, try it with you. Even if you've had five husbands, an Aries must be convinced he's the first man you've ever felt this way about. They can't stand to be Number Two, but they'll take it bravely . . . for about thirty seconds. Ah, yes . . . Aries is jealous, but remember it's a healthy sign. They know they're God's creatures, and you'd better treat them like it.

TAURUS's symbol is a bull with horns. Think of a baked potato when you look at the symbol and you have the best and the worst of Taurus—simplicity itself. "I have" is the state associated with Taurus; the happy ones have and the insecure ones do not. It is a stubborn, fixed earth sign, ruled by sweet Venus.

Taurus people have strong values. They're slow to make up their minds, but that doesn't make them stupid. Sigmund Freud and the Buddha were Taureans. Taurus is the sign of common sense. If you like something, do it again, says Taurus, and again and again. The Bull sees the god in good food, beautiful objects, and comfortable surroundings, but don't be misled: a Taurus won't trade in his values for those commodities unless those *are* his values, and unfortunately sometimes those are the only values Taurus feels safe in counting on. He has other values, but if his associates prove to be unreliable in the love or the business department, hot fudge sundaes and fancy cars will simply have to do. They have the highest standards and the healthiest values in the world, and they will wait patiently for people to come along who embody those standards. Meantime, they make themselves comfortable.

They may act like big cuddly bears or pussycats because a happy Taurus is sensual, patient, and while they may be big or stocky, they are gentle people. Taurus is the calm, no-nonsense mother who wipes away the tears and fixes you peaches and cream in bed.

What's the worst thing about Taurus? There is no boredom more exquisite than to sit seven nights a week parked in front of the idiot-box with a six-pack of Schlitz, unless you happen to be Taurus, and then you are in Valhalla. It's hard to get them to go anywhere. They're narrow-minded in odd ways, and the really low-life bulls will do anything for money, a particularly boring and banal vice. Ho hum!

Find the areas with Taurus in your chart. Here are the places where you want security. If Taurus is on the house of children and love affairs (fifth house), you'd rather have one steady girlfriend, and you won't marry until you're sure there's enough money to give the children the things they need. Taurus on the friend box (eleventh house) will attract you to sensible, prosperous pals; you intend to keep them as friends for life. Any place you find Taurus you will find these high standards, a yearning for security, possessiveness amounting to mania, and those good old-fashioned values we had before MacDonald's started cranking out hamburgers.

Curiously, you often find a *lack* in the areas where you find Taurus in a chart, especially when reading for a person under forty. Never mind. It's just another case of Taurus waiting to fulfill those high standards. Why settle for less?

I wish Taurus people weren't so ashamed of their greed. They can teach all of us a thing or two about how to slow down and relax, luxuriating like Ferdinand the Bull in the sweet flowers. There is no such thing as overindulgence when you have the very best.

GEMINI's symbol is the numeral two. It is the sign of the twins. This is a sign most beloved of the gods; when the gods got bored churning out Taureans, they invented Gemini, a flexible, mutable air sign.

Where is Gemini on your chart? This is the area where you make light of difficulties, tell a joke or two whilst handling three things at once. You need variety here. If Gemini is on the Midheaven (tenth house) you'll want more than one career, or a job in the communications industry—write a column, talk on the phone, run a mail-order business. Where you find Gemini you can do one thing *only* if it is smart enough. Gemini on the marriage box (seventh house) does *not* mean you must be a bigamist, nor need you marry more than once; but your partner had better be bright, social, and able to do a variety of things well.

Routine unnerves these people, and they're too nervous already. Nothing is more rattling than to see a Gemini burst into tears. Then you see their dear nerves sticking out like bedraggled porcupine quills, and you feel you would do anything in the world to help them. You can. Give them a million and one new things to do, give them books, turn on the television. Madness? Yes. But Geminis get *edgy* when there's nothing to do.

Male Geminis think they're cute little boys, even at age eighty-two. Female Geminis thrash about, eternally restless—usually with a fair lashing of self-pity—wondering what to do next. A committed Gemini is a glorious sight. They still aren't *relaxed,* but commitment to a project brings out the old wit and makes them pleased with themselves. They're good at so many things there's a danger they'll scatter those talents; it helps them to make a list and to narrow their specialties down to about three or five pursuits.

Class. It's a weird word to use in democratic times, but Geminis have *intellectual* class. Nothing impresses them more than brains. You won't find them stooping to low levels of conduct. Even Roderick, an original and charming mid-Atlantic con man client, amused his creditors with his apologetic, mellifluous lies.

Geminis are weird when they come in for chart readings. They all say the same thing: "Please level with me. Tell me the truth. But don't tell me if it's bad." Remember, they're fragile and nervous; they don't want to handle gory information. They create a situation where people "protect" them from certain truths, even vital information. Recent studies on stress show that one of the most effective ways of avoiding stress is to *ignore it.* In the life of every Gemini is at least one unpalatable truth, obvious to everyone but Gemini. They say they want to know, but they don't.

As far as your life goes, and everyone else's, though, they notice everything down to the quizzical look on the bridesmaid's face in the yellowing photograph. They're always asking questions. They expect to tell you about their friends and even realize deep down that their own lives, too, are grist for the mill. The high types would never betray a secret, but make sure you tell them it *is* a secret. They don't like to discuss important things on the telephone or in letters. Perhaps it's a hangover from the McCarthy era, when not even the mail was safe. They may even be right. Even Gemini babies are born sophisticated.

CANCER's symbol is curly-wurly. It's supposed to look like cuddly round bosoms. Here's a pushy, cardinal water sign, rushing in to protect and nourish itself and its children. Cancer is the sign of the mother; I know it's hard to take if you've got one as a friend, spouse, or business contact, but they see *everyone* as babies, and that means you. If a Cancer decides they like you, look out: they'll cluck and flibberty-gibbet over you until you're thoroughly spoiled. If you're a fire or air sign this may make you a wee bit nervous at first. You may not be accustomed to having your pillows fluffed up and your feelings explored. You might even be silly enough to try and make a run for it, straight back into the world of cold intellect or unthinking adventure, but you'll miss the point of living if you do.

It's no accident that the summer solstice marks the beginning of Cancer. The Druids still celebrate this day when the Sun is at its most powerful, the longest day of the year. Many Cancers don't realize how powerful they are. They are the givers of life, the nourishers of all creatures. Their mission is to take care of people, the most important job on earth. Cancers don't realize they scare people with their superior abilities to be intimate. It is a quiet, understated power, which is just as well: Cancer is the most powerful sign of the zodiac. Without food and love, life cannot go on.

Look up where Cancer is in your horoscope. Can you admit how moody you are in this area of your life? Are you in touch with how much you care? If you have Cancer on the friend box (eleventh house) you're wildly popular and probably unaware of the fact. Be careful not to *smother* the area where you have Cancer, give the thing room to breathe. Is Cancer on the Midheaven (tenth house)? Leave the running of the office to others once in awhile. It'll run without you. After all, if you're a good mother hen, you've brought your business up right and it can stand on its own feet.

Dr. Zipporah Dobyns, the clinical psychologist who uses astrology in her work all over the world, has a clever yardstick for measuring emotional health in a horoscope. She says that the house where you find Cancer in a chart is where you want to be *both* Mummy and baby. Say you have Cancer on the partnership box (seventh house). Make sure you're not doing all the nurturing. Kick back and let your partner take care of you too. This ability to switch back and forth between caring for and being cared for is a most reliable index of sound emotional adjustment.

Flaws? Claws. They hang onto old pain; they nurse old grudges. They collect hurts; the hurts fester, and they don't tell you about them—they make you guess. They're too shy to speak up. When they sulk or get moody, you can shovel on the cheer for hours and they never seem to fill up when they feel empty. This can cause them problems with food and drink. They're cunning.

They wear their vulnerabilities on their sleeves so you won't hurt them. Or they play the chameleon.

Money seems to run through their fingers, but it's an act. Cancers are accumulators and excel in business. They're the best bargain finders in the world. They love antiques. In fact, they love all old things, and that means you too, dear, when you get old and crotchety.

🦁 **LEO's** symbol is a lion's mane. Leo is ruled by the lucky old Sun, which, according to the soothsayers of yore, has nothing to do but roll around heaven all day. It is a fixed fire sign. Leos like you to orbit round them. The shy ones are just being classy. They expect you to zero in on their true greatness.

Leo women train themselves to hold back; princesses know who they are. They try like hell not to show off. It doesn't work—somehow they always manage to look beautiful. Catch a Leo lady in her holey undies cleaning out the toilet bowl . . . embarrassed? Yes. But she'll wield the mucky plunger like a sceptre and unclog the drain if it takes her all night. Only Scorpio has more will power than a Leo, and Leo can't bear to lose, even to a recalcitrant loo. Triumph is everything to these people.

Leo men want to be show-offs. There's no sadder sight than a Leo with nothing to be proud about. The biggest problem with Leos is this pride. If there's a deal cooking, they've just got to tell someone about it. Leos always have big deals cooking, lots of them. According to the law of averages, some of these deals fall through. Other signs accept this, but not Leo. Every mishap is a personal blow, decreed by an angry God. They take failure harder than anyone else. Sneaky Scorpios and cunning Capricorns get ahead in business by keeping *schtum* until they've got the deal wrapped up—then they leak the good news. They know that if they treat their triumphs as secrets, the gossip-hungry rabble will spread the secret like wildfire. Leo has too much faith in human nature. They trumpet their victories to the four winds. And if one of those deals falls through, they hope you'll never ask about it. They're ashamed. The worst extreme of this Leo pride is the braggart, the teller of tall tales. Nothing is ever big enough, magnificent enough, for Leo the Lion.

These warm, affectionate, noble people like to do things in a big way. They give magnificent parties and presents. Leo is the most creative sign of the zodiac—they can write, paint, make speeches, act, compose music, fix stereos, order in Chinese, and conquer every man or woman in sight as long as they have center stage, or love, or both. The ability to be creative expands exponentially with applause. What's important, then, for Leos is appreciation and adoring friends. It doesn't pay them to be snobbish if they need approbation in order to function, but they're snobs anyway.

Paul Stewart, a whizz-kid friend with an off-scale I.Q. and a Leo heart of gold to match, was dining with a business colleague one evening. After he ordered for both of them *in Szechuan* and lightly mentioned his most recent half-dozen triumphs, the colleague eyed him coldly:

"You think you're *better* than other people, that's your trouble," he said.

"I am," smiled Paul—and picked up the check.

Find the house where Leo is in your chart. This is how you light up a room. You're proud and stubborn and must have unswerving loyalty here. The house you find Leo in is important. It may even tell you what you should be doing for a living. It will always tell you what you're good at. Just remember that this house can also make you an empty braggart; that applause has to be *earned* you know. Even a king serves his people.

VIRGO's symbol is demure. See how modestly she curls her tail under herself. Just like a Bryn Mawr girl! This is a nervous, flexible earth sign, as in quicksilver— or quicksand. Virgo embodies the princess and the pea principle: she knows when something's wrong, and no one's going to get any rest until she fixes it.

This sign has a bad press. I can't understand it. Virgos do nag, yes . . . they show how much they love you by picking you to pieces, certainly . . . they're cruel, accurate gossips for sure, and nothing's ever perfect enough for them, but they're only human . . . aren't they? Have you ever staggered, bleary-eyed, into the breakfast nook and got your hands on the coffee before Virgo's inspected your daily attire? Nope. See how much friendly advice they give you, free of charge? Of course they love you. They just want to make you an eensy-weensy, tiddley-bit *better*, is all.

Turn the criticism around on them and they go to bits, get hysterical; tears form in their kindly eyes; they hang their sorry heads. How could you be so cruel? You've just uncovered Virgo's defense mechanism. They know they're not perfect, so they try to make up for it . . . by helping to make *you* perfect. Aarggh!

Where is Virgo in your chart? On the friend box (eleventh house)? On the lovers-and-children box (fifth house)? Think it over.

Virgos are superb craftsmen. They excel in the arts and the healing professions. They're ruled by Mercury, the planet of brains. Virgos and Geminis are the best mimics in the world. Peter Sellers was a Virgo. His meticulous timing and stagecraft made him one of the finest actors of the twentieth century.

Keep your gassy Sagittarians, spouting idealism while they chase the chambermaid and drink your brandy—when it comes to real idealism, the award goes to Virgo. They don't talk about it. They do it. They prefer to stay in the background while they work their miracles of healing and helping. No one bothers them if they're incognito, so they get a lot more done. Virgo gets it *all* done. And they do it better than anyone. Just don't mess with them while they're doing it. They have fine, analytical minds, and they never miss a detail.

Virgos have to be useful or life has no meaning for them. Work is a god to them; if you see a Virgo slopping around, avoiding work, be patient. She hasn't found a job yet that fulfills her high standards of service and improving the world. If she still slops around, breaks a leg, or keeps catching rare diseases like virus of the toenail, give her a push and a pep talk. The perfect job hasn't been invented yet.

LIBRA's symbol is the scales of justice. Libra's a machine, the only zodiac sign that isn't symbolized by an animal or human. It is also the best-looking damned machine you ever saw in your life. You can push and push a Libra. Then, one day, the scales spring right back—sproinnnnng. It may take years for the scales to deliver justice, but to every action by you, Libras have an equal and opposite reaction. You can't say it isn't fair.

The sad part of Libra's temperament is also what makes them sweet. They don't know how to speak up for themselves. In silence they take what you dish out; they want peace at any price. What they don't realize is the danger and psychological damage they do themselves—and others—by putting up with other people's nonsense. The Sun is weak in Libra, and it's hard for them to stand alone. Libras aren't here to be loners. They express their personalities best in company, preferably with their mate. They're here to bring people and ideas together, people and people together, and ideas with ideas. As such they make excellent diplomats, artists, designers, teachers and matchmakers. Hell for a Libra is to be alone for too long; even then they'll get out the books and start a dialogue with God.

Look for the part of your chart with Libra on the cusp. You see both points of view here. If Libra's on the religion box (ninth house) you're fair to all religions. You're a genius at playing chameleon here, pleading the Jewish cause with your Catholic friends, being Zenny with the Protestants. You pull it off, though, with charm and intellect. Libra's a pushy air sign. It doesn't matter to you which side you take in an argument as long as you push the ideas around a bit. In truth, you like to take the opposite side in a discussion, just to stir things up. If Libra's on the Midheaven, you prefer to work in a pretty place. If Libra's on the hospital box (twelfth house), you'll recuperate faster in a gorgeous setting.

Romantic, stylish, sentimental people are not what you'd expect to find in the middle of the war room or out in the trenches. Still we find Libra pronounced in the charts of generals (Ike) and Svengali-like, hypnotic dictators (Hitler had it rising). Libras know how to sandbag action. Their expert eyes figure out, fast, *how to contain a situation*. You're having a tantrum? You're the handsomest man at the party? Libras know just what to do with you. They'll flatter, negotiate, coerce—whatever the situation calls for, Libra will do it.

Rotters and eyelash-batters are found in this sign, it's true. Libras aren't usually afraid to mooch or wangle some way of getting themselves taken care of. Even the tramps are refined. My flatmate brought home a highly literate, charming, impoverished Libra musician one week.

"I say," he said to me one day at teatime, "do you fancy a sandwich?"

"Naw," I snapped, banging out a column hours before a deadline.

"Oh," he said. He reflected for a moment. Nothing is noisier than a Libran's gentle hesitation. I looked up from the typewriter. "Then would you mind terribly if I made myself one?"

I felt so embarrassed by this man's refinement that I made him the sandwich and French Onion soup under the grill. Libras can always teach Aries a thing or two about humanity.

The fatal flaw in Libra is their ability to gloss over anything that's ugly, mercenary, or cruel. Then there are the other Librans, like Jimmy Carter and Mahatma Gandhi, who aren't afraid of being laughed at while they humbly stick up for extraordinary, human, spiritual values.

SCORPIO's symbol looks like Virgo, with a telling difference; Scorpio sticks her tail right out and wiggles it at you. It's a fixed water sign, and these still waters run deep. People don't understand Scorpios. Scorpios like it that way. No one has more secrets than this sign, though they are detectives at heart—they'll have your motives worked out before you've realized what's happened.

Their secrets are simple; Scorpios love and hate with an intensity that lasts forever. They're afraid that if you know what they want, you'll take it away from them. They send out false signals, red herrings to see how much you care about them before they reveal themselves. "I dare you to figure me out" is the game they play. They cover *this* one up with a controlled, "I don't give a damn" demeanor. They'll reveal themselves, slowly, to you as you *earn* their trust. Their eyes bore into your heart as they check you out and make their steely assessment. What Scorpios greatly fear is being hurt in the one-to-one relationship, but they fear losing the relationship with their own self-respect more. If it's a choice between you and that self-respect, you go bye-bye. Scorpio knows that we all go alone into the pine box. If you haven't got your values, there's nothing else you can take with you. It's a hard philosophy, but they're right. No one is so loyal a friend, so dangerous an enemy as Scorpio, for they do forgive, but they never forget.

Oh, wishy-washy days of Age of Aquarius, you declare it's not "cool" to carry a grudge. Scorpio doesn't give a damn what philosophy is fashionable this millenium. Somebody attacks your child or sister and you go out and *get* them . . . it's a matter of honor. Scorpio doesn't act right away. Scorpio may wait forever. The higher types may never seek revenge, but Scorpios *remember*. They make sure your cruel act is recorded Up There, burnt into the Akashic Records with blood and passion. They leave it to God to straighten things out, and it doesn't take long. Their enemies trip themselves up.

Scorpios glide amongst their three spiritual levels: the scorpion, the eagle, and the dove.

The scorpion type gets revenge and enjoys the muck. They revel in the vulgar and sneaky. They shoplift and want to mess around with your wife. No one rationalizes actions better than this type; their eyes are so mud-covered they don't see the Big

Picture. Ultimately they only damage themselves in the eyes of others. They enjoy pulling you down to their level. Don't beg for mercy with these types—your suffering gives them a feeling of power.

The eagle wants to protect her loved ones. She won't pounce unless it's necessary. She is proud and independent, and she won't be told what to do. America uses the eagle as its symbol. Don't tread on me!

The dove type, too, wants power. Here is the power to control one's own desires. Doves practice the principle of *ahimsa*, harmlessness. One of the philosopher Ram Dass' teachers wrote on a slate, "Snakes Know Heart." The harmless yogi, a man of peace, need not fear life in the jungle, for all creatures sense he means no harm to any living being.

The house in your chart where you find Scorpio is where daily you have a choice between these three levels. Psychologists manipulate people to become better human beings. This is the function of Scorpio. Do you face your own power here? Do you clean up your own act or do you retreat to the gray slime and live in fear and paranoia? You can have your secrets here. Make sure they're guarding something worthwhile. Means never justify the ends.

SAGITTARIUS's symbol is the centaur, half man, half horse. He shoots off his arrows and his mouth. Sometimes the arrow stands for his high principles and higher spirits. At other times those arrows stand for the blunt remarks Sagittarians unconsciously use to hurt people. It's a flexible fire sign.

Hurt people? Never Sagittarius! They're too busy flying their planes, cheering at soccer games, working sixteen-hour days, and taking business trips to hurt people. They love religion, high morals, and educating themselves. These philosophers see the Big Picture all right, but they miss the frame-by-frame focus that comprises the movie of daily life. They don't mean to trample on your feelings, but they're too naïve and afraid of losing their freedom to notice the trouble others go to for them every day. If they noticed the messes they make, and this sign is too intelligent not to see clearly, they'd have to pitch in. Most Sagittarians, for all the fuss and bluster, are terrified of responsibility. Nero was a Sagittarian; he fiddled while Rome burned.

They make up for it by being funny. Nothing ever measures up to their "Ideal"; quickly Sagittarians learn to take life as it comes and laugh at imperfections. They roll with the punches.

Sagittarians grow more responsible with age, because *Sagittarians play to win,* and winners commit themselves. They read it in a book. Their honorable reputations stem from Sagittarius's big secret: there's a little club in their heads, and this club plays by the rules. It just doesn't occur to them that not everybody belongs to the club. They're shocked when you have *other* rules; no, they can't stand it. The dumb ones then preach at you, and the smart ones want to learn more. It's how you tell them apart. *They want to be hip* and run with In people, but unlike more frightened, less fiery folk, *they make their own In groups.* Female Sagittarians want to be a cheerleader, cha-cha queen, or the hippest beatnik on campus. The men try to stay bachelors as long as possible. It doesn't occur to them that freedom can include responsibility.

A woman with generous Sagittarius on the pet box (the sixth house, not the kitty litter bin) loves critters. She's a millionairess who thinks she's running the Bide-A-Wee home, taking in everyone's waifs and strays. Find the house on your horoscope with Sagittarius. Is it hip? Is it highly principled? Aren't you optimistic about it? Isn't it fun? Of course it is.

Guardian angels protect this lucky sign. Sagittarians may look like gamblers to you and me, but they play to win, and those risks are calculated. Stick around and learn from them awhile. They preach at you, but they'll inspire you and teach you too. No one is a better teacher. They *are* gross sometimes. They'll spill dinner on the carpet, scrape it up, and try to serve it to you anyway. When the Virgos start turning green, Sagittarians think it's funny . . . then they fart and announce the fact. A Leo would be mortified. Not a Sag. It's all part of life to them.

Sagittarians know where the action is, or they'll make it happen. If you want to see the world or have a hell of a time in your own living room, get a Sag. They were born knowing how to have fun, and they're better at it than anyone.

Think of Bugs Bunny when you think of Sagittarius. A surprising number of them look like rabbits.

Note well the symbol for **CAPRICORN.** Better yet, try and *draw* the sucker. Tough? You betcha. It's supposed to look like a goat with a fishtail. Capricorn is a pushy earth sign, so think of digging earth with a shovel, or breaking rocks in the old prison yard. Easy it isn't, but if you must, you must.

Want to move mountains? Capricorn can. Capricorns will grind anything that gets in their way down to dust. Time is on their side. It gets easier for them as they get older. They cheer up, too, when they age. Every passing year gets happier with Capricorn—nothing is ever as hard for them as it was when they were just starting out. You get wrinkles while Capricorn gets more youthful. Other signs run into trouble when they get older. Not Capricorns. They are the goats who grew up eating rusty tin cans and wind up with Cherries Jubilee. Saturn, the planet of adversity, is their friend. Saturn makes life so tough for these individuals that they learn to work longer and harder than anyone else for what they want, and what they want is Excellence.

The sign is a cross between a cockroach and a cash register if their values aren't screwed on straight. No one is more coldly opportunistic than this sign. They use people. They are so busy protecting their interests they cannot stop to care if you get stepped on. Your fault for not looking out for Number One, baby! Then they wonder why no one trusts them, why they're alone, why their money and power isn't enough to chase away the paranoia and melancholy. As the Sun sinks slowly over this futile horizon, we bid a fond farewell to this cucaracha side of Capricorn. There's another side to this sign, a side that embodies so much wisdom, beauty, loyalty, and depth it leaves you breathless.

What makes Sally run? Look at the house in your horoscope with Capricorn on the cusp. You feel hopeless and inadequate in this area. Beware! Do not succumb to negativity in this area, and don't stop trying. If you're smart, you'll *work* (Saturn's favorite word) and learn to compensate for your real and imagined flaws. You may feel touchy about this stuff, but you court disaster if you sit back and "give up" in this house.

If you have Capricorn on the communication box (third house), watch the news, read the papers, learn something new every day, and speak so people can understand you; sit back, or give up and never know how much your narrow world bores good people away. If Capricorn is your rising sign, don't despair if you walk with a limp. Make a big deal out of it—some people think it's cute, you know! You don't know, because you put yourself down with Capricorn here. Shine up your personality instead, and stop picking your nose in public. You can turn your scars into stars and *capitalize* (another Capricorn word) on your flaws. Maybe the wisest lesson Capricorn teaches us is that no one loves a perfect person—makes the rest of us feel itchy, you see.

It's a fine line between working madly to improve our flaws whilst accepting them at the same time. Accept them too much and you drag down every other area of your life. Hating your weaknesses does nothing to bring you peace of mind.

Chip away at your fears. Be gentle with yourself, but do the work. Fear is at the root of all Capricorn troubles. Capricorns, the wise ones, have learned to love those fears. It is those very terrors that spur folks on to greatness. Where you find Capricorn, you find the potential for being BETTER THAN OTHER PEOPLE, and to hell with democracy. You don't become superior in a particular field of endeavor because you feel comfortable with yourself. You have to be honest enough, wise enough, and want it badly enough to have a bash at it. Will you? Where is Capricorn in your chart?

That zappy symbol for **AQUARIUS** could be electricity. Every Aquarian has it, and magnetism; the public loves them. In the old days those wavy lines stood for the water the Water-Bearer pours from his jug to serve humanity. Take your pick. It's a stubborn air sign. These folks are stubborn with their ideas because they're new ideas. Aquarians stick to their guns to make sure their new ideas stick.

Aquarian women are wonderful. They don't talk about boys and clothes all the time. Aquarian men are a delight. They don't whisk you off to bed before they know your name. In "Sneakin' Sally Down the Alley" Robert Palmer sings, "I'd really like to get to know what's between your ears." God bless him.

If Aquarius is on your first house (the rising sign) you're a freaky dresser. If it's on your sex box (the eighth house) you have high ideals about sex. Aquarius on the Midheaven means you'd be happier being self-employed. Wherever you find Aquarius in your chart you need lots of space and freedom to experiment.

Remember too that there are two kinds of Aquarians, the conventional ones ruled by Saturn, and the fascinating radicals ruled by Uranus. Which way are you manifesting Aquarius in your chart?

Here is the sign of brotherhood, friendliness and curiosity. Science, technology, engineering, electronics all come under Aquarius's rule. This sign wants to give people a break. It's a pleasure to be around them. They practice what they preach—live and let live.

Before we drag out that well-documented soybean about 75 percent of the people in the Hall of Fame being Aquarians, it behooves us to learn why this is so. The Sun is weak in Aquarius, as it is in Libra. Aquarians have a shaky sense of who they are, so they're afraid to get personal.

Have you noticed how people with planets in Aquarius don't want to ride the bus? They don't want to go out Saturday night, either—it's when "the plebs" go out. Aquarians feel inferior and superior to other human beings; they feel intensely guilty about feeling different from other people. They're supposed to regard all people as equal, and they hide behind causes and revolutions.

Aquarius is the most lovable robot in the world, but there's a bolt missing. This tragic bolt is the capacity for intimacy. You can't have intimacy if you don't know what you are. If you keep it light, they're fine as friends, but they strike out in the one-to-one relationship. Put your nose up to their noses and ask "Who's in there?" They run a mile. This sign invented the line, "My wife doesn't understand me." It's a con. Their spouses understand them all too well and have long since given up on them.

Don't tell anybody this; the astrologers will bind and gag me, pour boiling molasses in my shoes, and force me to listen to Dane Rudhyar lectures for the rest of the fiscal year if you do. There is an awful secret that lies behind the bone-chilling detachment of Aquarians. They are aliens visiting from outer space. The galaxy they come from is probably run by IBM.

PISCES's symbol looks like Neptune, its ruling planet, lying drunk on its side. Or you might think of Pisces as the two fishes swimming in opposite directions. Two fishes is a queer way to regard Pisces, the sign of true love, faith, and inner peace. Perhaps one fish helps people and meditates while the other fish finds peace at the bottom of a bottle of Jack Daniel's. Pisceans enjoy this choice between saint and slut. It's a mutable water sign. They can take you to heaven and send you to hell; saintly Pisceans stay that way because they always know they have a choice.

This gentle sign cannot hurt you directly; it is their weaknesses that can scramble your brains. The majority of Pisces people are kind and gullible. Did you ever meet one of those people who sells you the Brooklyn Bridge and every once in a while buys it?

Depression gets them. Because they see life as a mystical whole, they take it as a sign that they're bad people when things go wrong. No other zodiac sign plans the evening on the basis of a reading from a fortune cookie.

Fish-faces are the ultimate romantics. They find love in ants, books, people, dustbins, flowers, weeds, or philosophy. Fine tuning is their bête noire; this sensitivity is a double-edged sword. Keep them away from horrible atmospheres, and they're free to help the helpless. Nothing cheers them up like someone to care of.

Self-pity is their vicious enemy. Self-pity turns off the people who would help them most. Many Pisceans enjoy wallowing in self-pity; they use their sensitivities to subtly dominate everyone around them. "I can't cope! Will you go to the shops for me?" Bat, bat, bat go the trembling little eyelashes. . . .

Pisceans are shy. Other people think they are mysterious, or just confused, but a Pisces can sort out other people's troubles. They believe in Fate, and like the most famous fish of them all, Albert Einstein, they retain a peaceful humility about their talents that would shame most Leos.

They'll lie to save your feelings, or just to stake out a little privacy for themselves. They don't like to be alone too much, just a little, to get the peace back. They can get addicted to booze, pills, or crackerjack, so they have to watch it.

The house in your chart with Pisces on the cusp is where you get by, often without visible means of support. You have faith, and you're kind there, so it comes back to you. If Pisces is on your money box (second house), you may not know where the cash will come from, but because you muddle through and help people, God always sends you just enough. If it's on the love box (fifth house), there's always someone around the corner who'd love it if you gave him a chance.

The Rising Sign: Your World View and the World's View of You, Too

"Beware, so long as you live, of judging men by their outward appearance."

—Jean de la Fontaine

"Men in general judge more from appearances than from reality. All men have eyes, but few have the gift of penetration."

—Niccolo Machiavelli

Don't let the rising sign fool you. It's the first impression a person makes, all right, and appearances are frequently deceptive. Psychologists call it the persona; psychiatrists call it the defense mechanism. Think of it as an eggshell surrounding the human spirit; the rising sign even describes what you look like, your body type, and what kinds of clothes look best on you.

What is your manner of meeting the world? The rising sign indicates your attitudes and styles of coping with people and things—it shows *how you get by.* No matter what you are feeling inside, your hopes, your desires, your hurts, your private quirks don't show until they pass through this sieve. If you're a giddy Gemini but your rising sign is Scorpio, you look like a Scorpio and act like a Scorpio. You don't chatter to strangers on the bus; you don't wear your favorite colors, green and yellow, because your Scorpio Ascendant won't let you. The Ascendant protects you at a cocktail party; people think you're mysterious. When they meet you at your home, they see the greens and yellows, and you talk their ears off. People take off their rising signs when they feel safe.

Yearning for the stuff of your Ascendant is healthy and typical. A Scorpio rising person thinks a good deal about sex,

PLANET	SIGN	LONG	HSE
SUN	Cpr	5 25.4	4
MOON	Leo	7 6.54	11
MERC	Cpr	2 17.8	4
VENU	Aqu	20 25.2	6
MARS E	Cpr	25 57.8	5
JUPI F	Cpr	20 25.8	5
SATU R	Cpr	17 12.8	5
URAN	Sag	18 11.8	4
NEPT	Gem	29 56.1R	10
PLUT	Gem	17 21.1R	10
ASC	Vir	4 8.4	1
MC	Tau	25 5.8	10
NODE*	Scp	12 7.1	3
PFOR	Ari	5 50.2	
VERTEX	Aqu	5 3.7	
EASTPT	Leo	20 20.5	

R=RULE   D=DETRIMENT
E=EXALTED   F=FALL
*TRUE NODE

	CARD	FIX	MUT		
FIRE	0	1	1	3	0
EARTH	5	0	0		
AIR	0	1	2	0	7
WATER	0	0	0		

*** NATAL ASPECTS ***

	ANGLE	ORB			ANGLE	ORB
CON=CONJUNCTION	0	10		TRI=TRINE	120	10
SSX=SEMISEXTILE	30	3		SQQ=SESQUIQUAD	135	4
SSQ=SEMI-SQUARE	45	4		BQT=BIQUINTILE	144	3
SXT=SEXTILE	60	6		QCX=QUINCUNX	150	3
QTL=QUINTILE	72	3		OPP=OPPOSITION	180	10
SQR=SQUARE	90	10		/ =PARALLEL OR	0	1

A=APPLYING   S=SEPARATING   CONTRAPARALLEL

	SUN	MOON	MERCURY	VENUS	MARS	JUPITER
MOON	QCX 1 42S	MOON				
MERC	CON 3 07A	BQT 1 11A	MERCURY			
VENU	SSQ 0 00A		SSQ 3 07A	VENUS		
MARS					MARS	
JUPI				SSX 0 01A	CON 5/32S	JUPITER
SATU					CON 8/45S	CON 3/13S
URAN	/	SQQ 3 55S		SXT 2 13S	/	SSX 2/14S
NEPT	OPP 5 29S		OPP 2 22S	TRI 9 31A		
PLUT	/			TRI 3 04S	BQT 2 37S	BQT 2 55A
ASC	TRI 1 17	SSX 2 59	TRI 1 51		BQT 2 11	SQQ 1 17
MC		QTL 0 01	BQT 1 12	SQR 4 41	TRI 0 52	TRI 4 40
NODE		SQR 5 00		SQR 8 18	QTL 1 51	

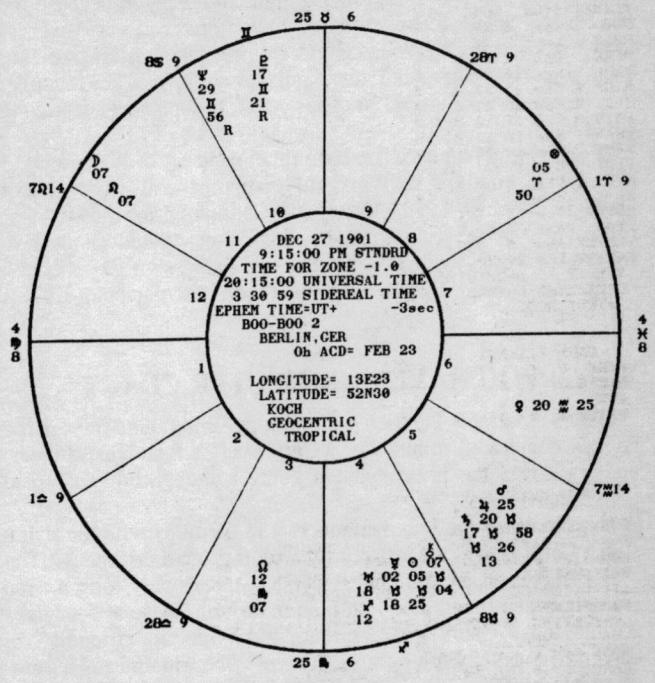

Marlene Dietrich

	SATURN	URANUS	NEPTUNE	PLUTO	ASC	MC
	SSX 0/59A					
	QCX 0 08A	OPP 0 51S				
	SQQ 1 56		SXT 4 12		SQR 9 03	
	TRI 7 53					
	SXT 5 06		SQQ 2 49	BQT 0 46		

psychology, and will power. Libra rising persons scheme for beauty, harmony with nature and their environments. They die without other people; they must have a rich social life.

You won't find a table of rising signs in this book because the rising sign degree changes *every four minutes*. Every twenty-four hours the twelve zodiac signs rise over the eastern horizon; each sign rises for about two hours every day. They change, too, depending on how far away your birthplace is from the equator.

If you can get an accurate birth time, send off to the computer and get it done *right*. That old computer will worry about Daylight Savings Time, War Time, latitudes, and nasty logarithms; it's more accurate than a human-calculated chart. I've seen some books with hokey round-off rising sign tables, but I don't want you to wind up with a boo-boo persona. Life is tough enough.

WHEN YOU HAVE A COMPUTER CHART

Here's Marlene Dietrich's horoscope. First note the rising sign, 4 degrees, 8 minutes of Virgo. She's a fastidious dresser, and she gives the impression of being a thoughtful, analytical perfectionist.

Next look for the Sun symbol. Is it in harmony with the rising sign? Look down the *aspect grid* of the chart to check. The "TRI" between the Sun and Ascendant means they form a trine angle between them. The Sun is in the fourth house at 5 degrees 25 minutes of Capricorn. Capricorn and Virgo are "friendly" to each other, as they are both earth signs. The trine means harmony. Marlene Dietrich's real self (hardworking Sun in Capricorn) is in harmony with your first impression of her. It's easy for her to create a smooth first impression, and she is pretty much what she seems to be.

Here is another kind of chart. The rising sign is Leo, and the Sun is Taurus, two signs that "fight" with each other. There is no connection between the Sun and the Ascendant on the aspect grid.

"How shall I act?" is often how this man feels when meeting people for the first time. He seems a warm, exuberant character who would like to put his arms around the earth and give it a big hug, which fits the Leo rising sign. Inwardly he is a dedicated writer who thrives on the routine of hard work and the comforts success brings him. That is his Sun in Taurus.

He is Trevor Ravenscroft, author of *The Spear of Destiny,* and you feel when you meet him that he must have written the book on charisma. People with conflict between the Sun and rising sign are more interesting characters; they generally have a lot of depth. You don't really get to know someone like this until you've met them at least five times; they show you a new facet of their personalities every day.

Disregard your first impressions when you meet people with conflicts between Sun and Ascendant. Take time to get to know them. If *you* have such a combination, you don't take people at face value, and you may need to polish up your first impression technique.

Harmony between the Sun and the Ascendant means you have so little difficulty making a smooth impression that you may not notice other people's social discomfort. It's easy for you to appear to be yourself.

If the rising sign is:

ARIES—Look for a walk with the head poked a couple of feet ahead of the body. They're Rams looking for trouble; the world's full of weaker people to rescue. Life's an adventure and a challenge; the challenge is mainly to keep people from telling them what to do. If you live near an Aries rising person, carry a "Don't Tread On Me" sign yourself. It's astonishing how blind are these innocent, warm, friendly folk when it comes to stepping on your toes. They turn up, unannounced, to watch your television. They get to feel free and dashing after you've cooked the dinner. No wonder they like rescuing weak people! It's the bravest rising sign in the world, though they don't even know it. The eminent astrologer Al H. Morrison exhibits the nobler qualities of this Ascendant: anyone may dine with him. Rich or poor, high born or low, makes no difference to him. He'll help anyone in trouble and he fixes it fast. Self-sacrifice is the loveliest character trait of Aries rising; shooting off one's own ego whilst embarrassing others close to oneself is the ugliest.

TAURUS—Gentle beyond belief, these folks may seem boring on first impression. They're biding their time. They're slow to form an opinion about you, or anything else. You'd do well to take your time in sizing them up, however . . . they *follow through on their promises*. Look for a strong, compact, even stocky body built to take life's shocks. A bull neck for the gentlemen, swan neck for the ladies, and a rich soothing radio announcer voice for both. They want comfort and security from life; this dominates their thoughts. Taurus rising makes a person

```
PLANET  SIGN  LONG    HSE
SUN     Tau   2 46 47  10
MOON  F Scp  17 11 52   4
MERC    Ari  15 23.2    9
VENU  R Tau   1 32.7R   9
MARS  D Tau  21  7.4   10
JUPI  D Vir   9 10.3R   1
SATU    Vir  18 36.2R   2
URAN    Pic   8 34.9    7
NEPT    Leo  10 57.7   12
PLUT    Can   7  0.6   11
ASC     Leo  18 35.5    1
MC      Tau   1 38.9   10
NODE*   Lib  27 10.3    3
PFOR    Pic   3  0.6
VERTEX  Cpr  10  9.1
EASTPT  Can  27 25.1
 R=RULE      D=DETRIMENT
 E=EXALTED   F=FALL
 *TRUE NODE
```

```
     CARD FIX MUT
FIRE   1   1   0      4 | 3
EARTH  0   3   2      -----
AIR    0   0   0      2 | 1
WATER  1   1   1
```

```
      *** NATAL ASPECTS ***
              ANGLE ORB              ANGLE ORB
CON=CONJUNCTION   0  10   TRI=TRINE      120  10
SSX=SEMISEXTILE  30   3   SQQ=SESQUIQUAD 135   4
SSQ=SEMI-SQUARE  45   4   BQT=BIQUINTILE 144   3
SXT=SEXTILE      60   6   QCX=QUINCUNX   150   3
QTL=QUINTILE     72   3   OPP=OPPOSITION 180  10
SQR=SQUARE       90  10   / =PARALLEL OR     0   1
A=APPLYING  S=SEPARATING   CONTRAPARALLEL
```

	SUN	MOON	MERCURY	VENUS	MARS	JUPITER
MOON						
MERC		QCX 1 49S				
VENU	CON 1 14S					
MARS		OPP 3 56A				
JUPI	TRI 6 23A		BQT 0 13S	TRI 7 38S		
SATU	SQQ 0 49A	SXT 1 24A		SSQ 2 03S	TRI 2 31S	CON 9 26A
URAN	SXT 5 48A	TRI 8 37S			QTL 0 32S	OPP 0/35A
NEPT	SQR 0 11A	SQR 6 14S	TRI 4 26S	SQR 9/25S		SSX 1 47S
PLUT	SXT 4 14A		SQR 8 23S	SXT 5 28S	SSQ 0 53A	SXT 2 10A
ASC		SQR 1/24	TRI 3 12		SQR 2 32	
MC	CON 1/08			CON 0 06		TRI 7 31
NODE	OPP 8 36			OPP 4 22		SSQ 3 00

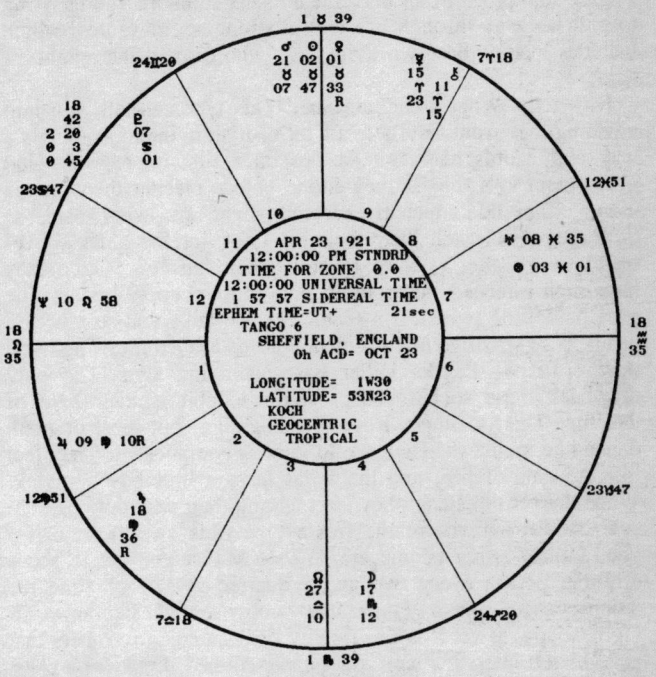

Trevor Ravenscroft

SATURN	URANUS	NEPTUNE	PLUTO	ASC	MC
	QCX 2 23A				
QTL 0 24S	TRI 1 34S	CON 7 38	SSQ 3 25		
SSX 0 01		SQR 9 19	SXT 5 22		
SQQ 1 57			TRI 9 50		OPP 4 29
	SQQ 3 35				

look placid. This same person goes to pieces without money, and the more insecure types will do almost anything to get their hands on the filthy lucre. Gloria Vanderbilt has this Ascendant. Money's no problem for her. She uses her stubborn Taurus rising to bull her way through life with a strong set of values, which includes making her own living . . . who cares if the neighbors beef!

GEMINI—What a car salesman! This type can talk you into anything they want to. There's a bit of Irish in them, as there's a way with words here that dazzles on a first impression. God made them kiss the Blarney Stone before placing them in the womb. They don't feel as charming, light, and witty inside as they seem, so watch their feelings. Look for the quick movements of a waiter as they go about their business. Often they have high foreheads to accommodate those slippery brains. The eyes have little twinkles in them. No one talks you so much to death, is so sensitive to your mental needs as Gemini rising. And they're funny—Phyllis Diller has this rising sign. The only drawback these socially adept spirits exhibit is their love of dancing. This is Ginger Roger's rising sign, but most of them dance like monkeys. Their world view is complicated. They feel like students of life, and the fellas have a little-boy complex. When danger threatens, they start talking their way out.

CANCER—If you're the fickle type, this sweetheart is for you. Cancer rising people are so moody that you get to see a different person every two and a quarter days, each time the moon changes signs. "Personable" doesn't sound like an exciting description; yet it is this quality of responding to others that gets the job interview won, the people calmed. Look for a chest bigger than the hips, a shambling walk, and sensitive skin that needs to stay out of the sun. Jayne Mansfield had this rising sign, as did Judy Garland. Each performer capitalized on different aspects of Cancer rising: Jayne with the famous Cancer rising chest, Judy with the ability to respond to the public and make them weep with empathy. All Cancer rising folks think food equals love, and even the wanderers have a home base they cannot bear to give up. The men and the women think they are mothers to the world and are afraid to show how cuddly they are, but they are. Their most destructive habit is letting opportunities go by because they aren't in the mood. They are lunatics on the quiet.

LEO—When this one walks into a room, POW! You notice them straight away. Leo rising people have *presence,* and uncommonly good posture. Even the funny-looking ones have a noble carriage. It's not just the well-proportioned body, the prominent eyes, the wide open, symmetrical face, pretty hair or the rubbable round head . . . they reek of self-assurance and dignity. Whatever inner doubts cloud their minds won't show. Here is the person everyone wants to wear on their arms at a premiere-razzle! Behind the gracious bonhomie is a will of steel, and a surprising, cold attitude with their close pals and spouses. They think the world's an audience, you see; many of these folks are afraid of intimacy, but it won't show up until you get to know them better. Fortunately their world view encompasses a "look on the bright side" attitude; they do trust people, and a "try harder" attitude in tough situations means they often win in no-win arenas. Kids love them. Leo rising people can turn your surly brat into Shirley Temple with a little razzle-dazzle. They wear out their opponents by turning up the drama knobs—no one cries louder, apologizes more profusely, and smiles more broadly than Leo rising.

VIRGO—Mary Mary Quite Contrary had this Ascendant. When they are good, they are very very good, and when they are bad, they are horrid. The most meticulous dressers and the most disgusting slobs are the Virgo risings. They're terribly busy or slacking off when you first meet them; this is a rising sign of extremes. In truth they go crazy if they don't feel they can be useful to the world; they will always find something to fix or fiddle with. Look for a pensive, worried expression, an oddly proportioned body, a quick walk, and a cool, rational, harshly intellectual first approach. Most Virgo rising people are slim from worrying—even the fat ones look slim from the back until you see the pot belly. Always learning something, they are great people to know if you're always getting into muddles with appliances or plane tickets or people. They'll spring right into action, take your problem apart, and put it together again. They prefer highly tailored clothes, with lots of pockets, and the military look. They create a classy intellectual first impression, laced with humility. Julie Andrews has it.

LIBRA—Even the ones who look like toads look like *good-looking* toads. The skin has an unearthly translucent quality, and there's often a bland, run-of-the-mill prettiness you see in the male and female models in television commercials. Real stunners, too, often have this rising sign, like Liz Taylor. Let a Libra ascending man tell the rest of the story: "It's easy for me to switch on a sort of public relations charm," he says, "Especially when I want to manipulate somebody. Oddly enough, it's never entirely cynical and insincere. I usually feel that we are two nice people having a friendly chat even when I've blatantly lied to someone. Lying for me is almost always motivated by the desire to keep personal relationships harmonious. I have no scruples or qualms about that at all. If I lie for personal gain or to escape the consequences of something, I feel very bad about it. A friend of a friend some months ago lent me a book of cartoons. I saw him about a week ago and he asked me if I had liked the cartoons. I said yes, although I thought in fact they were vulgar and unfunny. The motive for lying was not wishing to seem unappreciative of his gesture in lending me the book—*unsolicited by me.*'' This good-looking guy wouldn't even hurt a *stranger,* let alone a friend.

SCORPIO—Often there is a square jaw, quiet demeanor, and eyes that bore right through you. Theirs is a tough, jutting-out stance that says, "Don't mess with me." They take awhile to get to trust you, and they puff up like adders if threatened. I'll bet you were so busy being frightened of them you didn't notice how guarded and paranoid they were! Helen Keller, Diane Von Furstenberg, Chris Evert-Lloyd, Eva Braun, and Gloria Steinem all have Scorpio rising, and the common thread running through the vastly different lives of these women is the power to inspire others with respect, even awe, (or in Eva Braun's case, fear) and *unbreakable will power.* They're all obsessed with one-to-one relationships, whether it's sex, psychology, or power. Scorpio rising gives people sexy vibrations—you feel like brushing up against them. They give you a little buzz when they stroll by.

SAGITTARIUS—Regardez le walk boppy, ze cheerful-little-earful smile, ze love of things foreign. They walk as if they're wearing sneakers. There's a long, open face, clear eyes, a certain endearing clumsiness when they knock over the teacups. The nose is strong, long, and well formed. Sagittarius rising folks are more generous, trusting, and lucky than the rest of us. These sickening optimists appeal to everyone because of their happy-go-lucky approach to life. This leads them to take risks, so they get away with traffic violations, delicate border crossings, and messy bank balances. If they coast on this luck too long a subtle erosion of character can occur; too much "luck" isn't always lucky in the long haul. Recognize this rising sign from the chirpy, naïve, hopeful way they spout grandiose plans—they'll change these plans the way other mortals change the sheets, but they have a wonderful way of making many of their dreams come true. They love travel so passionately they frequently bump into things; they're accident-prone. Their secret peeve is not getting enough sympathy from others. They look so happy on the outside people forget to boost them up. It's Margaret Trudeau's rising sign. They can be a wee bit superficial.

CAPRICORN—Horrible posture, unless they work at it. There is usually a downcast look in the old goat's eye. Often these eyes were made beautiful through sadness; there was a tough, often downright rotten childhood they must rise beyond and forget. They played with the older kids and spent too much time with grown-ups. There's a big, beaky nose, a noticeable bump-bone on the wrist, pretty laugh lines round the mouth, and an annoying tendency to look more youthful and handsome with each passing year! Often they have a funny, vulnerable way of walking. They're racked with feelings of inferiority, suffer from melancholia, and may even have black-dog depressions. You wonder how they get through life in such a shambles. They look best in formal clothes, conservative, dark colors, but they don't seem to care much how they look. So you relax, and these ambitious schemers leap ahead to get the top honors, the best jobs, and your girl. Serves you right for judging a book by its cover, says Capricorn rising. Ari Onassis, Jean Paul Getty, and Billie Jean King have Capricorn rising. We all know who Clark Kent *really* is.

AQUARIUS—A cool, arm's-length kind of first impression they make, though they do try to display their eccentricities so you won't be bored. They're the best friends you could ask for, as they're more loyal and not as detached as they want you to think. Social and spiritual issues motivate them. This might make them superior to say the Scorpio rising type, who runs on lust and desire. Then again, Aquarius rising can sacrifice you or another loved one to a Higher Principle faster than you can open a new box of Cheerios. They're awfully psychic, and they like to think of themselves as the weirdos of the group, though they prefer to associate with archconservative people; it makes them feel more daring. In truth they are conventional in odd ways. Janis Joplin, Emmaline Pankhurst, Elisabeth Kubler-Ross, and Germaine Greer have Aquarius rising. Look for funny legs, a square jaw, and fine, wide eyebrows arched like MacDonald's. It's an even face, like Libra's, though not usually as prettified. The eyeballs themselves are a strange lopsided shape, which gives them the look of The Lost Children of Atlantis.

PISCES—Sweet and sour. Tender, brave, and cynical. It's a short body, inclined to *un bon pointe*. Their hair always looks invitingly mussed up, and here are the famous bedroom eyes of Raquel Welch and Princess Caroline of Monaco, both of whom have Pisces rising. These big bloopy eyes rank with Capricorn rising as the most gorgeous orbs of the zodiac. Pisces rising people look like fish-faces. These poetic, sneaky, imaginative, bright, dreamy, restless, sensitive people must be HIGHLY SELECTIVE in choosing environments and people; they soak up everything that goes on around them. Fortunately most of them are intuitive, and their insight helps them to avoid the sleaze. They can choose the wrong people and need to *check the facts*. They can be strong and brave enough to flow with God's plan; they can play victim and serve as ace martyrs; they're sharp con artists too. It's all in how they choose. Some of them are so unworldly they will swish around the department store until you find them the exit . . . but they can save your life.

Occult teachers say that we return to using the rising sign when we have fulfilled the purpose of our Sun signs. This usually does not occur until after the kids have grown and we've got time to muck about with nirvana. Then, say the sages, the Ascendant is your Ultimate Spiritual Path, and it has nothing to do with how you act at a cocktail party.

Those Shocking Squiggles in Your Chart: How to Read Them

Got squiggles in your chart? Those gizmos are the symbols for the planets. Learn them.

PLANETS

THE SUN. Rules the sign Leo. The most important planet in your chart, so always look at it first. It's who you are, and what you want to be, and what you're always struggling to improve. It represents major men in your life and how you express the "male" part of your psyche. No matter how hard it seems, do it big.

THE MOON. Rules the sign Cancer. It's shaped like a cup. Remember that. It shows what you receive from what you hear, the style in which you listen, so we call it the "female" part of your personality. It represents the important women in your life. Look at it second when you stare at a horoscope, for it shows what you need, what makes you comfortable, your emotional anchor. Do it and you'll calm down.

I know, I know; neither the Sun nor Moon are strictly planets, but astrology pretends they are. They look like pretty big deals to us on earth, and their influence on human affairs packs quite a wallop.

☿ MERCURY. Rules the signs Gemini and Virgo. It rules cold thinking and has no gender. It shows the style in which you speak, the rhythm of your thoughts (fast? slow? intuitive? superficial? practical? vague?) and indicates what your mind is really on when you gaze out of the window.

♀ VENUS. Rules the signs Taurus and Libra. Venus is, natch, female and shows your capacity for love and that feeling of contentment. It's fun, lazy, artistic, pretty, self-indulgent and always shows what turns you on—it's the receptive part of sex, how you respond to come-ons, the type of sensuality you have, and your style of expressing it. It shows your taste in women, sex, music, and clothes.

♂ MARS. Rules the signs Aries and Scorpio. It's pretty damned aggressive, this hunk of rock. It's masculine, pushy, and shows what kind of temper you have and how you get angry. It's the active, pursuing part of the sex drive; how much you drive and where you're driving is what Mars shows, gang-busters with zeal, impulsiveness, and enthusiasm. Where you leap before you look, and in which ways you are fearless.

♃ JUPITER. Rules the signs Sagittarius and Pisces. Look at the shape of this squiggle and then think of doctors shouting "Fore!" on the golf course, goofing off. Like Venus it is also fun, but it's a more rollicking generous fun. Jupiter is the planet of mercy, and it makes you lucky because you're not afraid to show what you enjoy. You like to give and in so doing get back so much more; trust and your trust is rewarded.

♄ SATURN. Rules the signs Capricorn and Aquarius. Grab it out of the chart right after you've looked at the Sun and the Moon. Saturn is where you're terrified . . . and ambitious. You want the very best, but you're afraid to go for it. You'll find ignorance and pain here, but this sucker gets luckier as you get older. It looks like a five; think of the fingers on your hand. Put those fingers to work and overcome that hopeless feeling of inadequacy. *If you work,* this planet becomes the wisest, most beautiful part of your personality.

♅ URANUS rules the sign Aquarius. Certainly it is an odd symbol. It looks like it would hurt if you stepped on it in the middle of the night. Think of it as a television aerial—

it has to do with all those rebellious, modern attitudes and achievements. Behind its off-beat facade you will always find someone thinking for themselves in a highly original manner. I have it in the sixth house of food. Once I asked my mother why the spinach she cooked always tasted gritty.

"Oh, that's the *iron* in it," said Mama, who had a master's degree in education.

I always feel safer eating in restaurants. TV dinners hold a certain nostalgic appeal.

NEPTUNE. It rules Pisces. Pitchfork power! Count on Neptune to make a clear issue vague. It's the planet of Rashomon, where all viewpoints are valid and no one opinion is the whole truth. It is the principle, too, of *ambivalence*. There will be one section in your chart where you will refuse to pin yourself down to one limiting point of view. It makes you *fascinated* with the house it's in, and through this delightfully addicting activity you can psychically merge with the *Zeitgeist*.

PLUTO rules Scorpio. Maybe it has something to do with ruling Aries too. Scorpios don't feel that way. They're jealous and want Pluto all to themselves; why, I'll never know. The introspective Aries types *do* transform themselves, getting rid of the garbage within, which is what Pluto is all about. The computer uses the P symbol, which stands for Percival Lowell, Pluto's discoverer. Astrologers prefer the other one, as it looks like a mushroom cloud. This baby gives you a lot of power, and it'll backfire on you if you're not wise. The house it's in is intense, or you don't play ball.

CHIRON. Its symbol is a key. They just discovered it. Do you hear yelling and screaming in the background? Those are the fuddy-duddies who don't believe it's a major planet. It is. Try it in your chart sometime and see what happens when it rolls over one of your stars. Meantime, use Al H. Morrison's dictum: "It breaks up an impasse situation or a stalemate. Hard lessons, but it's an inconvenient benefic. It always brings about a better situation afterwards." Let's hope so.

These next three aren't planets, but you may find them on your computer chart:

NORTH NODE OF THE MOON. This looks like a croquet wicket and shows you the lucky stuff to do and the best people for you. Like blueberry yogurt, it's delightful and good for you too.

SOUTH NODE OF THE MOON. It may not be on your computer chart, but its location is exactly opposite the North Node. Here is the real garbage bag of your chart. You have to look after it, but do it too much or mess with people on this point, and it all begins to reek. It's your line of least resistance.

PART OF FORTUNE. This too is a mathematical point, the ratio/blend of the Sun and Moon. It's lucky. You yearn for this stuff, and you do it well. You shine here.

Other horrors:

Uranian planets, planetary nodes, fixed stars, "unseen" planets like TransPluto, Pan, and Midas all have validity and add great dimension in interpreting a chart, but they're a pain in the ass if you're just beginning to learn astrology.

Not too many clients come in with questions on how to develop their telepathic powers, for which you would then look at their asteroids. Most clients want to know when they'll get laid, when to ask the boss for a raise, or when to sell their house. The "normal" planets will do for work of this ilk. Picasso did not need complicated tools to ply his art.

On the other hand these weird "extras" can clear up a specific question—they're fast and accurate.

Perhaps the happiest scheme is to spend the first 150 years studying the basic planets in the basic chart. *If you become an expert at understanding human nature and you truly have the measure of your client through understanding his natal chart, your predictions will gain an outstanding accuracy because you have guessed which way a particular person will jump when confronted with Stimulus X or Y or Z.*

Don't glop up your chart with extras when you don't have to. It looks a mess as it is.

That said, we'll have a fast swoop round the asteroid belt. These little suckers are *hot.* You can get information about where they are by ordering ephemerides for them. Write to CAO Times, Box 75, Old Chelsea Station, New York, N.Y. 10113 for information.

I've included the asteroids because they represent a break-through for professional astrologers. Each asteroid delineates a specific function, and we soothsayers are still learning about how they work and what they mean, so don't take these interpretations as gospel. These baby 'roids just started to get their own little ephemerides. Thanks are due to Mr. Brian G. Marsden, director of the Smithsonian Institute Astrophysical Observatory in Cambridge, Massachusetts; he was kind enough to make the orbits of these asteroids available to astrologers.

Out in the miserable snow are the "unseen" and "Uranian" planets. They do work in charts, but God only knows why. Take a photograph of the night sky and you won't find an "unseen" planet—they don't exist in physical form. Look for them if you want to! They ain't there. Their symbols are hard to draw. The symbols for the asteroids, below, are crawly enough.

ASTEROIDS

TORO. "Here's the bull in the China shop," says Al H. Morrison. "They have the knack of presenting themselves forcefully and consistently. Think of Roman soldiers. It doesn't occur to them anything's being destroyed." He's got a bizarre orbit. Toro goes round the earth for a while, then switches orbits to go round the Sun, then jumps to orbit round Venus. He's a three-timer, the only 'roid to act so outrageously. He stands for *blind pushiness*.

PSYCHE. If you have Psyche on somebody else's whatsis, you can read them like a book. Psyche seems to have little to do with events and everything to do with trauma in predictive work. It deals with the realm of telepathy known as *scrying*. Aw, go on . . . look it up.

HIDALGO. Go ahead. Go for broke. Unthinking, natural courage.

EROS. The smitten heart. If her Eros is on your whatsis, look out! Troo love funnies time. Bubbles forever.

ICARUS. Back to Al H. Morrison again: "Abrupt triumph and downfall. Like running into a pothole the size of a delivery van." It ascended at Pearl Harbor.

SAPPHO. Says Al: "Utter existentialist passion. Sharp like a more compressed Pluto. Being very explic Destiny. Deep intent."

URANIA. Al says: "Literal accuracy. Disgarding the ne essentials. Precision." We astrologers are hoping it m have some correlation with the ability to be an astrolog but the studies aren't in yet. Urania has to do with getti things right the first time, trying to understand the *cause* any matter.

PANDORA. "Where you make your magic and yo mischief," says Al. Dr. Lee Lehman finds it a rath sexy asteroid in the cases she's observed.

AMOR. Makes you friendly and amiable, eas going.

 LILLITH. Not to be confused with that other horror t "dark moon Lillith," which does not exist. I wonder wh astrologers of the old fogey school, especially in Englan use Lillith, especially as it does not exist and only brings b news. This Lillith is a real dead chunk of asteroid rock. symbol is a hayfork, poking you in the ass. Al says Lilli is "persnickety, jealous, territorial, teasing, capricious, wit holding—now you can have it, now you can't." Sounds li my landlord.

 **PALLAS.** Eleanor Bach writes in her ephemeris of t four asteroids, Pallas, Juno, Vesta, and Ceres: "Pall Athene sprang fully armed from Zeus' head." Nice lad that Pallas! She always wants to bring peace, so she starts o with war; *Pallas has the means to bring peace.* Pallas promine in your chart gives you highly developed political skills.

VESTA. A workaholic, and often a celibate. I gue the work is a compensation. Eleanor Bach says th when Vesta goes over a sensitive point in yo chart, you get insecure in a relationship and may turn off for little while to see if your sugar-poo still loves you without th sex. Be patient—it's a quick transit.

✳ **JUNO.** Helpless feelings. You can get away with it, too. If you have it in the third house, the car box, you can bat your lashes at the traffic cop and apologize in a foreign language. He'll more often than not let you go with a warning.

⌑ **CERES.** This one will always protect you, but too much can be smothering. It can keep you from accepting new ideas or changing yourself psychologically. It has a motherly influence—kind and nurturing and comforting.

Aren't these little 'roids cute? They're driving the professional astrologers crazy. We're a lazy lot. The technology boom keeps turning up new data, new 'roids, comets, sunspots, and research findings. It's a lot to keep up with. There are two kinds of astrologers: fuddy-duddies who stick to what they know and manic-depressives who live continually curious and clobbered by the boom in astrological discovery. Does your astrologer subscribe to the latest journals? Has he or she heard of Chiron? Does your astrologer have insomnia, worry about not knowing enough, use the Void of Course Moon, and have a nervous facial tic? These are sure signs that you have the right astrologer. He or she may live on the brink of insanity trying to assimilate the latest data, but this is the price an astrologer pays for being topnotch. Would you feel comfortable with a doctor who'd never heard of interferon?

Rulers: They Make the Horoscope Hang Together

Rulers are things that help you to read a chart in depth. The rul of Exxon is gasoline; the ruler of Kraft is cheese. A ruler is t symbol of the energy of a zodiac sign.

Mars—rules Aries and Scorpio
Venus—rules Taurus and Libra
Mercury—rules Gemini and Virgo
The Moon—rules Cancer
The Sun—rules Leo
Pluto—rules Scorpio
Jupiter—rules Sagittarius and Pisces
Saturn—rules Capricorn and Aquarius
Uranus—rules Aquarius
Neptune—rules Pisces
Chiron—we don't know yet what sign, if any, it rules.

Why do some signs get two rulers, others only one? Unt Uranus was discovered astrologers only knew about five plane plus the Sun and the Moon. The twelve zodiac signs had to share When Uranus, Neptune, and Pluto came along, astrologe observed them in charts and eventually assigned them to the proper signs. Oddly, the old rulers still work too. That is wh there are two sorts of Aquarians—fuddy-duddy, careful, conse vative Saturn types and Uranian freako types; there are two sor of Scorpios, too—the pugnacious, trouble types and the one involved in inner work and psychology. And there are two sor of Pisceans. One type is the *bon vivant* philanthropist, and the other type is more introverted, mystical, and escapist.

With better telescopes, "blink microscopes," and scanners, more planets are bound to come rolling along, changing the rulerships of the signs ruled by Venus and Mercury.

Let's look at Evel Knievel, the stunt man. We can use the "rulers" to understand his horoscope.

Find the money box, the slice of pie marked 2. The symbol for Sagittarius is on the cusp. Evel Knievel makes money by taking risks, and by travel. The ruler of Sagittarius is Jupiter, and Jupiter is in the slice of pie marked 3. Thus in his chart the money box and the movement/communication box are connected. Media coverage helps him make his money. Cars, motorbikes, and movement are all third house activities; they make him money. He could write a hundred different books, and they'd all bring him money, too. The third house has to do with writing.

Jupiter is the planet to watch in Evel's chart whenever we want to know about how he makes his money.

When we want to predict the times when he will make more money, or when he will have to watch his budget, we look at where the planets are in the sky now to see if any of them is making an angle to that Jupiter. Saturn making an angle to his Jupiter will slow the money down; Jupiter hitting it will bring in a Big Deal!

Back to his basic chart, we look at the angles other planets made to his Jupiter when he was born. There are plenty of planets hitting Jupiter. He has many ways of making good dough.

```
PLANET SIGN  LONG  HSE
SUN  F Lib 17 44 14 11
MOON E Tau 16 56  5  6
MERC   Lib 18 39.4   11
VENU D Scp 28 50.7   12
MARS   Vir 21 27.5   10
JUPI   Aqu 22 29.2R   3
SATU F Ari 14 20.9R   5
URAN F Tau 16 54.3R   6
NEPT D Vir 21 52.4   10
PLUT   Leo  1 24.5    9
ASC    Scp 29 34.9    1
MC     Vir 18 41.9   10
NODE*  Scp 17 57.3   12
PFOR   Gem 28 46.8
VERTEX Can 12 32.5
EASTPT Sag 20 27.1
R=RULE    D=DETRIMENT
E=EXALTED F=FALL
  *TRUE NODE
```

```
     CARD FIX MUT
FIRE  1   1   0      5 | 1
EARTH 0   2   2        |
AIR   2   1   0      1 | 3
WATER 0   1   0        |
```

*** NATAL ASPECTS ***

	ANGLE	ORB		ANGLE	ORB
CON=CONJUNCTION	0	10	TRI=TRINE	120	10
SSX=SEMISEXTILE	30	3	SQQ=SESQUIQUAD	135	4
SSQ=SEMI-SQUARE	45	4	BQT=BIQUINTILE	144	3
SXT=SEXTILE	60	6	QCX=QUINCUNX	150	3
QTL=QUINTILE	72	3	OPP=OPPOSITION	180	10
SQR=SQUARE	90	10	/ =PARALLEL OR	0	1

A=APPLYING   S=SEPARATING   CONTRAPARALLEL

	SUN	MOON	MERCURY	VENUS	MARS	JUPITER
MOON	QCX 0 48A	MOON				
MERC	CON 0/55S	QCX 1 43A	MERCURY			
VENU	SSQ 3 54S			VENUS		
MARS		TRI 4 31A	SSX 2 48A		MARS	
JUPI	TRI 4 45A	SQR 5 33A	TRI 3 50A	SQR 6 21S	QCX 1 02A	JUPITER
SATU	OPP 3 23S	SSX 2 35S	OPP 4 19S	SQQ 0 30A		
URAN	QCX 0 50S	CON 0/02S	QCX 1 45S		TRI 4 33S	SQR 5 35S
NEPT		TRI 4 56A			CON 0/25A	QCX 0 37A
PLUT		QTL 2 28A		TRI 2 34A		
ASC	SSQ 3 09			CON 0 44		SQR 7 06
MC	SSX 0 58	TRI 1 46	SSX 0 02	QTL 1 51	CON 2/46	
NODE	SSX 0 13	OPP 1 01	SSX 0 42		SXT 3 30	SQR 4 32

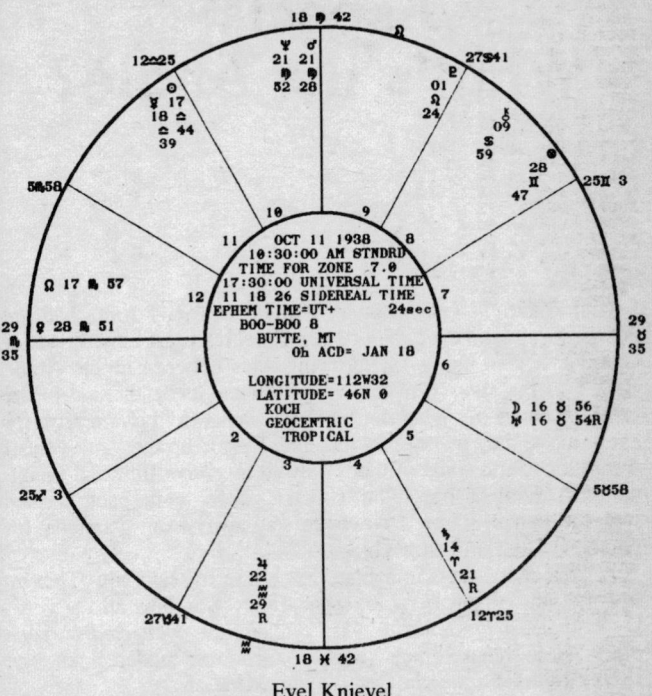

Evel Knievel

	SATURN	URANUS	NEPTUNE		PLUTO		ASC		MC
SATURN	SSX 2 33S								
URANUS		TRI 4 58S							
		QTL 2 30S							
NEPTUNE	SQQ 0 14				TRI 1 50				
PLUTO		TRI 1 48	CON 3/11	SSQ 2 17		QTL 1 07			
ASC	BQT 2 24	OPP 1 03	SXT 3 55					SXT 0 45	

Aspects:
What's the Angle?

I would have *flunked* geometry if my best friend Anita had not coached me. And even then I got a C, which must have stood for Charity. It was 'no sweat' drawing lines between points A and B; it was the *rules* that drove my thirteen-year-old mind to the brink of madness. What double Aries wants to give a reason for every move they make? Not this one. I made up the "rules" as I went along, and some of them showed inventive flair and imagination to rival Disney's, but still the papers came back slashed with red pencil marks. I vowed to stay away from geometry for good. So I became an astrologer.

Angles and aspects in a chart don't have to scare you. They're like the guts of an old radio; aspects show you how all the wires hook up. *Aspects tell you what planets are connected to each other.* How much voltage, loose connections, hidden links, and short circuits are the stuff aspects are made of.

Look at the terrifying grid below your computer chart. It's that boring stepladder thing that has the word SUN on top of the first column and all the other planets listed underneath. This wonderful grid saves you measuring the angles between all the planets. The computer has already done all the work.

We're not going into aspects much in this book, but the basics aren't hard to understand. You need to know how your own wires hook up. If you want to find out what makes you tick, study the aspects between your planets.

In the old days astrologers called the tough aspects "bad" and let it go at that. Better luck next life!

Modern astrologers say there are no "bad" or "good" aspects—it is all psychological. They let it go at that.

I say the "bad" aspects are the best friends you will ever have in your chart. The "bad" aspects are good. The "good" aspects are good, too, but they make you smug and boring to be around. The bad aspects are interesting.

The "bad" aspects are: squares, quincunxs, oppositions.
The "good" aspects are: trines, sextiles.

> CONJUNCTION—0 degrees apart
> SEMI-SEXTILE—30 degrees apart
> SEXTILE—60 degrees apart
> QUINTILE—72 degrees apart
> SQUARE—90 degrees apart
> TRINE—120 degrees apart
> QUINCUNX—150 degrees apart
> OPPOSITION—180 degrees apart

The conjunction is like locking two strangers up in a stalled elevator for a lifetime. Some planets get along on top of each other, and others don't. They're "good" and "bad," depending on which planets are stuck in the elevator.

The weird aspects are: semi-sextiles, quintiles, reptiles, bathroomtiles, sesquiquadrates, and Rob Hand's favorite, futiles. You don't have to bother with them in *this* book . . . let your astrology teacher explain them to you.

You can look for hook-ups between planets just by running your finger round the chart. Let's say you are looking for angles to the Sun. Look at the degree of the Sun in your chart. Say it's 24 degrees Scorpio. Now run your finger round the other planets and see where you find other 24s. If there aren't any 24s, try for 23s and 25s. With the Sun you have a leeway of, say, ten or twelve degrees either way. Which brings us to the old astrological hot-potato called *Orbs*.

Orbs. Astrologers fight like rabid dogs over how much "orb" or leeway to give a planet when it makes an aspect to another planet. If the Sun is 24 degrees Scorpio and Uranus is 24 degrees Pisces you have an *exact* trine. If Uranus is 23 degrees Pisces you have a *close* trine. How many degrees away from a perfect 120-degree angle can you have before it isn't a trine any more? Might as well ask how many angels dance on the head of a pin.

I prefer to give the Sun and Moon and Jupiter and Saturn an extra couple of degrees than most astrologers would give. If there's a talent or a trauma hanging about on the outskirts, say I, *reach for it*.

Here's the standard list of orbs for the aspects:

Conjunction, square, trine, opposition, 10 degrees.
Sextiles, 6 degrees.
Quincunxes, 3 degrees.

"I go for tight orbs, myself," says my 24 degrees Scorpio astrologer.

ASPECTS

Ready for the aspects? Let's go:

CONJUNCTION. Its symbol looks like a fizzing bomb, ready to go off at any moment. Conjunctions are *pure power*. It also looks like a Tootsie-Roll lollipop—strong, and always with a surprise in the center! Remember those strangers locked in the lift. Mars, the male planet, and the female planet, Venus, in conjunction get on fine together. But try locking the planet of craziness, Uranus, with the planet of love, Venus. Or the planet of fear, Saturn, with the planet of guilt, Neptune. Fun, isn't it? Not if you were *born* with these gems, sweetheart.

TRINE. A Great Pyramid, a super-lucky gift. You have talent here from other lives if you believe in that sort of thing. If you don't believe, you've still got the talent. You feel peaceful about this stuff. You blend these two planets easily. Say your talker, Mercury, is trine Saturn, planet of wisdom. You talk as if you had a lot of common sense. You take your talent for granted and you think it's nothing special, but other people admire you for it. You can use this stuff to make you lucky. You don't, because it bores you. You'd rather do your "bad" aspects.

SEXTILE. Like the trine, but you have to push it a little. Here are opportunities for you. These things make you grow and sparkle. They look like snowflakes. Like snowflakes, these aspects show ways in which you are unique.

☐ **SQUARE.** They say it is self-defeating, and if "they" are the ones who are always following us down shadowy streets, lurking around corners, spying on us, and snickering into their hats, "they" are right—squares make you *paranoid*. You try to squoosh one planet in favor of the other—repress, repress, repress! You *exaggerate* the two planets in a square and gross everybody out. You don't care, but you should, because you'll stab yourself in the back every time until you learn to use this aspect with kindness, not cruelty. You don't want to see how cruel you're being to other people and yourself. There's a war going on inside you between two conflicting urges. Don't try blending them. Do one, then the other. There is no hope of *not* exaggerating a square, so play it to the hilt, but do it with kindness. A man may have Mars square Saturn and be terrified he's not sexy and strong enough, so he shafts his friends and treats women like tissues; or he works hard to be a better, less-selfish lover to his one woman and works hard to let his friends know they can count on him for loyalty. Which is the real definition of a man?

⟍ **QUINCUNX.** A stick figure with no head, and no wonder! It's not the big things that drive you round the bend. It's the insidious thoughts, little guilts, the niggling loose ends of daily living that make you burst out crying when the shoelace snaps in your hands. The quincunx is an annoying aspect. It's unpronounceable for a start. You never feel satisfied with the way things are. You're always improving upon things.

Keep it to yourself, for the tendency is to project your annoyance onto others, *blaming them for your own imperfections*. You feel obliged to do things for others. Then you wind up feeling hurt when they let you down or resentful when they make a reasonable request. Niggling compulsions and delusions of persecution show up with the quincunx. The bores are perennial malcontents; they live with irreconcilable paradoxes.

Refined star-trippers learn to enjoy their subtle personalities. They ride life's bumps like master sailors, learning to shift and tack with the changing wind. A quincunx is a delicate gyroscope; at your best you can detect subtle shifts in the atmosphere, in world events, and in your loved ones. You then make the thoughtful adjustments in your own behavior to flow with the changes and behold the paradoxes with a chuckle.

OPPOSITION. Lifting barbells requires practice and a sense of balance. It makes you strong.

If you have an opposition in your chart you're a complex character. You seesaw between two extremes. Your friends are snobs or guttersnipes. Some years you're hardworking; other years you'd rather just pick your nose. You can have fun with this kind of stress because you can choose which end of the teeter-totter you want to ride on. When you're at your best you see both sides of an issue; the opposition will give you a bird's eye view of life, but not without considerable soul-searching! In this way you will develop depth, if not always inner peace.

Often we get stuck in one end of the opposition, so we choose associates who symbolize the other point of view. Say, for example, your name is Duncan, and women play you for a yo-yo. You have Venus, the love planet, opposite Uranus, the freedom planet. You fall in love with an airline stewardess; she is always leaving you, and you're miserable about it.

Duncan is playing Venus now, and his girl symbolizes Uranus. Maybe Duncan had an on-again, off-again relationship with his mother, so he unconsciously seeks cold girls. Maybe he fears intimacy, or he simply doesn't know how to be close. When he plays Uranus, he leaves other girls behind. Maybe Duncan's a good guy who picks weirdos, or he's a bad guy who pretends to get close and then rips away. But Duncan's smart. He picked an airline stewardess to fall in love with, so he can satisfy his opposing urges for snuggles and space. The chances are with an opposition that you *do* pick weirdos to give balance to your life. Just try not to get stuck in one end of your opposition.

Why are the "bad" aspects good? Let's look at Vanessa Redgrave's chart. Her Sun sign is Aquarius, and it makes a square to Uranus. We've a rebel on our hands here, a trouble-maker for sure, maybe even a crazy maniac, but as an actress she is a genius. Why did the good Lord put Vanessa on this earth? To be a sweet acquiescent piece of empty-headed Hollywood cheese-cake? Hell, no. God in her puzzling wisdom put her here to shock the baloney out of people, to *make us think*. She's here to raise hell. Her chart is in the Uranus section.

The trouble with squares is that you overdo them, and they always boomerang back on you. The square means you exaggerate a quality, and if you do it all over people by being too tactless or bizarre or manipulating or dictatorial or inconsiderate, you'll get a reaction. A kick in the teeth, perhaps? Fortunately squares have a built-in safety valve. When you push too far you get your teeth shoved down your throat. My girlfriend's husband has Venus square Pluto. He is so afraid she is more competent than he is, so terrified that she might leave him, that he "tests" her. He is a cruel tyrant in his home. He wants to feel in control all the time. In truth he wants passion and depth, but his petty undermining is starting to boomerang on him. She is becoming more independent of him by the day. She loves him, but putting up with torture won't prove it.

Search your chart for the "*hard angles*" first. The hard angles are conjunctions, squares, and oppositions. These are your outstanding characteristics.

Youngsters use their hard angles differently from the ways older folks use theirs. The teenage heartbreaker (Venus opposite Saturn) who dumps the football captain becomes a wise woman; cruelty sickens her. She grows to be loyal and learns that love is patient. The little dumb boy at school who can't do arithmetic (Mercury conjunct Saturn) grows up hollering, "E = MC squared!"

Here is the joy in astrology. Nothing is more awesome than the continuing proof that people's worst aspects can become their most beautiful characteristics.

Not everybody manages it; easy, it ain't. If you manage to turn a scar into a star you can light the way for everyone around you; hard angles make it possible. *You can have it if you want it badly enough.*

Retrogrades

If you see an Rx on your chart, the little planet isn't feeling well. It needs medicine.

We call a planet retrograde when it looks as if the planet is going *backward* in its orbit. The truth is that no planet goes bass-ackward in its orbit ever, but astrology is mostly concerned with what things look like from our perch on earth. During the year, different planets appear to backtrack for a few weeks or months. There isn't a damned thing anyone can do about it, either.

Backward is beautiful if you are willing to work at pulling out the real subtlety and depth of a retro planet in your chart. It shows an area in your character and upbringing where you're a bit bottled up, so you act with caution and reticence. In a refined character, reticence is often the wisest way of buying yourself extra time to choose which way to behave. People with retrograde planets usually have this subtlety and intelligence at their command, but they see more choices and more complexity in everyday situations. At one extreme is self-absorption and crippling shyness—at the other extreme is the wondrous ability to see the universe in a grain of sand.

The Sun and Moon never look backward to us on earth. They are never retrograde in a chart.

Mercury Rx shows a person who is more concerned with motive than plot. When these people go to the movies, they don't seem to be able to keep track of what side all the spies are on. They do notice the shaking hand of the man in the dark brown overcoat; he was supposed to be relaxed.

Everyday paper work is too much already for the Mercury retro gang; note their grateful sighs if you offer to make a couple of difficult phone calls for them or to help them with their tax forms. God created travel agents to ease their strain in dealing with the real world.

Different they are, but they ain't dumb. Dr. Jonas Salk, Ralph Nader, Arthur Miller, Mae West, Carl Sandburg, Frederic Chopin, and Ben Franklin were all born with Mercury retrograde. It gives the gift of digging deep, whether in research or in creative invention. Some folks born with this position are shy and even feel guilty about talking about how they feel. They do a considerable amount of their own thinking.

Venus Rx people sometimes do not know what they are feeling. The world of people and ideas is their first love. They don't value "things" much, though often there is a silent, almost fervent love of art. They resent giving presents, but do they give you experiences! They'll take you on trips abroad, to the theater, sightseeing, and you can bring your friends too. They go to extremes helping their fellow man because they don't know when to quit, then recoil, hurt, when people take advantage of their largesse. "You can't trust other people" is what they believe, and this goes a long way to explaining their cynicism towards expressing love and affection. Often the mother has an odd attitude and makes the Venus Rx person mistrust people and look for hidden motives; Venus Rx people expect women to fall short of the mark in personal relationships and treat them that way.

At its nicest, Venus Rx is a loyal style of loving, a sort of New Englandy, repressed type of relationship where a "Yep" substitutes for flamboyant declarations of love. Often these odd souls do not even know themselves how deeply their love runs until it is too late. At its worst, Venus Rx is like old Uncle George, whose kid came up to him one day and chirped, "Gosh, I really love you, Dad." Uncle George grinned. He looked at his son. "What's the angle, kid," he said. "You need a loan or something?"

Many of the world's best and worst humanitarians with Venus Rx: Winston Churchill, Yoko Ono, Adolf Hitler, Lizzie Borden, and the brilliant analyst, Alfred Adler.

Now Mars Rx folks have no little anxiety when it comes to expressing anger. They're terrified to stand up for themselves in open confrontation. They first try denying rage; they often turn it in on themselves, so they get depressed or sprout aches and pains. Obviously bottling up hurts or taking sly pokes at people from behind the bushes poisons relationships, but Mars Rx is thoughtful and introverted, and this gang needs time to discover their anger. They must get rid of the red demons *at the time they feel it,* not later.

Any retrograde planet makes you think more deeply about the stuff the planet represents. Mars retro people feel the clean outrage at the suffering caused by people's thoughtless anger, so they try not to use their anger; look out when they let it rip! The classiest Mars Rx produces an apt, mordant wit, a controlled rebelliousness, and a master strategist—especially for social causes. You will have to force them to fight, something I wouldn't recommend unless you like losing to a shrewd, relentless opponent. Nina Simone, Philip Roth, Nicolai Gogol, Betty Ford, Carol Burnett, Clark Gable, Jascha Heifetz, James Beard, and Rocky Marciano were all born with it.

Retro means complicated. You can be dramatically extreme in one opinion, then swing drastically the other way on that same issue, given enough proof and a little time!

The other planets retrograde aren't what we call *personal* planets, like Venus for love or Mars for war, but they are no less fascinating to watch if harder to define.

Jupiter retrograde people make their own luck; if they're born with privilege, they go out searching for life's meaning. Some of them are lazy; some of them believe charity begins at home; some of them make their own religions and ethics. The best of them enjoy a unique overview, preferring to enjoy life viewed from the balcony; it's inner things that matter to them, not the clothes on your back or the fine antiques in the window.

When grouchy old Saturn is retrograde, folks have a hard time protecting and defending themselves. They are morbidly sensitive, and the worst of them can shove off genuine aid. Tip-top Saturn Rx gives a thoughtful person profundity; they need to be alone a little bit every day to ponder. Once they make a stand on any issue, they won't back down even if their lives are at stake.

Uranus Rx people are subtle in the way they undermine everyday routine with their conservative act—and it's an act. Peep through their keyholes and you'll see one with a teakettle on his head, dancing the hootchy-kootchy in blue and yellow knickerbockers. Never in public!

When kindly Neptune is retrograde, there is a rich inner life. Here is the man with the fantasy lover, or the psychiatrists' joy—a patient with an endless stream of symbolic dreams. They're dreadful at concealing things or deceiving people—their hearts aren't in it, but they're shaky on reality testing. Let's hope they have a slew of commonsense friends and advisers. Neptune Rx ever knows where the "line" begins and ends. It's great if you want to be a mystic, but not in the subway car. Too many vibes!

Look to your routines when you encounter a person with Pluto etro; run like hell unless you want your life to change. Then again, hang about . . . the change may do you good. Depends on what the Pluto Rx person wants—if they want you to marry them, all right, but they may be the sorts to send you off to war. Astrologer John McCormick studied the charts of the World War I generals: they *all* had Pluto Rx! Here the Rx can dull the senses; these people bring drastic change in your life, and they do not realize until much later what they have done, for good or ill. Often there is a noble dedication to serving people, without realizing how many wonderful differences they've made in people's lives.

All retrograde positions make you hesitant and at best refined. It gives *class,* bustah!

Fire Signs, Air Signs, Jell-o and Dirt Signs— Elements and Qualities

ELEMENTS AND QUALITIES

Fire signs, air signs, jell-o and dirt signs—that's how the zodia is divided, into The Four Elements.

FIRE SIGNS

There's something terribly noble about fire signs, or ther should be.They're extroverted, enthusiastic and strike an upbea note. You can usually spot fire in a person by the twinkle in thei eyes. Fire is the symbol of warmth and spirit. Fire is chivalrous it has a code of honor. These folks heat you up with thei energy. They're self-centered, and may not be aware of othe folks' shyness in the social situations that fire signs handle s easily. Aries, Leo, and Sagittarius.

EARTH SIGNS

You get a feeling of practical, brass-tacks realism around earth sign people. They know how to get from A to B. These are the take-charge people, who get things done without fuss or bluster You can count on them when the chickens hit the fan. They wan to be comfortable with their surroundings. Earth signs want to feel useful. They care about how others see them so they tend to have a conventional, conservative attitude. Even wild, hard-drinking Janis Joplin, a Capricorn, wanted badly to be accepted by other people; it gave her the drive to become famous. They're introverts. Taurus, Virgo, and Capricorn.

WATER SIGNS

Look for a juicy quality to one of the lips, a baggy or come-hither cast to the eyes. Water signs are comforting, if moody, to be around. Often they try to hide their feelings, as they are impressionable and sensitive. Water signs *understand* and *feel*; they have strong intuition. They tend to cling to people and situations. Astrologer Bob Pike says that water sign men suffer most in Western society; they often feel out of place with their feminine sensitivities and hide them by attempting to become more "macho," as did Ernest Hemingway, a Cancer. They're introverts too. Cancer, Scorpio, Pisces.

AIR SIGNS

How cool they are, these intellectuals . . . they have the distinct edge in social gatherings because they're friendly and have the light touch with people. Look for even features and a bland courtesy. Logic is their most valuable asset; they don't get caught up in the soup of your emotional whirlpools, hence, they make the best advisers. It's amazing how *reasonable* these folks can be. They're social and extroverted. The only fly in the ointment is that they tend to intellectualize feelings instead of experiencing them. Gemini, Libra, and Aquarius.

Another way of grouping the zodiac signs is by Qualities.

CARDINAL SIGNS

Pushy people, good at starting things and getting out of ruts. Aries leaps up and yells, "Come on!" Cancer fusses and frets and feeds and fixes you up; Libra initiates social arrangements and brings people together with each other and with ideas; Capricorn organizes quietly and gets the job done *right*.

FIXED SIGNS

Stubborn people, who will mind the store in the middle of a typhoon. They are rocks, and when they move, they're steamrollers of strength and power. Taurus provides stability; Leo is a loyal, loving ally; Scorpio can wait forever; Aquarius is the stubborn fanatic and will stick with a cockeyed ideal despite all appeals to reason.

MUTABLE SIGNS

Flexible people, they are actors and can push you, mind the store, or move with the breeze. They know how to adapt to situations; they know the strength of the tree when it bends in the wind. Geminis consider all viewpoints and run to and fro communicating messages; Virgos serve humanity with practical hard work tailored to the needs of the moment; Sagittarians travel and preach; Pisces understands everything and becomes, chameleonlike, a vehicle for everyone's needs.

Go back to your chart and play. See if your love planet is pushy, stubborn, or flexible. Do the same with the rest of the planets. Count up how many planets are in fire, earth, air and water.

If you're missing an element, learn to compensate for your lack. No-air people need to develop detachment. No-water people need to learn to be sensitive to other people's feelings. No-fire people need inspiration. No-earth people must learn to be practical.

Work at it, and your lack will spur you on to *overcompensation*; you can become superior at the traits you lack. Don't work at it, and your shortcomings will hold you back in all areas of your life. Remember Demosthenes learning to overcome his lisp with stones in his mouth. Remember, too, the price you pay for not facing your lacks. No-air people are intellectual *bores*. No-fire people have no enthusiasm or loyalty to give. No-water people think they'll make it big in the world hurting people's feelings. No-earth people can't get it together. It's not always what we do in life that spells the difference between success and failure. It's the unseen effects we have on other people that make us win or lose. *Astrology gives us the tools to see the back of our own heads*. Cover yourself. Be the best you can be.

How to Read a Chart in Less Than Five Minutes

We're not talking about all the trimmings and subtle nuances and conflicting urges that make up a human being, though you'll uncover a surprising number of these things with this method. This is the five-minute, yank-the guts-out method of chart analy-,sis. It's all you'll need to get at all the basic motivations of the person whose chart you're looking at.

1) Always look first at the Sun in the chart. This shows you what this soul is here to do in this life. They must do the *house* the Sun is in, or they'll never be happy. What *style* (sign) is it in?

2) In which direction are they pointing? What's their means of getting there? What's their veneer, the defense mechanism? *Look at the sign the rising sign is in* to see.

3) What planet or planets rule the rising sign? *What houses are they in?* They have to cultivate these areas if they're going to express themselves properly. You don't shine unless you do the house your ruler is in. Do it to the max!

4) What do they need? Where do they run when they get the blues? Check the Moon out, by house and by sign.

5) Finally, what scares the dickens out of them? Saturn will tell you, by house and by sign.

Part
II

The Planets and Other Celestial Bodies

The Moon—
the Things You
Can't Live Without

What do you need? What can you not live without? What is your emotional anchor?

The Moon in your chart shows this. No one can live without fulfilling their emotional needs. Until you fix your Moon, you cannot go on to become what you want to be in this lifetime—the Sun is the symbol for that.

We all need an anchor or we drift, uneasy and directionless. How can people work if they don't have enough to eat? How can anyone eat if they don't have anyone to love? How can you love if you find no joy in your work?

Most of us use the Moon in our charts too much. Then the Moon's a balloon—blown up out of proportion. It is a demanding child. It will try to take over your chart until you are using up most of your precious time wallowing in moody needs. It gets greedy and you can't quit. This grasping need does not promote your growing or your happiness any more than giving too many sweets to a child helps the kid to grow up strong. We have to set limits on our moons while we honor our needs.

Look up the sign the Moon was in when you were born in the RED LIGHTS, GREEN LIGHTS tables. If you have a computer chart, notice what slice of pie the Moon is in.

The sign the Moon is in shows the style in which you need things. Moon in Aries, for example, wants everything NOW. You can't wait to have your needs fulfilled.

The house the Moon is in shows the kind of stuff you need in the world. Moon in the fifth house needs love, needs to be original and creative, and needs to be a little childish. If you have an eleventh house Moon and no friends, you're in trouble. You won't be able to fulfill your goals in life unless the emotional side of your life is satisfied first.

In some cultures women are brought up to be like their Moons more than their Suns. This is part and parcel of that old if-you-want-the-man-to-buy-you-a-house-and-a-burro-you'd-better-shut-up-and-listen-to-the-old-bore goulash. Is this why the statistics are so staggering on depression in middle-aged, married, non-working women? A *big* chunk of an astrologer's work is taken up in encouraging our housewife sisters to bring out the house and sign of the Sun. When you live through your Moon you're swamped; you never get enough and always hunger for more. Eat, eat, eat!

Your Moon tells *how you view your mother,* and not surprisingly, it shows what you inherit from her or in reaction to her, in emotional ways. Was Mama a protected, precious little vulnerable thing? Hell no, but *you* saw that side of her if you have a Moon in Pisces.

It follows then that the Moon also shows those instinctive habits you formed in childhood in order to feel safe. *That's often the trouble!* You don't have to do those things to death now you're a grown-up.

What kinds of women do you admire? Should they stay home with the kids? That's Moon in Cancer for you. Should they get out and make sparkling conversation? Moon in Gemini.

Here is where men can trip themselves up. In a man's chart the Moon is his anima, his so-called "feminine" receptive side. In order to become more well-rounded, a man needs to act out his Moon. Now London men seem to have little trouble with the softer sides of themselves. Spoiled brats of New York, take heed! *Why* bother to explore the soft side of yourself? You get more girls that way. Or even *the* girl. You won't be looking for someone to play out the aching, desperately emotional side of yourself you've tried so hard to hide.

A hot tip, ladies: where is the Moon on your man's chart? This is what he is looking for in a woman. Whatever you may be, *he will project* what he is looking for onto you. If you love him enough and you have the stuff in your chart that resembles this archetype, *emphasize* these parts of your nature.

Example time. A man with the Moon in Pisces is forever seeking a woman who combines the highest attributes of a saint and a harlot. It will be easier for him to find her if he displays these qualities himself. Like attracts like. Uh, yes, I know, opposites attract too. What the hell. But not for long.

Reincarnation freaks, this is your turn. If you want to buy into the idea of reincarnation, the Moon shows the kind of person you were in those lives that influence the present life you're living now. The only argument I have with reincarnation is that it presupposes that time moves in a straight line of past-present-future. Einstein disproved that idea a few decades ago. Aren't you sick of insecure bimbos bragging about how important they used to be when they were the Queen of Araby, the witch of the glen, the cap on the tube of toothpaste? Eecchhh. It is spooky, we will grant, how often fire and air Moon signs show a predominantly *masculine* background, and water and earth Moons suggest more feminine experiences from the past. People will say, "Yes, I do feel I was a woman in past lives."

If you believe in time as a straightforward past-present-future arrangement, which I certainly do when I have to hop on a bus to get to an appointment, the idea of reincarnation is indeed fascinating. I don't believe in straight time much, however, when sitting in the desert gawping at the starry night sky.

And oh Lordy, the Moon even shows what *foods* you like to eat; do you have a hot and spicy Aries Moon, or do you like plain sensible Virgo Moon stodge?

Its symbol is a big cup, like a radar dish. The Moon shows how the world listens to you. The house your Moon is in shows where you will find your eager public.

When you're staring at a chart and want to know what somebody's ordinary, wake-up-and-smell-the-coffee everyday needs are, *cherchez la moon*! If you're depressed, do the things of the house and the sign that the Moon is in. The Moon tells you what feels comfortable for you to do.

"*Desire affects perception,*" writes Ram Dass in *Be Here Now*. The most staggering secret about your Moon sign is that it shows the style in which you listen, and the way you are likely to respond. Knowing this extra information about your customers, patients, lovers, and children gives you the most effective method of all for influencing people favorably—insight. It's worth brushing up on other people's Moon signs. Learning to *respond* to people's needs is the biggest secret of success. It makes the difference between strained, unhappy communications and caring, pleasant relationships.

What are we waiting for? If you have a computer chart, find

the house and the sign the Moon is in. If you don't yet have a proper chart, look up the sign of your Moon in the RED LIGHTS, GREEN LIGHTS tables.

MOON IN ARIES, MOON IN THE FIRST HOUSE

Where's the fire? Aries Moon knows. Usually he's already there, a box of matches in one hand and a fire extinguisher in the other. He may have started that blaze himself, as it happens. He knows how to finish it, too, with firecrackers and exploding, bomb-bursting extravaganza. This Moon position loves trouble. The loftier types love to rescue folks in trouble. It's a Girl and Boy Scout Moon.

Hair-trigger reaction time makes this gang unique. In fact these guys feel that *life itself* is an emergency; they aim to get the ever-loving most out of every moment. No one is so ready to go to war for a Noble Cause—every one of them is a potential chivalrous soldier. And if you are lucky enough to be their friend, they will even fight a noble war for you . . . again and again.

Passion cooks in these people. Men with this Moon like their women hot and sassy, then invariably want to *tame* them. If the poor woman won't be tamed, the Aries Moon man stumbles about in a befogged state of exasperation; if he does manage to subdue her, he gets bored!

Aries Moon women are male chauvinists too. They're surprised when you tell them they're competitive. According to one astrological sage, they secretly want the man to take charge while they shout, "No!" He's right. These women like to keep on a selection of male "buddies" to joke around with. They are deeply horrified when outsiders misconstrue these friendships, believing there's romance in them. This is the most naïve Moon of the bunch. It's a Pollyanna Moon.

They are horrible listeners because they're always waiting to butt in with their tuppence worth. They need to learn that people will like them more if they SLOW DOWN and RESPOND to what you said before they go racing on to the next idea.

Aries Moon does hear you, though. They just think fast. They don't know they're being rude.

It's easy to sell them something if you remember that *their deepest need is for you to like them*. So just act as if you won't like them if they don't buy. They know you're just spooking them, but it rattles them just the same. They feel with their egos and live in the future; they're brave and restless and always have heroes and villians.

Restless, Lordy, are they restless. Egocentric? They are self-centered beyond belief. They take everything personally. Have them stand alone on a building top or let them brag about how cool they are when they feel blue. They'll soon be cheerful again.

Oh, the fire? They know its true location is in the heart.

MOON IN TAURUS, MOON IN THE SECOND HOUSE

The second-best listeners of the zodiac. You can say absolutely anything. Beat on their chests and scream, "You brute! You brute!"—they take it all calmly and quietly. There is something about the way they listen, something *solid,* like talking to a brick wall.

If they are ever shocked, they don't show it much. Nothing in their manner has ever yet proved that they are shockable as far as I can see. They soothe you the way they listen.

Moon in Taurus folks handle Scorpios very well. They are great to go to for a good sob. They have shocking friends.

You can ruffle them, though. Take away their comforts and their money and their food. Let it bleed!

This is Reliable Roger, whom you can generally trust for a meal or a place to stay. They try to telephone around the time they said they would and have a good reason if they don't.

Common sense appeals to them, so sell them the practical side of what you are proposing. They need a base of operations or they're lost. Don't talk fancy to them. You are the man in the street, and you know they want results from what you are proposing. Give them a lot of information. Stress how much easier and more comfortable they will be when they feel more *secure*.

When they get bluesy they need to have their *things* around them. They go mad when their bodies aren't comfortable. They get attached to their stuff, and buying things cheers them up. They see the God in beautiful objects. If you're a guest in their house, try not to handle all their stuff. They hate that; it brings out the possessive streak in them.

Pry them out of the house with a can opener if you can. It is of little use getting them to come to you. Nearly always they, especially the older ones, want you to go to their house instead. One way to get them to come to you is if you send a car to pick them up and promise them a huge dinner. Mention the potatoes you're serving on the side. Taurus' symbol is not really a bull's head, it is a baked potato.

Most of them are money magnets. They learn quickly how to get it and how to hang onto it too. Somehow they always have plenty, although it's not ever enough for them.

They need to sing and show off their good voices. Touching is an important part of their life's pleasures. Cuddling is the other part.

MOON IN GEMINI, MOON IN THE THIRD HOUSE

Omigawd, do they ever stop learning? This specimen does not merely *understand* media. They *are* little radios which jabber, jabber, jabber all day long. It's comforting mostly. Radios are handy to take along with you, and when you feel worn out, you can tune out for a bit. When you tune back in, there they still are, chirping away at amazing speed, fierce and furious. They simply need to express themselves.

Is your jabberwocky pal depressed? Get your friend to talk about it. That's all these folks need to do; it makes them feel better straight away. Putting them in motion works. Pop them on a bus or a plane, or stick them in a car and drive round in different neighborhoods for awhile.

Want to sell them something, even yourself? Variety will get you everywhere. Change topics every ninety seconds, three minutes at the most. If yours is a long spiel, pop in a wee item of unrelated trivia every so often. Their high-speed minds need those commercial breaks. Good talkers impress them. You have to be pretty good to keep up with them, and if you're not glib, kick back and listen. They won't even notice.

Gemini Moon people need a daily paper, telephone calls, magazines, a chat with the lady next door; they love to be known in their own neighborhood, and they get friendly fast with the local shopkeepers. They like the television on, even with the sound turned off. The more aesthetic ones find comfort in non-stop music. Thy trash and thy trivia, it comforts them.

And what an ear for accents, buzz-words, slang! They like to be up-to-date on the newest in everything.

How about their *friends*, then? Here we witness the famous "flexible value system." This Moon position shows a constantly expanding curiosity about how other people live their lives. It enables them to count among their friends priggish pastors, porn moviemakers, bankers, winos, saints, poodle breeders, the complete boiling range of human society. This ability to travel lightly amongst all walks of life is unique to them.

They take a risk though. Some of the more superficial or unsavory values of their buddies may—and usually do—rub off on them. They're flexible as oily eels though, and they know to keep their traps shut when amongst their gangster buddies. This does not do a lot for their Spiritual Evolvement, but it does keep them out of concrete overcoats. Weirdo friends keep their lives *piquant*.

Teachers, talkers, and writers they are, every one of them. They come by it so naturally, they usually take these gifts for granted. It surprises them that these skills are so special.

Cruel gossips are numbered among this Moon position. They think they are merely being witty and interesting. Why then are they so cagey about telling you the minutiae of their own private lives?

They must learn to listen without adding their choicest bon mots to your story. They do have empathy, lots of it, for the other guy's predicament, but sometimes their harsh witticisms belie this. You can say one thing for them, though. They're never dull. And they will even befriend a bore if the bore has some free time and a car to ride around in.

MOON IN CANCER, MOON IN THE FOURTH HOUSE

Consider this wry tract from an advertisement in California:

"Do you enjoy petting your dog? Do you enjoy playing with your children? Do you have a marriage and not a 'relationship'? Then you belong to the Dull Men's Club."

And they're *swamped* with requests from women wanting to join. So far no dice. Men only. Their happy motto is "Out of it and proud of it."

This here is a wonderful Moon position, the best listener of the zodiac. While a Taurus Moon will eventually try to hush you up, the Moon in Cancer native lets you cry and cry and then says sweet profound true things to you. Weep and they jump. They really care about people and spring into action fast when you're in distress. "I'll fix it up," they say, and they do.

They make excellent shrinks and parents because they *let you be*. Of course there's a catch. You have to belong to them.

Letting go is not their big virtue. Most of them have hang-ups that stem from childhood attachments to one of the parents. The men in particular seem to suffer more from this attachment, usually to the mother. God help any woman in a Cancer Moon man's life if he had a rotten relationship with his mother! No one is meaner to his woman than the man with Moon in Cancer, and he won't let go of her, either. Do these men ever live to regret it!

Men with this Moon need to learn to stop being ashamed of their sentimental, clingy emotions. Both sexes are moody and wrestle with themselves to avoid becoming too babyish and needy. When they act too slushy, others can see them as drips. It's a fine line, but better slush than toughing it out with a crabby shell to protect the old emotions. Those emotions always get out somehow, anyway. Cancer Moon people have the best shot of the Moon signs at expressing their feelings, and they should.

It's a shame so many of them are rooted in habits and traditions from the past that prevent them from breaking free of fears into a happier state of being. They get so brainwashed in childhood that many exhibit an irrational, "Do it because I say so" mentality. A pity because they are the best equipped of all the Moons to clear up their problems. They get their feelings hurt quickly, acutely and honestly—instant pain, and with help, instant *release* from pain. A little sensible help can relieve them from carrying around lifetimes of grief baggage.

The attachment to the old ways has to be broken consciously. Otherwise the women pout, and the men turn their wives into mothers.

I suppose they hang on to hurts because even the hurt is a part of the person they love, and their love runs deep. Love never dies for them either, no matter how the beloved treats them.

Home and family mean the world to them. They need to belong somewhere. They need to have a safe feeling in their homes. Owning land makes them feel secure too. Food or a drink will always stabilize their wiggly feelings.

Before you feel too sorry for these tender, touchy folk, one caveat—they always set their lives up *just the way they want them*.

When selling to them, sell them security. They just hate to think of anyone being insecure. *Just be yourself*. It doesn't hurt to walk into their office tapping your white stick, however.

MOON IN LEO, MOON IN THE FIFTH HOUSE

"There's something very naked about the bath water if you don't put bubbles in it," says the woman with the Moon in Leo.

Big baby Leo Moons got big baby needs. This baby need love, need attention, need respect, need applause, need human beings laugh at jokes. Big baby Leo Moon need never to grow up, need lovely music, need lobster thermidor, need small parties, need favorite drinks to drink, need tall outrageous tall tales, need mate to wait on baby Moon when baby feel sick. Wait on hand and foot for baby Moon. Baby need to act pompous and aloof when pride hurt; big baby Leo Moon got lots of pride to get hurt. Need loyal pals go hell and back to show love for big baby Leo Moon. Big baby Leo Moon need all these things or baby curl up and die *right now*!!!

So why isn't this Moon position crazy about kids?

CHORUS: *Because they ARE kids!!!*

Thank you. It is a dramatic Moon, you know. Regal, too. They have a way of inspiring loyalty in their subjects.

They like to keep a little distance at first. If someone wants to develop an intimacy, it develops slowly. They can and do hit it off with people right away. Just be honest about yourself or anything you're trying to sell them. They can't abide tall tales. They tell a few themselves, you see. Hate to see it in other people.

When hard times come, do they ever know how to cheer themselves up! They don't exactly enjoy pain, but there's something almost sensual about melancholy. Life gets profound, then it's the world's problem. It's raining just for them. Then they do the I Ching, buy themselves a little something, eat alone in restaurants, whatever pampers them *and* adds to the drama. They don't want strangers to know they're suffering—it's embarrassing. And they don't want pity from acquaintances! Sympathy from close friends is okay. But they won't talk about it unless you do.

This need for loyalty can work out a little strangely. A Leo Moon client, typically warm, loving and creative, told me about the last date she had with her lover. They were in bed.

"You know," she said prettily, "it doesn't really matter that you went to bed with somebody else."

"That's good," said her fellow. "Because I just spent the whole day making love with Evelyn."

My client sat up. "You know," she said prettily. "I was *wrong.*"

She waited until he turned round; then she slugged him in the jaw.

Moon in Leo is chivalrous. It's not fair, she said, to hit him from behind.

She gathered up her clothes and went downstairs to the telephone, called her friend, a man who had wanted her for months; then she got dressed. By the time she got her shoes on, the taxi was waiting.

Her friend was waiting too. Someone will always be waiting for this beautiful woman, for like her Moon position, she is beautiful inside and out.

MOON IN VIRGO, MOON IN THE SIXTH HOUSE

Ah, sweet obsession. *You* tell me why these guys grind over every achin' detail until their cronies turn to stone.

They need to pick it all apart, every last iota. They can't move on until they do, or until something or someone kicks their ass and hollers, "Get OFF it!"

Don't do it too soon, though. They need to pick, pick, pick at the problems of daily life the way you or I would pick at a nasty bit of needlepoint. And then Lo! the problem comes undone and the day saves itself.

Deep thinkers, these guys. They all love housework. It relieves them of the puritan work/guilt ethic that tells them they should always be doing something, and it frees their minds to do more thinking.

Oho, do they ever have secret disgusting habits! They'll never tell you what they are, of course, and perhaps they merely sniff the pits of their shirts and dresses before deciding whether or not to hang them back in the cupboard. Some of them, though, some of them, get caught with grotty handkerchieves or worse—like using the dishrag to wipe the kitchen floor, or collecting boogies on the sides of the bedsheets. Rare, thank God.

The opposite extreme is just as annoying. They may empty the ashtrays on the half hour or not let you have a bite of their lasagne. Well now, they do *hate* germs. They are awfully good at losing the cap to the toothpaste, and it is this that lands them in Divorce Court.

This need to analyze calms them. They prefer small cities and small towns too. They need to look at a bit of green grass. If they seem freaked out to you, throw them in the bath and some clean clothes. As soon as they've had their shower, they are ready for the Revolution.

Good luck with your sales pitch. Expect to make it more than once. Have all the details at hand. Let them worry over it for a while. Come back and start again. Shoot the breeze a little, too. Stress the practical benefits. When you see that worried look on their faces and the shaking of their heads, they're about to say "maybe."

Work is a god to them, and they love it best. Don't worry, they'll love you best too as long as you've got some worries for them to help with. *They need to help.* At worst, they'll pick on you until you need help. Then they turn 180 degrees and start fixing you up again.

Hypochondria keeps them going to a ripe old age. There's a delicate awareness of their bodies, and this fine tuning responds well to chiropractors, masseurs, and pizza.

Let them have their precious little routines. Once they've lined up all the toothbrushes *exactly right* every morning, they're just like you and me.

MOON IN LIBRA, MOON IN THE SEVENTH HOUSE

Most of all they need a mate. A best friend, business partner, or buddy will do. They spoil you with attention and are frightfully charming and frighteningly dependent upon having someone to love.

The men devastate women because they understand their own refined "feminine" feelings. In fact, they seem to relate *better* to women than to men. The women always have their pick of men; they seem to be able to present themselves in a fluffy, fascinated package. They are smart; they are soft, and they listen, listen, listen. This reminds me of Tom Wolfe's definition of what young ladies learn to do at finishing school: "Are you *rilly* an architect? Are you *rilly* a Senator?"

Oh, this gang picks up every subtle nuance of what you're talking about. Their radar is made of *feathers*. It's important to them to have a placid appearance, yet inside, a lot of the time, they feel hysterical. They feel as if their hearts are on springs. They not only react to you—they react to how *you* react.

These sweet people have only one horrifying vice: they make Minnie the Moocher look like a philanthropist. No other Moon sign matches this one's excellence at wheedling goodies out of you and making you think it was all your idea. You feel like a king when you pick up the check. And the next one. And the next one. They are successful where Moon in Capricorn fails— using people cleverly. They owe you a couple of grand? You'd feel like a *monster* for bringing the subject up. Deep down they're secretly convinced that you should feel honored to have their company. Deeper down they're depressed and frightened at how much they need you; dependency is the desperate racket they run to keep you under their thumbs. It's called the Tyranny of the Weak, and if you're close to a Libra Moon person, you have no doubt heard of it.

Selling something? Dress well, lots of jewelry too. Mention the big shots you know, hint at parties, but in an off-the-cuff, low-key manner. These guys love celebrities. In other cases you can stress the benefits of what you're selling to the rest of their families or associates. Libra Moons need to make other people happy. If you or your product is beautiful, *that* doesn't hurt, either.

Don't underrate this Moon sign when it comes to romance. They give you the best gift of all—themselves, wholeheartedly. They get stepped on for their kindnesses, so be kind and watch them blossom. They need compliments and flattery daily, but they give in return as well. They get to know you and tailor their praise to what they think you want to hear. They're right. Keep a Virgo, Capricorn, or a Scorpio around as a secondary sounding board or these Moons will softly lull you with a stream of adoring yesses. Sounds awful, doesn't it?

The line forms right here.

MOON IN SCORPIO, MOON IN THE EIGHTH HOUSE

Next to a Capricorn Moon, Scorpio is traditionally presumed to be one of the more twisted Moons you can buy.

If being passionate, caring, profound, creative, and sexy is twisted, I'm ready to leap into the pretzel machine in the next sixty seconds. This may be a *tough* Moon sign, because the challenge is nothing less than mastery of the self.

Ach, and here's the rub! So many of us are threatened by displays of deep emotion that Scorpio Moons learn to hide their feelings when they are young. By the time they grow up, they've gotten good at hiding their reactions from you. What's unfortunate is that they have also learned to hide their reactions from *themselves*. The men, especially, need a woman who's a bit of a psychologist, someone patient enough—and tough and fearless enough!—to help them to dig out the feelings they're so afraid to show.

The trickiest game they play boils down to a recurring, hidden script: "I dare you to guess what I need. I'll drag a red herring all over your path so you can't figure me out. And if you're not clever enough or caring enough to *guess*, I won't let you in."

Sometimes they use drugs, alcohol, or sneaky affairs to fool themselves that they are coping with themselves. Eventually their inherent intelligence decides to take over and in a swoop they give up their smoke-screen vices. You can't make them do it. But when they are ready, *this Moon has the most courage and more will power than all the other signs put together*. It isn't that they need courage to give up affairs or drugs or drink; it's the courage to look the fears in the face, fears that create the need for vices.

They're fun to sell to. Let it be noble, let it be bizarre. Hang in tough, present your wares in a matter-of-fact manner. A take-it-or-leave-it stance seems to work the best. This Moon thinks it's John Wayne. He likes anyone who acts proud, talks tough, and walks tall.

You can tell these hip-shooters anything. They keep secrets.

Crisis is their favorite hobby. Give them some extreme situation, and they're in their element—Rocks of Gibraltar. They will *create* a crisis, or at least burst into tears every so often, in order to release the steam that builds up inside. Police work, psychology, and rescue missions are all part of their talents.

Once they understand that they perceive even ordinary everyday occurrences as threats to their own authority, there is a chance of draining off some of the poisonous paranoia that plagues these frightened people. They need to feel in control so badly that they fail to see what's really going on. Then they strike out, cruelly, to let you know how badly you've hurt their feelings.

A day dawns when it occurs to them that it's okay to have vulnerable feelings and that sharing those feelings with someone you trust is the best protection against not getting hurt.

Until that day they live out their emotional lives alone.

MOON IN SAGITTARIUS, MOON IN THE NINTH HOUSE

That ol' debbil rubber Moon! God, you can do what you like to these soulful folks, but they'll always come bouncing back like boppo toys and praising your name to boot! Sock 'em in the jaw, pop them in the snot-box and they just roll on back *with that smile still on their faces*.

We should all be so lucky to have this big-hearted Moon; it's a guarantee of deep reservoirs of faith and resilience. Who can keep them down? Who'd be mean enough to try, especially as these folks are so much fun to be around? They're not afraid to throw their money around, either, when they've got it. They love to be generous to other people, and in return they are surrounded by a crowd of chattering, devoted loonies.

And funny? They invented comedy—timing is their forte. After a couple of beers they'll start improvising, and they're damned good at it too. It's no wonder they make friends fast and keep them a long time.

Drawbacks—well, there are a few. If something goes wrong, it's the other guy's problem. This Moon position is inclined to be a Grade A rationalization expert. They don't like things to, ah, *get heavy*. They're terrified of treadmills. As long as they feel they're *on their way* somewhere, they're okay. They dislike facing the truth about themselves and their childish refusal to act like responsible grown-ups. Let's just not look at *that*. What are you trying to *do*, spoil their fun? Let someone else carry the dull routine part of the work load. That's *life* after all—Scoobie-doo-bee-doo!

If there's a big problem, it makes sense to them to get their plimsoles on and scoot along to the next adventure. Some of them do. If they stay to work things through, it's usually because they have High-Minded Principles. This self-righteousness may bore you, but it's comforting to know that they care about doing The Right Thing. Being Right is their favorite pastime. They will tell you what's good for you before they've even gotten to know the problem! This Moon position needs to preach.

They are better salesmen than you are, but *they can never resist you if you ask for their advice.* I have never met one Moon in this sign or house who did not have an evangelical streak. If they don't want your product, they'll help you find another customer. They don't live unless they give. Their feelers are in the future, and "keep on trucking" is their credo.

If your favorite clown's got the blues, get him into a religious or ethical argument. Philosophy cheers them up. Pass the hat and take up a collection to buy them a plane ticket somewhere. Even reading foreign newspapers cheers this lot up. Perhaps their reach exceeds their grasp, but they think people get a lot farther with that philosophy. It's exasperating to admit it, but they're right *again*. They give good advice.

MOON IN CAPRICORN, MOON IN THE TENTH HOUSE

When somebody with the Moon in Capricorn starts being especially nice to you, *always* ask yourself *"What do they want?"* Might as well ask what a rabid crocodile wants when he licks his chops. The answer is the same in both cases. *He wants blood.*

I know it's nasty, but that's how these people operate. You'll save yourself a lot of confusion if you define the terms of the relationship from the start. It's the ugliest Moon sign of the lot. This specimen believes that the world is such a harsh place that the means justify the ends—and if that means taking something away from you, even if you are more deserving, that's just tough.

The most hideous effect they have on other people is this using capacity. Only the Moon in Capricorn acts this way—any other planet or point in Capricorn is fine. Why are these Moons so twisted? Mostly you can trace a cold, childish, selfish mother figure. Sometimes Mother died when the child was young. These people never got decent values or adequate emotional nurturing when they were children. They have all lost their mothers in some way. Parents wanted them to push, push, push in society and never mind whose head you have to walk on to get at the Big Chance. Only when you become a Big Shot, says Mummy, will I love you. Is it any wonder so many successful famous people have the Moon in Capricorn? And that the rest of the Capricorn Moons live desperate, fearful lives of isolation and failure? A Capricorn Moon may *seem* to be better at something than you are, but this isn't as likely as the cold fact that *they want it worse than anyone.* Adolf Hitler had this Moon.

Somewhere under that heart of cardboard is a *conscience*, though. Capricorn Moons always unconsciously set themselves up to get cracked right in the teeth by their nasty ambitious boomerangs. They always get clobbered badly, but you shouldn't hold your breath waiting. Stop them in their tracks before they rip too many people off, including you. They have a wide circle of "friends" (whom they secretly consider to be their inferiors) to whom they moan and groan about how depressing and hard life is. They don't have patience for your sad story, though—they might get sucked into your depression, and they've got better things to do!

Selling them is easy. Just find out what they want, and make them pay for it, like Mother did.

All right, there *is* another side to Moon in Capricorn. Those black-dog depressions lead to not a little profundity, even wisdom. If you don't mind waiting a couple of centuries for the buggers to trust you, they will reward you by acting loyal, hard-working, and responsible. They're not afraid of work.

These emotionally-guarded paranoids have a deep yearning for love, but they're not *giving* it away. You must earn it. When they fall in love, they give their hearts for life. Maybe their love goes deepest of all the signs, but they'd rather show it in material ways. They want *your* slush, but they'll be damned if they embarrass themselves showing their vulnerability. . . . *Chickens!!!* Forgive them—'twas the doing of Mommie Dearest.

Once in a while you find a sweetie with Moon in Capricorn; then you can be sure you're dealing with what the young bores over at the Unification Church call an "Old Soul." Charles and Susan, you're *okay*, sweethearts . . . but look out for the other, "Young Soul" types!

Abe Lincoln is the best example of the Moon in Capricorn's most surprising and endearing trait—a dry, wry sense of humor. Someone in a crowd heckled Abe one time, calling him two-faced.

"I leave it to you," quipped Abe, our finest stand-up comic President. "If I had two faces, would I be wearing this one?"

MOON IN AQUARIUS, MOON IN THE ELEVENTH HOUSE

The most unreasonable of "reasonable" people. These folks don't have blood in their veins, it's Xerox copy fluid. To say the feelings do not run deep here would not be entirely accurate. They do have feelings, and they do run deep. Deep as the kitchen sink!

Call this a Mr. Spock Moon and leave it at that. They think feelings are supposed to be "logical." Check their ears for points on the tips.

They are great friends and need to have friends that they would do anything for. You can tell them *anything*, and they'll understand. They are utterly honest and trustworthy, fair, reasonable, and straightforward . . . getting bored?

Most of them are awfully bright. They can talk for long periods without using the personal pronoun "I," which is why they have so many friends. They love to hear about science, *need* gadgets, and *have to have their own systems for doing things—their way.*

Once in a blue moon they get hysterical, and then no one around them can figure quite what went wrong. This is Moon in Aquarius suddenly getting in touch with their personal feelings. It is quite a sight, and everybody rushes to help out. Moon in Aquarius likes this, and calms down around friends.

Dreams are what they need badly. They can happily live in ah, *eccentric* surroundings if they have a Noble Rationale. Getting them to see how to get to this goal and not just talk about it is another thing. They love to talk and spin daydreams about the ideal world. The most beautiful side to this Moon is the need to make the world a better place, right here and now. They need to feel that all the people of the world are their brothers and sisters. The perverted Moon in Aquarius types are bigots, but they don't start out life that way.

If you have something to sell, approach them in a friendly, low-pressure manner. Soft sell is the only way to get these people to respond. If you can be funny, that's even better. They need quite a lot of weirdness and manage to have it one way or another. Emphasize your unique, even eccentric qualities, and *don't pressure.* Talk a lot about freedom. They love and need *space.* Don't get too personal at first. They regard it as a sign of bad breeding. A cool approach is best, and showing your brains never hurts.

The Moon in Aquarius gang aren't impressed by traditional male-female role models much. The women aren't much interested in cooking, and the men make a fairly good job of it. One couple I know, both with many planets in Aquarius including the Moon, keep a stack of paper plates in the kitchen, next to the plastic silverware. When they finish dinner, they just chuck the entire works away. Housework ain't their favorite hobby. They'd rather think and read.

Odd then, when you discover how irrationally loyal these folks can be. Cool and detached they may be, but they stick like glue to the people they love and respect. They stay in situations long past what others could handle and put up with—is it bravery or fear of intimacy?

MOON IN PISCES, MOON IN THE TWELFTH HOUSE

They are wells. And like wells, they have everything to give. A well runs deep. Don't expect to fathom it entirely. These people are complicated. They have odd ways of isolating themselves from the mainstream of life. They are too psychic for anybody's good. So they take the phone off the hook once in awhile. It's hell going out in the street when the world seems harsh. At these times they need an aide-de-camp just to accompany them. They're deeply frightened at such moments, but don't you be fooled. Underneath the fear is a curious bedrock courage. This is a flowing "water" sign Moon—water may be a drip, or it may be the mighty ocean, all-loving, sustainer of all life.

People overlook this Moon's neuroses for a number of reasons; this Moon is sweet, sympathetic, and so damned good in bed. Oh, they can even be faithful in love if they have people to help and a Spiritual Goal and if *you* have lots of wigs and accents and imagination. And even then, at the peak of intimacy, they just float out into a private Disneyland and leave you with the body, while the soul has Gone Elsewhere. They're *psychic,* y'know. Tarot cards, astrology, the I Ching all appeal to them. They like to talk to God, but it's got to be private.

Don't you go grinding them down with your troubles and then take these kindly souls for granted. They get depressed after friend No. 92 has rung up with her difficulties. Let them wallow in self-pity a little. They need lots of sympathy when they're depressed, that and reassurance. Remember the well. Fill them back up with barrelsful of confidence. Their biggest enemy is self-doubt.

Call them the bleeding hearts of the zodiac. Scruple-free manipulators see them as suckers for a sob story. Snake-oil salesmen love them: all they do is twirl out a subtle sad innuendo of inner torment and this Moon's hooked—or in love!

Would it surprise you to learn there is an extremely sneaky, downright tyrannical side to this Moon position?

"My Pisces Moon can't stand to see anyone suffering," says he, lurching out the door whilst you are in the middle of an asthma attack.

Do you know anybody who uses "sensitivity" to dominate the works? Ah, they're brokenhearted and can't be faithful! Oh, they're *tired* today and will you pick up a few things for them at the store? They rule the roost with their aches, pains, moans, groans, and alones. They just can't help themselves—so you go fetch!

Dare to gently enlighten them with a dab of commonsense psychology. Hold the mirror of reality to them and they twist and cringe like vampire bats backing off from the light. The game they play is "Victim," yet most of these Moons yearn to break loose from their brain confusion. Tolerate their more charming weaknesses, and don't give them an inch if you see them slithering away from taking responsibility for their own lives. They like to blame Fate, or the Other Guy, for their troubles—they are terrified to think they control their destiny. Curiously, they're never ever depressed when they recognize their own bottomless strength and take charge. So throw a rope down that well and help them climb out.

These folks make the world soft for you and shower you with a million small kindnesses. If you're truly a strong person and do not mistake their kindness for weakness, treat them with the gentle handling they so richly deserve.

Get the Moon
to Work for You
Every Day

Where is the Moon in the sky right now? If you live in a big city, swivel your head round the skyscrapers until you find it. There, now. Is it full? Then no wonder everyone you know is acting larger than life—good time for a party. Expect to break with routine and enjoy the lunacy.

No Moon in the sky? That's a new Moon. Shortly it will be a good time to begin new projects. Make sure it's a new Moon though. It may be up there all right, but you can't see it in Times Square.

What *sign* is the Moon in right now? Look it up in the RED LIGHTS, GREEN LIGHTS tables. The Moon visits each zodiac sign for about two and a half days each month.

If you bear in mind that the Moon's stay in each sign is fleeting, a general two-day wash of feeling that affects human behavior, you will begin to notice an unmistakable *tone* to newspaper headlines, events, people's feelings.

There's a wonderful thick section on this subject in Llewellyn's *Moon Sign Guide*. Pay attention to where the Moon is in the sky when planning events. We've included some hot tips.

When the Moon is in Aries—There's a lot of ego about, and razzle-dazzle. People are impatient, express themselves, and show sarcasm and quick tempers. *Aries people get their way;* Libras need rest—lay low.

When the Moon is in Taurus—People hold on to what they've got. They get greedy and sensual, wanting to eat big meals. A careful, conservative feeling in the streets. *Taurus people get their way;* Scorpios need rest and to stay out of new trouble.

When the Moon is in Gemini—Bring out the witty repartee, play it light, write letters, read and get the bus driver's opinion on the world crisis. Well, it's always a bloody crisis somewhere. *Gemini people get their way;* Sagittarians need rest and to stop preaching.

When the Moon is in Cancer—It's homey, so if you feel like crawling out of your shell go visit people in theirs. They don't want to go out. This Moon is good, however, for the restaurant business. *Cancer people get their way;* Capricorns need a rest from scheming about how to take over the world.

When the Moon is in Leo—What a bunch of show-offs! A fashion show in the streets. This is a theatrical Moon and good for parties. People feel warmhearted. See a play or a movie. *Leo people get their way;* Aquarians should take a hike, or rest, or both.

When the Moon is in Virgo—Clean the house, tidy your desk, do your taxes. *Don't* ask for a loan or take your driving test unless you are a Virgo or your uncle is David Rockefeller. People in charge are critical and want to see all the details. Bad for hitchhiking; you'll wait a long time between rides. Don't *nag! Virgo people get their way;* Pisces people should wrap themselves in cotton wool and rest.

When the Moon is in Libra—Lighten up. Hit the hairdresser or beauty parlor, then socialize. Good for meeting-people types of cocktail parties, art shows, decorating your house, bringing flowers. People are social and lazy now. *Libra people get their way;* you Aries people, shut up and lay back!

When the Moon is in Scorpio—Sexy! People act from the noblest motives or use scurrilous, sneaky tactics. People go to extremes as to what they put in their mouths. Be a little careful walking down those dark alleys. At least it is a weird and interesting night out. *Scorpio people get their way;* Taureans need to stop worrying and rest.

When the Moon is in Sagittarius—Good deals and good will abound. People feel generous, so go to court or see your bank manager about that loan, maybe tell him a leetle joke. Hit the streets with your tin cup and guide dog. If you see that guy selling pencils on the corner, slip him a buck. People tip generously on this Moon, and they like to gabble on about travel and philosophy late into the night. Parties now are gleeful at least, wildly abandoned at best. *Sagittarius people get their way;* Geminis need rest and carrot juice.

When the Moon is in Capricorn—Hard work is the order of the day. Get out your monkey suit and the good shirt to go with it. The jury's in a hanging mood, so no nonsense please. It's a whiney, depressive Moon, when people give in to the best or the worst in themselves. You can accomplish a lot. *Capricorn people get their way for a change;* Cancer people feel squooshy and should rest.

When the Moon is in Aquarius—A nice bland Moon, with the occasional shocking announcement or revolution. Good for talk parties, having friends get together, meeting new people, improving the world you live in. People seem more objective today. *Aquarius people get their own way;* Leo people need to rest, repair the light bulbs in their halos.

When the Moon is in Pisces—People seem more vulnerable now. A good time to get or give sympathy, especially to the bank's loan manager when you ask for another Big One. Music soothes everyone, and people are more likely to grant you favors— their hearts bleed for you. Parties go well, especially those with plenty of wine and weird cigarettes. *Pisces people get their way;* Virgos need a break. Tell them to rest.

Entering the Twilight Zone: Avoiding Trouble on the Void-of-Course Moon

> *"If it don't come out in the wash, it come out in the rinse."*
>
> —Arkansas proverb

That crusty genius Al H. Morrison has done more to publicize this weird Moon period than any astrologer in the four-thousand-year history of the art. Medieval soothsayers knew about it. William Lilly wrote about it in his 1600s book, *Christian Astrology*, and then it seems everybody shut up about it.

Then Al came along and started making trouble. He insisted that we pay attention to the times when the Moon is void of course. He swore that it worked at all levels of daily life. He nagged, he harangued, he cranked out tens of thousands of void-of-course Moon sheets; he demanded that astrologers and lay persons try it out.

People started writing in to his New York office. A wife persuaded her husband, a loan manager at a bank, to use the sheet for six months. Her husband reluctantly agreed to try the method. He did not grant loans to customers if they asked when the Moon was void of course. He asked them to go away and bring back more information.

Today that man is a vice-president of the bank. His loan record was remarkably superior to the records of other loan managers, and they promoted him.

Years ago I did not want to believe the void-of-course Moon worked. I went for part-time job interviews. I never got the job when the Moon was void of course. I made plans. The plans altered when the Moon was void of course. I bought clothes and never wore them when I bought them on a void Moon.

Astrologers wrote in to the astrology magazines, asking about this weird phase of the moon. One fuddy-duddy teacher, using the old "Truth by Proclamation" rhetoric, screeched that the ancient theory did not work, but people saw that it did. They kept writing to Al H. Morrison with their observations.

Other astrologers stole or copied his writings on the subject and did not give him the credit. Al kept printing void-of-course Moon sheets.

If you look at a copy of *The American Ephemeris* you will see a complete set of void-of-course Moon tables on every page. The publisher decided it was too important to leave out. No other book of planets' positions carries these tables yet: *The American Ephemeris* is the first, and for professional astrologers it is generally acknowledged to be the best, most complete, working tool-book available.

WHAT THE HECK IS THE VOID-OF-COURSE MOON?

Let the expert, Al H. Morrison, explain:

"Every couple of days there comes a time which is best used for subjective, spiritual non-material concerns, like prayer, yoga, play, psychotherapy or passive experience, sleep or meditation.

"This period may last a few seconds, or it may be three days and nights in a single session.

"It begins when the Moon in transit makes the last major aspect it will make before it changes from one sign of the zodiac to the next. It ends when the Moon enters the next sign. The name of this period is: Void-of-Course Moon. You may call it a silly season, or vacation from normal living.

"Decision making in such periods turns out later unrealistic. Creativity diverges into unplanned directions, improvisations, false starts, error. Business moves fail to generate profits or meet unexpected difficulties. If you buy any object it usually fails of its intended use.

"Human judgment is more fallible than usual during the time the Moon is void of course. This is the principal factor in all observed experience so far.

"Routine proceeds readily, but often requires an adjustment later. Defects or shortages come to light. Delay, frustration are commonly experienced while the Moon is void of course.

"Neurotic tendencies, bad habits are more open to change. ESP experiments show odd results.

"Historic events during such periods have a wild, Pandora's box impact on cultural evolution. The first two dozen successful space shots were all launched with the Moon void of course to open an all-new age in which old concepts and ideas are corrected or disproven.

"In every presidential election from 1900 through 1972 one of the two major party candidates was nominated with the Moon void of course. Every one of the candidates nominated with the Moon void of course lost.

"Jimmy Carter's 1980 nomination came in a void-of-course Moon.

"For those rare people born with the Moon void of course, life has a characteristic quality which differs from common experience.

"If you have a natal planet located very late in any sign, the Moon sometimes makes a major aspect to your natal planet after it has completed its last aspect to any transiting planet. This tends to sustain your effective action while the world in general experiences errors of judgment.

"Only observation can demonstrate what the void-of-course Moon indicates in your daily living. The scientific approach is to check it out. Design your own experiment.

"There is much more to selecting a 'good' time to act or decide material issues. Skipping the void-of-course Moon is just staying out of avoidable, obvious difficulties.

"Go out of business when the Moon makes its last aspect. Feed your soul until the time the Moon enters the next sign. Then, go back into business!"

All I can add to Mr. Morrison's observations is that void-of-course Moons are pretty jolly times to get sloshed on wine. A writer friend reports that comedy writing goes well on the void. If you're planning a trip, find out what time the plane or train will arrive, and *don't arrive in your destination town when the Moon is void* if you want to stick to the agenda. If you're happy to take what comes and you're not on business, the void's okay.

Use the RED LIGHTS, GREEN LIGHTS tables to find out when the Moon is void of course. Think of this time period as a tunnel. You enter the Lincoln tunnel in New York. When you drive through the tunnel, the radio doesn't work. The moment you leave the tunnel you are in a new state—New Jersey.

Look up January 4, 1984 in the RED LIGHTS, GREEN LIGHTS tables. Next to this date are two columns of times. *The first column tells you the moment you enter the tunnel.* This is when the Moon goes into the void, at 9:34 A.M. Greenwich Mean Time. If you live in the soggy British Isles you can read the times directly from the tables, but if you live elsewhere you will have to convert these times for your time zone. For New York, for example, you would subtract five hours from all the times in the tables; New York is five time zones away from England. In New York the Moon goes void at 4:34 A.M. on that day.

You can get a sheet of void-of-course Moon times adjusted for Eastern Standard Time by sending a couple of bucks donation to: CAO Times, Box 75, New York, N.Y. 10113. They do all the conversion for you, and there's a handy booklet edition which you can sneak into your wallet.

The second column tells you the moment you leave the tunnel and enter the new state, the next sign of the zodiac. On January 4, 1984 the Moon leaves the void at 4:31 P.M., the moment it enters Aquarius.

Our friends back in the Owld Sod have a void during business hours that day. Important meetings go cuckoo, appointments get switched around, major decisions are unrealistic on that day. Learn to make your schedules around void Moons; leave leeway for emergencies, cancellations and goof-off time. Do your routine tasks, and take a long lunch!

Born on a
Void-of-Course Moon

It's a gift. Sometimes it's a curse. They all bear the spark of greatness. People born when the Moon was making no aspects are "special." Therein lies the rub.

Void-of-course Moon people do not react to life, or life's happenings, in predictable ways. It is as if the inhibitory valve in the brain is somehow stuck, and the filter doesn't filter out all stimuli. When this open valve, or "brain-blood-flow" as Colin Wilson calls it, receives a series of impressions, *all* the impressions register simultaneously.

For example, void Moon folks may be getting on the bus like you and me, but they also have the birds singing and the clammy air and the distant siren and the red balloon in the sky and the blades of grass poking up through the pavement cracks and the sensation of basking in all eternity. They have to deal with these sensations on a constant minute-by-minute basis all their lives *and* have the exact change ready. Yes, it does give superior perception. Every time.

Do not expect them to react in "normal" ways to life's challenges. Oh, they love the word "normal." They'll tell you what is and what is not normal—as if they knew themselves! These unusual people like to stop and see the leaf fall. They live to make grand, extraordinary gestures.

Winston Churchill was one of the extraordinary ones born with the Moon void of course. Like most Moon void natives, his relationship with his mother was exceedingly odd. Most void Moon children have absentee mothers—sometimes the mother is eccentric, even crazy. Sometimes there is a good mother, but the nanny looking after the child is a little off beam. The child may

107

have a string of mother substitutes before the age of six, so the child is confused in how to model his behavior. In extreme cases too many mother substitutes and the lack of one constant maternal influence can cause "splitting off" of the personality, laying the groundwork for mental illness in later life. Other factors in the chart have to indicate this, however. Being born on a void Moon is not enough to make you crazy!

They drive everybody else crazy, though. If a Moon void person does not or cannot get in touch with his greatness soon enough, look out! They will affect the lives of dozens of other people with their negative attitude and irresponsible behavior. They like to question reality a little, so they run up huge debts or throw television sets out of hotel windows.

Sometimes I wonder if Moon void folks ever get in touch with their feelings, especially the ones that are here to give the world so much. Do they ever experience satisfaction? These people are so wide-eyed and vulnerable that it is essential for them to have a slew of trusted advisers to keep them on the earth plane: good lawyers, commonsense friends, a top-notch shrink, and plenty of money. They pay a price for their originality, even genius; theirs is a constant fight to keep from getting shafted. They simply cannot tell the difference between good companions and connivers. Some of them can act pretty slippery themselves—they're *not* dumb!

Drugs and alcohol are poison to them. They're *born* stoned, and need no additional stimulation. *Water* makes these people high.

New worlds open for us because of what these people give. Their lives are not "ordinary," "normal," or "easy." Lauren Bacall, Valerie Perrine, Shirley Temple Black, Judy Garland, Rod Stewart, Patti Smith, Christopher Columbus, Pope John-Paul II (and possibly the Ayatollah Khomeini) were born with the Moon void.

Let's not forget Winston Churchill. Late in his career his country threw him out of office. Who knew he was going to make the biggest comeback of the twentieth century and save the free world from the Nazis? What courage! What rhetoric! He even had astrologers working for him, to tell him what Hitler's astrologers were telling Hitler.

Crazy? It worked, didn't it?

Eclipses

Don't mess with eclipses. The newspaper will tell you when they are going to occur, or you can ring up a local astrologer, the Planetarium, or get an ephemeris and look it up there.

Those old eclipses will stir you up, all right. All sorts of feelings leap out of you. And if you regard an eclipse as a *period of instability* where new attitudes come up into view, you'll find they're wonderful for getting rid of old muck inside of you.

The trick is *not to act more than necessary* when an eclipse is operating. It may be necessary to act more than you would during normal times because of outside changes, but do not do more than you must. People are stirred up now.

Ten days before and three days after the eclipse is the unstable period. We call it the *shadow of the eclipse*. Big business deals and big love deals swirl about in the ethers; *don't initiate action or decide issues* until you count one, two, three days after the eclipse.

Ronald Reagan was inaugurated on January 20, 1980. It was the day of an eclipse. This was not a good sign for the President; many unpredictable difficulties cropped up for him. Prince Charles married Lady Diana Spencer in the shadow of the eclipse; married life will take unexpected highways for this lovely couple!

Do you want that new job badly? *Wait.* You've fallen madly in love? Fine. That's what eclipses are for, to stir you up. But keep your cotton-pickin' hands to yourself until you count one, two, three days after the eclipse if you want the romance to count. Well, you can *neck* a little bit.

The Sun—
Where Are You
Going in Life?

"Life will give you what you ask of her only if you ask long enough and plainly enough."

—Proverb

The Sun is the most important part of your chart. Know it, struggle with it, and you'll feel rich and happy inside. The Sun shows what you're good at already. You'll get better at it if you keep on practicing, for the Sun tells what you are *learning* to be. Ignore it and you'll never be happy. The catch is, it takes a whole lifetime to get it right. The Sun shows your pot of gold, the gifts and talents you have at your fingertips. Polish up your Sun thing every day.

Knowing where you're going is a big help. You can save yourself years of wasted tap-dance lessons.

Dig out these gifts by polishing the best of the sign your Sun is in. This gives you *style*. What's more important is the *house* of the Sun—you need a computer chart for this. Aries feel like cowards and are *learning* to be brave. Libras are *learning* to cooperate with other people. Pisceans may seem self-pitying, but remember, they are *learning* to be compassionate, and charity begins at home!

As you get older, you show more of your Sun position, but you can save yourself years of floating around by getting in touch with knowing what you *want*. Your Moon position can get in the way—be careful not to let it overwhelm what your soul craves. Fulfill your needs and get on with the Sun thing.

Signs are styles; the sign your Sun is in merely shows the style in which you approach your goals. The Sun signs are:

ARIES, born 21 March to 20 April; the leader
TAURUS, born 21 April to 20 May; the determined
GEMINI, born 21 May to 21 June; the intellectual

CANCER, born 22 June to 22 July; the nurturer
LEO, born 23 July to 23 August; the superstar
VIRGO, born 24 August to 23 September; the analyst
LIBRA, born 24 September to 23 October; the lover
SCORPIO, born 24 October to 22 November; the passionate
SAGITTARIUS, born 23 November to 21 December; the optimist
CAPRICORN, born 22 December to 19 January; the cautious
AQUARIUS, born 20 January to 18 February; the progressive
PISCES, born 19 February to 20 March; the compassionate

A computer chart will show you what house the Sun is in, and here is where we hit pay dirt. Look up the symbol for the Sun in your chart, find the house it's in, and *go for it*. Your life depends on it, by the way, if you want to live up to the best in yourself. This is where you shine. You're gifted here.

If the Sun is within five degrees of the *following* house, you can have both houses. That is, if your Sun is late in the eighth house, and within five degrees of the ninth house cusp, read both the eighth and ninth house definitions. Why not reach for it?

SUN IN THE FIRST HOUSE

> *"If I am not for myself, who will be for me? And if I am for mine own self, what am I? And if not now, when?"*
> —Hillel the Elder

You're a personality kid. That's what you came here to do this lifetime . . . shine. People admire your arrogance.

Oddly, it is one of the hardest positions for the Sun, because the work is self-improvement on every level. You can't afford to behave in any way less than a god. You affect people profoundly with the sheer force of your personality. You might be a teacher, a salesman, or run your own business, but people won't let you get away with less than noble behavior. Act selfishly, use other people to build up your ego, and the house you have built comes tumbling down; all that is left is ashes, and yourself, and a sorry self at that. You may have had troubles with Daddy—look yourself in the mirror and remind yourself you can be better than him. There are more people coasting on their slick egos who hate themselves with first house Suns than any other position. Learn to love yourself. The best way to do that is to be the brightest, shiniest, most self-confident character on the block. You don't do this by tearing other people down. Psychotherapy will help you.

A celebrity client with a first house Sun told his wife, "If you leave *me*, you'll never forgive yourself." She did leave him, and she did forgive herself.

There's a spark of god in you. Be brave and live up to it. Dare to throw off your neuroses! Remember too, that you're supposed to believe you're the Christ. Just don't forget everybody else is the Christ, too. There's a danger here of a self-centeredness bordering on Divine Right. Polish your character up each day, then show off. People look to you as an example. *Gulp!*

Here's the chart of a guru in India who makes miracles happen in front of your eyes. Other first house Sun folks are Rita Hayworth, James Joyce, John Milton, Renoir, Sophia Loren. Can you think of a more individualistic bunch?

Look for a big smile on a first house Sun person's face, resembling the grille of an Impala. Now here's the guru, Satya Sai Baba, and his sunny horoscope.

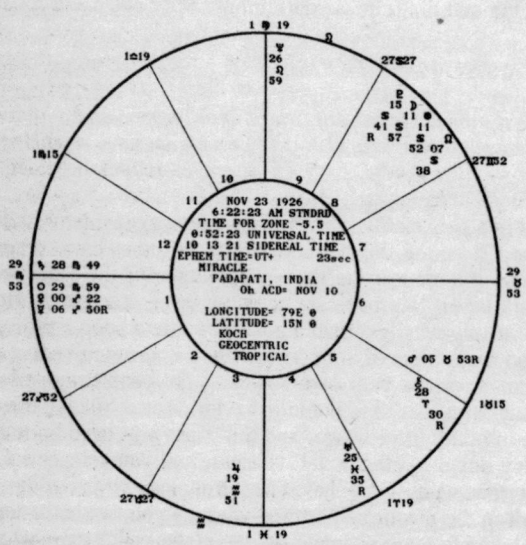

Satya Sai Baba

SUN IN THE SECOND HOUSE

> *"The greatest and the most amiable privilege which the rich enjoy over the poor is that which they exercise the least—the privilege of making others happy."*
> —Charles Colton

Huh? Anyroad, this is a wonderful place to have the Sun because your mission here is simple. The most spiritual thing you can do in this lifetime is make money. Quit trying to wrap your legs round your head, chuck out the Kalil Gibran jazz, and *get busy*.

Hold it . . . there's a qualifier. Have you ever known a time in the course of human events when there wasn't a catch? Yah, yah, it all depends on what you *do* with the money. Strangely, what you do with your money depends on your values. *People born with the Sun in the second house are here to build inner values*, of which dough-re-mi is the mere snivelling symbol.

You are the best equipped of all the Sun house positions to keep on keeping on when the going gets impossible. Look at the odd assortment of determined specimens with Sun in the second. There's Karl Marx, Harry Houdini, Thomas More, Helen Hayes, Thomas Jefferson, Frank Sinatra, Mark Twain, Joseph Kennedy (the Daddy), Joe Stalin, George Lincoln Rockwell (leader of the American Nazi Party), and Edgar Allen Poe.

Poor old Eddie Poe. Somehow he managed to fight off grief and melancholia, kept those digits writing, and left us a legacy. Jefferson helped begin a nation based on new values. These second house Sun folks can leave a lasting legacy behind them when they go, whether it's a fortune, a building, kids with high ideals or an enduring philosophy.

You are here to form your own stubborn values. You feel like imposing them on other people, usually. Whether you mean to or not, you're here to build an empire in the world or of the spirit. Take your time as you pick and choose your philosophies, for they will have a far-reaching effect even after your death.

I couldn't resist running two charts here to illustrate the second house Sun principle.

The first chart is of the late philosopher Alan Watts. He loved cigars and houseboats but his legacy was his thoughts and the courage he brought to his life. His book, *In My Own Way*, tells a colorful Capricorn story of his life.

I put in Telly Savalas' chart because he always seems to play characters with strong value systems. I got the correct *time* of his

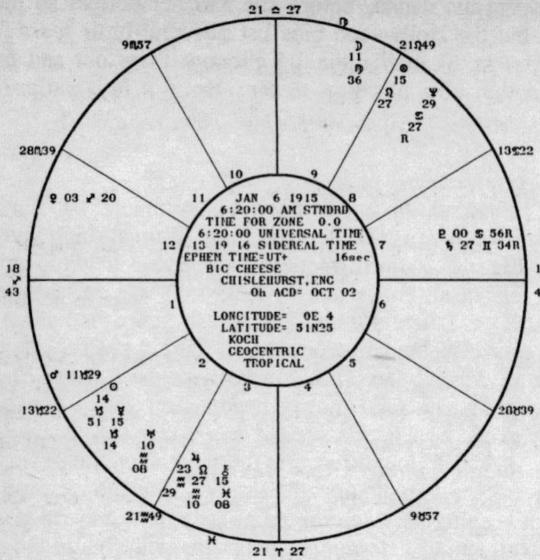

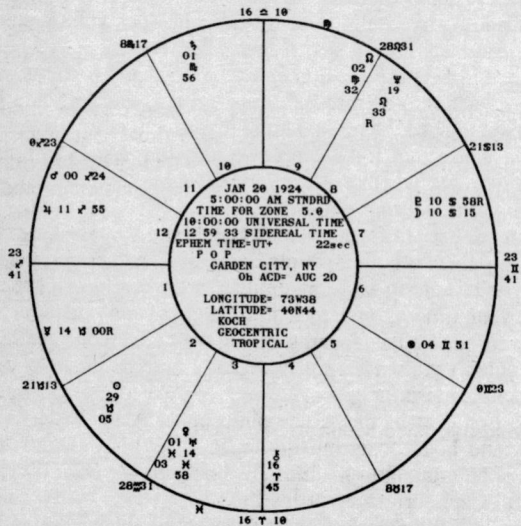

Alan Watts

Telly Savalas

birth from his mama, before she had her coffee, so the time's right, but the Hollywood bios list different birth *years* for Telly . . . you know movie stars! I checked them out and this chart looked the most like him to me. He is a long-suffering, kind man.

SUN IN THE THIRD HOUSE

> "*Perhaps each life has one sensational thought, if acted upon will bring great meaning.*"
> —Michael R. Baer

Student of life, when will you ever stop asking questions? You love to interview people, so people adore you. You know the secret of popularity—getting people talking about themselves. Let them give you half a chance and you'll talk them under the table—there's nothing boring about *you*.

You hear God on the radio, and you give great telephone. You're here to learn a little about a lot, crank it around for awhile, then spit it back out to the rest of us. You're the messenger, which makes you a writer, teacher, an actor purveying the ideas of other people. If you work on it a little, you're the master of words and can pick up languages too. One woman I know with a third house Sun can say "Where's the toilet?" in nineteen languages. Comes in handy.

This commercial ear and love of the everyday marketplace might make your thinking a little superficial, but you can avoid this trap by constant learning. Cary Grant with his impeccable romantic repartee and Picasso's shrewd commercial and artistic eye embody the third house Sun principle. Other third housers are Hugh Hefner, Abraham Lincoln, Eugene O'Neill, William Penn, Albert Schweitzer, Isaac Newton, Jerry Lewis, and Hermann Goering. You can't say they aren't original thinkers; even Goering was, the rotten one in the barrel.

Here's Rod Stewart's horoscope. He may just seem sexy and too much the wild rock-'n'-roller to you, but he's a hell of a songwriter. Listen to "Mandolin Wind" sometime. Note also the void-of-course Moon in his chart.

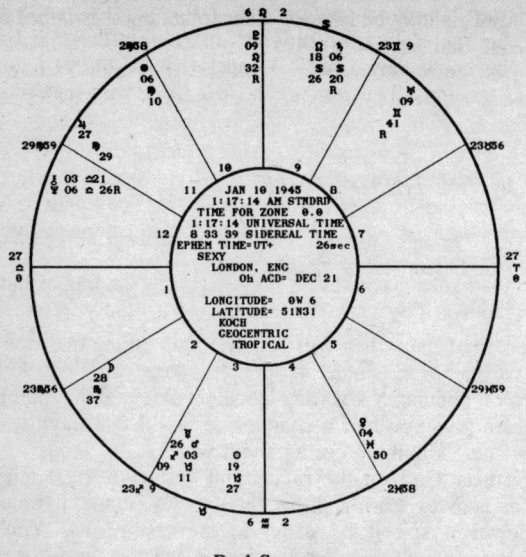

Rod Stewart

SUN IN THE FOURTH HOUSE

"One man with courage makes a majority."
—Andrew Jackson

You're a hoot owl. This is the house of midnight madness; there is no limit or bottom to your feelings or the depth of your soul. You feel as if you're pitted against tradition or the Establishment. You're *supposed* to feel that way if you have a fourth house Sun. *You are here to change society in a unique, personal way.* Yehudi Menuhin, Martin Luther, Leo Tolstoy, Kahil Gibran, T. E. Lawrence, Howard Hughes, Jesse James, and Joseph Goebbels have Sun in there. It seems to go with the kind of original thinking people do in the deep of the night.

This house is loaded with Freudian undertones. No one can fully plumb its depths, but shrinks have a ball with patients who have a planet or two there. Unhappy fourth house Sun folks get stuck in tradition and try to live their lives as Mummy and

Daddy did. This may be fine for other folks, but it is *lethal* for a fourth house Sun.

You must create your own emotional network. You regard your friends as family, introduce everyone to each other, then complain happily that you're living in Peyton Place. Make your own traditions. Tell society to go hang and stick to your own principles. What's important to you is emotional depth, and you'd feed or shelter anyone who deserved it. You ought to have a home, or a hunk of land, but the ideal crashpad comes later in life. You're good at real estate and agriculture.

Sun in the fourth gives you an intuitive understanding of human nature. Many of these folks are more than a little psychic. The example chart belongs to Al H. Morrison, who is possibly the world's greatest living astrologer. He lives in Manhattan, but he sneaks into churchyards to plant flowers when nobody's looking.

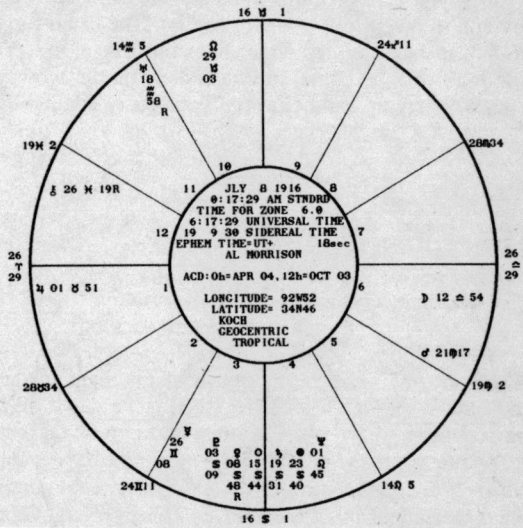

Al Morrison

SUN IN THE FIFTH HOUSE

> "If you would create something, you must be something."
>
> —Goethe

You're creative. Acting, painting, weaving, writing, lecturing, coloring Easter eggs and doodling on notepads come out of your ears and nostrils. You are the Pied Piper and can work miracles with children. You take the play apart in Darien and make it a hit on Broadway. You could learn to be a show-off and you should, for you're nothing until you love yourself. Grab the applause and live your life in a way that makes you proud. Then teach the rest of us how to love each other. You may have many lovers or a mate who is your pride and joy, but you must love.

Since you're such a big kid, you thrive in pleasure centers, resorts, pinball arcades, the social circuit, show biz, and anywhere you can speculate, like the Stock Exchange, which is full of big baby brokers. Folks with this Sun position enjoy playing the child; if you find your close ties playing "parent" roles, do remember you're here to be *creative*, not childish.

God stuck you here on earth to be sunny, damn it, to experience joy and to give it out to the rest of us. The catch for you is that the human race, by and large, does not live in joy. You've got to do it at work, at home, in Calcutta, or on the subway. We need you, so hurry up and believe in your many talents. Sing us a song, give us a cuddle, cheer us up, love us.

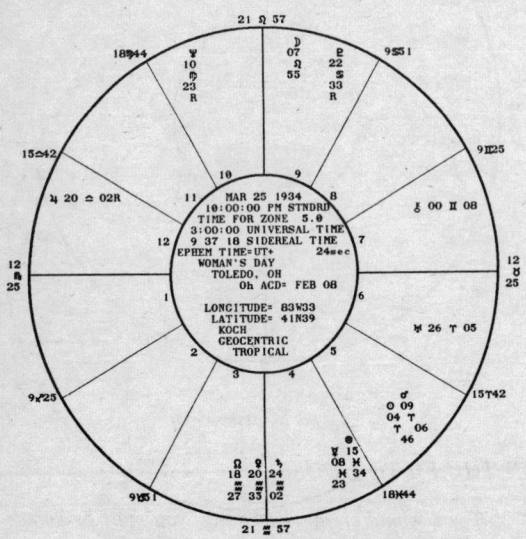

Gloria Steinem

Some famous fifth housers: Liberace, Clark Gable, Zsa Zsa
Gabor, Mozart, Shirley Temple, Maurice Ravel (he composed
Bolero), Will Rogers, Rasputin.

SUN IN THE SIXTH HOUSE

> *"Genius is infinite painstaking."*
> —Henry Wordsworth Longfellow

Oh, nobly born, you have the most underrated and most
misunderstood Sun position of them all. You deserve the Nobel
Prize, but you're too dearly humble and hard at work to go
looking for it. Give us a kiss!

You are the salt of the earth, a true idealist, here to make the
world better right here and now. Work is your god. You don't
use work as a way of avoiding your family or so the Joneses will
envy your new Mercedes—you work because you believe in
what you do with all your soul, and you do it better than anyone

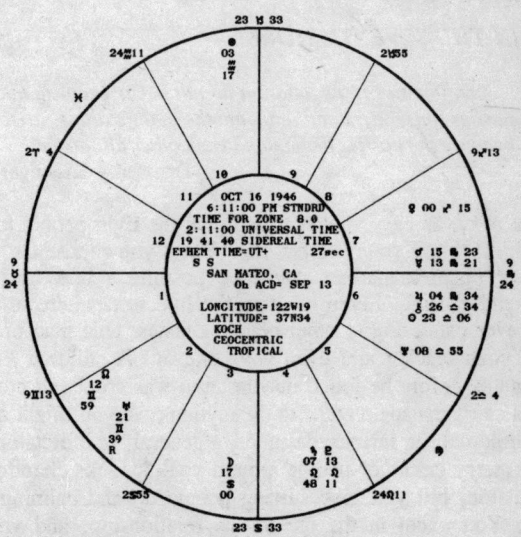

Suzanne Sommers

else. You put your ideals into practice every day. You want people to be healthy, to be educated, and to have enough to eat, and you can't rest until you've done your bit to improve the quality of life for humankind.

John Keats, John Lennon, Dr. Carl Jung, General Patton, and Alfred Hitchcock all had two things in common; they had the sixth house Sun and they worked like the devil. You can streamline a factory or make the perfect movie, fix Mrs. Castle's washing machine or teach first aid at the Y; and you can do more. Your talents are without limit. This worries you, because people with this Sun position are always looking for the perfect job, without realizing that they *are* the perfect job. They may change jobs often, but this is a strength, not a weakness.

You'll never find the one occupation that sums you up any more than a beautiful girl finds the one dress to live in all her life. You are Hanuman, the perfect servant of the Lord. Pat yourself on the back. You do a meticulous job wherever you go. Get vocational guidance if you're young or old, and realize that you're here to improve your surroundings. Great human beings are never satisfied.

SUN IN THE SEVENTH HOUSE

> *"Difficulties in negotiation do not occur because the parties misunderstand one another—difficulties arise because the parties understand each other all too well."*
> —Dr. Henry Kissinger

You're on an easy wicket if you pick the right people to hang out with if this is your Sun position. But if you choose the wrong mate or business partner you'll be pushing a boulder up the mountain, darling. Learn to draw the line somewhere or you'll be forever pandering to other people's tastes. One man picked a weird yoga teacher and even gave one of his children a weird yoga name before he found out the guru was cruel and crooked.

You can persuade anyone to do anything, so you might as well be a diplomat, an interior designer, a general, or a dictator. You like a merry circus of people around you. It looks chaotic from the outside, but you love stirring people up and calming them down. You excel in the one-to-one relationship, and you can have one-to-ones with three dozen people, and you prefer things that way. You're a social butterfly, and you must have a mate or

idea you're in love with or you can't feel fulfilled. You may
an artist; you are certainly an artist with other people.

Sigmund Freud, Patrick Henry, Bobby Kennedy, Adolf Hitler,
d Charles Manson are famous examples of seventh housers.
bout all they have in common is powerful charisma and the
ility to affect others deeply, changing other people's lives.
itler and Manson might have had a better crack at expressing
emselves had they learned in childhood how to form peer
lationships, which is the work of the seventh house. You're not
pposed to feel better than or lesser than other people. What
ou're here to do is to join with other people, to join people with
eas, or ideas with ideas.

You're a super organizer, a political animal, and can be wildly
pular. Here's Charles Manson's chart.

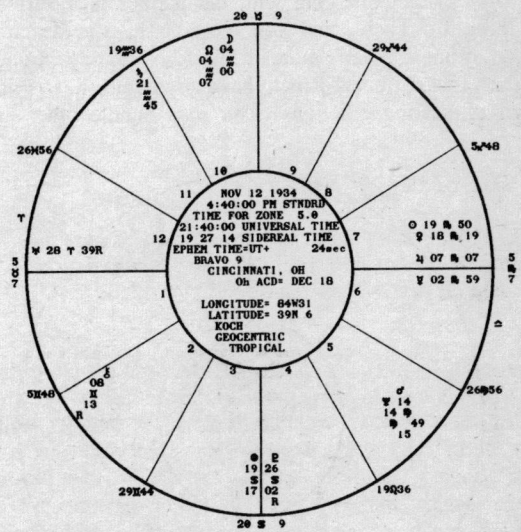

Charles Manson

UN IN THE EIGHTH HOUSE

> *"The thing was deep in him. He was too strong and
> alive for it to die lightly."*
>
> —F. Scott Fitzgerald

You eat crisis for breakfast. The aforementioned F. Scot
Galileo, John Glenn, Henry the Eighth, Helen Keller, Jac
Kennedy, James Pike, Rachmaninoff, and both Rockefeller
John D. and Nelson, are eighth house Sun types. Some a
tycoons, all are psychologists, some have conquered Self, and a
of them have *power*.

The house of many talents, of Destiny, of Fate, of mysterie
wondrous makes you feel alone. The eighth is the house of
self-reliance, the ability to stand alone with one's principle
Then the eighth house makes you give it all up to fully merge wit
Destiny. You blow it if you don't have a deep, one-to-one, full
committed relationship with one other person. The deep relation
ship is your Holy Grail. You attain by penetrating life's myster
ies; two people merge for a time, then stand alone, merge, the
stand alone. Each merging with the partner is a surrender t
Something Up There, and you must do it, and develop self
reliance to boot! What's more, it must be done again and agai
with the same partner if it is to have any depth. Sex is only on
symbol of sharing emotions. You may handle other people'

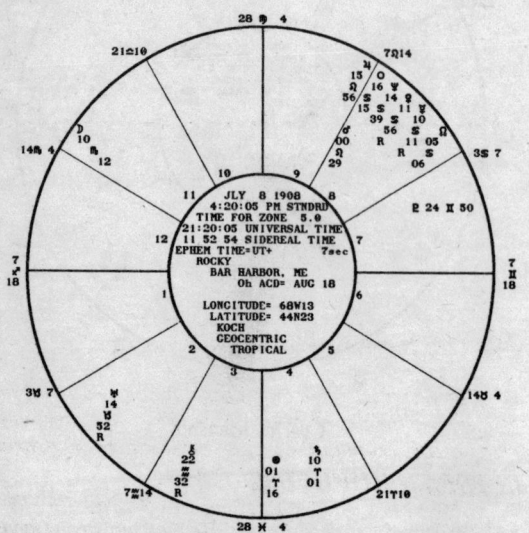

Nelson Rockefeller

money or other people's lives. But it is you who has the power
to change yourself and transform others.

Nelson Rockefeller has a *loaded* eighth house. He did inherit a
few bob, but a true eighth houser he was, so he made his own
merits and mistakes. The psychic Edgar Cayce was born here, too,
in this rarest time for people to be born, when the sun is slanting
sadly across park benches in late afternoon, when we contemplate
our own mortality. The eighth gives intuition and a direct pipe-
line to the Infinite. Cayce was convinced of our immortality.

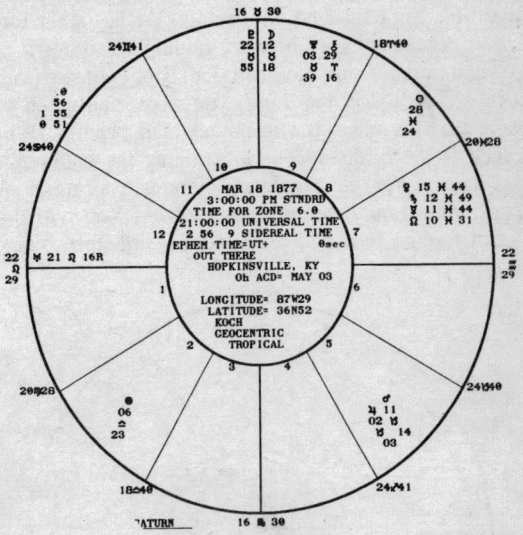

Edgar Cayce

SUN IN THE NINTH HOUSE

> "Free will is not the liberty to do whatever one
> likes, but the power of doing whatever one sees ought
> to be done, even in the face of otherwise overwhelming
> impulse. There lies freedom, indeed."
>
> —G. Macdonald

Two activities bring out the best in you; travel and mind
expansion. You might even be happier living in a foreign coun-

try, if other factors in your horoscope indicate this. At least you will travel widely, and if you're broke or paralyzed, these circumstances won't stop you. You'll study the world from your armchair, and pretty soon the kids will start coming around calling you Professor. You're a grand teacher when you get going.

This Sun position could make you a lawyer, a talk-show host, a travel agent, a hippie, a diplomat, or the local sage. It will give you a big mouth, but a well-considered, educated one!

Not too many people are born this time of day; chances are you'll have some rare experiences not often encountered in everyday life. Your life and your mind may be richer for being rarer; most people are born between midnight and dawn.

You want more from life than Joe Bloggs down the road. You'll take risks to get the things you want, and much of what you want can't be measured in pounds and pennies. What you really seek is the bird's-eye view, noticing the common thread that runs through varying people and cultures. Your mission in life is to study philosophy, religion, and ethics. You will probably eat a lot of foreign food and see a lot of weird stuff. Your job is

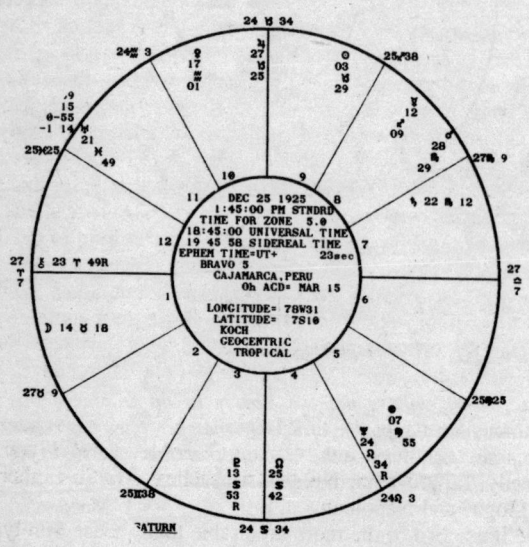

Carlos Casteneda

to digest it all, then broadcast it all back to us. We're waiting to hear about your discoveries in freedom.

Famous fearless ninth housers are Henry Miller, Nasser, Rudolf Nureyev (who leaps to freedom), Nostradamus, Princess Grace of Monaco, and Christine Jorgensen, the first transsexual.

SUN IN THE TENTH HOUSE

> "It is not titles that reflect honor on men, but men on their titles."
>
> —Machiavelli

> "I courted fame but as a spur to brave and honest deeds; who despises fame will soon renounce the virtues that deserve it."
>
> —Mallet

You choose to live your life in a goldfish bowl. You're here to set an example to us, so you become the pillar of the community. The price you pay for this stardom is not so high—the only thing you pay is living your life as if a television camera were trained on you twenty-four hours a day. You feel as if Someone Up There is watching you. She is. All you have to do is find a noble career, grow a bigger, nobler personality than any career could contain you with, and act as if the whole world is watching.

You asked to be a big shot, sweetheart, and you'll enjoy every minute of it *as long as you keep your actions exemplary*. Tenth house Sun people (or any planets in the tenth house, for that matter) can't get away with *nuthin'*. The gory details always leak out.

Don't be afraid to be the power broker you long to be. You're good at power if you had a sweet Mama. This is another loaded house for the psychologists to explore; tenth house Sun folks have to overcome their identification with their mothers before they can go on to success. Success is your birthright. As the good old I Ching says, "Shine like the sun at midday." That's when you were born.

Famous examples of this larger-than-life, living-example-to-the-masses condition are Ivan the Terrible, Errol Flynn, Rose Kennedy, Janis Joplin, Nikita Khrushchev, Martin Luther King, Van Gogh, and Napoleon.

We'll use two of the more admirable tenth house Sun types for you to study. Number one is Ben Franklin, and number two is the ever-delicious philosopher/sage, Ram Dass.

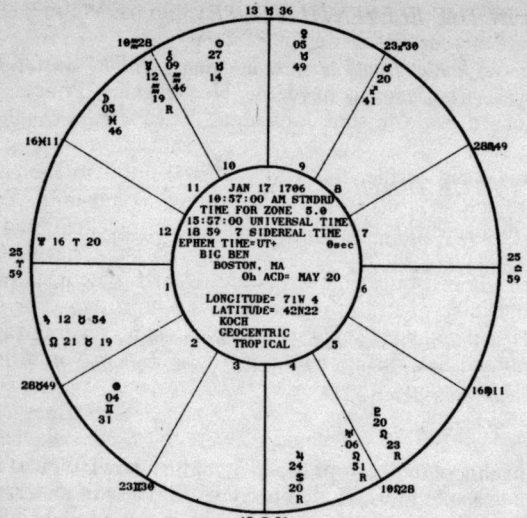

Ben Franklin

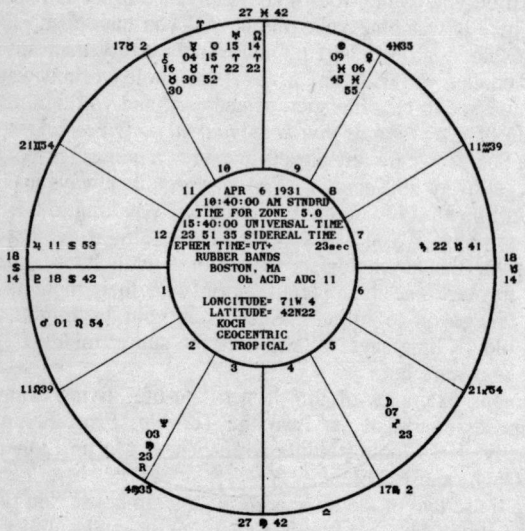

Ram Dass

SUN IN THE ELEVENTH HOUSE

> "A real friend is someone who sticks by you even
> when you become successful."
>
> —Fortune Cookie

Dream big or die, that's you. You believe to the core that you're here to affect what goes on in your community. You can. You're a superb team player (with a bit of practice), and you're never happier than when you pool in with your friends on a big project. Friends mean the world to you, and sometimes you have a rough time of it just to find friends who match your specific ideals, but you must keep trying to find them. You're okay about your blood ties, but it's more of a challenge to you to love the people you adopt, who are like family to you. At times you may feel as if you're living in a commune. Sometimes eleventh housers *do* live in a commune, like Allen Noonan the outer-space guru who communes with flying saucers. His chart is here. Eleventh housers aren't afraid to look into unorthodox subjects. If you're a little twisted, you can let your heavy influential

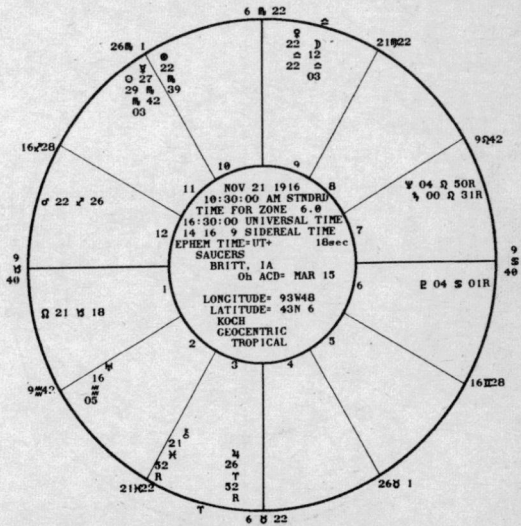

Allan Noonan

friends get the better of you. The trick here is to remember you're part of a group, neither better than or worse than the others. Remember how unique you are . . . in fact, you've a rare ability to project a particular character or image. In an actor or public figure the ability to be recognized instantly is an asset. Don't be fooled by your own stereotyped image—that public image can turn into a coffin that stifles your growing, changing personality if you let it. Surround yourself with unique oddballs, and be one yourself—to the hilt. Whether you're a corporate boy or a member of a rock-'n'-roll band, you feel more like you in a crowd. Social skills are important, as you'll spend considerable time convincing others to go along with your schemes. Don't let those dreams slip away. *Save* those whales.

Some world-saving eleventh housers: Jackie Gleason, Billy Graham, John Hancock, Marshal Tito, Eleanor Roosevelt, Douglas MacArthur, Bob Hope, Marconi, and Spiro Agnew, shown here.

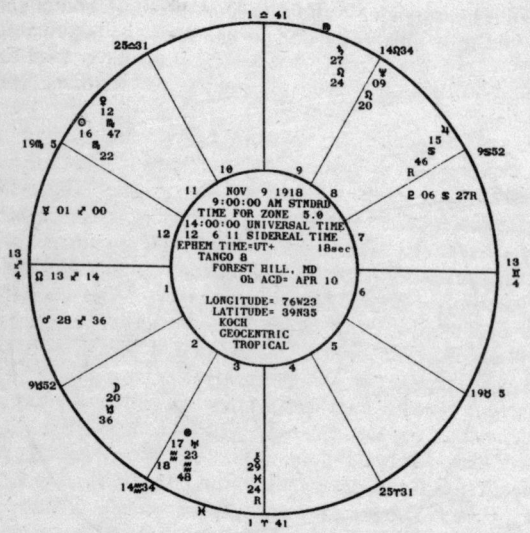

Spiro Agnew

SUN IN THE TWELFTH HOUSE

> *"When joyously led, the people forget their burdens;*
> *in wrestling joyously with difficulties, they even forget*
> *that they must die. Joy's greatest quality is the encourage-*
> *ment it affords the people."*
>
> —I Ching, Blofeld edition

There is a wind in Germany they call the *fuhrn*. It is an ill, dry wind, and when it blows, it makes you want to jump out of the windows and rip out the doors. I went to high school in Furth, a gray, hideously provincial suburb of Nuremberg, and a more goddamned depressing burg you'd never want to see. In winter the fog rolls low, in lumps, coming down the street at you in early morning. Henry Kissinger was born there, and he was glad to get out of there too. He was born with a twelfth house Sun. He gave me his birth time so I could make sure.

This is an extraordinary Sun position, for it bestows great power and prevents you from fully using it. Dr. Kissinger could never become president of the United States because he was born overseas. Criminals, sages and coo-coos have twelfth house Suns. You'll find philosophers, rabbis, psychiatrists, and saints here too.

Do you remember that old *Twilight Zone* one in which the guy gets captured by extra-terrestrial gorillas and they have a book called *To Serve Man* that no one can translate? The man thinks they're idealists and gets into the spaceship; at the last moment he discovers it's a cookbook. That's the predicament of the twelfth house Sun person. You get screwed unless you listen to the inner voice and help your fellow man. You don't feel like other people. It is as if you live in an eggshell, a spacesuit that subtly isolates you from other people. This isolation is a sign of your specialness. No other Sun position is better equipped for helping people with their emotional problems. You can get inside another person's skin and visit for a little while. Lawrence Olivier's twelfth house Sun helped him *become* his characters.

Mao Tse-Tung, Tchaikovsky, Steve McQueen, Audrey Hepburn, Henry Fonda, Havelock Ellis, Judy Garland, Robert Mitchum, William Randolph Hearst, Mahatma Gandhi . . . these are the twelfth housers. It is a distinguishing characteristic of the twelfth house Sun person to believe that he is here to serve humanity. Of course, you don't have to agree with them, but that's how these people feel!

Don't let the old-fogey astrology books scare you with lines like "the twelfth is the house of hospitals and self-undoing." Most of the folks born with this Sun position are as healthy as *horses*. The stars only make you sick if they have first tried every other way to get you to wake up and participate in loving humanity. You might *work* in a hospital or an institution, or you may just let your friends cry on your shoulder a lot.

The first chart is of Jean McArthur, a highly gifted psychic based in Washington D.C. She prefers to live in nearby Alexandria, away from the distracting nonsense of town. Her psychic abilities have been verified by scientists; her office is strewn with signed photos from people you and I would call Very Big Deals, she's got a mile-long waiting list. But McArthur somehow can always make time for the poor, the sick at heart, the man with no kidneys, the crippled girl who wants a family.

The other chart is of a fireman, a handsome young buck from Philadelphia. It doesn't occur to him that he's a hero, though he's in the business of saving lives every day. He's just your ordinary, common, garden-variety everyday saint, is all.

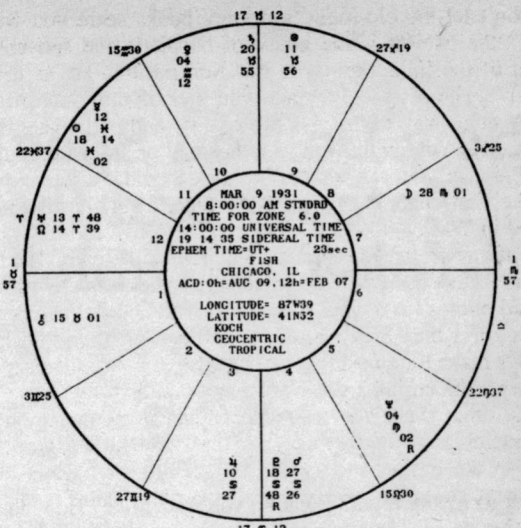

Jean McArthur

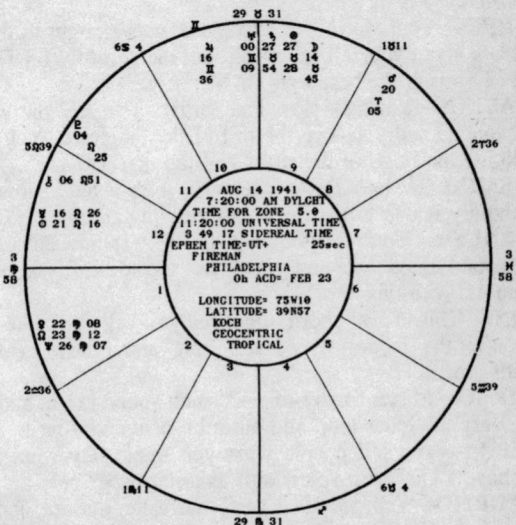

Fireman

How Do You Speak? Mercury and the Yak-Yak Tables

What's on your mind? What do you sound like? How do you talk to other people? Look up your Mercury in the YAK-YAK tables. Mercury is your talker.

If Mercury is in:

ARIES—Your warm, friendly voice gets straight to the point. You talk about yourself too much, but the goo-roos on The Other Side say this is the best sign for Mercury.

TAURUS—You talk slow and earthy. You feel the words on your tongue and you love the roll of the language. You're good at talking the lingo of the street and the marketplace.

GEMINI—A Bob Dylan Mercury, with a huge, imaginative vocabulary is one of the finest talkers you can buy.

CANCER—You're a good off-the-cuff, spontaneous speaker. You sound emotional, and you're not too logical; you can sway the public with this one.

LEO—This is a stubborn, dignified yak-yak. You like to brag. If you're the modest type, you brag about how heavy your friends are.

VIRGO—Mister Matter-of-Fact. You sound bright and analytical. Vary the tones a bit and put a bit of wonder in it.

LIBRA—You tell people what you think they want to hear. You have a charming voice, soft as toilet paper.

SCORPIO—Your speech is nasty, sarcastic, truthful, and always fascinating. You're good at digging out secrets and have fanatical, strong opinions.

SAGITTARIUS—You have a gorgeous, sexy speaking voice, Richard Burton! You can sell anyone anything with your cheerful philosophy.

CAPRICORN—Nixon's Mercury is here. You're a master of diplomacy if it suits you. Your mind is like a steel trap. This is an excellent place to have your talker—you see the Big Picture.

AQUARIUS—If you're not a member of some crazy fanatic cult, your ideas are way ahead of their time. You have an excitable, logical way of expressing yourself, with a slight stammer when rabid.

PISCES—Cute spoonerisms creep into your speech. You'd do anything to avoid hurting people's feelings—you are the heart and soul of tact. You'd even lie, but you forget the details. Witty.

1901	JAN	2	Cap	12:27		JUN	14	Gem	6:23
	JAN	21	Aqu	6:30		JUL	1	Can	22:13
	FEB	7	Pic	10:35		JUL	16	Leo	0:26
	APR	15	Ari	17:10		AUG	1	Vir	13:25
	MAY	3	Tau	13:57		AUG	28	Lib	8:16
	MAY	17	Gem	20:08		SEP	7	Vir	19:44
	JUN	1	Can	23:35		OCT	9	Lib	1:50
	AUG	10	Leo	4:45		OCT	26	Scp	20:15
	AUG	25	Vir	22:24		NOV	14	Sag	13:47
	SEP	11	Lib	6:21		DEC	4	Cap	14:14
	OCT	1	Scp	4:35	1905	FEB	9	Aqu	5:35
	DEC	6	Sag	23:38		FEB	27	Pic	22:08
	DEC	26	Cap	9:31		MAR	15	Ari	19:33
1902	JAN	13	Aqu	19:35		APR	1	Tau	18:20
	FEB	1	Pic	15:59		APR	28	Ari	13:10
	FEB	18	Aqu	7:00		MAY	15	Tau	20:06
	MAR	19	Pic	3:04		JUN	8	Gem	18:00
	APR	9	Ari	12:07		JUN	23	Can	9:54
	APR	25	Tau	8:41		JUL	7	Leo	22:07
	MAY	9	Gem	12:09		JUL	27	Vir	6:50
	MAY	29	Can	8:27		OCT	1	Lib	23:17
	JUN	26	Gem	6:44		OCT	19	Scp	7:45
	JUL	13	Can	9:31		NOV	7	Sag	16:27
	AUG	2	Leo	21:22		DEC	2	Cap	4:45
	AUG	17	Vir	16:34		DEC	10	Sag	0:43
	SEP	4	Lib	2:30	1906	JAN	12	Cap	20:56
	SEP	28	Scp	7:21		FEB	2	Aqu	12:04
	OCT	15	Lib	23:35		FEB	20	Pic	3:32
	NOV	10	Scp	15:08		MAR	8	Ari	2:10
	NOV	30	Sag	1:30		MAY	15	Tau	3:10
	DEC	19	Cap	3:01		MAY	31	Gem	22:49
1903	JAN	6	Aqu	19:31		JUN	14	Can	19:24
	MAR	14	Pic	21:52		JUN	30	Leo	21:27
	APR	2	Ari	0:25		SEP	7	Vir	21:54
	APR	16	Tau	21:51		SEP	24	Lib	3:26
	MAY	2	Gem	13:36		OCT	11	Scp	23:37
	JUL	10	Can	13:08		NOV	1	Sag	19:33
	JUL	25	Leo	12:11		DEC	6	Scp	22:38
	AUG	9	Vir	17:51		DEC	12	Sag	23:48
	AUG	29	Lib	5:36	1907	JAN	7	Cap	0:55
	NOV	4	Scp	4:56		JAN	26	Aqu	5:00
	NOV	22	Sag	19:22		FEB	12	Pic	8:38
	DEC	12	Cap	0:14		MAR	3	Ari	20:53
1904	JAN	2	Aqu	9:25		MAR	14	Pic	4:29
	JAN	14	Cap	3:24		APR	18	Ari	10:42
	FEB	15	Aqu	10:59		MAY	8	Tau	15:22
	MAR	7	Pic	8:05		MAY	23	Gem	10:39
	MAR	23	Ari	23:33		JUN	6	Can	16:43
	APR	7	Tau	19:13		JUN	27	Leo	8:05

1907	JUL	26	Can	14:50	NOV	19	Sag	8:12
	AUG	12	Leo	16:20	DEC	8	Cap	18:23
	AUG	31	Vir	6:54	1911 FEB	13	Aqu	4:03
	SEP	16	Lib	6:56	MAR	4	Pic	21:14
	OCT	5	Scp	4:36	MAR	21	Ari	3:30
	DEC	11	Sag	3:37	APR	5	Tau	9:04
	DEC	31	Cap	3:57	JUN	13	Gem	1:26
1908	JAN	18	Aqu	17:22	JUN	28	Can	23:59
	FEB	5	Pic	4:24	JUL	13	Leo	3:20
	APR	12	Ari	22:48	JUL	30	Vir	13:41
	APR	29	Tau	18:59	OCT	6	Lib	20:49
	MAY	13	Gem	20:52	OCT	24	Scp	6:34
	MAY	30	Can	4:34	NOV	12	Sag	4:56
	AUG	6	Leo	23:47	DEC	3	Cap	1:44
	AUG	22	Vir	1:31	DEC	27	Sag	16:53
	SEP	7	Lib	18:14	1912 JAN	15	Cap	7:15
	SEP	28	Scp	19:36	FEB	7	Aqu	2:25
	NOV	1	Lib	22:56	FEB	25	Pic	6:32
	NOV	11	Scp	17:52	MAR	12	Ari	1:26
	DEC	3	Sag	17:54	MAY	16	Tau	19:54
	DEC	22	Cap	22:31	JUN	5	Gem	5:10
1909	JAN	10	Aqu	9:00	JUN	19	Can	9:00
	MAR	17	Pic	11:31	JUL	4	Leo	9:00
	APR	6	Ari	1:27	JUL	26	Vir	8:13
	APR	21	Tau	10:00	AUG	21	Leo	3:21
	MAY	5	Gem	21:46	SEP	10	Vir	17:07
	JUL	13	Can	6:04	SEP	28	Lib	7:27
	JUL	30	Leo	0:39	OCT	15	Scp	18:59
	AUG	13	Vir	21:32	NOV	4	Sag	14:46
	SEP	1	Lib	0:05	1913 JAN	10	Cap	5:20
	NOV	7	Scp	18:06	JAN	30	Aqu	1:44
	NOV	26	Sag	15:00	FEB	16	Pic	10:44
	DEC	15	Cap	16:33	MAR	4	Ari	22:36
1910	JAN	3	Aqu	21:28	APR	7	Pic	16:42
	JAN	31	Cap	3:04	APR	14	Ari	2:46
	FEB	15	Aqu	13:10	MAY	12	Tau	6:15
	MAR	11	Pic	21:34	MAY	28	Gem	0:29
	MAR	29	Ari	6:52	JUN	10	Can	21:32
	APR	13	Tau	0:28	JUN	28	Leo	5:37
	APR	30	Gem	15:54	SEP	4	Vir	10:58
	JUN	1	Tau	23:43	SEP	20	Lib	10:03
	JUN	12	Gem	0:14	OCT	8	Scp	14:53
	JUL	7	Can	3:28	OCT	30	Sag	18:07
	JUL	21	Leo	12:38	NOV	23	Scp	12:31
	AUG	6	Vir	4:37	DEC	13	Sag	8:51
	AUG	27	Lib	6:42	1914 JAN	3	Cap	19:20
	SEP	28	Vir	13:48	JAN	22	Aqu	15:51
	OCT	12	Lib	4:35	FEB	8	Pic	19:11
	OCT	31	Scp	18:09	APR	16	Ari	16:06

1914	MAY	5	Tau	0:58
	MAY	19	Gem	10:03
	JUN	3	Can	5:53
	AUG	11	Leo	6:29
	AUG	27	Vir	10:46
	SEP	12	Lib	15:47
	OCT	2	Scp	5:54
	DEC	8	Sag	4:54
	DEC	27	Cap	17:41
1915	JAN	15	Aqu	4:28
	FEB	2	Pic	10:33
	FEB	23	Aqu	15:13
	MAR	19	Pic	8:46
	APR	10	Ari	19:22
	APR	26	Tau	21:41
	MAY	10	Gem	23:47
	MAY	29	Can	10:34
	AUG	4	Leo	8:59
	AUG	19	Vir	4:38
	SEP	5	Lib	9:03
	SEP	28	Scp	8:11
	OCT	21	Lib	1:11
	NOV	11	Scp	14:08
	DEC	1	Sag	9:18
	DEC	20	Cap	11:14
1916	JAN	8	Aqu	1:22
	MAR	15	Pic	0:08
	APR	2	Ari	11:00
	APR	17	Tau	11:00
	MAY	2	Gem	16:14
	JUL	10	Can	18:17
	JUL	26	Leo	1:42
	AUG	10	Vir	4:05
	AUG	29	Lib	4:53
	NOV	4	Scp	12:26
	NOV	23	Sag	3:40
	DEC	12	Cap	7:13
1917	JAN	1	Aqu	17:07
	JAN	18	Cap	4:21
	FEB	15	Aqu	3:21
	MAR	8	Pic	15:34
	MAR	25	Ari	11:35
	APR	9	Tau	5:43
	JUN	14	Gem	18:14
	JUL	3	Can	10:27
	JUL	17	Leo	13:26
	AUG	2	Vir	19:31
	AUG	26	Lib	22:51
	SEP	14	Vir	11:41

	OCT	10	Lib	4:48
	OCT	28	Scp	5:24
	NOV	15	Sag	21:29
	DEC	5	Cap	16:57
1918	FEB	10	Aqu	9:24
	MAR	1	Pic	7:53
	MAR	17	Ari	7:25
	APR	2	Tau	13:16
	JUN	10	Gem	1:22
	JUN	24	Can	23:50
	JUL	9	Leo	8:39
	JUL	28	Vir	1:28
	OCT	3	Lib	9:00
	OCT	20	Scp	16:48
	NOV	8	Sag	22:06
	DEC	1	Cap	16:20
	DEC	15	Sag	12:21
1919	JAN	13	Cap	18:13
	FEB	3	Aqu	19:27
	FEB	21	Pic	14:10
	MAR	9	Ari	10:43
	MAY	16	Tau	2:26
	JUN	2	Gem	11:06
	JUN	16	Can	8:45
	JUL	2	Leo	2:02
	SEP	9	Vir	3:43
	SEP	25	Lib	14:16
	OCT	13	Scp	7:26
	NOV	2	Sag	19:07
1920	JAN	8	Cap	5:56
	JAN	27	Aqu	13:49
	FEB	13	Pic	18:42
	MAR	2	Ari	19:25
	MAR	19	Pic	16:15
	APR	17	Ari	18:06
	MAY	8	Tau	23:56
	MAY	24	Gem	0:32
	JUN	7	Can	3:02
	JUN	26	Leo	12:30
	AUG	2	Can	22:31
	AUG	10	Leo	9:11
	AUG	31	Vir	18:29
	SEP	16	Lib	17:14
	OCT	5	Scp	9:27
	OCT	30	Sag	12:40
	NOV	10	Scp	19:01
	DEC	11	Sag	4:37
	DEC	31	Cap	11:23
1921	JAN	19	Aqu	2:29

921	FEB	5	Pic	10:14
	APR	14	Ari	2:12
	MAY	1	Tau	7:03
	MAY	15	Gem	10:09
	MAY	31	Can	5:12
	AUG	8	Leo	7:41
	AUG	23	Vir	13:54
	SEP	9	Lib	2:37
	SEP	29	Scp	16:02
	DEC	5	Sag	0:28
	DEC	24	Cap	6:45
922	JAN	11	Aqu	16:58
	FEB	1	Pic	17:48
	FEB	9	Aqu	3:39
	MAR	18	Pic	6:32
	APR	7	Ari	10:22
	APR	22	Tau	23:19
	MAY	7	Gem	7:04
	JUN	1	Can	3:07
	JUN	10	Gem	21:55
	JUL	13	Can	20:04
	JUL	31	Leo	13:26
	AUG	15	Vir	8:59
	SEP	2	Lib	4:20
	OCT	1	Scp	9:10
	OCT	5	Lib	1:05
	NOV	8	Scp	22:32
	NOV	27	Sag	23:06
	DEC	17	Cap	0:28
1923	JAN	4	Aqu	23:40
	FEB	6	Cap	17:09
	FEB	13	Aqu	23:25
	MAR	13	Pic	2:37
	MAR	30	Ari	18:09
	APR	14	Tau	12:58
	MAY	1	Gem	5:18
	JUL	8	Can	12:47
	JUL	23	Leo	2:08
	AUG	7	Vir	13:34
	AUG	27	Lib	22:30
	OCT	4	Vir	13:20
	OCT	11	Lib	22:25
	NOV	2	Scp	2:47
	NOV	20	Sag	16:26
	DEC	10	Cap	0:18
1924	FEB	14	Aqu	3:18
	MAR	5	Pic	5:53
	MAR	21	Ari	15:38
	APR	5	Tau	16:23
	JUN	13	Gem	1:42
	JUN	29	Can	13:23
	JUL	13	Leo	15:38
	JUL	30	Vir	16:49
	OCT	7	Lib	4:12
	OCT	24	Scp	15:59
	NOV	12	Sag	12:08
	DEC	2	Cap	23:42
	DEC	31	Sag	16:36
1925	JAN	14	Cap	7:16
	FEB	7	Aqu	8:13
	FEB	25	Pic	16:54
	MAR	13	Ari	12:36
	APR	1	Tau	15:22
	APR	15	Ari	23:09
	MAY	17	Tau	1:32
	JUN	6	Gem	15:23
	JUN	20	Can	23:07
	JUL	5	Leo	17:52
	JUL	26	Vir	11:46
	AUG	27	Leo	6:47
	SEP	11	Vir	5:09
	SEP	29	Lib	18:05
	OCT	17	Scp	3:52
	NOV	5	Sag	18:55
1926	JAN	11	Cap	7:28
	JAN	31	Aqu	10:05
	FEB	17	Pic	21:30
	MAR	6	Ari	2:57
	MAY	13	Tau	10:54
	MAY	29	Gem	13:51
	JUN	12	Can	10:08
	JUN	29	Leo	5:02
	SEP	5	Vir	20:33
	SEP	21	Lib	20:57
	OCT	9	Scp	21:59
	OCT	31	Sag	11:01
	NOV	28	Scp	5:28
	DEC	13	Sag	20:38
1927	JAN	5	Cap	1:59
	JAN	24	Aqu	1:13
	FEB	10	Pic	4:28
	APR	17	Ari	12:24
	MAY	6	Tau	11:29
	MAY	21	Gem	0:04
	JUN	4	Can	13:39
	JUN	28	Leo	19:34
	JUL	14	Can	3:51
	AUG	12	Leo	3:43

1927	AUG	28	Vir	23:08
	SEP	14	Lib	1:38
	OCT	3	Scp	8:39
	DEC	9	Sag	9:26
	DEC	29	Cap	1:48
1928	JAN	16	Aqu	13:35
	FEB	3	Pic	10:23
	FEB	29	Aqu	6:26
	MAR	18	Pic	2:45
	APR	11	Ari	1:55
	APR	27	Tau	10:35
	MAY	11	Gem	12:08
	MAY	28	Can	23:03
	AUG	4	Leo	20:00
	AUG	19	Vir	16:59
	SEP	5	Lib	16:20
	SEP	27	Scp	18:13
	OCT	24	Lib	21:46
	NOV	11	Scp	9:06
	DEC	1	Sag	16:58
	DEC	20	Cap	19:38
1929	JAN	8	Aqu	8:09
	MAR	16	Pic	1:08
	APR	3	Ari	21:21
	APR	19	Tau	0:24
	MAY	3	Gem	21:35
	JUL	11	Can	21:08
	JUL	27	Leo	15:12
	AUG	11	Vir	14:48
	AUG	30	Lib	6:01
	NOV	5	Scp	19:29
	NOV	24	Sag	12:07
	DEC	13	Cap	14:42
1930	JAN	2	Aqu	10:26
	JAN	23	Cap	0:32
	FEB	15	Aqu	15:09
	MAR	9	Pic	22:39
	MAR	26	Ari	23:37
	APR	10	Tau	17:06
	MAY	1	Gem	5:30
	MAY	17	Tau	10:47
	JUN	14	Gem	20:09
	JUL	4	Can	22:11
	JUL	19	Leo	2:44
	AUG	4	Vir	2:39
	AUG	26	Lib	18:05
	SEP	20	Vir	2:13
	OCT	11	Lib	4:45
	OCT	29	Scp	14:35
	NOV	17	Sag	5:32
	DEC	6	Cap	20:58
1931	FEB	11	Aqu	12:28
	MAR	2	Pic	17:28
	MAR	18	Ari	19:31
	APR	3	Tau	13:38
	JUN	11	Gem	7:27
	JUN	26	Can	13:49
	JUL	10	Leo	19:56
	JUL	28	Vir	23:25
	OCT	4	Lib	18:28
	OCT	22	Scp	2:09
	NOV	10	Sag	4:27
	DEC	2	Cap	0:01
	DEC	20	Sag	7:48
1932	JAN	14	Cap	12:47
	FEB	5	Aqu	2:37
	FEB	23	Pic	0:50
	MAR	9	Ari	20:21
	MAY	15	Tau	22:50
	JUN	2	Gem	23:05
	JUN	16	Can	22:31
	JUL	2	Leo	8:17
	JUL	27	Vir	20:38
	AUG	10	Leo	6:52
	SEP	9	Vir	7:20
	SEP	26	Lib	1:15
	OCT	13	Scp	15:42
	NOV	2	Sag	20:28
1933	JAN	8	Cap	10:25
	JAN	27	Aqu	22:40
	FEB	14	Pic	5:07
	MAR	3	Ari	10:50
	MAR	25	Pic	21:53
	APR	17	Ari	15:27
	MAY	10	Tau	7:43
	MAY	25	Gem	14:27
	JUN	8	Can	14:12
	JUN	27	Leo	1:12
	SEP	2	Vir	5:45
	SEP	18	Lib	3:48
	OCT	6	Scp	15:05
	OCT	30	Sag	4:27
	NOV	16	Scp	1:58
	DEC	12	Sag	3:44
1934	JAN	1	Cap	18:40
	JAN	20	Aqu	11:45
	FEB	6	Pic	17:24
	APR	15	Ari	4:14

1934	MAY	2	Tau	18:45		OCT	8	Lib	10:12
	MAY	16	Gem	23:44		OCT	26	Scp	1:14
	JUN	1	Can	8:22		NOV	13	Sag	19:26
	AUG	9	Leo	13:49		DEC	3	Cap	23:52
	AUG	25	Vir	2:18	1938	JAN	6	Sag	22:17
	SEP	10	Lib	11:30		JAN	12	Cap	22:32
	SEP	30	Scp	14:46		FEB	8	Aqu	13:18
	DEC	6	Sag	6:42		FEB	27	Pic	3:01
	DEC	25	Cap	15:00		MAR	15	Ari	0:03
1935	JAN	13	Aqu	1:20		APR	1	Tau	13:25
	FEB	1	Pic	11:17		APR	23	Ari	14:02
	FEB	15	Aqu	2:51		MAY	16	Tau	17:46
	MAR	18	Pic	21:54		JUN	8	Gem	0:32
	APR	8	Ari	18:40		JUN	22	Can	13:09
	APR	24	Tau	12:29		JUL	7	Leo	3:21
	MAY	8	Gem	17:21		JUL	26	Vir	22:55
	MAY	29	Can	19:27		SEP	3	Leo	3:41
	JUN	20	Gem	17:56		SEP	10	Vir	15:40
	JUL	13	Can	22:22		OCT	1	Lib	4:19
	AUG	2	Leo	1:48		OCT	18	Scp	12:44
	AUG	16	Vir	20:40		NOV	6	Sag	23:33
	SEP	3	Lib	9:33	1939	JAN	12	Cap	7:58
	SEP	28	Scp	15:53		FEB	1	Aqu	17:58
	OCT	12	Lib	17:22		FEB	19	Pic	8:10
	NOV	10	Scp	1:24		MAR	7	Ari	9:14
	NOV	29	Sag	7:06		MAY	14	Tau	13:43
	DEC	18	Cap	8:29		MAY	31	Gem	2:46
1936	JAN	6	Aqu	3:32		JUN	13	Can	23:02
	MAR	13	Pic	6:40		JUN	30	Leo	6:41
	MAR	31	Ari	5:09		SEP	7	Vir	4:58
	APR	15	Tau	1:45		SEP	23	Lib	7:48
	MAY	1	Gem	1:30		OCT	11	Scp	5:20
	JUL	8	Can	20:48		NOV	1	Sag	7:04
	JUL	23	Leo	15:40		DEC	3	Scp	8:24
	AUG	7	Vir	23:00		DEC	13	Sag	19:17
	AUG	27	Lib	17:43	1940	JAN	6	Cap	7:56
	NOV	2	Scp	11:00		JAN	25	Aqu	10:15
	NOV	21	Sag	0:39		FEB	11	Pic	14:01
	DEC	10	Cap	6:40		MAR	4	Ari	10:08
1937	JAN	1	Aqu	16:44		MAR	8	Pic	0:55
	JAN	9	Cap	20:50		APR	17	Ari	4:57
	FEB	14	Aqu	0:26		MAY	6	Tau	21:14
	MAR	6	Pic	14:07		MAY	21	Gem	13:59
	MAR	23	Ari	3:41		JUN	4	Can	22:29
	APR	7	Tau	1:10		JUN	26	Leo	14:33
	JUN	13	Gem	22:28		JUL	21	Can	1:40
	JUL	1	Can	2:21		AUG	11	Leo	17:06
	JUL	15	Leo	4:12		AUG	29	Vir	11:11
	JUL	31	Vir	21:07		SEP	14	Lib	11:34

1940	OCT	3	Scp	12:14	1944	FEB	12	Aqu	14:18
	DEC	9	Sag	12:45		MAR	3	Pic	2:46
	DEC	29	Cap	9:36		MAR	19	Ari	7:43
1941	JAN	16	Aqu	22:37		APR	3	Tau	17:29
	FEB	3	Pic	13:09		JUN	11	Gem	11:46
	MAR	7	Aqu	2:56		JUN	27	Can	3:40
	MAR	16	Pic	12:26		JUL	11	Leo	7:42
	APR	12	Ari	7:19		JUL	28	Vir	23:44
	APR	28	Tau	23:09		OCT	5	Lib	3:18
	MAY	13	Gem	0:51		OCT	22	Scp	11:34
	MAY	29	Can	17:33		NOV	10	Sag	11:10
	AUG	6	Leo	5:57		DEC	1	Cap	15:32
	AUG	21	Vir	5:18		DEC	23	Sag	23:22
	SEP	6	Lib	23:58	1945	JAN	14	Cap	3:05
	SEP	28	Scp	9:22		FEB	5	Aqu	9:21
	OCT	29	Lib	20:51		FEB	23	Pic	11:26
	NOV	11	Scp	20:11		MAR	11	Ari	6:45
	DEC	3	Sag	0:11		MAY	16	Tau	15:22
	DEC	22	Cap	3:54		JUN	4	Gem	10:30
1942	JAN	9	Aqu	15:24		JUN	18	Can	12:28
	MAR	17	Pic	0:11		JUL	3	Leo	15:39
	APR	5	Ari	7:07		JUL	26	Vir	14:48
	APR	20	Tau	13:43		AUG	17	Leo	8:36
	MAY	5	Gem	4:38		SEP	10	Vir	7:21
	JUL	12	Can	20:24		SEP	27	Lib	12:09
	JUL	29	Leo	4:24		OCT	15	Scp	0:14
	AUG	13	Vir	1:48		NOV	3	Sag	23:07
	AUG	31	Lib	8:28	1946	JAN	9	Cap	14:10
	NOV	7	Scp	1:45		JAN	29	Aqu	7:23
	NOV	25	Sag	20:26		FEB	15	Pic	15:43
	DEC	14	Cap	22:22		MAR	4	Ari	9:27
1943	JAN	3	Aqu	8:27		APR	1	Pic	18:46
	JAN	27	Cap	23:44		APR	16	Ari	14:55
	FEB	15	Aqu	19:00		MAY	11	Tau	14:29
	MAR	11	Pic	5:00		MAY	27	Gem	4:13
	MAR	28	Ari	11:20		JUN	10	Can	2:01
	APR	12	Tau	4:57		JUN	27	Leo	19:08
	APR	30	Gem	15:56		SEP	3	Vir	16:30
	MAY	26	Tau	10:22		SEP	19	Lib	14:34
	JUN	14	Gem	0:46		OCT	7	Scp	21:22
	JUL	6	Can	9:05		OCT	30	Sag	11:24
	JUL	20	Leo	16:08		NOV	20	Scp	20:10
	AUG	5	Vir	10:34		DEC	13	Sag	0:03
	AUG	27	Lib	0:37	1947	JAN	3	Cap	1:47
	SEP	25	Vir	10:09		JAN	21	Aqu	21:06
	OCT	11	Lib	23:27		FEB	8	Pic	1:32
	OCT	30	Scp	23:38		APR	16	Ari	4:31
	NOV	18	Sag	13:39		MAY	4	Tau	6:03
	DEC	8	Cap	1:48		MAY	18	Gem	13:34

1947	JUN	2	Can	13:41
	AUG	10	Leo	17:40
	AUG	26	Vir	14:51
	SEP	11	Lib	20:55
	OCT	1	Scp	15:26
	DEC	7	Sag	12:32
	DEC	26	Cap	23:18
1948	JAN	14	Aqu	10:07
	FEB	2	Pic	0:47
	FEB	20	Aqu	11:06
	MAR	18	Pic	8:14
	APR	9	Ari	2:26
	APR	25	Tau	1:39
	MAY	9	Gem	4:39
	MAY	28	Can	10:51
	JUN	28	Gem	18:24
	JUL	11	Can	20:57
	AUG	2	Leo	13:55
	AUG	17	Vir	8:44
	SEP	3	Lib	15:48
	SEP	27	Scp	7:19
	OCT	17	Lib	3:22
	NOV	10	Scp	2:19
	NOV	29	Sag	15:10
	DEC	18	Cap	16:47
1949	JAN	6	Aqu	8:53
	MAR	14	Pic	9:52
	APR	1	Ari	16:02
	APR	16	Tau	14:56
	MAY	2	Gem	2:19
	JUL	10	Can	3:19
	JUL	25	Leo	5:20
	AUG	9	Vir	9:05
	AUG	28	Lib	15:48
	NOV	3	Scp	18:58
	NOV	22	Sag	9:07
	DEC	11	Cap	13:38
1950	JAN	1	Aqu	12:41
	JAN	15	Cap	7:09
	FEB	14	Aqu	19:13
	MAR	7	Pic	22:05
	MAR	24	Ari	15:52
	APR	8	Tau	11:13
	JUN	14	Gem	14:33
	JUL	2	Can	14:57
	JUL	16	Leo	17:09
	AUG	2	Vir	2:44
	AUG	27	Lib	14:17
	SEP	10	Vir	18:42

	OCT	9	Lib	14:41
	OCT	27	Scp	10:37
	NOV	15	Sag	3:11
	DEC	5	Cap	1:58
1951	FEB	9	Aqu	17:51
	FEB	28	Pic	13:05
	MAR	16	Ari	11:54
	APR	2	Tau	3:28
	MAY	1	Ari	21:41
	MAY	15	Tau	1:40
	JUN	9	Gem	8:44
	JUN	24	Can	3:14
	JUL	8	Leo	13:39
	JUL	27	Vir	15:24
	OCT	2	Lib	14:26
	OCT	19	Scp	21:53
	NOV	8	Sag	4:59
	DEC	1	Cap	20:42
	DEC	12	Sag	11:32
1952	JAN	13	Cap	6:45
	FEB	3	Aqu	1:38
	FEB	20	Pic	18:55
	MAR	7	Ari	17:11
	MAY	14	Tau	14:44
	MAY	31	Gem	15:26
	JUN	14	Can	12:22
	JUN	30	Leo	10:28
	SEP	7	Vir	12:02
	SEP	23	Lib	18:46
	OCT	11	Scp	13:06
	NOV	1	Sag	5:35
1953	JAN	6	Cap	13:25
	JAN	25	Aqu	19:11
	FEB	11	Pic	23:57
	MAR	2	Ari	19:23
	MAR	15	Pic	21:02
	APR	17	Ari	16:48
	MAY	8	Tau	6:24
	MAY	23	Gem	3:59
	JUN	6	Can	8:24
	JUN	26	Leo	11:01
	JUL	28	Can	14:10
	AUG	11	Leo	14:04
	AUG	30	Vir	22:59
	SEP	15	Lib	21:45
	OCT	4	Scp	16:41
	OCT	31	Sag	15:52
	NOV	6	Scp	21:37
	DEC	10	Sag	14:49

	DEC	30	Cap	17:14
1954	JAN	18	Aqu	7:44
	FEB	4	Pic	18:04
	APR	13	Ari	11:35
	APR	30	Tau	11:26
	MAY	14	Gem	13:58
	MAY	30	Can	16:13
	AUG	7	Leo	14:44
	AUG	22	Vir	17:42
	SEP	8	Lib	8:06
	SEP	29	Scp	4:07
	NOV	4	Lib	14:18
	NOV	11	Scp	10:23
	DEC	4	Sag	7:03
	DEC	23	Cap	12:10
1955	JAN	10	Aqu	23:05
	MAR	17	Pic	20:50
	APR	6	Ari	16:15
	APR	22	Tau	2:58
	MAY	6	Gem	13:06
	JUL	13	Can	14:45
	JUL	30	Leo	17:23
	AUG	14	Vir	13:09
	SEP	1	Lib	12:07
	NOV	8	Scp	6:58
	NOV	27	Sag	4:35
	DEC	16	Cap	6:07
1956	JAN	4	Aqu	9:17
	FEB	2	Cap	13:17
	FEB	15	Aqu	6:35
	MAR	11	Pic	10:28
	MAR	28	Ari	22:42
	APR	12	Tau	17:10
	APR	29	Gem	22:42
	JUL	6	Can	19:02
	JUL	21	Leo	5:36
	AUG	5	Vir	19:07
	AUG	26	Lib	13:30
	SEP	29	Vir	21:41
	OCT	11	Lib	7:29
	OCT	31	Scp	8:20
	NOV	18	Sag	21:43
	DEC	8	Cap	7:12
1957	FEB	12	Aqu	14:30
	MAR	4	Pic	11:35
	MAR	20	Ari	19:49
	APR	4	Tau	23:38
	JUN	12	Gem	13:40
	JUN	28	Can	17:08

	JUL	12	Leo	19:42
	JUL	30	Vir	1:44
	OCT	6	Lib	11:09
	OCT	23	Scp	20:51
	NOV	11	Sag	18:01
	DEC	2	Cap	11:20
	DEC	28	Sag	17:55
1958	JAN	14	Cap	10:04
	FEB	6	Aqu	15:22
	FEB	24	Pic	21:44
	MAR	12	Ari	17:32
	APR	2	Tau	19:20
	APR	10	Ari	12:35
	MAY	17	Tau	1:53
	JUN	5	Gem	20:59
	JUN	20	Can	2:21
	JUL	4	Leo	23:47
	JUL	26	Vir	10:08
	AUG	23	Leo	14:37
	SEP	11	Vir	1:09
	SEP	28	Lib	22:46
	OCT	16	Scp	8:52
	NOV	5	Sag	2:36
1959	JAN	10	Cap	16:48
	JAN	30	Aqu	15:42
	FEB	17	Pic	2:15
	MAR	5	Ari	11:53
	MAY	12	Tau	19:48
	MAY	28	Gem	17:36
	JUN	11	Can	14:11
	JUN	28	Leo	16:32
	SEP	5	Vir	2:28
	SEP	21	Lib	1:20
	OCT	9	Scp	4:02
	OCT	31	Sag	1:17
	NOV	25	Scp	12:07
	DEC	13	Sag	15:43
1960	JAN	4	Cap	8:25
	JAN	23	Aqu	6:17
	FEB	9	Pic	10:14
	APR	16	Ari	2:23
	MAY	4	Tau	16:46
	MAY	19	Gem	3:27
	JUN	2	Can	20:31
	JUL	1	Leo	1:09
	JUL	6	Can	1:00
	AUG	10	Leo	17:49
	AUG	27	Vir	3:12
	SEP	12	Lib	6:30

1960	OCT	1	Scp	17:17
	DEC	7	Sag	17:31
	DEC	27	Cap	7:22
1961	JAN	14	Aqu	18:59
	FEB	1	Pic	21:40
	FEB	24	Aqu	20:31
	MAR	18	Pic	10:16
	APR	10	Ari	9:23
	APR	26	Tau	14:34
	MAY	10	Gem	16:35
	MAY	28	Can	17:23
	AUG	4	Leo	1:16
	AUG	18	Vir	20:52
	SEP	4	Lib	22:33
	SEP	27	Scp	12:17
	OCT	22	Lib	2:30
	NOV	10	Scp	23:54
	NOV	30	Sag	22:55
	DEC	20	Cap	1:05
1962	JAN	7	Aqu	15:08
	MAR	15	Pic	11:43
	APR	3	Ari	2:32
	APR	18	Tau	4:10
	MAY	3	Gem	6:05
	JUL	11	Can	7:37
	JUL	26	Leo	18:50
	AUG	10	Vir	19:30
	AUG	29	Lib	15:48
	NOV	5	Scp	2:21
	NOV	23	Sag	17:32
	DEC	12	Cap	20:51
1963	JAN	2	Aqu	1:11
	JAN	20	Cap	4:57
	FEB	15	Aqu	10:09
	MAR	9	Pic	5:27
	MAR	26	Ari	3:53
	APR	9	Tau	22:04
	MAY	3	Gem	4:14
	MAY	10	Tau	19:57
	JUN	14	Gem	23:21
	JUL	4	Can	3:00
	JUL	18	Leo	6:20
	AUG	3	Vir	9:21
	AUG	26	Lib	20:34
	SEP	16	Vir	20:18
	OCT	10	Lib	16:44
	OCT	28	Scp	19:55
	NOV	16	Sag	11:08
	DEC	6	Cap	5:18

1964	FEB	10	Aqu	21:31
	FEB	29	Pic	22:51
	MAR	16	Ari	23:55
	APR	2	Tau	0:59
	JUN	9	Gem	15:46
	JUN	24	Can	17:18
	JUL	9	Leo	0:39
	JUL	27	Vir	11:36
	OCT	3	Lib	0:13
	OCT	20	Scp	7:12
	NOV	8	Sag	11:03
	NOV	30	Cap	19:31
	DEC	16	Sag	14:02
1965	JAN	13	Cap	3:13
	FEB	3	Aqu	9:03
	FEB	21	Pic	5:40
	MAR	9	Ari	2:20
	MAY	15	Tau	13:20
	JUN	2	Gem	3:47
	JUN	16	Can	2:05
	JUL	1	Leo	15:56
	JUL	31	Vir	11:24
	AUG	3	Leo	4:59
	SEP	8	Vir	17:14
	SEP	25	Lib	5:50
	OCT	12	Scp	21:16
	NOV	2	Sag	6:05
1966	JAN	7	Cap	18:27
	JAN	27	Aqu	4:10
	FEB	13	Pic	10:18
	MAR	3	Ari	2:59
	MAR	22	Pic	2:34
	APR	17	Ari	21:32
	MAY	9	Tau	14:49
	MAY	24	Gem	18:00
	JUN	7	Can	19:12
	JUN	26	Leo	19:06
	SEP	1	Vir	10:36
	SEP	17	Lib	8:20
	OCT	5	Scp	22:03
	OCT	30	Sag	7:39
	NOV	13	Scp	3:04
	DEC	11	Sag	15:28
1967	JAN	1	Cap	0:53
	JAN	19	Aqu	17:06
	FEB	6	Pic	0:38
	APR	14	Ari	14:39
	MAY	1	Tau	23:27
	MAY	16	Gem	3:28

1967	MAY	31	Can	18:03
	AUG	8	Leo	22:09
	AUG	24	Vir	6:18
	SEP	9	Lib	16:54
	SEP	30	Scp	1:47
	DEC	5	Sag	13:42
	DEC	24	Cap	20:34
1968	JAN	12	Aqu	7:20
	FEB	1	Pic	12:59
	FEB	11	Aqu	18:14
	MAR	17	Pic	14:46
	APR	7	Ari	1:02
	APR	22	Tau	16:19
	MAY	6	Gem	22:57
	MAY	29	Can	22:44
	JUN	13	Gem	22:27
	JUL	13	Can	1:30
	JUL	31	Leo	6:11
	AUG	15	Vir	0:54
	SEP	1	Lib	16:59
	SEP	28	Scp	14:41
	OCT	7	Lib	22:26
	NOV	8	Scp	11:01
	NOV	27	Sag	12:48
	DEC	16	Cap	14:12
1969	JAN	4	Aqu	12:19
	MAR	12	Pic	15:20
	MAR	30	Ari	9:59
	APR	14	Tau	5:55
	APR	30	Gem	15:19
	JUL	8	Can	3:58
	JUL	22	Leo	19:12
	AUG	7	Vir	4:22
	AUG	27	Lib	6:51
	OCT	7	Vir	6:25
	OCT	9	Lib	17:14
	NOV	1	Scp	16:54
	NOV	20	Sag	6:01
	DEC	9	Cap	13:22
1970	FEB	13	Aqu	13:09
	MAR	5	Pic	20:11
	MAR	22	Ari	8:00
	APR	6	Tau	7:41
	JUN	13	Gem	12:46
	JUN	30	Can	6:23
	JUL	14	Leo	8:07
	JUL	31	Vir	5:22
	OCT	7	Lib	18:04
	OCT	25	Scp	6:17
	NOV	13	Sag	1:17
	DEC	3	Cap	10:15
1971	JAN	2	Sag	23:40
	JAN	14	Cap	2:17
	FEB	7	Aqu	20:52
	FEB	26	Pic	7:58
	MAR	14	Ari	4:46
	APR	1	Tau	14:12
	APR	18	Ari	21:48
	MAY	17	Tau	3:33
	JUN	7	Gem	6:45
	JUN	21	Can	16:25
	JUL	6	Leo	8:54
	JUL	26	Vir	17:04
	AUG	29	Leo	20:57
	SEP	11	Vir	6:44
	SEP	30	Lib	9:19
	OCT	17	Scp	17:50
	NOV	6	Sag	7:00
1972	JAN	11	Cap	18:19
	JAN	31	Aqu	23:47
	FEB	18	Pic	12:54
	MAR	5	Ari	17:00
	MAY	12	Tau	23:46
	MAY	29	Gem	6:46
	JUN	12	Can	2:56
	JUN	28	Leo	16:53
	SEP	5	Vir	11:37
	SEP	21	Lib	12:12
	OCT	9	Scp	11:11
	OCT	30	Sag	19:28
	NOV	29	Scp	7:47
	DEC	12	Sag	23:21
1973	JAN	4	Cap	14:42
	JAN	23	Aqu	15:24
	FEB	9	Pic	19:31
	APR	16	Ari	21:18
	MAY	6	Tau	2:55
	MAY	20	Gem	17:25
	JUN	4	Can	4:43
	JUN	27	Leo	6:42
	JUL	16	Can	7:48
	AUG	11	Leo	12:21
	AUG	28	Vir	15:23
	SEP	13	Lib	16:17
	OCT	2	Scp	20:13
	DEC	8	Sag	21:30
	DEC	28	Cap	15:15
1974	JAN	16	Aqu	3:57

1974	FEB	2	Pic	22:43		JUN	10	Gem	21:07
	MAR	2	Aqu	18:22		JUN	26	Can	7:08
	MAR	17	Pic	20:12		JUL	10	Leo	12:01
	APR	11	Ari	15:21		JUL	28	Vir	10:16
	APR	28	Tau	3:11		OCT	4	Lib	9:17
	MAY	12	Gem	4:56		OCT	21	Scp	16:24
	MAY	29	Can	8:04		NOV	9	Sag	17:21
	AUG	5	Leo	11:42		DEC	1	Cap	6:44
	AUG	20	Vir	9:05		DEC	21	Sag	7:17
	SEP	6	Lib	5:49	1978	JAN	13	Cap	20:08
	SEP	28	Scp	0:21		FEB	4	Aqu	15:55
	OCT	26	Lib	23:23		FEB	22	Pic	16:12
	NOV	11	Scp	16:06		MAR	10	Ari	12:11
	DEC	2	Sag	6:18		MAY	16	Tau	8:21
	DEC	21	Cap	9:17		JUN	3	Gem	15:27
1975	JAN	8	Aqu	21:59		JUN	17	Can	15:50
	MAR	16	Pic	11:51		JUL	2	Leo	22:29
	APR	4	Ari	12:29		JUL	27	Vir	6:10
	APR	19	Tau	17:21		AUG	13	Leo	6:40
	MAY	4	Gem	11:56		SEP	9	Vir	19:24
	JUL	12	Can	8:56		SEP	26	Lib	16:41
	JUL	28	Leo	8:05		OCT	14	Scp	5:31
	AUG	12	Vir	6:13		NOV	3	Sag	7:49
	AUG	30	Lib	17:21	1979	JAN	8	Cap	22:34
	NOV	6	Scp	8:59		JAN	28	Aqu	12:50
	NOV	25	Sag	1:45		FEB	14	Pic	20:39
	DEC	14	Cap	4:11		MAR	3	Ari	21:33
1976	JAN	2	Aqu	20:23		MAR	28	Pic	11:02
	JAN	25	Cap	1:36		APR	17	Ari	12:49
	FEB	15	Aqu	19:04		MAY	10	Tau	22:04
	MAR	9	Pic	12:03		MAY	26	Gem	7:44
	MAR	26	Ari	15:37		JUN	9	Can	6:33
	APR	10	Tau	9:30		JUN	27	Leo	9:52
	APR	29	Gem	23:12		SEP	2	Vir	21:39
	MAY	19	Tau	19:18		SEP	18	Lib	19:00
	JUN	13	Gem	19:20		OCT	7	Scp	3:56
	JUL	4	Can	14:19		OCT	30	Sag	7:07
	JUL	18	Leo	19:36		NOV	18	Scp	3:00
	AUG	3	Vir	16:42		DEC	12	Sag	13:35
	AUG	25	Lib	20:53	1980	JAN	2	Cap	8:04
	SEP	21	Vir	7:16		JAN	21	Aqu	2:20
	OCT	10	Lib	14:47		FEB	7	Pic	8:08
	OCT	29	Scp	4:56		APR	14	Ari	15:59
	NOV	16	Sag	19:03		MAY	2	Tau	10:56
	DEC	6	Cap	9:26		MAY	16	Gem	17:07
1977	FEB	10	Aqu	23:56		MAY	31	Can	22:07
	MAR	2	Pic	8:10		AUG	9	Leo	3:31
	MAR	18	Ari	11:57		AUG	24	Vir	18:48
	APR	3	Tau	2:47		SEP	10	Lib	2:01

1980	SEP	30	Scp	1:17
	DEC	5	Sag	19:46
	DEC	25	Cap	4:48
1981	JAN	12	Aqu	15:49
	JAN	31	Pic	17:36
	FEB	16	Aqu	7:49
	MAR	18	Pic	4:34
	APR	8	Ari	9:12
	APR	24	Tau	5:32
	MAY	8	Gem	9:43
	MAY	28	Can	17:05
	JUN	22	Gem	22:54
	JUL	12	Can	21:09
	AUG	1	Leo	18:31
	AUG	16	Vir	12:48
	SEP	2	Lib	22:41
	SEP	27	Scp	11:03
	OCT	14	Lib	1:57
	NOV	9	Scp	13:15
	NOV	28	Sag	20:53
	DEC	17	Cap	22:22
1982	JAN	5	Aqu	16:50
	MAR	13	Pic	19:12
	MAR	31	Ari	21:00
	APR	15	Tau	18:55
	MAY	1	Gem	13:30
	JUL	9	Can	11:27
	JUL	24	Leo	8:49
	AUG	8	Vir	14:08
	AUG	28	Lib	3:23
	NOV	3	Scp	1:11
	NOV	21	Sag	14:29
	DEC	10	Cap	20:05
1983	JAN	1	Aqu	13:33
	JAN	12	Cap	6:12
	FEB	14	Aqu	9:37
	MAR	7	Pic	4:25
	MAR	23	Ari	20:10
	APR	7	Tau	17:05
	JUN	14	Gem	8:07
	JUL	1	Can	19:19
	JUL	15	Leo	20:58
	AUG	1	Vir	10:23
	AUG	29	Lib	6:07
	SEP	6	Vir	2:00
	OCT	8	Lib	23:45
	OCT	26	Scp	15:48
	NOV	14	Sag	8:57
	DEC	4	Cap	11:24
1984	FEB	9	Aqu	1:52
	FEB	27	Pic	18:08
	MAR	14	Ari	16:28
	MAR	31	Tau	20:27
	APR	25	Ari	12:07
	MAY	15	Tau	12:34
	JUN	7	Gem	15:45
	JUN	22	Can	6:40
	JUL	6	Leo	18:57
	JUL	26	Vir	6:50
	SEP	30	Lib	19:45
	OCT	18	Scp	3:03
	NOV	6	Sag	12:10
	DEC	1	Cap	16:33
	DEC	7	Sag	20:53
1985	JAN	11	Cap	18:26
	FEB	1	Aqu	7:45
	FEB	18	Pic	23:42
	MAR	7	Ari	0:08
	MAY	14	Tau	2:11
	MAY	30	Gem	19:45
	JUN	13	Can	16:12
	JUN	29	Leo	19:35
	SEP	6	Vir	19:40
	SEP	22	Lib	23:14
	OCT	10	Scp	18:51
	OCT	31	Sag	16:45
	DEC	4	Scp	20:17
	DEC	12	Sag	11:05
1986	JAN	5	Cap	20:43
	JAN	25	Aqu	0:35
	FEB	11	Pic	5:23
	MAR	3	Ari	7:22
	MAR	11	Pic	16:38
	APR	17	Ari	12:34
	MAY	7	Tau	12:35
	MAY	22	Gem	7:27
	JUN	5	Can	14:07
	JUN	26	Leo	14:16
	JUL	23	Can	21:54
	AUG	11	Leo	21:10
	AUG	30	Vir	3:29
	SEP	15	Lib	2:29
	OCT	4	Scp	0:20
	DEC	10	Sag	0:35
	DEC	29	Cap	23:11
1987	JAN	17	Aqu	13:09
	FEB	4	Pic	2:32
	MAR	11	Aqu	23:05

1987	MAR	13	Pic	22:18		JUL	11	Leo	23:50
	APR	12	Ari	20:24		JUL	29	Vir	11:11
	APR	29	Tau	15:40		OCT	5	Lib	17:45
	MAY	13	Gem	17:51		OCT	23	Scp	1:47
	MAY	30	Can	4:22		NOV	11	Sag	0:08
	AUG	6	Leo	21:21		DEC	2	Cap	0:14
	AUG	21	Vir	21:37		DEC	25	Sag	23:01
	SEP	7	Lib	13:53	1991	JAN	14	Cap	8:03
	SEP	28	Scp	17:22		FEB	5	Aqu	22:22
	NOV	1	Lib	2:17		FEB	24	Pic	2:36
	NOV	11	Scp	21:57		MAR	11	Ari	22:41
	DEC	3	Sag	13:34		MAY	16	Tau	22:46
	DEC	22	Cap	17:41		JUN	5	Gem	2:25
1988	JAN	10	Aqu	5:29		JUN	19	Can	5:41
	MAR	16	Pic	10:10		JUL	4	Leo	6:06
	APR	4	Ari	22:05		JUL	26	Vir	13:01
	APR	20	Tau	6:43		AUG	19	Leo	21:39
	MAY	4	Gem	19:41		SEP	10	Vir	17:15
	JUL	12	Can	6:42		SEP	28	Lib	3:27
	JUL	28	Leo	21:20		OCT	15	Scp	14:02
	AUG	12	Vir	17:30		NOV	4	Sag	10:42
	AUG	30	Lib	20:26	1992	JAN	10	Cap	1:47
	NOV	6	Scp	14:58		JAN	29	Aqu	21:16
	NOV	25	Sag	10:06		FEB	16	Pic	7:05
	DEC	14	Cap	11:55		MAR	3	Ari	21:47
1989	JAN	2	Aqu	19:42		APR	3	Pic	23:54
	JAN	29	Cap	4:32		APR	14	Ari	17:37
	FEB	14	Aqu	18:13		MAY	11	Tau	4:11
	MAR	10	Pic	18:09		MAY	26	Gem	21:17
	MAR	28	Ari	3:17		JUN	9	Can	18:28
	APR	11	Tau	21:37		JUN	27	Leo	5:12
	APR	29	Gem	19:54		SEP	3	Vir	8:04
	MAY	28	Tau	23:00		SEP	19	Lib	5:42
	JUN	12	Gem	8:56		OCT	7	Scp	10:14
	JUL	6	Can	0:55		OCT	29	Sag	17:04
	JUL	20	Leo	9:06		NOV	21	Scp	19:43
	AUG	5	Vir	0:56		DEC	12	Sag	8:06
	AUG	26	Lib	6:15	1993	JAN	2	Cap	14:49
	SEP	26	Vir	15:49		JAN	21	Aqu	11:26
	OCT	11	Lib	6:11		FEB	7	Pic	16:21
	OCT	30	Scp	13:54		APR	15	Ari	15:19
	NOV	18	Sag	3:11		MAY	3	Tau	21:54
	DEC	7	Cap	14:31		MAY	18	Gem	6:54
1990	FEB	12	Aqu	1:13		JUN	2	Can	3:55
	MAR	3	Pic	17:16		AUG	10	Leo	5:51
	MAR	20	Ari	0:06		AUG	26	Vir	7:07
	APR	4	Tau	7:37		SEP	11	Lib	11:19
	JUN	12	Gem	0:30		OCT	1	Scp	2:11
	JUN	27	Can	20:47		DEC	7	Sag	1:05

	DEC	26	Cap	12:48		MAR	16	Ari	4:14
1994	JAN	14	Aqu	0:26		APR	1	Tau	13:46
	FEB	1	Pic	10:29		MAY	5	Ari	2:23
	FEB	21	Aqu	15:21		MAY	12	Tau	10:25
	MAR	18	Pic	12:05		JUN	8	Gem	23:26
	APR	9	Ari	16:31		JUN	23	Can	20:42
	APR	25	Tau	18:28		JUL	8	Leo	5:29
	MAY	9	Gem	21:09		JUL	27	Vir	0:43
	MAY	28	Can	14:53		OCT	2	Lib	5:39
	JUL	2	Gem	23:28		OCT	19	Scp	12:10
	JUL	10	Can	12:41		NOV	7	Sag	17:44
	AUG	3	Leo	6:10		NOV	30	Cap	19:13
	AUG	18	Vir	0:45		DEC	13	Sag	17:28
	SEP	4	Lib	4:57	1998	JAN	12	Cap	16:22
	SEP	27	Scp	8:52		FEB	2	Aqu	15:16
	OCT	19	Lib	6:09		FEB	20	Pic	10:23
	NOV	10	Scp	12:48		MAR	8	Ari	8:30
	NOV	30	Sag	4:40		MAY	15	Tau	2:11
	DEC	19	Cap	6:27		JUN	1	Gem	8:08
1995	JAN	6	Aqu	22:18		JUN	15	Can	5:34
	MAR	14	Pic	21:36		JUN	30	Leo	23:53
	APR	2	Ari	7:30		SEP	8	Vir	1:59
	APR	17	Tau	7:55		SEP	24	Lib	10:14
	MAY	2	Gem	15:19		OCT	12	Scp	2:46
	JUL	10	Can	16:58		NOV	1	Sag	16:04
	JUL	25	Leo	22:20	1999	JAN	7	Cap	2:05
	AUG	10	Vir	0:14		JAN	26	Aqu	9:33
	AUG	29	Lib	2:08		FEB	12	Pic	15:29
	NOV	4	Scp	8:52		MAR	2	Ari	22:52
	NOV	22	Sag	22:48		MAR	18	Pic	9:07
	DEC	12	Cap	2:58		APR	17	Ari	22:10
1996	JAN	1	Aqu	18:08		MAY	8	Tau	21:24
	JAN	17	Cap	9:18		MAY	23	Gem	21:23
	FEB	15	Aqu	2:46		JUN	7	Can	0:20
	MAR	7	Pic	11:54		JUN	26	Leo	15:40
	MAR	24	Ari	8:04		JUL	31	Can	19:18
	APR	8	Tau	3:18		AUG	11	Leo	4:24
	JUN	13	Gem	21:46		AUG	31	Vir	15:17
	JUL	2	Can	7:38		SEP	16	Lib	12:55
	JUL	16	Leo	9:57		OCT	5	Scp	5:14
	AUG	1	Vir	16:18		OCT	30	Sag	20:11
	AUG	26	Lib	5:18		NOV	9	Scp	19:26
	SEP	12	Vir	8:59		DEC	11	Sag	2:11
	OCT	9	Lib	3:14		DEC	31	Cap	6:50
	OCT	27	Scp	1:02	2000	JAN	18	Aqu	22:21
	NOV	14	Sag	16:37		FEB	5	Pic	8:10
	DEC	4	Cap	13:50		APR	13	Ari	0:19
1997	FEB	9	Aqu	5:55		APR	30	Tau	3:55
	FEB	28	Pic	3:56		MAY	14	Gem	7:12

2000 MAY 30 Can 4:28
     AUG 7 Leo 5:43
     AUG 22 Vir 10:12
     SEP 7 Lib 22:24
     SEP 28 Scp 13:29
     NOV 7 Lib 16:48
     NOV 8 Scp 23:49
     DEC 3 Sag 20:27
     DEC 23 Cap 2:04

Don't Sign, Don't Buy— Mercury Retrograde

Let's not get too *superstitious* here gang, but don't sign important stuff when Mercury is going backward. It does this backward boogie in a three-week stretch, three or four times a year.

Letters get delayed sometimes. If you're sending some Wedgwood to Uncle Nigel you're safer if you deliver it yourself—those packages will rattle just a touch too much otherwise.

Travel gets weird. Often the buses go on strike, or the plane's delayed. Your hosts said they'd meet you on the left side of Heathrow airport, and it's bigger than you thought, and you can't find their home phone number. Double check and have a back-up plan before you embark.

Contracts and leases that you sign now will need adjusting later. You may overlook an important clause. Or the landlord may forget to sign the thing, too. You will probably want to alter something in the contract later.

Writers, hacks, and editors beware! The stuff that gets handed in during a Mercury backward period needs redoing, if it gets handed in at *all*. Don't believe the deadlines you give your writers—those jaw-jerkers will promise you the Moon but they can't deliver on a Mercury retrograde.

Your new *stereo* will seem to be your pride and joy when you buy it on the backward boogaloo, but when that rewind button sticks for the twenty-eighth time you won't think it's so cute. Ditto for all the tape players, radios, electronic junk, computers, cars, and mechanical furshlugginers you buy now. *Don't buy* major appliances now. You can buy other things.

Cars and boats may perform surprisingly well on a retrograde Mercury, if you don't mind the sound of little bits and bobs rattling and squeaking and smoking.

Whatever gave you the impression that Mercury retrograde was *bad*? It's all in how you look at it. Use it to clean out the drawers and files, edit your book report, revise, rethink, retread, and tidy up. You *can* stall, you see, and hold off your decisions on major matters until Mercury goes direct again. It's cleverer to stall at these times because more information will come to you over the time period. Why push your affairs when the tide is out?

Geminis and Virgos please note: as Mercury rules your signs, this period is a gift to you to doubly slow down, rest, exercise, and clean up old muck. You Geminis can jabber for three weeks, while the Virgos happily analyze everything to pieces. It won't hurt you two to relax a little, as you normally get more done than the rest of us during normal times. And remember, there's a double-good blast of pushy energy going for you on the day Mercury goes straight again.

If you have a computer chart look around the wheel and find the house cusps with Gemini and Virgo on them. If Gemini is your second house (money) and Virgo is on the sixth house (work) it is hardly the time to push for a raise now, is it?

Not everything will go goo-goo when Mercury marches backward, but the odds are definitely in favor of Mr. Myxlptk. These are only timetables. You are free to use and abuse them as you wish. Don't sweat the small stuff, but if it's a big deal, check the MERCURY RETRO tables.

1980	FEB	26	1:34	TO	1980	MAR	19	14:03
	JUN	28	11:13	TO		JUL	22	16:41
	OCT	23	2:03	TO		NOV	12	11:08
1981	FEB	8	12:41	TO	1981	MAR	2	7:09
	JUN	9	11:37	TO		JUL	3	13:02
	OCT	6	9:19	TO		OCT	27	9:00
1982	JAN	23	5:54	TO	1982	FEB	13	7:22
	MAY	21	2:07	TO		JUN	13	23:22
	SEP	19	11:06	TO		OCT	11	5:28
1983	JAN	7	3:07	TO	1983	JAN	27	13:31
	MAY	1	16:36	TO		MAY	25	12:50
	SEP	2	6:43	TO		SEP	24	20:54
	DEC	22	0:44	TO	1984	JAN	11	0:35
1984	APR	11	20:24	TO		MAY	5	14:08
	AUG	14	19:34	TO		SEP	7	3:59
	DEC	4	21:42	TO		DEC	24	16:05
1985	MAR	24	19:03	TO	1985	APR	17	5:22
	JUL	28	0:51	TO		AUG	20	22:49
	NOV	18	16:17	TO		DEC	8	11:34
1986	MAR	7	10:56	TO	1986	APR	30	8:45
	JUL	9	20:28	TO		AUG	3	0:47
	NOV	2	6:42	TO		NOV	22	8:53
1987	FEB	18	16:04	TO	1987	MAR	12	21:22
	JUN	21	3:44	TO		JUL	15	7:51
	OCT	16	16:44	TO		NOV	6	7:50
1988	FEB	2	6:25	TO	1988	FEB	23	17:28
	JUN	1	22:46	TO		JUN	24	22:44
	SEP	28	21:36	TO		OCT	20	5:12
1989	JAN	16	1:37	TO	1989	FEB	5	20:06
	MAY	12	11:55	TO		JUN	5	8:08
	SEP	11	20:57	TO		OCT	3	23:48
1990	JAN	30	23:26	TO	1990	JAN	20	4:36
	APR	23	6:58	TO		MAY	17	2:02
	AUG	25	14:07	TO		SEP	17	12:10
	DEC	14	21:17	TO	1991	JAN	3	18:00
1991	APR	4	18:13	TO		APR	28	9:49
	AUG	7	24:00	TO		SEP	31	14:36
	NOV	28	16:55	TO		DEC	18	11:06
1992	MAR	17	0:33	TO	1992	APR	9	6:29
	JUL	20	0:55	TO		AUG	13	2:52
	NOV	11	9:56	TO		DEC	1	7:40
1993	MAR	27	23:01	TO	1993	MAR	22	13:43
	JUL	1	15:31	TO		JUL	25	20:50
	OCT	25	22:43	TO		NOV	15	5:29
1994	FEB	11	8:24	TO	1994	MAR	5	5:47
	JUN	12	17:50	TO		JUL	6	19:43
	OCT	9	6:41	TO		NOV	30	4:14
1995	JAN	26	1:20	TO	1995	FEB	16	5:05
	MAY	24	9:02	TO		JUN	17	6:58

	SEP	22	9:13	TO		OCT	14	0:39
1996	JAN	9	22:02	TO	1996	FEB	30	10:14
	MAY	3	22:44	TO		MAY	27	19:04
	SEP	4	5:46	TO		SEP	26	17:06
	DEC	23	19:40	TO	1997	JAN	12	20:39
1997	APR	15	0:00	TO		MAY	8	18:07
	AUG	17	19:52	TO		SEP	10	1:44
	DEC	7	17:05	TO		DEC	27	11:50
1998	MAR	27	19:44	TO	1998	APR	20	7:34
	AUG	31	2:29	TO		AUG	23	22:39
	NOV	21	11:39	TO		DEC	11	6:23
1999	MAR	10	9:13	TO	1999	APR	2	9:18
	JUL	12	23:35	TO		AUG	6	3:28
	NOV	5	3:04	TO		NOV	25	4:03
2000	FEB	21	12:54	TO	2000	MAR	14	20:43
	JUN	23	8:33	TO		JUL	17	13:24
	OCT	18	13:46	TO		NOV	8	2:19

Venus—Sleazy Sex and Eternal Love

"A woman whom we truly love is a religion."
—Émile de Girardin

"When I walk with you I feel as if I had a flower in my buttonhole."

—William Makepeace Thackeray

"The beauty seen is partly in him who sees it."
—Christian Nestell

Sex. Don't look at me. All that slurping and burping and bumping and grinding and sliding and wriggling and huffing and puffing the stuffing out of one another takes *time*. I don't even want to *think* about it, stuck in this luxury shoebox these bastards call a studio apartment in New York. How anyone can live in this sweltering 95 degree heat every summer is beyond me, let alone how anyone can make love with the constant pressure of the damned Picasso exhibits, little art gallery openings, auctions at Christies, drinkie-poos at Doran's, Armenian, Indian, Lithuanian, and Eskimo restaurants every couple of blocks, Japanese massage parlors, literary luncheons, and the constant gnawing anxiety of wondering what Mick is up to today and if Bianca still cares. Somebody is always up to something intense in New York at all moments. There is this grinding sense that somewhere out there wonderful rich wise and successful people are laughing gaily over ruby red goblets of tinkling iced water and making brilliant repartee. So who has time for sex?

When the editor cruelly, coldly refused my request for a suite at the Plaza for a three-month period in the interests of research for this section, she forced me to go begging to clients, friends, derelicts on the subway platform, and anyone who would speak to me about what they like—heterosexual, homosexual, and the few lucky ones who are polymorphously erotic. The results of this research, for better or worse, are here.

The delights of the sexually satisfied life do not need enumerating here. When you haven't got it, you spend an awful lot of time thinking about it, denying it, staring at the ceiling, working too hard, working too lazy, getting cranky, and being rotten to the people you fancy because they remind you of your mad craving for them. You get tired, you get energetic, you get crazy, I know. Finally you just pick out someone who looks okay on the subway, follow him home, and spend the rest of your life picking bugs out of your ears.

Don't do it. A happy love life frees you for other activities, like improving yourself, helping other human beings and making the world a better place. And there are so many kinds of love to choose from.

So many kinds of love! And some of the varieties may look *very strange* to you and me, but they are love all the same. John Alan Lee's book, *The Colors of Love*, explores this topic beautifully. Do read it.

The fastest way to understand what turns you on is to look up what sign Venus is in. As there are only twelve signs, consequently there are twelve basic *styles* of falling in love.

If you have a computer chart, this will tell you much more . . . check the *aspects* other planets make to Venus. See also what house Venus is in.

So first check the OOOH! tables to find the Venus sign of your quarry. Just this alone will give you a spooky insight into what they want, how to rope and tie and brand 'em, how to get them to fall in love, how to get them to fall out of love. This last bit is important if you want them forever and ever, or about six months at *least*.

Just to confuse you, you sort of can read these Venus signs to give you little tips on other bits of their chart. Like if your quarry is a Scorpio with Venus in Capricorn, you could look up Venus in Scorpio too. But you'd have to knock 40 percent off the definition. If he has Gemini rising, you could read Venus in Gemini for him too, knocking 40 percent off. And so on.

Some Venus signs are more demented than others. It is at home in Libra and Taurus, exalted in Pisces, and demented in Virgo, Scorpio, Aquarius, and Aries.

VENUS IN ARIES

They want you to say "I love you" first. Don't. Once they've completely conquered you it's all over. This is a weird warlike place for Venus to be in; they look for trouble in love, and they

find it. They need someone with a bigger ego than they have—
no mean feat! And only a big ego can stand up to the constant
battering and flirtatiousness of Venus in Aries—they don't realize how painfully transparent their behavior is to onlookers.
They badly need to impress you with their string of conquests.

Do they love to see you get jealous! If *you* display the teeniest
bit of interest in anyone else, however, they go banana-boats.
Don't.

Yes, ladies and gentlemen, here's the old double standard, and
the males and females with Venus in Aries are male chauvinists.
Imagine what this does to women with Venus here. They too
believe that woman's place is in the sack, being conquered, but
they love the hunt. Some people like fishin' and shootin'. Venus
in Aries likes conquering—just for the hell of it. The song
"Under My Thumb" by the Rolling Stones is their guiding
credo. These women are fiercely competitive.

Be aggressive. They love to be worshipped. But they do little
to earn your admiration in the sack because they are so selfish.
They will only strive to please you at the outset. When you feel
their insistent little hands forcing your head toward unknown
corners of the Universe, this is Venus in Aries every time.

They like you in red and black and white. Both sexes also go
for a frilly or dandified look in their partners, but they don't take
people who dress this way seriously. Wear jeans, tight ones.

Hammerlocks round the neck with your fist on their chins turn
them on. Muss up their hair. Touch their faces a lot. Rub the bit
between the eyebrows. There. Now they belong to you.

If you like passion, you'll love Venus in Aries, but keep it
new. If you're married to one, rehaul yourself every so often, be
a new person in some way, begin new projects, bring in new
people, or better yet, be an Aries yourself. Refuse to be crushed
by that overwhelming selfish ego of theirs. Don't take any guff
from them, stand up and fight with every shred of self-respect
and independence you can muster. Give 'em fire and brimstone.
Bite them. Pinch them. Scratch them. When they drag out the
old flame bit get them to stop acting like babies. They'll cut the
crap fast when you drag out a few memories of ex-paramours of
your own. They want to be Number One.

Then they are sweetly awestruck and happily devoted. And
that's how Mary had her little lamb.

VENUS IN TAURUS

Relax. People with Venus in Taurus are collectors, and if you go out with them, you become their property, as with Venus in the other earth signs, Virgo and Capricorn. They see God in material things—nice furniture, pretty boxes, your flesh and bones. They love to touch. The boys like their girls in dresses, and the girls want the boys dressed up real sharp—real fabrics, and no polyester! A moth-eaten pullover is okay with them if it's cashmere and *feels* good. Always wear clothes that feel sensual against *their* skin.

Venus likes to be at home in Taurus because real troo love tends to be at its best when it's reliable and *responsible*. Some people might find this boring. Venus in Taurus people do like doing the same thing again and again and again. Perhaps it all depends on what they're doing!

Here greed is seen as a delicious virtue. They love The Good Life. Their fantasy life is rich beyond belief. When they can't have a roll in the hay, a roll in the hand will do, complete with mayo, mustard, lettuce, tomato, and anything else on hand to construct a proper Dagwood Bumstead banquet. People who love good food are good in bed, and Venus in Taurus *loves* good food . . . your pleasure is important to them.

Talk dirty to them. Blow in the left ear. Blow in the right. Run an exhaustive search pattern in the area between the shoulder and the neck—there's a spot in the hollow there that is rather fond of being kissed. Wear pale icky colors, pinks and blues and yellows. Put on background music, especially music with a strong repetitive beat. (Rolling Stones). These folks need a lot of cuddling all the time, and theirs is a nice commonsense approach to the birds and bees: *more is better*. They are fantastically oral people—remember their food trip! Make them feel as comfortable, safe, and luxurious as you know how. Sex is raunchy, important, risky business to them, and if you hurt them, they act frostier than celibate polar bears, and they stay that way a lo-o-o-o-ong time. It takes a lot to get them to leave a relationship once they've committed themselves, and they put up with a lot.

They'll marry not so much for money but for security. (It takes a lot of money for them to feel secure.) Venus in Taurus people often marry fast, but they rarely marry each other, which is a pity. Often they waste their affections on people with lesser capacities to love, but who seem, for a time, to be exciting.

They need a secure comfortable setting, and for this reason the are easier to seduce in their homes with all their things aroun them. After, of course, a good meal.

VENUS IN GEMINI

Now here's a real firecracker in the sack! Still, as the relation ship continues they become more brotherly-sisterly—*shared inter ests* here are vital. The famous fickle reputation usually surface only when they are not mated with an intellectual equal. Goo talk keeps them hooked. Refinement is important to them, that and repartee.

When you talk to them look them straight in the eye. The don't trust you unless you do that. But they don't watch you eyes, they look at your mouth—every twitch and tremble of each lip tells them universes about your character. If you've eve played trumpet or saxophone, *tell them* so they'll know you're special kisser. They like kissing best of all. Venus in Gemini the all time make-out champion. Talk and run away from them lot.

Loud music gets in the way of their brains. They dislike noise Dark, stuffy places depress them. They love plants, and light airy roomy spaces. They love apple green, yellow, splash flowery patterns, off-beat hues like violet, sea green, and gentl gaudy colors and batiks.

Essentially they are intellectual in love and need "good talk' more than sex. Keep it light, warm, and friendly; stay *interestin* and don't devour them with passion as passion overrules thei most valued possession, *clear thinking*.

Oh ho! yes, they do kiss and tell—but usually only a close friend. Yes, they do compare lovers, and they can be in love with two, even three lovers at the same time. Yes, they can grow more restless as the years roll on. They like to stay friends with their exes, and they expect you to like them too. Better to have the old flame over to dinner with you, all friendly and out in the open, than to creep off for a coffee with you wondering wha they're up to—you're supposed to be gracious and *understand* One gal was so beautiful inside and out she encouraged three old flames to go into business together. It worked, for a while.

When they turn off sexually, they turn off for *life*. Maybe that's why they don't understand how their friendships with old lovers hurt your feelings. They do get terribly jealous themselves but can't see why *you* would be. Recovering from broken hearts seems to be easier for them than for most of us. Usually they replace the lover swiftly or sublimate their feelings into hearty intellectual discussions with their buddies.

What they really want is variety, though they act bewildered about "not knowing" what they want. Just keep changing the character you play in bed. Learn another language and talk to them in a weird accent. They are good at being faithful if you're *bright*. Once settled, they have an infinite capacity to "make do."

The women are too refined to say so, but they like big guys. You don't have to be tall, though. Just smart.

VENUS IN CANCER

The mmm and mmms of the zodiac. They are sweeties, each and every one of them. They have thousands of erogenous zones, nose-tips and auras included. They'll find yours, double-quick.

Pull out all the soppy old romantic tricks. Act strong but tragically in need of care and feeding. The women want you to look like a banker or a North Woodsman in flannel shirt and beard. The men want you in simpering flowered fabrics and long skirts and shocking erotic undies. The men are particularly fascinating as they are both masculine and feminine in nature—the way the rest of the world will become someday when the men start liberating themselves. Why wait another two hundred years? Venus in Cancer will cook you a meal and let you kiss him forcefully without his masculinity being threatened a noodge.

Ridicule terrifies these people. Don't tease please. Give them mementoes, send cards. Give them their place at the table, their shelf in the bathroom. Make them feel at home. Swoon a bit. They like green, silver, shiny and misty colors.

Now here's the catch. They're weird. They enjoy vengeful threesomes, infidelities—often embarrassingly flamboyant ones—and the role of slave in a relationship. You can be a little mean to them for awhile and they say nothing. They are terrified of rejection, so they will put up with coldness from you; the only trouble is, you wouldn't be cold to them in the first place if they didn't set you up for it. Perhaps that is why some of them fool around—so you'll treat them as slaves. The smart ones go for therapy and work out their massive Oedipal problems, for let's face it, the ones who aren't perverts make wonderful wives and husbands in equal-partner marriages. They just seem to need to be treated mean, and they don't see how they were mean in the first place. If you're dating someone with a negative Venus in Cancer and they hurt you consistently, insist they get help or drop them. Who needs S&M games when we can get it on the "Nine O'Clock News"?

Seduce them with the food of their own country. They can't take a regular diet of foreign fare. The way to their hearts is not through their stomachs, although food helps, but they are boob lovers, both sexes.

I'm told these people are fun to live with. They have many moods, experimental minds, and will play baby one day and parent the next. They like to mumble and fuss over you like big mother hens—they're great clucks!

VENUS IN LEO

Want to get their attention? Two direct routes are available. Watch them show off. Laugh at their jokes—they tell great jokes. Ask them to order for you at one of their favorite gourmet restaurants. Watch them as they cross the proverbial crowded room. Solicit their considered opinion. Praise them, praise them, praise them.

There's another way. Be a show-off yourself. Hurl yourself up on a pedestal. Then praise them, praise them, praise them.

Defer quietly to them. Chivalry, courtliness, and noblesse oblige surprises them. Live it. These are displaced knights in shining armor, love-lost queens in a democratic age they never made. Remember Camelot.

Who cares if you have another lover? They do. But pride is more important to them, so they may try to pretend the Other does not exist. They are sure they can drive out all the competition and win you back. They can, but most people with Venus in Leo are proud. Mental health has a way of raising its ugly, unwanted little head even when they are rapturously in love. So they let you go to the Other. It hurts, but it's cool with them— after all, it's not your fault if you want to slum with lesser mortals. It is the fault of the king or queen for choosing a commoner in the first place. And, hell, they always have a waiting list.

Back rubs are their excuse for getting to you, so you rub theirs for a change. Nipple rubs always work, but mind—they're sensitive! They love to sit around and have you bring them things.

They love you to sit around and go off to get you things. It doesn't matter who does what, as long as it's *regal*.

Aphrodisiacs for Venus in Leo include the lion's share of grand cuisine, fine drinks, lively companions, and attention. Happily, this is the Venus sign most likely to be loyal, loving, warm and emotionally healthy in love.

Dress for attracting a Venus in Leo can be outrageous or dramatic; rainbow-colored hair is fine, as are capes, boiler suits, kimonos, and flamboyant colors, especially gold.

Try to look like a millionaire or a rock star. Got it? *Act* like one, anyway.

Things You Will Have To Put Up With Department: constant need for praise and flattery to the point of suckerdom. Terrible bragging, white lies, and tall tales. They are honest people who only fib about their own accomplishments. They *fish* for compliments. A roving eye in both sexes—they appreciate the opposite sex, that's all. Perhaps it is the adulation of their subjects they crave. Inwardly they are snobs, so usually they don't let the riffraff get any closer to them than flirting. This is particularly true if you remind them of how special they are.

VENUS IN VIRGO

We are back in the land of dementia again, though it's a different variety from Venus in Aquarius or Aries. Venus in Virgo sees sex as a healthy function, something one does in order to be a tension-free, well-rounded person.

The kiddies like to play doctor. The grown-ups insist that you smell nice. Bathe often. No, even more often. These guys don't feel comfortable kissing you until they've brushed their teeth. They hate to make love in a messy room. You know they're in love with you when they don't mind getting sticky and dirty. Drop a melted Mars bar in their laps to see. It excites them to get dirty in a perverse way—daring! You know they're in love with you if they pick on you, as they are extremely critical and faultfinding.

Wear ethnic clothes and things that are hard to undo, things with millions of tiny buttons, laces, and cross straps. They want you to dress neatly, with a pulled-together look. Or dress like a ragbag; it'll get their attention and give them something to do, namely to make you over. They love turquoise jewelry.

Be wrapped up in your work. The women love cold bastards and workaholics. The men like meticulous models, chorus girls, and groupies, but the girl who loves her work is what the men are looking for. A whore in her mink is one image of Venus in Virgo. The well-scrubbed lady in the long skirt cooking health food is another. Work, work, work. Neither sex with Venus in Virgo wants someone hanging on them all the time. It interferes with *work*, which is this Venus sign's real love.

Deny it if you want to, but behind this clean-cut, slightly prissy Venus in Virgo mask is a heart yearning for emotional, sometimes even physical, *bondage*. They feel tied up to you, run your errands, fuss and carp over you. Even the shy ones secretly would love to be *forced* into maintaining the relationship. I said *secretly*, now, ladies and gentlemen . . . they may not even know themselves how kinky they can be. Their fantasies have exact details, which may even involve being snowed in in a log cabin from which there is no escape. They want and expect the most detailed, accurate and intricate forms of advanced lovemaking. They keep logs in their heads of all their amours. It keeps them happy to have a record during their long sexual deserts. When they come to the end of a desert they go wild, make up for lost time and binge, like camels filling up at an oasis.

Unfortunately this sex-equals-health maxim, extrapolated to its most extreme, decadent maximum, indicates a tendency to use lovers as other people use Kleenex. Oddly many of our current pop stars have Venus here; Mick Jagger, Shaun Cassidy, and Jackson Browne for starters. This fires my theory that the Woodstock generation (we all have Pluto in Leo) have a fairly perverted view of love. We use each other as catalysts, consider each other "learning experiences." We don't stick things out through thick and thin; our idols are twisted.

Once the men get over wanting bitches and both sexes learn to stop judging people in the first five minutes of a meeting, they generally find congenial partners who have good careers of their own.

When they love you, they show it through service. Often they had childhood experiences in which they felt they had to meet a certain standard to get any love at all.

VENUS IN LIBRA

If you're sick of slick dames or roving rotters, snuggle up with a Venus in Libra person, even if it's not for long. (They're always in demand!) Then anyone who comes after them will have to match the good treatment you get from these people. They just spoil you to delighted pieces.

Root beer in your favorite glass, sir? Squeeze your cheek on the way to the bathroom? Light your cigarette, milady? One courtly Venus in Libra man brings a single carnation to give the lady before dinner. The only thing they have trouble with is taking out the garbage. They'll do it for you, but it hurts their senses so much who would want to torture them?

You might look like an iguana, but a woman with Venus in Libra or Pisces genuinely believes you're the most handsome creature in God's universe. (Venus in Pisces women rather like their men to look like fish or iguanas, but that comes later. They're weird.) The men's archetypal woman wears lots of jewelry, dresses, and a pastel, fluffy look.

This Venus sign likes to do everything together. They love having their skin stroked with very light, feathery touches. They need to surround themselves with beauty, and they can feel *sick* in an ugly environment.

Catches? Of course, of course. *Convenience* is the watchword. Sure they'll go for it. The women dream of being idle wives eating chocolates on the chaise longue; the men wouldn't mind being gigolos. There is a scary coldness underlying the too-attentive mannerisms of Venus in Libra. No other position works so hard to attain the "easy life." Better to go out and win the daily bagels and come home to a more honest, equal relationship say, but this is not for Venus in Libra.

The artist's eye and the photographer's frame of reference is what Venus in Libra's got. They can teach you how to love fully and considerately. Just find out first if it's you they love or your crystal-filled house on the hill and your trendy friends. If you live in a tacky slum and they still pour you that root beer, grab 'em fast—it's real.

VENUS IN SCORPIO

So it's demented. They walk naked and alone in the world. They don't mind naked, it's the alone that gets them after some time. They are capable of going long times between affairs.

These cookies will put themselves through the Cuisinart of love, but they have only two speeds, fascinated detachment or to hell and back.

They have two styles in bed. When they're hung up on power and control, it stops them from letting go and letting things flow, and they're not much good. Once they've learned that it is themselves they must control, they are just fantastic with good staying power, lovely slithery body movements, cute sulks, stinging sarcasm, *and* they are surprisingly cuddly. At least that is what my "subway poll" tells me, those charming chaps who ride the "D" train. Thank you, boys and girls.

They're good secret keepers in love. Sometimes they find that duty compels them to be your secret lover whilst you're going through a bad patch in another relationship. If you're just recovering from a breakdown or, even better, *going* through a breakdown, they are even more intrigued. They love depth and craziness. And they're *loyal*, which means they don't tell their other lovers about you.

Extremes of coldness or masochism crop up in their relationships. They love excesses of any sort; purity is as great a turn-on as a lover with a twisted past.

You'll lose them in an instant if you discuss the intimate details of your relationship with your locker-room budzos. Do not ever. And you blow it if you snoop around in their stuff. All right, all right, they drive you to it, acting so mysterious all the time, but *be careful,* with the cloak and dagger routine.

Why not give them a thing or two to puzzle over? Mysteries enchant them, and it keeps them happily puzzled. They like exploring all the gaps in your mind and body. If there's a space, they just have to poke something in it.

Find out what their invisible line is. Usually it has to do with loyalty. Cross over that line and they go straight out the door. They will always call your bluff. Say to Venus in Scorpio, "There's a little blonde nurse following me around a lot lately, . . ." and she will coldly say, "Go for it!" She doesn't mean it, of course. She just wants to see if *you* do.

Murky colors suit them best—black, maroon, scarlet, midnight blue, lizard green—as long as it's velvet. They like foods with complicated cream sauces, garlic, and champagne. Wear what you like. A true Venus in Scorpio never judges a book by its cover.

VENUS IN SAGITTARIUS

Love starts out like Doctor Livingstone embarking on a great adventure—and so, pal, are you. They're reckless. They're aggressive. Romance is a glorious, all-embracing, mind-expanding, exuberant game with Venus in Sagittarius. It's a game they play by the rules. Who wrote the rules, anyway? I'll give you twelve guesses.

Starry-eyed and sparkling with magic, they're not above crawling up your drainpipe and sneaking in the bathroom window just to surprise you. You never know with them. It's a special gift they have, this magic, and they'll give you wild presents, flirt with everybody, and talk philosophy with you till the sun comes up. Loosen up a little and trip the light fantastic with them . . . you'll never forget it.

Snap one up, if you can, and you can. They just love hippies, foreigners, philosophers, "In" people, and anyone who's bright, but they'll gladly pal around with you, even if you're merely fun and wear casual or ethnic clothes. Keep changing your looks and keep them on the hop. They will if you don't do it first!

Expect anything. Most of them do a mean horse imitation. Not one of them is above telling you a joke or making like Groucho Marx in the midst of a passionate moment.

Drawbacks? Let's see now . . . one of their games is Wounding Honesty. Your friend tells you that you look a little like Liz Taylor and Venus in Sagittarius pipes up, "Oh, but your tits aren't big enough!" Yes, like that.

Consciously they see nothing wrong, till later, in blurting out the "truth." Good old unconscious mind is right in there, though, protecting them, creating a little distance here and there, yearning to breathe free. If you're *interesting,* though, (their favorite word) they're awfully loyal. If you're smart, you'll share their love of "space."

Game playing is what they do best, but the high types are extraordinarily noble and chivalrous when ending a relationship. They'll end it when they need a change, when they feel their precious "freedom" slipping away from them, but the high types don't turn off unless they lose respect for you and your ideals. Even then you can *earn back* that respect. Why should they carry a grudge?

So strong is their code of honor it does not occur to them that not everyone plays by the rules, their rules. In this way they are mere babes in the woods, and they can be deeply hurt. One sweet Venus in Sagittarius boy knew his ex-girlfriend was still crazy about him, so he met her twice a week for dinner and a movie until her craving subsided. They went to horror movies. It helped to exorcise their jumbled-up feelings about the parting, and his kind aftercare blew her mind. She is married now, to a bright, mild-mannered man she adores, but once in a blue moon she tells the story of a young man's gallantry, and there's a gleam in her eye when she tells it.

VENUS IN CAPRICORN

The connoisseur. Think of them as Englishmen or women in love—they still think sex is frightfully *naughty*! Men in pin-stripes and women in black stockings and garter belts feature in their guilty fantasies. Ask anyone riding on the London under-ground, if you dare.

There are two kinds of lovers for them: the saucy lower-class chambermaid or rough and ready gamekeeper, or the sort of specimen you take home to meet Daddy. If you've got both qualifications, they'll fall deeply in love with you. Don't ever show affection in public, and don't keep your hands off them in private. The men like long-legged ladies, oval faces, and lots of black clothing, and the women like their men with a six-inch bank account—or the prospect of same.

You can look like Bizarro if you've got money, power, or fame, so don't sweat the small stuff. Venus in Capricorn folks do have one odd kink, however. They are fascinated with bone structure. Your body is the way they like to study architecture, whereas the folks with Venus in Sagittarius just don't give a hang about your body as long as you like to boogie-woogie. Venus in Capricorns are attracted to moody loners, and you can never be too rich or too skinny. Remember Cassius' lean and hungry look.

Forget keeping them around unless you can be useful to them, especially in their work. Show them how you fix a doorknob, type, or Make Yourself Useful. Weirdly, they are more often exploited themselves because they feel inadequate about their own worth. So they may try to "buy" you in some way. The men may actually tell you to go away and come back when they've made their mark in the world; they'll live in barren conditions, though, telling you that's their way of keeping the gold-diggers away. They trust only the friends who stick with them in hard times. They get good at making money. Both sexes believe that the best partners won't be theirs unless they "earn" the partner's devotion. This pound-wise, penny-foolish attitude on their part wrecks many budding romances. People don't like to think of love in the same breath as worldly affairs. Venus in Capricorn people need two things only: a kick in the pants for being too worrisome and mercenary, and lots and lots of kisses along the spine. These weird, frosty people are lusty beyond belief. NEVER grab them in front of business or social acquaintances unless they want you to, as a status symbol. They will let you know, by post.

VENUS IN AQUARIUS

You know those adorable talking robots they sell for about eighty bucks?

These dear sweet souls wonder what goes wrong in their relationships. Why do people get sick of them so fast? Why does it seem they have to try so much harder than other people? How come they have to try so many *more* people when they're looking for a mate? We know Venus in Aquarius is demented, as in Aries, Virgo, or Scorpio, but in the other three signs Venus is at least gaudily selfish, exacting, or obsessive, in that order. Dear sweet friendly Venus in Aquarius people wonder and do not know that they are cold fish.

Oh, the old gonads run real good, and Venus in Aquarius people have fascinating friends, but it's rare that you take these people seriously as lovers. Their take-it-or-leave-it attitude might intrigue you at first, but these eminently beddable folks never seem to warm up emotionally unless you're not there.

If you like your lovers easy to get, like a newspaper, you can have them, and you can keep them too. Their faithful state comes not from the heart but from habit, though sexually they can be dynamite. It's a cover-up for the lack of feeling. Both sexes want romance to be unexpected, on the whim of the moment. They are most turned on when you don't want to be turned on, or where someone might catch you in the act. That old lightning just strikes when it strikes, and by God, you'd better be ready. In this way they can be Attila the Hun with your feelings, though they try . . . and they try . . . and they try . . . and they try . . .

Dress like a preppie or a hippie slut, crazy or conservative. For the ladies out to attract a Venus in Aquarius man, loafers and Peter Pan collars will do. You gentlemen, stick with the gray suit and the cool lady will love you for it. If you're broke, always dress like an idealist.

In general these fellas secretly think all women are the same. The women can take the whole romance thing or leave it, so their men cheat on them, desperately looking for emotion, and the women can take a deep breath and have "space" to potter about with their weird hobbies.

Oh, I guess they really do care a lot about you, it just comes out funny. They certainly never want to hurt anybody. Think of how difficult it must be for a robot to express passion and trust that somewhere deep in that hunk of gray gunmetal there is a power cell that pulses for you, pulses forever.

Beep! Beep!

VENUS IN PISCES

They're gooshy, mooshy, want always to be dominated in bed (though they'll pretend otherwise!), and they have an obsessive sweet directionless perversity in matters of romance. You must always tell them you love them and mean it (actions speak louder than words!) or they get hurt, silent, sweet, and pouty. Then they slip off and make a raving fool out of you.

So why, in the name of Jesus, is this the best of the love signs? Look what *happened* to Jesus. No one could stand his love. He paid a mighty high price for his ability to love boundlessly and forever, and the Big Guns lashed out at him. That's what happens to Venus in Pisces when they get mixed up with folks who can't love as well. Venus in Pisces gets crucified. It's the sucker of the zodiac. It's a great position for everybody whom Venus in Pisces loves.

Love is mixed up with religion for this gang. They see the God in you. They love everybody, but they love you special. Folks who feel inadequate or have little faith in themselves can't abide this high-quality Light. So they step on old Venus in Pisces and crawl off under their rocks. Venus in Pisces weeps for them and wishes the best for them, in life, genuinely sorry for these people.

In truth, a Venus in Pisces can't fall in love with you unless they feel a bit sorry for you. Affect a limp. You can be a lonely saint or a lonely whore but pick an extreme. Look dashing. Better still, look like a fish, with big bulging eyes, or a frog, with a little potbelly. I'm serious. Ugliness is merely a temporary setback. As soon as they fall in love with you, you're the handsomest man on God's green earth, the world's most tantalizing woman. If you're good-looking, practice looking like an iguana. It will help you.

Common sense, not to mention mental health, would dictate that people with Venus in Pisces should read to the blind twice a week and pick lovers who will appreciate and complement the astonishing range of their feelings.

How easily they slip in and out of sado-masochistic games! They'll be sadistic if it please you they should be. But given the choice, they'll take the route of kindness. Love reminds them that life is short, and Venus in Pisces knows that only good deeds survive the grave.

These simple/sophisticated people are breathtakingly varied in their love styles. Two men dating a Venus in Pisces woman will see entirely different sides of her psychedelic heart. As one Venus in Pisces gal complained to her man,

"I have 31 flavors and all you want is vanilla!"

Yes, there's the rare, low-rent, sleazy Venus in Pisces type. They lean on people, are unfaithful, rip you off in a million sneaky ways, and don't want to grow up. Even this type can be redeemed if they carry round the motto "No self-pity."

Venus in Pisces is the best place to have it. They can make a million sacrifices for you, and they feel honored to do so without losing a shred of dignity. They want you to have what you want, and they'll give you up, too, if they think that's what you want. Better reassure them a lot (they're touchy as hell), give them magic, and be kind to their dozen tragic friends. Some lovers make the mistake of interpreting this Venus sign's easygoing, tender, compassionate nature for weakness. Is the tree weak as it bends in the wind? Venus in Pisces will make a million excuses for you, and they'll love you in this and the next ten thousand lives, but they'll leave you when they run out of excuses for any cruel behavior on your part—*or if they see you deliberately trashing your life away.* Anybody who ever loved well encouraged the lover to live up to the highest ideals; kill the ideals, and you lose Venus in Pisces. God wouldn't have it any other way. They are the creme de la creme of lovers, and despite the occasional bout of masochism, these creatures seem to realize they deserve a mate who deserves *them.*

1901	JAN	16	Cap	11:29
	FEB	9	Aqu	13:06
	MAR	5	Pic	14:51
	MAR	29	Ari	18:03
	APR	22	Tau	23:34
	MAY	17	Gem	7:34
	JUN	10	Can	17:37
	JUL	5	Leo	5:22
	JUL	29	Vir	19:13
	AUG	23	Lib	12:33
	SEP	17	Scp	11:29
	OCT	12	Sag	19:15
	NOV	7	Cap	19:25
	DEC	5	Aqu	13:32
1902	JAN	11	Pic	17:47
	FEB	6	Aqu	22:52
	APR	4	Pic	19:31
	MAY	7	Ari	7:05
	JUN	3	Tau	23:59
	JUN	30	Gem	6:28
	JUL	25	Can	18:59
	AUG	19	Leo	18:28
	SEP	13	Vir	7:18
	OCT	7	Lib	12:06
	OCT	31	Scp	11:51
	NOV	24	Sag	9:06
	DEC	18	Cap	5:32
1903	JAN	11	Aqu	2:18
	FEB	4	Pic	0:47
	FEB	28	Ari	3:03
	MAR	24	Tau	11:53
	APR	18	Gem	6:41
	MAY	13	Can	16:23
	JUN	9	Leo	3:07
	JUL	7	Vir	20:36
	AUG	17	Lib	21:51
	SEP	6	Vir	2:17
	NOV	8	Lib	14:43
	DEC	9	Scp	14:42
1904	JAN	5	Sag	3:43
	JAN	30	Cap	9:28
	FEB	24	Aqu	3:07
	MAR	19	Pic	16:01
	APR	13	Ari	3:27
	MAY	7	Tau	14:52
	JUN	1	Gem	2:28
	JUN	25	Can	13:29
	JUL	19	Leo	23:01
	AUG	13	Vir	6:53
	SEP	6	Lib	13:50
	SEP	30	Scp	21:04
	OCT	25	Sag	5:37
	NOV	18	Cap	16:40
	DEC	13	Aqu	9:08
1905	JAN	7	Pic	14:39
	FEB	3	Ari	4:49
	MAR	6	Tau	5:26
	MAY	9	Ari	11:15
	MAY	28	Tau	11:16
	JUL	8	Gem	11:59
	AUG	6	Can	8:17
	SEP	1	Leo	20:16
	SEP	27	Vir	4:02
	OCT	21	Lib	18:32
	NOV	14	Scp	22:40
	DEC	8	Sag	21:31
1906	JAN	1	Cap	18:24
	JAN	25	Aqu	15:12
	FEB	18	Pic	13:13
	MAR	14	Ari	13:42
	APR	7	Tau	17:59
	MAY	2	Gem	3:13
	MAY	26	Can	18:17
	JUN	20	Leo	16:36
	JUL	16	Vir	1:19
	AUG	11	Lib	3:21
	SEP	7	Scp	15:33
	OCT	9	Sag	10:31
	DEC	15	Scp	12:53
	DEC	25	Sag	23:46
1907	FEB	6	Cap	16:28
	MAR	6	Aqu	20:44
	APR	2	Pic	1:28
	APR	27	Ari	12:29
	MAY	22	Tau	15:18
	JUN	16	Gem	13:14
	JUL	11	Can	6:42
	AUG	4	Leo	19:08
	AUG	29	Vir	2:30
	SEP	22	Lib	5:52
	OCT	16	Scp	6:55
	NOV	9	Sag	7:08
	DEC	3	Cap	7:26
	DEC	27	Aqu	8:53
1908	JAN	20	Pic	13:50
	FEB	14	Ari	2:55
	MAR	10	Tau	8:06
	APR	5	Gem	20:57

	MAY	5	Can	17:44		MAY	31	Gem	13:19
	SEP	8	Leo	22:32		JUN	25	Can	0:12
	OCT	8	Vir	6:13		JUL	19	Leo	9:44
	NOV	3	Lib	11:29		AUG	12	Vir	17:43
	NOV	28	Scp	10:43		SEP	6	Lib	0:54
	DEC	22	Sag	20:01		SEP	30	Scp	8:27
1909	JAN	15	Cap	23:20		OCT	24	Sag	17:25
	FEB	9	Aqu	0:41		NOV	18	Cap	5:04
	MAR	5	Pic	2:11		DEC	12	Aqu	22:24
	MAR	29	Ari	5:12	1913	JAN	7	Pic	5:28
	APR	22	Tau	10:35		FEB	2	Ari	23:22
	MAY	16	Gem	18:31		MAR	6	Tau	17:09
	JUN	10	Can	4:37		MAY	2	Ari	5:26
	JUL	4	Leo	16:32		MAY	31	Tau	9:44
	JUL	29	Vir	6:42		JUL	8	Gem	9:17
	AUG	23	Lib	0:35		AUG	5	Can	23:33
	SEP	17	Scp	0:21		SEP	1	Leo	9:20
	OCT	12	Sag	9:28		SEP	26	Vir	16:04
	NOV	7	Cap	12:12		OCT	21	Lib	6:02
	DEC	5	Aqu	13:01		NOV	14	Scp	9:55
1910	JAN	15	Pic	20:57		DEC	8	Sag	8:38
	JAN	29	Aqu	8:24	1914	JAN	1	Cap	5:26
	APR	5	Pic	9:53		JAN	25	Aqu	2:10
	MAY	7	Ari	2:27		FEB	18	Pic	0:05
	JUN	3	Tau	14:58		MAR	14	Ari	0:30
	JUN	29	Gem	19:32		APR	7	Tau	4:49
	JUL	25	Can	7:02		MAY	1	Gem	14:11
	AUG	19	Leo	5:56		MAY	26	Can	5:34
	SEP	12	Vir	18:30		JUN	20	Leo	4:26
	OCT	6	Lib	23:11		JUL	15	Vir	14:11
	OCT	30	Scp	22:54		AUG	10	Lib	18:12
	NOV	23	Sag	20:09		SEP	7	Scp	10:58
	DEC	17	Cap	16:38		OCT	10	Sag	1:50
1911	JAN	10	Aqu	13:28		DEC	5	Scp	23:23
	FEB	3	Pic	12:03		DEC	30	Sag	23:14
	FEB	27	Ari	14:29	1915	FEB	6	Cap	15:57
	MAR	23	Tau	23:36		MAR	6	Aqu	13:15
	APR	17	Gem	18:56		APR	1	Pic	15:19
	MAY	13	Can	5:43		APR	27	Ari	0:56
	JUN	8	Leo	18:48		MAY	22	Tau	2:56
	JUL	7	Vir	19:04		JUN	16	Gem	0:22
	NOV	9	Lib	0:55		JUL	10	Can	17:31
	DEC	9	Scp	9:23		AUG	4	Leo	5:47
1912	JAN	4	Sag	18:38		AUG	28	Vir	13:07
	JAN	29	Cap	22:45		SEP	21	Lib	16:31
	FEB	23	Aqu	15:29		OCT	15	Scp	17:42
	MAR	19	Pic	3:49		NOV	8	Sag	18:07
	APR	12	Ari	14:50		DEC	2	Cap	18:38
	MAY	7	Tau	1:57		DEC	26	Aqu	20:21

1916	JAN	20	Pic	1:41		APR	12	Ari	2:07
	FEB	13	Ari	15:24		MAY	6	Tau	12:55
	MAR	9	Tau	21:49		MAY	31	Gem	0:05
	APR	5	Gem	13:32		JUN	24	Can	10:54
	MAY	5	Can	20:37		JUL	18	Leo	20:26
	SEP	8	Leo	22:26		AUG	12	Vir	4:31
	OCT	7	Vir	22:12		SEP	5	Lib	11:53
	NOV	3	Lib	0:59		SEP	29	Scp	19:45
	NOV	27	Scp	23:07		OCT	24	Sag	5:11
	DEC	22	Sag	7:50		NOV	17	Cap	17:29
1917	JAN	15	Cap	10:46		DEC	12	Aqu	11:46
	FEB	8	Aqu	11:51	1921	JAN	6	Pic	20:33
	MAR	4	Pic	13:09		FEB	2	Ari	18:35
	MAR	28	Ari	16:01		MAR	7	Tau	9:19
	APR	21	Tau	21:17		APR	25	Ari	23:48
	MAY	16	Gem	5:09		JUN	2	Tau	4:20
	JUN	9	Can	15:16		JUL	8	Gem	5:57
	JUL	4	Leo	3:20		AUG	5	Can	14:42
	JUL	28	Vir	17:52		AUG	31	Leo	22:24
	AUG	22	Lib	12:20		SEP	26	Vir	4:09
	SEP	16	Scp	13:00		OCT	20	Lib	17:35
	OCT	11	Sag	23:34		NOV	13	Scp	21:11
	NOV	7	Cap	5:01		DEC	7	Sag	19:47
	DEC	5	Aqu	13:14		DEC	31	Cap	16:32
1918	APR	5	Pic	20:11	1922	JAN	24	Aqu	13:14
	MAY	6	Ari	20:58		FEB	17	Pic	11:07
	JUN	3	Tau	5:27		MAR	13	Ari	11:30
	JUN	29	Gem	8:13		APR	6	Tau	15:51
	JUL	24	Can	18:44		MAY	1	Gem	1:22
	AUG	18	Leo	17:06		MAY	25	Can	17:04
	SEP	12	Vir	5:24		JUN	19	Leo	16:33
	OCT	6	Lib	10:00		JUL	15	Vir	3:23
	OCT	30	Scp	9:44		AUG	10	Lib	9:30
	NOV	23	Sag	7:02		SEP	7	Scp	7:15
	DEC	17	Cap	3:34		OCT	10	Sag	22:34
1919	JAN	10	Aqu	0:29		NOV	28	Scp	21:51
	FEB	2	Pic	23:09	1923	JAN	2	Sag	7:26
	FEB	27	Ari	1:44		FEB	6	Cap	14:34
	MAR	23	Tau	11:08		MAR	6	Aqu	5:38
	APR	17	Gem	7:03		APR	1	Pic	5:16
	MAY	12	Can	18:59		APR	26	Ari	13:37
	JUN	8	Leo	10:35		MAY	21	Tau	14:51
	JUL	7	Vir	18:17		JUN	15	Gem	11:46
	NOV	9	Lib	8:05		JUL	10	Can	4:36
	DEC	9	Scp	3:29		AUG	3	Leo	16:43
1920	JAN	4	Sag	9:20		AUG	27	Vir	24:00
	JAN	29	Cap	11:55		SEP	21	Lib	3:29
	FEB	23	Aqu	3:47		OCT	15	Scp	4:49
	MAR	18	Pic	15:31		NOV	8	Sag	5:24

	DEC	2	Cap	6:06		FEB	22	Aqu	16:16
	DEC	26	Aqu	8:03		MAR	18	Pic	3:26
1924	JAN	19	Pic	13:46		APR	11	Ari	13:36
	FEB	13	Ari	4:10		MAY	6	Tau	0:04
	MAR	9	Tau	11:56		MAY	30	Gem	11:01
	APR	5	Gem	6:47		JUN	23	Can	21:43
	MAY	6	Can	1:49		JUL	18	Leo	7:16
	SEP	8	Leo	21:43		AUG	11	Vir	15:29
	OCT	7	Vir	14:17		SEP	4	Lib	23:06
	NOV	2	Lib	14:44		SEP	29	Scp	7:18
	NOV	27	Scp	11:48		OCT	23	Sag	17:13
	DEC	21	Sag	19:56		NOV	17	Cap	6:09
1925	JAN	14	Cap	22:29		DEC	12	Aqu	1:26
	FEB	7	Aqu	23:16	1929	JAN	6	Pic	12:02
	MAR	4	Pic	0:22		FEB	2	Ari	14:34
	MAR	28	Ari	3:05		MAR	8	Tau	7:30
	APR	21	Tau	8:14		APR	20	Ari	2:06
	MAY	15	Gem	16:04		JUN	3	Tau	9:47
	JUN	9	Can	2:15		JUL	8	Gem	2:00
	JUL	3	Leo	14:31		AUG	5	Can	5:40
	JUL	28	Vir	5:25		AUG	31	Leo	11:24
	AUG	22	Lib	0:29		SEP	25	Vir	16:14
	SEP	16	Scp	2:05		OCT	20	Lib	5:13
	OCT	11	Sag	14:11		NOV	13	Scp	8:35
	NOV	6	Cap	22:35		DEC	7	Sag	7:04
	DEC	5	Aqu	15:09		DEC	31	Cap	3:44
1926	APR	6	Pic	3:59	1930	JAN	24	Aqu	0:22
	MAY	6	Ari	15:13		FEB	16	Pic	22:12
	JUN	2	Tau	20:00		MAR	12	Ari	22:34
	JUN	28	Gem	21:05		APR	6	Tau	2:58
	JUL	24	Can	6:42		APR	30	Gem	12:37
	AUG	18	Leo	4:35		MAY	25	Can	4:37
	SEP	11	Vir	16:37		JUN	19	Leo	4:39
	OCT	5	Lib	21:08		JUL	14	Vir	16:35
	OCT	29	Scp	20:51		AUG	10	Lib	0:54
	NOV	22	Sag	18:12		SEP	7	Scp	4:06
	DEC	16	Cap	14:49		OCT	12	Sag	2:45
1927	JAN	9	Aqu	11:48		NOV	22	Scp	7:44
	FEB	2	Pic	10:34	1931	JAN	3	Sag	20:03
	FEB	26	Ari	13:17		FEB	6	Cap	12:25
	MAR	22	Tau	22:57		MAR	5	Aqu	21:46
	APR	16	Gem	19:26		MAR	31	Pic	19:04
	MAY	12	Can	8:34		APR	26	Ari	2:10
	JUN	8	Leo	2:52		MAY	21	Tau	2:39
	JUL	7	Vir	18:55		JUN	14	Gem	23:05
	NOV	9	Lib	13:26		JUL	9	Can	15:35
	DEC	8	Scp	21:26		AUG	3	Leo	3:30
1928	JAN	4	Sag	0:06		AUG	27	Vir	10:43
	JAN	29	Cap	1:13		SEP	20	Lib	14:15

	OCT	14	Scp	15:45		NOV	9	Lib	16:35
	NOV	7	Sag	16:33		DEC	8	Scp	14:36
	DEC	1	Cap	17:30	1936	JAN	3	Sag	14:17
	DEC	25	Aqu	19:44		JAN	28	Cap	14:01
1932	JAN	19	Pic	1:52		FEB	22	Aqu	4:15
	FEB	12	Ari	16:59		MAR	17	Pic	14:54
	MAR	9	Tau	2:07		APR	11	Ari	0:41
	APR	5	Gem	0:20		MAY	5	Tau	10:53
	MAY	6	Can	9:05		MAY	29	Gem	21:40
	JUL	13	Gem	11:23		JUN	23	Can	8:15
	JUL	28	Can	12:35		JUL	17	Leo	17:51
	SEP	8	Leo	19:45		AUG	11	Vir	2:12
	OCT	7	Vir	5:46		SEP	4	Lib	10:02
	NOV	2	Lib	4:02		SEP	28	Scp	18:36
	NOV	27	Scp	0:07		OCT	23	Sag	5:01
	DEC	21	Sag	7:43		NOV	16	Cap	18:36
1933	JAN	14	Cap	9:57		DEC	11	Aqu	14:52
	FEB	7	Aqu	10:30	1937	JAN	6	Pic	3:18
	MAR	3	Pic	11:25		FEB	2	Ari	10:40
	MAR	27	Ari	13:58		MAR	9	Tau	13:20
	APR	20	Tau	19:01		APR	14	Ari	4:15
	MAY	15	Gem	2:47		JUN	4	Tau	6:41
	JUN	8	Can	13:01		JUL	7	Gem	21:13
	JUL	3	Leo	1:30		AUG	4	Can	20:14
	JUL	27	Vir	16:46		AUG	31	Leo	0:08
	AUG	21	Lib	12:24		SEP	25	Vir	4:03
	SEP	15	Scp	14:55		OCT	19	Lib	16:34
	OCT	11	Sag	4:32		NOV	12	Scp	19:43
	NOV	6	Cap	16:03		DEC	6	Sag	18:06
	DEC	5	Aqu	18:01		DEC	30	Cap	14:43
1934	APR	6	Pic	9:22	1938	JAN	23	Aqu	11:16
	MAY	6	Ari	8:54		FEB	16	Pic	9:01
	JUN	2	Tau	10:11		MAR	12	Ari	9:21
	JUN	28	Gem	9:38		APR	5	Tau	13:47
	JUL	23	Can	18:22		APR	29	Gem	23:36
	AUG	17	Leo	15:45		MAY	24	Can	15:56
	SEP	11	Vir	3:32		JUN	18	Leo	16:38
	OCT	5	Lib	7:56		JUL	14	Vir	5:45
	OCT	29	Scp	7:37		AUG	9	Lib	16:27
	NOV	22	Sag	5:00		SEP	7	Scp	1:37
	DEC	16	Cap	1:39		OCT	13	Sag	18:50
1935	JAN	8	Aqu	22:44		NOV	15	Scp	15:58
	FEB	1	Pic	21:37	1939	JAN	4	Sag	21:49
	FEB	26	Ari	0:30		FEB	6	Cap	9:20
	MAR	22	Tau	10:30		MAR	5	Aqu	13:29
	APR	16	Gem	7:37		MAR	31	Pic	8:35
	MAY	11	Can	22:02		APR	25	Ari	14:29
	JUN	7	Leo	19:12		MAY	20	Tau	14:13
	JUL	7	Vir	20:34		JUN	14	Gem	10:11

	JUL	9	Can	2:25		APR	15	Gem	20:12
	AUG	2	Leo	14:12		MAY	11	Can	11:57
	AUG	26	Vir	21:25		JUN	7	Leo	12:09
	SEP	20	Lib	1:03		JUL	7	Vir	23:57
	OCT	14	Scp	2:42		NOV	9	Lib	18:25
	NOV	7	Sag	3:41		DEC	8	Scp	7:45
	DEC	1	Cap	4:52	1944	JAN	3	Sag	4:44
	DEC	25	Aqu	7:26		JAN	28	Cap	3:11
1940	JAN	18	Pic	14:01		FEB	21	Aqu	16:40
	FEB	12	Ari	5:51		MAR	17	Pic	2:47
	MAR	8	Tau	16:26		APR	10	Ari	12:10
	APR	4	Gem	18:10		MAY	4	Tau	22:04
	MAY	6	Can	18:47		MAY	29	Gem	8:40
	JUL	5	Gem	16:38		JUN	22	Can	19:12
	AUG	1	Can	2:19		JUL	17	Leo	4:47
	SEP	8	Leo	16:59		AUG	10	Vir	13:13
	OCT	6	Vir	21:10		SEP	3	Lib	21:17
	NOV	1	Lib	17:24		SEP	28	Scp	6:13
	NOV	26	Scp	12:32		OCT	22	Sag	17:08
	DEC	20	Sag	19:37		NOV	16	Cap	7:26
1941	JAN	13	Cap	21:30		DEC	11	Aqu	4:48
	FEB	6	Aqu	21:49	1945	JAN	5	Pic	19:19
	MAR	2	Pic	22:34		FEB	2	Ari	8:07
	MAR	27	Ari	0:58		MAR	11	Tau	11:18
	APR	20	Tau	5:54		APR	7	Ari	19:04
	MAY	14	Gem	13:37		JUN	4	Tau	22:58
	JUN	7	Can	23:53		JUL	7	Gem	16:21
	JUL	2	Leo	12:33		AUG	4	Can	11:00
	JUL	27	Vir	4:13		AUG	30	Leo	13:05
	AUG	21	Lib	0:30		SEP	24	Vir	16:07
	SEP	15	Scp	4:02		OCT	19	Lib	4:10
	OCT	10	Sag	19:22		NOV	12	Scp	7:05
	NOV	6	Cap	10:17		DEC	6	Sag	5:23
	DEC	2	Aqu	23:05		DEC	30	Cap	1:57
1942	APR	6	Pic	13:15	1946	JAN	22	Aqu	22:28
	MAY	6	Ari	2:26		FEB	15	Pic	20:12
	JUN	2	Tau	0:26		MAR	11	Ari	20:32
	JUN	27	Gem	22:19		APR	5	Tau	1:02
	JUL	23	Can	6:11		APR	29	Gem	11:00
	AUG	17	Leo	3:05		MAY	24	Can	3:40
	SEP	10	Vir	14:38		JUN	18	Leo	5:01
	OCT	4	Lib	18:58		JUL	13	Vir	19:23
	OCT	28	Scp	18:41		AUG	9	Lib	8:35
	NOV	21	Sag	16:08		SEP	7	Scp	0:17
	DEC	15	Cap	12:53		OCT	16	Sag	10:45
1943	JAN	8	Aqu	10:03		NOV	8	Scp	8:32
	FEB	1	Pic	9:02	1947	JAN	5	Sag	16:45
	FEB	25	Ari	12:05		FEB	6	Cap	5:42
	MAR	21	Tau	22:25		MAR	5	Aqu	5:09

	MAR	30	Pic	22:15	1951 JAN	7 Aqu	21:11
	APR	25	Ari	3:03	JAN	31 Pic	20:15
	MAY	20	Tau	2:06	FEB	24 Ari	23:27
	JUN	13	Gem	21:36	MAR	21 Tau	10:06
	JUL	8	Can	13:30	APR	15 Gem	8:34
	AUG	2	Leo	1:07	MAY	11 Can	1:42
	AUG	26	Vir	8:18	JUN	7 Leo	5:10
	SEP	19	Lib	12:01	JUL	8 Vir	4:54
	OCT	13	Scp	13:49	NOV	9 Lib	18:48
	NOV	6	Sag	14:59	DEC	8 Scp	0:19
	NOV	30	Cap	16:23	1952 JAN	2 Sag	18:45
	DEC	24	Aqu	19:13	JAN	27 Cap	15:58
1948	JAN	18	Pic	2:14	FEB	21 Aqu	4:43
	FEB	11	Ari	18:51	MAR	16 Pic	14:19
	MAR	8	Tau	7:00	APR	9 Ari	23:18
	APR	4	Gem	12:41	MAY	4 Tau	8:55
	MAY	7	Can	8:28	MAY	28 Gem	19:19
	JUN	29	Gem	8:11	JUN	22 Can	5:47
	AUG	3	Can	2:15	JUL	16 Leo	15:23
	SEP	8	Leo	13:41	AUG	9 Vir	23:58
	OCT	6	Vir	12:26	SEP	3 Lib	8:18
	NOV	1	Lib	6:43	SEP	27 Scp	17:37
	NOV	26	Scp	0:55	OCT	22 Sag	5:03
	DEC	20	Sag	7:29	NOV	15 Cap	20:03
1949	JAN	13	Cap	9:01	DEC	10 Aqu	18:31
	FEB	6	Aqu	9:06	1953 JAN	5 Pic	11:11
	MAR	2	Pic	9:39	FEB	2 Ari	5:55
	MAR	26	Ari	11:54	MAR	14 Tau	18:58
	APR	19	Tau	16:44	MAR	31 Ari	4:51
	MAY	14	Gem	0:26	JUN	5 Tau	10:34
	JUN	7	Can	10:48	JUL	7 Gem	10:30
	JUL	1	Leo	23:41	AUG	4 Can	1:09
	JUL	26	Vir	15:44	AUG	30 Leo	1:35
	AUG	20	Lib	12:39	SEP	24 Vir	3:48
	SEP	14	Scp	17:13	OCT	18 Lib	15:28
	OCT	10	Sag	10:19	NOV	11 Scp	18:13
	NOV	6	Cap	4:54	DEC	5 Sag	16:25
	DEC	6	Aqu	6:06	DEC	29 Cap	12:54
1950	APR	6	Pic	15:14	1954 JAN	22 Aqu	9:21
	MAY	5	Ari	19:20	FEB	15 Pic	7:02
	JUN	1	Tau	14:19	MAR	11 Ari	7:22
	JUN	27	Gem	10:45	APR	4 Tau	11:56
	JUL	22	Can	17:50	APR	28 Gem	22:04
	AUG	16	Leo	14:18	MAY	23 Can	15:04
	SEP	10	Vir	1:38	JUN	17 Leo	17:05
	OCT	4	Lib	5:51	JUL	13 Vir	8:43
	OCT	28	Scp	5:34	AUG	9 Lib	0:34
	NOV	21	Sag	3:04	SEP	6 Scp	23:29
	DEC	14	Cap	23:55	OCT	23 Sag	22:12

	OCT	27	Scp	7:30		OCT	3	Lib	16:45
1955	JAN	6	Sag	6:48		OCT	27	Scp	16:27
	FEB	6	Cap	1:16		NOV	20	Sag	14:00
	MAR	4	Aqu	20:22		DEC	14	Cap	10:56
	MAR	30	Pic	11:31	1959	JAN	7	Aqu	8:17
	APR	24	Ari	15:14		JAN	31	Pic	7:29
	MAY	19	Tau	13:36		FEB	24	Ari	10:53
	JUN	13	Gem	8:38		MAR	20	Tau	21:56
	JUL	8	Can	0:16		APR	14	Gem	21:08
	AUG	1	Leo	11:43		MAY	10	Can	15:46
	AUG	25	Vir	18:53		JUN	6	Leo	22:43
	SEP	18	Lib	22:41		JUL	8	Vir	12:09
	OCT	13	Scp	0:39		SEP	20	Leo	4:28
	NOV	6	Sag	2:03		SEP	25	Vir	8:08
	NOV	30	Cap	3:43		NOV	9	Lib	18:11
	DEC	24	Aqu	6:53		DEC	7	Scp	16:42
1956	JAN	17	Pic	14:23	1960	JAN	2	Sag	8:44
	FEB	11	Ari	7:47		JAN	27	Cap	4:46
	MAR	7	Tau	21:32		FEB	20	Aqu	16:48
	APR	4	Gem	7:23		MAR	16	Pic	1:54
	MAY	8	Can	2:18		APR	9	Ari	10:33
	JUN	23	Gem	12:14		MAY	3	Tau	19:56
	AUG	4	Can	9:49		MAY	28	Gem	6:12
	SEP	8	Leo	9:24		JUN	21	Can	16:34
	OCT	6	Vir	3:13		JUL	16	Leo	2:12
	OCT	31	Lib	19:40		AUG	9	Vir	10:54
	NOV	25	Scp	13:02		SEP	2	Lib	19:30
	DEC	19	Sag	19:07		SEP	27	Scp	5:14
1957	JAN	12	Cap	20:23		OCT	21	Sag	17:13
	FEB	5	Aqu	20:17		NOV	15	Cap	8:58
	MAR	1	Pic	20:40		DEC	10	Aqu	8:35
	MAR	25	Ari	22:47	1961	JAN	5	Pic	3:32
	APR	19	Tau	3:29		FEB	2	Ari	4:47
	MAY	13	Gem	11:09		JUN	5	Tau	19:25
	JUN	6	Can	21:35		JUL	7	Gem	4:33
	JUL	1	Leo	10:43		AUG	3	Can	15:29
	JUL	26	Vir	3:11		AUG	29	Leo	14:19
	AUG	20	Lib	0:45		SEP	23	Vir	15:43
	SEP	14	Scp	6:20		OCT	18	Lib	2:59
	OCT	10	Sag	1:16		NOV	11	Scp	5:33
	NOV	5	Cap	23:46		DEC	5	Sag	3:41
	DEC	6	Aqu	15:27		DEC	29	Cap	0:07
1958	APR	6	Pic	16:00	1962	JAN	21	Aqu	20:31
	MAY	5	Ari	11:59		FEB	14	Pic	18:09
	JUN	1	Tau	4:08		MAR	10	Ari	18:29
	JUN	26	Gem	23:09		APR	3	Tau	23:05
	JUL	22	Can	5:27		APR	28	Gem	9:24
	AUG	16	Leo	1:29		MAY	23	Can	2:47
	SEP	9	Vir	12:36		JUN	17	Leo	5:32

	JUL	12	Vir	22:33		JUN	26	Gem	11:41
	AUG	8	Lib	17:14		JUL	21	Can	17:12
	SEP	7	Scp	0:12		AUG	15	Leo	12:48
1963	JAN	6	Sag	17:36		SEP	8	Vir	23:41
	FEB	5	Cap	20:36		OCT	3	Lib	3:45
	MAR	4	Aqu	11:42		OCT	27	Scp	3:29
	MAR	30	Pic	1:00		NOV	20	Sag	1:07
	APR	24	Ari	3:40		DEC	13	Cap	22:09
	MAY	19	Tau	1:22	1967	JAN	6	Aqu	19:37
	JUN	12	Gem	19:57		JAN	30	Pic	18:54
	JUL	7	Can	11:19		FEB	23	Ari	22:30
	JUL	31	Leo	22:39		MAR	20	Tau	9:57
	AUG	25	Vir	5:49		APR	14	Gem	9:55
	SEP	18	Lib	9:43		MAY	10	Can	6:06
	OCT	12	Scp	11:50		JUN	6	Leo	16:49
	NOV	5	Sag	13:26		JUL	8	Vir	22:12
	NOV	29	Cap	15:22		SEP	9	Leo	12:29
	DEC	23	Aqu	18:54		OCT	1	Vir	18:07
1964	JAN	17	Pic	2:54		NOV	9	Lib	16:33
	FEB	10	Ari	21:10		DEC	7	Scp	8:49
	MAR	7	Tau	12:39	1968	JAN	1	Sag	22:38
	APR	4	Gem	3:04		JAN	26	Cap	17:35
	MAY	9	Can	3:16		FEB	20	Aqu	4:56
	JUN	17	Gem	18:15		MAR	15	Pic	13:32
	AUG	5	Can	8:53		APR	8	Ari	21:49
	SEP	8	Leo	4:54		MAY	3	Tau	6:57
	OCT	5	Vir	18:11		MAY	27	Gem	17:03
	OCT	31	Lib	8:55		JUN	21	Can	3:21
	NOV	25	Scp	1:26		JUL	15	Leo	13:00
	DEC	19	Sag	7:03		AUG	8	Vir	21:50
1965	JAN	12	Cap	8:01		SEP	2	Lib	6:40
	FEB	5	Aqu	7:42		SEP	26	Scp	16:46
	MAR	1	Pic	7:56		OCT	21	Sag	5:17
	MAR	25	Ari	9:55		NOV	14	Cap	21:48
	APR	18	Tau	14:31		DEC	9	Aqu	22:41
	MAY	12	Gem	22:09	1969	JAN	4	Pic	20:08
	JUN	6	Can	8:40		FEB	2	Ari	4:46
	JUN	30	Leo	22:00		JUN	6	Tau	1:49
	JUL	25	Vir	14:52		JUL	6	Gem	22:04
	AUG	19	Lib	13:07		AUG	3	Can	5:31
	SEP	13	Scp	19:51		AUG	29	Leo	2:48
	OCT	9	Sag	16:47		SEP	23	Vir	3:27
	NOV	5	Cap	19:37		OCT	17	Lib	14:18
	DEC	7	Aqu	4:38		NOV	10	Scp	16:41
1966	FEB	6	Cap	13:25		DEC	4	Sag	14:42
	FEB	25	Aqu	10:54		DEC	28	Cap	11:04
	APR	6	Pic	15:54	1970	JAN	21	Aqu	7:27
	MAY	5	Ari	4:34		FEB	14	Pic	5:05
	MAY	31	Tau	16:01		MAR	10	Ari	5:26

	APR	3	Tau	10:06		FEB	28	Aqu	14:25
	APR	27	Gem	20:34		APR	6	Pic	14:18
	MAY	22	Can	14:20		MAY	4	Ari	20:22
	JUN	16	Leo	17:50		MAY	31	Tau	7:19
	JUL	12	Vir	12:17		JUN	25	Gem	23:45
	AUG	8	Lib	10:00		JUL	21	Can	4:35
	SEP	7	Scp	1:54		AUG	14	Leo	23:47
1971	JAN	7	Sag	1:00		SEP	8	Vir	10:28
	FEB	5	Cap	14:58		OCT	2	Lib	14:28
	MAR	4	Aqu	2:25		OCT	26	Scp	14:13
	MAR	29	Pic	14:02		NOV	19	Sag	11:57
	APR	23	Ari	15:45		DEC	13	Cap	9:07
	MAY	18	Tau	12:49	1975	JAN	6	Aqu	6:40
	JUN	12	Gem	6:58		JAN	30	Pic	6:06
	JUL	6	Can	22:03		FEB	23	Ari	9:54
	JUL	31	Leo	9:16		MAR	19	Tau	21:43
	AUG	24	Vir	16:26		APR	13	Gem	22:26
	SEP	17	Lib	20:26		MAY	9	Can	20:12
	OCT	11	Scp	22:44		JUN	6	Leo	10:55
	NOV	5	Sag	0:31		JUL	9	Vir	11:07
	NOV	29	Cap	2:42		SEP	2	Leo	15:49
	DEC	23	Aqu	6:33		OCT	4	Vir	5:20
1972	JAN	16	Pic	15:02		NOV	9	Lib	13:53
	FEB	10	Ari	10:09		DEC	7	Scp	0:30
	MAR	7	Tau	3:26	1976	JAN	1	Sag	12:15
	APR	3	Gem	22:49		JAN	26	Cap	6:10
	MAY	10	Can	13:51		FEB	19	Aqu	16:51
	JUN	11	Gem	20:03		MAR	15	Pic	1:00
	AUG	6	Can	1:27		APR	8	Ari	8:57
	SEP	7	Leo	23:28		MAY	2	Tau	17:50
	OCT	5	Vir	8:34		MAY	27	Gem	3:44
	OCT	30	Lib	21:41		JUN	20	Can	13:57
	NOV	24	Scp	13:24		JUL	14	Leo	23:37
	DEC	18	Sag	18:35		AUG	8	Vir	8:37
1973	JAN	11	Cap	19:16		SEP	1	Lib	17:46
	FEB	4	Aqu	18:44		SEP	26	Scp	4:18
	FEB	28	Pic	18:46		OCT	20	Sag	17:23
	MAR	24	Ari	20:35		NOV	14	Cap	10:43
	APR	18	Tau	1:06		DEC	9	Aqu	12:54
	MAY	12	Gem	8:43	1977	JAN	4	Pic	13:02
	JUN	5	Can	19:21		FEB	2	Ari	5:55
	JUN	30	Leo	8:56		JUN	6	Tau	6:11
	JUL	25	Vir	2:14		JUL	6	Gem	15:10
	AUG	19	Lib	1:11		AUG	2	Can	19:19
	SEP	13	Scp	9:06		AUG	28	Leo	15:10
	OCT	9	Sag	8:09		SEP	22	Vir	15:06
	NOV	5	Cap	15:40		OCT	17	Lib	1:38
	DEC	7	Aqu	21:38		NOV	10	Scp	3:53
1974	JAN	29	Cap	20:01		DEC	4	Sag	1:50

	DEC	27	Cap	22:10		OCT	9	Sag	0:05
1978	JAN	20	Aqu	18:30		NOV	5	Cap	12:41
	FEB	13	Pic	16:08		DEC	8	Aqu	20:54
	MAR	9	Ari	16:30	1982	JAN	23	Cap	3:01
	APR	2	Tau	21:15		MAR	2	Aqu	11:26
	APR	27	Gem	7:55		APR	6	Pic	12:21
	MAY	22	Can	2:05		MAY	4	Ari	12:27
	JUN	16	Leo	6:20		MAY	30	Tau	21:03
	JUL	12	Vir	2:15		JUN	25	Gem	12:14
	AUG	8	Lib	3:09		JUL	20	Can	16:22
	SEP	7	Scp	5:09		AUG	14	Leo	11:10
1979	JAN	7	Sag	6:39		SEP	7	Vir	21:39
	FEB	5	Cap	9:16		OCT	2	Lib	1:34
	MAR	3	Aqu	17:19		OCT	26	Scp	1:20
	MAR	29	Pic	3:19		NOV	18	Sag	23:08
	APR	23	Ari	4:03		DEC	12	Cap	20:21
	MAY	18	Tau	0:30	1983	JAN	5	Aqu	17:59
	JUN	11	Gem	18:14		JAN	29	Pic	17:33
	JUL	6	Can	9:03		FEB	22	Ari	21:36
	JUL	30	Leo	20:08		MAR	19	Tau	9:52
	AUG	24	Vir	3:17		APR	13	Gem	11:27
	SEP	17	Lib	7:22		MAY	9	Can	10:58
	OCT	11	Scp	9:49		JUN	6	Leo	6:05
	NOV	4	Sag	11:51		JUL	10	Vir	5:26
	NOV	28	Cap	14:21		AUG	27	Leo	11:51
	DEC	22	Aqu	18:36		OCT	5	Vir	19:36
1980	JAN	16	Pic	3:38		NOV	9	Lib	10:53
	FEB	9	Ari	23:41		DEC	6	Scp	16:16
	MAR	6	Tau	18:55	1984	JAN	1	Sag	2:01
	APR	3	Gem	19:47		JAN	25	Cap	18:52
	MAY	12	Can	20:53		FEB	19	Aqu	4:54
	JUN	5	Gem	5:28		MAR	14	Pic	12:36
	AUG	6	Can	14:25		APR	7	Ari	20:14
	SEP	7	Leo	17:58		MAY	2	Tau	4:55
	OCT	4	Vir	23:08		MAY	26	Gem	14:41
	OCT	30	Lib	10:39		JUN	20	Can	0:50
	NOV	24	Scp	1:36		JUL	14	Leo	10:32
	DEC	18	Sag	6:22		AUG	7	Vir	19:41
1981	JAN	11	Cap	6:50		SEP	1	Lib	5:08
	FEB	4	Aqu	6:09		SEP	25	Scp	16:06
	FEB	28	Pic	6:03		OCT	20	Sag	5:47
	MAR	24	Ari	7:44		NOV	13	Cap	23:56
	APR	17	Tau	12:09		DEC	9	Aqu	3:28
	MAY	11	Gem	19:46	1985	JAN	4	Pic	6:25
	JUN	5	Can	6:30		FEB	2	Ari	8:30
	JUN	29	Leo	20:21		JUN	6	Tau	8:53
	JUL	24	Vir	14:05		JUL	6	Gem	8:02
	AUG	18	Lib	13:46		AUG	2	Can	9:11
	SEP	12	Scp	22:52		AUG	28	Leo	3:40

	SEP	22	Vir	2:54		JUN	29	Leo	7:22
	OCT	16	Lib	13:05		JUL	24	Vir	1:33
	NOV	9	Scp	15:09		AUG	18	Lib	1:59
	DEC	3	Sag	13:01		SEP	12	Scp	12:24
	DEC	27	Cap	9:19		OCT	8	Sag	16:01
1986	JAN	20	Aqu	5:37		NOV	5	Cap	10:14
	FEB	13	Pic	3:12		DEC	10	Aqu	4:56
	MAR	9	Ari	3:33	1990	JAN	16	Cap	15:20
	APR	2	Tau	8:20		MAR	3	Aqu	17:52
	APR	26	Gem	19:11		APR	6	Pic	9:14
	MAY	21	Can	13:47		MAY	4	Ari	3:53
	JUN	15	Leo	18:53		MAY	30	Tau	10:15
	JUL	11	Vir	16:24		JUN	25	Gem	0:15
	AUG	7	Lib	20:47		JUL	20	Can	3:42
	SEP	7	Scp	10:16		AUG	13	Leo	22:06
1987	JAN	7	Sag	10:21		SEP	7	Vir	8:22
	FEB	5	Cap	3:04		OCT	1	Lib	12:14
	MAR	3	Aqu	7:56		OCT	25	Scp	12:04
	MAR	28	Pic	16:21		NOV	18	Sag	9:59
	APR	22	Ari	16:08		DEC	12	Cap	7:20
	MAY	17	Tau	11:57	1991	JAN	5	Aqu	5:04
	JUN	11	Gem	5:16		JAN	29	Pic	4:46
	JUL	5	Can	19:51		FEB	22	Ari	9:03
	JUL	30	Leo	6:51		MAR	18	Tau	21:46
	AUG	23	Vir	14:01		APR	13	Gem	0:12
	SEP	16	Lib	18:13		MAY	9	Can	1:30
	OCT	10	Scp	20:50		JUN	6	Leo	1:17
	NOV	3	Sag	23:05		JUL	11	Vir	5:07
	NOV	28	Cap	1:52		AUG	21	Leo	15:05
	DEC	22	Aqu	6:30		OCT	6	Vir	21:16
1988	JAN	15	Pic	16:05		NOV	9	Lib	6:38
	FEB	9	Ari	13:05		DEC	6	Scp	7:22
	MAR	6	Tau	10:22		DEC	31	Sag	15:20
	APR	3	Gem	17:09	1992	JAN	25	Cap	7:15
	MAY	17	Can	16:28		FEB	18	Aqu	16:41
	MAY	27	Gem	6:37		MAR	13	Pic	23:58
	AUG	6	Can	23:25		APR	7	Ari	7:17
	SEP	7	Leo	11:38		MAY	1	Tau	15:43
	OCT	4	Vir	13:16		MAY	26	Gem	1:19
	OCT	29	Lib	23:21		JUN	19	Can	11:24
	NOV	23	Scp	13:35		JUL	13	Leo	21:08
	DEC	17	Sag	17:57		AUG	7	Vir	6:27
1989	JAN	10	Cap	18:09		AUG	31	Lib	16:10
	FEB	3	Aqu	17:16		SEP	25	Scp	3:33
	FEB	27	Pic	17:00		OCT	19	Sag	17:48
	MAR	23	Ari	18:33		NOV	13	Cap	12:49
	APR	16	Tau	22:54		DEC	8	Aqu	17:51
	MAY	11	Gem	6:29	1993	JAN	3	Pic	23:55
	JUN	4	Can	17:19		FEB	2	Ari	12:38

	JUN	6	Tau	10:04		MAY	10	Gem	17:22
	JUL	6	Gem	0:22		JUN	4	Can	4:19
	AUG	1	Can	22:39		JUN	28	Leo	18:39
	AUG	27	Leo	15:49		JUL	23	Vir	13:18
	SEP	21	Vir	14:24		AUG	17	Lib	14:32
	OCT	16	Lib	0:14		SEP	12	Scp	2:18
	NOV	9	Scp	2:08		OCT	8	Sag	8:27
	DEC	2	Sag	23:55		NOV	5	Cap	8:52
	DEC	26	Cap	20:10		DEC	12	Aqu	4:41
1994	JAN	19	Aqu	16:29	1998	JAN	9	Cap	20:57
	FEB	12	Pic	14:06		MAR	4	Aqu	16:15
	MAR	8	Ari	14:29		APR	6	Pic	5:39
	APR	1	Tau	19:22		MAY	3	Ari	19:17
	APR	26	Gem	6:25		MAY	29	Tau	23:33
	MAY	21	Can	1:28		JUN	24	Gem	12:29
	JUN	15	Leo	7:24		JUL	19	Can	15:18
	JUL	11	Vir	6:34		AUG	13	Leo	9:21
	AUG	7	Lib	14:38		SEP	6	Vir	19:26
	SEP	7	Scp	17:14		SEP	30	Lib	23:15
1995	JAN	7	Sag	12:08		OCT	24	Scp	23:07
	FEB	4	Cap	20:13		NOV	17	Sag	21:08
	MAR	2	Aqu	22:12		DEC	11	Cap	18:34
	MAR	28	Pic	5:11	1999	JAN	4	Aqu	16:27
	APR	22	Ari	4:08		JAN	28	Pic	16:18
	MAY	16	Tau	23:23		FEB	21	Ari	20:51
	JUN	10	Gem	16:20		MAR	18	Tau	10:01
	JUL	5	Can	6:40		APR	12	Gem	13:18
	JUL	29	Leo	17:33		MAY	8	Can	16:30
	AUG	23	Vir	0:44		JUN	5	Leo	21:26
	SEP	16	Lib	5:02		JUL	12	Vir	15:19
	OCT	10	Scp	7:49		AUG	15	Leo	14:02
	NOV	3	Sag	10:20		OCT	7	Vir	16:52
	NOV	27	Cap	13:25		NOV	9	Lib	2:20
	DEC	21	Aqu	18:24		DEC	5	Scp	22:43
1996	JAN	15	Pic	4:32		DEC	31	Sag	4:55
	FEB	9	Ari	2:32	2000	JAN	24	Cap	19:54
	MAR	6	Tau	2:02		FEB	18	Aqu	4:45
	APR	3	Gem	15:27		MAR	13	Pic	11:37
	AUG	7	Can	6:15		APR	6	Ari	18:39
	SEP	7	Leo	5:08		MAY	1	Tau	2:50
	OCT	4	Vir	3:23		MAY	25	Gem	12:16
	OCT	29	Lib	12:03		JUN	13	Can	22:16
	NOV	23	Scp	1:36		JUL	13	Leo	8:04
	DEC	17	Sag	5:35		AUG	6	Vir	17:34
1997	JAN	10	Cap	5:33		AUG	31	Lib	3:37
	FEB	3	Aqu	4:29		SEP	24	Scp	15:27
	FEB	27	Pic	4:02		OCT	19	Sag	6:20
	MAR	23	Ari	5:27		NOV	13	Cap	2:16
	APR	16	Tau	9:44		DEC	8	Aqu	8:50

Mars—How You Drive People Crazy

> " 'Tis in my head; 'tis in my heart; 'tis everywhere; it rages like a madness, and I must wonder how my reason holds."
>
> —Thomas Otway

Hey, bay-bee! Want a good time? Fight maybe? Step a little closer, tell you what I'm going to do. Introduce you to Mister Mars, ol' fireball glowing red in the sky—the most macho planet in the whole universe!

Mars likes war. Mars makes enthusiasm too, though it'll settle for trouble. Mars is your energy, what you put your energy into, your drive and your courage. Mars stands for lust and drive and passion. Mars burns for things. If someone has Mars on your Venus, they burn for *you*.

The sign Mars is in shows what kind of special sparkle you have. Think of a peacock showing off in courtship. Some Mars signs strut more successfully than others.

Things that make you angry are Mars things. If Mars is in Virgo, for example, *dirt* drives you crazy. If Mars is in Pisces you go wild when the druggist is late.

Your Mars sign even indicates the style in which you rip up the joint—nagging and picking in Virgo, a whining, sneaky self-pitying fool in Pisces.

Find the sign Mars was in at your birth in the ZAP! tables. If you have a proper computer chart, the *house* Mars is in indicates those areas in life where you focus all your drive and enthusiasm—go for it!

Make everyone else crazy with your Mars if you want to, but you're inviting a punch on the nose. If your friends are the refined sort, perhaps they'll confine themselves to spitting in the soup when you're not looking.

Want to blow off steam? Look up your Mars, and all your friends' Marses here. Then get out some ugly plates and toss them about the room for a bit. Boppo toys work well too. I had one once, but it busted when it found itself carving a foot-long *hole* in the wall one evening. A most unruly toy.

MARS IN ARIES

Confidence! Get some. When you feel competitive or aggressive, you look awfully sexy. You look cute in a baseball cap. When you feel zappy, you can win anyone on this earth. Mars *loves* to be in Aries. You're popular. People admire your unique, honest personality, and you have courage, a clean enthusiasm, and endless sparkle. People can tell when you're in love with them, for you're direct without meaning to be, and you're fun, always willing to try new places, new foods, and new ideas. You have heroes and villains. You invented chivalry. You're not afraid to take a stand, nor will you back away when it's time to zap the unjust. You are sexier than you think and braver than you know. You would be surprised at how many people want to drag you off to a deserted haystack. Why do you get paranoid?

You've a hair-trigger temper. You seem always to be irate about something or other. If you've an image of yourself as a long-suffering sweetie pie, you get depressed a lot, which really means you're mad as a starving Brachiosaurus. You've still got the best Mars of the lot, however, for you do get in touch with your anger, get it off your chest, and forget about it. People envy your good sportsmanship, and hate you for it.

MARS IN TAURUS

Not everyone appeals to you, nor do you appeal to all people. You're one hell of a snob. You love the people and the things that you love, and the rest can go fish. Good food is big with you. Good duds to wear too. People think they must be quality folks if you let them hang around with you. This appeals to *their* secret snobberies. You never put up with nonsense; folks have to toe the line with you. You're wizard at giving a hearty welcome, though, to those you care about. You work terribly hard, but you move slowly and deliberately, with the suggestion of laziness. You ooze an earthy sexiness and seem as if you would be willing to put down whatever you were doing in favor of a little huggin' and squeezin'. You would be.

Muhammed Ali has Mars in Taurus. Why does traditional

strological lore deplore this position? Here is a stubborn, persis-
ent, fighter. You see a barney where there is only an inkling of
misunderstanding, and make it worse by coming out punching.
At worst you are a meretricious measurer of a person's worth by
he size of their bank balance. You will fight for your values,
hough those values reflect a pig's-eye view of things, unless you
re lucky enough to have a sprinkling of brains along with your
logmatism. True, you *are* generous, and you get furious when
people are cheap with *you*. You do love to stir it up, though it
lways looks to you as if it's the other guy who's being
unreasonable.

MARS IN GEMINI

Kinky! You want to try all sorts of experiences. Yours is a
dignified, cerebral way of flirting. You are so sophisticated that
often folks don't even know you are flirting with them. That's
okay with you—weeds out the dumbbells. Watch the gossip, as
you are capable of inflicting subtle mental cruelty on a mate just
or the fun of things. You know people in all walks of life. You
ove to drag your dear ones out to new neighborhoods, and you
want them to do the same to you. Variety is your god, but you
can be faithful to a multifaceted partner. Mind you don't drive
your sweetie schizophrenic with your little tests and games. The
mind is, after all, the biggest sex organ. You do a lot of your
own original thinking. This turns people on, even if they don't
understand you. Do you?

You sometimes use cruel words on purpose, and you think
you're getting by with it in the name of being witty. You talk,
talk, talk people to death until they smother in a sea of knock-
knock jokes. Shut up.

MARS IN CANCER

Oh, you're cute all right, darlin' . . . you are *so* coy, and you
pout and everything . . . you do a sort of swivelling aw-shucks
thing. Where *did* you learn those cuteness lessons? Of course,
some of you come on too strong. You do that when you're
covering up your shyness about sex, and you *could* turn people
off by acting like a drip. Stick with the coy, it works better.
Some men with Mars in Cancer are still psychologically tied to
their families, resenting their women for no damned good reason

and taking their anger out on their relationships. The way to you
heart is through your belly, and you enjoy feeding the foll
you're with. You are acutely sensitive to your mate's emotion
needs because you are genuinely kind, so you are better *
keeping a mate than any other Mars position. Relax. Give your
self credit for sneaking up on people with your suave, subtle
sweet understanding—the good old Sideways School of Seduction

And what about your temper? Why can't you ever ask fo
what you want directly, instead of sneaking up on people all th
time? We haven't got all *day,* you know . . . Mama's darling!

MARS IN LEO

Precious angel, you do so love to show off! How proud an
devastating you are! Could this be why you always have
waiting list of would-be sweethearts? You know *exactly* how t
ride in taxis and send roses and pick the lint off your lover'
coat. You are particularly grand at restaurantishness, that rare a
of treating the waiter with just the proper mixture of consider
ation and condescension. You tell wonderful jokes. You ar
loyal until someone treats you shabbily for too long. You knov
how to impress anyone you've a mind to impress, and you ar
good with children and in-laws until they get too disgusting
Then you draw yourself up proudly, swish your mane, and walt
off back to the castle.

But when you get mad, you go *bonkers* in the grand style—
sock in the jaw, a small but effective lawsuit, or the healthies
outlet, *you do things better than they do*: a better car, an ecstati
relationship, a successful life. You don't care how long it takes
and it never takes you long to top them whilst never losing you
style, or grace, or chivalry. Maddening.

MARS IN VIRGO

Hard to get! You're so fussy hardly anyone appeals to you
sexually, though many—*too* many, you sniff—fancy you. Occa
sionally you do meet someone who meets your kinky standard
and then you go ga-ga rubbing his or her back, running errands
and catering to the tiniest sexual whim. No one would drean
how imaginative you can be in the sack, but you usually work
out your fantasies through emotional bondage. You want your
relationships to be clean, healthy, happy, and holy. If hurt in

ove, you'll turn to decadence and love among the sickos. You
urn people on by your analytic skills and your willingness to
work at things.

You like to brush your teeth before you get cuddly, and you
never smell like tuna fish. You're a fine, long-term bet as a
over, so spare some pity for the one who must live with your
quirky, cantankerous temper.

Nag, nag, nag! You're a porcupine. You can take people
apart, but you're not too hot at putting them together again. They
sense that you're rating them on a scale of one to ten in a dozen
different categories. Learn to describe a thing without the windy
criticism. At work, no one can do the job as well as you can, so
they tell you to shove it and do it all yourself. Then you worry,
worry, worry.

MARS IN LIBRA

You like me? I like you. You like me? I like you. You like
me? Sheesh, do you get everyone going billing and cooing and
flirting like that all day long? You *are* a big flirt, or maybe you
just like a lot of feedback from attractive people. Is this why so
many sexy celebrities have Mars in Libra? Richard Burton,
Richard Burton, Richard Burton, and Richard Burton have Mars
here. You're a thoughtful dresser—you know how to cut a pretty
picture without seeming to go to a lot of fuss. You know how to
look people in the eye and ask them a million questions about
themselves, don't you? You're another popular lover with a
waiting list, but you are far too charming and refined to trumpet
your conquests. You just get on with it, and get away with it,
too.

Then again, people end up screaming at you while you sit,
sweetly wide-eyed and wondrous. You're a sneaky passive-
aggressive type, and you get your jollies when other people react
to you. You act out your anger in flirting, fishing for compliments, driving people nuts, and acting innocent when they accuse
you. You coast on your tangible charm, but this is a tough
complex for you to crack because you can't bear to look at how
angry you are or how you set other people up to blow up at you.
You play emotional barter games, stretching people out to see
how much more they love you. Ick!

MARS IN SCORPIO

Some folks are afraid of you, but you realize it's not really you they're afraid of, it's passion. Passion is your middle name. You have no trouble getting lovers, for you ooze sex appeal because you are a deep person too, you have little trouble getting the right mate. You know what you want, and you know what you don't want. People get turned on by your magnificent obsessions—your work, some odd hobby, your true love, the #&!*% government. You dare to show your passions. Weirdness appeals to you, but let no one forget that you have a clear code of honor, unique to yourself, that you have constructed, painstakingly, over the years. Anyone who loves you won't mess with that code. Not twice, anyway.

You're a loyal friend, a bitter enemy, and never forget betrayal. You're slow to venom, yet you can carry out the kill with frightening detachment. You enjoy doing very little, sitting back and watching your enemies royally screw themselves. You then permit yourself a shrug and a chuckle.

MARS IN SAGITTARIUS

Mr. and Mrs. Leave It To Beaver, that's you! You've got that clean-cut twinkle in your eye, and you're kind and funny. You like to pretend you're an animal in bed. You are. You joke a bit much at romantic moments, but your honey thinks you're adorable, a philosopher. Travel excites you. You turn people on with generosity, bonhomie, and natural love of the underdog. You are nothing if not charitable. You'll turn people on with a rousting debate, but your most successful sexual asset is that laugh. Your laugh burbles up from a place somewhere deep inside of you, and your laugh is the sound of pure joy. You will har-dee-har har anyone to the casbah, and you always have a good laugh when you leave a loved one. You like having the last laugh, too.

And when the going gets tough, the tough get going. It's not that your leaving upsets people, it's how you leave. So intent are you on the new goal and the Wide Horizon that you blind yourself to the unholy mess you leave behind and the long-term effects of your actions on other people. You don't want responsibility and force others to be responsible for you. At your worst, your worm's-eye view allows you to laugh at other folks' serious attempts at maturity. You love animals. It's the people who detest you when you act like a schmuck.

MARS IN CAPRICORN

You're not cute, or helpless, or weak, although at times you believe you should seem to be these things. You are probably gorgeous (Capricorn rules the bone structure), and you don't believe you are a knockout. This makes you gloomy, but you are jolly good value as you are the height of responsibility in a relationship. Do you play Mother or Father in love? Do you like wearing dark colors? Do weird age gaps with lovers appeal to you? Do you like to control in bed? Mars in Capricorn, as with Mars in Aries and Scorpio, is among the best Marses on the market. Love lasts a long time with you. Your power turns people on. They think of you as a Big Shot.

You manipulate people, and yet it's usually for their own good. This is a fine place for Mars in business, as you start out as coffee boy and two years later end up owning the joint. You think you're superior to other people, though, and tell them their faults in a calm, caring effective style—but they'd better not tell you anything! This fear of authority bogs down your whole life; you need to learn to play and work *by the rules*. You resent this so-called intrusion on your "freedom," which is actually a narrower, more immature kind of life than if you played things straight. You love to be In Charge, and no matter how odd your life may look to others (you are terribly image conscious) your life is just the way you want it. You've a chip on your shoulder, and nobody had better mess with *you*.

MARS IN AQUARIUS

High on technique—when you *bother*—but you are mucho low on understanding. Passion is *nice* (your favorite word), but it scares the living cucarachas out of you to fall in love. You long to fall, desperately, yet beyond a certain point intimacy terrifies you. Then you get involved with married folks looking for side flings, or tepid, passive, not-too-well-organized lovers. This keeps you nice and safe, and damned lonesome. More than the other Mars signs, you have trouble *getting* lovers in the first place. You turn off any quality, special people by your machine-gun spray technique of looking for a mate. You try all the people in the room, one after the other. Then you wonder why no one likes you. You're bright, and you need an intelligent mate, but with your bizarre take-it-or-leave-it attitude, only idiots bother with *you*. There is an answer. Stop looking. Turn to some Good Cause. When you glow with zeal for making the world a better place and mean it, you're the biggest turn-on of the lot. Then someone worthy of your lofty goals will find *you*. Guaranteed. Don't rush intimacy.

You may have guessed this is an unfortunate Mars. You make your own miseries. You break appointments, forget to return items and sneer when anyone asks you to behave properly. You're a cool rebel, you think, and you're hostile to doing the things people expect of you in polite society. You think that stuff's corny. What you don't realize is that you hurt people and act like a boor. If you're such a rebel, why then do you seek out the company of responsible people? Others, let down and disappointed by you, dismiss you as being unstable and weak. Pull your socks up! Buy your hostess some soap!

MARS IN PISCES

There's a sexy, helpless streak to you—just a touch—and this brings out everybody's urge to nurse you. Just a tinge of sweet martyred sadness. Clever! You use intuition to get a fix on what turns a lover on, then out comes the actor you. You know which roles to play, and in a sense you're not acting, for your personality is diverse and imaginative. You do want to please your amours as long as they keep playing nursemaid, shrink, or doctor. You begin a love affair tentatively, testing the water, and after a time you get a rather brilliant hang of things. You make love as if you are two stars in a ballet; subtle, graceful, sophisticated, and affectionate. Then again, you can be shy and a bit passive at times, careful before you make any moves. You are kind, and can let yourself in for hurts when a partner is not sensitive enough to appreciate your gentleness or spot your glamour, riding roughshod over your feelings instead. Practice finding a partner worthy of you—that one will be the lucky one to have you.

As for making people crazy, you make a profession out of being a poor misunderstood baby. Then everyone has to let you walk all over them and you do as you please.

GAMES YOU CAN PLAY WITH THE ZAP! TABLES

Big Red takes two years to go round the sun one orbit. Look up what sign Mars is in right now. Then pencil in the Mars symbol on the outside of the circle that is your chart, in the area of that sign. Mars will stir up your activities and make you enthusiastic about that area of your chart.

Let's say Mars is in Sagittarius in the sky right now. You have the sign Sagittarius on the second house cusp of your chart. At some point Mars will enter that area and make you ambitious to make more money. It can make you impulsive and temperamental in that area too, so watch it!

The ZAP! tables don't tell you the details of exactly what *degree* Mars is in, only the sign. Chances are that Mars will be in the house *before* the one with Sagittarius on the cusp for a while. So it'll stir up, say, your first house for a while and give you lots of energy and a chip on your shoulder. Then it'll swing into your second house and stir up your greed.

If you want to know exactly where Mars is now, and the day it enters your money box, get a proper ephemeris. If you have 15 degrees of Sagittarius on the money box, look up Mars and find the date when it will be at fifteen degrees Sagittarius. That's all there is to it.

Watch your speech when Mars is going through the sign of your Mercury. You think you're being witty, but they think you're being obnoxious. You are. You'll do some fast thinking.

Lurch out to parties when Mars is in the sign of your Venus. You're likely to meet a good-looking stranger. This is a romantic time if you're married, and sweet William will ignore the telly if you stand naked in front of the set.

1901	MAR	1	Leo	19:31		MAY	22	Can	14:14
	MAY	11	Vir	6:05		JUL	8	Leo	3:54
	JUL	13	Lib	19:59		AUG	24	Vir	6:44
	AUG	31	Scp	18:13		OCT	10	Lib	6:05
	OCT	14	Sag	12:48		NOV	25	Scp	14:18
	NOV	24	Cap	4:44	1909	JAN	10	Sag	3:55
1902	JAN	1	Aqu	23:54		FEB	24	Cap	2:13
	FEB	8	Pic	23:53		APR	9	Aqu	20:34
	MAR	19	Ari	4:31		MAY	25	Pic	22:54
	APR	27	Tau	10:49		JUL	21	Ari	8:37
	JUN	7	Gem	11:19		SEP	26	Pic	21:22
	JUL	20	Can	17:44		NOV	20	Ari	20:47
	SEP	4	Leo	14:48	1910	JAN	23	Tau	1:54
	OCT	23	Vir	22:54		MAR	14	Gem	7:18
	DEC	20	Lib	3:33		MAY	1	Can	20:49
1903	APR	19	Vir	20:53		JUN	19	Leo	3:31
	MAY	30	Lib	17:21		AUG	6	Vir	0:58
	AUG	6	Scp	16:27		SEP	22	Lib	0:15
	SEP	22	Sag	13:52		NOV	6	Scp	13:39
	NOV	3	Cap	5:31		DEC	20	Sag	12:17
	DEC	12	Aqu	9:56	1911	JAN	31	Cap	21:30
1904	JAN	19	Pic	15:50		MAR	14	Aqu	0:07
	FEB	27	Ari	3:12		APR	23	Pic	8:28
	APR	6	Tau	18:05		JUN	2	Ari	21:48
	MAY	18	Gem	3:35		JUL	15	Tau	16:01
	JUN	30	Can	14:56		SEP	5	Gem	15:21
	AUG	15	Leo	3:22		NOV	30	Tau	4:12
	OCT	1	Vir	13:52	1912	JAN	30	Gem	21:02
	NOV	20	Lib	6:24		APR	5	Can	11:31
1905	JAN	13	Scp	19:27		MAY	28	Leo	8:16
	AUG	21	Sag	19:33		JUL	17	Vir	2:43
	OCT	8	Cap	0:06		SEP	2	Lib	17:04
	NOV	18	Aqu	4:15		OCT	18	Scp	2:39
	DEC	27	Pic	13:50		NOV	30	Sag	7:41
1906	FEB	4	Ari	23:45	1913	JAN	10	Cap	13:43
	MAR	17	Tau	11:54		FEB	19	Aqu	8:00
	APR	28	Gem	17:00		MAR	30	Pic	5:53
	JUN	11	Can	19:39		MAY	8	Ari	3:00
	JUL	27	Leo	14:13		JUN	17	Tau	0:38
	SEP	12	Vir	12:53		JUL	29	Gem	10:31
	OCT	30	Lib	4:26		SEP	15	Can	17:18
	DEC	17	Scp	12:07	1914	MAY	1	Leo	20:31
1907	FEB	5	Sag	9:30		JUN	26	Vir	4:48
	APR	1	Cap	18:33		AUG	14	Lib	14:10
	OCT	13	Aqu	14:29		SEP	29	Scp	10:38
	NOV	29	Pic	4:30		NOV	11	Sag	10:47
1908	JAN	11	Ari	4:39		DEC	22	Cap	3:49
	FEB	23	Tau	3:25	1915	JAN	30	Aqu	6:13
	APR	7	Gem	4:06		MAR	9	Pic	12:56

	APR	16	Ari	20:42		SEP	13	Cap	13:03
	MAY	26	Tau	3:08		OCT	30	Aqu	18:55
	JUL	6	Gem	6:23		DEC	11	Pic	13:10
	AUG	19	Can	9:10	1923	JAN	21	Ari	10:07
	OCT	7	Leo	20:48		MAR	4	Tau	0:42
1916	MAY	28	Vir	18:42		APR	16	Gem	2:55
	JUL	23	Lib	5:23		MAY	30	Can	21:19
	SEP	8	Scp	17:44		JUL	16	Leo	1:26
	OCT	22	Sag	2:58		SEP	1	Vir	0:58
	DEC	1	Cap	17:10		OCT	18	Lib	4:18
1917	JAN	9	Aqu	12:56		DEC	4	Scp	2:11
	FEB	16	Pic	13:34	1924	JAN	19	Sag	19:06
	MAR	26	Ari	17:40		MAR	6	Cap	19:03
	MAY	4	Tau	22:15		APR	24	Aqu	15:59
	JUN	14	Gem	20:58		JUN	24	Pic	16:28
	JUL	28	Can	4:01		AUG	24	Aqu	15:39
	SEP	12	Leo	10:52		OCT	19	Pic	18:42
	NOV	2	Vir	11:01		DEC	19	Ari	11:10
1918	JAN	11	Lib	8:56	1925	FEB	5	Tau	10:18
	FEB	25	Vir	18:49		MAR	24	Gem	0:42
	JUN	23	Lib	19:20		MAY	9	Can	22:44
	AUG	17	Scp	4:16		JUN	26	Leo	9:08
	OCT	1	Sag	7:42		AUG	12	Vir	21:12
	NOV	11	Cap	10:13		SEP	28	Lib	19:01
	DEC	20	Aqu	9:06		NOV	13	Scp	14:02
1919	JAN	27	Pic	11:21		DEC	28	Sag	0:36
	MAR	6	Ari	18:48	1926	FEB	9	Cap	3:35
	APR	15	Tau	5:00		MAR	23	Aqu	4:40
	MAY	26	Gem	9:38		MAY	3	Pic	17:04
	JUL	8	Can	17:14		JUN	15	Ari	0:51
	AUG	23	Leo	6:18		AUG	1	Tau	9:15
	OCT	10	Vir	3:53	1927	FEB	22	Gem	0:43
	NOV	30	Lib	12:11		APR	17	Can	1:29
1920	JAN	31	Scp	23:19		JUN	6	Leo	11:36
	APR	23	Lib	20:29		JUL	25	Vir	7:48
	JUL	10	Scp	18:15		SEP	10	Lib	14:19
	SEP	4	Sag	20:27		OCT	26	Scp	0:21
	OCT	18	Cap	13:22		DEC	8	Sag	11:01
	NOV	27	Aqu	13:38	1928	JAN	19	Cap	2:03
1921	JAN	5	Pic	7:40		FEB	28	Aqu	6:31
	FEB	13	Ari	5:21		APR	7	Pic	14:27
	MAR	25	Tau	6:26		MAY	16	Ari	21:35
	MAY	6	Gem	1:45		JUN	26	Tau	9:04
	JUN	18	Can	20:35		AUG	9	Gem	4:10
	AUG	3	Leo	11:01		OCT	3	Can	3:47
	SEP	19	Vir	11:40		DEC	20	Gem	5:24
	NOV	6	Lib	16:13	1929	MAR	10	Can	23:19
	DEC	26	Scp	11:49		MAY	13	Leo	2:33
1922	FEB	18	Sag	16:16		JUL	4	Vir	10:04

	AUG	21	Lib	21:52		SEP	26	Vir	14:52
	OCT	6	Scp	12:27		NOV	14	Lib	14:53
	NOV	18	Sag	13:30	1937	JAN	5	Scp	20:40
	DEC	29	Cap	10:45		MAR	13	Sag	3:17
1930	FEB	6	Aqu	18:21		MAY	14	Scp	22:50
	MAR	17	Pic	5:55		AUG	8	Sag	22:14
	APR	24	Ari	17:27		SEP	30	Cap	9:08
	JUN	3	Tau	3:16		NOV	11	Aqu	18:31
	JUL	14	Gem	12:55		DEC	21	Pic	17:46
	AUG	28	Can	11:28	1938	JAN	30	Ari	12:45
	OCT	20	Leo	14:44		MAR	12	Tau	7:48
1931	FEB	16	Can	14:43		APR	23	Gem	18:40
	MAR	30	Leo	3:48		JUN	7	Can	1:29
	JUN	10	Vir	14:58		JUL	22	Leo	22:27
	AUG	1	Lib	16:38		SEP	7	Vir	20:23
	SEP	17	Scp	8:44		OCT	25	Lib	6:20
	OCT	30	Sag	12:47		DEC	11	Scp	23:26
	DEC	10	Cap	3:11	1939	JAN	29	Sag	9:49
1932	JAN	18	Aqu	0:35		MAR	21	Cap	7:26
	FEB	25	Pic	2:37		MAY	25	Aqu	0:20
	APR	3	Ari	7:02		JUL	21	Cap	19:30
	MAY	12	Tau	10:53		SEP	24	Aqu	1:14
	JUN	22	Gem	9:20		NOV	19	Pic	15:56
	AUG	4	Can	19:53	1940	JAN	4	Ari	0:06
	SEP	20	Leo	19:44		FEB	17	Tau	1:54
	NOV	13	Vir	21:26		APR	1	Gem	18:41
1933	JUL	6	Lib	22:03		MAY	17	Can	14:46
	AUG	26	Scp	6:34		JUL	3	Leo	10:32
	OCT	9	Sag	11:35		AUG	19	Vir	15:58
	NOV	19	Cap	7:19		OCT	5	Lib	14:22
	DEC	28	Aqu	3:43		NOV	20	Scp	17:16
1934	FEB	4	Pic	4:14	1941	JAN	4	Sag	19:43
	MAR	14	Ari	9:09		FEB	17	Cap	23:33
	APR	22	Tau	15:40		APR	2	Aqu	11:46
	JUN	2	Gem	16:21		MAY	16	Pic	5:05
	JUL	15	Can	21:33		JUL	2	Ari	5:17
	AUG	30	Leo	13:44	1942	JAN	11	Tau	22:21
	OCT	18	Vir	4:59		MAR	7	Gem	8:05
	DEC	11	Lib	9:32		APR	26	Can	6:18
1935	JUL	29	Scp	17:33		JUN	14	Leo	3:56
	SEP	16	Sag	12:59		AUG	1	Vir	8:28
	OCT	28	Cap	18:22		SEP	17	Lib	10:11
	DEC	7	Aqu	4:34		NOV	1	Scp	22:37
1936	JAN	14	Pic	14:00		DEC	15	Sag	16:52
	FEB	22	Ari	4:09	1943	JAN	26	Cap	19:10
	APR	1	Tau	21:30		MAR	8	Aqu	12:42
	MAY	13	Gem	9:17		APR	17	Pic	10:26
	JUN	25	Can	21:54		MAY	27	Ari	9:26
	AUG	10	Leo	9:43		JUL	7	Tau	23:05

	AUG 23	Gem	23:58		NOV 6	Cap	6:41
1944	MAR 28	Can	9:55		DEC 15	Aqu	8:59
	MAY 22	Leo	14:17	1951	JAN 22	Pic	13:06
	JUL 12	Vir	2:55		MAR 1	Ari	22:04
	AUG 29	Lib	0:24		APR 10	Tau	9:37
	OCT 13	Scp	12:10		MAY 21	Gem	15:33
	NOV 25	Sag	16:12		JUL 3	Can	23:42
1945	JAN 5	Cap	19:32		AUG 18	Leo	10:56
	FEB 14	Aqu	9:58		OCT 5	Vir	0:21
	MAR 25	Pic	3:44		NOV 24	Lib	6:12
	MAY 2	Ari	20:29	1952	JAN 20	Scp	1:34
	JUN 11	Tau	11:53		AUG 27	Sag	18:54
	JUL 23	Gem	9:00		OCT 12	Cap	4:45
	SEP 7	Can	20:56		NOV 21	Aqu	19:40
	NOV 11	Leo	21:06		DEC 30	Pic	21:36
	DEC 26	Can	14:51	1953	FEB 8	Ari	1:08
1946	APR 22	Leo	19:32		MAR 20	Tau	6:54
	JUN 20	Vir	8:32		MAY 1	Gem	6:08
	AUG 9	Lib	13:18		JUN 14	Can	3:49
	SEP 24	Scp	16:35		JUL 29	Leo	19:26
	NOV 6	Sag	18:23		SEP 14	Vir	18:00
	DEC 17	Cap	10:56		NOV 1	Lib	14:19
1947	JAN 25	Aqu	11:45		DEC 20	Scp	11:23
	MAR 4	Pic	16:47	1954	FEB 9	Sag	19:18
	APR 11	Ari	23:03		APR 12	Cap	16:29
	MAY 21	Tau	3:40		JUL 3	Sag	7:28
	JUL 1	Gem	3:35		AUG 24	Cap	13:23
	AUG 13	Can	21:26		OCT 21	Aqu	12:03
	OCT 1	Leo	2:31		DEC 4	Pic	7:42
	DEC 1	Vir	11:45	1955	JAN 15	Ari	4:34
1948	FEB 12	Leo	10:24		FEB 26	Tau	10:23
	MAY 18	Vir	20:54		APR 10	Gem	23:09
	JUL 17	Lib	5:26		MAY 26	Can	0:50
	SEP 3	Scp	13:59		JUL 11	Leo	9:23
	OCT 17	Sag	5:44		AUG 27	Vir	10:14
	NOV 26	Cap	21:59		OCT 13	Lib	11:20
1949	JAN 4	Aqu	17:50		NOV 29	Scp	1:34
	FEB 11	Pic	18:06	1956	JAN 14	Sag	2:28
	MAR 21	Ari	22:03		FEB 28	Cap	20:05
	APR 30	Tau	2:33		APR 14	Aqu	23:40
	JUN 10	Gem	0:57		JUN 3	Pic	7:52
	JUL 23	Can	5:55		DEC 6	Ari	11:24
	SEP 7	Leo	4:52	1957	JAN 28	Tau	14:19
	OCT 27	Vir	0:59		MAR 17	Gem	21:35
	DEC 26	Lib	5:24		MAY 4	Can	15:22
1950	MAR 28	Vir	11:08		JUN 21	Leo	12:19
	JUN 11	Lib	20:27		AUG 8	Vir	5:28
	AUG 10	Scp	16:48		SEP 24	Lib	4:32
	SEP 25	Sag	19:49		NOV 8	Scp	21:04

	DEC 23	Sag	1:30		NOV 6	Vir	3:21
1958	FEB 3	Cap	18:57	1965	JUN 29	Lib	1:13
	MAR 17	Aqu	7:11		AUG 20	Scp	12:17
	APR 27	Pic	2:31		OCT 4	Sag	6:47
	JUN 7	Ari	6:21		NOV 14	Cap	7:20
	JUL 21	Tau	7:04		DEC 23	Aqu	5:37
	SEP 21	Gem	5:26	1966	JAN 30	Pic	7:02
	OCT 29	Tau	0:02		MAR 9	Ari	12:56
1959	FEB 10	Gem	13:58		APR 17	Tau	20:35
	APR 10	Can	9:47		MAY 28	Gem	22:08
	JUN 1	Leo	2:26		JUL 11	Can	3:16
	JUL 20	Vir	11:04		AUG 25	Leo	15:53
	SEP 5	Lib	22:47		OCT 12	Vir	18:38
	OCT 21	Scp	9:41		DEC 4	Lib	0:56
	DEC 3	Sag	18:10	1967	FEB 12	Scp	12:22
1960	JAN 14	Cap	5:00		MAR 31	Lib	5:59
	FEB 23	Aqu	4:12		JUL 19	Scp	22:57
	APR 2	Pic	6:25		SEP 10	Sag	1:45
	MAY 11	Ari	7:20		OCT 23	Cap	2:15
	JUN 20	Tau	9:05		DEC 1	Aqu	20:13
	AUG 2	Gem	4:32	1968	JAN 9	Pic	9:50
	SEP 21	Can	4:07		FEB 17	Ari	3:18
1961	FEB 5	Gem	0:47		MAR 27	Tau	23:44
	FEB 7	Can	5:15		MAY 8	Gem	14:15
	MAY 6	Leo	1:14		JUN 21	Can	5:04
	JUN 28	Vir	23:48		AUG 5	Leo	17:08
	AUG 17	Lib	0:42		SEP 21	Vir	18:40
	OCT 1	Scp	20:03		NOV 9	Lib	6:10
	NOV 13	Sag	21:51		DEC 29	Scp	22:08
	DEC 24	Cap	17:51	1969	FEB 25	Sag	6:22
1962	FEB 1	Aqu	23:07		SEP 21	Cap	6:36
	MAR 12	Pic	7:59		NOV 4	Aqu	18:51
	APR 19	Ari	16:59		DEC 15	Pic	14:23
	MAY 28	Tau	23:48	1970	JAN 24	Ari	21:30
	JUL 9	Gem	3:51		MAR 7	Tau	1:29
	AUG 22	Can	11:38		APR 18	Gem	18:59
	OCT 11	Leo	23:55		JUN 2	Can	6:51
1963	JUN 3	Vir	6:31		JUL 18	Leo	6:44
	JUL 27	Lib	4:15		SEP 3	Vir	4:58
	SEP 12	Scp	9:12		OCT 20	Lib	10:58
	OCT 25	Sag	17:32		DEC 6	Scp	16:35
	DEC 5	Cap	9:04	1971	JAN 23	Sag	1:35
1964	JAN 13	Aqu	6:14		MAR 12	Cap	10:12
	FEB 20	Pic	7:34		MAY 3	Aqu	20:58
	MAR 29	Ari	11:25		NOV 6	Pic	12:32
	MAY 7	Tau	14:41		DEC 26	Ari	18:05
	JUN 17	Gem	11:43	1972	FEB 10	Tau	14:05
	JUL 30	Can	18:23		MAR 27	Gem	4:31
	SEP 15	Leo	5:23		MAY 12	Can	13:15

	JUN	28	Leo	16:09
	AUG	15	Vir	1:00
	SEP	30	Lib	23:24
	NOV	15	Scp	22:18
	DEC	30	Sag	16:13
1973	FEB	12	Cap	5:52
	MAR	26	Aqu	21:00
	MAY	8	Pic	4:10
	JUN	20	Ari	20:54
	AUG	12	Tau	14:57
	OCT	29	Ari	22:59
	DEC	24	Tau	8:10
1974	FEB	27	Gem	10:12
	APR	20	Can	8:19
	JUN	9	Leo	0:55
	JUL	27	Vir	14:05
	SEP	12	Lib	19:09
	OCT	28	Scp	7:06
	DEC	10	Sag	22:06
1975	JAN	21	Cap	18:50
	MAR	3	Aqu	5:33
	APR	11	Pic	19:16
	MAY	21	Ari	8:15
	JUL	1	Tau	3:54
	AUG	14	Gem	20:48
	OCT	17	Can	8:45
	NOV	25	Gem	18:18
1976	MAR	18	Can	13:16
	MAY	16	Leo	11:11
	JUL	6	Vir	23:28
	AUG	24	Lib	5:56
	OCT	8	Scp	20:24
	NOV	20	Sag	23:54
1977	JAN	1	Cap	0:43
	FEB	9	Aqu	11:58
	MAR	20	Pic	2:20
	APR	27	Ari	15:47
	JUN	6	Tau	3:01
	JUL	17	Gem	15:14
	SEP	1	Can	0:21
	OCT	26	Leo	18:57
1978	JAN	26	Can	2:01
	APR	10	Leo	18:51
	JUN	14	Vir	2:39
	AUG	4	Lib	9:08
	SEP	19	Scp	20:58
	NOV	2	Sag	1:21
	DEC	12	Cap	17:40
1979	JAN	20	Aqu	17:08

	FEB	27	Pic	20:26
	APR	7	Ari	1:09
	MAY	16	Tau	4:26
	JUN	26	Gem	1:56
	AUG	8	Can	13:30
	SEP	24	Leo	21:22
	NOV	19	Vir	21:37
1980	MAR	11	Leo	20:51
	MAY	4	Vir	2:28
	JUL	10	Lib	18:00
	AUG	29	Scp	5:51
	OCT	12	Sag	6:28
	NOV	22	Cap	1:44
	DEC	30	Aqu	22:31
1981	FEB	6	Pic	22:49
	MAR	17	Ari	2:41
	APR	25	Tau	7:18
	JUN	5	Gem	5:27
	JUL	18	Can	8:55
	SEP	2	Leo	1:53
	OCT	21	Vir	1:58
	DEC	16	Lib	0:16
1982	AUG	3	Scp	11:47
	SEP	20	Sag	1:21
	OCT	31	Cap	23:06
	DEC	10	Aqu	6:18
1983	JAN	17	Pic	13:11
	FEB	25	Ari	0:21
	APR	5	Tau	14:04
	MAY	16	Gem	21:45
	JUN	29	Can	6:55
	AUG	13	Leo	16:55
	SEP	30	Vir	0:13
	NOV	18	Lib	10:27
1984	JAN	11	Scp	3:21
	AUG	17	Sag	19:52
	OCT	5	Cap	6:03
	NOV	15	Aqu	18:10
	DEC	25	Pic	6:39
1985	FEB	2	Ari	17:20
	MAR	15	Tau	5:08
	APR	26	Gem	9:14
	JUN	9	Can	10:42
	JUL	25	Leo	4:05
	SEP	10	Vir	1:33
	OCT	27	Lib	15:17
	DEC	14	Scp	19:01
1986	FEB	2	Sag	6:28
	MAR	28	Cap	3:48

	OCT	9	Aqu	1:02	SEP	27	Scp	2:16
	NOV	26	Pic	2:36	NOV	9	Sag	5:30
1987	JAN	8	Ari	12:22	DEC	20	Cap	0:35
	FEB	20	Tau	14:45	1994 JAN	28	Aqu	4:07
	APR	5	Gem	16:38	MAR	7	Pic	11:03
	MAY	21	Can	3:02	APR	14	Ari	18:03
	JUL	6	Leo	16:48	MAY	23	Tau	22:38
	AUG	22	Vir	19:53	JUL	3	Gem	22:31
	OCT	8	Lib	19:28	AUG	16	Can	19:16
	NOV	24	Scp	3:20	OCT	4	Leo	15:50
1988	JAN	8	Sag	15:26	DEC	12	Vir	11:33
	FEB	22	Cap	10:16	1995 JAN	22	Leo	23:48
	APR	6	Aqu	21:46	MAY	25	Vir	16:11
	MAY	22	Pic	7:43	JUL	21	Lib	9:22
	JUL	13	Ari	20:01	SEP	7	Scp	7:01
	OCT	23	Pic	22:28	OCT	20	Sag	21:04
	NOV	1	Ari	12:54	NOV	30	Cap	13:59
1989	JAN	19	Tau	8:12	1996 JAN	8	Aqu	11:03
	MAR	11	Gem	8:53	FEB	15	Pic	11:51
	APR	29	Can	4:39	MAR	24	Ari	15:13
	JUN	16	Leo	14:11	MAY	2	Tau	18:17
	AUG	3	Vir	13:37	JUN	12	Gem	14:44
	SEP	19	Lib	14:39	JUL	25	Can	18:33
	NOV	4	Scp	5:30	SEP	9	Leo	20:03
	DEC	18	Sag	4:58	OCT	30	Vir	7:14
1990	JAN	29	Cap	14:12	1997 JAN	3	Lib	8:12
	MAR	11	Aqu	15:55	MAR	8	Vir	19:46
	APR	20	Pic	22:10	JUN	19	Lib	8:31
	MAY	31	Ari	7:12	AUG	14	Scp	8:44
	JUL	12	Tau	14:45	SEP	28	Sag	22:23
	AUG	31	Gem	11:41	NOV	9	Cap	5:34
	DEC	14	Tau	8:03	DEC	18	Aqu	6:38
1991	JAN	21	Gem	1:16	1998 JAN	25	Pic	9:28
	APR	3	Can	0:50	MAR	4	Ari	16:19
	MAY	26	Leo	12:21	APR	13	Tau	1:06
	JUL	15	Vir	12:37	MAY	24	Gem	3:43
	SEP	1	Lib	6:39	JUL	6	Can	9:01
	OCT	16	Scp	19:06	AUG	20	Leo	19:17
	NOV	29	Sag	2:20	OCT	7	Vir	12:30
1992	JAN	9	Cap	9:48	NOV	27	Lib	10:12
	FEB	18	Aqu	4:39	1999 JAN	26	Scp	12:01
	MAR	28	Pic	2:05	MAY	5	Lib	21:35
	MAY	5	Ari	21:37	JUL	1	Scp	4:01
	JUN	14	Tau	15:57	SEP	2	Sag	19:31
	JUL	26	Gem	19:00	OCT	17	Cap	1:37
	SEP	12	Can	6:06	NOV	26	Aqu	6:58
1993	APR	27	Leo	23:42	2000 JAN	4	Pic	3:02
	JUN	23	Vir	7:44	FEB	12	Ari	1:05
	AUG	12	Lib	1:12	MAR	23	Tau	1:27

```
MAY   3 Gem 19:20
JUN  16 Can 12:31
AUG   1 Leo  1:22
SEP  17 Vir  0:21
NOV   4 Lib  2:02
DEC  23 Scp 14:39
```

Jupiter—
Merciful Fatso

"Surely goodness and mercy shall follow me all the days of my life, and I shall dwell in the house of the Lord for ever."

—Twenty-third Psalm

"Roll them dice!"

—Twentieth-century folk expression

Ho, ho, ho! Has the Cosmos got a planet for *you*! We don't call them the WOW! tables for nothing. When the shrink says "bounty" do you think of a chocolate bar? Think again. Jupiter is bringing you good luck right now if you know where to look. *Big* time luck, kid!

Look around the solar system. You can't miss him. Jupiter is the biggest planet we've got. He wears big stripes on his belly, and a Great Red Spot. Jupiter is made of gas, and he *is* a gas. He is Santa Claus, the golden goose, and the sacred cow rolled into a Big One. His motto is, "Be big about it" and his principle is *mercy*. Jupe is a fatso, and he tends to expand everything he touches. Fatso brings you healing, help, and lucky protection, even in the worst of times.

Look up the sign Jupiter was in when you were born in the WOW! tables. Check the house it's in in your chart. Exaggerate these areas in your daily life to increase your luck.

There's another way to increase your luck with Jupiter. You can look up where it is in the sky right now and see what house it's affecting in your horoscope. More on that later.

Jupiter shows how and when you trust; it shows the things you enjoy and the ways that you are kind. Oh, generous soul, it is no accident that you are lucky in the areas where you like to give, take risks and trust; Jupiter gives you a sense of humor, too.

JUPITER IN ARIES OR THE FIRST HOUSE

Personality kid. You prefer to die rather than wait, and it costs you money. The heck you care! You are honest, usually, and your personality brings you luck when you take risks on impulse, which is often. Your greatest luck comes to you when you use your charisma and your cheerfulness and zest. Whether you are selling a product, making a presentation, pleading a case or giving a heartfelt and accurate compliment, always sell *yourself* and you won't go wrong. You're good to yourself in many little ways, though you may miss the broader ways of making yourself happier through slavery to passing compulsions. You taste the chili and tell everybody what a wonderful cook you are. Then you wonder why you don't get enough compliments. Count to forty before you give yourself that public pat on the back; let others have a chance to praise you, and they will. You lavish your love on rugged individualists.

JUPITER IN TAURUS OR THE SECOND HOUSE

Money cheers you up. You hate to think of yourself as a materialist because generally you have higher values than the camel-hair coat brigade, but when the loot rolls in, you love to count it. You love to give presents, and you'll spend more money on other people than on yourself because it makes you happy to do so. You have a knack for picking out the right clothes and colors for your loved ones, and in return you attract wonderful presents because you're not afraid to delight in displaying your greed. If you're poor, you have the proverbial champagne taste on the beer budget, but you get by somehow and "getting by" includes regular luxuries that you consider to be essential. When you're well off (and you *will* be eventually) you can easily become naïve regarding the financial struggles of others.

Resist the temptation to hold yourself back in a "steady" job or a "safe" marriage that offers you filthy lucre and precious little else. You love to spend your energies making people comfortable; you'd make a fine nurse to a sick friend, and you love to give folks a roof over their heads. You're generous in the sack, too.

JUPITER IN GEMINI OR IN THE THIRD HOUSE

You love to talk, and it's no wonder—when you talk you always win. You probably have a lot of telephones. Education never stops with you, and when you're feeling generous, you love to teach people, and you do it in a manner so entertaining they don't even realize how much they're learning from you.

Languages come easy to you, and you learn by osmosis, plunking yourself down amongst the natives and mimicking their sounds until you get it right. Three days later you're speaking Swahili. Stay there six months and your friends will notice that you're speaking English with an African accent, so watch it! Newspapers, magazines, short school courses, and gossip keep the sparkle in your eye and the tongue sharp; the flotsam and jetsam of everyday life buoys you up.

JUPITER IN CANCER OR IN THE FOURTH HOUSE

Mother to the world—that's you. And you are lucky in real estate, so you'll always have a place to put Auntie Alivia and baby Jesse. People offer to put you up wherever you go; you'd rather stay with somebody than in some old formica-slabbed motel. You're funny in hotels; you like them, but you rearrange everything when you get into the room. You're soft and kind in your better moments, and have the art of making folks feel at home in every situation.

Even if Daddy was Quasimodo, and Mum was down at the bar every evening, you've inherited the better traits of your parents and make a super, if overindulgent, parent yourself. You love to cook, and food will make you money if you ever need it. Better brush up on the antique business too. You're a wheeler-dealer if there ever was one.

JUPITER IN LEO OR IN THE FIFTH HOUSE

Romance is fun for you, and no matter how the hussies or creeps have burned you in the past, you can't help being grand to your new lover. You hope it'll work out this time. Foreigners turn you on the most. Old flames still dream about you years later; they send you sexy psychic vibes to make you lucky in love—if you will learn to curb your excesses! Harems are too expensive for you, emotionally and financially, and by thirty you generally have outgrown this phase, though you'll dream a little of the Ones That Got Away. Jupiter is excess, and Leo is the child, so you of all the sign positions must make a concerted effort to Grow Up. Don't worry that life will grow gray—you'll never entirely stop being childish. People like your playful side, and your children will love you for it and grow up to be people you admire. You're kind to kids, and your luck comes from them, along with pursuits to do with the entertainment industry. Buy gold. You'll know when.

JUPITER IN VIRGO OR IN THE SIXTH HOUSE

You love to work, and you've high principles about what's fair and isn't fair to the boss. You're usually on the side of the employees, which is lucky if you rise to become the boss—a likely occurrence. Medicine fascinates you, and if you're ever ill, you're temporarily glum, but you'll never turn into a "health bore" and you rally fast; you don't have time to be sick.

People offer you jobs out of nowhere because you can handle anything. When they pile too much work on you, you're savvy enough to delegate tasks—even the kids and the baby-sitter pitch in gleefully, thrilled you trust them enough to use their skills. You know you have high standards in love, in work, in life; you make every phase of your life successful because you're willing to tote that barge with a sense of joy. You're willing to work for what you want, so you get it.

JUPITER IN LIBRA OR IN THE SEVENTH HOUSE

Sometimes you think you're luckier for other people than they are for you, but it isn't so. People even promote you behind your back. You're a good matchmaker, and your friends can generally dig up important connections for you; lovers, mentors, even employers. They do this for you because you flatter people so with the attention you lavish upon them. Even your enemies remember you with affection—you were so sweet before you turned into a worm, Lizzie!

You wither without a good social life, but you're rarely without a suitor waiting in the wings or a party to go to. Maybe you're so lucky with people because at your best you're so tolerant. You really love to watch people cut loose and express themselves. They reward you with grandiose praise.

JUPITER IN SCORPIO OR IN THE EIGHTH HOUSE

You're as horny as a three-balled tomcat—people can just tell you're brilliant in bed. You turn on to the powerful, competent, well-known people in your circle, and you usually get them into business or bed. You like the decadence, the booze, and the smoke, and when the mood hits you, you like to rise above all that. When you tire of purity you enjoy fantasizing about your more debauched options, but more often than not, the fantasies will do.

Al H. Morrison says this is the "do it big or bust" place for Jupiter. You love excesses in business, religion, or love. You're a natural-born armchair psychiatrist and will spend all kinds of time and money on Tarot cards, horoscopes, sex manuals, body-language books, Rorschach tests, and, of course, wine, sweet-smelling oils, candles, and fancy cigarettes.

JUPITER IN SAGITTARIUS OR IN THE NINTH HOUSE

No stingy bones in your skeleton! Somebody's in need? You've got the cash, or a lily pad they can sleep on. Your favorite hobby is philanthropy. This means you're awfully popular. Your associates come in three varieties: tough taskmasters who grumble and need your good humor, fun people, and Big Shots. Your big-hearted philosophy makes you pretend you're wiser than most folks, which you probably are, but you do love the "In" crowd. You loathe that restricted feeling, and even when you settle down, there's always a happy loophole—you need to do your thing.

You are the teacher's pet at school, and you can just as easily educate yourself on the farm or in the street; learning is lucky for you. You're lucky in travel, with cars and with horses, and you probably number a couple of writers in your circle of friends. You trust people and give them more rope than others might think wise, but you don't see it that way. You couldn't shake that code of honor even if you wanted to. This attitude saves you in the long run, and it protects you from those who would take unfair advantage of your generous spirit.

JUPITER IN CAPRICORN OR IN THE TENTH HOUSE

Boy, do you love power! You get it, too, because you don't mind making sacrifices for it. You know how to connect with the right people, talk them into deals, and make them like your weirdness. No one glides through the Old Boy Network better than you do. Politics, in the world or in the office, intrigues you. You're a whizz-bang wheeler-dealer.

People do business favors for you that would stagger other get-ahead types; you do some pretty outrageous favors yourself, liberally scattering freebies about. You believe that bread cast upon the waters comes back to you tenfold. You present yourself with a cocky cheerfulness and an ambition that turns on the Ones in Charge. You love hard work and beg for more. You know exactly how to suck up to the boss. No wonder people keep offering to kick you upstairs.

JUPITER IN AQUARIUS OR IN THE ELEVENTH HOUSE

You have lucky friends, and you'll keep them, too. Your friendships withstand knocks that would leave other people on nonspeaking terms. It's because you *like* people, and you'll happily send a bit of luck your friends' way. No matter how infuriating your behavior (or theirs!) people can't bear to be without you. You care about them. You especially flower in groups, dashing around, promoting fellowship and the greater good.

This is a lucky place for Jupiter if you want to steadily increase your income. You can job hop or keep suggesting improvements to the boss. You're good at organizing systems and cutting out the deadwood. You have so many grand dreams that by the sheer weight of averages, most of them come true. Honesty is your religion, yet you're attracted to the weird and unorthodox in people and things: robots and computer games appeal to you. You may invent a few gizmos yourself before your number's up.

JUPITER IN PISCES OR IN THE TWELFTH HOUSE

You're Snow White, and if you don't keep your Good Works out of your private life, you come home to a ringing phone and a houseful of pleading dwarfs. You're patient with the blind, the lame, and the helpless. The sight of a bum lying in a doorway on a rainy night tweaks your kind heart, and you feel guilty until you do something about him. The only people you don't feel sorry for are those you haven't met yet. Oh, that bleeding heart!

People poke fun at you because you're so emotional, but they stick around for their fair share of understanding. Learn to discriminate a little. Why waste deep sympathy on jerks? But you do.

Charity is your middle name. All this kindness (much of it unseen by anyone but The Great One) brings you luck and protection on every level. Something out there keeps an eye on you. The kinder you are, the more psychic you get. You can trust this gift of intuition. Go with it.

WINNING WITH JUPITER

Old happy fatso takes about twelve years to sashay once around the Sun. This means he spends about a year in each zodiac sign. You can get a rough idea of where he is in your chart by checking the WOW! tables to see what house he's in right now. You've got luck there. Get out there and roll them dice.

By and by, he'll pass over every one of the planets in your chart, bringing good will and protection as well as opportunity for you too. For example, when Jupiter is in the sign of your Venus, your social and love life will pick up. If you think I'm going to give you examples of when it hits each one of your planets, you're wrong. . . . You can look up the planets and the houses in this book yourself. Would you ask a wretched shell of what was once a human being to bang out *another* list in a sweltering shoebox at five A.M.? You would, I know. Clients phone me at eight o'clock on a Sunday morning too. Nobody cares if a soothsayer gets any sleep at all. Why should they, when Saturn's always kicking someone in the ass and Jupiter's giving other people too many lovers to choose from? Anyway, *combine* the idea of Jupiter giving opportunity with the idea of the planet or house it's hitting. Oh, hell, this one's too special to pass up: when Jupiter in the sky goes into the sign your Saturn is in, something deep and wonderful happens to you. You get cured in some way. You begin to understand that what you thought was an ugly hang-up can be something to be proud of. Your fears are not as abnormal, nor are your flaws as bad, as you thought they were.

Big time luck occurs on two occasions: when Jupiter crosses over your rising sign, and when it returns to its own place. One lady won the million dollar lottery when Jupiter hit her rising sign. Most people travel or come into money.

The most bizarre case I've ever seen was that of a woman *who had a nervous breakdown* when Jupiter crossed her rising sign. This is rare. *Very* rare. I couldn't figure it out until she came in to see me one year later. She said the nervous breakdown was the luckiest thing that could have happened. She had had a severe drinking problem for several years, much of it based on the twisted way her father had treated her. Her father died shortly before Jupiter crossed her rising sign; all the years of love and guilt and grief and anger came pouring out in a rush. She doesn't drink anymore. If she hadn't had the breakdown, her liver would have said enough—she would be dead. She's healthier *now* than I've ever seen her.

Jupiter returns to its own place every twelve years. This is called, oddly enough, the Jupiter Return. It's the luckiest of the bunch. This is a "bumper crop" year for you. You have opportunities now that can raise your standard of living and happiness for the rest of your life. You can plan for your Jupiter Return years in advance . . . work like the devil, brush up on being kind and merciful, and plan to be at the right place when the Jupiter Return occurs. This might be your big trip to China, the time you get out of medical school, or the time you start your own business, depending on what house Jupiter was in when you were born.

It's a good idea to check in with an astrologer a few months or years before your Jupiter Return, so the stargazer can tell you the date it becomes exact. Jupiter is an expansive planet, and the luck can come up to eight weeks earlier than the exact date. I got stuck in Philadelphia six weeks before my Jupiter Return and never made it to New York—the luck started breaking all over the place, bringing some of the best friends I've ever had, sixteen shrinks who sent their patients in for readings, and some of the most bizarre and colorful clients any astrologer could ask for. You'd be surprised at what goes on behind the discreet velvet drapes in Philadelphia. Next Jupiter Return, though, I'm making it Rio, six weeks before the exact date.

1901	JAN	19	Cap	8:33	1939	MAY	11	Ari	14:08
1902	FEB	6	Aqu	19:31		OCT	30	Pic	0:48
1903	FEB	20	Pic	8:35		DEC	20	Ari	17:03
1904	MAR	1	Ari	3:01	1940	MAY	16	Tau	7:54
	AUG	8	Tau	20:16	1941	MAY	26	Gem	12:48
	AUG	31	Ari	13:18	1942	JUN	10	Can	10:37
1905	MAR	7	Tau	18:29	1943	JUN	30	Leo	21:47
	JUL	21	Gem	0:23	1944	JUL	26	Vir	1:05
	DEC	4	Tau	22:30	1945	AUG	25	Lib	6:07
1906	MAR	9	Gem	21:49	1946	SEP	25	Scp	10:20
	JUL	30	Can	23:13	1947	OCT	24	Sag	3:01
1907	AUG	18	Leo	23:15	1948	NOV	15	Cap	10:39
1908	SEP	12	Vir	10:02	1949	APR	12	Aqu	19:19
1909	OCT	11	Lib	23:33		JUN	27	Cap	18:25
1910	NOV	11	Scp	17:04		NOV	30	Aqu	20:09
1911	DEC	10	Sag	11:36	1950	APR	15	Pic	8:59
1913	JAN	2	Cap	19:46		SEP	15	Aqu	2:25
1914	JAN	21	Aqu	15:13		DEC	1	Pic	19:58
1915	FEB	4	Pic	0:45	1951	APR	21	Ari	14:58
1916	FEB	12	Ari	7:12	1952	APR	28	Tau	20:51
	JUN	26	Tau	1:32	1953	MAY	9	Gem	15:34
	OCT	26	Ari	14:53	1954	MAY	24	Can	4:45
1917	FEB	12	Tau	15:59	1955	JUN	13	Leo	0:08
	JUN	29	Gem	23:52		NOV	17	Vir	4:01
1918	JUL	13	Can	5:54	1956	JAN	18	Leo	1:59
1919	AUG	2	Leo	8:39		JUL	7	Vir	19:03
1920	AUG	27	Vir	5:30		DEC	13	Lib	2:19
1921	SEP	25	Lib	23:11	1957	FEB	19	Vir	15:28
1922	OCT	26	Scp	19:17		AUG	7	Lib	2:13
1923	NOV	24	Sag	17:32	1958	JAN	13	Scp	12:54
1924	DEC	18	Cap	6:26		MAR	20	Lib	19:07
1926	JAN	6	Aqu	1:01		SEP	7	Scp	8:53
1927	JAN	18	Pic	11:44	1959	FEB	10	Sag	13:48
	JUN	6	Ari	10:14		APR	24	Scp	14:03
	SEP	11	Pic	3:43		OCT	5	Sag	14:41
1928	JAN	23	Ari	2:55	1960	MAR	1	Cap	13:12
	JUN	4	Tau	4:51		JUN	10	Sag	1:51
1929	JUN	12	Gem	12:20		OCT	26	Cap	3:03
1930	JUN	26	Can	22:42	1961	MAR	15	Aqu	8:03
1931	JUL	17	Leo	7:53		AUG	12	Cap	8:57
1932	AUG	11	Vir	7:17		NOV	4	Aqu	2:51
1933	SEP	10	Lib	5:12	1962	MAR	25	Pic	22:09
1934	OCT	11	Scp	4:56	1963	APR	4	Ari	3:21
1935	NOV	9	Sag	2:57	1964	APR	12	Tau	6:54
1936	DEC	2	Cap	8:39	1965	APR	22	Gem	14:34
1937	DEC	20	Aqu	4:06		SEP	21	Can	4:42
1938	MAY	14	Pic	7:46		NOV	17	Gem	3:02
	JUL	30	Aqu	3:00	1966	MAY	5	Can	14:54
	DEC	29	Pic	18:35		SEP	27	Leo	13:21

Year				
1967	JAN 16	Can	3:48
	MAY 23	Leo	8:23
	OCT 19	Vir	10:53
1968	FEB 27	Leo	3:33
	JUN 15	Vir	14:46
	NOV 15	Lib	22:46
1969	MAR 30	Vir	21:36
	JUL 15	Lib	13:32
	DEC 16	Scp	15:57
1970	APR 30	Lib	6:44
	AUG 15	Scp	18:01
1971	JAN 14	Sag	8:51
	JUN 5	Scp	2:11
	SEP 11	Sag	15:35
1972	FEB 6	Cap	19:39
	JUL 24	Sag	16:47
	SEP 25	Cap	18:23
1973	FEB 23	Aqu	9:30
1974	MAR 8	Pic	11:13
1975	MAR 18	Ari	16:49
1976	MAR 26	Tau	10:26
	AUG 23	Gem	10:27
	OCT 16	Tau	20:18
1977	APR 3	Gem	15:44
	AUG 20	Can	12:44
	DEC 30	Gem	23:49
1978	APR 12	Can	0:14
	SEP 5	Leo	8:32
1979	FEB 28	Can	23:33
	APR 20	Leo	8:34
	SEP 29	Vir	10:26
1980	OCT 27	Lib	10:12
1981	NOV 27	Scp	2:21
1982	DEC 26	Sag	2:00
1984	JAN 19	Cap	15:06
1985	FEB 6	Aqu	15:37
1986	FEB 20	Pic	16:06
1987	MAR 2	Ari	18:42
1988	MAR 8	Tau	15:45
	JUL 22	Gem	0:00
	NOV 30	Tau	20:55
1989	MAR 11	Gem	3:27
	JUL 30	Can	23:51
1990	AUG 18	Leo	7:32
1991	SEP 12	Vir	6:02
1992	OCT 10	Lib	13:29
1993	NOV 10	Scp	8:18
1994	DEC 9	Sag	10:56
1996	JAN 3	Cap	7:25

Year				
1997	JAN 21	Aqu	15:14
1998	FEB 4	Pic	10:53
1999	FEB 13	Ari	1:24
	JUN 28	Tau	9:30
	OCT 23	Ari	5:50
2000	FEB 14	Tau	21:41
	JUN 30	Gem	7:36

Saturn—
What's Stopping You
From Getting There?

> *"If you do what you should not, you must bear what you would not."*
> —Benjamin Franklin

> *"Life is like one of those computer games. By the time you learn the rules, the game is over."*
> —Batya Stark

> *"Turn your scars into stars."*
> —Dr. Robert Schuller

Now here is Saturn. Saturn, green glowing specter of the night skies with its rings shining, is the most beautiful of all our planets.

Oh, slow beauty of preternatural mysteries, you spin, serene, gliding your sure, measured orbit round the Sun. It takes you twenty-nine years to go round once, yet I could gladly gaze at you forever . . . why are you such a pain in the ass?

Ironic, isn't it, that the planet of greatest beauty is associated with discipline, caution, hard work, wisdom, sorrow, loneliness, depression, trials, "bad luck," delays, ignorance, inadequacy, great suffering, fear, Fate, and Time. . . ?

Take Fate for a start. How else are we to explain why one child fears the dark while another is born blind?

Every newborn baby has Saturn somewhere in its chart. A wise parent studies this chart, and notes the fears and weaknesses of the tiny human being. The wise parents then take care not to aggravate the fears; they take steps to help the child overcome the weaknesses. Here is astrology at its most golden. I wish more parents used it.

Curiously, most of us want to give our children what we did

not have—or we are trying like the devil not to give our children what our parents dished out to us. We don't see the child as an individual with talents and fears that may be light-years away from our own feelings. Perhaps a day is coming when more parents will look at their babies' horoscopes. Those bald, drooling blobs deserve better than to be treated as blank slates for their ancestors' desires and frustrations. Nip terror in the bud!

Saturn is the symbol of all the things that scare the living daylights out of you. Astrologers call it The Great Teacher, but they're jiving if they neglect to inform you of the pain that comes with the lessons. Most of this pain comes from ignorance. Saturn shows what got distorted in youth. It shows the things we never got or what we got too much of. Worse still, if someone offers those things we want most now, we don't know what to do with the goodies. Psychologists and astrologers are constantly astonished at how human beings push away the very things that could make us feel secure. We're afraid to want the things of our Saturn, so we pretend we can do without them. We *do* do without them, but at a cost to our willingness to gently work on facing our fears.

If you want to stretch your character, take Saturn slowly and gently. As you overcome your fears, Saturn becomes the shining jewel in your chart—the wisest, deepest, most generous planet you've got.

Lazy bones this lifetime? Don't work on your stuff. Saturn will gradually deliver to you a depressing horror show of emptiness. But Saturn is wise, and ever patient; he gives you a lifetime to try. It's amazing how patient Saturn is—he lets us screw up a lot. He doesn't care as long as we keep trying.

Think you've got it licked, eh? Saturn is the *relentless* Great Teacher. As soon as you've mastered one level, he sneaks back to teach you on more subtle areas.

If you don't care about self-improvement, Saturn will at least show where other people are tsk-tsking behind your back. "Why doesn't he go back to school?" for a Saturn in Gemini; "She's not fooling anyone with that promiscuous act—she's got a sexual problem," of a second house Saturn; "Why does he always wear horrible clothes?" for a Capricorn rising. If you've worked on your fears, the murmuring turns to praise: "He's smart! Well-read, too," "She's worked hard on her sense of self-worth, and she makes her boyfriend feel secure," and "What a snappy dresser!" You pays your karma and you takes your choice.

Most of us don't want to discuss our Saturn positions. We

hope nobody will notice. We think we don't deserve better. We feel like losers here anyway, and even if we're winning, we *know* it's only temporary . . . and negative thinking can make it so.

I work with over two dozen psychiatrists, psychologists, and psychoanalysts. They send their patients in for chart readings. We tape the charts and the patients go back and listen to them with the shrinks. I often phone the shrink after the session, noting the Saturn positions in a client's chart, and say, in effect, "Drill here and *here*, Doc." This can save up to six months in costly therapy, as the therapist learns quickly where it hurts and where the patient needs to build up self-esteem. It's like an X-ray, and you can do this yourself if you have a computer chart.

Be careful doing it with anyone else. Saturn is good at an "I don't care" stance, and your boss will not thank you for pointing out his sore spots. Shut up. Saturn may seem stern and boring, but it is the essence of responsibility, and *duty* to one's fellow man. As for the "New Age," there's nothing new about it. Compassion never goes out of style.

DON'T CROSS THAT LINE!

These secrets of Saturn are not intended as twelve tiddledy-winks for a *Who's Afraid of Virginia Woolf* parlor game. The "silly fear" to me may be your big sacred secret special thing, and if I tread on your toes in the area of your Saturn, you will close the door on me, usually in hurt silence, sometimes in violent outrage and sorrow.

If you want to *keep* your job, your lover, your children, your friends, it is *vital* to learn what is important to these people and to avoid harming them at all costs. It is never good policy to mess with another person's Saturn area. They are probably wiser, through their suffering and hard work and experience, in these things than *you*.

It is enough for you to quietly know where your associates feel shaky and to build up their confidence where you can. Compliment them too much and they mistrust your words, although if they've worked on their Saturns, they probably *are* superior in those areas of their lives. When you receive contempt for your heartfelt praise, chalk this up to the old Groucho Marx school inferiority complex: "I wouldn't want to belong to a club that would have me as a member."

EVERYBODY HAS THREE "LINES"

Saturn in a sign. You can look anyone up in the OUCH! tables.

Saturn in a house. You need a computer chart for this. It is a deeper, more personal hurt, than the sign position.

The house or houses with Capricorn on the cusp—it hurts just as much as Saturn in a house.

Don't jump to conclusions when reading a Saturn position. Your subject may have suffered much; he may be handling it wisely. Before you tell someone that Mummy was mean to them, a rejecting parent, find out how old your subject was when she died. Saturn is Fate, too. Find out how your subject grew up. What fears has he already overcome? You will learn far more about Saturn, its humility, its courage, its grace under pressure, by *listening* than by talking.

Saturn is how you can be mean to other people, too. We rationalize our behavior—or we're too scared to notice someone's bleeding from our behavior.

Protect yourself. Don't hide your Saturn. Let people *close to you* know where the line is, what your limits are. Tell them what you can take and what you will not tolerate. Yell and scream and holler that nobody's going to step on you in this area. It sounds foolhardy, but we are all wrapped up in our personal fogs. No one who truly cares for you will willingly hurt you in a Saturn area if you have explained it carefully, and you'll save many friendships this way, avoiding tragic accidents of hurt feelings. You can't blame them for hurting you if they didn't know what hurt. People who knowingly hurt you in your Saturn area are called sadists, and you're better off not giving them your birth date.

Everybody's different. What fazes Aunt Katy may be sheer mirth to Uncle Igor!

The truth is, you may always carry a scar from Saturn. Will you let blindness crush you, or will you be Stevie Wonder? This *stunting* Saturn causes creates the urge for great compensations. Not everyone rises to the challenge, but many do. Perhaps that is why Saturn is our most beautiful planet.

SATURN IN ARIES, THE FIRST HOUSE, OR CAPRICORN RISING

> *"The definition of cowardice is to see what is right and not do it."*
>
> —Confucius

So many comedians are born with Saturn here. I guess they're afraid people will laugh at them anyway, and Saturn, always practical, might as well get paid for it. These are very serious folks, but they try their damnedest to hide the fact.

In childhood they weren't allowed a normal, healthy, show-off ego. The parents said, "Don't be selfish—share." Parents played with your presents before you got them, and it was rare that you ever got the luxury of pure, new "vibes" on anything.

People with this Saturn are afraid of the things Aries is afraid of—that you won't like them. They want to come first in your life, but they're afraid to ask or act like they have the right. You can win them forever by treating them as Number One. They burn to be leaders—inwardly they yearn to be Superman. They're terrified to show how much they want it. They have terrible guilt complexes about their egos; often this is the position of the oversheltered but neglected child. Parents force them to be grown-up too fast.

No wonder so many of these folks stay single, or even become priests to breathe the heady air of self-hood, which their parents taught them was obscene. The loner image is a sham—they're greedily desperate to prove their independence . . . to themselves. They're afraid they can't do it all themselves.

No one ever taught them how to build up their charisma, how to dress right, how to please themselves first. Past lifetimes, if you buy them, have given them quiet courage, wisdom beyond their years, and the memory of having been pushed around a lot by other people. They remember being pushed out of the spotlight, being passed over, and they're not going to let that happen this time. It is sheer hell getting them to let go of power—as bosses they're awful at delegating authority. Or they get so bossy they forget what leadership really is. Then they see everybody as a threat to their own seat.

They are anxious about their bodies or looks in some way. They've been crippled or limited in their movements in the past, and they're touchy about it.

Once there were two friends. One was known as a maverick, and the other friend was known as a "yes-man." He had Saturn in this position. One night the maverick stood up before their club and mentioned the corruption that was creeping in; the group had been acting cruelly and breaking rules. The maverick pushed for some reforms, while Martin, his friend, let the group tear the maverick to pieces. Privately he supported his friend's cause, but he was unable to act with the wild, jazzy, you're-terrific-even-if-you're-a-madman courage. No one had ever taught him how.

If they avoid the two extremes of "yessing" people to death or monopolizing the whole show, they're doing A-OK.

Nudge them, but don't push them. Praise their appearance lavishly. Note their wise courage. Let them lead whenever possible. They were starved of the chance as children. Cheer them up—they get depressed. Gently show them that if they allow you to work in your own way you are freeing them of details so they

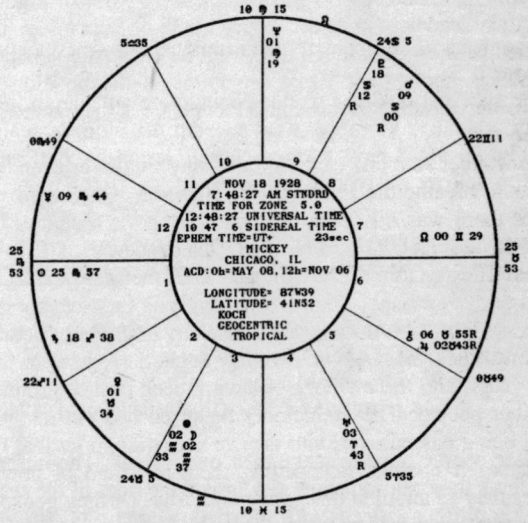

Mickey Mouse

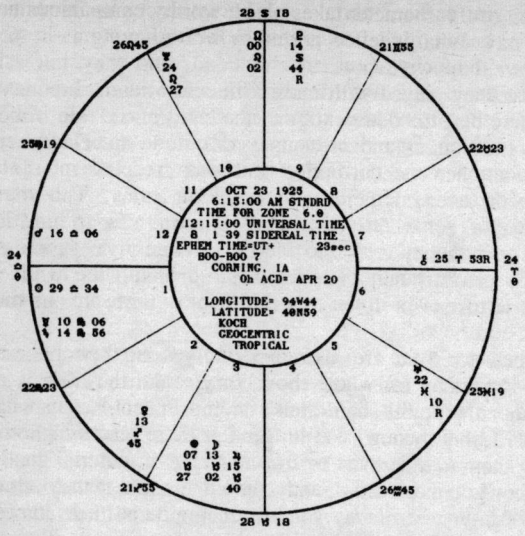

Johnny Carson

can be leaders. Emphasize their uniqueness—they've worked hard for it.

The sweetest qualities of this position are wit, depth, dependability, chivalry, humility, wisdom, and the ultimate realization that one does not have to *take* oneself seriously, but one must *treat* oneself seriously and with respect.

SATURN IN TAURUS, THE SECOND HOUSE, OR CAPRICORN ON THE CUSP OF THE SECOND HOUSE

> "It is a funny thing about life; if you refuse to accept
> anything but the best, you often get it."
> —W. Somerset Maugham,
> *The Mixture As Before* (Doubleday-Doran, 1940)

These people have to make their own values. The unfortunate ones think they can somehow slip around the rules of the system— they shoplift, or sleep with married women, or rip off the telephone company in the name of a holy cause. Saturn lets them get away with it for awhile; he's patient. Over the years, a steady erosion of the character takes place; worthy companions begin to slip away. What is left is not much worth having.

Often they were poor in childhood, and they felt ashamed because they played with more affluent children. Frequently we find here too, the other extreme; the child of the rich, fobbed off with quick kisses and presents as Mummy and Daddy zoomed out to another cocktail party. Both extremes take presents seriously; they regard them as symbols of love. See how embarrassed they get when you give them something to hold in their hands! Often they criticize the gift, or even give it back to you. Shabby presents hurt their feelings, so remember to give them the best tokens of love you can afford. It means so much to them.

The lucky ones are almost puritanical in their honesty and generosity: they offer you their homes, and the door is always wide open. They'll share their last can of lentil soup with you, and still they worry you'll think they're greedy. Somebody taught them to hide their greed, their love of material goods. The lucky ones believe it is more blessed to give than to receive— you'd be surprised at how this openhanded attitude comes back to them, multiplied tenfold. This honesty, the unwillingness to take paper clips or make personal calls at the office because it's stealing from the company, gives them a timbre, a trustworthy quality not found in any other Saturn position.

This is one of the harder positions of Saturn to deal with because it tends to extremes. Reincarnationists link it with past lives spent starving to death or feelings that poverty is holy and noble. These people often have weight problems or problems in handling money. They may want money too much, selling their souls in order to prove (to whom?) their "worth." Or they may be afraid to let it rip and admit how much they want money, eschewing the game for a life of genteel poverty to prove theirs is a better "value system" than other people's. Or they may simply feel they don't deserve better.

What's beautiful about the wiser ones is that they truly do see the God in material things. They have exquisite taste. They love beauty. They are tolerant of other people's views (sometimes because their own are so shaky, but that's a secret!), and they have more common sense in their pinkies than the whole United Nations put together.

You can tell their level of evolution, oddly, by what they're like in bed. The stingy ones, concerned only with their own pleasure, have a long road to go.

Boost them up. Give them presents, tell them how much they do give with no thought of return, bolster them. Deep down their feelings of worthlessness terrify them. Remind them, if they're moneygrubbing, that *people count more than things*. What's more important, love or money? Tell them not to be afraid to spend a little extra for the thing they want. Sympathize when the thing breaks.

Remind these insecure people that theirs is a priceless asset; *the ability to give others a feeling of security*. Help them to find their own security, with good, sound, down-home, loving values. It comes when they value themselves.

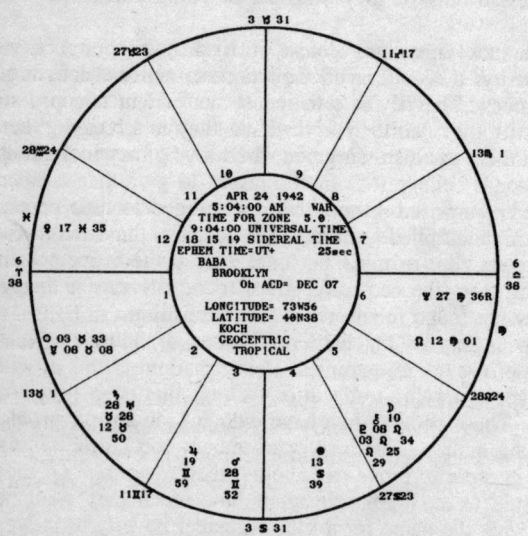

Barbra Streisand

SATURN IN GEMINI, THE THIRD HOUSE, OR CAPRICORN ON THE CUSP OF THE THIRD HOUSE

> *"It is the mark of an educated mind to be able to entertain a thought without accepting it."*
>
> —Aristotle

"The greatest pains are those you can't tell others."
—Jewish proverb

Saturn here, like all the other positions, has good news and bad news.

The good news is that these people are often found in the high I.Q. zone, they tell the truth, have a firm sense of right and wrong, are diplomats par excellence, and are blessed with limitless curiosity. They are loyal to their brothers and sisters; they know how to keep a secret, and they're polished conversationalists. This gang sparkles.

The bad news is they're afraid of going crazy. Let's look at how this works.

Combine a crushing sense of right and wrong, a worried nature, and a deeply instilled parental taboo on discussing deep, personal stuff. They're terrified to confide in anyone, so they bottle it all up, tell themselves if a situation's bugging them that the fault is their own, and then wonder why they feel like they're coo-coo.

These people are blessed, as the solution to their problems is simple, and they are gifted with enough brainpower to think of ways round their problems. They need to talk about their personal stuff with a secret-keeping friend, or pay a therapist to keep their secrets for them. Perhaps they ought to light a candle before they spill the beans—it makes them feel they're banishing the taboo on talking heart-to-heart.

They can't bear to give bad news, so they just try not to tell you. Or they drive you crazy as you watch them loyally denying everyday abuse and frustration, telling you everything's "fine" when you know it isn't. They'll fight you off, too, if you probe too fast, so take it easy.

Most of them are terrified of being thought stupid. Some of them may have mild learning disabilities; remind them these have nothing to do with intelligence.

Telephones bring out their feelings of vulnerability. If you said you'd phone, you'd better.

Trips away, even for the day, cheer them up. They never get enough of them. Perhaps it is easier to pour out your story to a stranger on a train than to talk turkey with your closest associates.

When you get sick of talking about the weather, or the cricket scores, you may talk about someone else's problems if they bear a similarity to those of your friend, but don't confront them directly. It's amazing how they'll fight off help and see it as a threat to their intelligence.

Their most infuriating habit is this sense of right and wrong. Being wrong destabilizes them, so they make a God of Being Right. They are usually right, but what drives you up the wall is the feeling that you can't tell them anything—they don't want to hear it. Then they wonder why their lives run stuck in boring little narrow circles. They are afraid of widening their horizons because someone will make them look stupid. Or perhaps they more deeply sense that to reach out from their normal spheres will open up a Pandora's box of intellectual restlessness. At the same time, routine terrifies them, and still they wonder why they're bored.

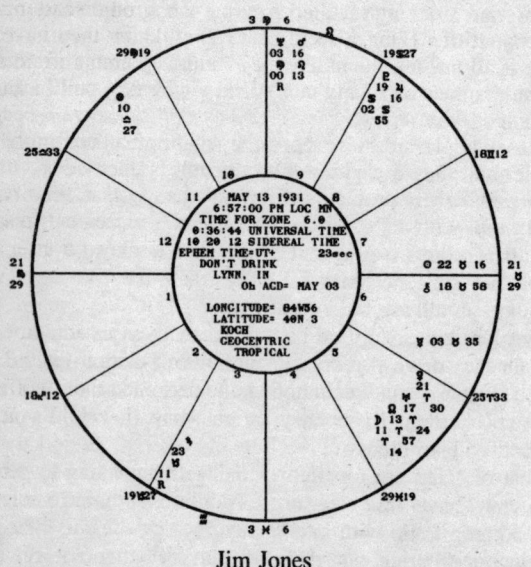

Jim Jones

SATURN IN CANCER, IN THE FOURTH HOUSE, OR CAPRICORN ON THE CUSP OF THE FOURTH HOUSE

"Be thou thine own home, and in thy self dwell."
—John Donne

"Good-bye, proud world! I'm going home;
Thou art not my friend and I'm not thine."
—Ralph Waldo Emerson

Many of these people dimly remember Atlantis, according to the past-life readers. Who's to know? Certainly they act as if they're searching for their lost home, and they're scared of dedicating themselves to a real home now—it might crumble on them, as it did so long, long ago.

Bums lying out in the rain shake them up. They're terrified of ending up like that. And yet unless they examine their fears of committing themselves to a home and family, they'll wander and wander, sorrowfully visiting other people's homes and families, noses pressed up against the windowpane.

The wise ones plant their feet on the ground and make a religion out of having a solid base. They know they have high standards to make a "dream home," and they aren't afraid to put up with cramped or lonely conditions while they build a base of security for themselves. They fear they don't deserve a beautiful place to live, and they've got to fight this fear continually, or they'll come home to a depressing mess that adds to their feelings of worthlessness. They'll rationalize that they can do without a lovely nest, or life insurance, or a retirement fund, but they'll feel a lot better about themselves if they go after these things.

It's a secret, maybe even to them, but they yearn for a Daddy-figure who will take care of them, even as adults. Shh!

Often one of the parents of this Saturn position let the child down badly. It's usually Daddy who undermined their feelings of competence, either by neglect or belittling the child's accomplishments. They grow up feeling like creeps, or jerks. Often they have struggles overcoming self-hate, or wanting to get back at Daddy. The easiest way to get back at Daddy is to screw up their careers. It's curious how many people with this placement of Saturn or Capricorn have emotional problems that get in the way of earning a decent living. More subtly, living on the breadline is also a way of pleasing Daddy's expectations—Daddy treated them as jerks, so they'll live up to the prophesy.

Nowhere else is it so vital to *fight back at Saturn's undermining* as in the fourth house. The antidote? An all-out, can't bust 'em, to-hell-and-back attitude of "I'll *show* them!"

This bunch has to make their own feelings of safety. The idea of being chained to the kitchen sink, surrounded by screaming babies is a silver dagger in their hearts, yet they yearn for emotional security. They're fine parents once they've resolved their own feelings of worthlessness, and they're excellent counselors, making their friends into "family" too. No other position of Saturn is as quick or as kind to offer shelter to the needy.

I've yet to meet a male or female with this position who didn't need to act "macho" in public. They all love to talk baby talk in private, but they won't unless they trust you *well*. They can't bear to be criticized in public, and they will let you do it only *once*.

What makes these people beautiful is a rare, hard-won integrity that develops over the years. The wise ones don't give a fig about what the world thinks of them, but that's after they've established a place in the world. Only then can they snuggle up, turn their backs on the world, and mean it. Without that success to back them up, they're kind, nurturing people, but they're not free of the gnawing hunger for self-love they so richly merit.

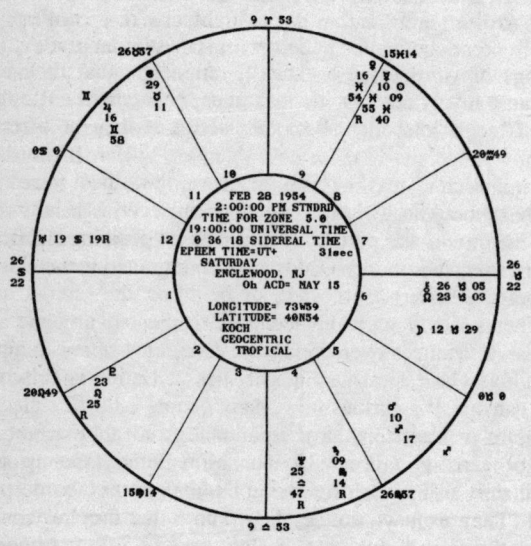

John Travolta

SATURN IN LEO, IN THE FIFTH HOUSE, OR CAPRICORN ON THE CUSP OF THE FIFTH HOUSE

> *"To be loved for what one is, is the greatest exception. The great majority love in another only what they lend him, their own selves, their version of him."*
>
> —Goethe

There's no business like show business. No matter how these people feel inside, they've got to stick a mask on "to meet the faces that they meet," to borrow from T. S. Eliot.

Some of them are terrified of children. There are good reasons for this, too many to go into now. Some of the reasons have to do with past lives (if you believe in linear time), not wanting to grow up, not feeling worthy enough to duplicate themselves, memories of a lousy childhood, not knowing how to have fun, not knowing how to love, wanting to be the Big Shot at home, etc.

When they do have children, they take the whole business seriously, often expecting the kids to act like grown-ups before they're ready. They can be strict parents, and they can be downright *rotten* parents, too. They are jealous of the kids being allowed to be kids. Often they ignore the child. They're still hungry, and want all the goodies and attention for themselves, not for their kids. Make a note of this position. If you have it, you might be a shocking parent and would do well to read up on the baby books and talk to other parents. With hard work and dedication you'll learn the art of adequate parenting. Ignorance is no excuse when human lives are forming. Now *there's* Saturn for you . . . tsk! tsk!

What makes these people beautiful is their loyalty and a rather endearing quality of arrogance that demands to be worshipped in love. They were big shots in other lives, you see, and they never forgot it.

Secretly these folks feel unlovable, and they can make it worse by telling you all the wonderful things other people say about them. They fish for the compliments they so desperately need. They want you to let them know that they're wonderful, wonderful, wonderful.

You see this Saturn position often in the charts of public relations personnel and managers of stars. Here they impart their past life memories of Being Out There In the Limelight to

gently guide their celebrity charges, and to keep them from
making public mistakes. These folks are afraid of the spotlight;
something wise in there tells them they've already done that trip
before. If you can get them to loosen up some evening their
ability to entertain and be creative will knock you backwards.
Saturn in Leo or the fifth house is a gifted position, but it makes
the natives shy. They suffer agonizing creative blocks and doubt
themselves so regularly it's surprising they attempt any creative
work at all. Yet if they give up on creativity, love or originality,
something dies inside. They need to chip away at these fears and
practice, practice, practice! The fear of expressing oneself is
nonsense, of course, and people with Saturn in the fifth sign or
house are without exception multitalented—they can take photo-
graphs, sew, dance, sing, play instruments, invent things, write,
act—if only they'd believe in themselves.

Sneaky tricks come into play when these folks want attention.
And their thirsty souls demand to be treated with respect—or
else. One of their biggest ruses is Being Tired. The world is
supposed to stop for them then. If you love them and build them
up a lot, presto! The energy suddenly returns. They feel so guilty

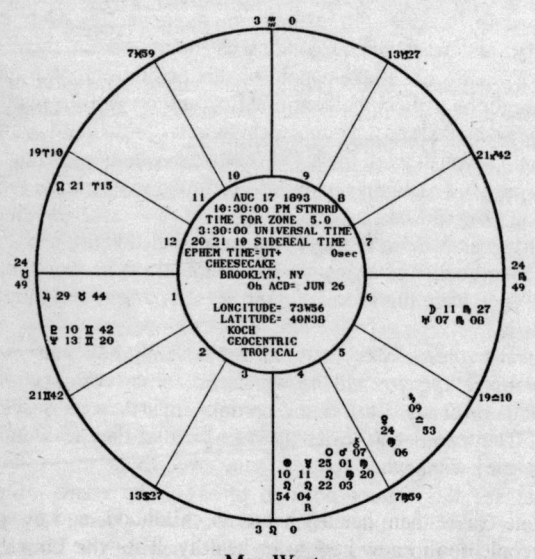

Mae West

nd unworthy about needing lots of love and attention that one
wonders about what kind of people their parents were.

One more point here, speaking of parenting. This position of
Saturn pops up frequently in the charts of parents who neglect or
abuse their children. Saturn in this position is heavier than many
other Saturns because it is how we deal with the humans of the
next generation. The kid grows up and pays you back in spades
for the rest of your life.

Cruel? Yes. Just? A matter of opinion. How many rotten
parents do you know who wonder why their husbands/wives/girl-
friends/boyfriends/best friends don't love them enough? Does it
ever occur to people with Saturn in Leo or in the fifth house that
*nobody is ever going to love you if you're rotten to your own
flesh and blood?*

Necessary? *Never.* This Saturn position produces conscien-
tious parents, the best, if people are willing to work at it.
Astrology is prevention, more often than not.

SATURN IN VIRGO, IN THE SIXTH HOUSE, OR CAPRICORN ON THE CUSP OF THE SIXTH HOUSE

> "Monotony is the awful reward of the careful."
> —English proverb

No worries here, Guv! These people make a *religion* out of
attempting to be careful, reliable, hardworking and healthy. No
position is more consumed with guilt over whether they're working hard enough and whether their work is up to snuff.

When the guilt gets too much for them, they trash their bodies
with junk food, don't return phone calls on time, take injudicious
risks, and let their work go to blazes. At its worst, this position
produces the health bore, or the hypochondriac.

They're touchy about health. Perhaps they saw illness in their
homes; certainly their bodies are more frail in youth than other
children's. Fate is at work here. Saturn will force them to watch
their health. Prevention is the best course, so encourage them to
take their vitamins (they don't), exercise, and become health
nuts. If they take Saturn's wise course, they will be healthy until
the day they die—when a truck runs over them while they're
jogging.

No one taught them healthy habits in childhood, and many of
these people don't know how to be healthy. The wise ones glow

with energy—they've learned how to organize themselves so well they make *you* feel sick. Weird waves of fatigue wash over them; they need to learn how to quit for a few minutes and then get back on the job. Without useful work they ooze quickly into dark periods of depression, and work is the only cure.

This bunch is queasy. They're not big on vomit or blood. They think burps are disgusting, not cute, and most of them exhibit odd phobias about germs and food. Cleanliness means a lot to them. Ask before you drink from their glass.

Drudgery terrifies them. In past lives they were maids and slaves. In the present life they think they're doing you a favor if they cook you a meal or clean their own house. They certainly don't want to help you clean up yours. The only exception to this observation is if they adore you or you're sick. They're beautiful when you're sick. But when you feel better, you can pick up your own socks and while you're at it, will you pick up theirs?

Some of them are irresponsible, even cruel, to animals. These are the people who slip through the grating of civilized human society, and we'll be there to say good-bye to them as they slip away. The wise ones think twice before taking on the care of a

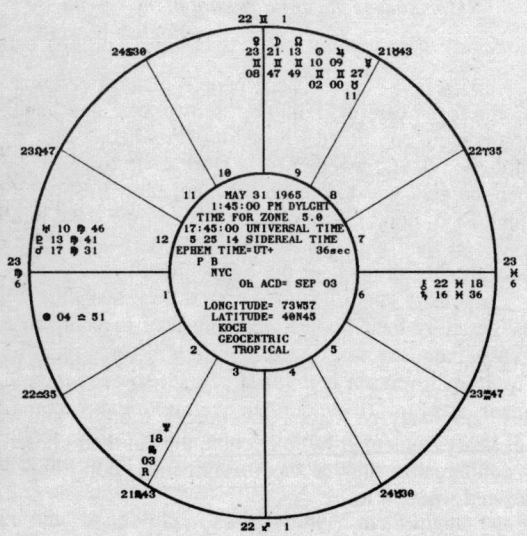

Brooke Shields

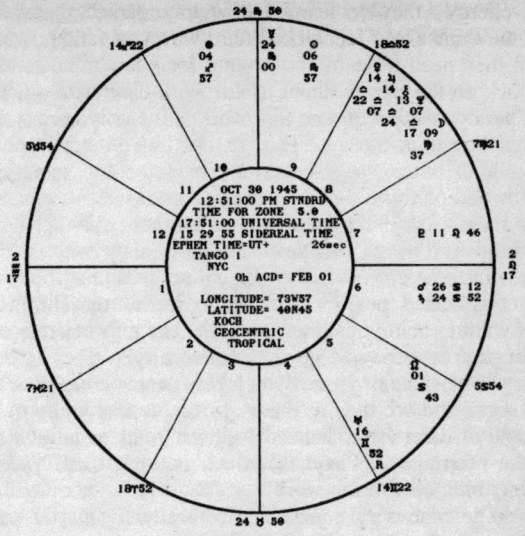

Henry Winkler

pet, and they'll go without rather than have the thing cooped up and bored in a cage or apartment.

What they fear most is chaos. They don't like surprises. The unexpected makes them nervous. They have to know what's going to happen before it happens. They read *The Economist* and go to astrologers. This kills spontaneity for everybody else, but it soothes these folks. They want to know what's going on down the pike. They want to know what's for dinner hours in advance so they can set their little dials. Sometimes the fear of chaos is so great that they stay in dumb jobs that make them feel safe instead of stretching their capabilities.

They must have reasons for everything, and if you don't explain yourself, they go mad. Bolts from the blue do not work well with these folks. Most of them are slobs, but the nicer ones are brilliant analysts. Given the proper training and constant praise, many of them grow to become tops in their chosen fields. They don't realize they're superb craftsmen, don't expect much praise, and *whine* a lot.

SATURN IN LIBRA, IN THE SEVENTH HOUSE, OR CAPRICORN ON THE CUSP OF THE SEVENTH HOUSE

"By all means marry; if you get a good wife you'll become happy; if you get a bad one, you'll become a philosopher."

—Socrates

"I'm Okay—You Suck!"
—New York proverb

A complicated position for Saturn means these folks work harder on their hang-ups; their problems are more visible to other people, and other people never let them forget it!

They'll be happier if they obey one simple rule: they should never marry before they're thirty. If they wait a while to tie the knot, they've the best chance of all the signs to have a happy, "dream marriage" of equals, which is what they crave more than anything else in the world.

These romantics take marriage so seriously that if an early marriage bums out on them, they'll wait years to take the risk again. Many of them are perfectionists and choose not to marry at all, forever seeking an impossible mixture of closeness and "space." Being single forever is a cop-out, however, as these folks do better as married people, once they've outgrown their babyish—and outrageous—illusions as to what marriage is all about.

The mistake of marrying too young aggravates a tendency to give too much or too little in a relationship; they put their mates on pedestals and give until they're drained dry, or they're afraid to share completely, freezing their partner out completely.

Often they select unequal partnerships: the mailman who marries a movie star or the tycoon who marries a pizza waitress are common examples. It is essential that they select a relationship of *peers*.

They're afraid of peer relationships. They secretly evaluate all their close ties as being "better than" or "lower than" they are. It's a cover-up for a terror of merging.

No one taught them how to merge. Most folks with this Saturn position had parents who presented themselves as an idealized, distant unit; the child never had the opportunity to watch how two people fight and make up, agree and disagree, compromise and negotiate. Often one parent ruled the roost, but the child sensed an unequal power between the parents, and he feared he would repeat the pattern of "unfairness" in his adult life.

The challenge is to live, as the Buddha said, in "the middle path." Moderation becomes a religion. Henry Kissinger has Saturn here. He worked hard on learning how to negotiate. He licked his fear of other people, paid Saturn's heavy dues when his first marriage failed, and succeeded by waiting before he married Nancy. She has made him happy.

Powerful and "heavy" people are drawn to this group. Saturn here does not allow you to do anything without criticism or a challenge from somewhere; whether you like it or not, you learn to stand on your own feet. Perhaps people would challenge and criticize less if these folks did not walk about with an unconscious chip on their shoulders—"I'm as good (or better) than anybody." It's an act. The silly ones choose associates with money, sex, drug, or booze problems; people they can comfortably feel superior to.

The wise ones are loyal beyond the call of duty, feel responsible for the well-being of all, and are always willing and open to

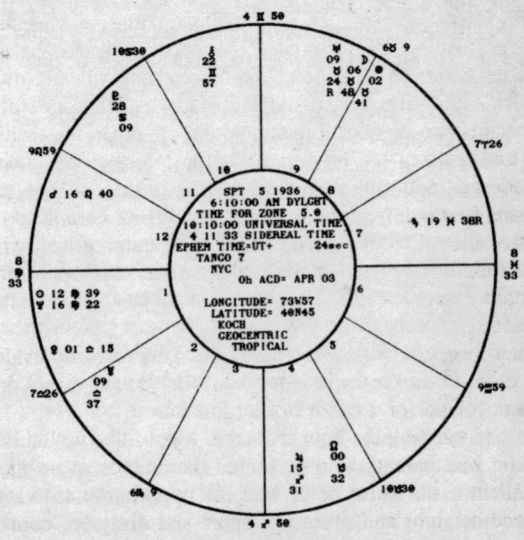

Joan Kennedy

work out relationship problems as they arise. They're a good bet to marry, if you can only drag them to the preacher. The best mates are usually worth the time and the chase, even if they do throw up the night before the wedding. Better bring handcuffs.

SATURN IN SCORPIO, IN THE EIGHTH HOUSE, OR CAPRICORN ON THE CUSP OF THE EIGHTH HOUSE

> "I count him braver who overcomes his desires than him who conquers his enemies; for the hardest victory is the victory over self."
>
> —Aristotle

> "Infidelity will not pass current with any heart that loves truly, or any head that thinks correctly. It is a fearful blindness of the soul."
>
> —Thomas Chalmers

When the weather's hot and sticky, ain't no time for acting tricky with these strong, lonesome souls. They can't handle emotional or sexual infidelity. Once it occurs something breaks in them; the depth is gone, and they can never get it back. They'll act like it's okay; Saturn is famous for an "I don't care" pose. They're not squares, just magicians. They believe that sex is magic.

Sex is only one *cause celebre* for these people. The root force is emotional betrayal in childhood. Often these children lose parents through separation or death or emotional neglect. No one seems to take the time to sit down and do a little armchair psychology with them. They feel alone. When a crisis comes, no one reaches out to them. The smart ones learn early to put their considerable pride in their back pockets and reach out for help.

Helping them is hard. They are terrified of their own passion, instead of learning to be proud of it. No one taught them how. But their deepest fear is *surrender*. The silly ones have one-night stands, avoid psychologists, pick unsuitable mates—all in order to keep control of their feelings. It takes them a long time to learn to trust people—longer if the people they pick let them down. Again, it's their own fault. They expect people to hear their silent screams for help, but pride keeps getting in the way.

It's also annoying to others, who sense that this Saturn position doesn't trust them. Saturn here doesn't know how to lean, because no one ever gave them that chance. They must make their own fortunes, and their "I don't need anybody" attitude doesn't help them get the emotional or financial backing they need.

They make excellent psychologists, giving out what they don't get. When a crisis or a big change occurs, they cash in their "stamps" and lean *too* hard on whoever's nearest, exhausting their associates.

Oddly, they're great in bed. They got that way out of pure fear, one of the luckier compensations. They're afraid they're not sexy, so tend to overdo a good thing. More curiously, they can go for long periods as celibates, like camels in the desert. Past-life speculators link these extremes with lifetimes spent as monks, nuns, yogis and belly dancers. They know how to channel the sex drive into *other* channels, like acquiring money and power.

They loathe the feeling of being financially dependent on anyone, and will usually feel safer if you are in their debt. They expertly rationalize away what they owe you in emotional terms.

No other position of Saturn drives shrinks crazy as expertly as

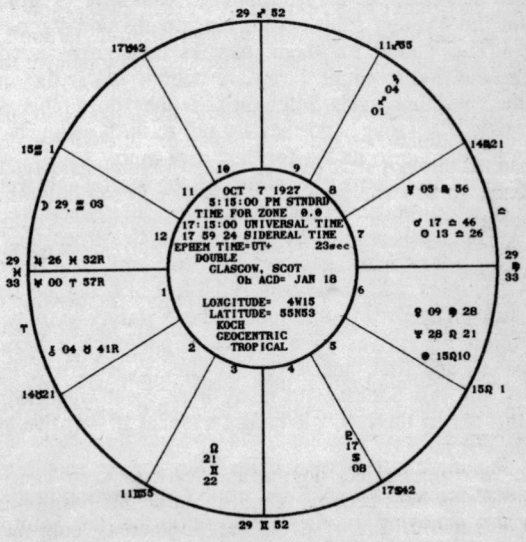

R. D. Laing

this gang; they resist therapy and change, but the wise ones keep on trying to understand themselves, because the thing they fear most is also what they crave—they want to merge deeply with one other person they can trust. It's getting them to trust that takes forever!

Love them or leave them; they remind you of heaven and send you to hell.

SATURN IN SAGITTARIUS, THE NINTH HOUSE, OR CAPRICORN ON THE CUSP OF THE NINTH HOUSE

"The narrower the mind, the broader the statement."
—Old saw

"It is the day of no judgement that I am afraid of."
—Edmund Burke

High ethics and a fanatical love of honesty marks this bunch out for a merry, roller-coaster ride of life. Sure they're maniacs, judgmental, seeing issues in black-and-white terms, with no gray areas in between, but they mean well. God save us from these people, the "young souls" with big mouths and "good intentions"! Thank God for them, too, as they grow in wisdom. They're the first to admit they were wrong, and as they mellow out, their wisdom rivals Solomon's. If they do wrong, at least they know it's wrong, and they try not to do it again. No other Saturn position is so lucky, for they love truth.

The catch is that they're afraid of the stuff Sagittarians are afraid of—too much freedom and losing their freedom. These folks get themselves into sticky mental binds. Often they avoid or screw up their marriages because "freedom" is a big deal to them. The other side of the coin is the fear of being too free—so they stick themselves in dull jobs and call it duty, or they refuse to commit themselves to a home, a philosophy, a mate, a profession, and find themselves less free than before. Past-life readers link this Saturn with many lives spent wandering; perhaps this is why these people hardly travel at all—or live in boats and airplanes.

The wise ones reject dogma and learn to keep their minds open; the silly ones become fanatics, but as this position usually gives a superior brain, even the dogmatists outgrow their philosophies.

They're afraid of foreign countries, and they're fascinated by them. These folks just have to learn to take their mind expansion slowly and seriously. You will not see one of these natives jumping up and down on the dance floor with a head full of mushrooms. They don't like to drive when they've had a few, either. They're careful where they take their impressionable heads.

It's such a sterling position for Saturn that most of them have only two problems. They must be made to see how their fear of being "tied down" to a job they love, a mate, or even to a schedule where they just check in with their loved ones is a prison. Then they need somebody to boot them out of their own culture, *often*, so they can sharpen those brains exploring relative truths, relative customs, and new restaurants. At its worst, this is the fear of expanding the mind. Let them take it at their own pace. As the psychiatrists say, "Before you knock down a fence, find out why it was built in the first place."

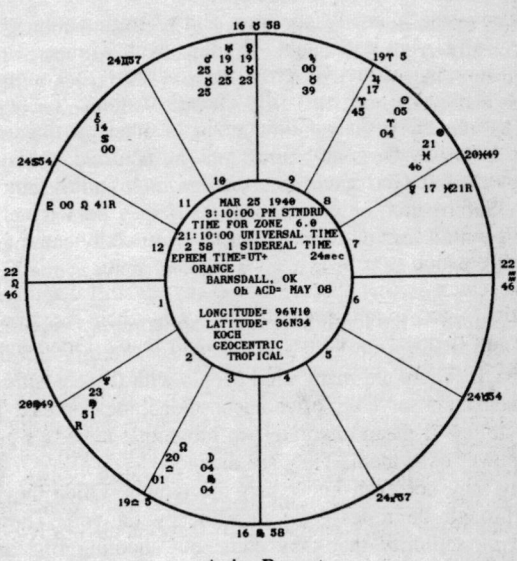

Anita Bryant

SATURN IN CAPRICORN, IN THE TENTH HOUSE, OR CAPRICORN ON THE CUSP OF THE TENTH HOUSE

"Cruelty and fear shake hands together."
—Balzac

"No man was ever written out of reputation but by himself."

—Monk

"'Tis not in mortals to command success,
But we'll do more, Sempronius, we'll deserve it."
—Joseph Addison

Sticky wicket, here. We must make a distinction between Saturn in Capricorn, a fine, upstanding, noble position, and Saturn or Capricorn involved with the tenth house, which can make a person *as mean as they come*.

Saturn is the ruler of Capricorn, and when this unlucky planet relaxes in his own home sign, he shines with wisdom. He wants status, has an instinctive knowledge of how to connect with people in power, and isn't silly enough to think that a title or fame means more than a little grain of sand on the beach of Allah. Certainly he is ambitious; yes, he *is* afraid of his hunger for power, but God gave him wisdom as his birthright. At its worst, Saturn in Capricorn shows the way a person will *delay* himself with a fear of success, but he'll generally come to terms with this when he's grown up a bit and make a mark on the world.

But Saturn *in* the tenth house, or Capricorn *on* the tenth house cusp, tells a story too long and twisted for the limits of a paltry paperback. There are many kind people with these positions, but they have an observable, often unconscious, mean streak. They'll do anything—I mean *anything*—to prove that nobody's going to have power over them. They are dictators.

They may not even know they are tyrants. Often they dominate through their desperate dependency on you. They're so scared of authority that they come out shooting first and ask questions later. But they must dominate, even if it means giving up the things or people that mean the most to them. They feel as if it is a life or death struggle.

Where did these poor souls learn to behave this way? The

general rule of thumb is to ask about the relationship with the parents, and particularly with the mother. While the kind, lucky people with Saturn connected with the tenth house may have merely had an older mother or a kindly grandmother who raised them and gave them wisdom and tenderness, many of these subjects lost a parent before sixteen years of age. The awful truth here is that the mother may have had severe problems in her ability to love; this gets passed on to the child. Sometimes he never quite makes up for it. A cold, twisted, or rejecting parent marks the child before he is seven. A man rejected by his mother has severe difficulties later in life; he may treat women as objects or choose women who will reject him (he doesn't see that he is behaving badly or shirking his responsibilities), or he substitutes career ambition for mother's love. A woman rejected by her mother may exhibit similar responses with men and her career, but she is more likely to take out her rage on herself. Here the fear of success is strong, as is the fear of being bossed.

Is there a "cure"? Therapy helps enormously if the native does not see the shrink as another hated authority figure and has the wisdom enough to go for help. An understanding mate helps too. While it is impossible to make up for early deprivation, the person can compensate by becoming a *benevolent* Big Shot. I stress the word benevolent because most of these people are grand at being Big Shots without the niceties.

The deepest fear here, and often the reason they avoid soul-searching, is that mother didn't really love them. No one can stomach that one, but perhaps it is closer to the truth that mothers are human beings, have problems of their own, and love imperfectly.

Don't panic if you've fetched out your child's chart and found Capricorn on the tenth house cusp or Saturn in there. Become instead that wise, steady, sensible, practical parent that is the archetypal ideal of Saturn. Be sure you give lots of love. You may not be doing the job you thought you were!

Good news if these folks keep plugging away at their problems with authority and careers with an open heart and mind; this position *guarantees* success later in life—Big Success. The only time these people fall from grace is when they're mean to other people, in which case Saturn, the Lord of Karma, will strip their reputations. They are hated beyond the grave, as with Hitler.

If this is your horoscope, Superstar, be nice! Everyone will remember you with love, as we do with Ram Dass.

They both belong in this section. Ram Dass was more fortunate, born with Saturn in Capricorn. Hitler had it in the tenth house. Can you feel the difference?

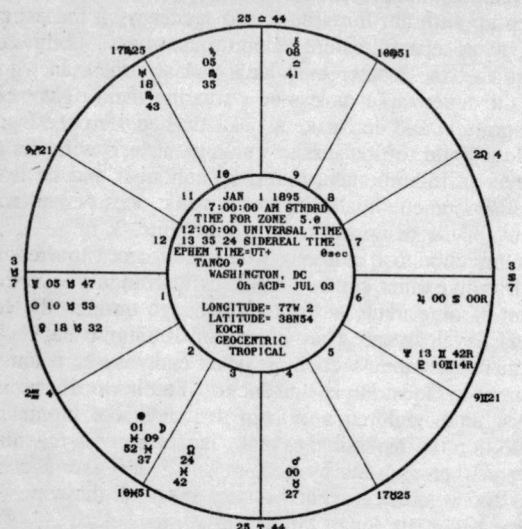

J. Edgar Hoover

SATURN IN AQUARIUS, IN THE ELEVENTH HOUSE, OR CAPRICORN ON THE CUSP OF THE ELEVENTH HOUSE

> "When a person identifies himself with a group his critical faculties are diminished and his passions enhanced by a kind of emotive resonance. The individual is not a killer; the group is; and by identifying with it, the individual becomes one. This is the infernal dialectic reflected in man's history."
>
> —Arthur Koestler

These people are special. They lacked something when they were growing up that their parents never thought about—world visionary goals. They compensate for it in displaying an astonishing dedication to improving society when they're older.

The eleventh house is the realm of peer group pressure, and it is here we detect the weakness of this position. These people are desperately trying to prove they're normal, whatever that is. They yearn to be just like the rest of the gang. Perhaps they grew up in families that practiced a secret snobbery, a family that had to keep up with the Joneses, or surpass them, at the expense of other, more eternal values. Conformism was subtly rammed down their tiny throats. At its worst, this is the man who can't go to the supermarket unless he's wearing the "right" clothes. He's secretive and defensive about being "different" from others. He's afraid to find out he's unique. If he's wise, he slowly discovers there's no such thing as "normal," and he learns to revel in his unique qualities. At his worst, this person will sell his soul for the group and talk the party line.

Another childhood extreme is the child forced to dress differently from the other children or the child who has never had the comfort of his parents' allowing him to go through the copycat stage of development. They name him Rainbow, but they send him to a conservative school. He never feels like he belongs with the rest of the kids. He is "different," and it worries him.

When these children grow up, they feel like hippies at the D.A.R.—or the man in the gray flannel suit in the midst of chanting Ubangis. Theirs is a yearning for and aversion to groups and organizations, and it's love-hate all the way.

In truth they are loners who wish to change society, so must work within it. They join IBM or declare war on the Establishment. The opinion of the world means more to them than is healthy for their sense of personal well-being; they must first find their own humanitarian goals and work toward them in a practical fashion, immune to the applause or the boos.

Friendship is their religion. They give far more to their friends than they get, and it hurts. But in subtle ways they make it hard for their friends to give them anything back. If you can sneak in a few good deeds to them when they're off-guard they go all slushy inside. What runs them is a fear that they have very few true friends. Sometimes they secretly feel that their friends are of a somewhat "lower level" than themselves. They're often right! The wise ones understand that to have a friend, you must first be a friend and give your friends a chance *to prove their worth to you*.

Real friends don't care what you look like, whether you're "normal" or not, or how much money you have, or how much garlic you've eaten. They'll tell you when it's time to go brush your teeth.

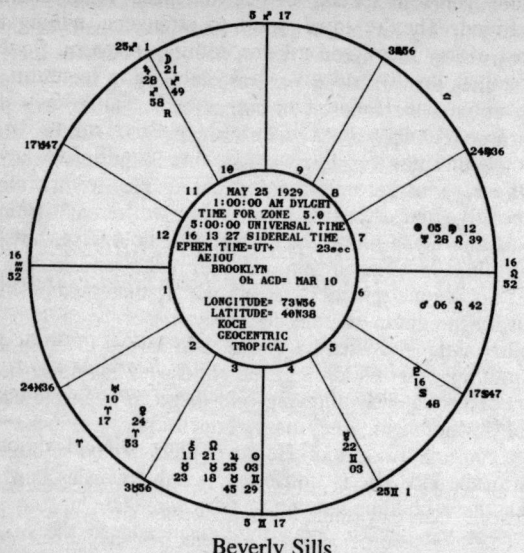

Beverly Sills

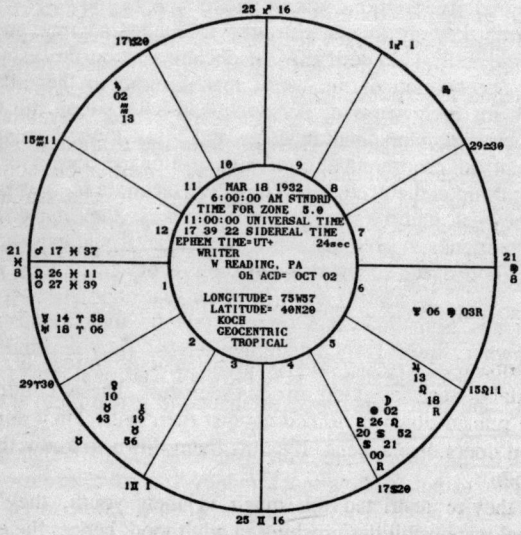

John Updike

Count yourself special if one of these folks counts *you* as a friend. They're loyal, kind to strangers, willing to bail you out of any mess, and ask for nothing in return. Fool them. Return their loyalty and give them everything in return. Make them take it and like it. One day they'll realize they deserve it. In the meantime they'll struggle with trying to be equal in an unequal world—it's the only way they'll find any inner peace.

SATURN IN PISCES, IN THE TWELFTH HOUSE, OR CAPRICORN ON THE CUSP OF THE TWELFTH HOUSE

> *"It is as though he had penetrated someone's left side and perceived a darkened heart (as clearly as if that heart had been abstracted) from its dwelling place."*
>
> —I Ching, Blofeld edition

We all have skeletons in our closets. What makes these people different is that they think their skeletons are worse than anybody else's—no bones about it, sometimes they *are*. But you don't solve anything by jumping down into the bottle of Scotch or taking "blue boys" every night to get to sleep and avoid those lonely, crazy feelings you fear. Nevertheless, that's what these folks often do. Their parents made them feel it was taboo to explore their fears. "Don't be afraid!" or even more destabilizing, "You're not really afraid" invalidates the child's feelings. They grow up fearing the irrational. This fear can include analysis, astrology, hypnosis, meditation, counseling and any form of personal introspection. No one taught them how. Often this fear of reality testing starts young. The parents talk about you as if you're not there, and you're standing in the middle of the room. The result: these folks sometimes feel so cut off from other people they wonder if they really exist.

Karma-watchers say this position denotes a fear of prison, hospitals, and any kind of confinement. These children are often pinned down or forced against their will. They don't like closed doors or playpens. It calms them down to know they can escape.

If they're restricted too much in their youth, they'll find normal responsibilities crushing in adulthood; hence, the escapist

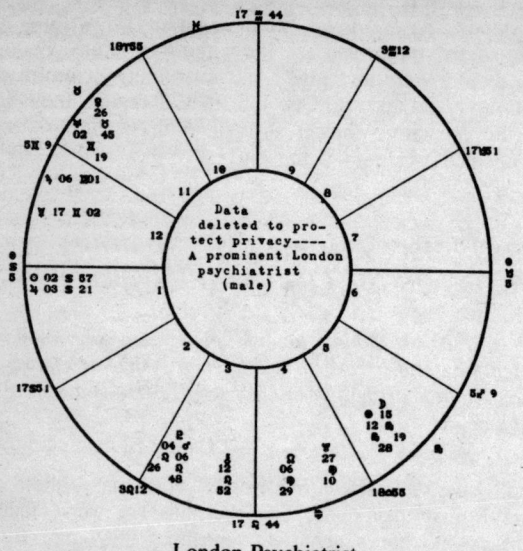

London Psychiatrist

behavior. At its most extreme, they may experience mild feelings of claustrophobia.

They are lonely, lonely souls. Often their faith is shot. What makes matters worse is that they are generally kind people. People come to them, cry on their shoulders, even have nervous breakdowns with them. These kind souls feel as if they are living in the middle of the Emergency Room at Bellevue; suffering moves them deeply. They can't bear to fob people off with platitudes; they feel responsible and roll up their sleeves and give their all. They cannot bear to sit by, or preach, when someone is in pain. I've never met one who didn't have someone close to him become quite ill. These people fear sickness, and they make fine nurses and helpers, but they need to learn to give themselves a break. They are more sensitive than any other sign position of Saturn. The weak ones see you suffering and walk out. They can't bear it.

No one knows better than these people how soul destroying Acts of God can be. They fear sudden cruelty, irrational behavior, lightning. Perhaps that is what gives them their wisdom and kindness. They make their own religion.

The worst of them deceive themselves. They weave tall tales and avoid responsibilities. Fate always seems to have a way of catching up with them, and one day they must face themselves.

Their terror is this introspection, but it is their lifeline. They learn to understand themselves by serving others, too. Their biggest problem is finding *positive* escapes, such as music, travel, and steam baths. Their greatest asset is in showing people how to help themselves and in being proud of their vulnerability. It is a gift given only to the strong. They can be stronger than they know.

1903	JAN	19	Aqu	22:17	1959	JAN	5	Cap	13:36
1905	APR	13	Pic	8:40	1962	JAN	3	Aqu	19:05
	AUG	17	Aqu	0:39	1964	MAR	24	Pic	4:22
1906	JAN	8	Pic	12:48		SEP	16	Aqu	20:59
1908	MAR	19	Ari	14:24		DEC	16	Pic	5:45
1910	MAY	17	Tau	7:31	1967	MAR	3	Ari	21:36
	DEC	14	Ari	23:08	1969	APR	29	Tau	22:26
1911	JAN	20	Tau	9:26	1971	JUN	18	Gem	16:12
1912	JUL	7	Gem	6:14	1972	JAN	10	Tau	3:42
	NOV	30	Tau	18:18		FEB	21	Gem	15:03
1913	MAR	26	Gem	13:08	1973	AUG	1	Can	22:24
1914	AUG	24	Can	17:29	1974	JAN	7	Gem	20:24
	DEC	7	Gem	6:45		APR	18	Can	22:38
1915	MAY	11	Can	21:24	1975	SEP	17	Leo	5:01
1916	OCT	17	Leo	15:36	1976	JAN	14	Can	13:11
	DEC	7	Can	19:12		JUN	5	Leo	5:13
1917	JUN	24	Leo	13:54	1977	NOV	17	Vir	2:51
1919	AUG	12	Vir	13:53	1978	JAN	5	Leo	0:35
1921	OCT	7	Lib	17:23		JUL	26	Vir	12:06
1923	DEC	20	Scp	4:27	1980	SEP	21	Lib	10:53
1924	APR	6	Lib	8:32	1982	NOV	29	Scp	10:34
	SEP	13	Scp	22:01	1983	MAY	6	Lib	19:25
1926	DEC	2	Sag	22:36		AUG	24	Scp	12:01
1929	MAR	15	Cap	13:53	1985	NOV	17	Sag	2:14
	MAY	5	Sag	4:07	1988	FEB	13	Cap	23:57
	NOV	30	Cap	4:24		JUN	10	Sag	5:15
1932	FEB	24	Aqu	2:49		NOV	12	Cap	9:31
	AUG	13	Cap	11:14	1991	FEB	6	Aqu	18:57
	NOV	20	Aqu	2:13	1993	MAY	21	Pic	5:15
1935	FEB	14	Pic	14:11		JUN	30	Aqu	7:56
1937	APR	25	Ari	6:31	1994	JAN	28	Pic	23:49
	OCT	18	Pic	3:40	1996	APR	7	Ari	8:55
1938	JAN	14	Ari	10:34	1998	JUN	9	Tau	6:14
1939	JUL	6	Tau	5:49		OCT	25	Ari	18:33
	SEP	22	Ari	5:10	1999	MAR	1	Tau	1:34
1940	MAR	20	Tau	9:43	2000	AUG	10	Gem	2:39
1942	MAY	8	Gem	19:41		OCT	16	Tau	0:34
1944	JUN	20	Can	7:51					
1946	AUG	2	Leo	14:44					
1948	SEP	19	Vir	4:38					
1949	APR	3	Leo	3:40					
	MAY	29	Vir	13:03					
1950	NOV	20	Lib	15:53					
1951	MAR	7	Vir	12:07					
	AUG	13	Lib	16:47					
1953	OCT	22	Scp	15:38					
1956	JAN	12	Sag	18:49					
	MAY	14	Scp	3:41					
	OCT	10	Sag	15:14					

Chiron

*"Either you pursue or push, O Sisyphus, the stone
destined to keep rolling."*

—Ovid

Chiron is the new baby in the family. It's making some astrologers mighty unhappy. They wish it would go away, and they don't want to take it seriously. The rest of us want to raise a ruckus and dance in the streets. We've never had a planet like this one before. It is a genuine *maverick*.

Even the astronomers don't know what to do with it. Chiron is too far away from the asteroid belt to be classified as a 'roid; it's so small the astronomers wonder if we can call it a planet. To add to the confusion, there exists no rule in astronomy that stipulates how large a planet is supposed to be.

Worse still, Chiron wasn't born here, according to the latest scientific theory. We captured it; it is now visiting us, and eventually Chiron will leave us. It has a strange orbit round the Sun, where it actually commutes between staid, uptight Saturn and all-hell-breaking-loose Uranus, like a weekend hippie.

What does Chiron mean in a chart? Nobody knows yet. Charles Kowal discovered it on November 1, 1977. You can join the Association for Studying Chiron and they will send you a regular newsletter and a form to fill out with your observations about what happened when Chiron passed over different areas of your chart. Zane B. Stein founded the association in order to get feedback quickly on the new planet; data pours into the ASC from all over the world, and Zane collates the observations and cranks them out. He is presently the world's expert on this planet, so we'll give him the floor:

"From 1955 to 1960 was a time of beatniks, mergers of vast unions such as the AFL and CIO, and exploring the sky with the first satellites. All of these fit the sign Aquarius, which Chiron then occupied.

"The sixties were largely under Chiron in Pisces. It was an extremely chaotic time with such Piscean things as a major drug culture, the search for spiritual truths, an influx of mystical

243

religion from the East, and the confusion of fighting a war that divided our country and brought disillusionment.

"In 1969, however, Chiron entered Aries, and we began a period which has been called the 'Me' decade. That in itself is a good Aries picture.

"In 1977 Chiron entered Taurus, and there were shifts in Man's attitude from 'Me' to 'My.' People became concerned with major shortages; money became much tighter, and economizing became a household word. By the way, the stock market crash of 1929 came right in the midst of the last Chiron in Taurus period; then we had depression."

Zane Stein thinks Chiron is connected with pregnancy and birth. Look at the strong position of the key symbol for Chiron in Louise Brown's horoscope. You remember Louise Brown, *the first test-tube baby*?

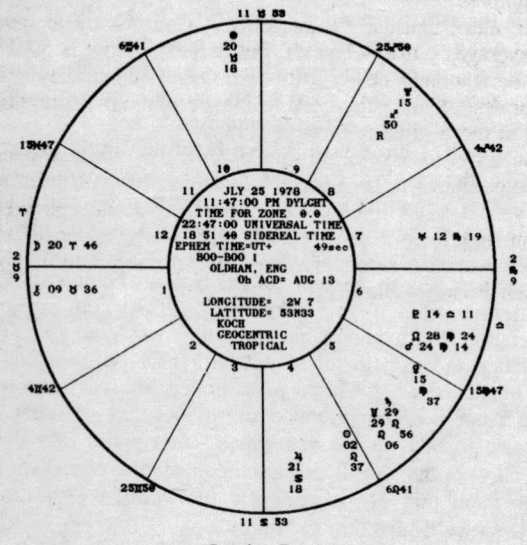

Louise Brown

Chiron is *rising* in the chart.

I'm wildly prejudiced in favor of using Chiron in your horoscope. It crossed over the Moon in my chart when my mother died. It hit my Sun and my *father* died. When it crossed over my talk planet, Mercury, I lost my voice for a week, delighting Tom and Jill and Robin and Elizabeth and Kate and Alice. Each time it brought unholy chaos, but every change brought unexpected mental clarity, *good luck in the extreme*, and forced sudden growth.

Al H. Morrison calls it "an inconvenient benefic," summing up in three words the essence of Chiron's behavior in your chart. In the years to come we will be learning more about this planet that some say has to do with healing.

Even the lousiest transit of Chiron—when it hits Saturn in your chart—will heal you if you aren't afraid to face your flaws and do a little work on changing your state of ignorance. Here the process takes longer, and it may involve psychotherapy. If you're brave, you can clear up a lot of bits of junk at these times, and they all have to do with how you screw up your life. Avoid the challenge and you wind up with a sandstorm of unhappiness.

One more unusual "coincidence": Chiron's cycle round the Sun averages out to 47 years, but its period now is 50.7 years. This corresponds neatly with the famed Kondratiev cycle in economics, which stipulates that an economic depression will occur at the beginning of each cycle.

You have to ask for Chiron as an extra when you order a computer chart—those grumpy astrologers don't *all* want to look at it yet. Ask for it—it's free—or get a special ephemeris for Chiron and look it up yourself. See what happened when it crossed over your rising sign, your Venus, your Saturn. Then tell yourself it isn't a Big Wheel, major planet!

The Outer Planets

When these babies roll across your chart you really feel them; because they move slowly, they take two to three years to effect all the necessary changes in your attitudes.

Too bad if you didn't want to change in the first place! Uranus, Neptune, and Pluto insist that you see beyond your little world whether you wanted to or didn't.

Uranus makes you free, nervous and can bring that mental and spiritual clarity we call Enlightenment, or if you are stupid, you can burn your bridges behind you with little to show for the bonfire.

Neptune can bring you everlasting love and the compassion of Christ and the insight of Buddha; on the other hand it can shatter dreams and leave you confused, disillusioned, and sneaky.

Pluto is God's way of lending you Divine Power. Will you use it to wrench out your weaknesses and manifest your God-given inner strength? Or will you use it to bully people and, in abusing your power, lose it?

Astrologers call these planets The Big Three. They brought you Jesus, Buddha, Nagasaki, Woodstock, and the Industrial Revolution. These guys stay in the same signs for a long time. Astrologers call them "generational planets" because each time one of the Big Three enters a new sign a new crop of attitudes emerges in society.

People who are interested in the evolution of the human race have angles between their Suns and one or more of the Big Three. Without an angle between the Sun and Uranus, Neptune, or Pluto there is no interest in the Big Picture. You are more interested in the gossip columns or in collecting knick-knacks to glorify your home or pocket. Nothing wrong with finding God in your hot fudge sundae, but nobody would call you *cosmic!!!*

Uranus— Rude Awakener

"Your Cadillac ain't no hipper than my bus stop,
Your champagne ain't no better than my soda pop.
Your social life ain't no better than my hot dog
*   stand,*
Your ejemuckation ain't no hipper than
*   what you understand . . ."*
—Dr. John the Nighttripper alias Mac Rebbenack

On an April night in 1978 an Aquarian, ruled by this crazy planet Uranus, won an Oscar, the Academy Awards' highest honor. So what did Vanessa Redgrave do when she got up there on the stage?

She did a Uranus thing. She grabbed the air time and let it rip in front of a hundred jillion zillion television viewers all over the world. She ignored that award for *Julia* and made wild political statements. The big plastic show full of phonies has never been the same since the night Vanessa Redgrave put Oscar's left foot in the bathtub and his right foot in the electric socket.

Who cares if anybody agreed with her opinions? Here was a real human being who had the guts to stand up and Defend A Cause Greater Than Oneself.

Vanessa Redgrave was fulfilling her life trip. Look at her horoscope. See the square angle Uranus makes to her Sun? Vanessa came here to make trouble, to do things her way, to make people stop and think, to shock people out of their Bulgari Necklaces. It's infuriating for those of us who don't agree with her beliefs to admit that she is a genius of an actress. That's independent, unpredictable Uranus for you. Comforting it ain't.

Even on the (rare) occasions when Uranus-type people are right, the style is often "wrong" or offbeat. You can count on Uranus to shoot off its mouth in a shocking manner. Above all else, Uranus *must* shock, (it rules electricity, you see) and the devil take the hindmost.

```
PLANET SIGN  LONG     HSE
SUN  D Aqu 10 27 32    6
MOON   Vir 29  3 29    2
MERC   Cpr 16 35.4     5
VENU E Pic 27 11.9     8
MARS R Scp 12 53.3     4
JUPI F Cpr 13 29.2     5
SATU   Pic 20  0.3     7
URAN F Tau  5 44.6     9
NEPT D Vir 18 31.7R    1
PLUT   Can 27 21.8R   11
ASC    Leo 24 31.4     1
MC     Tau 11 53.4    10
NODE*  Sag 23  7.6     4
PFOR   Ari 13  7.3
VERTEX Cpr 19  2.9
EASTPT Leo  7  3.0
 R=RULE      D=DETRIMENT
 E=EXALTED F=FALL
  *TRUE NODE
```

```
      CARD FIX MUT
FIRE   0   0   0      1 | 3
EARTH  2   1   2     ---+---
AIR    0   1   0      2 | 4
WATER  1   1   2
```

*** NATAL ASPECTS ***

	ANGLE	ORB			ANGLE	ORB
CON=CONJUNCTION	0	10		TRI=TRINE	120	10
SSX=SEMISEXTILE	30	3		SQQ=SESQUIQUAD	135	4
SSQ=SEMI-SQUARE	45	4		BQT=BIQUINTILE	144	3
SXT=SEXTILE	60	6		QCX=QUINCUNX	150	3
QTL=QUINTILE	72	3		OPP=OPPOSITION	180	10
SQR=SQUARE	90	10		/ =PARALLEL OR	0	1
A=APPLYING S=SEPARATING				CONTRAPARALLEL		

	SUN	MOON	MERCURY	VENUS	MARS	JUPITER
MOON	SQQ 3 36S					
MERC						
VENU	SSQ 1 44S	OPP 1 52S	QTL 1 24A			
MARS	SQR 2 26A	SSQ 1 10S	SXT 3 42S	SQQ 0 41A		
JUPI			CON 3 06S	QTL 1 43S	SXT 0 36A	
SATU		OPP 9 03S	SXT 3 25A	CON 7 12S	TRI 7 07A	
URAN	SQR 4 43S	BQT 0 41A			OPP 7 09S	TRI 7 45S
NEPT	BQT 2 04A		TRI 1 56A	OPP 8 40S	SXT 5 38A	TRI 5 03A
PLUT		SXT 1 42S		TRI 0 10A		
ASC			BQT 1 56	QCX 2 40	/	SQQ 3 58
MC	SQR 1 26	SQQ 2 10	TRI 4 42	SSQ 0 18	OPP 0 60	TRI 1 36
NODE	SSQ 2 20	SQR 5 56		SQR 4 04		

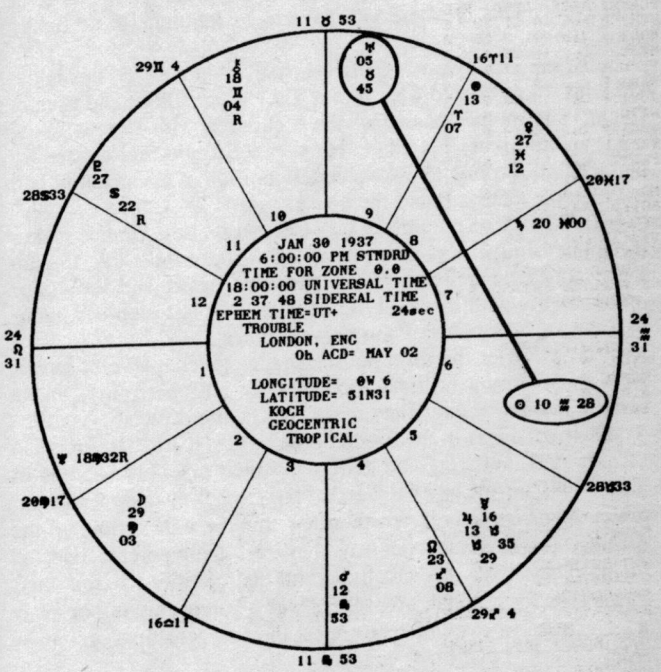

Vanessa Redgrave

	SATURN	URANUS	NEPTUNE		PLUTO	ASC	MC
SSQ 0 44A		SQQ 2 13S					
OPP 1/29S		SQR 8 23S					
TRI 7 22A					SSX 2 50		
			CON 6 09	TRI 6 38			
SQR 3 07		SQQ 2 23	SQR 4 36		BQT 1 46	TRI 1 24	SQQ 3 46

Now this kind of attitude is hardly likely to win any popularity contests, nor does it bode well for lifelong relationships. It *is*, as Commander Whitehead used to say in the Schweppes adverts, "curiously refreshing," though.

Uranus is *smart*; it's unique, and it's honest. Where is it in your chart? This is where you have to be let alone to do things your way.

In the personality box (the first house) or in ARIES, this is the kid who won't be told what to do. They're rebellious and usually bright. The mother of one of these children with Uranus rising came in to discuss his chart. He was a Scorpio and apparently had a habit of trying to poke a certain portion of his anatomy into the electric sockets round the house.

In TAURUS or the money box (second house), Uranus makes the money roll in and go as in a flash. These folks like to earn their money on a free-lance or part-time basis, and they cope quite happily with instability in general. Our last crop of Uranus in Tauruses were Depression or war babies.

In GEMINI or the third house, Uranus gives a love of television and radio, a brilliant, occasionally unstable mind, and a love of rushing about. They make fine racing drivers!

When Uranus is in the fourth house or CANCER, the Freudian shrinks start muttering and getting out their notebooks. Some of these folks go on odd food fads. They rebel against a conventional home structure, which often implies a rejection of the parents, for in some odd way they feel their parents rejected them. They have friends living in their homes or run their businesses from home; often there was a parent missing or away a lot. The most extreme types reject their citizenship to get away from "the ties that bind."

You have an unusual child on your hands if Uranus is in your fifth house. As a parent you aren't much, but you are a real friend to your kids. You want them to develop in their own unique ways and teach them early to stand on their own. This isn't a hot position for Uranus, nor is Uranus in the fifth sign, LEO. The Uranus in Leo generation are a little too honest with their kids, expecting them to be too grown-up for their ages. These people feel ashamed of their jealous feelings and rationalize that they are mentally loyal to their lovers even when physically unfaithful, then they are astonished when the people they love do not seem to go along with their ideals. The trick is to be loyal (Leo) to someone bright enough, idealistic enough, and unique enough to hold your interest. Get the head engaged and the body (with a little gentle arm twisting!) follows!

If you have Uranus in the sixth house you'd be happier with a weird boss or in a self-employed job. It's difficult to keep to a schedule. Uranus in VIRGO is similar. Both are attracted to weird pets but basically believe that critters should be free. They hate to see a bird in a cage. Sickness comes on suddenly, and just as quickly goes away. So many of their illnesses are psychosomatic.

Everybody knows about Uranus in LIBRA or in the partnership box. This is Elizabeth Taylor's position. They just get jumpy when a partner tries to tie them down too much. They want a bright relationship of peers. This one works out better after the age of forty-two on when people are more mature and less apt to blame a partner on their own feeling of personal freedom. Look at the tables for when Uranus was in Libra and compare this period with the divorce statistics. If Uranus is in your seventh house, you can be happy in a love relationship if you'll *grow up* and respect your partner's individuality. It isn't the other guy's fault if you're not developing your uniqueness!

Uranus in SCORPIO tells us we are all bisexual, though we can play this out mentally or emotionally without getting sticky about the issues. It is a psychic position. Uranus in the eighth house is similar. They hate to pay taxes more than anyone, even you.

You'll find a mind-expansion freak when Uranus is in the ninth house—the ones with it in SAGITTARIUS are just starting to get born. These folks just cannot abide the old dogma. This attracts them to all kinds of travel—space included! They have amazing mental-telepathy abilities, and this talent gets stronger if they take the interest to develop it. Slow planets such as Uranus show shifts in social thinking; by the end of the Eighties we shall have been exposed to the harm, as well as good, that religious dogma can cause. Make-your-own, do-it-yourself religion will be commonplace. Most of us will take the best bits from various religions, add a thing or two from our own experiences, and enjoy unique freedom to practice whatever belief system works for us.

What rebels we find when Uranus is in CAPRICORN, the tenth house! Like their sixth house Uranus buddies, these guys are happiest working for themselves or without direct supervision. Sure they are dictators! How else, they feel, will they protect themselves and their precious freedom? This position occasionally produces a great revolutionary or, at least, a fascinating boss. He may be crazy on the job, but an electric current runs through him to his underlings; they'll work like maniacs to please him. Here you get a controversial public image, one that comes across best on television. They cut through the plastic smiles with a realer-than-real magnetism. Kiddies with Uranus in Capricorn haven't been born yet, but each one will cultivate a unique public image, and all of them will be happily at odds with society; they're going to change the status quo or die trying.

Uranus loves to be in AQUARIUS or the eleventh house. Here the ideal is a wide sweep of friends from all walks of life. These folks dream odd dreams of improving the world—not all of them practical. Perhaps it is enough that they share and shock with their theories. They get everybody thinking. They are the world's best experts at letting you be as eccentric as you like. They'll encourage their associates to blossom; they selflessly pitch in when there's work to be done.

In PISCES or the twelfth house, Uranus imparts a strange emotional quirkiness. My mother had this one. She was a fragile-looking woman, five feet four inches tall, with huge green fish eyes that set off her vulnerable beauty. She never seemed to know how impressionable she was nor how psychic. This tender woman had trouble finding the exit in Macy's, yet she fearlessly walked all over New York, Paris, Madrid, Rome, Barcelona, at all hours of the day and night.

"Aren't you ever scared of being attacked?" I remember Uncle Henry asking her once over a beer.

"Oh, no," said my pretty Mama. "If I see anyone coming I'm ready for them," she cackled, pulling out a *can opener* from her purse. Maybe would-be muggers sensed that here was a woman with formidable weaponry loose on the streets; maybe Mama had such fine psychic tuning she always knew where not to go, who knows? Uranus in Pisces or the twelfth house is in the position of lightning radar, and this eccentric sensitivity is both a blessing and a curse to all the folks who have it.

Do you know where your Uranus is? This is where you are honest, sometimes brilliant. It is the part of your life where you race—the house it is in shows the things you can accomplish with lightning speed. You appear to be detached, even coldly calculating, in the area where Uranus is; in truth this is an area of pure *fascination* with you. In fact your cooly-cool attitude here often puts you in a superior negotiating position—you can take or leave the deal.

Herschel's discovery of Uranus coincided with the American Revolution *and* the Industrial Revolution. Nobody wanted to be enslaved to housework, taxes, ignorance, or boring old British cooking. Science took off like a rocket. Giuseppe invented the pizza.

Tables of URANUS

1904	DEC	20	Cap	13:37
1912	JAN	30	Aqu	22:41
	SEP	4	Cap	16:56
	NOV	12	Aqu	8:43
1919	APR	1	Pic	1:48
	AUG	16	Aqu	22:06
1920	JAN	22	Pic	18:33
1927	MAR	31	Ari	17:28
	NOV	4	Pic	10:33
1928	JAN	13	Ari	8:53
1934	JUN	6	Tau	15:45
	OCT	10	Ari	0:32
1935	MAR	28	Tau	3:01
1941	AUG	7	Gem	15:45
	OCT	5	Tau	1:53
1942	MAY	15	Gem	4:10
1948	AUG	30	Can	15:51
	NOV	12	Gem	13:09
1949	JUN	10	Can	4:13
1955	AUG	24	Leo	18:08
1956	JAN	28	Can	1:52
	JUN	10	Leo	1:53
1961	NOV	1	Vir	16:04
1962	JAN	10	Leo	5:44
	AUG	10	Vir	1:21
1968	SEP	28	Lib	16:09
1969	MAY	20	Vir	21:03
	JUN	24	Lib	10:34
1974	NOV	21	Scp	9:33
1975	MAY	1	Lib	17:47
	SEP	8	Scp	5:18
1981	FEB	17	Sag	9:35
	MAR	20	Scp	22:39
	NOV	16	Sag	12:13
1988	FEB	15	Cap	0:35
	MAY	27	Sag	0:50
	DEC	2	Cap	15:53
1995	APR	1	Aqu	13:04
	JUN	9	Cap	0:43
1996	JAN	12	Aqu	7:40

Neptune—
Ecstasy Express

> *"I find good people good,*
> *And I find bad people good*
> *If I am good enough;*
> *I trust liars*
> *If I am true enough;*
> *I feel the heartbeats of others*
> *Above my own*
> *If I am enough of a father,*
> *Enough of a son."*
>
> *"Though heaven prefer no man,*
> *A sensible man prefers heaven."*
> —Lao Tzu

> *"The tyrant dies and his rule is over;*
> *the martyr dies and his rule begins."*
> —Soren Kierkegaard

There's a book that glares out at me from the shelves at Watkins' bookshop in London, a navy blue book with white letters on the cover. It's called *Glamour—A World Problem*.

Ahhh, glamor is a world problem indeed. There isn't enough of it during the daytime for a start. All those awful blue suits and ties the men wear. Crikey!

I tried to read the book, but I couldn't. It's one of those dull, long-winded Alice Bailey books where this dead Tibetan lays the rap down about how it all runs on the Other Side.

We can't even get things to run so hot on *this* side, sez I, and the thought of a Spiritual Hierarchy with a review board the size of the Sony Corporation makes me want to stick my head in the garbage compactor, *now*. Why mess around? Crrrrruuuuunnnch! Okay, Alice, here's what an Aries thinks of joining your ranks and files! And hey, if it's so hot out there in the Land of Light, how come you gooroos can't write in plain English? *Hah?*

It simply won't do . . . we're not being spiritual, or kind, or compassionate, and these are the things Neptune is made of.

255

Neptune is the god of the sea. Neptune is a world full of unconditional love and plenty of time, tropical music and blue lights and Pina Coladas, tiki gods breathing fire, and a wishing pond. You know, like Trader Vic's. When I die, Neptune's going to be the first stop before heading out to the good old White Light for a well-earned *rest*.

Ecstasy is what Neptune's all about. (Jes' a touch 'fore I go, Lawd, jes' a touch . . .) Glamor is merely one of a million pathways to ecstasy, the most sure and direct route being Love of That Which Lies Beyond Oneself.

Show me the house where Neptune is in your chart, and I'll show you what makes you high. Drag out a chart where the subject has a "hard angle" (square, opposition, conjunction) of their Sun or Moon or Venus with Neptune, and I'll show you an everyday saint, an artist, or a con artist.

Yes, a con artist. They reverse the usual Neptune process of wanting to see the best in others, so they exploit the noble human urge to trust. Most con victims see what they want to see, and the confidence trickster knows this. Neptune rules get-rich-quick schemes, deception, and trickery.

This is the cheap-and-easy side of Neptune, and a pretty sight it isn't. Herein lies the realm of lies, betrayal, treachery, self-deception, escapism, masochism, refried confusion, "I don't know what I want," and all the myriad forms of self-defeating behavior.

If Neptune aspects a planet harshly in your chart, you'll have a struggle to see clearly about some aspect of your behavior. You'll have to resist acting sneaky, cheap, and weak on the one hand and avoid being an unappreciated doormat on the other. Sidestep both extremes and you're a candidate for not merely a happy life, but *bliss,* that caviar of human emotions.

It's hard to keep friends when your pals hate each other's guts. If Mercury aspects Neptune, you may be inclined to feel compassion for both parties, but you don't keep a friend by being two-faced. You can keep both, sometimes, with love.

It's hard to say your husband is your best friend and go out and cheat on him. That's what often happens when Neptune aspects Venus, and the cheater only confuses herself the more.

Down with confusion! Slay the dragons of Neptune and get hip to the trip of consciousness! If Neptune is strong in your chart you can achieve Nirvana *now* if you're willing to pay the price. The price? Well, madam, we are discussing the Rolls Royce class of human endeavor—honesty, causing hurt to no one, compassion, service, sacrifice, empathy, humility, subtlety— Madam? Madam? Where's she gone?

As one head-in-the-sand Neptunian client remarked, "I like *some* of the ten commandments." He wonders why everything he touches turns to bat guano, but he'd rather stay confused and avoid seeing how he hurts everyone around him, including, naturally, himself. There are clear steps to personal happiness in every religion and psychology, so why do Neptunians so often think they can "take the easy way" and shoplift inner peace?

The best antidote to a mixed-up Neptune is to tell yourself that you are worthy of good treatment from others and to stop feeling sorry for that old drunk on the corner when you could be helping your best friend with her tulip garden. Be reliable yourself and check out your acquaintances a couple of times before you give your all. They may turn out to be irredeemable derelicts.

And yet, and yet . . . if you really believe that the criminal about to attack you is really a Buddha, sometimes you communicate this feeling to your attacker, and he gives you a break. It has happened. Neptune rules miracles, and the concept of Grace.

Psychedelic, guilt-producing, compassionate, kind, yearning, alcoholic, side-tracking, druggie, ecstatic, psychic, glamorous, impressionable, sneaky, misunderstood, creative, imaginative, socialistic, martyred, subtle vibes all go into the sign and house where you find Neptune in a chart. This multifaceted planet is too bighearted and complex for us to do justice to it here, but a whip round the signs and houses will at least start your imagination working.

Neptune in:

ARIES or the first house: An impressionable person who doesn't like you to figure out who they are.

TAURUS or the second house: A "soft touch" who will give you the shirt off his back.

GEMINI or the third house: Someone who spent a childhood surrounded by people talking funny or foreign.

CANCER or the fourth house: A weak or absentminded parent did not give them the support they needed. They like to have a boat, or a home by the water, or at least a fish tank at home.

LEO or the fifth house: Great in the sack, artists in some way, probably music.

VIRGO or the sixth house: Natural healers, but they are terrifyingly disorganized about their working conditions.

LIBRA or the seventh house: They choose foreign, crazy, pitiful or superior associates who are symbols to them.

SCORPIO or the eighth house: They have rich sexual fantasies, and are extremely psychic. Don't try to fool them!

SAGITTARIUS or the ninth house: Outer space freaks. They dream of foreign climes and prefer mystical religions.

CAPRICORN or the tenth house: A glamor or helping profession suits them best.

AQUARIUS or the eleventh house: They dream beautiful dreams of saving the world. Their buddies are weirdos and artists.

PISCES or the twelfth house: A real martyr trip, or unsung, noble helping of people without tooting their horns about it.

Hang on to the idea that the sign and house of Neptune is where you'll be happiest if you purify your life in some way. Clean up and enjoy the Jungian oceanic feelings.

Misunderstood? Neptune is often misunderstood. It is the ache we feel when we look at a sunset. It is the silence of the six million who entered the gas chambers. It is show biz and excitement and tinsel and neon, and it is people looking for that *rush*, folks who cannot live without that charged, higher awareness. Without real love to back up the tinsel, however, chameleon Neptune turns into another one of its archetypes, the chimera, the empty sham. Cynicism sets in. Life loses meaning. Peace is out of grasp; the taste of ashes on the tongue. The angels weep.

1901	JUL	19	Can	23:58
	DEC	25	Gem	13:29
1902	MAY	21	Can	13:35
1914	SEP	23	Leo	20:26
	DEC	14	Can	20:34
1915	JUL	19	Leo	13:35
1916	MAR	19	Can	15:32
	MAY	2	Leo	10:51
1928	SEP	21	Vir	12:08
1929	FEB	19	Leo	11:19
	JUL	24	Vir	15:09
1942	OCT	3	Lib	16:59
1943	APR	17	Vir	11:02
	AUG	2	Lib	19:10
1955	DEC	24	Scp	14:56
1956	MAR	12	Lib	2:20
	OCT	19	Scp	9:14
1957	JUN	15	Lib	20:58
	AUG	6	Scp	7:44
1970	JAN	4	Sag	19:02
	MAY	3	Scp	2:37
	NOV	6	Sag	15:49
1984	JAN	19	Cap	1:25
	JUN	23	Sag	3:16
	NOV	21	Cap	11:46
1998	JAN	29	Aqu	0:36
	AUG	23	Cap	4:22
	NOV	27	Aqu	21:47

Pluto—Below the Boom Boom Room

"Heat not a furnace for your foe so hot that it do singe thyself."

—William Shakespeare

"Revenge is a dish best eaten cold."

—American proverb

Permit me to introduce Pluto. He is the god of the underworld. Hell is his realm. He feasts on the rotting flesh of broken mortals. His hunger and his greed are insatiable.

Pornography, not sex, is Pluto. That which enjoys power for its own sake is Pluto. The feel of the whip in the hand is the feel of Pluto, and the crack of the whip is the sound of Pluto.

Can one man change the world? Hitler thought so. He came to power when Pluto was discovered.

Could anyone stop him? Einstein thought so. Then there was the bomb.

Some say that Pluto is like Janus, the god with two faces. One face is evil, and the other face is good.

Charles and Vivia Jayne think the Hindu idea of God best describes Pluto. The Hindus say that everything in life either creates, preserves, or destroys. These are God's three ways of amusing himself.

Certainly Pluto is creative. You only have to notice the house Pluto is in in a chart to see how deep and purifying you want to be. Pluto in the partnership box (seventh house) means you have a Svengali complex. You want to bring out the best in those twisted, moody loners. So what if your friends don't like his tatty black leather jacket! Pluto in the religion box (ninth house) says you have an obsessive mind. This is the merde-detector. You will have the truth no matter how much it costs, and it costs you plenty.

Pluto lived in the underworld. He lived there with the dead

people. He thought he was so unlovable that he lived there for aeons without a mate. When he fell in love with Persephone, he had to steal her. She saw how aloof and lonely he was and perhaps that made her love him all the more. Still even the god Pluto had to compromise and let his wife go home for half of the year. In the sky, the planet Pluto travels ahead in its orbit for six months, and for the other half of the year it looks like it is traveling backward. Men get crazy when their wives go away, and when the wives come back, things seem to straighten out again. You see it happen all the time.

In your chart Pluto shows the area in which you will endure hell to attain heaven. You will strive against all odds and logic to achieve rare depth and understanding. It takes some will power, but you have it. If you want it badly enough. Pluto shows you where you will find your treasure, for it is the Ultimate Jackpot. You must aim very high and act with noble intentions and a will of steel. Make a mistake and Pluto will French fry you. It is not a planet that tolerates wishy-washy feelings.

Pluto is that part of yourself that must work doggedly to transform the ugly into the priceless jewel. Pluto *must have its way* even at his own expense.

Especially at his own expense.

Do not misunderstand. Pluto helps the weak. He is the god of transformation.

Ram Dass writes about this process in *Be Here Now*. He calls it "the crisp trip." Your ego goes through the Van Allen belt and life wipes out the impurities in your life. You might become an overnight success or lose a loved one. Wars and LSD trips, too, have a way of getting people back down to basics. Pluto burns through the garbage. What you have left to work with is what you are. It hurts sometimes. Not everyone survives ego loss.

Nothing disgusts this planet. He has a lot to do with research because he digs deeply. He is unafraid of muck and gunge.

Psychology is another of Pluto's gifts. We cannot be free of the cucarachas in our souls unless we get a good look at them first. If you have connections between Pluto and other planets in your chart, you are probably doing a lot of things you don't know about. Pluto rules the unconscious functions. Do you give the house Pluto is in too much power over you? Is it a compulsion? Will it benefit you or will it be your undoing? You will always be safer if you examine the Pluto areas regularly.

Pluto saves lives. He is the monster who saves the girl from marrying a wimp. He is the radiation machine that burns the cancer cells from the bodies of the one quarter of the cases who suffer from this disease. Radiation treatment is harsh, but its function is to preserve life.

Pluto loves longest. Boris Karloff in *The Mummy* waited 3,500 years to meet his love again. His crumbling flesh and shuffling, bandaged figure did not amuse his love object. The girl did not want to die with him in order to live with him forever. Her boyfriend saved her life and the mummy died. No doubt he is still waiting for her, out there in the afterlife.

And whether you like it or not, Pluto transforms everything and everyone he touches. If you are young, the house that your Pluto is in will bring you bigger surprises than you think. If you are old, this house is like a book of short stories, with distinct and separate chapters.

Pluto stays in each sign a long time. He won't go through all the zodiac signs in your lifetime. Some astrologers say that Pluto does not say anything personal about you. They say he only counts as a symbol of the generation you are in, and that he shows what was going on in the world when you were born. Those astrologers are wrong. You can look up the sign Pluto was in when you were born in this book. We'll cover the signs Pluto affects for this century in a moment, but remember that Pluto is in the houses in your chart, and the house in which you find Pluto is more important than the sign he's in. Apply the ideas of passion, strength, will power and the choice between degradation and purity to the house in your chart containing Pluto. With a bottle of Ripple and thirty-seven hours to spare, we could go over the twelve house positions of Pluto, but we wouldn't do it justice, so instead we'll look at the signs he affects this century.

If you have Pluto in the sign CANCER you have deep, sentimental feelings. Life forced you to examine and uproot phony family obligations and reach for a purer idea of family life. Sometimes you may have had to make your own family, choosing friends to make up your nest. You are obsessed with giving and getting emotional understanding. People with Pluto in Cancer have made wonderful, slushy, emotional movies. They love their country obsessively and learned the joys and dangers of patriotism. They loved their children to the point of obsession and wanted to give them everything; some were too busy protecting their own stake to join in the family of man. As Pluto likes to be in Cancer, or any water sign, this was a good time to be born. It gave folks a deep feeling nature and maturity.

Pluto in LEO is the Woodstock Nation. Pluto does not like to be in Leo. We behave obnoxiously to our parents and our children do not stand a chance . . . we even call them Moonbeam and Zowie . . . the kids just have to put up with whatever we dish out to them. We are obsessed with being the center of attention, *we are the Superkids*. Our generation is huge in number; we're used to getting our own way, and we always will. We will sit in the old folk's home in our blue jeans, smoking dope and playing backgammon. We think love is a training course, and we use each other as catalysts for our own self-centered transformation. Who cares if a few hearts get broken as long as we have *growth*, brother? We have a lot to learn about love and loyalty. You have to admit it, though. We've done a hell of a lot with fun and music. Rock and roll forever!

People born with Pluto in VIRGO want to be perfect, which is tough going when you look out the window. They are specialists, and work is a god to them. Look at the riots in England in the eighties—*the kids wanted to work*. Give them half a chance and they'll do the job perfectly if it takes all night. Moog synthesizers came in around this time, making smooth, perfect, electronic, throbbing music. Micro chips are taking over industry. Computers do a better job than people. It all leaves people out of work. That's okay too—Pluto in Virgo people will let the machines do it. There are new jobs people do better. Aren't there?

Keep an eye on the other guy. Pluto in *LIBRA* will. They do their own thinking in the marriage department. The ones that marry at all will work harder at it than Pluto in any other sign. It's got to be deep and pure or it's nothing. There's no middle path with this sign position of Pluto, you either come clean in a relationship with them, or they just nuke you. They like partners vastly different from themselves, and you'll see some odd couples here.

Soon Pluto will go home into his own sign, SCORPIO. He likes to get home and relax. Some folks are afraid of what will happen when Pluto starts feeling his oats again. They say he will bring us weird plagues and diseases that resist medicines, or nuclear leaks and terrorism. Don't worry about old Pluto. He will see that we eat our vegetables. We will learn lessons, grow strong, and clean up our feelings. Pluto will teach us just what is worth getting passionate about. He will find a cure for cancer. He will show us a combination of love and sex and passion to make us forget what came before. He will bring us a deeper psychology and the truth about what's important—like passion, life, and death. Of course, Pluto will not stand for any drag-assing in his home. He cracks the whip.

When Pluto goes into SAGITTARIUS people will be constantly thinking about life in outer space. Why?

1912	SEP	10	Can	17:50	
	OCT	20	Gem	6:46	
1913	JUL	9	Can	22:50	
	DEC	28	Gem	3:46	
1914	MAY	26	Can	21:11	
1937	OCT	7	Leo	11:44	
	NOV	25	Can	9:21	
1938	AUG	3	Leo	17:54	
1939	FEB	7	Can	12:59	
	JUN	14	Leo	4:51	
1956	OCT	20	Vir	8:17	
1957	JAN	15	Leo	0:23	
	AUG	19	Vir	5:48	
1958	APR	11	Leo	11:29	
	JUN	10	Vir	22:22	
1971	OCT	5	Lib	7:18	
1972	APR	17	Vir	6:05	
	JUL	30	Lib	13:17	
1983	NOV	5	Scp	18:52	
1984	MAY	18	Lib	18:41	
	AUG	28	Scp	1:14	
1995	JAN	16	Sag	19:31	
	APR	21	Scp	19:07	
	NOV	10	Sag	10:06	

Part
III

Astrology in Daily Living:
From A to X

Astrological Birth Control

Is like playing Russian Roulette. It isn't foolproof yet.

It is great for cutting down the odds of pregnancy. You find the angle between the Sun and Moon when you were born. When this angle repeats itself once a month, you are most likely to be fertile. If you were born on a full Moon, you're fertile then.

Don't risk it. If you want to study astrological birth control more deeply, a computer service will make a chart for you, and you can watch it yourself.

What does seem to work is your choosing the sex of your children. The computer chart will tell you that. And if you're trying to have children, the fertility tables will increase your chances a great deal.

The Chart of a . . . Building???

I had a friend once who was in love with the G. P. O. (Post Office) Tower. She used to draw pictures of it, dream of it, and everything.

This eyesore lights up a lurid green at night and juts out of the London skyline, out of sync with the Houses of Parliament, Big Ben, and St. Paul's, glowing gaudily and ruining the stately picture as far as the eye can see. And yet Jude loved it, this tall, inappropriate canister with little wheelie things sticking out of the top. We suspected it was what Her Majesty's Post Office used to tap all the phones in the London area. Certainly it ensures the phones will not work too well, but that's another tale . . .

It is hard getting a birthday for a building because you have so many dates to choose from. Do you take it from when they put the first shovel in the ground to excavate, when the cornerstone goes on, or when they cut the ribbon?

Louise Duncan knocked herself out foraging through the old clippings and came up with the official birthday for the Empire State Building. This extraordinary building even celebrates its birthday *every year*, as befits its unique personality. The building had a bumpy start—Jimmy Walker was mayor of New York then, but everybody wanted Al Smith, the old mayor, to cut the ribbons, so they got him instead. Smith wanted his two grandchildren to cut the ribbons to symbolize the future generations, but the kids couldn't get the scissors to work, so Smith ripped the ribbons himself at exactly 11:15 A.M. on May 1, 1931.

People born in 1931 are extraordinary, every one of them. They have terrible conflicts within themselves (see all the big squares in the Empire State Building's chart), and as a result of

he pressure they often achieve eminence in some way. Like the
building, they learn to bend and sway while still retaining their
unique character, head and shoulders above the crowd. Newsman
Dan Rather and Cosmicman Ram Dass both spring from the crop
of '31.

The Empire State Building is no longer the tallest building in
the world. It isn't even the tallest building in New York anymore—
the soulless twin monstrosities downtown took care of that. But
for most folks who come to visit from all over the world it is still
their favorite, the structure with a soul and a heart . . . and a
lurid past. As of this writing fourteen people have hurled themselves to their deaths from the Empire State Building. In 1945 a
B-25 bomber got lost and crashed into the building. One guy
jumped off and the winds were so high he was *blown back onto
the building*. It surprised him so much he decided to live and
crawled back in through a window.

The Sun is in the tenth house of the ESB's chart, so it fulfills itself best by being in the limelight, a pillar of the
community.

The Moon is in the fourth house, so it feels very insecure
about being moved. It wants the people in its hometown to
accept it, and it loves its home very much.

The Midheaven is in Aries, so it wants to be Number One,
and it wants to be original, unique, and a big shot. Uranus
is there at the top, too, so it looks unlike anything then or
since. It's one of a kind. Remember the shape of Uranus?
The top of the Empire State Building is a big television
aerial.

Venus is square Jupiter in the ESB's chart, so it makes people
happy and it's popular. The trine between Venus and Mars
denotes a lasting sex-appeal. The ESB is beautiful and has an art
deco lobby. People even get married up there. Even junkies love
it, as it looks to them like a giant needle in the sky. On
Halloween the building glows orange, at Christmas it is red and
green, and on the Fourth of July they light it up red, white, and
blue. There's a great souvenir stand on top. This building knows
how to have fun. Even King Kong liked it.

What's it like in bed? Well, with Aquarius on the eighth house
cusp, it has very high ideals. It might even like groups. The ruler
of its eighth house is Uranus, which has to do with sudden, sharp
excitement, and it's got some squares to it, so it may have some
sexual problems.

```
PLANET  SIGN  LONG      HSE
SUN     Tau   10 16 50  10
MOON F  Scp    2 20  1   4
MERC    Tau    8 18.8R 10
VENU D  Ari    6 37.8   9
MARS    Leo   10 45.9   1
JUPI E  Can   14 56.1  12
SATU R  Cpr   23 16.5   6
URAN    Ari   16 45.5  10
NEPT D  Vir    3  2.5R  2
PLUT    Can   18 51.8  12
ASC     Can   29 41.9   1
MC      Ari   14 30.3  10
NODE*   Ari   14 16.2   9
PFOR    Cpr   21 45.1
VERTEX  Sag   15 36.5
EASTPT  Can   12 17.1
   R=RULE      D=DETRIMENT
   E=EXALTED   F=FALL
   *TRUE NODE
```

```
      CARD FIX MUT
FIRE   2   1   0       5 | 1
EARTH  1   2   1      ---+---
AIR    0   0   0       2 | 2
WATER  2   1   0
```

*** NATAL ASPECTS ***

	ANGLE	ORB			ANGLE	ORB
CON=CONJUNCTION	0	10	TRI=TRINE		120	10
SSX=SEMISEXTILE	30	3	SQQ=SESQUIQUAD		135	4
SSQ=SEMI-SQUARE	45	4	BQT=BIQUINTILE		144	3
SXT=SEXTILE	60	6	QCX=QUINCUNX		150	3
QTL=QUINTILE	72	3	OPP=OPPOSITION		180	10
SQR=SQUARE	90	10	/ =PARALLEL OR		0	1
A=APPLYING		S=SEPARATING	CONTRAPARALLEL			

	SUN	MOON	MERCURY	VENUS	MARS	JUPITER
MOON	OPP 7 57A					
MERC	CON 1/58S	OPP 5/59A				
VENU			SSX 1 41A			
MARS	SQR 0 29A	SQR 8 26A	SQR 2 27S	TRI 4 08A		
JUPI	SXT 4 39A			SQR 8 18A		
SATU		SQR 9 04S		QTL 1 21S	TRI 5 60A	OPP 8 20A
URAN						SQR 1 49A
NEPT	TRI 7 14S	SXT 0 42A	TRI 5 16A	BQT 2 25A		SSQ 3 06A
PLUT			QTL 1 27A			CON 3/56A
ASC		SQR 2 38	SQR 8 37	TRI 6 56	/	
MC				CON 7 53	TRI 3 44	SQR 0 26
NODE				CON 7 38	TRI 3 30	SQR 0 40

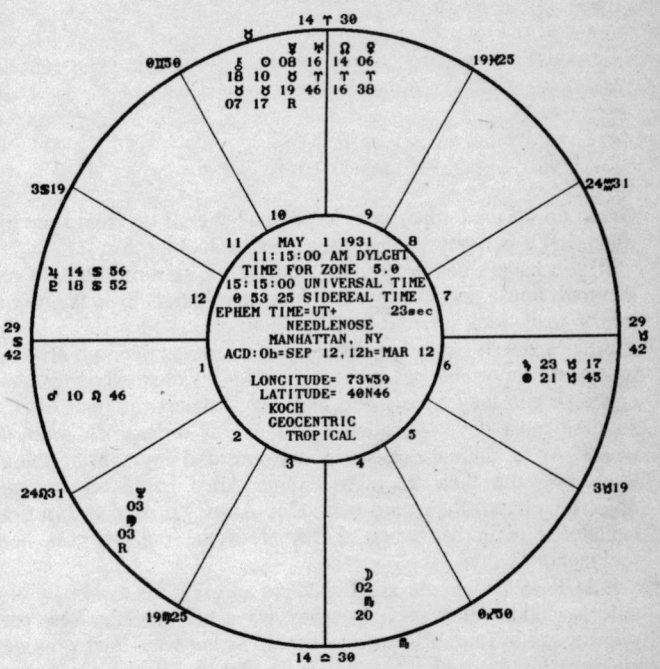

Empire State Building

SATURN					
SQR 6 31A	URANUS				
	SQQ 1 17A	NEPTUNE			
OPP 4 25A	SQR 2 06A	SSQ 0 49S	PLUTO		
OPP 6/25				ASC	
SQR 8 46	CON 2/15	SQQ 3 32	SQR 4 21		MC
SQR 9 00	CON 2 29	SQQ 3 46	SQR 4 36		CON 0 14

Critters

Given up on the human race, have you? We all do from time to time, and a pet may be the answer you're looking for.

If you have a computer chart, look at the sign on the cusp of the sixth house and look up that definition here below. If you're a lazy snail, look up your Sun sign below.

ARIES doesn't care for slobbering critters, as they are always in a rush—a portable pet is best. They don't like smelly creatures either. When they have a pet, they may exhaust the poor beast, so they must develop patience and *let the animal do what it wants*. Aries' animals are sheep and rams and any adoring thing that buoys up their big egos. Some Aries fixate on strange objects and turn them into pets. One Aries gal used to bring a cantaloupe with her when she went to the pub—it was her meloncholy baby.

TAURUS people are good cuddlers and will always be available to cuddle their pets. In many ways they are the best pet owners, as a Taurus is sure to be set in his ways and provide stability for an animal. Just look at Queen Elizabeth and her famous corgis! Perhaps Taurus is so devoted to pets because animals will return unbridled devotion where humans would if only Taureans weren't so boring. They like a nice normal conservative pet and will never let the thing go hungry. Dogs and cats, cows and bulls, camels, two-toed things, sloths, bears, racoons, rabbits, weasels, and anything that stinks, like skunks, come under the rulership of Taurus.

GEMINIS will never subject a pet to isolation on purpose. But sometimes they need a friend to point this out, as Geminis always have a lot on their minds and can be unthinkingly mentally cruel. Just remind them that a pet needs somebody of its own species to talk to—that should do it! Apes, gorillas, hamsters, squirrels, and even ants fascinate them. Insects come under the rulership of Gemini. Perhaps their favorite creatures are birds, creatures that elicit all their tender feelings best. Bright, fidgety monkeys also come under Gemini, but a monkey would make most Geminis nervous as the two are too much alike.

CANCER people like furry things in need of protecting. Cats, bunny rabbits, and old faithful dogs tug at the old heartstrings. If the creature slobbers, so much the better. Crabs, lobsters, oysters, hippos, walruses, and armadillos appeal to them, and many Cancers relate well to tropical fish. They like to muck about with fish tanks, to ensure a nice "home" for their finny friends. Snails, too. They can watch them inch along and feel content. You have to watch them, though. They have a habit of crawling up to the ceiling and hanging there.

LEOS have a soft streak for any critter in distress, but given the choice they will choose a pet they can be proud of. It doesn't have to be the best breed, but a Leo has to feel that his pet is special, with extraordinary qualities. They are good to their animals, playing weird games with their pets, squashing down the cat's ears and making him cruise through the air like a Bonzai flyer. They adore cats, all cats—lions, tigers, cheetahs, pumas, and kitties.

VIRGOS prefer cats too, but this is due to their innate dislike of dirt and smells and to a rather cool attitude that wants the darned critter out of the way when there's work to do. They can be very happy with little turtles. They're fascinated by tiny things—other Virgos crawlies are porcupines, minks, squirrels, mice, rats, hamsters, rabbits, and bats. Yes, bats. Servile dogs work well with them. An ant farm is the closest thing to a Virgo's life—work, work, work! A flea circus is another timely gift idea, though Virgos are also phobic about cleanliness. If you ever need to get even with a Virgo, just tip the ant farm on its side and leave the honey jar open.

LIBRA is another cold sign when it comes to living with animals. They admire creatures most in their natural habitat, where they're happiest. Libras generally make their partners into their pets, and if the partner is doing his utmost to be a mature adult, *Libra* becomes the pet. Think I'm joking? Just try to remember how much fussing and errand running Libra requires. It is the only zodiac sign with a *machine* for a symbol. Tis true—their things are their pets—usually a camera or automobile. They're too involved with people to have much time to lavish on a creeping thing.

SCORPIO thinks hard before taking on the responsibility of a critter, but when they commit themselves, they are the best of masters. Typical animals for Scorpios include arachnids, frogs, bees, anything poisonous or with a stinger, weasels, gorillas, and scorpions, natch. Once in every Scorpio's life they get a fish tank. They like to play God in there, watching the cycle of birth, death, and gobbling up; when they tire of their fancies, which they usually do, they can coolly hand the beasts over to a new, kind, responsible owner. They think snakes and tame fuzzy tarantulas are cute; or maybe they like to watch other people's horrified reactions to the creepers.

SAGITTARIANS love their dogs and horses. They're not too good at correct feeding schedules, but they have hearts of gold for all beasts. This sign "rules" all large animals, one-toed things, whales, elephants, walruses, deer, hippos, giraffes. They go for quirky animals, like kangaroos. One Sagittarian I knew had an otter who ate nothing but chicken necks. He used to roll around on the sofa and swim in the bathtub. The otter did too.

Perhaps CAPRICORN has the most complex relationship with his pets of all the signs. People have disappointed them so often that they develop deep, caring relationships with their animals. Remember Nixon and his "Checkers" speech? Even the dog was put to work. Capricorns love it when the dog fetches the paper, but nothing tops the feeling of understanding Capricorn's experience when, Capricorn in the midst of a "black dog" depression, feels the sympathetic sniveling snout of his loyal bulldog on his kneecap. These stuffy, lonely people delight in exotic beasties. Perhaps they identify with the strange savage beauty of their sign's own creatures: iguanas, crocodiles, alligators, dinosaurs, lizards and the reptiles with legs, ants, and that most industrious of ambitious beasts, the beaver.

AQUARIUS doesn't like cats much. Cats are cold and don't need him, and that's Aquarius' game. He doesn't like it much when it's played on him. Give him at least a bright Siamese cat or a smart Labrador retriever. Aquarians love smart, loyal dogs who obey their every command. They have no time for dumb bunnies. Bears are also Aquarian—they're big and clumsy and always experimenting. Birds (they must be free, you see), bats, and pterodactyls are their other favorite thingies. If there's a beast in pain, trust Aquarius to calm it—he has a sixth sense with critters. It's the people he can't connect with.

Ah, PISCES, Pisces, what a softie you are. Your house may not smell so nice, but at least the strays have a place to stay, eh?

This sign will have a three-legged dog, a turtle kidnapped from a cruel owner, and always leaves a little milk out on the back porch for the froggie. Pisces rules the fishes, worms, legless slithering things, bacteria, night creatures, whales, elephants, dolphins, seals, sharks, and dogs that look like Walter Matthau. They like things that drool and things that go squish.

Enemies

This time they've gone too far. Drive any sign stark, slobbering loony in seconds by following this guide.

ARIES—Be kind to their enemies. Display no passion. Act like you don't *like* them.

TAURUS—Spend their money, eat their food, borrow stuff, don't return it, and tell them to hurry. Change the objects around in their house when they're not looking; just move everything a few inches from their normal spots.

GEMINI—Bore them to tears with long monologues about your emotional life. Don't talk to them at all. Monopolize them at a party so they can't move about and talk to anyone else.

CANCER—Insult their mothers. Criticize their homes; warn them that they might lose their jobs or that a highway is going to be built running through the house.

LEO—Teach them something they don't know about. Ignore them. Forget to introduce them. Chuckle at their taste.

VIRGO—*Whine* a lot. Mess up their homes, wreck their schedules, rip off the box tops, lose the cap to the toothpaste. Smell bad.

LIBRA—Say "It's up to you" a lot. Take them to ugly places. Act gross in public, wipe your nose on your sleeve in full view. Criticize their mates. Refuse to argue with them.

SCORPIO—Ask personal questions. Know too much. Be more successful than they are and don't brag about it; it kills them.

SAGITTARIUS—Give them lots of responsibility. Travel more than they do. Point up the lack of realism in their philosophies. Invite them to bogus social functions. Make them wear clothes they hate.

CAPRICORN—*You* organize everything—they feel useless. Remind them of their lowly position. Embarrass them in public.

AQUARIUS—Show off. Get personal and intimate. Insist they phone in thirteen times a day to inform you of their exact movements. Take them for granted.

PISCES—Tell them to get a grip on themselves, that they're wallowing in self-pity. Meet them in bright, noisy, crowded places, like the underground or Times Square.

Food

The sneakiest way to understand someone fast is to watch how
and what they eat. Nothing is more revealing except, perhaps,
how they go to the bathroom, which is disgusting and boring to
watch. With a few guidelines you can work out quickly what
will charm your dinner companions, or how to rid yourself of a
guest who has outstayed his welcome.

IF YOU KNOW THE BIRTHDAY ONLY: Look up their
zodiac sign below, and take it as a general guide.

IF YOU HAVE A COMPUTER CHART: Find the slice of pie
marked 6. This is the food box. Look at the sign on the cusp of
the sixth house and look up this sign instead of the Sun sign.

Next see if there are planets in the sixth house. Look them up,
too, below. Do they tell a contradictory story about your eating
habits? Now you know what the astrologer goes through when
reading a chart. People are contradictory.

ARIES OR MARS WITH THE SIXTH HOUSE

Hungry in a hurry, they always want their food NOW, on the
double. One is cautioned to feed them before their tempers
erupt—don't mess with them when they're starving. They like
bright colors on the plate, so don't forget to add the purple food
dye to their scrambled two—it cheers them up—and a couple of
green pickles on the side. They have an extreme aversion to, or
wildly adore, pizza, Chinese food, Indian curries, cauliflower,
celery, crunchy pickles, and most anything with unusual spices
and garlic.

They have no patience for a lot of preparation and burn things,
so many of them live on convenience foods. When the meal is
over, they want to push away from the table fast. Lingering over
congealed egg yolk is not their cuppa.

TAURUS OR VENUS WITH THE SIXTH HOUSE

Most people think that the symbol for Taurus is a bull's head with horns. Actually, it is a baked potato. Folks with this position crave all kinds of spuds—mashed, smashed, chips with everything, and the more the merrier. If you're out of potatoes, you had better pull out some starch—rice or noodles will do, even cold macaroni or potato salad. Simple food always succeeds with this lot. They are slow cooks and are so stubborn they will slow down if you try to rush them. Actually they are slow coaches in everything. They like a nice restaurant with booths or big soft chairs and big pig helpings. They eat vast quantities of food and like a full-bull feeling. It helps if you think of pigs or cave men. In any area of life where Taurus is concerned, they like meat and potatoes on the table and a comfortable body in the bed. They love simple gravies and sauces. They don't like sour cream.

GEMINI OR MERCURY WITH THE SIXTH HOUSE

You'd get jumpy too if you ran on your nerves as these folks do. They like small portions and prefer to choose their foods from a buffet. They need variety, else they ain't hungry. Most of them like at least two drinks at a meal, at the same time too. They are fiends for salad and raw crunchies. I once actually witnessed a Gemini being seduced by a big avocado salad. (It was the most beautiful pear he had ever seen.) The Eastern custom of many different dishes at the same time relaxes these creatures; they don't then feel intimidated or bored and can pick and choose at will. If you set it up like a smorgasbord, they will return, birdlike, to the groaning board again and again. As cooks they will invariably surprise you, pouring jam and orange juice over the ham, mixing frozen vegetables with the eggs.

CANCER OR THE MOON WITH THE SIXTH HOUSE

Start out with nice hot buns and then a soup to comfort them. Goulash, stew, lasagne, and anything thick and hot and *motherly* should turn the trick. They're not all that turned on by a lot of foreign muck. When they're sick, find out what Mother used to make for them and, by God, make it. They are childish about food, and at times it's hard to get them to leave their homes. Promise them a nice home-cooked meal at your place. Better yet, let *them* cook for you and you bring the wine. That assures them they'll get to eat what they want. They're good cooks—the best! I used to visit with an elderly friend who had lost most of her sight, hearing, and mobility. I brought her Cheddar, crackers, and fruit yogurts. One day her face lit up as if illumined. "You know, dearie," she shouted, "I think God is *cheese*." They are terrified of starving to death. They will even finish your food for you at a fancy restaurant if no one taught them otherwise.

LEO OR THE SUN WITH THE SIXTH HOUSE

Let them take you out. Let them cook their gourmet dishes for you. These golden hearts love to show off, so don't accept their dinner invitation if you know they're broke. They spend a fortune on goodies. Here are your natural gourmets, and they'll start with sherry and finish with brandy and cigars if they can. Flaming dishes like Cherries Jubilee or Christmas Pudding sway them into a reverent frame of mind. They don't care what they eat as long as it's *extraordinary*—these folks suffer an identity crisis unless you fuss. Dining out, they will inform the waiter if something is wrong with the meal; like true royalty they do not make the servants feel small in the telling. If you're cooking them dinner, croon over them, stick them at the head of the table, and pop a paper parasol in their beer. Bow low before them as you present their beans on toast.

VIRGO OR MERCURY WITH THE SIXTH HOUSE

The food bore. A hand-pottered bowl of brown rice and a bottle of organic apple juice sends these poor buggers into paroxysms of ecstasy. They're easy to please, though; a cheap health food joint impresses them. Spices send them on an eight-hour acid trip. They will happily munch their lives away on Granola and yogurt. Admittedly, it's the healthiest of diets. They are fussy, so find out first if they have any food preferences. They're ashamed of how finicky they are, and they should be; if you want to coddle them, you must devote time on drawing these shy folks out about their likes and dislikes. Offer Vitamin C tablets as a special after-dinner treat and watch them light up like neon signs.

LIBRA OR VENUS WITH THE SIXTH HOUSE

See Taurus, but with fewer potatoes. Snobs they are; they're delighted to eat with chopsticks or with only the right hand in an Indian restaurant. They're peculiar with food they think is squishy or squidgy; they love or hate Japanese and Chinese dishes. Eating alone depresses them; at those times they grab a sandwich and feel sorry for themselves. Libra's life is comprised of little touches, so place a pot of chutney or Worchestershire sauce on the table. Librans like mayonnaise; they love desserts that combine two or more textures, like raspberries and ice cream, zabaglione with a cookie, or a box of Twinkies. It makes them feel sexy to handle pretty silverware and goblets. If the view is good from the dining room, so much the better. If they cook for you, they'll add the sprig of parsley on the side and doctor the beans with herbs. It's the only sign I know that can make spinach taste like the Elysian Fields.

SCORPIO OR PLUTO WITH THE SIXTH HOUSE

Who's afraid of garlic or sushi? Not this bunch. They regard food with utter detachment or burning zeal. This group doesn't mind starving all day until the fish restaurant opens, if fish is what they fancy. They're the same in love. Movies are a delight with them, as you can hold the Dots up to the screen and give them all the black ones; they love licorice. Mushrooms, sour foods, spices, and booze make up their favorite meals. Oddly, they believe they need massive lumps of protein to survive, wolfing down eggs, cheese, milk, and meat as if they were preparing for World War III. They are. If one of this lot goes vegetarian, give him full marks for conquering his insatiable food lust. Take him to someplace sleazy or dark to eat. No tofu or alfalfa sprouts should be served at any time.

SAGITTARIUS OR JUPITER WITH THE SIXTH HOUSE

Bring in the dump truck, fellas! We'll need it to carry lunch in for this crew. They love food, but they love it a million times more if you tell 'em jokes and stories at the table. A weird guilt complex compels them to serve small portions when you visit them; they can't stop eating, so they think they're doing you a favor by cutting down for you. They'll eat you out of house and home when they're over by you, so hide your smallest children

. . . nothing is safe when they're hungry. They adore Mexican and Spanish food, with the rice and the shrimps and the shells all making a merry clatter on the plate. Anything expensive, untried, or foreign in the food department delights them, the more elegant the better. Barbequed food is their favorite, as it's cooked in their world, out of doors.

CAPRICORN OR SATURN WITH THE SIXTH HOUSE

More than other eaters, these guys have to be good to themselves at mealtimes because they put their hearts and souls into their work, and it's work that extracts every drop of blood. Vitamins should be the habit and not the whim. They like grim, no-nonsense cafeterias with low prices and *hot food*. Dairy products give them comfort and sustenance now that Mummy and Daddy aren't there to feed them, and they can gulp down three lemon yogurts before the meal begins.

They're funny about food. If you arrive unexpectedly, they'll count out what noodles they have and share them with you, no matter how poor they are. Of course, there is another side to their natures; one Capricorn got caught sneaking the only Granola bar into the closet and eating it in there when she thought no one was looking. Don't stick them with Cote de Veau a la Sauge Lyonnaise—even the millionaires would rather dig boil-in-the-bag broccoli and a hamburger with french fries. If you're going there for dinner, bring a dessert. They often omit this course as they think it's frivolous. Cold food is bad for them, as is gloom or work talk at dinner. Most of these people will shyly try caviar, 100-year-old Benedictine and champagne truffles if you force them to give up their usual monotonous fare. If you're entertaining them, try sewing Gucci labels on the ravioli.

AQUARIUS OR URANUS WITH THE SIXTH HOUSE

Let them loose at the salt lick for a couple of days. They love salt, even if it's not so good for them.

Haphazard gourmets is what they are; they like weird food and are terribly sensitive to all the nuances of what they eat. Many of them live in restaurants, hate breakfast, and would rather not cook except as recreation. When they bother, they are spectacular chefs, and it's usually foreign fare. They throw tantrums in restaurants mainly because when they're hungry it's sudden, and they can't help turning into Jaws. They had weird eating habits in childhood, and when grown up they'll go *miles* for the food they crave. They can live on sardines and Boursin for days; then they go on runs of root beer and brown rice and Marlboros. They'll survive; they believe that if the food makes them happy, the mind will keep them healthy, and generally it does. As Aquarius or Uranus anywhere in the chart indicates thinking ahead of one's time, many of these people are vegetarians. They don't like killing.

PISCES OR NEPTUNE WITH THE SIXTH HOUSE

Picture them on the terrace at sunset, gazing at nature while they put away a refined meal of fresh fish, and you'll have these folks clocked. The stuff doesn't go down into their bellies right unless they feel soothed when they eat. They prefer seafood, particularly oysters and salmon, to red meat. Champagne, soda pop, and beer please them more than any other drinks; they just love those bubbles!

Turn them on with food just grabbed from the field, still warm from the sun. Turn them off with a meal where all the food is the same color; undercook and overboil the main ingredients, and make them feel guilty if they don't clean every bit off their plates. They'll never darken your doorstop again. They don't want you to think they're vulgarians, so they'll never tell you their awful secret: they love to listen to Muzak while they eat.

Gifts

Waesuck! What does one get for the battle-ax's Halloween present? A crate of dead bats for a Scorpio? A rubber woman for an Aquarius?

Most of us give presents that *we* like. Unless your friends are irredeemable clots, this is the *wrong* way to give gifts.

You give them what *they* want, of course. If you feel lazy, just look up the things that go with their Sun sign. If you do have a computer chart, look at the sign on the second house cusp and give them *that* stuff instead.

Give to their Sun, their Moon, ascendant or Venus sign. It's hard to go wrong with the Venus sign, especially when you're trying to pick out a *color*.

ARIES—They can't wait, so don't tell them you have a present for them. Aries are great readers, but somehow they just cannot decipher "Do Not Open Til Christmas" labels. If you tell them, they will pester you until you are out of your mind, so always hide something for the Big Day or they will crumple up like tissue paper if there's nothing to look forward to.

A pure Aries type hates antiques and old stuff. They like new vibes. Don't read the book or feel the thing before you give it—they have to be the first owner. *Your* old stuff is okay to give them, they like *you*. Never give old clothes, unless they are yours. Someone could have *died* in them, for Gawd's sake.

Most of them love glass, especially diamonds. Custom-made things, or things that appeal directly to their egos, work well. Those tacky placemats with a smiling lion or dog or something that has their name on the top might be just the ticket. I had the misfortune once to have a lodger, an Aries slip of a girl built like the Nimitz, who insisted on sticking her orange plastic "April's Room" sign up on the Victorian door.

Their colors are red, black and white, and see-thru.

Not one of them will ever tell you this, but you'd better wrap it in magic-looking paper. These babies never really forgive you if you don't wrap it up properly. *Shiny* paper is best, with lots of ribbon. They will love an old used gumball if you wrap it right.

TAURUS—You don't have to give the gift on time, and you may combine Christmas with birthday presents if you like. In fact you should, for they go for quality and the expensive stuff.

Pay particular attention to texture. There is nothing ruder than a Taurus who paws the object and finds it wanting. Things have to feel good or smell good. Avoid polyester *anything*. They are snobs about texture and can spot the best every time.

Outrageous foods, like champagne truffles, will do nicely while you're saving up to get them that Rolls Royce. Dinner at a hearty restaurant that serves potatoes is a safe gift. Flowers always choke them up.

Every Taurus would rather receive things as presents than experiences, though breaking out of the rut is good for them. They see things as symbols of what you feel about them; you will have to hunt endlessly for the right gift.

Expect them to act a little disappointed when they receive your gift. It's a cover-up. They're embarrassed by their own greed. They seem to choose better gifts than the gifts they get. Such is the ephemeral pleasure of the material world. Colors are pastels and any shade of blue.

GEMINI—What a joy to shop for these people! Geminis bore easily and are interested in *everything*. They are modest and don't like to show to people how important the day is, so don't be late or these sensitive, nervy souls feel lost.

They are too bright to care about the wrapping. Ostentatious wrapping quite frightens them, and they're jumpy enough. It really doesn't matter if you wrap the thing or not, but do stick it in a bag so there's a five-second mystery.

Green and yellow are their favorites; they like all bright colors and loathe murky shades.

It's best to give them a collection of assorted little gifts. They like this grab-bag effect and are thrilled to bits when there's a variety of prezzies.

Jokey items tickle the Twins. The kids like magic tricks. They like neckwear, especially colored beads and scarves. All Geminis like seashells. Yo-yos that run well. Books, books, books, and magazine subscriptions. Theater tickets. Gift certificates for new services or shops. Take them to the best salad joint in town. If you're not in town, a telegram gives them a monster of a buzz.

CANCER—Wrap the thing up nicely in icky flowered paper if you wish to serve their sentimental streak. Be sure to give them a soppy card as well. Cancers are so mushy and moodily insecure that they save these cards way past the occasion. They pull them out and look at them sometimes. Give them a photograph of you.

Make their world soft. Clothes do. They are partial to shawls and ponchos. They love to get gifts for the home. Candles, cooking stuff, bedspreads, quilts, *extra* pillows, antique jewelry. Anything old or antique does fine with these guys.

Watch them get misty when you give them something from your own family, or something from you with a "story" connected with it.

Come to think of it, a bag of groceries makes a most unusual gift this time of year . . . or a grand meal out on the town. God and food are One to these children of the Moon. Even a great lump of green cheese will do, so long's you don't forget the card.

Cancer colors can all be found on the inside of the shell of an abalone.

LEO—Better make it big. Even if you're broke, make a big fuss of them. Always err on the side of flamboyance. Gold gift wrap, big ribbons, and royal treatment are the least they deserve.

Vain about their manes, they are generally happy to receive things for their hair. You can't fail with good time presents. This would include theater tickets, a luxurious dinner, a bop out to a nightclub, records, tapes, or a singing telegram. You might consider giving your local starving astrologer a break—we have to eat too you know!—and give your Leo a gift horoscope reading. Leo gets its ego bathed in attention—always a plus with this crew—and Leo may well get a bit of the guidance it's too proud to ask for.

I know it sounds hokey, but their favorite color really is gold. Flame reds, blazing oranges, and dead blacks bring out the dramatic beast in their souls. They like kimonos. They like lions, a lot.

Give them a lot of love and attention. That's the best present you can give them. Laugh at their old jokes.

Go wild. Be a devil. Give them a mug with their name on it. Or a mirror.

VIRGO—Little Miss and little Mister Fussbudget will surprise you here. They're not at all fussy about what you give them. Sweet humble souls! A casual meal will do nicely, if you cook it yourself. They get nervous if they think you've spent a lot of money on them, so simple, well-researched gifts are best.

Cult magazines fascinate them. Get them subscriptions to *Mother Earth News, The Economist, Vampire Monthly, Mother Jones.* They love those how-to psychology books, especially those on body language, behind the scenes in politics or advertising, books that sharpen their analytic skills.

They love natural fibers, woven things, and baskets. A basket filled with flowers and assorted weirdnesses from the health food store starts them oohing and aahing.

Virgos like functional colors. To me electric blue is highly useful—it makes my eyeballs pop out of their sockets when I wake up in the afternoon—but to these guys functional means brown, cream, wheat, khaki. You know, the colors brown rice comes in.

See their sweet soft humble eyes light up when you give them a calculator or a computer game.

LIBRA—Ach, we're back to *cards* again. Libras love romance, and they simply must have a flowery card. Say something squooshy on it. Say something squooshy on the flyleaf of the book, too.

Make sure they have a partner or friend to be with on the day. The kind that jumps out of a cake at you is best, but you'll do fine.

Oddly, they don't make a big deal out of special days but they feel it inside. Flowers, clothes, and jewelry are their favorites. For the girls: art, a cameo on a black velvet ribbon, makeup, and perfume. For the boys: booze glasses, crystal, a transistor radio, or maybe a nice gold disco chain.

Their colors are pastels, especially pink and mauve, blues and purples, and, weirdly, red.

SCORPIO—These birds are so hard to shop for that I asked the Magus to give us the dirt on what a real double Scorpio wants to receive. I do not wish to be held responsible for the suggestions here.

"They can pull it out of a brown paper bag," he said with a leer. "The wrapping is so quickly forgotten.

"Carte blanche at a whorehouse relieves us of guilt, because we can't refuse the gift. Dig up a girl. We like a bit of cheesecake."

"Sir," I importuned, "What if the man is *married*?"

"Probably then give him dirty pictures of his wife," said the Magus.

"What if he's *old*?" I persisted.

"Probably a *young* girlfriend," said he with a faint sneer of contempt.

"Anything else?" I said.

"Oh, a 300-foot yacht, a 707, waterbeds, firecrackers, rifles, booze, rock-'n'-roll, a chemistry set, books on the occult, a mushroom kit, anything with a mystery in it . . ."

"That makes you guys pretty hard to shop for."

"There's really no way to tell, Kempton."

"What about colors, then?" I pleaded.

"Black and blue." (Actually, maroon and poison green are good too.)

"Is there any guiding philosophy one should bear in mind whilst shopping for you?"

"Just remember—a Scorpio respects consistency."

"Thank you."

"Don't mention it."

Mots amoku, pyyzer toevoo. (Good luck.)

SAGITTARIUS—Things that glow in the dark. Driving gloves. Beach towels. Sporting equipment. Tickets to games. Practical joke kits. Horse books. Lottery tickets. Whiskey. Space stuff. Magazine subscriptions. A real show-stopper: something smashing to wear that they look good in because *you* picked it out, not them. They like some foreign things and hate others. Depends on the country. Find out.

They always need another baggy sweater.

Their colors are purple, royal and dark blue, and white.

They like to party. Constantly.

CAPRICORN—Take them to your club.

Scheme-your-way-to-the-top books, people-watching books, body-language books are required reading for these lonely souls if they're ever going to stop being lonely. Biographies appeal to them, as Capricorns are always comparing themselves with their "betters." Ensure that the subject of the biography lived a twisted, miserable life. This makes Capricorns feel better.

Goats are easy to shop for. They like the best, or what people think is the best: Gucci, Chanel, Vuitton, Rolls Royce are a few brand names to remember.

They *need* a massage, but you must force them by giving them a massage gift certificate. They get depressed, so a balloon will cheer them up for a couple of hours. For colors see Virgo, but add dark green, black, and silver. Gray is often their favorite. It goes with the complexion.

Stuff that will help them with their work will impress them the most; a briefcase or a filing cabinet will give them endless hours of delight.

AQUARIUS—Find out what the current passion is first. They always have at least one peculiar hobby. Ask them what they like; they have a ready, mile-long list in their heads if they can only remember where they put it.

Gizmos excite them, anything in good humor and good taste. Try pyramids, Chinese cooking tools, beanbag chairs, robots, and things made out of modern materials like acrylic. They love velcro and zippers. Break out and get 'em a boxful. They like to build their own ships, and gardens in a bottle will keep them happily crazed.

Aquarian colors are shocking shades, white, blue, yellow sometimes, green always, and *stripes*.

Toss a dirty book or magazine in with their present. They do need reminding they're made of flesh from time to time. All those robots, you understand.

PISCES—Magic is what they want every time, and they want it *bad*. Give these sensationalists what they want!

Clothes should be velvety, chiffony, soft, and flowing. Or give them things to sniff and sip to make them feel that way. I've never met a Pisces who did not find delight in turning his or her brains to custard on the crest of some aesthetic experience. So take them out to a place with a view or to a pub full of groovers grooving; drag them to a gypsy to get their fortune read; give them candles, incense, good luck charms, a magic looking glass, they like glass, and movies and the cha-cha-cha. Peacock feathers appeal to them, and those are their colors, plus purple.

You can give them poetry and mystical books. They love the pre-Raphaelite period of painting and old, whimsical music—Irish folk tunes, the Incredible String Band and medieval music. If your Pisces pal is shy, give him or her a pair of dark glasses or a floppy hat. They like coconuts.

Astrology
and Health

See your doctor.

If you need an operation, follow two rules:

One, look up the times when you will be under a good Moon in the RED LIGHTS, GREEN LIGHTS tables. You heal faster near your good Moon. Avoid surgery on your low Moon.

Two, avoid operations when the Moon in the sky is in the sign that "rules" the bit of your body that needs repair. If, for example, you are going in for foot surgery, don't do it when the Moon is in Pisces, which "rules" the feet. If you are a Pisces and that's your good Moon, get it done *near but not on* the Pisces Moon. And don't let them operate when the Moon will be void of course.

Follow the above rules and you'll get well sooner than average. Give yourself the best shot and you'll be pleased with the results.

Bits of the body ruled by the signs:

ARIES—Face, sinuses, brain, eyes, ears, and all the things that hang on your head.

TAURUS—Throat, tonsils, glands in the neck, larynx.

GEMINI—Allergies, mouth, arms, hands, lungs, nervous system.

CANCER—Stomach, digestive system, body fluids, lymph glands, gooshy bits in your middle.

LEO—Circulatory system, heart, spine.

VIRGO—Intestines, some lymph glands, assimilative system.

LIBRA—Kidneys, female sex organs, skin, adrenal glands.

SCORPIO—Male sex organs, eliminative system.

SAGITTARIUS—Thighs, sciatic nerves, hips, arteries, liver.

CAPRICORN—Bones, back, spine, knees, teeth.

AQUARIUS—Calves and ankles, Achilles tendon, circulatory system.

PISCES—Feet, alimentary canal, glands, body fluids.

Astrologers are not doctors, yet doctors still take the Hippocratic Oath and Hippocrates was an astrologer. One day soon some foundation or university someplace will cough up the money to run the charts of ten thousand heart attack victims through a computer; we'll be able to see and predict the weak links in a person's body through the horoscope. Clues to the mystery of DNA are in the horoscope, but we badly need research before we can begin to practice preventive medicine using astrology.

In the meantime, many doctors ask the advice of prominent psychics when they're baffled by a medical problem. It's one of the best-kept secrets of the century, and while scientists don't broadcast this practice for fear of being shunned by the medical establishment, top doctors and surgeons don't make it to the top by having closed minds. You would recognize some of these brilliant men's names.

Horary:
Burning Questions

Got a question? Do you want all the fine details? Horary is the branch of astrology where you make a chart for the time you asked the question.

Pick up the books by William Lilly, Barbara Watters, and Geraldine Davis on horary and study them for five years or so. Then go back to your chart and question. By then you will be well-versed enough in horary to have a correct answer, or at least it won't matter anymore. It's a tough study, horary, and you'd do better to go to an astrologer with a background in horary than try to do it yourself. A good one will cost you.

Personally, I prefer the I Ching. It's fast, wise, cheap, and there are no ugly logarithms to do. The Ching is the sneakiest book you will ever buy. The more you use it, the less you need it. You may not like what it says to you, but it cannot fail to give wise advice and make us wiser in the process. Even when the damned book gives you the *opposite* response you'd expect, it stirs you up to do more of your own original thinking. The uncanny book is like a mirror—it mocks you, soothes you, questions you, puzzles you, guides you, but it's better than having a twenty-four hour guru service because you can shut it up whenever you want to.

Still want to take a crack at horary? We'll get you started.

"Will I marry Custis?" Fast! Now! Note down what time it is. Is it British Summer Time, Daylight Savings Time, Yukon Time; in other words, what kind of time are they observing in the place you're asking the question? You'll need this information.

Write that question down. Will I marry Custis differs from *should* I, or will Custis marry me, or will he ask, or what would be like to be married to him? The horary is a precision tool for prediction—define your question exactly. Keep it simple.

Now, send the shebang out to the computer—time, place, day, month, and year—and wait for it to come back. Haul out the books and weep. Horary is hard, but you'll win if you keep at it. Try the following hot tips instead:

1) Is the Moon void of course? You can check this out, now, in the RED LIGHTS, GREEN LIGHTS tables.

If the Moon's not void, you can advance to the next rule. If the Moon *is* void, *stop right there*. The chart is not "fit to read." Don't look at me—I didn't make these succotash rules. Something is wrong with the question. Faulty judgment is at work. It may seem harsh, but the question will be irrelevant in the long run. The stars want you to forget the issue or at least put it to one side at the moment. Other factors are at work. For all we know, Custis is at this very moment saying "I do" to that red-hot mama he met at Interferon, or maybe you really know that you can't possibly marry Custis because the children would look like toads.

2) Now you're ready for the computer chart. Look at the degree on the rising sign.

Is it zero, one, two, or three degrees of whatever sign rising? Anything up to three degrees is "too soon to tell." You still have a great proportion of free will to influence events.

Forget the rest of the too-soon-to-tell chart. It's not valid to read it; too much is still hanging in the air. Place the chart on the bottom of the birdcage and paint your toenails in the colors Custis likes, instead.

Is the rising sign 27, 28, or 29 degrees plus? Anything from 27 degrees on to zero means "it is already too late." A Philadelphia client came for a horary. Her sister had just died. The girl wanted to know if it was a suicide. The chilling answer came back with a late-degree rising sign: the chart unfit to read. "It is already too late" was the stars' way of protecting the client from the answer, negative or positive. The stars wanted her to put the matter behind her, and for her, maturity's toughest lesson would be learning to live with an unanswered question for the rest of her life.

So the Moon isn't void; the rising sign degrees aren't too soon or too late; you're sitting there with the astrologer waiting for the answer, and the astrologer says Saturn is in the seventh house. This usually means the *astrologer* is not fit to read the chart.

```
PLANET SIGN   LONG    HSE
SUN    Gem   5 51 10   7
MOON F Scp   2 40 30  11
MERC R Gem  21 15.3    7
VENU   Can   2 29.7R   8
MARS   Vir   7 58.4    9
JUPI D Vir   1 37.5    9
SATU   Vir  20 12.6   10
URAN E Scp  23  1.8R  12
NEPT   Sag  21 43.9R   1
PLUT   Lib  19 15.6R  11
ASC    Sag   2 35.0    1
MC     Vir  18 34.6   10
NODE*  Leo  23 44.1    9
PFOR   Ari  29 24.4
VERTEX Can  16 40.3
EASTPT Sag  20 20.9
   R=RULE    D=DETRIMENT
   E=EXALTED F=FALL
   *TRUE NODE
```

```
     CARD FIX MUT
FIRE   0   0   1      4 | 5
EARTH  0   0   3
AIR    1   0   2      1 | 0
WATER  1   2   0
```

*** NATAL ASPECTS ***

	ANGLE	ORB		ANGLE	ORB
CON=CONJUNCTION	0	10	TRI=TRINE	120	10
SSX=SEMISEXTILE	30	3	SQQ=SESQUIQUAD	135	4
SSQ=SEMI-SQUARE	45	4	BQT=BIQUINTILE	144	3
SXT=SEXTILE	60	6	QCX=QUINCUNX	150	3
QTL=QUINTILE	72	3	OPP=OPPOSITION	180	10
SQR=SQUARE	90	10	/ =PARALLEL OR	0	1
A=APPLYING S=SEPARATING			CONTRAPARALLEL		

	SUN	MOON	MERCURY	VENUS	MARS	JUPITER
MOON	BQT 2 49S	MOON				
MERC		SSQ 3 35A	MERCURY			
VENU		TRI 0 11S		VENUS		
MARS	SQR 2 07A	SXT 5 18A		SXT 5 29S	MARS	
JUPI	SQR 4 14S	SXT 1 03S	QTL 1 38S	SXT 0 52A	CON 6 21S	JUPITER
SATU		SSQ 2 32A	SQR 1 03S			
URAN			QCX 1 47A			SQR 8 36
NEPT	/		OPP 0 29A			TRI 9 54
PLUT	SSQ 1 36S	/	TRI 1 60S		SSQ 3 43S	SSQ 2 38
ASC	OPP 3/16	SSX 0 05		QCX 0 05	SQR 5 23	SQR 0 57
MC		SSQ 0 54	SQR 2 41			
NODE			SXT 2 29			CON 7 53

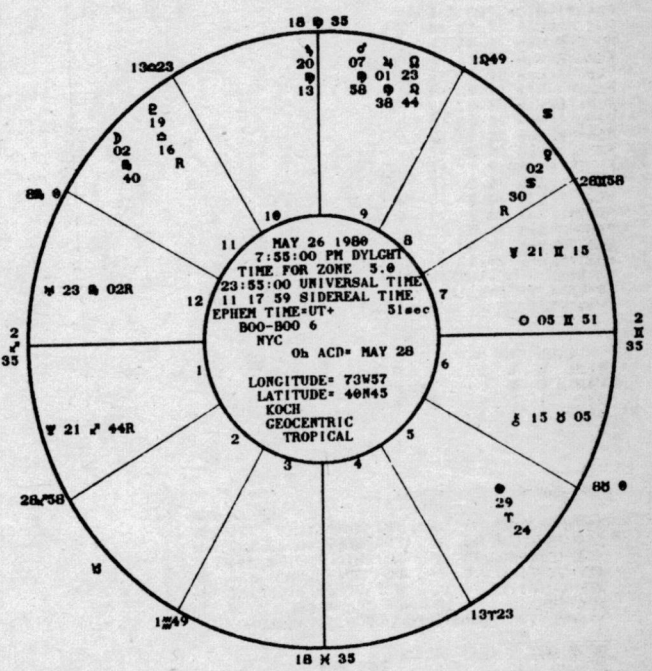

"Will I Marry Custis?"

	SATURN	URANUS	NEPTUNE	PLUTO	ASC	MC
SXT 2 49A						
SQR 1 31A	SSX 1 18A					
SSX 0 57S		SXT 2 28A				
QTL 0 22	CON 9 33		SSQ 1 41			
CON 1 38	SXT 4 27	SQR 3 09	SSX 0 41	QTL 2 00		
	SQR 0 42	TRI 2 00	SXT 4 29	SQR 8 51		

PLANET		SIGN	LONG	HSE
SUN		Scp	14 37 18	12
MOON		Gem	28 24 54	8
MERC	D	Sag	5 33.2	1
VENU		Sag	3 56.5	1
MARS		Leo	24 11.6	9
JUPI	D	Vir	6 39.8	9
SATU		Vir	23 56.5	10
URAN	E	Scp	20 53.4	12
NEPT		Sag	18 56.7	1
PLUT		Lib	20 7.9	11
ASC		Scp	28 36.2	1
MC		Vir	8 52.9	10
NODE*		Vir	5 43.3	9
PFOR		Can	12 23.8	
VERTEX		Can	16 40.2	
EASTPT		Sag	11 59.4	

R=RULE D=DETRIMENT
E=EXALTED F=FALL
*TRUE NODE

	CARD	FIX	MUT		
FIRE	0	1	3		
EARTH	0	0	2	4	3
AIR	1	0	1	3	0
WATER	0	2	0		

*** NATAL ASPECTS ***

	ANGLE	ORB			ANGLE	ORB
CON=CONJUNCTION	0	10		TRI=TRINE	120	10
SSX=SEMISEXTILE	30	3		SQQ=SESQUIQUAD	135	4
SSQ=SEMI-SQUARE	45	4		BQT=BIQUINTILE	144	3
SXT=SEXTILE	60	6		QCX=QUINCUNX	150	3
QTL=QUINTILE	72	3		OPP=OPPOSITION	180	10
SQR=SQUARE	90	10		/ =PARALLEL OR	0	1

A=APPLYING S=SEPARATING   =CONTRAPARALLEL

	SUN	MOON	MERCURY	VENUS	MARS	JUPITER
MOON	SSQ 1 12A	MOON				
MERC			MERCURY			
VENU			CON 1 37A	VENUS		
MARS	SQR 9 34A	SXT 4 13S		SQR 9 45S	MARS	
JUPI			SQR 1 07A	SQR 2 43A		JUPITER
SATU		SQR 4 28S	QTL 0 23A	QTL 1 60A	SSX 0 15S	
URAN	CON 6 16A	BQT 1 31S			SQR 3 16S	QTL 2 14A
NEPT		OPP 9 28S		/	TRI 5 15S	
PLUT		TRI 8 17S	SSQ 0 25S	SSQ 1 11A	SXT 4 04S	SSQ 1 32S
ASC		QCX 0 11	CON 6 57	CON 5 20	SQR 4 25	SQR 8 04
MC	SXT 5 44	QTL 1 32	SQR 3 20	SQR 4 56		CON 2 13
NODE			SQR 0 10	SQR 1 47		CON 0 57

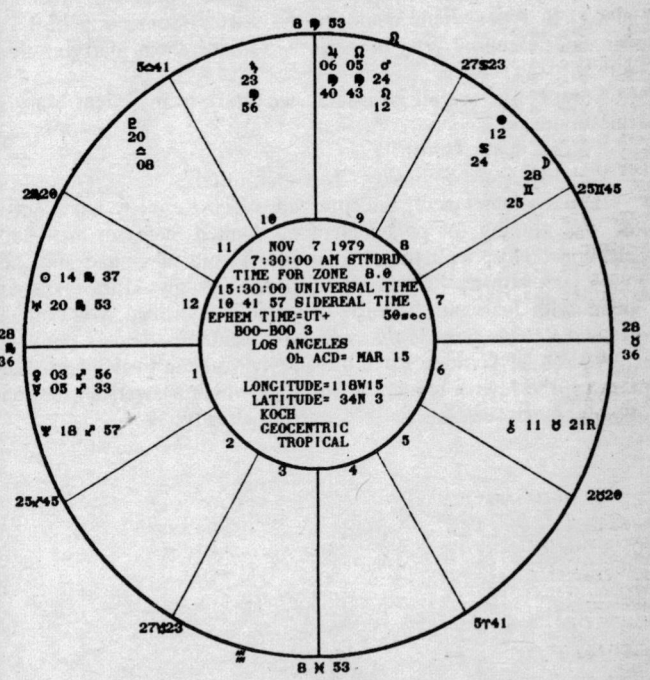

8 ♍ 53

5 ♎ 41

27 ♋ 23

♃ ☊
06 05   ♂
♃ ♀ 24
40 43   ☊
12

♇
20
♎ 08

12
♄ 24

28
♊ 25

28 ♍ 20

10

11

9

8

25 ♋ 45

NOV 7 1979
7:30:00 AM STNDRD
TIME FOR ZONE 8.0
15:30:00 UNIVERSAL TIME
10 41 57 SIDEREAL TIME
EPHEM TIME=UT+   50sec
BOO-BOO 3
0h ACD= MAR 15

☉ 14 ♏ 37
♆ 20 ♏ 53

7

28
♉ 36

28 ♌
36

☿ 03 ♐ 56
♋ 05 ♐ 33

LONGITUDE=118W15
LATITUDE= 34N 3
KOCH
GEOCENTRIC
TROPICAL

6

♄ 11 ♉ 21R

♀ 18 ♐ 57

1

2

3   4

5

28 ♉ 20

25 ♐ 45

27 ♐ 23

5 ♈ 41

♅
8 ♓ 53

Ted Announces

SATURN					
SXT 3 03S	URANUS				
SQR 4 60S	SSX 1 57S	NEPTUNE			
	SSX 0 46S	SXT 1 11S	PLUTO	ASC	
SXT 4 40	CON 7 43				
	QTL 0 01		SSQ 3/45		MC
			SSQ 0 35	SQR 7 07	CON 3 10

When a good soothsayer sees Saturn here, they usually forget the whole deal.

Go back to the RED LIGHTS, GREEN LIGHTS tables and see what sign the Moon is in. Aquarius is a freedom sign. Perhaps the woman in question would be better off breezing along. In Aries? This could be the start of something big! In Pisces or Gemini? Why is she in two minds about marrying this guy?

Now, before we all go insane, we return to my client Mary's question;

"Will I marry Curtis?"

We shall see, baby-cakes. Too soon to tell.

Here's another gem, the time when Ted Kennedy announced he was running for president of the United States in the 1980 elections. Note well the elegant Moon void of course and the "too late, already" rising sign degree. You should have stayed home with Joan and the kids, choochie-pie! Instead, you helped Ronald Reagan win. Is *that* what you wanted?

And no, if you don't like the answer you can't ask again. For *horary*, the Jewish branch of astrology which answers a question with another question, once is enough already.

Horoscopes of Nations

*"THERE IS NO PITY FOR THOSE WHO DO NOT
SEEK LISA'S HELP. 46200 EAST 55 STREET. OPEN
9 AM to 9 PM. SPECIALIZING IN SAND AND WAX
READINGS. AVAILABLE FOR SOCIAL
GATHERINGS."*

—Sign in a telephone booth

I got news for you, Lisa . . . there is precious little pity for any of us slobbering, ragged mortals on the third stone from the Sun. If you want to scare yourself witless, honey, study the horoscopes of nations and the poor politicians who try to run them. Put the sand away like a good child and start lighting those candles.

Consider, for example, the chart of Indira Gandhi. Regardez the Moon void of course, and in Capricorn. It is hard to predict how a Moon void person will react to any outside stimulus, though a Capricorn Moon is, shall we say, tenacious of power? Mrs. Gandhi has lucky old Jupiter in the public image box (tenth house). She is popular with the masses, relying on the famous short memory of the public.

Mundane astrology is a special branch of soothsaying, as brain surgery is to medicine. We study the maps of eclipses, equinoxes, prime ministers and nations, making predictions where we can. The biggest problem is getting accurately timed 'scopes; who really knows when a nation began or if the president is lying? We'd be better predictors if we had better data, but we have sneaky ways of getting data: we write letters, hit the library, and look at our watches when there's a revolution. The charts of nations here are *known to work;* there are other charts for these nations, but these are generally acknowledged to be the cream of the crop. I don't care what Dane Rudhyar said, America's got Gemini rising! Check it out.

Spare yourself the rules of mundane astrology, unless you've

```
PLANET SIGN   LONG   HSE
SUN      Scp 26 50 23  4
MOON  D  Cpr 28 18 11  6
MERC  D  Sag  5 57.1   4
VENU     Cpr 13 43.1   5
MARS     Vir  9 .5.7   1
JUPI  D  Gem  7 43.0R 10
SATU  D  Leo 14 30.1  12
URAN  R  Aqu 19 58.0   6
NEPT     Leo  7  5.0R 12
PLUT     Can  5 10.4R 11
ASC      Leo 20  4.4   1
MC       Tau 17 43.5  10
NODE*    Cpr  1 55.1   5
PFOR     Lib 21 32.2
VERTEX   Sag 15 18.6
EASTPT   Leo 12 47.6
  R=RULE     D=DETRIMENT
  E=EXALTED  F=FALL
   *TRUE NODE
```

```
     CARD FIX MUT
FIRE   0   2   1       4 | 0
EARTH  2   0   1         |
AIR    0   1   1       1 | 5
WATER  1   1   0
```

```
        *** NATAL ASPECTS ***
              ANGLE ORB                    ANGLE ORB
CON=CONJUNCTION    0  10    TRI=TRINE        120  10
SSX=SEMISEXTILE   30   3    SQQ=SESQUIQUAD   135   4
SSQ=SEMI-SQUARE   45   4    BQT=BIQUINTILE   144   3
SXT=SEXTILE       60   6    QCX=QUINCUNX     150   3
QTL=QUINTILE      72   3    OPP=OPPOSITION   180  10
SQR=SQUARE        90  10    / =PARALLEL OR   0   1
A=APPLYING  S=SEPARATING    CONTRAPARALLEL
```

	SUN	MOON	MERCURY	VENUS	MARS	JUPITER
MOON	SXT 1 28S	MOON				
MERC	CON 9 07S		MERCURY			
VENU	SSQ 1 53S			VENUS		
MARS				SQR 3 09A	TRI 4 37S	MARS
JUPI		TRI 9 25A		OPP 1 46A	BQT 0 00S	SQR 1 23S	JUPITER
SATU				TRI 8 33A	QCX 0 47A	
URAN	SQR 6 52S			QTL 2 01A		
NEPT			OPP 8/47A	TRI 1 08A		SSX 2 01S	SXT 0 38A
PLUT		BQT 2/20A	/	QCX 0 47S	OPP 8 33S	SXT 3 55S	SSX 2 33A
ASC		SQR 6 46			BQT 0 21		QTL 0 21
MC		OPP 9 07			TRI 4 00	TRI 8 38	
NODE						TRI 7 11	

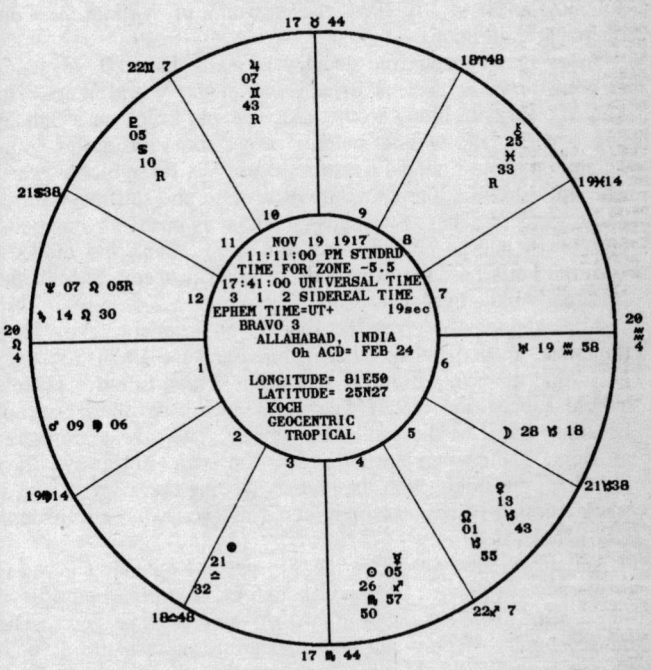

Indira Gandhi

SATURN						
OPP 5 28S	URANUS					
CON 7 25S		NEPTUNE				
	SQQ 0 12A	SSX 1/55S	PLUTO			
CON 5 34	OPP 0/06		SSQ 0 06	ASC		
SQR 3/13	SQR 2 15		SSQ 2 27	SQR 2 21	MC	
SQQ 2 25	SSQ 3 03	BQT 0 50	OPP 3 15	SQQ 3 09	SQQ 0 48	

got about five years to spare. You might like to compare your chart with these countries. You might want to compare them with each other.

Who says you can't read a nation's chart like a person's? Are you ready to have a go? Here's England's chart, cast for the Julian calendar in A.D. 1066, the crowning of William the Conqueror at high noon.

Aries rising means the country is really happiest when it's fighting—how marvelous Britain was in the World Wars! The Sun in Capricorn clings to the past; you can't pick up a Sunday paper in England without coming across some old duffer going on and on about England's history, especially those bloody wars. The English are a funny mixture of warmth and stuffiness, Aries and Capricorn. These two signs are about as pushy as the zodiac gets. They had an empire once, you know. Capricorn thinks it knows what's best for everybody. The British empire built the best roads India ever had, or has.

Aries rising also gives the English an insatiable ego. They think they're better than other nations, and the English smugly *know* that the Sun will never set on the British Empire. There's an old superstition that if the ravens ever leave the Tower of London, that'll be the end of the empire. The ravens are *there*, all right. Their wings are clipped so they can't fly away. They look happy enough, with the tourists feeding them seven days a week, though I doubt anybody could tell you what an unhappy raven looks like.

Actually, I have yet to see the Sun *rise* in England. The sky is nearly always gray in England, though the Sun pokes out just at sunset, and there's a week or two of summer some years. The entire country is gray sky and a magnificent lush green, both Capricorn colors. Yet everywhere you look there are surprising dots of red—telephone kiosks, post boxes, guards' uniforms. That's the Aries rising.

Mercury is in Capricorn, a stuffy, clipped, organized way of speaking. It makes a soft angle, a trine, to Neptune, and another trine to Jupiter and Saturn. It's a gorgeous, sweet, formal, imaginative, subtle, and ever-changing accent, like the language.

The girls a country fancies show in the Venus position. Venus in Capricorn denotes the English ideal—the perfect lady, understated, never-flashy beauty, slim, with perfect skin and lots of leg (Capricorn rules the knees). England invented style, understated elegance, and it lives with the understanding that while the outside appearance may be somewhat shabby (Capricorn) the inner stuff is the best. They don't go for the pair of 44s and the mouth full of teeth. They don't want women to look like rubber dolls or Cadillacs.

Outsiders envy the English health system. I like it too, though waiting up to four years in a queue for an operation on the National Health Service may not be your cuppa.

My doctor looks like a kindly Captain Hook. I caught him one day in the local coffee bar. He was chain-smoking Gauloises as usual.

"Oh, doctor," I burbled, "I'm so glad to run into you! I've been wondering—it's seventeen years since I've had a thorough physical checkup. Do you think you could recommend a clinic where I could have it done?"

The doctor smiled gently and put down his Gauloise. "Now Miss Smith," he said. "I don't know if that is such a good idea. . . . After all, there's *bound* to be something wrong with you, *isn't* there, and you'd only worry about it afterwards. Sometimes I think it's better not to know about these things."

He was right, you know. I've never felt better in my life. England has Saturn in the health box. It may be madness, but Saturn is also the planet of wisdom and common sense. Saturn in the sixth screws up efficiency, productivity, and industry—problems that plague England. At the same time Saturn there is the mark of the craftsman; who is better at making China, hand-joined wooden furniture, and Rolls Royces?

Contrast England's chart with that of the United States. One's a Capricorn and the other is Cancer, born on the Fourth of July. They're opposites, and they need each other.

POW! Dig the Uranus right on the rising sign of the United States chart. Uranus is the planet of science and *revolution*. We'll be damned if anyone tells *us* what to do! Our earliest flags said, "Don't Tread On Me."

Gemini rising makes us a nation of yakkers. We have the best telephone system in the world. We may seem superficial to onlookers, but our technology is unrivaled. When foreigners look beyond the first impression of the loud, childlike American, they discover the four planets in warm, home-loving Cancer. Americans think they are mothers to the world, and they're lucky, with fatso Jupiter near the Sun. This gives Americans what Rob Hand calls our "Santa Claus complex." We really want to be generous.

PLANET	SIGN	LONG	HSE
SUN		Cpr 9 54 50	10
MOON		Pic 29 3 56	12
MERC		Cpr 16 36.7	10
VENU		Cpr 29 51.6	10
MARS		Aqu 8 28.0	11
JUPI	D	Vir 7 56.7R	6
SATU		Vir 16 49.7R	6
URAN		Sag 28 26.6	9
NEPT		Tau 22 12.0R	1
PLUT	E	Pic 3 17.4	11
ASC		Ari 22 0.1	1
MC		Cpr 8 34.8	10
NODE*		Vir 19 25.4	6
PFOR		Can 11 9.2	
VERTEX		Lib 7 34.2	
EASTPT		Ari 10 10.9	

R= RULE   D= DETRIMENT
E= EXALTED F= FALL
*TRUE NODE

	CARD	FIX	MUT		
FIRE	0	0	1	6	1
EARTH	3	1	2		
AIR	0	1	0	1	2
WATER	0	0	2		

*** NATAL ASPECTS ***

	ANGLE	ORB		ANGLE	ORB
CON= CONJUNCTION	0	10	TRI= TRINE	120	10
SSX= SEMISEXTILE	30	3	SQQ= SESQUIQUAD	135	4
SSQ= SEMI-SQUARE	45	4	BQT= BIQUINTILE	144	3
SXT= SEXTILE	60	6	QCX= QUINCUNX	150	3
QTL= QUINTILE	72	3	OPP= OPPOSITION	180	10
SQR= SQUARE	90	10	/ = PARALLEL OR	0	1
A= APPLYING S= SEPARATING			CONTRAPARALLEL		

	SUN	MOON	MERCURY	VENUS	MARS	JUPITER
MOON						
MERC	CON 6 42S	QTL 0 27S				
VENU		SXT 0 48A				
MARS	SSX 1 27S			CON 8 36A		
JUPI	TRI 1 58S		TRI 8 40S	BQT 2 05A	QCX 0 31S	
SATU	TRI 6 55A		TRI 0 13A	SQQ 1 58A	BQT 2 22A	CON 8 53S
URAN	/	SQR 0 37S	/	SSX 1 25S		TRI 9 30A
NEPT	SQQ 2 43S		TRI 5 35A	TRI 7 40S		
PLUT	/		SSQ 1/41A			OPP 4 39A
ASC				SQR 7 52	QTL 1 32	SQQ 0 57
MC	CON 1/20	SQR 9 31	CON 8 02	SQR 5 23	SSX 0 07	TRI 0 38
NODE	TRI 9 31	OPP 9 39	TRI 2 49			

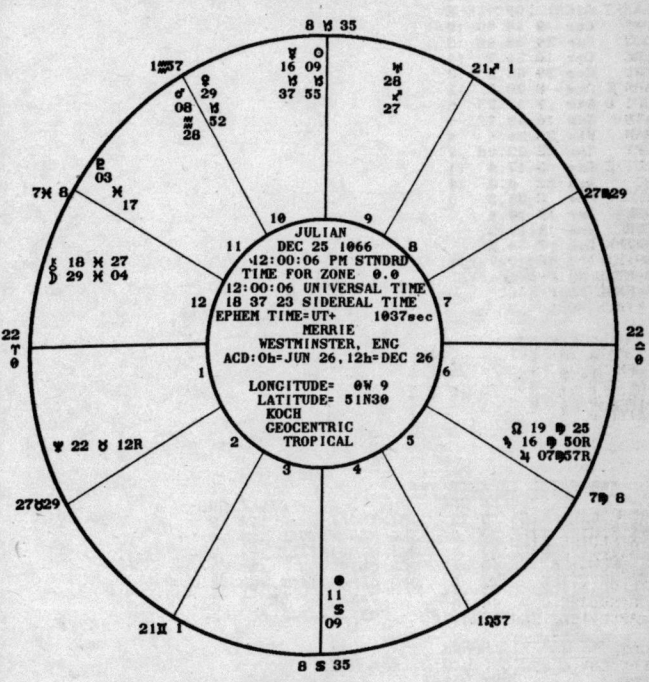

England

SATURN	URANUS	NEPTUNE	PLUTO	ASC	MC
TRI 5 22A	BQT 0 15S				
	SXT 4/51A				
BQT 0 50	TRI 6 26	SSX 0 12	SSQ 3 43		
TRI 8 15	/	SQQ 1 23	SXT 5/17		
CON 2 36	SQR 9 01	TRI 2 47		QCX 2 35	

```
PLANET SIGN  LONG    HSE
SUN    Can 12 43 49   2
MOON   Aqu 18 10 43  10
MERC   Can 24 28.4R   3
VENU   Can  2 21.5    1
MARS   Gem 20 58.0    1
JUPI E Can  5 47.7    2
SATU E Lib 14 47.2    5
URAN   Gem  8 53.4    1
NEPT D Vir 22 24.3    4
PLUT   Cpr 27 22.7R   9
ASC    Gem  7 43.5    1
MC     Aqu 14  4.2   10
NODE*  Leo  6 35.7    3
PFOR   Cpr 13 10.4
VERTEX Scp  3 16.2
EASTPT Tau 19  0.3
  R= RULE      D= DETRIMENT
  E= EXALTED   F= FALL
    *TRUE NODE
```

```
      CARD FIX MUT
FIRE   0   0   0        1 | 1
EARTH  1   0   1          |
AIR    1   1   2        6 | 2
WATER  4   0   0          |
```

*** NATAL ASPECTS ***

	ANGLE	ORB		ANGLE	ORB
CON= CONJUNCTION	0	10	TRI= TRINE	120	10
SSX= SEMISEXTILE	30	3	SQQ= SESQUIQUAD	135	4
SSQ= SEMI-SQUARE	45	4	BQT= BIQUINTILE	144	3
SXT= SEXTILE	60	6	QCX= QUINCUNX	150	3
QTL= QUINTILE	72	3	OPP= OPPOSITION	180	10
SQR= SQUARE	90	10	/ = PARALLEL OR	0	1
A= APPLYING S= SEPARATING		CONTRAPARALLEL			

	SUN	MOON	MERCURY	VENUS	MARS	JUPITER
MOON	BQT 0 33A					
MERC						
VENU	/	SQQ 0 49S				
MARS	/	TRI 2 47A		/		
JUPI	CON 6/56S	SQQ 2 37A		CON 3/26A		
SATU	SQR 2 03A	TRI 3 23S	SQR 9 41A		TRI 6 11S	SQR 8 60A
URAN		TRI 9 17S	SSQ 0 35A			
NEPT	QTL 2 19S	BQT 1 46S	SXT 2 04A	SQR 9 57S	SQR 1 26A	
PLUT	/		OPP 2 54S	/	BQT 0/25A	/
ASC			SSQ 1 45			SSX 1 56
MC	QCX 1 20	CON 4/06	/	SQQ 3 17	TRI 6 54	BQT 2 17
NODE					SSQ 0 38	SSX 0 48

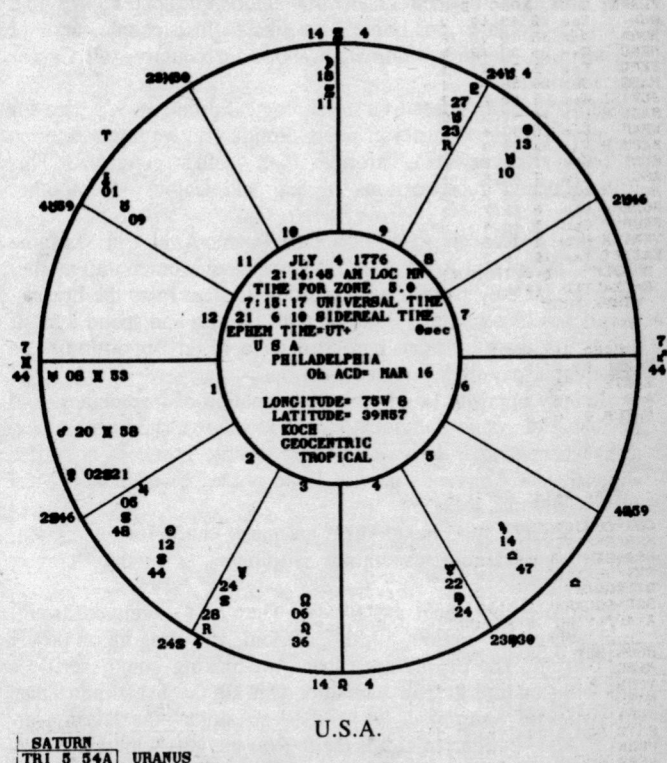

U.S.A.

SATURN							
TRI 5 54A	URANUS						
		NEPTUNE					
	SQQ 3 29A	TRI 4 58A	PLUTO				
TRI 7 04	CON 1/10				ASC		
TRI 0 43	TRI 5 11	BQT 2 20			TRI 6 21		NC
	SXT 2 18	SSQ 0 49	OPP 9 13		SXT 1 08	OPP 7 29	

Sun and Jupiter in the money box does give the United States luck and love with money—"Land of Opportunity." The funkier side of the USA is that money has become a God to many Americans; the spiritual meaning of this placement is that it is a nation founded on *strong emotional values*. We like to invite people to our homes, we like to feed people, and we get terribly, sloppily sentimental about our country—all Cancer characteristics.

Saturn in Libra poses us a psychological problem. It's hard for us to meet other countries as peers. Politically, we think in terms of being "better than, stronger than" other countries. This attitude brings repercussions of fear and jealousy from other nations.

Venus in Cancer gives us a clue to the American feminine ideal—"Mom and Apple Pie." We make our women into mother figures, and they must have big titties. Cancer rules the breasts. Americans like women (Venus is with Jupiter) and spend a lot of money on them; women here still have better opportunities to make equal pay than in other countries.

Mercury opposite Pluto makes us a nation of insomniacs, and we're big on round-the-clock television shows. The harsh American accent sounds harsher to those people living in countries which resent America's power. Pluto is the power planet, Mercury is how we speak.

The Soviet Union next. There are many charts for this nation, and a lot of arguments among astrologers as to the "correct chart."

Scorpio is the USSR's Sun sign. They're a secretive, strong, stubborn, moody nation, a little paranoid, and hung up on power and control. The people are capable of making grand sacrifices and withstanding greater hardship. One of the overriding characteristics of Scorpio is its need to be alone—the "Iron Curtain." Another Scorpio trait is the urge to merge—with whatever's next door, like Afghanistan!

We won't dwell on the rising sign or the house positions because there are so many "correct times" for the USSR chart, and they're all different.

Look at the Sun making a square aspect to Saturn, a sure indicator of an inferiority complex so grinding that the nation must overcompensate until it is powerful. A majority of successful businessmen have the Sun square Saturn—they work hard to show Daddy they're good enough.

Saturn in Leo shows the strict concern the Soviets have for

their children. They screen and test their kids to bring out their talents and abilities to the maximum. Saturn in Leo is also hung up on not being lovable; the Soviets are so afraid their own citizens won't love them that they forbid their citizens to leave the USSR. A rather extreme example of enforced fidelity, denoting what past-life hobbyists would call a "young soul" or "unevolved being." Let's hope they grow up soon.

Here's the chart of the Palestine Liberation Organization. A rather violent first impression they make, too, with both Uranus (revolutionary, shocking, and sudden) and Pluto (the underground, power, and manipulation of the masses) straddling the rising sign.

New baby Chiron is in the seventh house, breaking up impasses. The seventh house in mundane astrology has to do with partners, enemies, and negotiations.

The PLO are determined not to take "no" for an answer. Libra Moon insists on being treated as an equal. Yet the opposition between Saturn and Uranus/Pluto indicates they're not so hot at cooperating. "Let's *compromise*," they say. "Do it my way."

Mars the warrior, Jupiter the risk-taker, and Mercury of what's on their minds are all in stubborn Taurus. They're not the kind of social club to easily change their minds—or their tactics.

Lastly, and least most, here is the chart of the revolution in Iran when the Ayatollah Khomeini took power.

How clearly the chart reflects a country torn in two! The Sun, ruling the country's goals, is in the tenth house of power. Psychologically we interpret this as a problem with a parent figure—disgust with the Shah, yet the pull for a new Daddy, the terrifying Khomeini.

The Moon is opposite the Sun, and as the Moon in mundane studies governs the needs and feelings of the people, we find a conflict between the people in power and the hungry bellies of the masses. The Moon was nearly full when the revolution took place. Full Moons can be crazy-making times, but when Uranus makes a square angle to both points we get nothing less than unbridled hysteria.

Despite the apparent stability of a stubborn Taurus rising sign, the Sun-Moon-Uranus angles do not indicate a stable, orderly regime. Chiron in the twelfth house whispers that underground movements and secret enemies would be constantly at work behind the scenes to change the status quo. Chiron receives two trines, one from Saturn, which rules the foreign sector (ninth

```
PLANET SIGN  LONG   HSE
SUN    Scp 14 28 14  9
MOON   Leo 22 36 24  8
MERC   Scp 16 43.3   9
VENU   Cpr  0 16.6  12
MARS   Vir  2 42.1   8
JUPI D Gem  9 14.2R  4
SATU D Leo 14 12.8   8
URAN R Aqu 19 49.2   2
NEPT   Leo  7  6.5   7
PLUT   Can  5 20.3R  6
ASC    Cpr 13 10.0   1
MC     Sag  2 52.6  10
NODE*  Cpr  2 47.0  12
PFOR   Lib 21 18.2
VERTEX Vir  4 42.3
EASTPT Aqu 28 40.5
 R=RULE    D=DETRIMENT
 E=EXALTED F=FALL
   *TRUE NODE
```

```
      CARD FIX MUT
FIRE   0   3   0      1 | 6
EARTH  1   0   1      --|--
AIR    0   1   1      1 | 2
WATER  1   2   0
```

```
        *** NATAL ASPECTS ***
                ANGLE ORB              ANGLE ORB
CON=CONJUNCTION    0  10   TRI=TRINE      120  10
SSX=SEMISEXTILE   30   3   SQQ=SESQUIQUAD 135   4
SSQ=SEMI-SQUARE   45   4   BQT=BIQUINTILE 144   3
SXT=SEXTILE       60   6   QCX=QUINCUNX   150   3
QTL=QUINTILE      72   3   OPP=OPPOSITION 180  10
SQR=SQUARE        90  10   / =PARALLEL OR   0   1
A=APPLYING  S=SEPARATING  CONTRAPARALLEL
         SUN
MOON SQR 8 08S   MOON
MERC CON 2/15S SQR 5 53S  MERCURY
VENU SSQ 0 48S TRI 7 40A SSQ 1 27S   VENUS
MARS QTL 0 14A            QTL 2 01S TRI 2 25A  MARS
JUPI          QTL 1 22S                    SQR 6 32A  JUPITER
SATU SQR 0 13S CON 8 24S SQR 2/31S SSQ 1 04S          SXT 4 59S
URAN SCR 3/21A OPP 2 47S SQR 3 06A
NEPT SQR 7 22S            SQR 9 32S BQT 0 50A          SXT 2 08A
PLUT TRI 9 08S SSQ 2 16S SQQ 3 37A OPP 5 04A SXT 2 38A
ASC  SXT 1 18             SXT 3 33                     BQT 2 04
MC                                 SSX 2 36  SQR 0 11  OPP 6/22
NODE SSQ 3 19            SSQ 1 04  CON 2 30  TRI 0 05
```

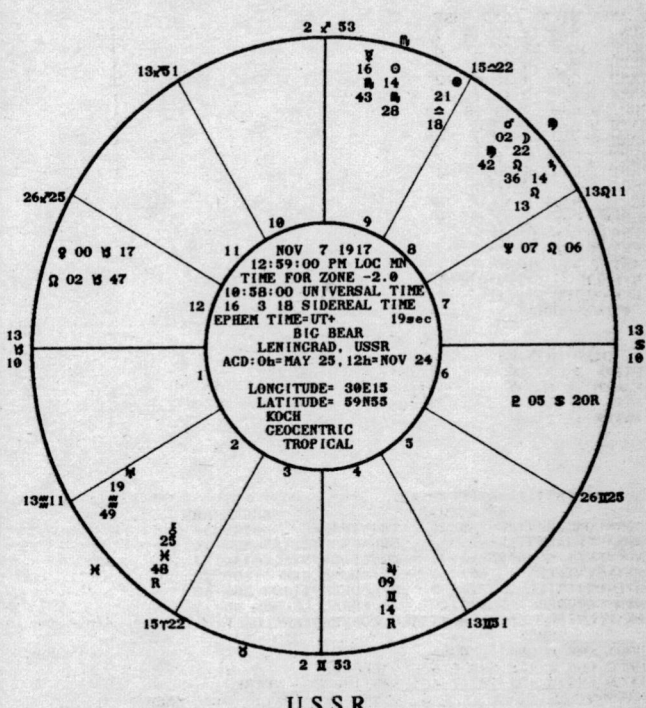

U.S.S.R.

SATURN				
OPP 5 36A	URANUS			
CON 7 06S		NEPTUNE		
	SQQ 0 31A	SSX 1/46S	PLUTO	
QCX 1 03			OPP 7 50	ASC
		TRI 4 14	QCX 2 28	MC
SQQ 3 34	SSQ 2 02	BQT 1 40	OPP 2 33	SSX 0 06

```
PLANET SIGN  LONG    HSE
SUN    Gem  1 19 46   9
MOON   Lib 17 17 52   2
MERC   Tau  6 34.6    8
VENU   Can  5 57.4   10
MARS D Tau 11  3.6    9
JUPI   Tau  9 32.1    9
SATU   Plc  4 34.6    6
URAN   Vir  5 57.0   12
NEPT   Scp 16  3.5R   3
PLUT F Vir 11 35.2R   1
ASC    Vir  9  0.1    1
MC     Gem  7 17.5   10
NODE*  Can  2 27.1   10
PFOR   Cpr 24 58.2
VERTEX Cpr 24 53.9
EASTPT Vir  3 33.9
 R=RULE    D=DETRIMENT
 E=EXALTED F=FALL
  *TRUE NODE
```

```
     CARD FIX MUT
FIRE   0   0   0      2 | 4
EARTH  0   3   2
AIR    1   0   1      3 | 1
WATER  1   1   1
```

*** NATAL ASPECTS ***

	ANGLE	ORB		ANGLE	ORB
CON=CONJUNCTION	0	10	TRI=TRINE	120	10
SSX=SEMISEXTILE	30	3	SQQ=SESQUIQUAD	135	4
SSQ=SEMI-SQUARE	45	4	BQT=BIQUINTILE	144	3
SXT=SEXTILE	60	6	QCX=QUINCUNX	150	3
QTL=QUINTILE	72	3	OPP=OPPOSITION	180	10
SQR=SQUARE	90	10	/ =PARALLEL OR	0	1
A=APPLYING S=SEPARATING CONTRAPARALLEL					

	SUN	MOON	MERCURY	VENUS	MARS	JUPITER
MOON	SQQ 0 58S					
MERC						
VENU			SXT 0 37S			
MARS			CON 4 29A	SXT 5 06S		
JUPI			CON 2 57A	SXT 3 35A	CON 1 32S	
SATU	SQR 3 15A	SQQ 2 17A	SXT 2/00S	TRI 1 23S		SXT 4 57S
URAN	SQR 4 37A	SSQ 3 39A	TRI 0/38S	SXT 0 00S	TRI 5 07S	TRI 3 35S
NEPT		SSX 1 14S	OPP 9 29A		OPP 4/60A	OPP 6 31A
PLUT	/		TRI 5 01A	SXT 5 38A	TRI 0 32A	TRI 2 03A
ASC	SQR 7 40		TRI 2 25	SXT 3 03	TRI 2 04	TRI 0 32.
MC	CON 5 58		SSX 0 43	SSX 1 20		SSX 2 15
NODE	SSX 1 07		SXT 4 08	CON 3 30		

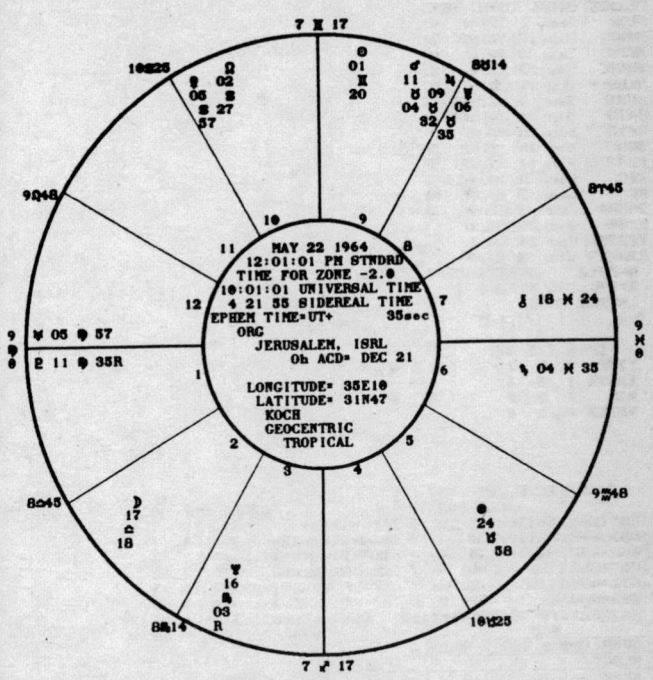

P.L.O.

SATURN					
OPP 1 22A	URANUS				
	QTL 1 54S	NEPTUNE			
OPP 7 01A	CON 5 38A	SXT 4 28A	PLUTO		
OPP 4 25	CON 3 03		CON 2 35	ASC	
SQR 2 43	SQR 1 20		SQR 4 18	SQR 1 43	MC
TRI 2 08	SXT 3 30	SQQ 1 24	QTL 2 52		

```
PLANET SIGN  LONG     HSE
SUN   D Aqu 21 59 45  10
MOON    Leo 13 35 33   4
MERC  E Aqu 23 36.5   10
VENU    Cpr  6 37.4    8
MARS    Aqu 16 58.5   10
JUPI    Leo  1 45.8R   3
SATU    Vir 11 58.4R   4
URAN  E Sep 20 55.3    6
NEPT    Sag 20  3.5    7
PLUT    Lib 19  6.3R   5
ASC     Tau 29 37.6    1
MC      Aqu  9 46.9   10
NODE*   Vir 17 33.6    5
PFOR    Sep 21 13.4
VERTEX  Lib 28 34.8
EASTPT  Tau 14 41.4
  R=RULE     D=DETRIMENT
  E=EXALTED  F=FALL
  *TRUE NODE
  ☉☽ ANGLE=171.60°
```

```
     CARD FIX MUT
FIRE   0   2   1        3   2
EARTH  1   0   1        ___
AIR    1   3   0        1   4
WATER  0   1   0
```

NATAL ASPECTS

	ANGLE	ORB	♂		ANGLE	ORB	♂
CON=Conjunction	0	10	5	TRI=Trine	120	10	6
SSX=Semisextile	30	3	4	SQQ=Sesquiquad	135	4	1
SSQ=Semi-Square	45	4	4	BQT=Biquintile	144	3	3
SXT=Sextile	60	6	7	QCX=Quincunx	150	3	2
QTL=Quintile	72	3	1	OPP=Opposition	180	10	5
SQR=Square	90	10	8	∕ =Parallel or	0	1	8
A=Applying S=Separating			Contraparallel				

TOTAL ASPECTS = 54

	SUN	MOON	MERCURY	VENUS	MARS	JUPITER
MOON	OPP 8/24A					
MERC	CON 1 37S					
VENU	SSQ 0 22A	BQT 0 58S	SSQ 1 59S			
MARS	CON 5 01S	OPP 3 23A	CON 6 38S			
JUPI				∕		
SATU		SSX 1 37S		TRI 5 21A		
URAN	SQR 1 04S	SQR 7 20A	SQR 2 41S	SSQ 0 42S	SQR 3/57A	
NEPT	SXT 1 56S	TRI 6 28A	SXT 3 33S	∕	SXT 3 05A	SQQ 3 18S
PLUT	TRI 2 53S	SXT 5 31A	TRI 4 30S			TRI 2 08A
ASC	SQR 7 38	QTL 1 58	SQR 6 01	BQT 0/60		SXT 2/08
MC		OPP 3 49			CON 7 12	OPP 8 01
NODE					QCX 0 35	SSQ 0 48

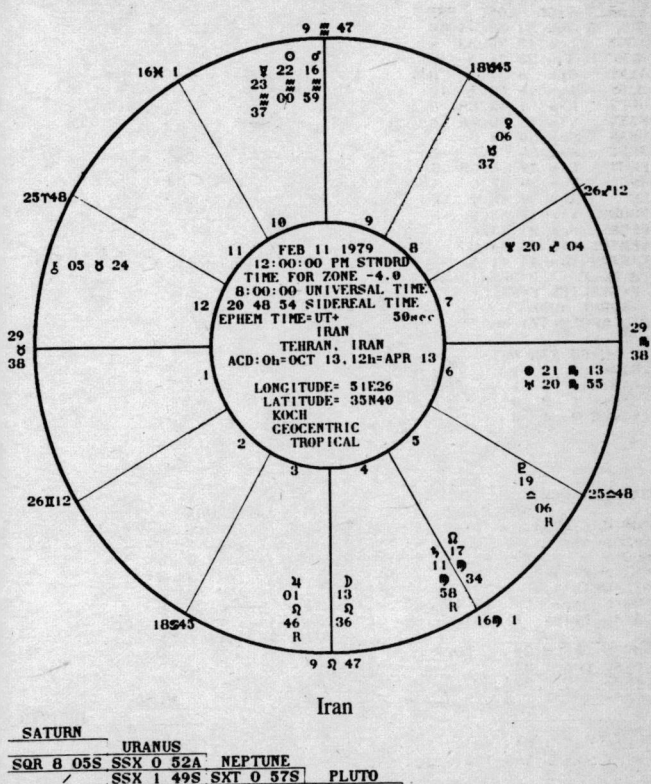

Iran

SATURN						
	URANUS					
SQR 8 05S	SSX 0 52A	NEPTUNE				
	SSX 1 49S	SXT 0 57S	PLUTO			
	OPP 8 42			ASC		
QCX 2 12			TRI 9 19		MC	
CON 5 35	SXT 3 22	SQR 2 30	SSX 1 33		BQT 1 47	

house), and the other from Venus, which rules the everyday workers (sixth house). Eventually the workers and foreign powers will work in tandem to undermine the present regime.

Saturn's work is slow, but it is sure. Saturn is the delicatessen planet. He delivers.

How Do You Make the World A Better Place?

What are you doing to make the world a better place? What are you going to leave behind you when your soul gets on that Greyhound bound for Buffalo?

Maybe you care about the world, and yet your hands are full making a living, raising a family, or planning how you'll make it through the day. You don't have time right now to join groups or organize a No Nukes meeting.

My hat is off to you. More trouble in this world has been caused by people who think they know better than you do what is best for you. Last week I noticed a travel poster in the London underground. There was a huge picture of Moscow. It said "Visit the Soviet Union." Someone had scrawled underneath, "Before the Soviet Union visits you . . ."

The eleventh house of your chart shows your hopes and wishes, your wildest dreams, your urge to cooperate with others, the kind of friend you are, and what you want to do that benefits the world *outside and beyond your personal needs*.

Yank out that computer chart. Obviously planets in this house will make idealism important for you. No planets here do not indicate a lack of idealism; look at the sign on the eleventh house cusp and see what planet rules that sign. If that planet makes big aspects and angles in your chart, you're ready to Save the Whale.

Here is the chart of a woman who wanted to make the world a better place. I doubt she ever sat down and thought about it, for

```
PLANET SIGN  LONG   HSE
SUN    Gem  5  4 45  11
MOON D Cpr 28 29 11   7
MERC R Gem 27 59.2   12
VENU D Arl 21 28.6   10
MARS D Tau 22  0.3   10
JUPI   Aqu 17  6.1    7
SATU R Cpr 27 30.7R   7
URAN   Sag 19 53.5R   5
NEPT E Can  0 11.6   12
PLUT   Gem 17 51.1   11
ASC    Can 23 46.2    1
MC     Arl  4 58.7   10
NODE*  Scp  3 55.8    4
PFOR   Plc 17 10.7
VERTEX Sag 10  9.5
EASTPT Can  4 11.6
  R=RULE    D=DETRIMENT
  E=EXALTED F=FALL
  *TRUE NODE
```

```
      CARD FIX MUT
FIRE   1   0   1        6 | 3
EARTH  2   1   0          |
AIR    0   1   3        0 | 1
WATER  1   0   0
```

```
       *** NATAL ASPECTS ***
                  ANGLE ORB              ANGLE ORB
CON=CONJUNCTION     0   10   TRI=TRINE     120  10
SSX=SEMISEXTILE    30    3   SQQ=SESQUIQUAD 135   4
SSQ=SEMI-SQUARE    45    4   BQT=BIQUINTILE 144   3
SXT=SEXTILE        60    6   QCX=QUINCUNX   150   3
QTL=QUINTILE       72    3   OPP=OPPOSITION 180  10
SQR=SQUARE         90   10   / =PARALLEL OR   0   1
A=APPLYING  S=SEPARATING   CONTRAPARALLEL
```

	SUN	MOON	MERCURY	VENUS	MARS	JUPITER
MOON	TRI 6 36A					
MERC		QCX 0 30S				
VENU	SSQ 1 24S	SQR 7 01S				
MARS		TRI 6 29S		SSX 0 32A		
JUPI		/		SXT 4 22S	SQR 4 54S	
SATU	TRI 7/34S	CON 0 58S	QCX 0 28S	SQR 6 02A	TRI 5 30A	
URAN			OPP 8 06S	TRI 1 35S	QCX 2 07S	SXT 2 47A
NEPT		QCX 1 42A	CON 2 12A			SSQ 1 54A
PLUT				SXT 3 38S		TRI 0 45A
ASC	SSQ 3/41	OPP 4 43		SQR 2 18	SXT 1 46	
MC	SXT 0 06		SQR 6 59			SSQ 2 02 SSQ 2 53
NODE	QCX 1 09	SQR 5 27	TRI 5 57			

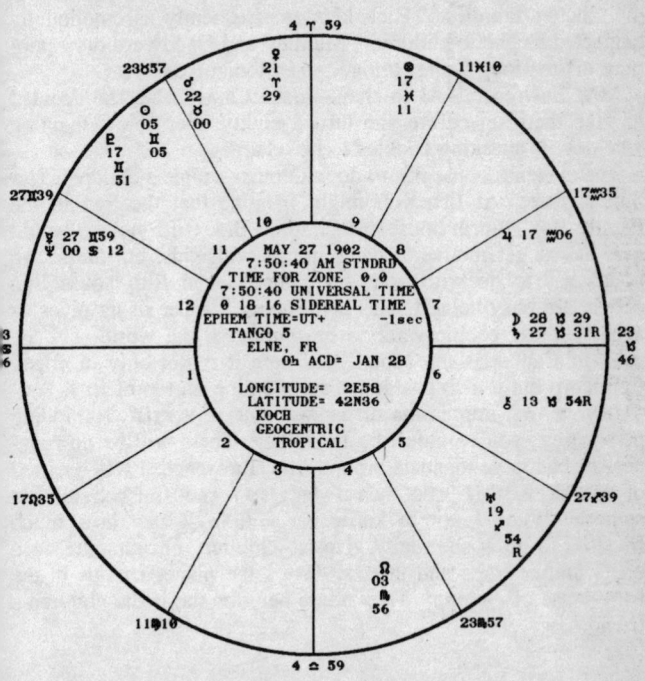

Mrs. Lawrence

	SATURN	URANUS	NEPTUNE	PLUTO	ASC	MC
	QCX 2 41S	/				
	OPP 3/44	OPP 2 02A	/			
		BQT 2 07		PLUTO		
			SQR 4 47	QTL 0 52		
	SQR 6 25	SSQ 0 58	TRI 3 44	SQQ 1 05		QCX 1 03

she was too busy doing it. Mrs. Lawrence is known in her circles as the World's Best Baby-sitter—she is a Nanny in the finest old-fashioned tradition. She has raised two well-adjusted children of her own, one a West Point graduate, and she has raised many little monsters of what the Main Line Philadelphians call the "better families." Rich kids are frequently as emotionally neglected as ghetto children—Mummy and Daddy are busy popping off to Hong Kong, bridge, and Bloomingdales.

Mrs. Lawrence used to chain-smoke Camels, but she decided to give them up before she turned eighty. Her sole remaining vice now is sneaking cookies to her charges.

The eleventh house has to do with other people's children. Her Sun is there. At first you might imagine that the Sun in the Family Box (fourth house) or Children Box (fifth house) would give a stronger motive to hang around with kids, but the fourth house has to do with your own family, and fifth house Sun people are busy being babies themselves. Cancer rising gives us a clue—these people want to be mother to the world, but the ruler of Cancer is the Moon, and here it is not only in crusty Capricorn but it also has dour Saturn sitting on top of it.

If your first impression of her was that of a strict, forbidding personality, you wouldn't be far wrong. There will be no rudeness or bad table manners around Mrs. Lawrence. I was terrified of her at first (I was then twenty-six) and finished all my spinach. When I got to know her a little, I saw how much freedom to grow she really gives to children, encouraging each one's unique traits and talents. That's the planet Uranus in the fifth house of children. They adore her, for she is the children's friend.

Maniacs

"There is nobody who is not dangerous for someone."

—Marquis de Sevigne

Have you ever felt like a maniac? Where will we get one this time of night???

You can easily spot a maniac in any group. He has a crazed glint in his eyes. Nothing is ever happening fast enough or hard enough for him. And you're a better goony bird than I am if you can keep up with him, too.

Two things in a chart show if you are a maniac or not. One of these is Mars, and the other Uranus. You need a hard angle (conjunction, square, quincunx, or opposition) with one of these *to any other planet in your chart*. Does either planet hit your Venus? Then you are a maniac of love. Do Mars or Uranus hit your Sun or Moon? You attack your whole life with the gusto of a rabid wolverine.

Taken alone, Uranus in a hard angle makes you hard as hell to get along with. You're not especially tactful. This goes double if Uranus makes a hard angle with your talker, Mercury. It is truth at all costs with you. At least you think it is the truth! Any aspect with Uranus makes you way ahead of your time or just plain crazy. Uranus with Jupiter gives you a wonderfully clever streak. Check the houses they're both in if they make any angle at all to one another; more than likely you're brilliant in those areas of your life.

You're no picnic to work next to if Uranus makes a hard angle with Saturn in your chart. To begin with you want to learn from more experienced people; then suddenly you want to do things your way or you throw a tantrum. When you're minding the store, you're a maniac for discipline, but the boss had better look out if she says "Boo" to *you*.

Any strong angle with Mars means you want everything to

323

happen NOW, come on already, it should have been done yesterday. You're a feisty son-of-a-gun. Put up your dukes, everyone!

Sex maniacs have a strong angle between Mars and Venus. You fight and compete to prove you have the most sex appeal. This makes you popular with the opposite sex, but you compete with your same sex buddies, and they resent it. You chalk it off as jealousy, usually, but if you want more close friends, you may wish to examine this competitive streak in yourself. Once you have a mate, your constant romantic demands can lead to fights. There's a fine line between being a sexpot and a crude vulgarian, but when all's told, people like sex maniacs. Just not on the subway. Have a little respect . . . *please*.

You're a talk maniac if Mars hits your Mercury. Your mind is sharp and fast; you wish people would hurry up and get to the point of their long-winded stories. Just watch the sharp tongue, will you? Not everyone learns as fast as you do.

Mars to Pluto makes you a workaholic, celibate for periods, and a sex maniac at other times. You're a power maniac, with superhuman stamina. You're a fanatic. Better note the houses these planets are in if they make an aspect to each other. No one can change your mind about a thing unless they bop you on the head, but you're too agile to let them get a chance. So you wait until your power trips boomerang on you; *then* you change your mind—maybe. You'd rather screw yourself up than have anybody else do it, believing in the motto "Better the enemy you know," even if it's you.

And what if Mars *and* Uranus are in hard angles to each other? You're a hothead, and you'd better watch it. Next time you get an attack of The Furies remember this: not everybody in this round world does things as fast or as smart as you do. Have a little patience with the poor SOBs. You may well be a genius, you know. Remember that too before you rip the eyeballs out of Ronald MacDonald's french-fried face.

Do you have a friend or relative with Uranus rising or strong in the chart? Weird, aren't they? In their own way, they are geniuses at *something*.

Are you strongly Uranian? Well, *you* may be going crazy, but I'm not going with you.

Marriage

Whom should you marry? Look at the seventh house of your horoscope. If you have planets in there, you'll want a partner with qualities like those planets.

Jane Fonda has Mars in the marriage box. She wants a pushy partner, brave and chivalrous, a mate who stands up to be counted. Someone who stirs up trouble for an ideal. Mars is in Pisces, so he has to care about less fortunate people and be emotional too. She found all of these qualities in Tom Hayden.

What *sign* is on Jane Fonda's marriage box? Aquarius. These people marry for friendship. The *ruler* of Aquarius, Uranus, is on the Midheaven. She wants a partner who is famous in his own right.

Don't worry if your marriage box is empty. You can still marry if you want to and have a happy marriage. You'll have to work at it, though. Marriage is not the goal of your existence.

With an empty marriage box, study the sign on the cusp. Go back to the zodiac zone section and see what your attitudes are to a potential partner. The more you give that stuff to your mate, the more you'll get it back. The sign on your marriage box *rarely describes* the sign you should marry. Taurus on the marriage box means you want someone you feel comfortable with, someone upon whom you can depend. Libra on the marriage box means you can only marry for love, and your mate is probably a creative type. Capricorn on the marriage box means that moody loners turn you on. You've got the idea.

Now find the planet that rules the sign on your marriage box. What sign is it in? What house is it in? That's the person you're looking for.

Once every miracle, you'll find someone whose chart agrees with yours—with something extra. They have an important,

```
PLANET SIGN  LONG    HSZ
SUN    Sag 29 46 13   5
MOON   Leo 28 15 44   1
MERC   Cpr 15 28.4R   5
VENU   Sag 19 13.2    5
MARS   Pic  0 13.0    7
JUPI   Aqu  0 24.6    6
SATU   Pic 28 42.8    8
URAN F Tau 10  1.6R  10
NEPT D Vir 21  9.2    2
PLUT   Can 29 36.3R  12
ASC    Leo 13  9.2    1
MC     Tau  2 40.3   10
NODE*  Sag  5 51.8    4
PFOR   Ari 11 38.8
VERTEX Cpr  0 13.7
EASTPT Can 28 21.5
  R=RULE    D=DETRIMENT
  E=EXALTED F=FALL
   *TRUE NODE
```

```
      CARD FIX MUT
FIRE   0   1   2      2 | 2
EARTH  1   1   1
AIR    0   1   0      2 | 4
WATER  1   0   2
```

*** NATAL ASPECTS ***

	ANGLE	ORB		ANGLE	ORB
CON=CONJUNCTION	0	10	TRI=TRINE	120	10
SSX=SEMISEXTILE	30	3	SQQ=SESQUIQUAD	135	4
SSQ=SEMI-SQUARE	45	4	BQT=BIQUINTILE	144	3
SXT=SEXTILE	60	6	QCX=QUINCUNX	150	3
QTL=QUINTILE	72	3	OPP=OPPOSITION	180	10
SQR=SQUARE	90	10	/ =PARALLEL OR	0	1
A=APPLYING	S=SEPARATING	CONTRAPARALLEL			

	SUN	MOON	MERCURY	VENUS	MARS	JUPITER
MOON	TRI 1 30A					
MERC	/	SQQ 2 13A				
VENU	/	TRI 9 02S				
MARS	SXT 0 27A	OPP 1 57A	SSQ 0 15A	QTL 1 00S		
JUPI	SSX 0 38A	QCX 2 09A		SSQ 3 49S	SSX 0 12A	
SATU	SQR 1 03S	QCX 0 27A	QTL 1 14S	SQR 9 30A	SSX 1 30S	SXT 1 42S
URAN			TRI 5 27A		QTL 2 11S	SQR 9 37A
NEPT	SQR 8 37S		TRI 5 41S	SQR 1 56A		TRI 9 15S
PLUT	QCX 0/10S	SSX 1 21A	/	/	QCX 0 37S	OPP 0 48S
ASC	SQQ 1 37		QCX 2 19	TRI 6 04		
MC	TRI 2 54	TRI 4 25		SQQ 1 33	SXT 2/27	SQR 2 16
NODE		SQR 7 36			SQR 5 39	SXT 5 27

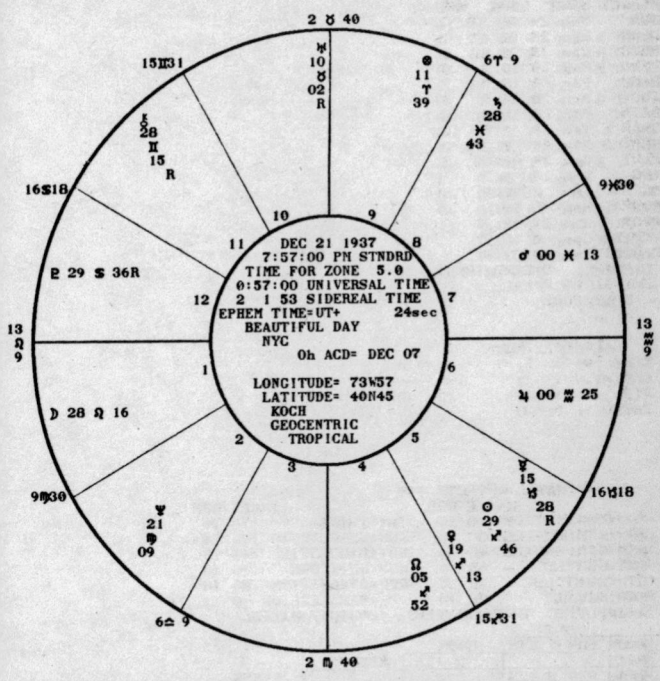

2 ♉ 40

15♊31 10 ♅ ♉ 02 R ⊕ 11 ♈ 39 6♈9

♋ 28 ♊ 15 R ♄ 28 ♓ 43

16♋18 9♓30

♇ 29 ♋ 36R 10 9 8 ♂ 00 ♓ 13

11 DEC 21 1937 7:57:00 PM STNDRD TIME FOR ZONE 5.0 0:57:00 UNIVERSAL TIME 2 1 53 SIDEREAL TIME EPHEM TIME=UT+ 24sec BEAUTIFUL DAY NYC 0h ACD= DEC 07 LONGITUDE= 73W57 LATITUDE= 40N45 KOCH GEOCENTRIC TROPICAL 7

13♌9 12 1 6 13♒9

☽ 28 ♌ 16 2 5 ♃ 00 ♒ 25

3 4

9♍30 ☿ 15 ♐ 28 R

♆ 21 ♍ 09 ⊙ 29 ♐ 46 16♑18

☊ 05 ♐ 52 ♀ 19 ♐ 13

6♎9 15♐31

2 ♏ 40

Jane Fonda

	SATURN	URANUS	NEPTUNE	PLUTO	ASC	MC
SATURN	SSQ 3 41S					
URANUS	OPP 7 34S	SQQ 3 52A				
NEPTUNE	TRI 0 54A					
PLUTO	SQQ 0 34	SQR 3 08				
		CON 7 21	SQQ 3 29	SQR 3 04		
ASC	TRI 7 09		QTL 2 43	TRI 6 16	TRI 7 17	BQT 2 48

PLANET	SIGN	LONG	HSE
SUN	Gem	24 12 18	11
MOON R	Can	0 11 22	11
MERC R	Gem	4 18.9	11
VENU R	Tau	8 30.6	10
MARS	Sag	5 10.0R	5
JUPI D	Vir	26 53.5	3
SATU	Tau	5 22.3	10
URAN	Vir	29 53.9	3
NEPT	Scp	26 37.3R	4
PLUT F	Vir	22 27.0	3
ASC	Leo	1 24.8	1
MC	Ari	15 51.2	10
NODE*	Pic	25 48.0	9
PFOR	Leo	7 23.9	
VERTEX	Sag	17 49.7	
EASTPT	Can	13 26.7	

R= RULE D= DETRIMENT
E= EXALTED F= FALL
*TRUE NODE

	CARD	FIX	MUT		
FIRE	0	0	1	5	0
EARTH	0	2	3	3	2
AIR	0	0	2		
WATER	1	1	0		

*** NATAL ASPECTS ***

	ANGLE	ORB			ANGLE	ORB
CON=CONJUNCTION	0	10		TRI=TRINE	120	10
SSX=SEMISEXTILE	30	3		SQQ=SESQUIQUAD	135	4
SSQ=SEMI-SQUARE	45	4		BQT=BIQUINTILE	144	3
SXT=SEXTILE	60	6		QCX=QUINCUNX	150	3
QTL=QUINTILE	72	3		OPP=OPPOSITION	180	10
SQR=SQUARE	90	10		/ =PARALLEL OR	0	1
A=APPLYING	S=SEPARATING		CONTRAPARALLEL			

	SUN	MOON	MERCURY	VENUS	MARS	JUPITER
MOON	CON 5 59S	MOON				
MERC			MERCURY			
VENU	SSQ 0 42S			VENUS		
MARS				OPP 0 51A	MARS	
JUPI	SQR 2 41A	SQR 3 18S	TRI 7 25S	SQQ 3 23A		JUPITER
SATU	SSQ 3 50S	SXT 5 11A	SSX 1 03A	CON 3 08S	QCX 0 12S	BQT 2 29S
URAN	SQR 5 42A	SQR 0 17S	TRI 5 25S	BQT 2 37S	SSX 5 16A	CON 3 00A
NEPT	QCX 2 25A	BQT 2 26A	OPP 1 29S	/	CON 8 33A	SXT 0 16S
PLUT	SQR 1 45S	SQR 7 44S	/	SQQ 1 05S	QTL 0 43A	CON 4 27S
ASC		SSX 1 13	SXT 2 53	SQR 7 00	TRI 3 45	SXT 4 31
MC		QTL 2 20	SSQ 3 28			
NODE	SQR 1 36	SQR 4 23		SSQ 2 17	TRI 5 22	OPP 1 05

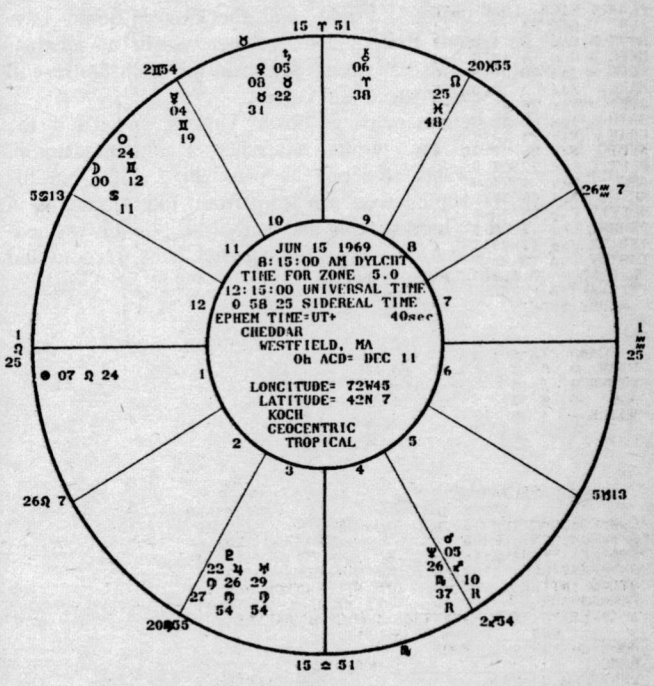

Peter Simm

	SATURN	URANUS	NEPTUNE	PLUTO	ASC	MC
	BQT 0 32A	SXT 3 17S				
	SQQ 2 05A	CON 7 27S	SXT 4/10A			
	SQR 3 57	SXF 1 31	TRI 4 48			
		OPP 4 06	TRI 0 49	OPP 3 21	TRI 5 37	

personal planet, like the Sun or Moon or Mercury or Venus or Mars on the ruler of your seventh house. You've found a soul mate; rope and tie and brand 'em.

Here's the chart of a young boy, Peter Simm, with an empty seventh house. He has Aquarius, too, on the marriage box. He wants someone unusual, bright, and shocking in some way. They will be friends first, and his partner will be an idealist. She'll have to be, as that strong Saturn in his tenth house will keep him busy with a successful career.

The ruler of Peter's marriage box is Uranus, and it's in the third house. She'll be a writer, a teacher, a communicator in some way. He wants someone he can jabber with, but his someone will be someone he can learn from, too. Uranus is in Virgo, so she'll be hardworking and analytical, possibly a scientist. He won't marry too young, as Aquarius likes freedom and he wants someone awfully bright.

Megabucks, Tycoonery, and Moolah

> *"Money never made a man happy yet, nor will it. There is nothing in its nature to produce happiness."*
>
> —Benjamin Franklin

Come *on*, now . . . tell it to the big boys in the cowboy hats down at the Stock Exchange and see how far it gets you, Ben baby. Money can't buy happiness, but if you are clever and own it rather than having it own you, it can buy an astonishing amount of freedom. You can tell the Boss to take his job and shove it. It buys you a week in the sun when you feel poorly. You can give it to friends. It is stomachs you can feed in Calcutta and Harlem, it is books and theater, it is a wide variety of *options*.

And it is sexy. Money is the ultimate Capitalist Tool. It is safer than raw power and slightly less corrupting. It is warm in the winter and cool in the summer. It can even buy you a husband or a wife, if you are desperate enough.

What words were you expecting from the daughter of a Keynsian economist who made millions for corporations and departed from this world without a dime? We had movies and restaurants and books and lived in a dozen countries. Every time a corporation offered him a vice-presidency, Dad quit the rat race and went fishing. Then he'd go out and get another Big Shot job. They loved him in his huge, tatty Burberry, and they loved his inventions and his crazy brain. I doubt any of the big corporations he fixed up knew why he always quit. How could a man with a big fancy salary walk out? The big fancy salary *enabled* him to walk out—to freedom at the end of a fishing line. Dad knew he couldn't take it with him.

```
PLANET SIGN  LONG    HSE
SUN     Sag 24  9 33  12
MOON F  Scp 13 24 45  10
MERC D  Sag 16 15.3R  12
VENU D  Scp 21  6.2   10
MARS    Pic 22  1.6    3
JUPI    Ari 15  2.6    3
SATU E  Lib 11 37.5    9
URAN E  Scp  9  9.8   10
NEPT    Gem  9 30.4R   5
PLUT    Gem  8 32.5R   5
ASC     Cpr  6  8.5    1
MC      Scp  4 27.9   10
NODE*   Tau  7 11.0    4
PFOR    Scp 25 23.7
VERTEX  Leo 16 21.1
EASTPT  Aqu  0  0.9
  R=RULE     D=DETRIMENT
  E=EXALTED  F=FALL
    *TRUE NODE
```

```
      CARD FIX MUT
FIRE   1   0   2      5 | 1
EARTH  0   0   0
AIR    1   0   2      2 | 2
WATER  0   3   1
```

*** NATAL ASPECTS ***

	ANGLE	ORB		ANGLE	ORB
CON=CONJUNCTION	0	10	TRI=TRINE	120	10
SSX=SEMISEXTILE	30	3	SQQ=SESQUIQUAD	135	4
SSQ=SEMI-SQUARE	45	4	BQT=BIQUINTILE	144	3
SXT=SEXTILE	60	6	QCX=QUINCUNX	150	3
QTL=QUINTILE	72	3	OPP=OPPOSITION	180	10
SQR=SQUARE	90	10	/=PARALLEL OR	0	1
A=APPLYING S=SEPARATING			CONTRAPARALLEL		

	SUN	MOON	MERCURY	VENUS	MARS	JUPITER
MOON						
MERC	CON 7 54S	SSX 2 51A				
VENU		CON 7/41A				
MARS	SQR 2 08S	TRI 8 37A	SQR 5 46S	TRI 0 55A		
JUPI	TRI 9 07S	QCX 1 38A	TRI 1 13A	BQT 0 04S	/	
SATU	QTL 0 32S	SSX 1 47S	SXT 4 38A			OPP 3 25A
URAN	SSQ 0 00A	CON 4 15S			SSQ 2 08A	SXT 5 32S
NEPT			OPP 6/45A			
PLUT		/	OPP 7 43A			
ASC	/			SSQ 0 02		SQR 8 54
MC		CON 8 57	SSQ 3 13		SSQ 2 34	
NODE	SSQ 1 59	OPP 6 14			SSQ 0 09	

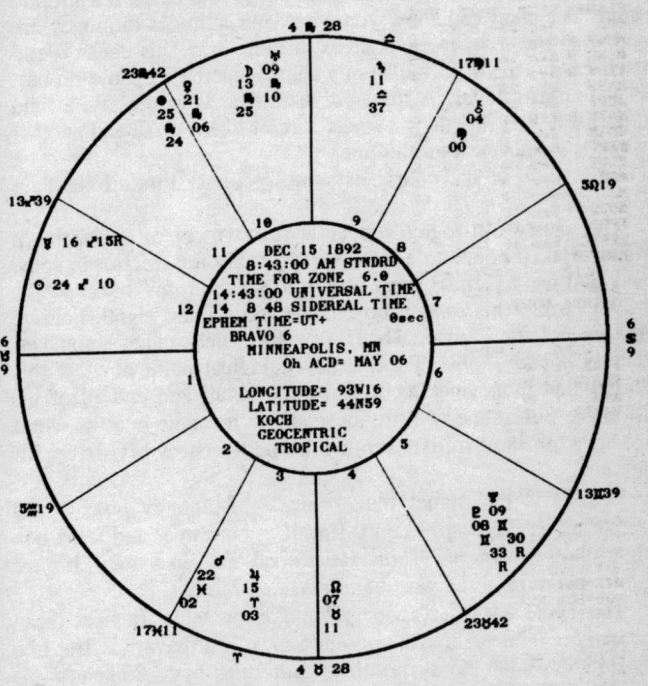

John Paul Getty

	SATURN	URANUS	NEPTUNE	PLUTO	ASC	MC
SATURN	SSX 2 28S					
URANUS	TRI 2 07S	QCX 0 21A				
NEPTUNE	TRI 3 05S	QCX 0 37S	CON 0 58A			
PLUTO	SQR 5 29	SXT 3 01		QCX 2 24		
ASC		CON 4 42	BQT 0 57	BQT 1 55	SXT 1 41	
MC		OPP 1 59	SSX 2 19	SSX 1 22	TRI 1 02	OPP 2 43

The only other thing money won't get you, besides happiness, is a decent system of values. Funny how the house ruling money (the second house) and one's value system are the same.

Now whether you are going to have a lot of money or not depends more on your greed and need than your chart. It's a subtle thing. The chart can show you what your attitudes to money are and what the most likely sources of lucre are. This doesn't lend itself easily to E-Z formulae in a cheap paperback; you'd do best to see an astrologer. A *financial* astrologer is better. It's a field unto itself. It's one thing to read a chart like a pizza and another when it's your cash on the line.

Let's look at the charts of some tycoons. First, John Paul Getty.

The crusty old-fogey veneer is just typical of a Capricorn rising sign. It points to a man who probably felt inferior in some way and had to amass great wealth to make up for it.

We look at his money boxes, the second and eighth houses, and except for Chiron, which we don't know much about yet, there's *nobody home*. From a psychological point of view this shows that moneymaking was not the be-all and end-all of his life. The Sun in the twelfth house shows he came into the world to be a philanthropist; money helped ensure his drive for privacy.

Uranus is the planet that ''rules'' his money box (it has Aquarius on the cusp). You'll find it in his career and fame box (tenth house) *with his Moon*. He needed that old money. It gave him a position in the world and placated Mother.

The house of big tycoonery has Chiron in it. It must mean *something*. Chiron breaks up impasses. It is a maverick. But Leo is on the eighth house, and *the Sun* rules that. Somehow his soul's purpose for being here was linked with making big bucks. You wouldn't notice these things if you just looked at those almost empty money boxes.

Getty's eccentricities, like his famous doll house collection, show up in the limelight because wild Uranus in the tenth house gave him a weird public image. We all have our weirdnesses, but Getty never got away with his—they're right out there for all to see.

Next is Ari Onassis's chart. Ye gods, another Capricorn rising! Don't let anyone tell you that a miserable childhood and a fearful demeanor never gets you anywhere! Here's another tycoon who had to compensate for feeling like a schmucky-looking guy.

Even if they're handsome or beautiful, Capricorn rising people never fully believe it. Perhaps this is their wisdom. Ari Onassis could never bank on being tall, dark, and handsome to get by in life.

Look at Ari's second and eighth houses. We get the Moon in the tycoon box (eighth) so he needed that money more than J. P. Getty did.

His second house is a mess. It has the two Big Trouble planets in it; Saturn for pain and Mars for burning drive. See what can be done with those horrible planets? Ari was so terrified of being poor it made him rich. He worked relentlessly for it. He has terrible mean old Saturn to thank for it. Saturn's in Pisces, by the way, and Pisces is connected with the sea, ships, and oil. Interesting, no?

What's intriguing about both these charts is that the Sun rules the eighth house. On a spiritual level it means their lives' purposes were bound up in being catalysts for other people. The eighth house rules death. Their deaths left museums, and fortunes to their relatives. They were the movers for institutions and governments affecting millions of people. Had they lived in the future, when life-spans will be much longer, they would both have probably gone back to school and studied psychology . . . the Lord knows they needed it.

Now here's John Maynard Keynes' chart. Look at all that stuff in Gemini—no wonder his ideas are currently out of fashion and misunderstood. The planets in the sky right now are attacking his chart. Dead men get no rest in astrology!

Check out that Sun and Moon both in the money box; both the need and the life purpose are connected with dough. Taurus is the rising sign, so the man would never feel comfortable without *some* money, but Sagittarius is on his tycoon box (the eighth) and its ruler, Jupiter, is in the talk box (third house). He had more fun talking and writing about money than making back-room deals for it. Along with Adam Smith and Karl Marx, Keynes left behind him a system of thought, *foundations* of economics. The second house shows the stuff that endures after you die, and with Gemini there, Keynes left *ideas*.

Karl Marx has a packed money box too. I did not wish to dignify him with a chart here. It's in so many astrology books already. He, like Keynes, has the Sun and Moon in the second house, but they're in heavy-handed Taurus. Marxism has sticky fingers and can't help getting its hands on your stuff. Taurus is

```
PLANET SIGN  LONG     HSE
SUN    Cpr 24 10 33    1
MOON   Vir 20  0  3    8
MERC   Cpr  3  6.5    12
VENU   Cpr 16 56.0    12
MARS   Plc 14 15.6     2
JUPI   Tau 26 31.9R    4
SATU   Plc  0 41.3     2
URAN   Cpr  5 31.7    12
NEPT E Can  8 36.0R    6
PLUT   Gem 21  8.4R    5
ASC    Cpr 22  2.3     1
MC     Scp 14 37.3    10
NODE*  Leo 21  5.8     7
PFOR   Vir 17 51.8
VERTEX Leo 26 26.5
EASTPT Aqu  9 42.8
  R=RULE      D=DETRIMENT
  E=EXALTED   F=FALL
   *TRUE NODE
```

```
      CARD FIX MUT
FIRE   0   0   0      3 | 1
EARTH  4   1   1
AIR    0   0   1      3 | 3
WATER  1   0   2
```

*** NATAL ASPECTS ***

	ANGLE	ORB		ANGLE	ORB
CON=CONJUNCTION	0	10	TRI=TRINE	120	10
SSX=SEMISEXTILE	30	3	SQQ=SESQUIQUAD	135	4
SSQ=SEMI-SQUARE	45	4	BQT=BIQUINTILE	144	3
SXT=SEXTILE	60	6	QCX=QUINCUNX	150	3
QTL=QUINTILE	72	3	OPP=OPPOSITION	180	10
SQR=SQUARE	90	10	/=PARALLEL OR	0	1

A=APPLYING S=SEPARATING CONTRAPARALLEL

	SUN	MOON	MERCURY	VENUS	MARS	JUPITER
MOON	TRI 4 11A	MOON				
MERC			MERCURY			
VENU	CON 7 14A	TRI 3 04S	/	VENUS		
MARS		OPP 5/44S	QTL 0 51S	SXT 2 40S	MARS	
JUPI	TRI 2 21A	TRI 6 32A	BQT 0 35S	TRI 9 36A	QTL 0 16A	JUPITER
SATU				SXT 2 25S	SSQ 1 15S	SQR 4 09S
URAN				CON 2/25A	/	BQT 2 60S
NEPT	/	QTL 0 36A	OPP 5/29A	OPP 8/20S	TRI 5 40S	SSQ 2 56S
PLUT	BQT 2 58A	SQR 1 08A			SQR 6 53A	
ASC	CON 2/08	TRI 2 02		CON 5 06		TRI 4 30
MC	QTL 2 27	SXT 5 23	SSQ 3 29	SXT 2 19	TRI 0 22	
NODE		SSX 1 06	SQQ 2 59	BQT 1 50		SQR 5 26

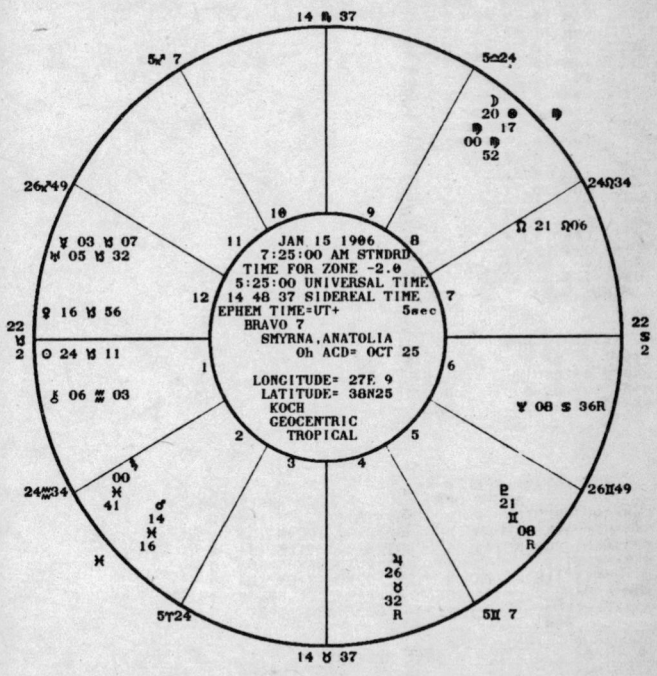

Ari Onassis

	SATURN	URANUS	NEPTUNE	PLUTO		ASC	MC
SXT 4 50A							
TRI 7 55A		OPP 3 04A					
TRI 9 33S							
				QCX 0 54			
			TRI 6 01	BQT 0 31			
OPP 9 36	SQQ 0 34	SSQ 2 30	SXT 0 03	QCX 0 57	SQR 6 28		

```
PLANET SIGN  LONG      HSE
SUN    Gem 14  2 47      2
MOON   Gem 11 47 20      2
MERC R Gem 18 39.9R      2
VENU R Tau 15 31.5       1
MARS D Tau  4 22.9      12
JUPI E Can  6 22.6       3
SATU   Gem  1 29.0       1
URAN   Vir 19 14.6       5
NEPT   Lib 19 29.6       ;
PLUT   Gem  0  3.6       1
ASC    Tau  8 51.1       1
MC     Cpr 13  1.1      10
NODE*  Sep 11  2.0       7
PFOR   Tau  6 35.7
VERTEX Lib 13 24.0
EASTPT Ari 17 40.9
  R=RULE     D=DETRIMENT
  E=EXALTED  F=FALL
   *TRUE NODE
```

```
      CARD FIX MUT
FIRE    0   0   0        1 | 0
EARTH   0   3   1
AIR     0   0   5        8 | 1
WATER   1   0   0
```

*** NATAL ASPECTS ***

		ANGLE	ORB			ANGLE	ORB
CON=CONJUNCTION		0	10	TRI=TRINE		120	10
SSX=SEMISEXTILE		30	3	SQQ=SESQUIQUAD		135	4
SSQ=SEMI-SQUARE		45	4	BQT=BIQUINTILE		144	3
SXT=SEXTILE		60	6	QCX=QUINCUNX		150	3
QTL=QUINTILE		72	3	OPP=OPPOSITION		180	10
SQR=SQUARE		90	10	/ =PARALLEL OR		0	1
A=APPLYING	S=SEPARATING		CONTRAPARALLEL				

	SUN	MOON	MERCURY	VENUS	MARS	JUPITER
MOON	CON 2 15A	MOON				
MERC	CON 4 37A	CON 6 53A	MERCURY			
VENU	SSX 1 29S			VENUS		
MARS			SSQ 0 43S		MARS	
JUPI	/				SXT 1 60A	JUPITER
SATU		/			SSX 2 54S	
URAN	SQR 5 12A	SQR 7 27A	SQR 0 35S	TRI 3 43A	SQQ 0 08S	QTL 0 52A
NEPT			SSX 0 50S	CON 3 58A		SSQ 1 53S
PLUT						
ASC		SSX 2 56		CON 6/40	CON 4 28	SXT 2 29
MC	QCX 0/58	BQT 2 46		TRI 0 30		OPP 8/39
NODE	BQT 2 59	QCX 0 45	BQT 1 38	OPP 4 29	OPP 6 39	TRI 4 39

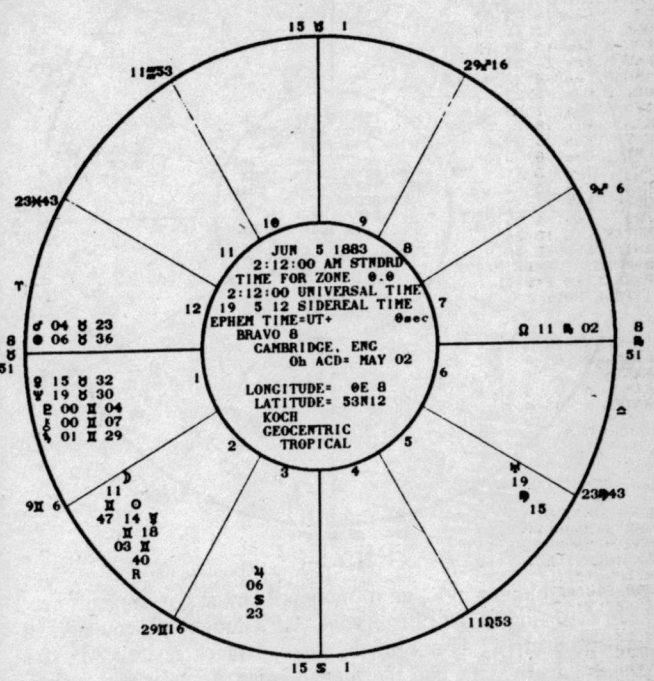

John Keynes

SATURN						
SSQ 1/05A	URANUS					
SQR 1 45S	SQQ 2 50S	NEPTUNE				
SQR 0/41S	SQQ 1/46S	CON 1 04A	PLUTO			
TRI 1 23		BQT 2 53	QCX 2 03	ASC		
SXT 5 41	CON 8 14	BQT 2 04	BQT 0 60			MC
	TRI 4 47					SQQ 1 59

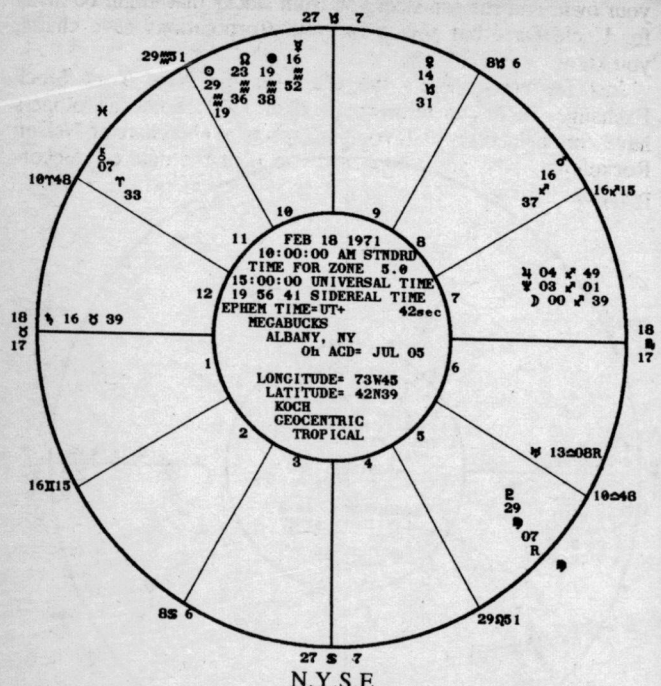

N.Y.S.E.

greedy and loathe to let go of money. Marxist governments can't keep their fingers out of everyone else's dough, and low agricultural productivity is one of the heavy-handed results. Marxism *sounds* ideal (Marx had the humanitarian Aquarius for a rising sign first impression) but it ain't fun, or free.

If you have a savvy astrologer working for you, and you want to go into business for yourself, the astrologer will set up an *electional chart* for you. This will cost you plenty, but it's worth it. First the astrologer studies your chart. Then the astrologer goes out of her mind, yanking out all the books and tries to find a ''perfect'' day and time for you to legally incorporate. As no perfect days exist in our solar system, this is no mean feat, but if your soothsayer knows her stuff, she'll cook up a chart to give you excellent odds on going into business successfully.

Like to play the stock market? Mad, impetuous *fool*, you! Bring a list of your favorite stocks to your financial astrologer. She can help you choose companies with charts compatible with your own, and she can steer you from stocks that might be lucky for Uncle Dave but poison for you. Corporations have charts, you know.

Just for grins, here's the chart for the New York Stock Exchange, as it was reincorporated in 1971. Some astrologers have commented on its favorable aspects to the chart of Nelson Rockefeller, who just "happened" to pick the date of reincorporation.

Old Age

What will we do when we're old and creaky? Old means you can't bend down to put on your roller skates for the disco anymore, but we hope by then to have found other ways of having fun. It is supposed to be the time when we celebrate the achievement of kindliness and wisdom, and if not, there are always drugs.

The fourth house has to do with old age, and we look at the sign on the cusp of the fourth to tell us the conditions we will find at the end of life.

Colonel Sanders had Taurus there, indicating a comfort and stability in his later years that most of us would envy. The ruler of Taurus is Venus, and instantly we see something unusual—it is on the Midheaven, smack at the top of the chart. This means career success, prestige, and even fame in later years.

Now check the angles to Venus and notice another stand-out quality: an almost exact square angle between Venus and Jupiter. Squares exaggerate a quality, and Jupiter is good luck and happiness, so the Colonel experienced great good fortune and happiness.

Old people sometimes forget they have a duty to the young; what they are now we soon shall be, and we need role models to follow.

With Jupiter in the first house of ego, Colonel Sanders made a fortune out of emphasizing his generous personality. His life reflected the Capricorn rising sign perfectly—he rose above terrific disappointment, struggled all his life, and never gave up. Capricorn gets success late, and when they get it, they loosen up and get silly.

I saw him in the lobby of the Sheraton-Universal hotel one day, giggling with somebody's children. When I asked him for his birth time he was courtly, warm, and diplomatic. The white suit he wore was fresh as the Arctic snows. Virgo, you know.

```
PLANET SIGN  LONG     HSE
SUN     Vir 17  4  5   8
MOON R  Cen 28  2 57   7
MERC    Lib 13  0.9    9
VENU D  Scp  2 56.4   10
MARS    Sag 21 31.9   12
JUPI    Aqu  2 53.4R   1
SATU    Vir  8 33.8    8
URAN    Lib 24 39.2    9
NEPT    Gem  6 49.2R   5
PLUT    Gem  7 53.2R   5
ASC     Cpr  9 56.5    1
MC      Scp  2 52.8   10
NODE*   Gem 19 52.2    6
PFOR    Scp 20 55.4
VERTEX  Leo 18 21.6
EASTPT  Cpr 28 32.9
R=RULE      D=DETRIMENT
E=EXALTED  F=FALL
 *TRUE NODE
```

```
     CARD FIX MUT
FIRE   0   0   1        2 | 5
EARTH  0   0   2
AIR    2   1   2        1 | 2
WATER  1   1   0
```

*** NATAL ASPECTS ***

	ANGLE	ORB			ANGLE	ORB
CON=CONJUNCTION	0	10	TRI=TRINE		120	10
SSX=SEMISEXTILE	30	3	SQQ=SESQUIQUAD		135	4
SSQ=SEMI-SQUARE	45	4	BQT=BIQUINTILE		144	3
SXT=SEXTILE	60	6	QCX=QUINCUNX		150	3
QTL=QUINTILE	72	3	OPP=OPPOSITION		180	10
SQR=SQUARE	90	10	/ =PARALLEL OR		0	1
A=APPLYING	S=SEPARATING		CONTRAPARALLEL			

	SUN	MOON	MERCURY	VENUS	MARS	JUPITER
MOON						
MERC		QTL 2 58A				
VENU	SSQ 0 52S	SQR 4 53A				
MARS	SQR 4 28A	BQT 0 31S		SSQ 3 35A		
JUPI	SSQ 0 49A	OPP 4 50A		SQR 0 03S	SSQ 3 39S	
SATU	CON 8 30S			SXT 5 37A		BQT 0 20A
URAN		SQR 3 24S	/	CON 8 17S	SXT 3 07A	SQR 8 14A
NEPT			TRI 6 12S	BQT 2 07S		TRI 3/56S
PLUT	SQR 9 11S		TRI 5 08S	BQT 1 03S		TRI 4 60S
ASC	TRI 7 08	/	SQR 3 04			
MC	SSQ 0 49	SQR 4 50		CON 0 04	SSQ 3 39	SQR 0 01
NODE	SQR 2 48		TRI 6 51	SSQ 1 56	OPP 1 40	SSQ 1 59

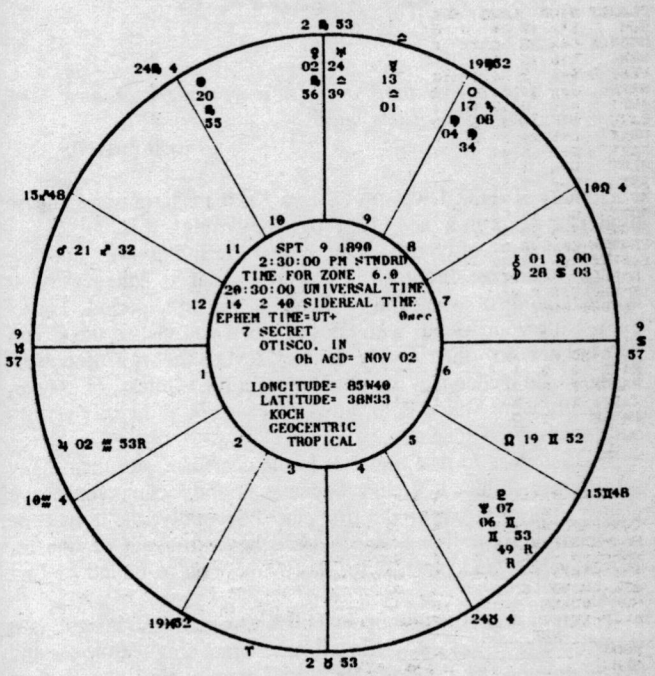

Inner chart text:
```
SPT  9 1890
2:30:00 PM STNDRD
TIME FOR ZONE  6.0
20:30:00 UNIVERSAL TIME
14  2 40 SIDEREAL TIME
EPHEM TIME=UT+        0sec
7 SECRET
OTISCO, IN
       0h ACD= NOV 02

LONGITUDE= 85W40
LATITUDE= 38N33
KOCH
GEOCENTRIC
TROPICAL
```

Colonel Sanders

SATURN	URANUS	NEPTUNE	PLUTO	ASC	MC
CON 1 25S	TRI 0 15S				
SQQ 1 28	TRI 4 14	TRI 4 29	SQQ 0 03	TRI 6 10	SXT 3 59
		OPP 8 28		OPP 2 11	

Past Lives

"The less we think of the next world, the greater mess we make of this one."

—Irish proverb

Personally, I think I was probably a Kraft macaroni and cheese dinner-in-a-box in a past life. Prove me wrong!

What counts, of course, is the life you're living now. Looking for clues to past lifetimes is constructive if it enhances your understanding of what you're doing in *this* life, period. Forget impressing your friends with tales of when you visited the Orient as Marco Polo—that merely denotes severe feelings of power-lessness and inadequacy about the present life. Unless, of course, you really were Marco Polo, in which case you'd do jolly well to cut down on the spaghetti.

Finding clues to past lifetimes in the chart is easier than many astrologers think. It's easy because nobody can ever prove you're right or wrong in the first place. Secondly, the horoscope is a complicated, living map. You'll never run out of houses, angles, signs, and patterns to play with. You're bound to find *something*.

"Even if what comes up is bullshit, you'll get insight into your life now," says Roy Alexander, a practicing astrologer and psychotherapist in London. He comes from a trained scientific background, neither believing nor disbelieving in past lives. He started fooling around with the idea of taking people back to other lifetimes in their imaginations. Then he applies whatever comes out to the chart and their present life fears. I blame him for many a refreshing, sometimes scary, spooked-out rainy after-noon in Swiss Cottage.

There are pitfalls, like the afternoon Roy went back to a life on the farm where he was Martha, a patient, hardworking woman leading a boring life. Her husband, Jonathan, was not an affec-tionate, understanding man.

"Jonathan and Martha, Jonathan and Martha," I said to myself. Where had I heard those names before? Later, Roy and I walked through the rain to grab a bite to eat, and it suddenly hit me.

"Roy," I said. "Jonathan and Martha were Superman's foster parents. Have you just recently seen the movie?"

He had.

On the whole, though, Roy Alexander has had more successes than failures with this intriguing technique. In one session he took me back to Finland, where I was a young man living in the wild. I had apparently run away from my home and family in Westphalia out of fear of being involved in the continuous battles that went on there. It was a coward's life, living on nuts and berries and squirrels. My companions and I rationalized that we were preserving Higher Ideals by keeping ourselves safe and far away, but in truth we had no ideals to protect, and it was a fruitless, empty life. I had not protected my sisters or my parents against the brutality that raged in my homeland, nor did I feel any pangs of guilt or loneliness for them. All these feelings had to be blocked in the service of my fear, for in truth I had loved them very much.

The experience explained why, in this life, I feel great discomfort when I hear people talking about ideals at the expense of personal love. Living in the wild suggests unendurable boredom and futility when there is so much to be done in this world; and while I have bopped all over the globe I have never ever wanted to go to Finland or any of the Scandinavian countries. Under this indifference I discovered aversion—you couldn't drag me there!

Certainly any psychologist or drinking buddy can have a field day with this material; yet the sessions I had with Roy Alexander made me look at and define feelings I had no hope of exploring without using my imagination.

I owe a debt, too, to Liz Greene, another astrologer who now practices in London. She started me thinking about digging past lives out of the chart as if it were a treasure hunt. Liz dared to look at the chart in startling, original ways. The material on sex stereotypes relating to past lives originates with her.

A few guidelines, then, to start you on the search, with a reminder: *there are no rules*. For all you and I know, we are all living several lifetimes at once. Perhaps we checkerboard back and forth through time dimensions. What you may be seeing in your chart is future lives. Maybe the only life we ever get is this one, and when it's over your soul goes to a garage in Buffalo.

Go back to the Moon section. Study your Moon position by house and sign. This is where you have *many talents* from other lives. You do these things as automatically as breathing. Look for all the angles other planets make to the Moon if you have a computer chart. Each angle tells you about another series of natural gifts you have.

In fact, *all* the angles in your chart to *everything else* give you clues to past lifetimes. The old-time astrologers felt that tough angles (conjunction, square, opposition, quincunx) represented bad habits you acquired in the past, even bad deeds you did to other people—you're paying for them now, kid!

This kind of thinking makes me choke, especially because there may be more than a grain of truth in it! It feels cruel and futile that we have to pay for stuff we can't even *remember*.

In yoga theory we find a more compassionate explanation of sorts. The yogis call our habits *samskaras*; each time you do something, it's like making a wave on a lake. Each time you make a wave, it shifts a little sand down on the bottom of the lake. Soon you build up a sand dune, and the dune makes it easier for you to make more waves identical to the ones you made before. The chart merely shows where the sand dunes are, and how lumpy!

Most of us take our good qualities for granted. Comb your chart now for every "easy" angle in it (conjunctions, sextiles, and trines). Wallow in all the talents, good deeds, and good luck you earned in other lifetimes. It makes you happy, why not?

Sorry—it's time to break the rules again. Some of the toughest, most god-awful angles in your chart may show great spiritual qualities, and exquisite strength of character. Here's the chart of the writer Arthur Koestler, definitely one of the twentieth century's "Hot One Hundred" minds. The chart's a mess. Capricorn rising for a traumatized childhood and melancholy outlook . . . it's not a "lucky" rising sign. Saturn, which rules his rising sign and hence his life, was going *backward* when he was born. See the nasty little oversensitive Rx on the symbol for Saturn? That sucker opposes the planet of writing, Mercury, which *also* is going backward. The Moon, what he was in a past life, is square what he is supposed to do in this life, the Sun. No inner peace with that one! Keep going round the chart and you'll wonder how he ever got out of bed in the morning—yet here is one of our most valued deep thinkers.

No horoscope will ever show the level of development of a person. Upbringing, education, evolution are all a mystery as far as the chart is concerned. No one can ever judge another soul. Too many hidden sand dunes!

Arthur Koestler's chart boggles the mind. No one writes more simply and sharply about nebulous issues—politics, gurus, physics, psychology; the list of his topics is endless. There is nothing in his chart to indicate that he would use his talents as well as he has done. Nothing in his chart indicates that he would be imprisoned and sentenced to death in the Spanish Civil War. Many souls would have been crushed by a prison experience; having Saturn opposite Mercury, the planet of writing, is enough to crush any would-be writer's confidence, yet something made him keep trying. He got out of jail, too, and he is still cranking out books. He lives happily in London, behind Harrods.

This is the grand "X-factor" that astrology does not deal with. One chart may be brimming with potential, yet the man resorts to petty cruelties and a useless, lonely life running away from himself. Another chart, like Koestler's, may be riddled with worry, obstacles, and a dangerous amount of introspection; yet the person triumphs over difficulties and is an inspiration to the rest of the world, to boot.

It's lucky that astrology can't distinguish a "new" soul from an "old" soul. If we could, astrologers would swiftly become the New Age Inquisitors. You can get a *feel* for it, though, by listening a lot and watching people. One notices that the people who are the most rigid about using words like "karma" are also those who have not experienced what you are suffering. A lack of compassion, a lack of drive to understand anyone but oneself are the clearest indicators of the "new" boy in town.

And what about Martha? She is a well-educated Scorpio, smart, pretty, and a devout student of Eastern philosophy. She came in for her chart reading very upset. A year earlier, some two-bit astrologer in Washington, D.C. had told her it would take her exactly five more lifetimes to work out her karma. I told her it must have been her bad karma to meet that astrologer. She had probably burned off the five lifetimes worrying about it in the past twelve months.

Babies are born blind; your best friend gets mugged; you run out into the road to catch a football, and a steamroller runs over

```
PLANET SIGN  LONG   HSE
SUN      Vir 12 20  9  8
MOON     Sag  4 57 23 11
MERC R   Vir  1 14.1R  8
VENU     Leo  4 23.7   7
MARS     Sag  8 38.4  11
JUPI D   Gem  5 50.2   5
SATU R   Aqu 28 32.2R  2
URAN     Cpr  0 15.0R 12
NEPT E   Can 10  0.4   6
PLUT     Gem 22 41.1   6
ASC      Cpr 12  6.2   1
MC       Scp 13  3.7  10
NODE*    Vir  0 11.4   8
PFOR     Ari  4 43.4
VERTEX   Leo 21 42.9
EASTPT   Aqu  8 11.2
  R=RULE      D=DETRIMENT
  E=EXALTED F=FALL
   *TRUE NODE
```

```
      CARD FIX MUT
FIRE   0   1   2        3 | 3
EARTH  1   0   2          |
AIR    0   1   2        1 | 3
WATER  1   0   0          |
```

*** NATAL ASPECTS ***

	ANGLE	ORB			ANGLE	ORB
CON=CONJUNCTION	0	10		TRI=TRINE	120	10
SSX=SEMISEXTILE	30	3		SQQ=SESQUIQUAD	135	4
SSQ=SEMI-SQUARE	45	4		BQT=BIQUINTILE	144	3
SXT=SEXTILE	60	6		QCX=QUINCUNX	150	3
QTL=QUINTILE	72	3		OPP=OPPOSITION	180	10
SQR=SQUARE	90	10		/ =PARALLEL OR	0	1
A=APPLYING S=SEPARATING				CONTRAPARALLEL		

	SUN	MOON	MERCURY	VENUS	MARS	JUPITER
MOON	SQR 7 23A					
MERC		SQR 3 43S				
VENU		TRI 0 34S				
MARS	SQR 3 42S	CON 3 41A	SQR 7 24S	TRI 4 15A		
JUPI	SQR 6 30S	OPP 0 53A	SQR 4 36S	SXT 1 26A	OPP 2 48S	
SATU		SQR 6 25S	OPP 2 42A			SQR 7 18S
URAN			TRI 0 59A	BQT 1 51A	/	
NEPT	SXT 2 20S	BQT 0 57S			QCX 1 22A	
PLUT		/		SSQ 3 17A		
ASC	TRI 0 14					BQT 0 16
MC	SXT 0 44	/	QTL 0 10	SQR 8 40		
NODE		SQR 4 46	CON 1 03		SQR 8 27	SQR 5 39
```
```

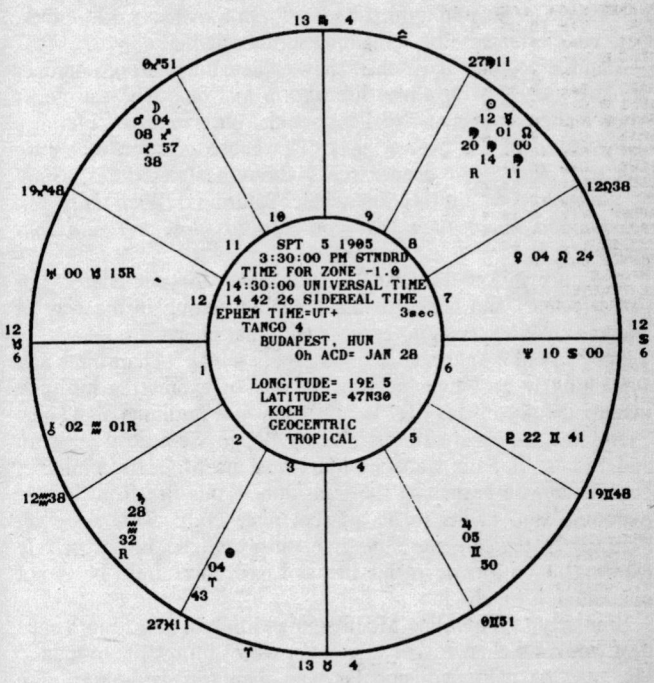

Arthur Koestler

SATURN						
SXT 1 43S	URANUS					
SQQ 3 32A	OPP 9 45S	NEPTUNE				
TRI 5 51A	OPP 7 34A		PLUTO			
SSQ 1 26		OPP 2/06		ASC		
	SSQ 2 11	TRI 3 03		SXT 0 58	MC	
OPP 1 39	TRI 0 04			SQQ 3 05	QTL 0 52	

your hands. Why is it that even the chart of a newborn child already shows what the baby fears?

I think we make a mistake when we look for reasons. You have to be pretty wise or very foolish to chalk it all up to the Will of God, just shrug and walk away, when harsh or senseless events occur. Searching for reasons doesn't always work, either. Perhaps there has to be something in the middle.

Saturn's position in the chart shows where the pain, or improper thinking, started—in a past life *and in this one!* The astrologer Marc Robertson has an excellent booklet out about past lifetimes with Saturn in the twelve signs. The house position of Saturn can give you even deeper hints about past lifetimes. Stare at your chart in the section where Saturn is. *What hurt you so damned much then that you had to close off and quit trying?*

If Saturn makes nasty angles to a planet in your chart, your past-life fears and hang-ups are probably getting in the way of whatever you're trying to express with that planet.

For example, Saturn attacking Mars in a man's chart hints that something in past lives gets in the way of expressing his sexy manhood fully in this life. Is his Moon in a feminine sign? The "feminine" signs are Taurus, Cancer, Virgo, Scorpio, Capricorn and Pisces. If Saturn attacks Mars *and* the Moon is feminine, chances are he is making the transition in this life from female memories and habits to his present male body. *This does not necessarily indicate the man is homosexual*; he is desperately learning to be a man in this life and is deeply afraid he is not man enough for the job.

Similarly, a masculine Moon sign and Saturn attacking Venus in a woman's chart reveals a woman who "thinks like a man." She may be extremely popular with men friends *because she feels like one of them*. These women desperately want to feel pretty and successful at being women; the motivated ones work hard at it, the terrified ones drop out of the male-female games and avoid makeup, weight control, coquettishness, and the million and one pleasurable and harmless games that come with the battle of the sexes. Many of these women have surgeons cut their faces with knives so that they may look more like the plastic faces (which were also, many of them, privately butchered) on the magazine covers. Successful types develop both inner and outer resources to compensate for their fears.

That Grand Old Man of Reincarnation, Manly Palmer Hall, has written and spoken volumes on finding clues in the horoscope. According to him, the sign on the twelfth house cusp of your computer chart tells what kind of person you used to be.

If Capricorn is on the twelfth cusp, for example, you remember hard work, responsibility, and hard times. You have a feeling you don't deserve a lot of help when you're blue. Now look to see where the planet that "rules" Capricorn, Saturn, is located. This tells what area of life you feel guilty about. If the planet ruling the twelfth is in, say, the third house, you feel frightened and guilty about the way you speak or what you say.

Taking another example, say you have Sagittarius on the twelfth house cusp, so Jupiter is the "ruler." It is in the money box (second house). You may not be rich, but you will always have enough to get by. You're lucky, according to the past-life theory, because you were generous in other lives.

Think of past-life searching as ketchup is to a main meal. Don't drown your meat and potatoes with it!

Rock-'N'-Roll Horoscopes

"He made Little Richard look like a stockbroker."
    —H. Craig Merrell

"I don't believe in astrology. It's a lot of crap. I think that's another thing you should throw out the window. Mysticism. Cheap. It's amazing that people still hang onto that after all these years."
    —Mick Jagger in 1980, *High Times* magazine June 1980

Guess he had a lousy astrologer.

What's fascinating is that his chart responds to the transits of the planets beautifully. I'm a Mick watcher from 'way back, but he's entitled to his privacy.

I chose The Who and The Kinks for this section because I thought you'd like to see what makes the few, rare pop groups that stick together for over a decade fit together. We'll start with The Kinks. Their Mummies supplied the information.

Can we describe a pop group by studying the members' horoscopes? Run your finger round the four charts of the Kinks. Note the preponderance of the signs Cancer and Aquarius. Cancer is a sign that can't bear to give up the past. Cancers don't like to let go of people. The Aquarius thrust means the Kinks believe in what they sing. Their songs reflect a social conscience, as in "Dedicated Follower of Fashion," "Shangri-La," "Lola," "Superman," and "Sunny Afternoon." It is music for the brain instead of the crotch. They never lose touch with the plight of everyday people in their music, and in their personal lives The Kinks help many people, quietly, with no strings attached.

This compassionate note leaps out of Ray Davies' chart. See the tight "square" aspect between his Sun and Neptune? Ray Davies is the kingpin of the band, singer, actor, and composer of 95 percent of their music. His Midheaven is Sagittarius, and its

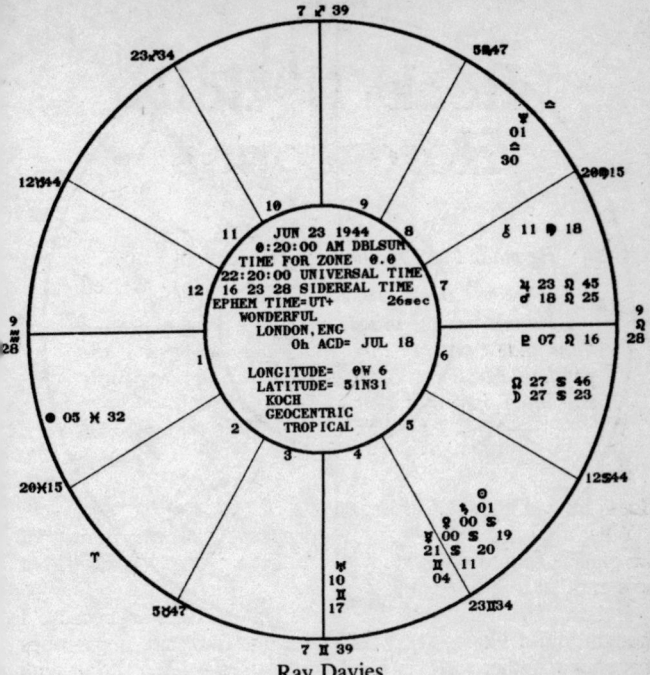

Ray Davies

ruler, Jupiter, is in showy Leo. Mars is on top of it, adding to his drive; when Mars and Jupiter get together we have the big risk-taker. Both are in the seventh house of the Vast Public. A Kinks concert is a music festival, but it is more like a dramatic event. You never know what Ray Davies will do next.

Take away the public image of the Midheaven and look to the personal planets, the Moon in Cancer and the Sun there too. How does a sensitive, whimsical, subtle double Cancer stay in show business? Don't ask me. Ray Davies isn't crazy about giving interviews. He keeps his private life strictly private. Remember the Sun squaring Neptune—it gives the music he writes a haunting, sadly humorous quality. His music uplifts people.

Dave Davies gives most of the interviews. His Sun is in the third house, a double-edged sword as the third house gives him bags of song-writing talent, the gift of being able to give a fascinating, off-beat interview, and a Big Wheel brother. Dave's

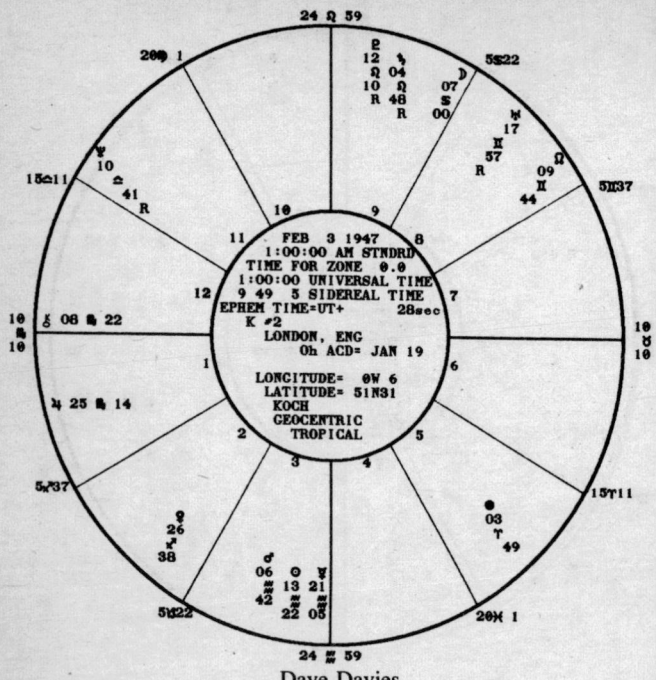

Dave Davies

brainy enough to have solved this paradox long ago; he adores his big brother Ray and makes his own music in his own right. He's growing increasingly prolific.

Mick Avery has that croquet-wicket-looking thingy, the North Node of the Moon in the eleventh house, so joining groups turns out lucky for him. Virgo rising in his chart means he is the meticulous one, always improving, filling in the details. His Sun is in the sixth house of service, which is like having the Sun in the sixth sign, Virgo, anyway. He doesn't care about throwing his ego around onstage; he just wants the band to be the best group in the world. He's like the band's doctor and editor, as well as being a key musician.

Jim Rodford has the Moon right there on the borderline of the eleventh house; he has a powerful need to work with groups, in a situation where he can be individual but equal with his friends. The Sun is in the fifth house. He is intensely creative—we will be hearing more from him. Look at the 26-degree rising sign in

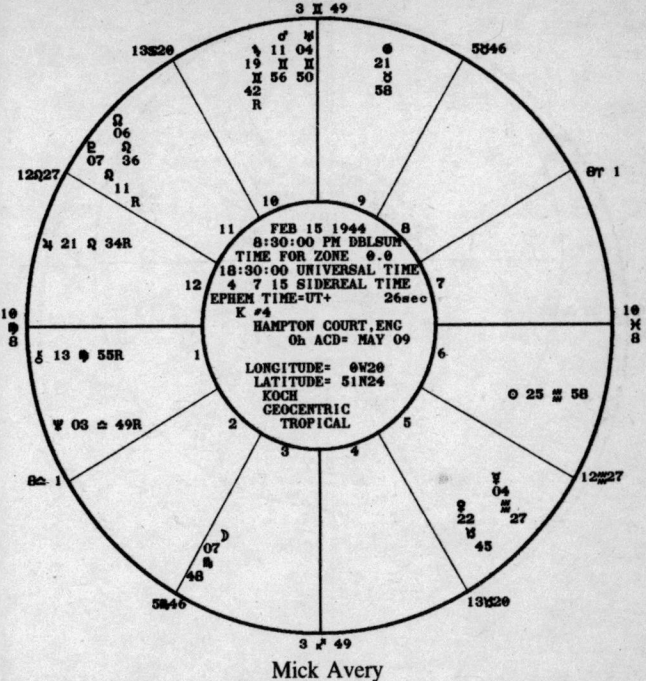

Mick Avery

Aquarius. See how it fits Mick Avery's 26-degree Aquarius Sun? There's one chance in 360 of that happening. Obviously the two are fated to work together, each enhancing the other.

When charts clash in pop groups, you find an ego and power struggle. The groups split up. The Kinks are Aquarian enough to let each other be themselves. The Beatles were Libra, Gemini, Cancer and Pisces. Each Beatle's personality was so different from the others that it gave a zillion little girls four distinct male archetypes to swoon on and choose from, but it didn't keep them together as long as The Kinks, whose personalities blend gracefully.

Next, The Who. I fell in love with Pete Townshend's nose when I was fifteen, stuck in school in Nuremberg. Pete Townshend's song, "My Generation," ripped through the hearts of *every* grown-up. It makes New Wave and Punk sound like Muzak. Townshend composes and arranges most of The Who's music. He wrote *Tommy*, the rock opera that became a film. It was an international smash success. If you haven't seen it, go for the

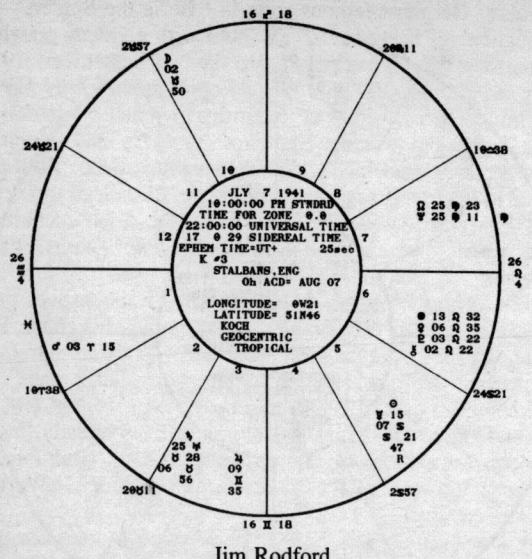

Jim Rodford

music, and go to see Ann-Margret crawling in an ocean of baked beans. Unbelievable.

Townshend has Sun in the ninth house. He is a visionary and a philosopher. He sees the bird's-eye view. He captured the spirit of London's "youthquake" in the sixties. "My Generation" was our rallying anthem.

Roger Daltrey has the Moon smack on Townshend's Sun. Daltrey responds to Pete Townshend's vision and puts it before the public—he's the sexy singer. I don't know if you'd call him the "front man." He is, but Townshend's no slouch with his leaps, his guitar playing, and his genius for composing music. My eyes keep drifting back to that marvelous nose. Look at all the planets Daltrey has in the public box (seventh house) and the fame box (ninth house). He is an actor in his own right.

John Entwhistle's chart does not link as closely with Townshend's chart or Daltrey's chart. He *looks* different onstage, stands there like a *rock*. Mars in Scorpio gifts him with a love of he macabre. His most famous song is "Boris the Spider," the lassic vignette of being stuck in a room with a creepy crawly.

Keith Moon was different too. He died in September, 1978, ne beloved, outrageous "wild man of pop" as the *Daily Mirror* alled him. Not one to disturb mourning parents, I left out his irth time and ran a solar chart for him. He had Moon in corpio, a rowdy placement. Rod Stewart has it too. Both pop tars used to love smashing things up; I guess it helped to release ension. Find the croquet wicket on Keith Moon's chart. It onnects with Townshend and Daltrey in late Taurus. Fated natch again!

Look down below Keith Moon's chart at the aspect grid. Mercury, the planet of intellect, hits *everything* in his chart. This s as rare as astrology ever gets. It is the mark of an extremely right, nervous soul, never content with an ordinary pace, the rain spinning on overdrive all the time.

"I know I have had about seventy-eight lives already," said Keith Moon shortly before his accidental death. "But I never hink about my own mortality. *Immortality* I consider." We will ot see *his* like again.

Kenny Jones joined The Who then, as the new drummer. His aturn is on Keith Moon's Sun, showing that he took over Moon's responsibilities. He is more sober than Moon, which nust come as a relief to the other members, but the feel is lifferent now. *His* Moon is on Daltrey's Sun. He responds to Daltrey more than to Townshend. His links with the group are ood. The Who grew up.

```
PLANET  SIGN  LONG    HSE
SUN     Tau 28 11 23   9
MOON    Vir  5 22 48  12
MERC    Tau  3 44.6    8
VENU D  Ari 20  3.7    7
MARS R  Ari 12 48.2    7
JUPI D  Vir 17 33.6   12
SATU D  Can  8 25.7   10
URAN    Gem 12 18.8    9
NEPT    Lib  3 50.0R   1
PLUT    Leo  8  5.6   11
ASC     Vir 22 25.4    1
MC      Gem 20  7.3   10
NODE*   Can 10  4.6   10
PFOR    Sag 29 36.8
VERTEX  Pic 12 19.3
EASTPT  Vir 18 18.7
 R=RULE      D=DETRIMENT
 E=EXALTED   F=FALL
  *TRUE NODE
```

```
      CARD FIX MUT
FIRE    2   1   0        4 | 5
EARTH   0   2   2       ---+---
AIR     1   0   1        1 | 0
WATER   1   0   0
```

*** NATAL ASPECTS ***

	ANGLE	ORB		ANGLE	ORB
CON=CONJUNCTION	0	10	TRI=TRINE	120	10
SSX=SEMISEXTILE	30	3	SQQ=SESQUIQUAD	135	4
SSQ=SEMI-SQUARE	45	4	BQT=BIQUINTILE	144	3
SXT=SEXTILE	60	6	QCX=QUINCUNX	150	3
QTL=QUINTILE	72	3	OPP=OPPOSITION	180	10
SQR=SQUARE	90	10	/ =PARALLEL OR	0	1
A=APPLYING S=SEPARATING		CONTRAPARALLEL			

	SUN	MOON	MERCURY	VENUS	MARS	JUPITER
MOON	SQR 7 11S					
MERC		TRI 1 38S				
VENU		SQQ 0 19S				
MARS	SSQ 0 23S	BQT 1 25A		CON 7 16A		
JUPI			SQQ 1 11S	QCX 2 30S		
SATU		SXT 3 03A	SXT 4 41A		SQR 4 22S	QTL 2 32S
URAN		SQR 6 56A			SXT 0 29S	SQR 5 15S
NEPT	TRI 5 39A	SSX 1 33S	QCX 0 05A		OPP 8 58S	
PLUT	QTL 2 06S	SSX 2 43A	SQR 4 21A		TRI 4 43S	
ASC	TRI 5 46		SQQ 3 41	QCX 2 22		CON 4 52
MC			SSQ 1 23	SXT 0 04		SQR 2 34
NODE	SSQ 3 07	SXT 4 42		SQR 9 59	SQR 2 44	

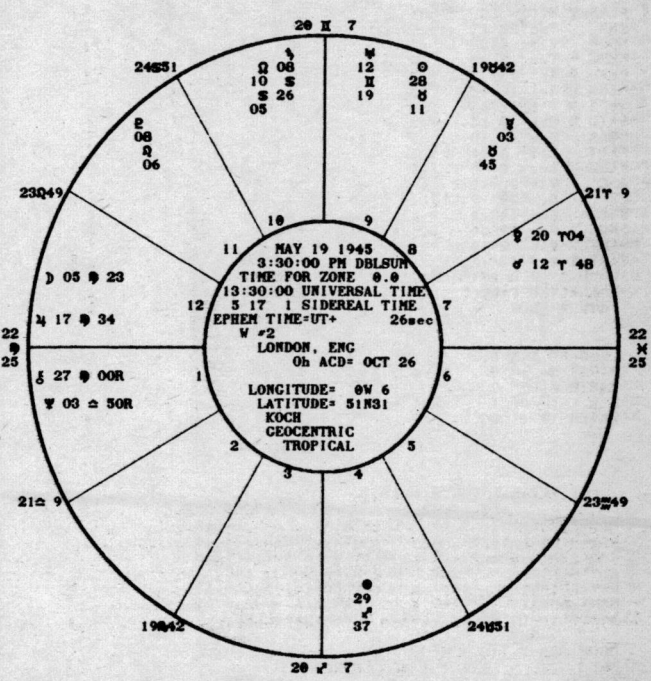

Pete Townshend

SATURN						
	URANUS					
SQR 4 36S	TRI 8 29S	NEPTUNE				
SSX 0 20S	SXT 4 13S	SXT 4 16S	PLUTO			
QTL 1 60			SSQ 0 40	ASC		
	CON 7/49		SSQ 2/58	SQR 2 18	MC	
CON 1 39	SSX 2 14	SQR 6 15	SSX 1 59	QTL 0 21		

```
PLANET SIGN   LONG     HSE
SUN    Pic 10 17 41    4
MOON E Tau 29 56 53    7
MERC E Aqu 26 27.3     3
VENU   Aqu 10 12.5     3
MARS   Gem 17 20.9     8
JUPI   Leo 19 46.7R    9
SATU   Gem 19 45.9     8
URAN   Gem  4 57.6     7
NEPT   Lib  3 29.1R   11
PLUT   Leo  6 53.6R    9
ASC    Scp 18  5.1     1
MC     Vir  6 50.4    10
NODE*  Leo  6 16.6     9
PFOR   Aqu  7 44.3
VERTEX Gem 28 50.4
EASTPT Sag 10 11.9
  R=RULE    D=DETRIMENT
  E=EXALTED F=FALL
   *TRUE NODE
```

```
       CARD FIX MUT
FIRE    0    2   0      1 | 6
EARTH   0    1   0
AIR     1    2   3      2 | 1
WATER   0    0   1
```

*** NATAL ASPECTS ***

	ANGLE	ORB		ANGLE	ORB
CON=CONJUNCTION	0	10	TRI=TRINE	120	10
SSX=SEMISEXTILE	30	3	SQQ=SESQUIQUAD	135	4
SSQ=SEMI-SQUARE	45	4	BQT=BIQUINTILE	144	3
SXT=SEXTILE	60	6	QCX=QUINCUNX	150	3
QTL=QUINTILE	72	3	OPP=OPPOSITION	180	10
SQR=SQUARE	90	10	/ =PARALLEL OR	0	1
A=APPLYING S=SEPARATING	CONTRAPARALLEL				

	SUN	MOON	MERCURY	VENUS	MARS	JUPITER
MOON						
MERC	SQR 3/30S					
VENU	SSX 0 05A					
MARS	SQR 7 03A	TRI 9 06S	TRI 7 08A			
JUPI		/	OPP 6 41S	OPP 9 34A	SXT 2 26A	
SATU	SQR 9 28A		TRI 6 41S	TRI 9 33A	CON 2 25A	SXT 0 01A
URAN	SQR 5 20S	CON 5 01A	SQR 8 30A	TRI 5 15S		QTL 2 49A
NEPT		TRI 3 32A	BQT 1 02A	TRI 6 43S		SSQ 1 18A
PLUT	BQT 2 36A			OPP 3 19S		
ASC	TRI 7 47		SQR 8 22	SQR 7/53	QCX 0 44	SQR 1 42
MC	OPP 3 27	SQR 6 53				
NODE	BQT 1 59			OPP 3 56	SSQ 3 56	

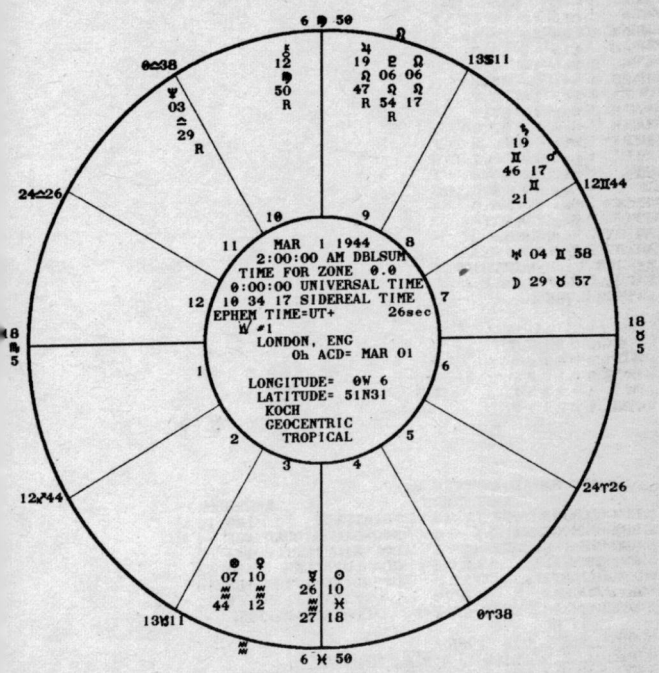

Roger Daltrey

SATURN	URANUS	NEPTUNE		PLUTO	ASC	MC
	TRI 1 29S					
SSQ 2 08A	SXT 1 56A	SXT 3 25S				
QCX 1 41		SSQ 0 24				
	SQR 1 53			SSX 0 03	QTL 0 45	
SSQ 1 31	SXT 1 19	SXT 2 48		CON 0 37		SSX 0 34

```
PLANET SIGN  LONG      HSE
SUN  F Lib 16 13 45    7
MOON R Can 23 18 46    5
MERC   Lib  7 59.3     7
VENU D Scp 14  1.5     8
MARS D Lib 27 25.6     8
JUPI D Vir 16  3.7     7
SATU D Can 10 37.0     5
URAN   Gem 12 57.0R    3
NEPT   Lib  4 26.8     7
PLUT   Leo 10  1.7     6
ASC    Pic  2 26.4     1
MC     Sag 19  0.3    10
NODE*  Can 23 56.0     5
PFOR   Sag  9 31.4
VERTEX Vir 20 18.8
EASTPT Pic 17  0.1
R=RULE      D=DETRIMENT
E=EXALTED F=FALL
  *TRUE NODE


      CARD FIX MUT
FIRE   0    1   0      0 | 6
EARTH  0    0   1       |
AIR    4    0   1      1 | 3
WATER  2    1   0
```

*** NATAL ASPECTS ***

	ANGLE	ORB			ANGLE	ORB
CON=CONJUNCTION	0	10		TRI=TRINE	120	10
SSX=SEMISEXTILE	30	3		SQQ=SESQUIQUAD	135	4
SSQ=SEMI-SQUARE	45	4		BQT=BIQUINTILE	144	3
SXT=SEXTILE	60	6		QCX=QUINCUNX	150	3
QTL=QUINTILE	72	3		OPP=OPPOSITION	180	10
SQR=SQUARE	90	10		/ =PARALLEL OR	0	1
A=APPLYING S=SEPARATING			CONTRAPARALLEL		

	SUN	MOON	MERCURY	VENUS	MARS	JUPITER
MOON	SQR 7 05S					
MERC	CON 8 14A	QTL 2 41A				
VENU	SSX 2 12A	TRI 9 17S				
MARS		SQR 4 07A				
JUPI	SSX 0/10S			SXT 2 02A	SSQ 3 38A	
SATU	SQR 5 37S	/	SQR 2 38A	TRI 3 24S		SXT 5 27S
URAN	TRI 3 17S		TRI 4 58A	QCX 1 05S	SQQ 0 31A	SQR 3 07S
NEPT		QTL 0 52S	CON 3 32S			
PLUT			SXT 2 02A	SQR 3 60S		
ASC	SQQ 1 13		BQT 0 27		TRI 5/01	
MC	SXT 2 47	BQT 1 41	QTL 0 59			SQR 2 57
NODE	SQR 7 42	CON 0 37	QTL 2 03	TRI 9 54	SQR 3 30	

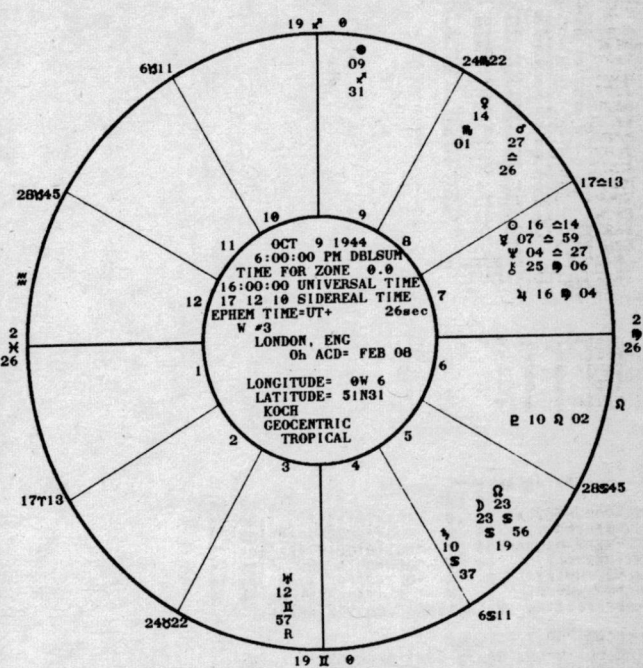

John Entwhistle

	SATURN	URANUS	NEPTUNE	PLUTO	ASC	MC
	SSX 2/20A					
	SQR 6 10A	TRI 8 30A				
	SSX 0 35S	SXT 2/55A	SXT 5 35A			
	TRI 8 11		QCX 2 00			
	/	OPP 6/03	QTL 2 33	TRI 8/59	QTL 1 26	
			QTL 1 29		BQT 2 30	BQT 1 04

PLANET		SIGN	LONG		HSE
SUN	R	Leo 29	13	56	1
MOON	F	Sep 25	37	13	4
MERC	F	Leo 23	12.2		12
VENU		Leo 26	8.0		12
MARS	F	Can 6	5.6		11
JUPI		Scp 19	48.6		4
SATU	D	Leo 14	40.0		12
URAN		Gem 25	28.8		10
NEPT		Lib 9	4.3		2
PLUT		Leo 13	28.7		12
ASC		Leo 29	9.1		1
MC		Tau 18	32.4		10
NODE*		Tau 27	54.9		10
PFOR		Scp 25	32.3		
VERTEX		Cpr 26	24.8		
EASTPT		Leo 13	36.8		

R=RULE D=DETRIMENT
E=EXALTED F=FALL
*TRUE NODE

	CARD	FIX	MUT
FIRE	0	5	0
EARTH	0	0	0
AIR	1	0	1
WATER	1	2	0

6	0
2	2

*** NATAL ASPECTS ***

	ANGLE	ORB			ANGLE	ORB
CON=CONJUNCTION	0	10		TRI=TRINE	120	10
SSX=SEMISEXTILE	30	3		SQQ=SESQUIQUAD	135	4
SSQ=SEMI-SQUARE	45	4		BQT=BIQUINTILE	144	3
SXT=SEXTILE	60	6		QCX=QUINCUNX	150	3
QTL=QUINTILE	72	3		OPP=OPPOSITION	180	10
SQR=SQUARE	90	10		/ =PARALLEL OR	0	1
A=APPLYING S=SEPARATING				CONTRAPARALLEL		

	SUN	MOON	MERCURY	VENUS	MARS	JUPITER
MOON	SQR 3 37A	MOON				
MERC	CON 6 02A	SQR 2 25S	MERCURY			
VENU	CON 3 06A	SQR 0 31A	CON 2 56A	VENUS		
MARS			SSQ 2 07S		MARS	
JUPI	SQR 9 25S	CON 5 49S	SQR 3 24S	SQR 6 19S	SSQ 1 17S	JUPITER
SATU			CON 8 32S			SQR 5/09A
URAN	SXT 3 45S	QCX 0 08S	SXT 2 17A	SXT 0 39S	/	BQT 0 20S
NEPT		SSQ 1 33S	SSQ 0 52A	SSQ 2 04S	SQR 2 59A	
PLUT			CON 9 44S			SQR 6 20S
ASC	CON 0/05	SQR 3 32	CON 5 57	CON 3 01		SQR 9 20
MC		OPP 7 05	SQR 4 40	SQR 7 36	SSQ 2 33	OPP 1/16
NODE	SQR 1 19	OPP 2 18	SQR 4 43	SQR 1 47		OPP 8 06

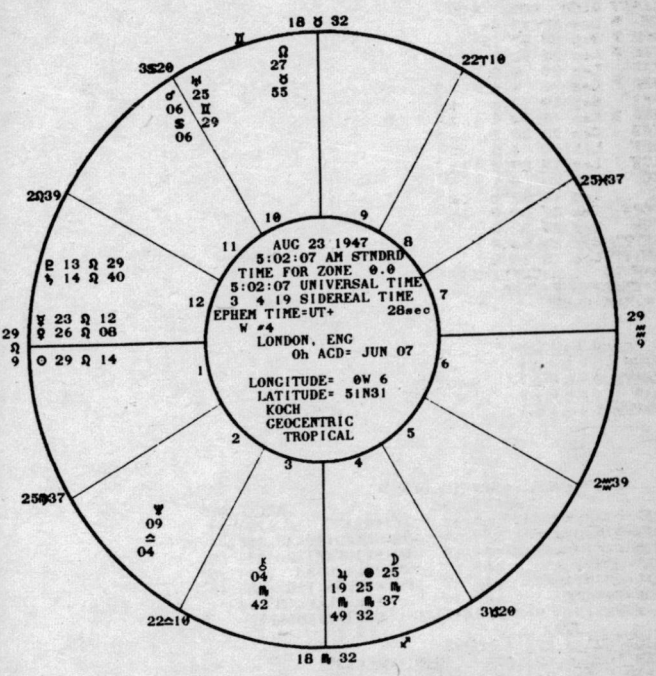

Keith Moon—Solar Chart

	SATURN	URANUS	NEPTUNE	PLUTO	ASC	MC
SXT 5 36S						
CON 1 11S		SSQ 2/60A	SXT 4 24A			
		SXT 3 40				
SQR 3/52				SQR 5 04		
		SSX 2 26	SQQ 3 51		SQR 1 14	CON 9 22

PLANET	SIGN	LONG	HSE
SUN	Vir	23 50	3 5
MOON	Pic	6 39 26	11
MERC	Lib	18 34.9	6
VENU	Leo	8 29.2	4
MARS R	Scp	8 50.8	6
JUPI R	Sag	20 37.6	8
SATU D	Leo	29 43.1	5
URAN	Can	0 24.7	2
NEPT	Lib	12 1.5	6
PLUT	Leo	15 43.4	4
ASC	Tau	20 49.4	1
MC	Cpr	22 30.9	10
NODE*	Tau	5 37.0	12
PFOR	Scp	3 38.8	
VERTEX	Lib	19 39.8	
EASTPT	Ari	26 13.3	

R=RULE D=DETRIMENT
E=EXALTED F=FALL
*TRUE NODE

	CARD	FIX	MUT
FIRE	0	3	1
EARTH	0	0	1
AIR	2	0	0
WATER	1	1	1

1	1
1	7

*** NATAL ASPECTS ***

	ANGLE	ORB			ANGLE	ORB
CON=CONJUNCTION	0	10		TRI=TRINE	120	10
SSX=SEMISEXTILE	30	3		SQQ=SESQUIQUAD	135	4
SSQ=SEMI-SQUARE	45	4		BQT=BIQUINTILE	144	3
SXT=SEXTILE	60	6		QCX=QUINCUNX	150	3
QTL=QUINTILE	72	3		OPP=OPPOSITION	180	10
SQR=SQUARE	90	10		/ =PARALLEL OR	0	1
A=APPLYING	S=SEPARATING			CONTRAPARALLEL		

	SUN	MOON	MERCURY	VENUS	MARS	JUPITER
MOON		MOON				
MERC		SSQ 3 04S	MERCURY			
VENU	SSQ 0 21A	QCX 1 50A	QTL 1 54A	VENUS		
MARS	SSQ 0 01A	TRI 2 11A		SQR 0 22A	MARS	
JUPI	SQR 3 12S		SXT 2 03A	SSQ 2 52S	SSQ 3 13S	JUPITER
SATU		OPP 6/56S	SSQ 3 52S		QTL 2 52A	TRI 9 05S
URAN	SQR 6 35A	TRI 6 15S			TRI 8 26S	OPP 9/47A
NEPT	/	BQT 0 38S	CON 6 33S	SXT 3 32A		
PLUT			SXT 2 52S	CON 7 14A	SQR 6 53A	TRI 4/54S
ASC	TRI 3 01	QTL 2 10	QCX 2 14			QCX 0 12
MC	TRI 1 19	SSQ 0 52	SQR 3 56		QTL 1 40	SSX 1 53
NODE	SSQ 3 13	SXT 1 02		SQR 2 52	OPP 3 14	SSQ 0 01

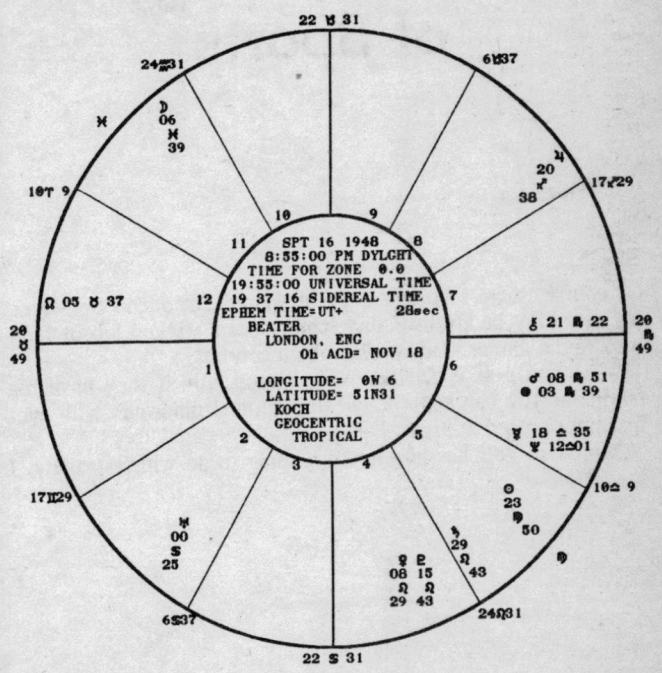

Kenny Jones

	SATURN	URANUS	NEPTUNE	PLUTO	ASC	MC
	SXT 0 42A					
	SSQ 2 42S					
		SSQ 0/19S	SXT 3 42A			
			BQT 2 48	SQR 5 06		
	SQR 8 54				TRI 1 42	
	BQT 1 12					
	TRI 5 54	SXT 5 12				

The Astrology
of Sports

Of course, there's an astrology of sports. Dr. Jacob Schwartz, my astrology buddy in Philadelphia, does a wicked job of forecasting the games. Talk to *him* about sports.

Miniature golf is another matter, especially if they have big pumpkins you can shoot a ball through and dinosaurs with eyes that light up red at night.

Miniature golf has absolutely nothing to do with astrology. I love it.

Synastry: The Sinister Art of Getting Along With Human Beings

This delicate art is beyond the scope of this cheap paperback. It's a branch of astrology all to itself. The astrologer makes a list of all your planets. Then the astrologer compares each one of your planets to each one of the other party's planets. This detailed work easily takes up an entire session, but it can save you a *fortune* if you're in marriage counseling. The kinks come out right away!

Psychiatrists often send couples in to have their planets compared, and we tape record the session. The jolliest part of this kind of work is that you can explain to Peter that he's driving Ellen mad when he expresses his individuality by playing video games all night. Then you explain to Ellen that it isn't a personal attack; that's how he's always expressed himself. Then we go back to Peter and explain that Ellen isn't the clingy type at all—she just doesn't like it when he doesn't ring when he says he will. She is vulnerable in the telephone box (Saturn in the third house). Then we talk to Ellen some more. She drives Peter crazy when she throws tantrums in restaurants. Her restaurant planet makes a square angle to his public image box. And so on.

Travel

"When the going gets tough, the tough get going."
—American proverb

No problem is too big to escape from. Life is precious. Sometimes your life may feel more precious someplace else.

All my life I've been plagued and blessed with crazy dreams. Seven-legged creatures made out of grape Jell-o with celery eyes have stalked me through subways; cruel brain surgeons try to strap me down for unsolicited lobotomies, but I fly away; I ride, alone and full of awe and wonder in that calm black night in a rowboat by the Taj Mahal. You know, the usual nighttime follies . . .

The ninth house rules the dreams that ooze through the gray matter in the sleeping hours. It rules consciousness. It rules travel. I travel a lot. It's harder for the grape Jell-os to find you if you keep lurching about the globe.

We'll leave the dreams to the analysts. Check your ninth house if you want to do some traveling. Planets here give you insatiable wanderlust. No planets here doesn't mean you're stuck. Look at the sign on the cusp of the ninth, and find the planet ruling it. If it makes a lot of angles to other planets you'll do your share of dragging the suitcases around.

Now here's a funny-looking chart. It belongs to singer/songwriter Electra Briggs. It's a map of the world, and a computer has drawn funny lines on it to tell her where she's lucky and where she's not. The computer does it from the day, month, year, time, and place she was born. It's called Astrocartography, or Astrolocality. You can send away for one. Your astrologer will help you to figure it out.

(If you order the map from Astrocartography in San Francisco, they'll give you a fascinating booklet that lets you find all the places yourself. It saves you money on going to an astrologer.)

When you take the chart to an astrologer, it saves hours of figuring out how to relocate the horoscope. At a glance you can tell where to go for romance or pleasure and where to avoid violence. For example, the Pluto line shows places where powers

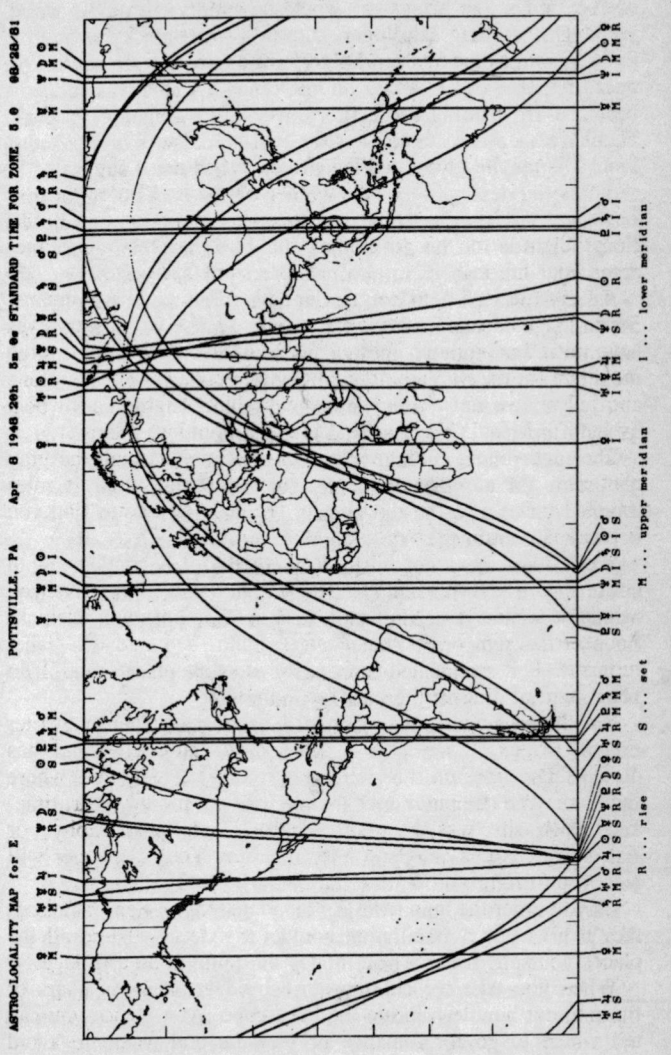

ASTRO-LOCALITY MAP for E   POTTSVILLE, PA   Apr 6 1948 20h 5m 0s STANDARD TIME FOR ZONE 5.0 98/28/81

I ... lower meridian

M ... upper meridian

S ... set

R ... rise

beyond your control hold sway. J.F.K.'s Pluto line runs through Dallas.

The Venus line brings the would-be suitors out of the wood-work. One dashing astrologer, cute in a smart-alecky way, used to be known as the Warren Beatty of the astrology network. One year he took a trip to a city on his Venus line and was suddenly beseiged by panting, sometimes weeping, women. He broke about five hearts in three days, and all he did was *breathe*. Our would-be playboy was terrified. It got so bad that I suggested he write a brief description of the women on the backs of all of their business cards, so he could remember them apart when he got home. As soon as he got home, off his Venus line, everything returned, regrettably, to normal. Verily I say unto you, the Venus line *works*! You don't even have to go there; people born around your Venus line fancy you too. Arabs always follow me around at conventions, though up to now I have refused their kind offers of trips, camels, and fancy joo-ells.

Are you currently living over two hundred miles away from your birthplace? You may need two charts, then, your real chart (which never changes) and your *relocated* chart. The planets stay the same on a relocated chart, but the Rising Sign and the Midheaven change, so the planets go into other houses. If you see that Saturn in the sky is about to sit on your Ascendant, for example, you may not wish to be in the place where that is occurring. Shift yourself elsewhere, and you'll still have hard work to do, but it needn't clobber you with full power—you'll have a new, temporary Ascendant.

Remember, a relocated chart never takes the place of your real chart, but it can shift the luck around a bit!

Another way to travel is to compare your chart with the country or cities you plan to visit. Is Japan's Mars on your Venus? The men will be crazy about you. Is the USA's Saturn opposite your Rising Sign? People are always criticizing you here. Is Brazil's Jupiter on your Sun? You may have a wonderful business or pleasure opportunity there. A good astrologer can look it all up for you. Cities and countries have charts too.

Have you lived your whole life in your hometown? Do you like it that way? Generally planets like the Moon or Saturn in the fourth house (the home box) make you feel a strong tie to your home with many responsibilities. Also generally speaking, it will be better for you psychologically to live elsewhere. The Moon often turns negative, fostering too many sick emotional ties that hold back your self-confidence, and Saturn can depress the living daylights out of you. Often Jupiter in the fourth house means you're lucky in some way if you stick near to home.

Pluto, Uranus, and Neptune often show up in the fourth house where a person has left his country altogether, sometimes even changing citizenship. As the fourth house is connected with feelings about family, particularly Dad, it's not surprising that the country of one's birth is rejected along with the memories. Pluto shows up so often in the charts of merry expatriates I've started calling it the Australian aspect—they're all in *London*!

For travel tips, check RED LIGHTS, GREEN LIGHTS to avoid jet lag. If you're going on a specific mission, take care not to arrive when the Moon is void of course, unless you like merry chaos and the unexpected. It's fine for a holiday if you like surprises.

Travel agents hang their heads and cry when Mercury is going backward—everybody changes their tickets or grumps about delays. Check the DON'T SIGN, DON'T BUY section too if this is the world cruise of your life, but Mercury backward is fine if you are prepared to be philosophical about little hitches.

In general big trips go more smoothly after an eclipse, even if only by a few hours. Then again, the eclipse may be the only Act of God to jolt you out from the beer can and the telly, so use your intuition, and roll with the compulsion if you must. Usually destiny is at work here, but you may not know how for another six months from the time you left home.

If you only know your Sun sign, you can still get a feel for everybody's traveling *style*.

ARIES—Want places that bring out challenge. They want to act like Action Man. They want to act like babies. They loathe organized tours. Free time is the only way they go.

TAURUS—Love nature, and quiet, boring holidays. They want good food, massages, and comfort. A farm or the Ginza sound right.

GEMINIS—Get nervy, so a few trees don't hurt. They're experts in the new language in ninety minutes and love to show it off. They can't bear to be stuck in one place. Bring books and keep moving.

CANCER—Isn't crazy about travel. They'd rather stay home. If they must travel, they like other people's homes. Let them bring a few mementos and stuffed toys with them. Distract them with good comforting food.

LEO—First class all the way! Sun worshippers.

VIRGO—They want to know they can get a bath when they want one, and safe, clean food. Usually they're drawn to places connected with their work or obsessions.

LIBRA—They don't like to go alone. Ever.

SCORPIO—They need a feeling of power in a strange place. A car satisfies this illusion in most cases.

SAGITTARIUS—Will go anywhere, anytime, and learn more than anyone, eat anything and go native fast.

CAPRICORN—Doesn't feel entitled to pleasure, so they need a two-hour business excuse on holiday. Then they can goof off. They do best on hot deserted beaches, where they practice doing nothing seriously. It takes them a few days to unwind.

AQUARIUS—People like places full of gadgets and weird people; they always find the off-beat place. An uptight, trains-run-on-time, fidgety place drives them *nuts*.

PISCES—Love the sea. They are not too keen on places where there is a great deal of human suffering. They all love France, but who can tell why?

X-ray Relationship Charts

This sneaky chart is like an X ray of a relationship. John Townley and Rob Hand made it famous, but I thought I'd seen everything until Lynn Schaffer pulled out her files and told me how she uses these charts to help her clients. Lynn Schaffer is a New York astrologer; a large portion of her clientele is single people. Lynn Schaffer started experimenting with the X-ray chart to see if she could help her love-lorn clients through the ups and downs of their romances. I laughed. She laughed right back.

She showed me the system. With it you can see what day *he* will phone, what day *they* will fight, and what day *she* can plan that weekend in the Poconos with the heart-shaped bathtubs. It *works*. I stopped laughing.

Ask your astrologer to do a composite chart for you. Then ask the astrologer to check the transits (where the planets are in the sky now) to the composite chart.

If your relationship is solid, you might not need this sort of service, but when it's new and you're goo-goo for the girl, you'd be amazed how useful this service can be.

A composite chart is your chart and the other party's chart put together, divided by two, then adjusted for the latitude where you two live.

It's handy to have a composite chart made up for you and any business partners or intended spouses. Occasionally this X-ray chart will spot a serious obstacle to the relationship, like a lack of ribs or something.

Part
IV

How to Use
the Tables
in This Book

What Time Zone
Do You Live In?

RED LIGHTS, GREEN LIGHTS, OOOH!, OUCH!, WOW!, and all the other tables here will tell you what signs all your blablas are in. These tables even tell you the *exact minute* each planet enters a new sign.

This can be a tremendous help if you must know whether the new fella wants to be treated like a king (Mars in Leo) or will be willing to fix your stereo (Mars in Virgo).

ALL the tables here are calculated for Greenwich Mean Time. If you live in England you can take the tables straight from the book. Astronomers and astrologers work to GMT, also called Time Zone Zero.

First, what time zone were you born in? See how many hours it differs from Time Zone Zero. This table will tell you. If you live in Chicago that's Central Standard Time, six hours away from Zero. You would *subtract* six hours from *all* the tables in this book. If you were born in Paris, you would *add* one hour to the tables.

Don't forget good old Daylight Savings Time, or War Time either, if you were born during one! If your birth hour was recorded in these times, you subtract one hour from your birth time, then compare this new birth time with GMT. Or kick back and get a computer service to do a chart for you. Chances are, you won't have to bother with time zones at all.

In fact, most of the planets move slowly enough so that you may not need these time zone tables at all, except for the void of course Moon when you do your daily business planning in the RED LIGHTS, GREEN LIGHTS tables. They're the only

Just remember that when it's New Year's Eve in London, it's 7 p.m. in New York. London gets it first. Always SUBTRACT the number of hours away from GMT for these locations:

For places East of Greenwich Mean Time, always ADD the number of hours from GMT. The sun rises in Baghdad *before* it gets to London. It's a round world.

Time Zones of the World

STANDARD TIME NAME	ABBREV	MERIDIAN	h m
GREENWICH	GMT	0° W	0
WEST AFRICA	WAT	15	1
AZORES	AT	30	2
BRAZIL ZONE 2		45	3
NEWFOUNDLAND	NST	52° W 30'	3:30
ATLANTIC	AST	60	4
EASTERN	EST	75	5
CENTRAL	CST	90	6
MOUNTAIN	MST	105	7
PACIFIC	PST	120	8
YUKON	YST	135	9
ALASKA-HAWAII	AHST	150	10
HAWAIIAN	HST	157° W 30'	10:30
NOME	NT	165	11
BERING	BST	165	11
INT'L DATE LINE		180° W	12

STANDARD TIME NAME	ABBREV	MERIDIAN	h m
CENTRAL EUROPEAN	CET	15°E	1
MIDDLE EUROPE	MET	15	1
EASTERN EUROPEAN	EET	30	2
BAGHDAD	BT	45	3
USSR ZONE 3		60	4
USSR ZONE 4		75	5
INDIAN	IST	82°E 30'	5:30
USSR ZONE 5		90	6
NORTH SUMATRA	NST	97°E 30'	6:30
SOUTH SUMATRA	SST	105	7
JAVA	JT	112°E 30'	7:30
CHINA COAST	CCT	120	8
JAPAN	JST	135	9
SOUTH AUSTRALIA	SAST	142°E 30'	9:30
GUAM	GST	150	10
NEW ZEALAND	NZT	165	11
		180°E	12

Reprinted with permission from *The American Ephemeris*, P.O. Box 16430, San Diego, California 92116 tables you'll need to use frequently. If you live in the United States, give yourself a break and send off to the CAO Times, Box 75, Old Chelsea Station, New York, N.Y. 10113. For a nominal sum they'll send you a sheet good for one year with all the voids calculated for your own time zone. It saves a lot of fussing every two days and is well worth the money. It's too easy to make mistakes on time zone corrections otherwise, and don't tell anybody, but it's what all the astrologers use because it's easy and lazy. It's worth the two bucks.

How to Win at Nearly Everything, Achieve Nirvana, and Screw Your Enemies With Black Magic Astrology

Shhh . . . we don't want those astrologers to hear us. You are about to learn one of the most well-kept Classified Cosmic Secrets of our galaxy. It is a wonderfully dangerous secret, so powerful it will insidiously change your life.

And still you *laugh*—ha! ha!—but your eyes will bleed when they first espy these tables. And when you at last comprehend their utter simplicity your brains will turn to Noodle-O's.

There are dark and terrible reasons why astrologers do not shout this stuff from the chimney tops. So proceed with *caution*, meinem Damen und Herren.

I never do. The price I pay for this starry recklessness is high, too high . . . there is a manic circus quality to my life, and the circus belongs to Charles Finney's Dr. Lao. Even a double Aries goes too far sometimes in the hell-or-high-water sweepstakes. When that happens I board a Short Line bus, fast, to Monroe, New York. Charles and Vivia Jayne, the Mr. and Mrs. Merlin of the stargazing world, do their best to lead a quiet life there, but they rarely live in peace; they are probably in the Top Five, worldwide, as far as astrologers go.

Charles Jayne is so smart that the Department of Defense had to build NORAD just to keep an eye on him. He is a spiritual math freak, outspoken, fearless, charming, endlessly kind and crazy. (When you do astrology as long as Charles Jayne has, you get crazy. We all do.) With Charles it is a crazed love of ideas and people. For his own twisted reasons he has helped and taught more astrologers than you've had hot dinners.

Vivia Jayne is a dangerous red-haired woman. She knows too much astrology for anybody's comfort, and she knows how to keep her mouth shut. There's a waiting list to have her do your 'scope. On the side she paints, sculpts, fixes cars, makes her own rugs, and makes sure Charles puts food in his body while his head juggles black hole formulae and the light bill.

When my first invitation came to one of the Jayne's infamous parties, Rob Hand, no slouch himself as far as astrologers go, gave me a ride up to Monroe. As we wheeled into the driveway, he stopped the car and let the engine idle for a moment.

"Before you go in there you'd better look out for Vivia," he warned me. "She keeps it very quiet, but she's the best chart reader in the country."

Nice one, Rob. I just love walking into parties paralyzed with awe.

Fortunately Vivia is one of the funniest astrologers around too. She actually *tells you the truth about your chart*. Oh, she's awfully nice about it. She puts the chart on the table and out come a stream of gentle snickers, oohs and ahhs.

"This guy ought to be working in Disneyland," she'll say. Or, "Oh, honey, these bitchy women in your seventh house are really nasty to you. You don't even see they're jealous of you, and you're so sweet to them." A reading with Vivia is better than five koala bears nuzzling you while you collect the Nobel Prize.

So of course Charles and Vivia Jayne taught me this RED LIGHTS, GREEN LIGHTS stuff, as Carl Payne Tobey taught them many years ago. Carl Payne Tobey had a mail order business and discovered that he always got lots of orders during the "lunar high" and felt like he was swimming through oatmeal on the "lunar low."

Actually they sort of *forced* the system down my throat, Charles patting my hand on one side and Vivia hollering, "Don't rush into it!" on the other. They had to do it more than once, too. It seemed like craziness to me, but it always worked and it kept me out of a lot of trouble. It has never let me down, and this system has brought me so many goodies, worldly and spiritual, that I want to share it with you. Share it with your friends and watch losers turn into winners. It's an unbeatable feeling.

Here comes the voodoo.

Red Lights,
Green Lights

"This sublime success comes only to those who follow what is right, namely the will of heaven or of those whose will embodies it."
—I Ching, Blofeld edition

GREEN LIGHTS—WHEN TO GET YOUR WAY

It's simple. Grab your calendar or appointment book. Then look up your GREEN LIGHTS days and pop them into your schedule. We'll show you how to find them in a minute.

Ready to win? These are your "best" days of the month. Now, "best" doesn't necessarily promise that these days will be fun or easy, but they are lucky. You're more likely to get your way . . . you have more power, more influence than at any other time of the month. Think of what you can accomplish if you dust off your zoot suit and steam ahead on these days:

Sign contracts
Begin important projects
Conclude deals
Ask the boss for a raise
Start love affairs with hard-to-get humans
Go for job interviews
Move into your new home
Apply for loans and credit cards
Approach "important people"
Arrive at your destination
Return home from a trip
Buy important clothes for business or pleasure
Argue with the telephone company
End something
Talk anyone into anything

You may have a headache, a hangover, or feel that your ego is sagging round your ankles. It doesn't matter. Get out there anyway. *Things will work out to your advantage*.

You will not do a jig in the subway car (unless somebody gooses you). And let's not blame astrology if the Thames does not part at the sight of your golden feet. You can screw up royally on a GREEN LIGHTS day, yet even then there is an element of lucky Fate at work. Maybe the boss screwed up, too, and you find yourself in good company. Perhaps the error of the moment turns out better for you in the long run. The great Mahabubu is steering you in a better direction.

If you're married, let your partner argue with the landlord on your *partner's* GREEN LIGHTS day. Double your luck!

Another advantage of GREEN LIGHTS days is that they appear to correspond with biorhythm cycles. People seem to heal up faster when they seek treatment on a GREEN LIGHTS day. If you've a medical problem, check the Astrology and Health section. Use it with your GREEN LIGHTS days.

What makes you win on these days? Is it dumb luck? Do you shine a little more than usual? Is the public in the mood to buy your wares? Nobody knows. There's no rational reason why these days should be luckier for you, but *this stuff works*.

Experiment. Say your buddies want Japanese food tonight and you're sick of the slimy stuff. You want Italian food. Tell them what you want on a GREEN LIGHTS night, then enjoy your pizza.

Do you think you're the vampiest woman who ever wriggled down the road? Experiment. You have more stamina on GREEN LIGHTS days. Try out the new dress today.

Lounge lizards, rejoice! Burn the candle at both ends! Think of how you can tax your strength and health beyond endurance! Party down on the GREEN LIGHTS days. Not so at the lunar low, when you may feel you need to hire a crane to lift the fork to your mouth.

RED LIGHTS—WHEN THEY GET THEIR WAY ALL OVER YOU

The secret of staying high on your "low" is simple. Kick back and let it roll over you. You need rest, for sure.

Things that happen on your low are not in your best *personal* interest. In a *broader* view however, it is in humanity's best interests to give our neighbor a helping hand. And help humanity you must, if they ask you on a RED LIGHTS day. It is a good time to be kind and spiritual. After all, it is only two days out of the month!

Give yourself a break. Have a swim, a massage, get a couple of early nights, and do favors for everyone.

Obviously this is the worst time of the month for the closing of your house sale, making deals, signing anything, starting a new job, or telling your honey about his bald spot. If you must decide something—don't. At least consult with experts. Listen to advice, but don't act unless you have to. Wait until the moon gets out of the RED LIGHTS district.

When the moon enters the next sign you'll be surprised at how easy it is to work out what your best course of action is.

Don't arrive in important locations on your RED LIGHTS days if you can help it. You'll be tired and jet lagged. You recuperate more slowly than on GREEN LIGHTS times. Pack the vitamins if you must go. The ball is in everyone's court but yours.

Even new restaurants and beauty parlors, if you're trying them for the first time, will disappoint you. RED LIGHTS days are tough tides to sail on if you are trying to get your way. That said, RED LIGHTS days have nothing to do with your spirits. You can be happy as a clam on these days. Just make like a clam. Watch one for a while. *Right.*

How to Use the Red Lights, Green Lights Tables

What is your Sun sign? That's all you need to know to find your "high" and "low" days. These tables tell you what sign the Moon is in in the sky, NOW.

If you're an Aquarius, your "high" is when the Moon enters Aquarius each month. Your "low" moon is Leo, the sign opposite Aquarius. If your daughter is a Gemini, her "high" is when the Moon goes into Gemini. Her "low" occurs when the moon enters Sagittarius, the sign opposite her Sun sign.

> ARIES is opposite LIBRA
> TAURUS is opposite SCORPIO
> GEMINI is opposite SAGITTARIUS
> CANCER is opposite CAPRICORN
> LEO is opposite AQUARIUS
> VIRGO is opposite PISCES

Forget the first column in the RED LIGHTS, GREEN LIGHTS tables when you want to know what sign the Moon is in. That first column won't tell you; it is for the void of course Moon, which appears in another section.

Use column two only for now. This second column tells you the precise moment when the Moon enters a new sign. The new sign is right there in the middle.

Let's take some examples for practice:

1982 RED LIGHTS, GREEN LIGHTS (Tables of the MOON)

JAN	1	21:51	2 Aries	6:34	JUL 30	20: 0	2 Sagittar	14:26
	4	7:18	4 Taurus	11: 3	4	17:31	5 Capricrn	3:16
	5	11:56	6 Gemini	12:49	7	4:12	7 Aquarius	16: 4
	8	7:55	8 Cancer	13: 2	9	17:58	10 Pisces	3:36
	10	8:11	10 Leo	13:22	12	3:32	12 Aries	12:50
	12	10:13	12 Virgo	15:38	14	10: 9	14 Taurus	19: 1
	14	13:14	14 Libra	21:18	16	11:25	16 Gemini	22: 4
	17	0:40	17 Scorpio	6:47	18	19: 9	18 Cancer	22:47
	19	17:39	19 Sagittar	19: 1	20	18:57	20 Leo	22:36
	22	1:39	22 Capricrn	7:52	22	14:44	22 Virgo	23:21
	24	17:33	24 Aquarius	19:26	24	17:30	25 Libra	2:46
	26	23: 4	27 Pisces	4:50	27	2: 9	27 Scorpio	9:59
	29	5:49	29 Aries	11:59	28	3:15	29 Sagittar	20:48
	31	11:44	31 Taurus	17: 4	AUG 1	7: 5	1 Capricrn	9:37
FEB	2	11:35	2 Gemini	20:21	3	11: 0	3 Aquarius	22:18
	4	17:13	4 Cancer	22:19	6	0:20	6 Pisces	9:24
	6	18:44	6 Leo	23:51	8	8: 4	8 Aries	18:21
	8	20:58	9 Virgo	2:16	10	16:44	11 Taurus	11: 2
	11	0:38	11 Libra	7: 3	13	2:33	13 Gemini	5:23
	13	9:14	13 Scorpio	15:17	14	22:45	16 Cancer	7:41
	15	20:22	16 Sagittar	2:46	16	23:58	17 Leo	8:41

Look up August 8, 1982 in the RED LIGHTS, GREEN LIGHTS tables. Isolated from the rest of the tables, we break it down this way:

AUG 8	**8:4**	**8**	**Aries 18:21**
(Date)	(This is the first column; skip it unless you want the Void Moon.)	(Date again)	(This is the time the moon entered Aries. Use this column.)

At 18:21 hours, or 6:21 P.M. Greenwich Mean Time, the Moon entered ARIES. Computers use the 24-hour clock so they don't have to fool with A.M. and P.M.. REMEMBER THAT ALL THE TIMES IN THIS BOOK ARE FOR GREENWICH MEAN TIME; you can use this book wherever you go. Just remember to convert the times for your time zone. If you live in Munich, add one hour to all the times in this book. If you live in Miami, subtract five hours to all the times in this book. A special page for looking up how many time zones you are away from Greenwich Mean Time is on page 382.

The Moon stayed in ARIES until it entered TAURUS, at 1:01 hours on August 11. It stayed in TAURUS until 5:23 hours, August 13, when it hit GEMINI. Run your finger down column two to see the times that the Moon changes signs every couple of days. Then stick it in your ear.

What if you want to make plans for January 3, 1984, and you see no date listing in the tables? No date listing means you can go right ahead and plan. There's no void that day. The moon is in Capricorn. Get down to some hard business.

JAN	2	19:29	2 Sagittar	21:33
	5	1: 7	5 Capricrn	10:25
	7	14: 1	7 Aquarius	22:54
	10	1:42	10 Pisces	10: 0
	12	2:24	12 Aries	18:49
	14	17:48	15 Taurus	0:39
	16	21:51	17 Gemini	3:26
	18	22:22	19 Cancer	4: 2
	20	22:37	21 Leo	3:59
	23	1:31	23 Virgo	5: 8
	24	7:49	25 Libra	9:10
	27	12: 1	27 Scorpio	17: 2
	29	7:12	30 Sagittar	4:19
FEB	1	13: 9	1 Capricrn	17:11
	4	2:17	4 Aquarius	5:32
	6	13:35	6 Pisces	16: 3
	8	19:47	9 Aries	0:18
	11	5:20	11 Taurus	6:22
	12	23:23	13 Gemini	10:24
	15	5:52	15 Cancer	12:46
	17	12:52	17 Leo	14:12
	18	19: 6	19 Virgo	15:54
	20	21: 0	21 Libra	19:22
	23	3:16	24 Scorpio	1:59
	25	12:19	26 Sagittar	12:11
	28	0:29	29 Capricrn	0:46
MAR	1	4:39	2 Aquarius	13:15
	4	1:13	4 Pisces	23:31
	6	5:18	7 Aries	6:55
	9	2:35	9 Taurus	12: 2
	11	11:32	11 Gemini	15:47
	13	7: 0	13 Cancer	18:52
	15	13:44	15 Leo	21:44
	17	18: 8	18 Virgo	0:50
	20	4:45	20 Libra	4:58
	22	10:27	22 Scorpio	11:19
	23	23:54	24 Sagittar	20:44
	26	21:17	27 Capricrn	8:52
	28	23:44	29 Aquarius	21:35
APR	31	12:20	1 Pisces	8:13
		7:45	3 Aries	15:23
	5	2: 4	5 Taurus	19:30
	7	8:25	7 Gemini	21:59
	9	16: 2	10 Cancer	0:17
	12	0:46	12 Leo	3:17
	13	21:15	14 Virgo	7:20
	15	13:46	16 Libra	12:37
	18	17:43	18 Scorpio	19:36
	20	10:37	21 Sagittar	4:59
	22	21:26	23 Capricrn	16:48
	25	18:13	26 Aquarius	5:43
	28	10:45	28 Pisces	17: 7
MAY	30	21:14	1 Aries	0:56
	2	13: 0	3 Taurus	4:55
	4	15: 8	5 Gemini	6:24
	6	16: 2	7 Cancer	7:15
	8	16:32	9 Leo	9: 2
	11	0:32	11 Virgo	12:42
	13	15:58	13 Libra	18:28
	15	8:55	16 Scorpio	2:17
	18	7:36	18 Sagittar	12:10
	20	5:31	21 Capricrn	0: 2
	23	7:32	23 Aquarius	13: 1
	25	9:57	26 Pisces	1: 8
	28	4:18	28 Aries	10: 9
	29	23:16	30 Taurus	15: 3
JUN	1	6: 9	1 Gemini	16:35
	3	2: 4	3 Cancer	16:31
	5	7:49	5 Leo	16:46
	7	10:23	7 Virgo	18:58
	9	15:49	9 Libra	24: 0
	12	2:16	12 Scorpio	7:56
	14	11:32	14 Sagittar	18:19
	17	1:51	17 Capricrn	6:28
	19	14:47	19 Aquarius	19:27
	22	4:26	22 Pisces	7:53
	24	15:41	24 Aries	17:57
	26	7:24	27 Taurus	0:20
	29	2:35	29 Gemini	3: 0

JUL	30	11:48	1 Cancer	3:10
	2	21:37	3 Leo	2:39
	4	22:27	5 Virgo	3:20
	7	1:58	7 Libra	6:48
	9	4:11	9 Scorpio	13:49
	11	20:30	12 Sagittar	0: 7
	13	16: 3	14 Capricrn	12:29
	16	21:49	17 Aquarius	1:28
	19	10:38	19 Pisces	13:45
	21	23: 9	22 Aries	0:10
	23	22:12	24 Taurus	7:45
	26	10:21	26 Gemini	12: 3
	27	20:19	28 Cancer	13:31
	30	02:19	30 Leo	13:25
AUG	1	12:35	1 Virgo	13:28
	3	14:51	3 Libra	15:32
	5	18:57	5 Scorpio	21: 5
	8	6:59	8 Sagittar	6:31
	9	20:16	10 Capricrn	18:45
	11	6: 3	13 Aquarius	7:44
	15	5:14	15 Pisces	19:42
	16	19:59	18 Aries	5:45
	20	9:15	20 Taurus	13:32
	22	18:52	22 Gemini	18:56
	24	7:58	24 Cancer	22: 1
	26	14:12	26 Leo	23:18
	28	4:45	28 Virgo	23:56
	31	1:22	31 Libra	1:34
SEP	1	12:24	2 Scorpio	5:56
	4	1:35	4 Sagittar	14: 9
	6	22:27	7 Capricrn	1:48
	8	10:28	9 Aquarius	14:46
	11	20:10	12 Pisces	2:35
	13	19:38	14 Aries	12: 1
	16	18:51	16 Taurus	19: 6
	18	17:32	19 Gemini	0:23
	21	1:29	21 Cancer	4:17
	23	3:59	23 Leo	7: 1
	25	1:34	25 Virgo	9: 3
	26	3:45	27 Libra	11:23
	28	16:53	29 Scorpio	15:31
OCT	30	22:43	1 Sagittar	22:51
	3	8: 4	4 Capricrn	9:43
	5	12:35	6 Aquarius	22:34
	8	8:56	9 Pisces	10:37
	11	1:10	11 Aries	19:52
	13	8:54	14 Taurus	2: 7
	16	6:18	16 Gemini	6:20
	18	1: 2	18 Cancer	9:38
	20	12:16	20 Leo	12:43
	22	15:13	22 Virgo	15:53
	24	18:35	24 Libra	19:31
	26	1: 4	27 Scorpio	0:24
	29	6: 5	29 Sagittar	7:41
	31	13:44	31 Capricrn	18: 3
NOV	3	5:38	3 Aquarius	6:42
	5	16:27	5 Pisces	19:14
	8	2: 5	8 Aries	5: 3
	10	5: 8	10 Taurus	11:13
	12	11:13	12 Gemini	14:28
	13	18:52	14 Cancer	16:22
	16	14:31	16 Leo	18:20
	18	17: 4	18 Virgo	21:16
	20	23:46	21 Libra	1:36
	22	8:19	23 Scorpio	7:34
	25	9:53	25 Sagittar	15:34
	27	0:58	28 Capricrn	1:58
	30	7:05	30 Aquarius	14:27
DEC	3	0:52	3 Pisces	3:24
	5	7:27	5 Aries	14:18
	7	20:23	7 Taurus	21:28
	9	18: 1	10 Gemini	0:51
	11	14:16	12 Cancer	1:50
	13	19: 5	14 Leo	2:10
	15	19:58	16 Virgo	3:31
	18	0:42	18 Libra	7: 2
	20	11: 8	20 Scorpio	13:13
	22	12:29	22 Sagittar	21:58
	24	10: 4	25 Capricrn	8:55
	27	10:53	27 Aquarius	21:26
	29	23:48	30 Pisces	10:28

```
JAN  1  2:58    1 Cancer    8:16     JUL  3  3:22    3 Pisces    4:35
     3  7:35    3 Leo      10:32          4  7:26    5 Aries    11:22
     5 11:32    5 Virgo    15:50          7 10: 7    7 Taurus   15:23
     7 11: 8    8 Libra     0:54          9 14:10    9 Gemini   17: 1
    10  6:33   10 Scorpio  12:50         11 16:38   11 Cancer   17:28
    12  5:46   13 Sagittar  1:24         13  2:25   13 Leo      18:27
    15  6:44   15 Capricrn 12:30         14 20:56   15 Virgo    21:40
    17 15:50   17 Aquarius 21:12         17 18:29   18 Libra     4:20
    19 22:45   20 Pisces    3:41         20  9: 1   20 Scorpio  14:31
    22  0:35   22 Aries     8:26         23  2:29   23 Sagittar  2:49
    24 10:26   24 Taurus   11:53         24  9:52   25 Capricrn 15: 9
    26  9:45   26 Gemini   14:30         26 23: 6   28 Aquarius  1:55
    28 12:53   28 Cancer   16:58         29  8:57   30 Pisces   10:28
    30 16:17   30 Leo      20:17    AUG  1 16: 4    1 Aries    16:48
FEB  1 21:41    2 Virgo     1:38          3 19:13    3 Taurus   21:10
     4  6:19    4 Libra     9:57          5 21:36    5 Gemini   23:58
     6 17:23    6 Scorpio  21: 7          7  0:44    8 Cancer    1:54
     9  8: 2    9 Sagittar  9:39         10  3: 2   10 Leo       3:56
    11 20:40   11 Capricrn 21:11         11 11:10   12 Virgo     7:23
    14  3:32   14 Aquarius  5:58         13 15:31   14 Libra    13:25
    16  9:42   16 Pisces   11:41         16 21:13   16 Scorpio  22:41
    18  9:43   18 Aries    15: 7         19  6: 7   19 Sagittar 10:33
    20 16:12   20 Taurus   17:30         21 19:37   21 Capricrn 23: 0
    21 21:37   22 Gemini   19:55         23 22:14   24 Aquarius  9:50
    24 22:29   24 Cancer   23:10         26  9:32   26 Pisces   17:51
    27  3:25   27 Leo       3:45         28 17:42   28 Aries    23:10
MAR 28  5:19    1 Virgo    10: 6         31  0:40   31 Taurus    2:42
     2  7: 0    3 Libra    18:35    SEP  2  4:47    2 Gemini    5:26
     4 22:44    6 Scorpio   5:23          3 15: 1    4 Cancer    8:11
     7 14:39    8 Sagittar 17:47          5 13:24    6 Leo      11:30
    10 10:41   11 Capricrn  5:55          7 20:32    8 Virgo    15:58
    13  3:34   13 Aquarius 15:33         10  0:34   10 Libra    22:17
    15 15:41   15 Pisces   21:31         12  9:39   13 Scorpio   7: 9
    17 18:49   18 Aries     0:14         15 15:25   15 Sagittar 18:36
    19  1: 8   20 Taurus    1:10         17 20: 7   18 Capricrn  7:15
    21 20:53   22 Gemini    2: 6         20 13: 5   20 Aquarius 18:39
    23 20:12   24 Cancer    4:34         22 10:39   23 Pisces    2:52
    25 21:47   26 Leo       9:23         24  8:28   25 Aries     7:35
    27 13:46   28 Virgo    16:35         26 22:34   27 Taurus    9:52
    30  9: 3   31 Libra     1:50         29  2: 1   29 Gemini   11:22
APR  1  8:39    2 Scorpio  12:50    OCT  1  6: 9    1 Cancer   13:32
     4  7: 2    5 Sagittar  1: 8          3 12:54    3 Leo      17:14
     6 21: 8    7 Capricrn 13:40          5 20:15    5 Virgo    22:41
     9 18: 7   10 Aquarius  0:25          7 17:28    8 Libra     5:53
    12  7: 3   12 Pisces    7:36         10  5:35   10 Scorpio  15: 2
    14  4:54   14 Aries    10:47         11 21:43   13 Sagittar  2:19
    16  4:23   16 Taurus   11: 8         15 12:50   15 Capricrn 15: 5
    17 12:56   18 Gemini   10:40         17 15: 1   18 Aquarius  3:19
    20 11:23   20 Cancer   11:28         20  5:54   20 Pisces   12:34
    21 14:33   22 Leo      15: 7         22  4:25   22 Aries    17:43
    23 20:58   24 Virgo    22: 5         24 19: 6   24 Taurus   19:34
    26  4:15   27 Libra     7:47         26 14:23   26 Gemini   19:34
    28 21: 8   29 Scorpio  19:14         28 18:56   28 Cancer   20:10
MAY  1  4:36    2 Sagittar  7:37         30 21: 1   30 Leo      22:48
     4 10:38    4 Capricrn 20:13    NOV  2  1:44    2 Virgo     4: 8
     7  6:46    7 Aquarius  7:41          4  2: 4    4 Libra    11:58
     9 14: 2    9 Pisces   16:17          6 18: 2    6 Scorpio  21:47
    11  3:52   11 Aries    20:54          8  5:58    9 Sagittar  9:16
    13 18: 0   13 Taurus   21:57         11 16:54   11 Capricrn 22: 1
    15 12: 6   15 Gemini   21: 8         14  5: 9   14 Aquarius 10:47
    17 15: 5   17 Cancer   20:40         16 15:32   16 Pisces   21:22
    19 19:52   19 Leo      22:38         18 21: 5   19 Aries     3:58
    21 20:15   22 Virgo     4:16         21  0:43   21 Taurus    6:27
    23 10:38   24 Libra    13:30         23  2:25   23 Gemini    6:15
    26 14:57   27 Scorpio   1: 6         24 23:21   25 Cancer    5:30
    28 21: 9   29 Sagittar 13:38         26 23:37   27 Leo       6:20
JUN 31 15:55    1 Capricrn  2: 7         29  4:29   29 Virgo    10:12
     3  8:39    3 Aquarius 13:38    DEC 30 19:12    1 Libra     17:30
     5 18:27    5 Pisces   23: 2          3 23: 4    4 Scorpio   3:09
     7  4:21    8 Aries     5: 9          6  2:30    6 Sagittar 15:28
    10  2:28   10 Taurus    7:45          8 18:36    9 Capricrn  4:15
    11 10:35   12 Gemini    7:49         11  7:15   11 Aquarius 17: 0
    14  3:21   14 Cancer    7:15         13 18:47   14 Pisces    3:59
    16  4:40   16 Leo       8: 8         16  0:51   16 Aries    12:31
    18  9:11   18 Virgo    12:13         18 10: 4   18 Taurus   16:46
    20 18:14   20 Libra    20:11         19 22:48   20 Gemini   17:40
    23  5:37   23 Scorpio   7:19         22  9: 4   22 Cancer   16:53
    25 17:51   25 Sagittar 19:52         24  8:32   24 Leo      16:33
    28  8:12   28 Capricrn  8:13         26 10: 8   26 Virgo    18:35
    30 16:37   30 Aquarius 19:20         28 18:52   29 Libra     0:15
                                         31  3:35   31 Scorpio   9:37
```

JAN	1 21: 8	2 Pisces 9:57	JUL	3 7:35	3 Scorpio 11:46
	4 11:10	4 Aries 12:44		5 19: 9	5 Sagittar 23:25
	6 14:26	6 Taurus 15:53		8 4:34	8 Capricrn 8:28
	8 18:23	8 Gemini 19:43		10 11:16	10 Aquarius 14:53
	10 20:46	11 Cancer 0:44		12 3:49	12 Pisces 19:23
	13 6:39	13 Leo 7:46		14 19:26	14 Aries 22:46
	15 8:24	15 Virgo 17:32		16 19:52	17 Taurus 1:34
	18 4:55	18 Libra 5:45		19 1: 1	19 Gemini 4:19
	20 17:58	20 Scorpio 18:35		21 4:20	21 Cancer 7:44
	23 5: 1	23 Sagittar 5:26		23 9:14	23 Leo 12:49
	25 8:27	25 Capricrn 12:40		25 14:57	25 Virgo 20:35
	27 16:23	27 Aquarius 16:28		28 3: 3	28 Libra 7:15
	29 15:55	29 Pisces 18: 9		30 16:14	30 Scorpio 19:45
	31 14: 7	31 Aries 19:22	AUG	2 4: 2	2 Sagittar 7:49
FEB	2 20:47	2 Taurus 21:26		4 12:46	4 Capricrn 17:19
	4 5: 9	5 Gemini 1:10		6 19: 0	6 Aquarius 23:32
	6 7:59	7 Cancer 6:58		8 18:48	9 Pisces 3: 5
	8 17:29	9 Leo 14:58		11 0:26	11 Aries 5:11
	11 10:24	12 Virgo 1:11		13 6:53	13 Taurus 7: 5
	13 16:21	14 Libra 13:18		15 4:19	15 Gemini 9:47
	16 22:15	17 Scorpio 2:14		17 7:57	17 Cancer 13:56
	19 10:26	19 Sagittar 13:57		19 18:49	19 Leo 20: 2
	21 6: 9	21 Capricrn 22:31		22 2: 4	22 Virgo 4:22
	23 17: 1	24 Aquarius 3:11		24 14:59	24 Libra 15: 3
	25 8:42	26 Pisces 4:43		27 3:16	27 Scorpio 3:26
	27 23:26	28 Aries 4:43		29 15:40	29 Sagittar 15:56
MAR	2 1:58	2 Taurus 5: 1	SEP	31 16:58	1 Capricrn 2:24
	4 6:45	4 Gemini 7:16		3 8:57	3 Aquarius 9:22
	6 5:10	6 Cancer 12:28		5 9:56	5 Pisces 12:49
	7 23:33	8 Leo 20:47		7 13:24	7 Aries 13:54
	10 10: 6	11 Virgo 7:36		9 13:44	9 Taurus 14:17
	13 4:35	13 Libra 19:59		11 15: 4	11 Gemini 15:41
	15 12: 4	16 Scorpio 8:52		13 7:48	13 Cancer 19:21
	18 16:46	18 Sagittar 20:57		16 1: 0	16 Leo 1:49
	20 12:30	21 Capricrn 6:45		17 10:58	18 Virgo 10:53
	22 20:30	23 Aquarius 13: 3		20 20:59	20 Libra 21:58
	25 0:51	25 Pisces 15:44		23 9:19	23 Scorpio 10:23
	26 11: 3	27 Aries 15:50		25 22: 0	25 Sagittar 23: 6
	29 2: 0	29 Taurus 15: 7		28 3:42	28 Capricrn 10:31
	31 5:30	31 Gemini 15:38		30 18:27	30 Aquarius 18:54
APR	2 12:23	2 Cancer 19:11	OCT	2 18:28	2 Pisces 23:24
	4 14:35	5 Leo 2:37		4 23:35	5 Aries 0:33
	7 4:41	7 Virgo 13:26		6 23:27	6 Taurus 23:58
	8 19:31	10 Libra 2: 5		8 22:45	8 Gemini 23:45
	12 14:16	12 Scorpio 14:57		10 22:38	11 Cancer 1:49
	13 23:11	15 Sagittar 2:53		13 6:18	13 Leo 7:26
	17 7:33	17 Capricrn 13: 6		14 23:55	15 Virgo 16:33
	19 19:54	19 Aquarius 20:42		18 2:51	18 Libra 4: 3
	21 15:32	22 Pisces 1: 7		20 15:26	20 Scorpio 16:37
	23 7:35	24 Aries 2:32		23 4: 8	23 Sagittar 5:17
	25 18: 6	26 Taurus 2:10		24 18:59	25 Capricrn 17: 6
	27 14:48	28 Gemini 1:56		30 2:25	28 Aquarius 2:45
	29 20:21	30 Cancer 3:58		30 8:21	30 Pisces 8:59
MAY	2 6:38	2 Leo 9:50	NOV	1 11: 1	1 Aries 11:28
	4 11:50	4 Virgo 19:48		3 10:29	3 Taurus 11:13
	6 13:12	7 Libra 8:20		5 9:30	5 Gemini 10:12
	9 14:20	9 Scorpio 21:11		7 9: 2	7 Cancer 10:40
	11 16: 6	12 Sagittar 8:49		9 13:53	9 Leo 14:34
	14 17:43	14 Capricrn 18:40		11 20: 1	11 Virgo 22:38
	16 21:54	17 Aquarius 2:31		14 9:23	14 Libra 9:59
	19 4:36	19 Pisces 8: 4		16 22:12	16 Scorpio 22:42
	21 7:45	21 Aries 11: 7		19 10:50	19 Sagittar 11:14
	23 9:14	23 Taurus 12: 7		21 18:53	21 Capricrn 22:46
	25 2:16	25 Gemini 12:26		24 8:35	24 Aquarius 8:44
	27 11:44	27 Cancer 13:59		26 12:11	26 Pisces 16:15
	29 18:10	29 Leo 18:39		28 0:57	28 Aries 20:35
JUN	1 2:25	1 Virgo 3:22		30 17:54	30 Taurus 21:54
	3 5: 9	3 Libra 15:18	DEC	2 3:44	2 Gemini 21:31
	6 3:29	6 Scorpio 4: 7		4 17: 8	4 Cancer 21:29
	8 7: 1	8 Sagittar 15:35		6 19: 7	6 Leo 23:56
	10 17: 9	11 Capricrn 0:51		9 1: 2	9 Virgo 6:22
	13 1: 4	13 Aquarius 8: 4		11 16:31	11 Libra 16:44
	15 2:39	15 Pisces 13:32		13 23:11	14 Scorpio 5:17
	17 11:34	17 Aries 17:24		15 21:34	16 Sagittar 17:48
	19 16:49	19 Taurus 19:48		18 22:51	19 Capricrn 4:56
	21 16:25	21 Gemini 21:27		21 8:19	21 Aquarius 14:18
	23 18:47	23 Cancer 23:40		23 15:57	23 Pisces 21:46
	25 23:12	26 Leo 4: 5		25 11:23	26 Aries 3: 5
	28 1: 6	28 Virgo 11:55		28 0:42	28 Taurus 6: 6
	30 22:58	30 Libra 23: 6		29 19:23	30 Gemini 7:23

JAN

1	1: 3	1	Libra	2:33
3	7:12	3	Scorpio	13: 3
5	14:14	5	Sagittar	19:28
7	16:44	7	Capricrn	21:56
9	17:34	9	Aquarius	22: 1
10	5:28	11	Pisces	21:52
13	20:17	13	Aries	23:23
16	1:20	16	Taurus	3:41
18	9:28	18	Gemini	10:54
20	20:15	20	Cancer	20:30
23	3:11	23	Leo	7:51
25	18: 1	25	Virgo	20:27
28	5: 3	28	Libra	9:22
30	16:51	30	Scorpio	20:49

FEB

2	2:25	2	Sagittar	4:52
3	6:23	4	Capricrn	8:46
6	6:30	6	Aquarius	9:22
7	15: 7	8	Pisces	8:35
10	5:48	10	Aries	8:30
12	8:12	12	Taurus	10:57
14	14: 6	14	Gemini	16:54
16	22:57	17	Cancer	2:14
19	11:11	19	Leo	13:53
21	12:18	22	Virgo	2:39
24	13: 1	24	Libra	15:24
27	2:50	27	Scorpio	2:58

MAR

1	10: 7	1	Sagittar	12: 2
2	9:38	3	Capricrn	17:40
5	18:27	5	Aquarius	19:56
6	12: 5	7	Pisces	19:58
9	19: 0	9	Aries	19:34
11	19:24	11	Taurus	20:38
13	23:36	14	Gemini	0:49
16	3:32	16	Cancer	8:52
18	19: 1	18	Leo	20: 9
21	21:55	21	Virgo	9: 0
23	20:42	23	Libra	21:36
26	7:56	26	Scorpio	8:43
28	17: 1	28	Sagittar	17:41
30	19:32	31	Capricrn	0: 8

APR

2	3:34	2	Aquarius	4: 0
3	5:45	4	Pisces	5:43
6	5:59	6	Aries	6:20
8	7: 2	8	Taurus	7:21
10	10:11	10	Gemini	10:29
12	7:35	12	Cancer	17: 4
15	3: 9	15	Leo	3:23
17	10:52	17	Virgo	16: 1
20	4:28	20	Libra	4:37
22	15:13	22	Scorpio	15:20
24	23:27	24	Sagittar	23:33
26	9:52	27	Capricrn	5:33
29	9:47	29	Aquarius	9:51

MAY

30	19: 5	1	Pisces	12:51
3	14:56	3	Aries	15: 0
5	17: 1	5	Taurus	17: 5
7	20:17	7	Gemini	20:22
10	1:23	10	Cancer	2:14
12	11:26	12	Leo	11:34
14	10:56	14	Virgo	23:44
17	12:15	17	Libra	12:28
19	22:58	19	Scorpio	23:13
22	6:36	22	Sagittar	6:52
23	21: 1	24	Capricrn	11:52
26	15: 1	26	Aquarius	15:21
28	4:11	28	Pisces	18:19
30	20:52	30	Aries	21:19

JUN

2	0:10	2	Taurus	0:40
4	4:21	4	Gemini	4:56
6	1:16	6	Cancer	11: 3
8	19:25	8	Leo	19:59
10	15:25	11	Virgo	7:44
13	19:36	13	Libra	20:36
16	6:48	16	Scorpio	7:52
18	15: 6	18	Sagittar	15:40
20	19:10	20	Capricrn	20: 3
22	21:12	22	Aquarius	22:21
24	10:48	25	Pisces	0:10
27	1:18	27	Aries	2:40
29	4:55	29	Taurus	6:24

JUL

1	9:59	1	Gemini	11:36
3	2: 3	3	Cancer	18:34
6	1:46	6	Leo	3:46
7	20:45	8	Virgo	15:23
11	2: 1	11	Libra	4:22
13	13:58	13	Scorpio	16:21
15	22:43	15	Sagittar	1: 3
17	17:46	18	Capricrn	5:46
20	5:13	20	Aquarius	7:30
22	5:25	22	Pisces	8: 1
24	6:34	24	Aries	9: 4
26	10:35	26	Taurus	11:54
28	14: 9	28	Gemini	17: 5
30	7:48	31	Cancer	0:39

AUG

2	7: 2	2	Leo	10:28
4	10:12	4	Virgo	22:16
7	7:28	7	Libra	11:18
9	19:59	9	Scorpio	23:51
12	6: 1	12	Sagittar	9:46
14	9: 2	14	Capricrn	15:43
16	16:11	16	Aquarius	17:59
18	10:56	18	Pisces	18: 2
20	14:14	20	Aries	17:46
22	18:26	22	Taurus	18:58
24	18:52	24	Gemini	22:57
26	11: 8	27	Cancer	6:12
29	11:36	29	Leo	16:20

SEP

31	7:31	1	Virgo	4:28
3	12:27	3	Libra	17:31
6	1: 7	6	Scorpio	6:11
8	12: 0	8	Sagittar	16:55
10	21:57	11	Capricrn	0:24
12	23:47	13	Aquarius	4:11
14	13:11	15	Pisces	5: 0
17	0:12	17	Aries	4:26
18	23:58	19	Taurus	4:22
21	3:32	21	Gemini	6:39
22	15: 0	23	Cancer	12:34
25	17:51	25	Leo	22:13
28	9:44	28	Virgo	10:28
30	18: 9	30	Libra	23:33

OCT

3	6:23	3	Scorpio	11:58
5	17:19	5	Sagittar	22:44
7	7:15	8	Capricrn	7: 5
10	7:37	10	Aquarius	12:30
11	20: 1	12	Pisces	15: 0
14	10:57	14	Aries	15:26
16	10:47	16	Taurus	15:17
18	11:46	18	Gemini	16:27
20	15:53	20	Cancer	20:46
23	4:49	23	Leo	5:11
24	17:44	25	Virgo	17: 0
28	0:35	28	Libra	6: 6
30	12:57	30	Scorpio	18:16

NOV

1	23:24	1	Sagittar	4:28
4	10:49	4	Capricrn	12:32
6	15:43	6	Aquarius	18:34
8	22:12	8	Pisces	22:36
10	20:35	11	Aries	0:45
12	21:43	13	Taurus	1:46
14	23: 2	15	Gemini	3: 6
16	3:36	17	Cancer	6:33
19	9:11	19	Leo	13:39
21	23:59	22	Virgo	0:34
24	8:58	24	Libra	13:30
26	21:27	27	Scorpio	1:44
29	7:32	29	Sagittar	11:29

DEC

30	18: 8	1	Capricrn	18:39
3	20:30	3	Aquarius	23:39
5	6: 3	6	Pisces	4: 8
8	4:16	8	Aries	7:25
10	8:23	10	Taurus	10: 1
12	9:40	12	Gemini	12:36
14	14:41	14	Cancer	16:26
16	20:55	16	Leo	22:59
19	3:35	19	Virgo	9: 1
21	18:43	21	Libra	21:36
24	7:30	24	Scorpio	10: 8
26	17:48	26	Sagittar	20: 8
28	11:41	29	Capricrn	2:49
31	5: 8	31	Aquarius	6:59

Month				
JAN	2 1:19	2 Gemini	2:30	
	3 17:54	4 Cancer	14:57	
	7 2:55	7 Leo	3:31	
	9 0:33	9 Virgo	15:30	
	12 1:54	12 Libra	1:56	
	14 7:36	14 Scorpio	9:31	
	16 5:39	16 Sagittar	13:26	
	17 23:21	18 Capricrn	14:8	
	20 12:52	20 Aquarius	13:16	
	21 5:2	22 Pisces	13:3	
	24 7:54	24 Aries	15:38	
	26 14:6	26 Taurus	22:17	
	29 0:15	29 Gemini	8:44	
	31 5:1	31 Cancer	21:12	
FEB	3 1:35	3 Leo	9:47	
	5 5:23	5 Virgo	21:23	
	8 5:32	8 Libra	7:31	
	10 8:36	10 Scorpio	15:36	
	12 17:10	12 Sagittar	20:59	
	14 22:48	14 Capricrn	23:31	
	16 18:15	17 Aquarius	0:1	
	18 23:31	19 Pisces	0:10	
	20 20:6	21 Aries	1:59	
	23 0:57	23 Taurus	7:9	
	25 9:46	25 Gemini	16:15	
	27 18:21	28 Cancer	4:11	
MAR	1 10:27	1 Leo	16:48	
	3 23:38	4 Virgo	4:14	
	6 8:0	6 Libra	13:41	
	8 15:44	8 Scorpio	21:6	
	10 21:28	11 Sagittar	2:33	
	13 0:52	13 Capricrn	6:9	
	15 3:38	15 Aquarius	8:16	
	16 2:26	17 Pisces	9:51	
	19 10:46	19 Aries	12:16	
	21 12:12	21 Taurus	17:0	
	24 0:4	24 Gemini	1:0	
	26 9:11	26 Cancer	12:7	
	28 22:19	29 Leo	0:38	
	31 5:46	31 Virgo	12:16	
APR	2 20:26	2 Libra	21:27	
	4 23:41	5 Scorpio	3:58	
	7 4:16	7 Sagittar	8:22	
	8 17:6	9 Capricrn	11:31	
	11 10:14	11 Aquarius	14:10	
	13 6:7	13 Pisces	17:1	
	15 16:43	15 Aries	20:44	
	17 22:50	18 Taurus	2:6	
	20 5:36	20 Gemini	9:55	
	22 4:36	22 Cancer	20:26	
	25 4:13	25 Leo	8:45	
	27 14:33	27 Virgo	21:6	
	30 2:42	30 Libra	6:28	
MAY	2 12:54	2 Scorpio	12:44	
	4 13:47	4 Sagittar	16:6	
	6 9:30	6 Capricrn	17:55	
	8 15:54	8 Aquarius	19:40	
	10 17:8	10 Pisces	22:30	
	12 22:57	13 Aries	3:1	
	15 5:24	15 Taurus	9:26	
	17 13:22	17 Gemini	17:49	
	20 0:55	20 Cancer	4:17	
	22 11:40	22 Leo	16:29	
	25 0:41	25 Virgo	4:59	
	27 15:53	27 Libra	15:34	
	29 18:8	29 Scorpio	22:31	
JUN	31 21:33	1 Sagittar	1:44	
	2 17:59	2 Capricrn	2:30	
	4 22:34	5 Aquarius	2:46	
	6 21:25	7 Pisces	4:20	
	9 4:0	9 Aries	8:24	
	11 10:9	11 Taurus	15:12	
	13 18:57	14 Gemini	0:17	
	16 1:37	16 Cancer	11:9	
	18 17:35	18 Leo	23:23	
	20 5:3	21 Virgo	12:8	
	23 17:51	23 Libra	23:38	
	26 2:24	26 Scorpio	7:55	
	28 6:50	28 Sagittar	12:2	
	30 6:12	30 Capricrn	12:48	

Month				
JUL	2 7:4	2 Aquarius	12:6	
	3 11:27	4 Pisces	12:8	
	6 8:59	6 Aries	14:43	
	8 14:31	8 Taurus	20:44	
	10 23:15	11 Gemini	5:53	
	12 23:49	13 Cancer	17:9	
	16 4:36	16 Leo	5:32	
	18 8:6	18 Virgo	18:17	
	21 3:36	21 Libra	6:15	
	23 12:55	23 Scorpio	15:44	
	25 14:48	25 Sagittar	21:25	
	27 9:44	27 Capricrn	23:18	
	29 16:39	29 Aquarius	22:48	
	31 19:49	31 Pisces	22:1	
AUG	2 16:52	2 Aries	23:6	
	5 0:12	5 Taurus	3:34	
	7 3:51	7 Gemini	11:50	
	8 20:9	9 Cancer	22:58	
	12 2:51	12 Leo	11:30	
	14 7:35	14 Virgo	0:8	
	17 3:17	17 Libra	11:56	
	19 16:4	19 Scorpio	21:51	
	22 3:37	22 Sagittar	4:49	
	24 5:50	24 Capricrn	8:23	
	26 1:52	26 Aquarius	9:11	
	26 19:2	28 Pisces	8:50	
	30 1:37	30 Aries	9:16	
SEP	1 4:7	1 Taurus	12:20	
	3 11:45	3 Gemini	19:9	
	4 19:7	6 Cancer	5:30	
	8 16:27	8 Leo	17:55	
	9 4:39	11 Virgo	6:29	
	13 15:41	13 Libra	17:52	
	15 18:6	15 Scorpio	3:21	
	18 2:19	18 Sagittar	10:32	
	20 11:24	20 Capricrn	15:13	
	22 17:39	22 Aquarius	17:40	
	23 23:53	24 Pisces	18:44	
	26 11:33	26 Aries	19:47	
	28 13:47	28 Taurus	22:25	
OCT	30 21:8	1 Gemini	4:2	
	3 11:47	3 Cancer	13:25	
	5 15:23	6 Leo	1:13	
	7 11:23	8 Virgo	13:50	
	10 15:17	11 Libra	1:1	
	13 0:29	13 Scorpio	9:47	
	15 7:13	15 Sagittar	16:8	
	17 10:51	17 Capricrn	20:38	
	19 18:10	19 Aquarius	23:52	
	22 0:31	22 Pisces	2:23	
	23 20:31	24 Aries	4:51	
	26 5:53	26 Taurus	8:12	
	28 11:45	28 Gemini	13:35	
	28 17:11	30 Cancer	21:57	
NOV	1 23:35	2 Leo	9:17	
	3 9:48	4 Virgo	21:58	
	7 0:15	7 Libra	9:30	
	9 9:24	9 Scorpio	18:3	
	11 15:20	11 Sagittar	23:27	
	13 6:19	14 Capricrn	2:45	
	15 21:33	16 Aquarius	5:15	
	18 1:10	18 Pisces	8:1	
	20 8:39	20 Aries	11:35	
	22 15:16	22 Taurus	16:13	
	24 14:21	24 Gemini	22:21	
	26 7:23	27 Cancer	6:38	
	29 9:3	29 Leo	17:31	
DEC	1 22:23	2 Virgo	6:12	
	4 10:19	4 Libra	18:24	
	6 20:12	7 Scorpio	3:40	
	9 2:10	9 Sagittar	9:0	
	10 20:22	11 Capricrn	11:16	
	13 6:1	13 Aquarius	12:15	
	15 9:57	15 Pisces	13:45	
	17 10:33	17 Aries	16:56	
	19 18:52	19 Taurus	22:11	
	21 22:44	22 Gemini	5:18	
	24 7:30	24 Cancer	14:15	
	26 20:3	27 Leo	1:10	
	28 4:39	29 Virgo	13:46	

Month	Day	Time	Day	Sign	Time
JAN	2	17:59	2	Aquarius	18:40
	4	21:14	4	Pisces	21:50
	7	4:27	7	Aries	4:57
	9	7:51	9	Taurus	15:59
	12	4:43	12	Gemini	4:58
	13	0: 2	14	Cancer	17:21
	16	20:45	17	Leo	3:37
	18	10:48	19	Virgo	11:40
	21	11:59	21	Libra	17:55
	23	22: 7	23	Scorpio	22:33
	26	0:12	26	Sagittar	1:38
	28	1: 1	28	Capricrn	3:27
	30	0:21	30	Aquarius	5: 4
FEB	1	3: 7	1	Pisces	8: 6
	3	11:22	3	Aries	14:13
	5	19:20	6	Taurus	0:10
	8	8: 4	8	Gemini	12:45
	10	12:24	11	Cancer	1:18
	13	7:43	13	Leo	11:32
	15	12:16	15	Virgo	18:53
	17	20:55	18	Libra	0: 1
	20	1: 5	20	Scorpio	3:56
	22	4:35	22	Sagittar	7:14
	23	14:41	24	Capricrn	10:12
	26	10:58	26	Aquarius	13:15
	28	18:45	28	Pisces	17:17
MAR	2	21:26	2	Aries	23:31
	5	6:52	5	Taurus	8:51
	7	19: 7	7	Gemini	20:56
	9	19:47	10	Cancer	9:41
	12	19:11	12	Leo	20:29
	14	0:22	15	Virgo	3:55
	17	7:27	17	Libra	8:19
	19	10:11	19	Scorpio	10:53
	21	12:23	21	Sagittar	12:58
	23	5:25	23	Capricrn	15:32
	25	18:49	25	Aquarius	19:11
	27	23:50	28	Pisces	0:19
	30		30	Aries	7:27
APR	1	7:56	1	Taurus	17: 0
	3	19:32	4	Gemini	4:50
	6	18:46	6	Cancer	17:41
	8	20:25	9	Leo	5:17
	10	20:12	11	Virgo	13:40
	13	10:39	13	Libra	18:21
	15	14:14	15	Scorpio	20:14
	17	13:38	17	Sagittar	20:52
	19	20:47	19	Capricrn	21:55
	22	0:38	22	Aquarius	0:39
	24	5:45	24	Pisces	5:52
	26	13:29	26	Aries	13:42
	28	15: 9	28	Taurus	23:54
MAY	1	11:22	1	Gemini	11:54
	3	7:39	4	Cancer	0:46
	6	12:12	6	Leo	12:56
	8	21:46	8	Virgo	22:34
	11	3:40	11	Libra	4:31
	12	23:31	13	Scorpio	6:54
	15	6: 2	15	Sagittar	6:59
	17	0:36	17	Capricrn	6:37
	19	0:48	19	Aquarius	7:40
	21	11:37	21	Pisces	11:41
	23	17:38	23	Aries	19:14
	25	20:34	26	Taurus	5:47
	28	18: 8	28	Gemini	18: 8
	30	18: 9	31	Cancer	7: 0
JUN	2	17: 5	2	Leo	19:18
	5	3:32	5	Virgo	5:47
	7	11: 1	7	Libra	13:14
	9	17: 3	9	Scorpio	17: 4
	11	17:44	11	Sagittar	17:51
	13	8:10	13	Capricrn	17: 6
	15	16:35	15	Aquarius	16:53
	17	16:39	17	Pisces	19:14
	20	0:54	20	Aries	1:30
	22	10:49	22	Taurus	11:36
	24	23: 4	25	Gemini	0: 3
	27	2:11	27	Cancer	12:57
	29	23:44	30	Leo	1: 3

Month	Day	Time	Day	Sign	Time
JUL	2	8: 8	2	Virgo	11:36
	4	18:50	4	Libra	19:56
	6	23:44	6	Scorpio	1:20
	9	2: 0	9	Sagittar	3:39
	10	19:23	11	Capricrn	3:44
	13	1:30	13	Aquarius	3:22
	15	1:15	15	Pisces	4:38
	17	6:58	17	Aries	9:24
	19	15:34	19	Taurus	18:21
	22	4:12	22	Gemini	6:24
	24	8: 8	24	Cancer	19:17
	27	3:44	27	Leo	7: 8
	29	13: 8	29	Virgo	17:13
AUG	31	21:53	31	Libra	1:24
	3	3:58	3	Scorpio	7:30
	5	7:44	5	Sagittar	11:15
	7	4:21	7	Capricrn	12:53
	9	9:58	9	Aquarius	13:29
	11	11:10	11	Pisces	14:47
	13	14:50	13	Aries	18:42
	15	21:42	16	Taurus	2:26
	18	9:22	18	Gemini	13:41
	20	21: 6	21	Cancer	2:25
	23	10: 5	23	Leo	14:14
	25	19:55	25	Virgo	23:51
	28	5: 8	28	Libra	7:16
	30	7:42	30	Scorpio	12:52
SEP	1	13:31	1	Sagittar	16:58
	3	15:45	3	Capricrn	19:46
	5	20:12	5	Aquarius	21:48
	7	20:54	8	Pisces	0: 9
	10	0:55	10	Aries	4:15
	12	5:16	12	Taurus	11:22
	14	18:16	14	Gemini	21:49
	16	21:10	17	Cancer	10:17
	19	19: 2	19	Leo	22:20
	22	5: 0	22	Virgo	8: 2
	24	12: 3	24	Libra	14:51
	26	13:26	26	Scorpio	19:21
	28	20: 4	28	Sagittar	22:31
OCT	30	8:34	1	Capricrn	1:11
	3	1:44	3	Aquarius	4: 0
	5	5:23	5	Pisces	7:36
	7	10:32	7	Aries	12:42
	9	18:50	9	Taurus	20: 6
	12	4: 5	12	Gemini	6:11
	13	22:21	14	Cancer	18:21
	17	5: 1	17	Leo	6:47
	19	15:40	19	Virgo	17:12
	21	22:58	22	Libra	0:16
	23	22:28	24	Scorpio	4: 8
	26	5: 0	26	Sagittar	5:57
	27	12:24	28	Capricrn	7:16
	30	8:41	30	Aquarius	9:24
NOV	1	12:42	1	Pisces	13:18
	3	18:53	3	Aries	19:22
	5	21:43	6	Taurus	3:36
	8	15:47	8	Gemini	13:56
	10	2: 1	11	Cancer	1:58
	13	8:50	13	Leo	14:38
	15	11:41	16	Virgo	2: 3
	18	5:23	18	Libra	10:19
	20	10:14	20	Scorpio	14:41
	22	15:44	22	Sagittar	15:57
	24	9:34	24	Capricrn	15:57
	26	12:19	26	Aquarius	16:16
	28	16:30	28	Pisces	19: 0
DEC	30	20:46	1	Aries	0:52
	3	5:35	3	Taurus	9:41
	5	16:36	5	Gemini	20:36
	7	20:37	8	Cancer	8:45
	10	17:50	10	Leo	21:25
	12	23:51	13	Virgo	9:27
	15	16:19	15	Libra	19:10
	17	22:41	18	Scorpio	1: 8
	20	1: 8	20	Sagittar	3:14
	22	2:23	22	Capricrn	2:47
	24	0: 9	24	Aquarius	1:53
	25	23:36	26	Pisces	2:46
	28	5:33	28	Aries	7: 7
	30	13:57	30	Taurus	15:22

	Date	Time		Date	Sign	Time
JAN	1	15:17		1	Virgo	20:16
	3	18:43		3	Libra	23:32
	5	22:13		6	Scorpio	2:30
	8	1:39		8	Sagittar	5:35
	10	5:40		10	Capricrn	9:17
	12	9:47		12	Aquarius	14:26
	14	19: 3		14	Pisces	22: 5
	17	3:48		17	Aries	8:43
	19	20:28		19	Taurus	21:23
	22	8: 5		22	Gemini	9:36
	24	18: 2		24	Cancer	18:56
	26	23: 1		27	Leo	0:39
	28	23:58		29	Virgo	3:40
	31	1:59		31	Libra	5:35
FEB	1	20:47		2	Scorpio	7:50
	4	7:37		4	Sagittar	11:15
	6	1:31		6	Capricrn	16: 3
	8	18:13		8	Aquarius	22:17
	11	2:53		11	Pisces	6:24
	12	12:53		13	Aries	16:50
	15	23:21		16	Taurus	5:21
	18	17:48		18	Gemini	18: 6
	20	5:37		21	Cancer	4:28
	23	7:27		23	Leo	10:49
	25	10:19		25	Virgo	13:28
	27	11: 2		27	Libra	14: 7
MAR	1	6:47		1	Scorpio	14:44
	3	13:39		3	Sagittar	16:55
	5	19: 4		5	Capricrn	21:25
	8	3:10		8	Aquarius	4:16
	10	9:26		10	Pisces	13:10
	12	20: 7		12	Aries	24: 0
	15	6:36		15	Taurus	12:28
	18	0:34		18	Gemini	1:30
	20	12:15		20	Cancer	12:55
	22	17: 1		22	Leo	20:40
	24	20:48		25	Virgo	0:15
	26	21:27		27	Libra	0:47
	28	17:44		29	Scorpio	0:16
	30	21: 9		31	Sagittar	0:42
APR	1	9:36		2	Capricrn	3:38
	4	5:39		4	Aquarius	9:46
	6	14:27		6	Pisces	18:52
	9	4:30		9	Aries	6:10
	11	11: 3		11	Taurus	18:49
	14	7: 6		14	Gemini	7:49
	16	12:24		16	Cancer	19:42
	19	2:35		19	Leo	4:46
	21	5:33		21	Virgo	9:59
	23	7:25		23	Libra	11:41
	25	10:12		25	Scorpio	11:19
	27	6:26		27	Sagittar	10:49
	28	3:33		29	Capricrn	12: 6
MAY	1	11:27		1	Aquarius	16:35
	3	19:12		4	Pisces	0:48
	6	6: 4		6	Aries	12: 2
	8	17:21		9	Taurus	0:51
	11	7:28		11	Gemini	13:44
	13	9:48		14	Cancer	1:28
	16	4:54		16	Leo	10:59
	18	12:51		18	Virgo	17:32
	20	20:31		20	Libra	20:55
	22	20:33		22	Scorpio	21:52
	24	16:10		24	Sagittar	21:44
	26	18:53		26	Capricrn	22:18
	28	19: 2		29	Aquarius	1:20
	31	1:11		31	Pisces	8: 4
JUN	2	11: 7		2	Aries	18:32
	4	22:49		5	Taurus	7:15
	7	12:19		7	Gemini	20: 4
	9	8:27		10	Cancer	7:23
	12	10: 9		12	Leo	16:30
	14	16: 4		14	Virgo	23:17
	16	20:48		17	Libra	3:49
	19	2:22		19	Scorpio	6:21
	21	0:45		21	Sagittar	7:33
	22	3:46		23	Capricrn	8:38
	25	3:51		25	Aquarius	11:11
	27	8:50		27	Pisces	16:45
	29	20:24		30	Aries	2: 8

	Date	Time		Date	Sign	Time
JUL	2	4: 9		2	Taurus	14:24
	4	18:18		5	Gemini	3:13
	7	13:14		7	Cancer	14:18
	9	14:25		9	Leo	22:44
	11	20:45		12	Virgo	4:49
	14	1:21		14	Libra	9:16
	16	3: 5		16	Scorpio	12:36
	18	7:33		18	Sagittar	15:10
	19	11: 2		20	Capricrn	17:31
	22	20:17		22	Aquarius	20:39
	24	17:28		25	Pisces	1:57
	27	1:28		27	Aries	10:32
	29	9:52		29	Taurus	22:14
AUG	1	2:35		1	Gemini	11: 6
	3	14: 8		3	Cancer	22:23
	6	3:44		6	Leo	6:32
	8	3:31		8	Virgo	11:43
	10	7:52		10	Libra	15: 8
	12	13:13		12	Scorpio	17:57
	14	12:55		14	Sagittar	20:54
	16	20:20		17	Capricrn	0:19
	18	20:23		19	Aquarius	4:35
	21	6:48		21	Pisces	10:28
	23	10: 2		23	Aries	18:56
	25	16: 4		26	Taurus	6:14
	28	9:52		28	Gemini	19: 8
	30	17:11		31	Cancer	7: 1
SEP	2	10:31		2	Leo	15:38
	4	16: 6		4	Virgo	20:34
	6	15:38		6	Libra	22:58
	8	12:16		9	Scorpio	0:27
	10	19: 7		11	Sagittar	2:26
	12	11:35		13	Capricrn	5:45
	15	3: 6		15	Aquarius	10:43
	17	9:44		17	Pisces	17:32
	19	20: 2		20	Aries	2:31
	22	9:47		22	Taurus	13:48
	24	18:31		25	Gemini	2:42
	25	17:30		27	Cancer	15:13
	29	19:47		30	Leo	0:56
OCT	2	0: 3		2	Virgo	6:40
	4	8:41		4	Libra	8:57
	5	21:10		6	Scorpio	9:23
	8	3:53		8	Sagittar	9:48
	9	12: 7		10	Capricrn	11:45
	12	9:56		12	Aquarius	16:10
	14	16:55		14	Pisces	23:19
	17	2:27		17	Aries	8:57
	19	19:16		19	Taurus	20:35
	22	3: 3		22	Gemini	9:29
	24	9:59		24	Cancer	22:16
	27	3:25		27	Leo	9: 6
	29	11:14		29	Virgo	16:22
	31	15: 8		31	Libra	19:47
NOV	2	8:52		2	Scorpio	20:20
	4	15:36		4	Sagittar	19:47
	6	12: 4		6	Capricrn	20: 3
	8	18:54		8	Aquarius	22:49
	11	0:37		11	Pisces	5: 5
	13	10:14		13	Aries	14:45
	15	13: 2		16	Taurus	2:45
	18	11:26		18	Gemini	15:42
	20	14:21		21	Cancer	4:22
	23	11:53		23	Leo	15:34
	25	20:51		25	Virgo	0:10
	28	2:26		28	Libra	5:23
	30	1:37		30	Scorpio	7:22
DEC	2	4:47		2	Sagittar	7:14
	4	3: 8		4	Capricrn	6:43
	6	6:43		6	Aquarius	7:52
	8	12: 3		8	Pisces	12:25
	10	18:42		10	Aries	21: 4
	12	21:40		13	Taurus	8:57
	15	19:55		15	Gemini	22: 1
	18	7:24		18	Cancer	10:26
	20	19:36		20	Leo	21:14
	23	4:37		23	Virgo	6: 2
	25	11:16		25	Libra	12:28
	27	8:12		27	Scorpio	16:18
	29	16:54		29	Sagittar	17:47
	30	6:27		31	Capricrn	17:58

Day	Time	Day	Sign	Time
JAN 2	14:32	2	Taurus	17:31
4	16: 7	5	Gemini	1:43
6	7:44	7	Cancer	6:11
8	23:27	9	Leo	7:50
11	0: 7	11	Virgo	8:21
13	1: 8	13	Libra	9:31
15	4: 2	15	Scorpio	12:43
17	13:54	17	Sagittar	18:31
19	4:43	20	Capricrn	2:47
22	3:31	22	Aquarius	13: 1
24	15:11	25	Pisces	0:48
27	3:53	27	Aries	13:29
29	4:52	30	Taurus	1:38
FEB 1	9:21	1	Gemini	11:16
3	2:48	3	Cancer	16:57
5	11:25	5	Leo	18:52
7	11:18	7	Virgo	18:30
9	10:42	9	Libra	17:59
11	6:53	11	Scorpio	19:24
13	15:58	14	Sagittar	0: 9
16	3:30	16	Capricrn	8:21
18	10:12	18	Aquarius	19: 6
20	22:12	21	Pisces	7:13
23	10:49	23	Aries	19:51
25	17:55	26	Taurus	8:12
28	10:19	28	Gemini	18:53
MAR 2	14:54	2	Cancer	2:17
4	22:15	5	Leo	5:41
6	22:49	7	Virgo	5:53
8	21:45	9	Libra	4:47
10	19:30	11	Scorpio	4:40
12	23:39	13	Sagittar	7:34
15	4:47	15	Capricrn	14:29
17	19:21	18	Aquarius	0:53
20	3:54	20	Pisces	13:12
22	16:32	23	Aries	1:52
25	5:54	25	Taurus	14: 0
27	17:26	28	Gemini	0:49
30	2:40	30	Cancer	9:15
APR 1	6: 9	1	Leo	14:22
3	11: 4	3	Virgo	16:11
5	8:16	5	Libra	15:55
7	11: 4	7	Scorpio	15:33
9	12:45	9	Sagittar	17:11
11	17:59	11	Capricrn	22:25
14	3:42	14	Aquarius	7:37
16	15:31	16	Pisces	19:33
18	23:52	19	Aries	8:15
21	16:58	21	Taurus	20: 9
24	3:44	24	Gemini	6:28
26	12:27	26	Cancer	14:46
28	11:10	28	Leo	20:40
MAY 30	22:23	1	Virgo	0: 1
MAY 2	16:23	3	Libra	1:21
5	0:47	5	Scorpio	1:58
7	2:33	7	Sagittar	3:35
9	6:58	9	Capricrn	7:52
11	4:46	11	Aquarius	15:45
14	2:19	14	Pisces	2:51
16	6:31	16	Aries	15:25
19	3: 9	19	Taurus	3:17
21	1:43	21	Gemini	13: 8
22	21:54	23	Cancer	20:39
25	15:17	26	Leo	2: 4
27	19:13	28	Virgo	5:47
29	22:23	30	Libra	8:19
JUN 1	7:57	1	Scorpio	10:23
3	2:11	3	Sagittar	13: 2
5	16:13	5	Capricrn	17:27
7	12:29	8	Aquarius	0:40
9	22: 2	10	Pisces	10:58
12	9:55	12	Aries	23:15
15	2: 2	15	Taurus	11:20
17	15: 4	17	Gemini	21:13
20	1:53	20	Cancer	4: 6
21	23:26	22	Leo	8:27
23	23:47	24	Virgo	11:19
26	9: 3	26	Libra	13:46
28	13: 2	28	Scorpio	16:38
30	20:27	30	Sagittar	20:29

Day	Time	Day	Sign	Time
JUL 3	1:39	3	Capricrn	1:49
5	7:51	5	Aquarius	9:15
7	18:38	7	Pisces	19:10
9	22:40	9	Aries	7:12
12	18:37	12	Taurus	19:38
15	4:56	15	Gemini	6: 8
17	11:48	17	Cancer	13: 9
19	11:25	19	Leo	16:48
21	16:47	21	Virgo	18:25
23	7:44	23	Libra	19:40
25	19:53	25	Scorpio	22: 1
27	23:46	28	Sagittar	2:14
30	5:38	30	Capricrn	8:28
AUG 1	3:45	1	Aquarius	16:37
3	23: 4	4	Pisces	2:44
6	7:25	6	Aries	14:40
8	23:44	9	Taurus	3:23
11	14:14	11	Gemini	14:48
13	18: 3	13	Cancer	22:47
15	14:34	16	Leo	2:44
17	23: 3	18	Virgo	3:42
19	16: 7	20	Libra	3:36
22	2:52	22	Scorpio	4:28
24	1:53	24	Sagittar	7:46
26	7:28	26	Capricrn	13:59
28	9: 7	28	Aquarius	22:43
31	1:40	31	Pisces	9:19
SEP 2	7:14	2	Aries	21:22
5	1:35	5	Taurus	10:10
7	13:34	7	Gemini	22:17
10	3:24	10	Cancer	7:38
12	1: 9	12	Leo	12:52
14	6:33	14	Virgo	14:21
16	3:12	16	Libra	13:45
18	6:47	18	Scorpio	13:15
20	12:41	20	Sagittar	14:54
22	19:33	22	Capricrn	19:55
25	1:42	25	Aquarius	4:20
27	4:24	27	Pisces	15:14
29	14:39	30	Aries	3:30
OCT 2	4:29	2	Taurus	16:14
4	16:42	5	Gemini	4:28
7	3:19	7	Cancer	14:43
9	10:50	9	Leo	21:35
11	14:43	12	Virgo	0:37
13	20:36	14	Libra	0:48
15	15:16	16	Scorpio	0: 2
17	14:56	18	Sagittar	0:24
19	21:34	20	Capricrn	3:43
22	8:53	22	Aquarius	10:50
24	14: 8	24	Pisces	21:18
26	22:42	27	Aries	9:40
29	17:19	29	Taurus	22:21
NOV 31	23:54	1	Gemini	10:14
NOV 3	17:44	3	Cancer	20:26
6	2:29	6	Leo	4: 7
8	8: 4	8	Virgo	8:48
10	2:46	10	Libra	10:43
12	1: 7	12	Scorpio	11: 1
14	3:42	14	Sagittar	11:21
16	13: 6	16	Capricrn	13:35
18	12: 6	18	Aquarius	19: 9
21	2: 4	21	Pisces	4:28
23	7:45	23	Aries	16:31
25	17:49	26	Taurus	5:15
28	8:43	28	Gemini	16:49
DEC 30	16: 6	1	Cancer	2:18
3	2:25	3	Leo	9:34
5	10:34	5	Virgo	14:44
7	11:42	7	Libra	18: 4
9	12: 2	9	Scorpio	20: 5
11	15:40	11	Sagittar	21:40
13	16:20	13	Capricrn	0: 7
15	22:38	16	Aquarius	4:52
18	10:42	18	Pisces	13: 0
20	22:27	21	Aries	0:20
23	5:25	23	Taurus	13: 6
25	18:41	26	Gemini	0:47
28	3:33	28	Cancer	9:47
30	10:45	30	Leo	16: 0

Month	Day	Time	Day	Sign	Time		Month	Day	Time	Day	Sign	Time
JAN	31	16: 7	1	Sagittar	7:31		JUL	1	6:50	1	Leo	22:16
	3	10:16	3	Capricrn	19:10			3	7: 1	3	Virgo	22:38
	5	16:12	5	Aquarius	8: 0			5	8:11	6	Libra	0:28
	8	20: 2	8	Pisces	20:53			7	15:12	8	Scorpio	4:54
	10	17:29	11	Aries	8:23			10	3:39	10	Sagittar	12:18
	13	2:33	13	Taurus	17: 1			11	20:54	12	Capricrn	22:17
	15	12:43	15	Gemini	21:56			14	19: 7	15	Aquarius	10: 4
	17	7:38	17	Cancer	22:58			17	9:38	17	Pisces	22:45
	19	21:29	19	Leo	22:58			20	6:45	20	Aries	11: 8
	21	15:12	21	Virgo	22:23			21	21:16	22	Taurus	21:37
	23	20:44	23	Libra	23:43			25	2:43	25	Gemini	4:45
	25	16:24	26	Scorpio	4:33			26	8:39	27	Cancer	8: 9
	28	8:33	28	Sagittar	13:21			28	16:59	29	Leo	8:40
	29	15:27	31	Capricrn	1: 8			30	17:23	31	Virgo	8: 2
FEB	1	23:31	2	Aquarius	14:10		AUG	1	16:15	2	Libra	8:18
	4	12:28	5	Pisces	2:52			4	4:40	4	Scorpio	11:17
	7	0:19	7	Aries	14:16			6	16:38	6	Sagittar	17:58
	9	11: 6	9	Taurus	23:37			8	1:36	9	Capricrn	4: 1
	11	21:38	12	Gemini	6: 9			10	8:29	11	Aquarius	16: 7
	14	2:56	14	Cancer	9:32			13	10:28	14	Pisces	4:52
	16	8: 0	16	Leo	10:16			15	21:40	16	Aries	17:12
	18	8: 5	18	Virgo	9:48			18	20:41	19	Taurus	4:11
	19	22:35	20	Libra	10: 5			21	10: 2	21	Gemini	12:37
	21	16:23	22	Scorpio	13:12			22	23:38	23	Cancer	17:37
	24	7: 7	24	Sagittar	20:27			25	6:31	25	Leo	19:16
	26	9: 0	27	Capricrn	7:34			27	3:45	27	Virgo	18:47
	28		29	Aquarius	20:35			29	14: 6	29	Libra	18:11
								31	10:37	31	Scorpio	19:39
MAR	2	19: 5	2	Pisces	9:12		SEP	2	23:38	3	Sagittar	0:51
	5	6:26	5	Aries	20: 8			5	1:56	5	Capricrn	10: 7
	7	14:16	8	Taurus	5: 6			7	7:42	7	Aquarius	22: 9
	10	3:30	10	Gemini	12: 4			10	8:45	10	Pisces	10:57
	12	13:49	12	Cancer	16:51			12	11: 2	12	Aries	23: 3
	14	9:31	14	Leo	19:21			14	8: 4	15	Taurus	9:48
	16	8:40	16	Virgo	20:14			17	12:58	17	Gemini	18:41
	18	18:19	18	Libra	20:56			19	19:54	19	Cancer	1: 0
	20	13:19	20	Scorpio	23:21			22	3:17	22	Leo	4:20
	22	21:17	23	Sagittar	5:14			24	3:10	24	Virgo	5: 9
	25	11: 7	25	Capricrn	15: 9			25	23:58	26	Libra	4:56
	27	12:52	28	Aquarius	3:45			27	7: 0	28	Scorpio	5:45
	30	1:39	30	Pisces	16:24			30	5:54	30	Sagittar	9:34
APR	1	13:27	2	Aries	3: 5		OCT	2	14:14	2	Capricrn	17:30
	3	14:44	4	Taurus	11:19			5	2:34	5	Aquarius	4:54
	6	16:11	6	Gemini	17:34			7	0:14	7	Pisces	17:39
	8	20: 8	8	Cancer	22:19			10	5:29	10	Aries	5:37
	10	23:52	11	Leo	1:47			11	18:35	12	Taurus	15:49
	12	16:30	13	Virgo	4:10			14	12:30	15	Gemini	0: 9
	14	17:20	15	Libra	6:11			16	19:18	17	Cancer	6:37
	17	4:43	17	Scorpio	9:11			19	10:23	19	Leo	11: 2
	19	0:28	19	Sagittar	14:41			21	10:38	21	Virgo	13:28
	21	1:33	21	Capricrn	23:41			23	1:43	23	Libra	14:40
	23	19:39	24	Aquarius	11:39			25	0:27	25	Scorpio	16: 5
	26	11:32	27	Pisces	0:21			27	15:24	27	Sagittar	19:30
	29	1: 6	29	Aries	11:14			28	16:33	30	Capricrn	2:19
MAY	30	22:53	1	Taurus	19:10		NOV	31	22:40	1	Aquarius	12:44
	3	21:49	3	Gemini	0:29			3	9:52	4	Pisces	1:14
	5	13:12	6	Cancer	4:10			6	2:14	6	Aries	13:20
	7	22:22	8	Leo	7: 8			8	13:53	8	Taurus	23:20
	10	7:34	10	Virgo	9:57			10	22:47	11	Gemini	6:50
	11	22:41	12	Libra	13: 6			13	12:17	13	Cancer	12:20
	13	21:38	14	Scorpio	17:16			15	10:16	15	Leo	16:24
	16	16: 4	16	Sagittar	23:23			17	11:40	17	Virgo	19:29
	18	9:54	19	Capricrn	8:14			19	18: 8	19	Libra	22: 4
	21	8: 5	21	Aquarius	19:44			21	20:14	22	Scorpio	0:53
	24	3:43	24	Pisces	8:26			24	0:32	24	Sagittar	5: 2
	26	19:36	26	Aries	19:53			25	4:37	26	Capricrn	11:39
	28	7:15	29	Taurus	4:17			28	16:39	28	Aquarius	21:20
	30	17:51	31	Gemini	9:20		DEC	30	20:50	1	Pisces	9:24
JUN	1	20: 2	2	Cancer	11:59			3	16:47	3	Aries	21:50
	4	0:32	4	Leo	13:36			6	3: 5	6	Taurus	8:17
	6	4:58	6	Virgo	15:29			8	15:25	8	Gemini	15:38
	8	14:23	8	Libra	18:34			9	23:42	10	Cancer	20: 6
	10	18:17	10	Scorpio	23:28			12	16:37	12	Leo	22:48
	13	13:18	13	Sagittar	6:30			14	14:58	15	Virgo	0:57
	15	5:44	15	Capricrn	15:51			16	19:45	17	Libra	3:34
	17	8:30	18	Aquarius	3:20			19	2:54	19	Scorpio	7:21
	20	15: 2	20	Pisces	16: 1			21	2:22	21	Sagittar	12:43
	22	14:43	23	Aries	4: 4			22	18:27	23	Capricrn	20: 5
	25	8:38	25	Taurus	13:29			25	18:50	26	Aquarius	5:44
	27	2:34	27	Gemini	19:15			28	6:25	28	Pisces	17:29
	29	1:22	29	Cancer	21:43			30	21:52	31	Aries	6: 8

JAN					JUL				
1	23:17	2	Leo	2:55	1	3:48	1	Pisces	17:52
4	1:10	4	Virgo	4:58	4	3:10	4	Aries	3:34
6	6:41	6	Libra	10:34	6	3:58	6	Taurus	9:53
8	13:13	8	Scorpio	20:0	8	9:43	8	Gemini	12:43
11	4:44	11	Sagittar	8:7	10	12:22	10	Cancer	13:4
13	20:1	13	Capricrn	21:1	11	19:7	12	Leo	12:36
16	7:15	16	Aquarius	9:5	14	12:10	14	Virgo	13:12
18	18:30	18	Pisces	19:24	16	4:35	16	Libra	16:35
20	23:51	21	Aries	3:28	18	15:12	18	Scorpio	23:42
23	6:3	23	Taurus	9:2	21	6:20	21	Sagittar	10:17
25	9:42	25	Gemini	12:7	23	17:32	23	Capricrn	22:56
27	9:46	27	Cancer	13:24	25	10:41	26	Aquarius	11:50
29	12:30	29	Leo	14:4	28	3:51	28	Pisces	23:36
30	23:23	31	Virgo	15:45	30	9:43	31	Aries	9:21
FEB					**AUG**				
2	19:13	2	Libra	20:3	2	2:52	2	Taurus	16:33
5	3:40	5	Scorpio	4:2	4	6:24	4	Gemini	20:55
6	19:58	7	Sagittar	15:24	6	9:41	6	Cancer	22:48
9	8:6	10	Capricrn	4:17	8	3:16	8	Leo	23:10
11	21:13	12	Aquarius	16:17	10	12:1	10	Virgo	23:36
14	17:33	15	Pisces	2:0	12	4:49	13	Libra	1:53
16	20:53	17	Aries	9:12	14	20:13	15	Scorpio	7:34
18	22:36	19	Taurus	14:25	17	6:6	17	Sagittar	17:12
21	16:45	21	Gemini	18:11	20	5:3	20	Capricrn	5:35
23	20:9	23	Cancer	20:57	22	5:29	22	Aquarius	18:28
25	7:7	25	Leo	23:13	25	1:43	25	Pisces	5:52
27	9:30	28	Virgo	1:51	27	9:9	27	Aries	15:2
					29	16:45	29	Taurus	22:1
MAR					**SEP**				
1	13:3	2	Libra	6:4	1	2:52	1	Gemini	3:3
3	11:22	4	Scorpio	13:9	3	3:2	3	Cancer	6:20
6	4:27	6	Sagittar	23:36	4	12:21	5	Leo	8:14
9	0:41	9	Capricrn	12:15	7	7:52	7	Virgo	9:36
11	6:2	12	Aquarius	0:32	8	15:39	9	Libra	11:52
13	22:54	14	Pisces	10:12	11	16:30	11	Scorpio	16:43
16	8:11	16	Aries	16:38	13	7:54	14	Sagittar	1:15
18	20:35	18	Taurus	20:41	15	22:2	16	Capricrn	13:5
20	23:22	20	Gemini	23:38	18	16:24	19	Aquarius	1:59
22	16:28	23	Cancer	2:28	20	21:54	21	Pisces	13:21
24	15:31	25	Leo	5:44	23	5:7	23	Aries	21:57
27	3:24	27	Virgo	9:42	25	16:53	26	Taurus	4:0
29	10:30	29	Libra	14:50	27	23:22	28	Gemini	8:26
31	19:51	31	Scorpio	22:2	30	4:59	30	Cancer	11:59
APR					**OCT**				
2	12:17	3	Sagittar	8:0	1	22:5	2	Leo	14:59
5	18:14	5	Capricrn	20:20	4	15:15	4	Virgo	17:46
8	5:44	8	Aquarius	9:1	6	11:50	6	Libra	21:1
10	14:8	10	Pisces	19:19	8	16:10	9	Scorpio	2:1
12	7:37	13	Aries	1:50	10	13:4	11	Sagittar	9:59
14	19:46	15	Taurus	5:6	13	17:0	13	Capricrn	21:11
16	13:39	17	Gemini	6:42	16	9:33	16	Aquarius	10:5
19	6:8	19	Cancer	8:18	18	11:17	18	Pisces	21:54
20	18:31	21	Leo	11:5	20	10:53	21	Aries	6:34
22	20:55	23	Virgo	15:30	23	11:9	23	Taurus	11:56
25	2:20	25	Libra	21:37	24	21:27	25	Gemini	15:10
27	7:1	28	Scorpio	5:35	26	18:56	27	Cancer	17:38
29	18:42	30	Sagittar	15:43	29	5:4	29	Leo	20:21
					31	14:16	31	Virgo	23:48
MAY					**NOV**				
2	13:0	3	Capricrn	3:55	3	0:40	3	Libra	4:13
4	19:49	5	Aquarius	16:52	4	5:54	5	Scorpio	10:10
8	1:58	8	Pisces	4:5	7	15:5	7	Sagittar	18:22
9	18:7	10	Aries	11:36	8	14:53	10	Capricrn	5:17
12	6:52	12	Taurus	15:8	11	22:16	12	Aquarius	18:7
14	4:37	14	Gemini	16:3	14	14:2	15	Pisces	6:34
16	15:41	16	Cancer	16:15	17	5:37	17	Aries	16:9
18	12:38	18	Leo	17:31	19	1:37	19	Taurus	21:50
20	19:47	20	Virgo	21:1	21	22:57	22	Gemini	0:23
22	23:20	23	Libra	3:9	23	12:53	24	Cancer	1:26
25	10:30	25	Scorpio	11:42	25	22:57	26	Leo	2:38
27	1:59	27	Sagittar	22:22	28	4:5	28	Virgo	5:13
28	15:16	30	Capricrn	10:41	29	23:13	30	Libra	9:48
JUN					**DEC**				
1	14:29	1	Aquarius	23:42	2	8:4	2	Scorpio	16:34
4	8:52	4	Pisces	11:37	4	8:30	5	Sagittar	1:33
5	22:43	6	Aries	20:26	6	14:18	7	Capricrn	12:42
8	2:32	9	Taurus	1:14	9	7:48	10	Aquarius	1:28
10	7:28	11	Gemini	2:37	11	21:3	12	Pisces	14:20
12	12:7	13	Cancer	2:17	14	9:33	15	Aries	1:7
14	7:2	15	Leo	2:11	16	22:19	17	Taurus	8:11
16	19:50	17	Virgo	4:4	18	21:30	19	Gemini	11:22
19	4:20	19	Libra	9:2	21	10:24	21	Cancer	11:55
21	16:59	21	Scorpio	17:19	22	22:36	23	Leo	11:39
23	4:16	24	Sagittar	4:17	24	23:12	25	Virgo	12:24
25	17:25	26	Capricrn	16:50	27	6:27	27	Libra	15:38
28	7:22	29	Aquarius	5:48	29	6:52	29	Scorpio	22:4

JAN	31	6:54	1 Pisces	6:11	JUL	1	4: 2	1 Scorpio	18: 2
	3	2:12	3 Aries	10:57		3	16: 7	4 Sagittar	6:36
	5	2:51	5 Taurus	14: 5		6	10:19	6 Capricrn	18:40
	7	1:25	7 Gemini	16: 3		9	0:26	9 Aquarius	5: 7
	8	17: 2	8 Cancer	17:53		11	12: 7	11 Pisces	13:30
	11	4:58	11 Leo	21: 3		13	5:39	13 Aries	19:37
	13	5:32	14 Virgo	2:58		15	14:10	15 Taurus	23:30
	16	4: 0	16 Libra	12:18		17	17: 3	18 Gemini	1:33
	18	21:29	19 Scorpio	0:17		20	2:39	20 Cancer	2:45
	21	7: 3	21 Sagittar	12:45		22	2:55	22 Leo	4:30
	23	15:15	23 Capricrn	23:28		23	16:41	24 Virgo	8:18
	25	21:30	26 Aquarius	7:26		26	5:50	26 Libra	15:19
	28	11:27	28 Pisces	12:52		29	0:22	29 Scorpio	1:40
	30	4: 2	30 Aries	16:35		31	6: 4	31 Sagittar	14: 1
FEB	1	5:53	1 Taurus	19:28	AUG	1	7:49	3 Capricrn	2: 9
	3	7:44	3 Gemini	22:13		5	6:58	5 Aquarius	12:20
	5	1:25	6 Cancer	1:28		6	18:42	7 Pisces	19:55
	7	20:11	8 Leo	5:52		9	22: 4	10 Aries	1:14
	9	19:17	10 Virgo	12:14		12	2:39	12 Taurus	4:56
	12	4:12	12 Libra	21:10		14	6:15	14 Gemini	7:42
	15	0:41	15 Scorpio	8:35		15	22: 6	16 Cancer	10:13
	17	18:49	17 Sagittar	21: 8		18	0:56	18 Leo	13:12
	18	15:51	20 Capricrn	8:31		20	12:40	20 Virgo	17:34
	22	6:43	22 Aquarius	16:53		22	15:42	23 Scorpio	0:17
	24	0:40	24 Pisces	21:50		24	13:15	25 Scorpio	9:57
	26	19: 4	27 Aries	0:17		27	18: 8	27 Sagittar	21:58
MAR	28	22:42	1 Taurus	1:44		29	19:46	30 Capricrn	10:24
	3	2:56	3 Gemini	3:38	SEP	1	4:26	1 Aquarius	20:52
	4	2: 6	5 Cancer	7: 3		3	20:21	4 Pisces	4: 7
	7	6:33	7 Leo	12:25		5	13:26	6 Aries	8:24
	9	20:52	9 Virgo	19:48		7	16:21	8 Taurus	10:56
	11	15:40	12 Libra	5:10		9	18:25	10 Gemini	13: 5
	14	2:54	14 Scorpio	16:26		11	20:54	12 Cancer	15:54
	16	20:52	17 Sagittar	4:57		14	4:19	14 Leo	19:53
	19	15:40	19 Capricrn	17: 2		15	23:42	17 Virgo	1:19
	21	14:54	22 Aquarius	2:32		19	0:47	19 Libra	8:35
	23	10:18	24 Pisces	8: 9		20	20:10	21 Scorpio	18: 7
	26	0:34	26 Aries	10:16		23	9:33	24 Sagittar	5:53
	28	1:10	28 Taurus	10:27		26	5:19	26 Capricrn	18:37
	30	1:27	30 Gemini	10:43		28	23:51	29 Aquarius	5:55
APR	1	3:49	1 Cancer	12:50	OCT	30	12:29	1 Pisces	13:43
	3	15:44	3 Leo	17:51		3	11:10	3 Aries	17:43
	6	1: 3	6 Virgo	1:43		5	0:53	5 Taurus	19: 7
	8	1:28	8 Libra	11:45		7	1:41	7 Gemini	19:48
	10	13: 0	10 Scorpio	23:19		8	20:58	9 Cancer	21:30
	13	1:35	13 Sagittar	11:46		11	5:59	11 Leo	1:17
	15	16:23	16 Capricrn	0:16		13	12:58	14 Virgo	7:22
	18	7: 3	18 Aquarius	10:54		15	18:54	16 Libra	15:27
	20	17:43	20 Pisces	17:58		18	15:38	19 Scorpio	1:25
	22	13: 5	22 Aries	20:59		20	15:43	21 Sagittar	13:10
	24	13:34	24 Taurus	21:41		23	22: 2	24 Capricrn	2: 4
	26	12:46	26 Gemini	20:13		25	17:33	26 Aquarius	14:15
	28	10: 8	28 Cancer	20:40		27	23:27	28 Pisces	23:23
MAY	30	17:22	1 Leo	0: 9		30	15:48	31 Aries	4:15
	2	6: 9	3 Virgo	7:19	NOV	1	13:20	2 Taurus	5:32
	5	8:18	5 Libra	17:29		3	16:36	4 Gemini	5: 7
	7	20: 0	8 Scorpio	5:23		5	1:31	6 Cancer	5: 8
	10	8:29	10 Sagittar	17:57		7	23:28	8 Leo	7:25
	12	1:49	13 Capricrn	6:22		10	11:20	10 Virgo	12:49
	15	8:18	15 Aquarius	17:31		12	6:25	12 Libra	21: 9
	17	19:46	18 Pisces	1:55		14	13:41	15 Scorpio	7:40
	20	4:43	20 Aries	6:32		17	17:59	17 Sagittar	19:40
	21	23:53	22 Taurus	7:43		18	22:47	20 Capricrn	8:32
	23	23:15	24 Gemini	7: 1		22	4: 7	22 Aquarius	21: 8
	26	0:19	26 Cancer	6:35		24	12:18	25 Pisces	7:33
	28	4:35	28 Leo	8:30		27	2:36	27 Aries	14: 7
	29	12:15	30 Virgo	14: 9		29	11:19	29 Taurus	16:38
JUN	1	13:14	1 Libra	23:32	DEC	1	4:21	1 Gemini	16:23
	4	0:34	4 Scorpio	11:22		2	20:48	3 Cancer	15:28
	6	12:55	7 Sagittar	0: 0		5	4: 1	5 Leo	16: 1
	8	11: 2	9 Capricrn	12:13		7	8:40	7 Virgo	19:40
	11	22:58	11 Aquarius	23:10		9	21:15	10 Libra	3: 1
	13	17:58	14 Pisces	8: 1		12	0:29	12 Scorpio	13:29
	16	4:49	16 Aries	13:56		15	1:23	15 Sagittar	1:45
	18	11:45	18 Taurus	16:44		17	4:23	17 Capricrn	14:36
	20	8:27	20 Gemini	17:15		20	0:38	20 Aquarius	3: 0
	21	21:14	22 Cancer	18:26		22	10:48	22 Pisces	13:49
	24	17:54	24 Leo	18:26		24	18:26	24 Aries	21:46
	26	18:29	26 Virgo	22:43		26	23:55	27 Taurus	2:10
	28	17:43	29 Libra	6:48		28	23:58	29 Gemini	3:27
						30	19: 8	31 Cancer	3: 3

JAN

1	18:35	1	Scorpio	21:35
4	0:45	4	Sagittar	7:13
6	3: 4	6	Capricrn	13:15
8	10:21	8	Aquarius	16:31
10	12:18	10	Pisces	18:32
12	14:13	12	Aries	20:36
14	19:19	14	Taurus	23:37
16	22:16	17	Gemini	3:58
18	0:30	19	Cancer	9:58
21	10:37	21	Leo	18: 3
23	20:51	24	Virgo	4:33
26	9:13	26	Libra	17: 2
29	5:41	29	Scorpio	5:50
31	12:53	31	Sagittar	16:31

FEB

1	16:28	2	Capricrn	23:31
4	21: 2	5	Aquarius	2:52
6	22:25	7	Pisces	3:53
8	23: 2	9	Aries	4:19
11	1:33	11	Taurus	5:46
13	7:27	13	Gemini	9:23
15	9:33	15	Cancer	15:41
17	19:37	18	Leo	0:34
20	6:57	20	Virgo	11:35
22	19:54	23	Libra	0: 6
25	5:51	25	Scorpio	12:58
27	21:36	28	Sagittar	0:30

MAR

1	7:38	2	Capricrn	8:59
4	12: 4	4	Aquarius	13:37
6	13:58	6	Pisces	15: 0
8	14: 3	8	Aries	14:37
10	14: 0	10	Taurus	14:26
12	1:48	12	Gemini	16:17
14	10:12	14	Cancer	21:28
16	23: 3	17	Leo	6:14
18	11:35	19	Virgo	17:40
22	2:10	22	Libra	6:25
23	9: 9	24	Scorpio	19:11
27	3:10	27	Sagittar	6:55
28	2:51	29	Capricrn	16:26
30	19:34	31	Aquarius	22:46

APR

2	0: 1	3	Pisces	1:38
4	1:21	5	Aries	1:52
6	6:40	7	Taurus	1: 8
8	0:17	9	Gemini	1:32
11	1:58	11	Cancer	4:59
13	3:32	13	Leo	12:32
15	20:59	15	Virgo	23:40
17	22:23	18	Libra	12:32
20	14:35	20	Scorpio	1:14
22	17:55	23	Sagittar	12:39
25	18:16	25	Capricrn	22:16
28	1:58	28	Aquarius	5:34
29	8:46	30	Pisces	10: 4

MAY

1	16:33	2	Aries	11:51
3	10: 9	4	Taurus	11:56
5	1:41	6	Gemini	12: 4
7	6: 2	8	Cancer	14:20
10	19:19	10	Leo	20:24
12	14:20	13	Virgo	6:31
15	7:52	15	Libra	19: 8
16	23:40	18	Scorpio	7:49
20	18:17	20	Sagittar	18:53
21	22:13	23	Capricrn	3:55
24	8:47	25	Aquarius	11: 2
26	21:16	27	Pisces	16:14
29	18:49	29	Aries	19:26
31	12:35	31	Taurus	21: 0

JUN

2	19:24	2	Gemini	22: 3
4	2:45	5	Cancer	0:18
7	2:19	7	Leo	5:29
9	12:10	9	Virgo	14:30
12	2:15	12	Libra	2:32
14	12:37	14	Scorpio	15:12
15	18: 1	17	Sagittar	2:13
19	6:58	19	Capricrn	10:42
20	22:46	21	Aquarius	16:58
23	7:14	23	Pisces	21:37
25	17:43	26	Aries	1: 7
28	1:12	28	Taurus	3:46
29	0:48	30	Gemini	6: 9

JUL

1	22:27	2	Cancer	9:20
3	7:11	4	Leo	14:38
6	12:56	6	Virgo	23: 5
9	1: 3	9	Libra	10:31
11	14:50	11	Scorpio	23:10
13	17:33	14	Sagittar	10:32
16	13:26	16	Capricrn	19: 2
18	18:40	19	Aquarius	0:36
21	0:35	21	Pisces	4: 8
23	3:57	23	Aries	6:41
25	7:11	25	Taurus	9:11
27	4:17	27	Gemini	12:16
29	16: 4	29	Cancer	16:33
30	14:39	31	Leo	22:42

AUG

3	7: 0	3	Virgo	7:20
4	9:59	5	Libra	18:29
6	23:38	8	Scorpio	7: 6
9	23:59	10	Sagittar	19: 3
12	16:17	13	Capricrn	4:17
13	3:56	15	Aquarius	10: 0
17	3: 7	17	Pisces	12:46
18	23:36	19	Aries	14: 0
21	12:35	21	Taurus	15:11
23	12:19	23	Gemini	17:40
25	21:31	25	Cancer	22:14
27	1:15	28	Leo	5:12
29	6:15	30	Virgo	14:30

SEP

1	2: 4	2	Libra	1:48
3	17:32	4	Scorpio	14:24
6	9:52	7	Sagittar	2:52
5	5:59	9	Capricrn	13:14
11	18:31	11	Aquarius	20: 3
12	18:48	13	Pisces	23: 8
15	19:45	15	Aries	23:39
16	14:57	17	Taurus	23:23
19	18:58	20	Gemini	0:17
22	2:11	22	Cancer	3:51
23	4: 0	24	Leo	10:45
25	15:45	26	Virgo	20:33
29	3:40	29	Libra	8:16

OCT

30	3:40	1	Scorpio	20:54
4	0:57	4	Sagittar	9:30
6	13:37	6	Capricrn	20:46
9	1:17	9	Aquarius	5: 7
10	11:37	11	Pisces	9:38
12	9: 2	13	Aries	10:42
14	20:33	15	Taurus	9:53
16	8:14	17	Gemini	9:20
19	3:53	19	Cancer	11:10
21	13:20	21	Leo	16:48
23	10:56	24	Virgo	2:16
25	15:24	26	Libra	14:12
28	21:12	29	Scorpio	2:57
30	8:50	31	Sagittar	15:24

NOV

3	1:15	3	Capricrn	2:47
4	7:47	5	Aquarius	12:10
6	15:54	7	Pisces	18:26
8	22:42	9	Aries	21: 9
10	14:22	11	Taurus	21:10
13	8:25	13	Gemini	20:19
15	8:25	15	Cancer	20:52
18	0:27	18	Leo	0:46
20	4:45	20	Virgo	8:55
21	15:45	22	Libra	20:26
24	9: 4	25	Scorpio	9:14
27	2:21	27	Sagittar	21:31
29	7:29	30	Capricrn	8:27

DEC

2	7:29	2	Aquarius	17:43
4	16:53	5	Pisces	0:49
7	4: 7	7	Aries	5:12
9	6: 2	9	Taurus	7: 0
10	23:14	11	Gemini	7:16
12	16:31	13	Cancer	7:50
15	7:10	15	Leo	10:42
17	16:40	17	Virgo	17:20
23	23:55	20	Libra	3:46
21	19:35	22	Scorpio	16:19
24	13:58	25	Sagittar	4:38
25	16:49	27	Capricrn	15:11
29	15:44	29	Aquarius	23:39

JAN	2	19:56	3	Cancer	0:17
	5	7:21	5	Leo	11:48
	7	23:43	8	Virgo	0:36
	10	9:44	10	Libra	13:18
	12	20:34	12	Scorpio	23:40
	15	5: 0	15	Sagittar	5:59
	17	6: 0	17	Capricrn	8:16
	19	5:27	19	Aquarius	8: 3
	21	5:34	21	Pisces	7:27
	23	6:44	23	Aries	8:32
	25	10:54	25	Taurus	12:37
	27	10:57	27	Gemini	20: 3
	30	4:47	30	Cancer	6:12
FEB	1	4:55	1	Leo	18: 7
	4	5:58	4	Virgo	6:55
	6	18:54	6	Libra	19:37
	9	6:14	9	Scorpio	6:43
	10	23:51	11	Sagittar	14:37
	13	18:35	13	Capricrn	18:37
	15	12:38	15	Aquarius	19:26
	17	15:55	17	Pisces	18:45
	19	15:34	19	Aries	18:36
	21	20:10	21	Taurus	20:51
	24	19:14	24	Gemini	2:43
	26	7:45	26	Cancer	12:13
	28	20:37	29	Leo	0:13
MAR	2	10:33	2	Virgo	13: 7
	3	16: 2	5	Libra	1:33
	7	12: 0	7	Scorpio	12:28
	9	5:18	9	Sagittar	21: 0
	11	16:27	12	Capricrn	2:32
	13	18:12	14	Aquarius	5: 9
	16	5:18	16	Pisces	5:43
	18	2: 3	18	Aries	5:46
	19	10:21	20	Taurus	7: 6
	21	15:52	22	Gemini	11:22
	23	4:28	24	Cancer	19:28
	26	15:40	27	Leo	6:55
	29	9: 0	29	Virgo	19:50
APR	1	3: 1	1	Libra	8: 6
	3	14:11	3	Scorpio	18:27
	6	1:27	6	Sagittar	2:30
	7	10:45	8	Capricrn	8:20
	9	19:22	10	Aquarius	12:11
	12	1:46	12	Pisces	14:25
	13	9:43	14	Aries	15:48
	16	12: 1	16	Taurus	17:32
	17	13:10	18	Gemini	21:11
	19	23:41	21	Cancer	4: 5
	22	2: 3	23	Leo	14:35
	25	4:30	26	Virgo	3:17
	27	21:10	28	Libra	15:38
MAY	30	11:22	1	Scorpio	1:40
	3	3: 7	3	Sagittar	8:53
	5	5:44	5	Capricrn	13:55
	6	18:20	7	Aquarius	17:38
	9	16:25	9	Pisces	20:40
	11	20:39	11	Aries	23:24
	14	0:51	14	Taurus	2:23
	15	23:19	16	Gemini	6:32
	18	8:21	18	Cancer	13: 6
	19	20:51	20	Leo	22:52
	22	22:18	23	Virgo	11:13
	25	14:16	25	Libra	23:50
	28	10: 1	28	Scorpio	10: 7
	29	21:18	30	Sagittar	16:58
JUN	1	20:37	1	Capricrn	20:59
	3	6:51	3	Aquarius	23:35
	6	1:23	6	Pisces	2: 1
	8	4:17	8	Aries	5: 5
	10	9: 2	10	Taurus	9: 3
	11	23:56	12	Gemini	14:15
	14	20:42	14	Cancer	21:20
	16	17:22	17	Leo	6:58
	19	17:39	19	Virgo	19: 4
	22	6:11	22	Libra	7:58
	24	16:57	24	Scorpio	18:59
	26	17:41	27	Sagittar	2:19
	29	3:49	29	Capricrn	6: 1

JUL	1	1: 4	1	Aquarius	7:30
	3	6: 9	3	Pisces	8:34
	5	8: 0	5	Aries	10:38
	7	11:35	7	Taurus	14:28
	9	16:42	9	Gemini	20:17
	12	3:51	12	Cancer	4: 9
	14	11:34	14	Leo	14:12
	17	0:32	17	Virgo	2:18
	19	14:32	19	Libra	15:23
	22	2:15	22	Scorpio	3:14
	23	16: 0	24	Sagittar	11:43
	26	12:15	26	Capricrn	16: 8
	28	16:47	28	Aquarius	17:26
	30	13:32	30	Pisces	17:24
AUG	1	13:51	1	Aries	17:54
	3	16: 4	3	Taurus	20:25
	4	22: 8	6	Gemini	1:44
	8	4:51	8	Cancer	9:53
	9	4:56	10	Leo	20:27
	13	3:14	13	Virgo	8:46
	15	16:13	15	Libra	21:53
	18	4:38	18	Scorpio	10:13
	20	15:52	20	Sagittar	19:56
	22	20:50	22	Capricrn	1:50
	24	12:18	25	Aquarius	4: 6
	26	23:25	27	Pisces	4: 2
	28	23: 5	29	Aries	3:30
	30	23:29	31	Taurus	4:23
SEP	1	21:54	2	Gemini	8:12
	4	10: 1	4	Cancer	15:38
	7	1:21	7	Leo	2:15
	9	8:49	9	Virgo	14:49
	11	21:54	12	Libra	3:52
	14	10:20	14	Scorpio	16: 8
	16	14:53	17	Sagittar	2:26
	19	4:36	19	Capricrn	9:46
	21	11:32	21	Aquarius	13:44
	23	10:20	23	Pisces	14:30
	25	10: 6	25	Aries	14:30
	27	10: 2	27	Taurus	14:30
	29	6:20	29	Gemini	16:44
OCT	1	17:42	1	Cancer	22:59
	3	23:35	4	Leo	8:32
	6	15:51	6	Virgo	21: 2
	9	5: 4	9	Libra	10: 4
	11	17:15	11	Scorpio	21:59
	12	20:40	14	Sagittar	7:59
	16	11:40	16	Capricrn	15:45
	18	13: 2	18	Aquarius	21: 6
	20	20:40	20	Pisces	23:59
	22	22: 1	23	Aries	1: 0
	24	22:40	25	Taurus	1:23
	27	2:45	27	Gemini	2:56
	29	7:17	29	Cancer	7:29
	31	15:59	31	Leo	16: 4
NOV	3	2:14	3	Virgo	4: 3
	5	15:46	5	Libra	17: 5
	8	3:59	8	Scorpio	4:47
	9	14:21	10	Sagittar	14: 7
	12	19:16	12	Capricrn	21:13
	14	13:13	15	Aquarius	2:37
	17	5: 7	17	Pisces	6:35
	19	7:59	19	Aries	9:13
	21	10: 0	21	Taurus	11: 3
	23	7:34	23	Gemini	13:12
	25	16:38	25	Cancer	17:20
	26	17:40	28	Leo	0:53
	30	11:45	30	Virgo	12: 0
DEC	3	0:22	3	Libra	0:57
	4	4:50	5	Scorpio	12:52
	7	20:16	7	Sagittar	21:56
	9	14:27	10	Capricrn	4: 8
	12	5:58	12	Aquarius	8:26
	14	9: 2	14	Pisces	11:54
	16	12:27	16	Aries	15: 4
	18	12:47	18	Taurus	18:12
	20	17:39	20	Gemini	21:44
	22	0:27	23	Cancer	2:36
	25	4:45	25	Leo	9:58
	27	14:35	27	Virgo	20:28
	30	2:46	30	Libra	9:10

Month	Day	Time		Day	Sign	Time
JAN	1	3:48		1	Aquarius	11:54
	3	6: 8		3	Pisces	12:37
	5	13:42		5	Aries	16:52
	7	13:37		8	Taurus	1:14
	9	14:31		10	Gemini	12:40
	12	13:42		13	Cancer	1:19
	15	6: 4		15	Leo	13:46
	17	14:32		18	Virgo	1:16
	20	10:52		20	Libra	11:10
	22	9: 8		22	Scorpio	18:31
	24	8:34		24	Sagittar	22:36
	26	15:42		26	Capricrn	23:43
	28	11:32		28	Aquarius	23:18
	30	15:36		30	Pisces	23:25
FEB	1	19:47		2	Aries	2:10
	4	7: 9		4	Taurus	8:54
	6	8:20		6	Gemini	19:24
	8	23: 3		9	Cancer	7:56
	11	11:30		11	Leo	20:22
	13	23:18		14	Virgo	7:27
	16	10:30		16	Libra	16:45
	18	23:42		19	Scorpio	0: 5
	21	1:14		21	Sagittar	5:10
	23	5: 1		23	Capricrn	7:58
	25	7: 4		25	Aquarius	9: 9
	27	3:58		27	Pisces	10: 8
MAR	1	12: 7		1	Aries	12:38
	3	11:31		3	Taurus	18:12
	4	19:55		6	Gemini	3:27
	8	8:18		8	Cancer	15:25
	10	6: 6		11	Leo	3:55
	13	14:53		13	Virgo	14:56
	15	17:18		15	Libra	23:35
	17	23:58		18	Scorpio	5:58
	20	9:13		20	Sagittar	10:33
	22	8:12		22	Capricrn	13:49
	24	2: 4		24	Aquarius	16:19
	26	14:35		26	Pisces	18:46
	28	16:31		28	Aries	22:13
	30	21:48		31	Taurus	3:47
APR	2	7:56		2	Gemini	12:17
	4	17: 0		4	Cancer	23:34
	6	17:57		7	Leo	12: 5
	9	17: 3		9	Virgo	23:29
	12	6:27		12	Libra	8: 6
	14	7:51		14	Scorpio	13:42
	16	3:45		16	Sagittar	17: 2
	18	16:10		18	Capricrn	19:22
	20	17:50		20	Aquarius	21:46
	22	19: 3		23	Pisces	1: 3
	24	23:27		25	Aries	5:42
	27	5:33		27	Taurus	12: 7
	28	4: 9		29	Gemini	20:44
MAY	2	0:21		2	Cancer	7:40
	3	13:15		4	Leo	20: 7
	7	0:39		7	Virgo	8: 8
	9	10:19		9	Libra	17:30
	11	16:20		11	Scorpio	23:10
	13	12:51		14	Sagittar	1:42
	15	23:43		16	Capricrn	2:37
	17	21:52		18	Aquarius	3:43
	20	5:24		20	Pisces	6:25
	22	3:42		22	Aries	11:24
	24	10:30		24	Taurus	18:40
	25	13: 4		27	Gemini	3:56
	29	13:10		29	Cancer	15: 0
JUN	31	8:33		1	Leo	3:26
	3	6:29		3	Virgo	15:57
	5	17:14		6	Libra	2:25
	8	0:26		8	Scorpio	9: 7
	10	10:19		10	Sagittar	11:54
	12	4: 0		12	Capricrn	12: 6
	14	0:56		14	Aquarius	11:46
	16	4: 8		16	Pisces	12:55
	18	11: 3		18	Aries	16:57
	20	22:22		21	Taurus	0:10
	22	16:26		23	Gemini	9:55
	25	11:37		25	Cancer	21:23
	28	0:46		28	Leo	9:53
	30	14:17		30	Virgo	22:35

Month	Day	Time		Day	Sign	Time
JUL	3	5:38		3	Libra	9:56
	5	17:53		5	Scorpio	18: 4
	6	19:10		7	Sagittar	22: 6
	9	18: 8		9	Capricrn	22:44
	11	17:39		11	Aquarius	21:50
	13	17:39		13	Pisces	21:37
	15	15: 0		16	Aries	0: 1
	18	2:25		18	Taurus	6: 5
	20	10: 1		20	Gemini	15:33
	23	0:11		23	Cancer	3:14
	25	13:12		25	Leo	15:51
	28	2:13		28	Virgo	4:26
	30	2:36		30	Libra	16: 0
AUG	1	23:42		2	Scorpio	1:10
	3	21:36		4	Sagittar	6:48
	6	7:57		6	Capricrn	8:52
	8	7:51		8	Aquarius	8:38
	10	7:22		10	Pisces	8: 2
	11	21:17		12	Aries	9:10
	14	13: 5		14	Taurus	13:39
	16	14:21		16	Gemini	22: 0
	19	8:47		19	Cancer	9:20
	21	21:25		21	Leo	21:59
	24	9:48		24	Virgo	10:24
	26	7:25		26	Libra	21:36
	29	6: 3		29	Scorpio	6:50
	30	12:47		31	Sagittar	13:25
SEP	2	16: 6		2	Capricrn	17: 5
	4	17:16		4	Aquarius	18:23
	6	17:21		6	Pisces	18:38
	8	7:34		8	Aries	19:35
	10	21: 5		10	Taurus	22:58
	12	20:48		13	Gemini	5:55
	15	13:32		15	Cancer	16:23
	18	1:30		18	Leo	4:51
	20	13:28		20	Virgo	17:14
	23	3: 9		23	Libra	3:59
	25	8: 6		25	Scorpio	12:31
	27	5:35		27	Sagittar	18:50
	29	12:24		29	Capricrn	23: 9
OCT	1	20:37		2	Aquarius	1:52
	3	22: 3		4	Pisces	3:40
	6	2:41		6	Aries	5:36
	8	3: 0		8	Taurus	8:58
	9	3: 1		10	Gemini	15: 4
	12	15:40		13	Cancer	0:32
	15	2:46		15	Leo	12:35
	17	14:43		18	Virgo	1: 7
	19	23:43		20	Libra	11:51
	22	17:29		22	Scorpio	19:42
	24	1: 6		25	Sagittar	0:58
	26	18:16		27	Capricrn	4:34
	28	20: 8		29	Aquarius	7:28
	31	2: 9		31	Pisces	10:20
NOV	2	10:24		2	Aries	13:41
	4	13:58		4	Taurus	18: 3
	5	16:47		7	Gemini	0:17
	9	5:36		9	Cancer	9:11
	11	20:40		11	Leo	20:46
	13	23: 6		14	Virgo	9:30
	16	11: 6		16	Libra	20:49
	18	22:39		19	Scorpio	4:48
	21	6:34		21	Sagittar	9:17
	23	10:48		23	Capricrn	11:33
	24	21:27		25	Aquarius	13:13
	27	14:42		27	Pisces	15:41
	29	12: 6		29	Aries	19:37
DEC	1	17:36		2	Taurus	1: 6
	2	21:17		4	Gemini	8:14
	6	9:50		6	Cancer	17:21
	8	8:23		9	Leo	4:41
	11	10:14		11	Virgo	17:31
	13	22:56		14	Libra	5:41
	16	8:40		16	Scorpio	14:42
	18	11:33		18	Sagittar	19:34
	20	18:26		20	Capricrn	21:21
	22	5: 3		22	Aquarius	21:21
	24	17:36		24	Pisces	22:11
	26	20:30		27	Aries	1: 6
	29	2: 3		29	Taurus	6:37
	31	3:51		31	Gemini	14:30

JAN	2	12:0	2 Libra	20:46	JUL	2	19:42	3 Gemini	10:33
	4	22:40	5 Scorpio	0:45		5	8:47	5 Cancer	23:20
	6	9:20	7 Sagittar	2:48		7	20:49	7 Leo	10:57
	8	11:20	9 Capricrn	3:43		10	18:54	10 Virgo	20:51
	10	12:23	11 Aquarius	5:2		12	15:36	12 Libra	4:41
	12	16:31	13 Pisces	8:40		14	20:11	15 Scorpio	9:59
	15	6:10	15 Aries	16:4		17	3:6	17 Sagittar	12:35
	17	22:14	18 Taurus	3:14		19	1:37	19 Capricrn	13:11
	20	0:57	20 Gemini	16:13		21	10:41	21 Aquarius	13:18
	22	14:37	23 Cancer	4:15		22	20:16	23 Pisces	15:0
	25	4:47	25 Leo	13:48		25	17:48	25 Aries	20:3
	27	14:49	27 Virgo	20:52		28	0:11	28 Taurus	5:12
	29	22:43	30 Libra	2:11		30	9:59	30 Gemini	17:20
FEB	31	22:11	1 Scorpio	6:20	AUG	1	16:44	2 Cancer	6:5
	3	2:24	3 Sagittar	9:32		4	10:17	4 Leo	17:27
	5	5:50	5 Capricrn	12:2		6	5:8	7 Virgo	2:45
	6	0:24	7 Aquarius	14:36		9	6:10	9 Libra	10:5
	9	13:51	9 Pisces	18:33		11	15:12	11 Scorpio	15:37
	11	9:32	12 Aries	1:21		13	4:30	13 Sagittar	19:18
	14	8:38	14 Taurus	11:39		15	8:32	15 Capricrn	21:23
	16	22:28	17 Gemini	0:18		17	7:45	17 Aquarius	22:45
	19	12:7	19 Cancer	12:40		19	18:55	20 Pisces	0:53
	22	22:16	21 Leo	22:26		21	12:20	22 Aries	5:28
	23	14:35	24 Virgo	4:59		23	15:24	24 Taurus	13:37
	26	0:15	26 Libra	9:8		26	10:22	27 Gemini	1:1
	27	22:38	28 Scorpio	12:7		29	10:56	29 Cancer	13:41
MAR	2	14:2	2 Sagittar	14:52	SEP	31	13:1	1 Leo	1:9
	4	7:39	4 Capricrn	17:57		3	2:59	3 Virgo	10:7
	6	16:22	6 Aquarius	21:43		4	20:14	5 Libra	16:34
	8	12:52	9 Pisces	2:49		7	1:2	7 Scorpio	21:13
	10	19:33	11 Aries	10:4		9	6:51	10 Sagittar	0:41
	13	4:53	13 Taurus	20:5		11	17:21	12 Capricrn	3:29
	16	1:31	16 Gemini	8:24		14	3:15	14 Aquarius	6:8
	18	16:39	18 Cancer	21:5		15	13:39	16 Pisces	9:28
	20	17:1	21 Leo	7:39		18	5:35	18 Aries	14:34
	23	10:22	23 Virgo	14:40		20	4:48	20 Taurus	22:26
	25	16:16	25 Libra	18:23		22	16:57	23 Gemini	9:14
	27	19:50	27 Scorpio	20:6		24	22:53	25 Cancer	21:45
	29	1:38	29 Sagittar	21:21		27	22:22	28 Leo	9:40
	31	20:10	31 Capricrn	23:26		30	9:1	30 Virgo	18:58
APR	2	6:48	3 Aquarius	3:12	OCT	2	19:14	3 Libra	1:54
	4	19:7	5 Pisces	9:4		5	0:58	5 Scorpio	4:36
	7	2:38	7 Aries	17:13		7	5:10	7 Sagittar	6:49
	9	12:26	10 Taurus	3:37		8	14:37	9 Capricrn	8:53
	12	4:36	12 Gemini	15:52		10	18:34	11 Aquarius	11:46
	14	23:0	15 Cancer	4:43		12	22:53	13 Pisces	16:4
	17	10:36	17 Leo	16:11		15	4:40	15 Aries	22:14
	19	23:43	20 Virgo	0:25		17	19:23	18 Taurus	5:38
	21	18:24	22 Libra	4:51		19	22:23	20 Gemini	17:16
	23	17:25	24 Scorpio	6:16		23	4:34	23 Cancer	5:38
	26	5:9	26 Sagittar	6:17		25	9:20	25 Leo	18:3
	27	17:36	28 Capricrn	6:29		27	23:31	28 Virgo	4:21
	29	9:43	30 Aquarius	9:7		30	8:38	30 Libra	11:5
MAY	1	23:42	2 Pisces	14:31	NOV	31	21:42	1 Scorpio	15:20
	4	7:17	4 Aries	23:2		3	13:47	3 Sagittar	15:20
	7	9:32	7 Taurus	10:0		5	0:3	5 Capricrn	15:49
	8	22:11	9 Gemini	22:27		7	12:32	7 Aquarius	17:29
	11	18:13	12 Cancer	11:19		9	12:50	9 Pisces	21:30
	14	10:5	14 Leo	23:16		11	14:29	12 Aries	4:15
	17	1:1	17 Virgo	8:46		13	21:43	14 Taurus	13:25
	19	11:34	19 Libra	14:42		16	12:43	17 Gemini	0:27
	21	2:39	21 Scorpio	17:3		19	3:20	19 Cancer	12:47
	23	3:25	23 Sagittar	16:58		22	0:12	22 Leo	1:26
	25	2:9	25 Capricrn	16:16		24	10:36	24 Virgo	12:47
	27	3:57	27 Aquarius	17:1		26	5:22	26 Libra	21:0
	29	9:43	29 Pisces	20:55		28	10:57	29 Scorpio	1:14
JUN	31	14:46	1 Aries	4:44	DEC	30	6:21	1 Sagittar	2:9
	3	6:50	3 Taurus	15:46		2	12:37	3 Capricrn	1:29
	5	14:19	6 Gemini	4:27		4	13:27	5 Aquarius	1:24
	7	23:2	8 Cancer	17:17		6	20:13	7 Pisces	3:49
	10	17:23	11 Leo	5:12		9	8:1	9 Aries	9:50
	12	23:26	13 Virgo	15:19		11	4:17	11 Taurus	19:11
	15	12:1	15 Libra	22:39		13	0:40	14 Gemini	6:42
	17	20:27	18 Scorpio	2:37		16	7:5	16 Cancer	19:10
	19	15:25	20 Sagittar	3:37		18	2:36	19 Leo	7:45
	21	14:39	22 Capricrn	3:1		21	18:45	21 Virgo	19:31
	23	22:36	24 Aquarius	2:51		23	16:8	24 Libra	5:6
	25	11:44	26 Pisces	5:13		26	0:26	26 Scorpio	11:7
	27	21:36	28 Aries	11:35		28	0:13	28 Sagittar	13:21
	30	2:57	30 Taurus	21:55		30	2:43	30 Capricrn	12:55

Date	Time	Day	Sign	Time		Date	Time	Day	Sign	Time
JAN 31	16:33	1	Taurus	0:37		JUL 30	18:54	1	Capricrn	18:23
3	10:12	3	Gemini	12: 1		3	16:42	3	Aquarius	21:37
5	5:50	5	Cancer	20:18		6	3:17	6	Pisces	3:41
7	17:24	8	Leo	1:29		7	21: 6	8	Aries	13:21
10	0:56	10	Virgo	4:40		10	6: 5	11	Taurus	1:45
12	0: 0	12	Libra	7:14		12	22:29	13	Gemini	14:24
14	0:45	14	Scorpio	10: 8		15	4: 3	16	Cancer	0:55
16	7: 3	16	Sagittar	13:49		18	0: 1	18	Leo	8:26
17	21:18	18	Capricrn	18:30		20	0:55	20	Virgo	13:30
20	18: 3	21	Aquarius	0:39		22	16:51	22	Libra	17:11
23	2:27	23	Pisces	9: 3		24	19:54	24	Scorpio	20:17
25	14:31	25	Aries	20: 6		26	15: 8	26	Sagittar	23:13
28	4:27	28	Taurus	8:54		28	18:18	29	Capricrn	2:22
30	17:54	30	Gemini	21: 1		30	15:30	31	Aquarius	6:26
FEB 2	5:48	2	Cancer	6: 0		AUG 2	1:57	2	Pisces	12:34
4	10:10	4	Leo	11: 3		4	5:17	4	Aries	21:43
6	8:54	6	Virgo	13:10		6	16:33	7	Taurus	9:42
8	10: 6	8	Libra	14:11		9	5:39	9	Gemini	22:32
10	1:12	10	Scorpio	15:50		11	11:44	12	Cancer	9:29
12	15: 7	12	Sagittar	19:10		14	2: 6	14	Leo	16:58
14	17:11	15	Capricrn	0:28		16	10: 6	16	Virgo	21:16
17	3:35	17	Aquarius	7:37		18	10:14	18	Libra	23:45
19	12:36	19	Pisces	16:39		20	22:12	21	Scorpio	1:52
21	23:40	22	Aries	3:43		22	17:43	23	Sagittar	4:37
23	15:21	24	Taurus	16:28		24	14:12	25	Capricrn	8:25
27	1:20	27	Gemini	5:12		27	12:10	27	Aquarius	13:32
MAR 28	19:22	1	Cancer	15:24		29	6:31	29	Pisces	20:26
3	18:12	3	Leo	21:29		SEP 31	15:14	1	Aries	5:43
5	20:40	5	Virgo	23:43		3	8:53	3	Taurus	17:28
7	20:49	7	Libra	23:48		6	4:12	6	Gemini	6:29
9	17:20	9	Scorpio	23:48		8	16:29	8	Cancer	18:11
11	22:17	12	Sagittar	1:30		10	14: 2	11	Leo	2:28
14	4:35	14	Capricrn	5:55		12	19:32	13	Virgo	6:53
16	9:33	16	Aquarius	13:12		14	21:57	15	Libra	8:35
18	18:59	18	Pisces	22:51		16	23: 0	17	Scorpio	9:18
21	6:16	21	Aries	10:21		19	4:46	19	Sagittar	10:41
23	3:46	23	Taurus	23: 7		21	12:34	21	Capricrn	13:50
26	7:41	26	Gemini	12: 3		23	8:40	23	Aquarius	19:12
28	0:22	28	Cancer	23:14		25	16:15	26	Pisces	2:51
31	6:52	31	Leo	6:52		28	2: 8	28	Aries	12:43
APR 2	6:24	2	Virgo	10:26		OCT 29	17:34	1	Taurus	0:36
4	6:56	4	Libra	10:55		3	3:33	3	Gemini	13:37
5	15: 8	6	Scorpio	10:11		5	8:47	6	Cancer	2: 0
8	5:55	8	Sagittar	10:18		8	3:50	8	Leo	11:34
9	19:31	10	Capricrn	12:58		10	16:58	10	Virgo	17:10
12	13:40	12	Aquarius	19: 5		12	12:41	12	Libra	19:13
14	22:34	15	Pisces	4:31		14	4:34	14	Scorpio	19: 6
17	9:53	17	Aries	16:19		16	13:19	16	Sagittar	19: 6
19	4: 8	20	Taurus	5:13		18	12:17	18	Capricrn	20:36
22	12:36	22	Gemini	18: 1		20	20:14	21	Aquarius	0:55
24	5: 3	25	Cancer	5:27		23	8:13	23	Pisces	8:28
27	7: 8	27	Leo	14:11		25	16:22	25	Aries	18:48
29	12:33	29	Virgo	19:25		28	2: 5	28	Taurus	7: 0
MAY 1	14:40	1	Libra	21:23		30	17:28	30	Gemini	20: 0
3	1: 9	3	Scorpio	21:18		NOV 1	12:11	2	Cancer	8:32
5	13:53	5	Sagittar	20:57		4	16:18	4	Leo	19: 4
7	6:39	7	Capricrn	22:12		7	0:12	7	Virgo	2:19
9	18: 8	10	Aquarius	2:39		9	4:19	9	Libra	5:53
12	5:43	12	Pisces	10:57		10	8:47	11	Scorpio	6:32
14	12:13	14	Aries	22:26		13	5:10	13	Sagittar	5:53
16	8:37	17	Taurus	11:24		14	8:19	15	Capricrn	5:54
19	21:42	20	Gemini	0: 2		16	22:59	17	Aquarius	8:26
21	10: 8	22	Cancer	11: 6		19	9: 4	19	Pisces	14:43
24	9: 6	24	Leo	19:55		21	23:59	22	Aries	0:43
26	15:32	27	Virgo	2: 7		23	11: 8	24	Taurus	13: 8
28	23:18	29	Libra	5:41		26	7:44	27	Gemini	2: 9
30	21:53	31	Scorpio	7: 8		28	18:37	29	Cancer	14:24
JUN 1	21:13	2	Sagittar	7:34		DEC 1	20:59	2	Leo	1: 0
4	5:23	4	Capricrn	8:35		3	20:49	4	Virgo	9:15
6	0: 8	6	Aquarius	11:53		6	13: 1	6	Libra	14:34
8	17:54	8	Pisces	18:47		8	10:30	8	Scorpio	16:57
10	16:35	11	Aries	5:25		10	15:54	10	Sagittar	17:14
13	1:56	13	Taurus	18:12		12	14:51	12	Capricrn	17: 0
15	16:10	16	Gemini	6:46		14	18:14	14	Aquarius	18:16
18	11:59	18	Cancer	17:23		16	12:56	16	Pisces	22:51
20	11:36	21	Leo	1:33		19	1:59	19	Aries	7:37
22	17:55	23	Virgo	7:33		21	19:28	21	Taurus	19:41
24	22:24	25	Libra	11:48		23	5:10	24	Gemini	8:46
27	7:56	27	Scorpio	14:38		26	19:18	26	Cancer	20:45
29	16: 9	29	Sagittar	16:31		27	12: 4	29	Leo	6:45
						30	22:51	31	Virgo	14:44

Mon	Day	Time	Day	Sign	Time
JAN	2	4:59	2	Capricorn	6: 8
	4	9:34	4	Aquarius	16:31
	7	3:44	7	Pisces	4:35
	9	16:36	9	Aries	17:16
	12	4: 9	12	Taurus	4:37
	13	23:57	13	Gemini	12:41
	16	16:40	16	Cancer	16:48
	18	14: 6	18	Leo	17:50
	20	6:54	20	Virgo	17:36
	22	11:28	22	Libra	18: 8
	24	18:57	24	Scorpio	21: 5
	26	0:54	27	Sagittar	3:13
	28	2:37	29	Capricrn	12:13
	30	22: 0	31	Aquarius	23:12
FEB	2	7: 6	3	Pisces	11:23
	5	13:54	6	Aries	0: 5
	8	10:14	8	Taurus	12: 6
	10	4: 0	10	Gemini	21:40
	12	15:23	13	Cancer	3:21
	14	20:30	15	Leo	5:10
	17	0:42	17	Virgo	4:33
	19	3:34	19	Libra	3:40
	22	17:57	21	Scorpio	4:45
	25	10: 1	23	Sagittar	9:23
	27	11: 8	25	Capricrn	17:50
			28	Aquarius	5: 3
MAR	1	1: 6	1	Pisces	17:30
	3	15:26	4	Aries	6: 8
	5	20:55	6	Taurus	18:10
	8	17:25	9	Gemini	4:30
	11	4:26	11	Cancer	11:49
	13	11:12	13	Leo	15:22
	15	9:14	15	Virgo	15:48
	17	10:11	17	Libra	14:52
	18	12:19	19	Scorpio	14:49
	21	12:32	21	Sagittar	17:42
	22	22:35	24	Capricrn	0:37
	26	6:38	26	Aquarius	11:10
	28	19:34	28	Pisces	23:38
	31	8:16	31	Aries	12:15
APR	1	15:13	2	Taurus	23:56
	5	6:56	5	Gemini	10: 5
	7	17:47	7	Cancer	18: 0
	9	20: 0	9	Leo	23: 2
	11	22: 5	12	Virgo	1:12
	13	22:10	14	Libra	1:30
	15	19:12	16	Scorpio	1:42
	17	23:15	18	Sagittar	3:44
	19	4: 7	20	Capricrn	9:11
	22	11:42	22	Aquarius	18:28
	24	22:21	25	Pisces	6:27
	27	9:44	27	Aries	19: 3
	30	1:37	30	Taurus	6:31
MAY	2	4:39	2	Gemini	16: 3
	4	16:47	4	Cancer	23:27
	6	22:24	7	Leo	4:44
	9	2:38	9	Virgo	8: 3
	10	19: 8	11	Libra	9:55
	13	9: 5	13	Scorpio	11:23
	15	4:30	15	Sagittar	13:51
	16	11: 3	17	Capricrn	18:44
	20	2:53	20	Aquarius	2:56
	22	13:59	22	Pisces	14: 9
	24	22:32	25	Aries	2:40
	27	13:51	27	Taurus	14:14
	28	19: 3	29	Gemini	23:24
JUN	1	5:23	1	Cancer	5:54
	3	9:45	3	Leo	10:20
	5	12:50	5	Virgo	13:28
	6	16:43	7	Libra	16: 4
	9	18: 4	9	Scorpio	18:49
	10	15:46	11	Sagittar	22:27
	14	2:54	14	Capricrn	3:49
	16	10:40	16	Aquarius	11:42
	18	21:11	18	Pisces	22:19
	21	6:10	21	Aries	10:41
	23	22:36	23	Taurus	22:39
	24	21:46	26	Gemini	8: 5
	28	13:55	28	Cancer	14:10
	30	16:24	30	Leo	17:31

Mon	Day	Time	Day	Sign	Time
JUL	2	19: 3	2	Virgo	19:28
	4	20:56	4	Libra	21:27
	6	23:51	7	Scorpio	0:29
	8	16:31	9	Sagittar	5: 4
	11	10:31	11	Capricrn	11:24
	13	18:25	13	Aquarius	19:42
	16	5: 0	16	Pisces	6:11
	18	17: 7	18	Aries	18:27
	21	5:37	21	Taurus	6:53
	23	10:26	23	Gemini	17:11
	25	23: 4	25	Cancer	23:45
	28	1:44	28	Leo	2:42
	30	2:36	30	Virgo	3:30
AUG	1	2:31	1	Libra	4: 4
	3	5:13	3	Scorpio	6: 5
	5	4:45	5	Sagittar	10:30
	7	17:11	7	Capricrn	17:25
	10	1:40	10	Aquarius	2:26
	12	12:31	12	Pisces	13:14
	14	23:39	15	Aries	1:29
	17		17	Taurus	14:14
	19	19:41	20	Gemini	1:32
	22	9: 6	22	Cancer	9:21
	24	12:52	24	Leo	13: 1
	26	13:29	26	Virgo	13:33
	28	10:54	28	Libra	12:58
	30		30	Scorpio	13:24
SEP	31	8:46	1	Sagittar	16:30
	3	20:26	3	Capricrn	22:56
	4	22:36	6	Aquarius	8:12
	8	16:44	8	Pisces	19:25
	11	5: 4	11	Aries	7:47
	13	17:52	13	Taurus	20:34
	15	18:49	16	Gemini	8:26
	18	15:10	18	Cancer	17:37
	20	19:24	20	Leo	22:50
	22	22:15	23	Virgo	0:20
	24	21:41	24	Libra	23:42
	26	21: 3	26	Scorpio	23: 5
	28	18:13	29	Sagittar	0:33
OCT	1	3:15	1	Capricrn	5:29
	2	8:23	3	Aquarius	14: 4
	5	23: 1	6	Pisces	1:20
	8	11:36	8	Aries	13:52
	11	0:19	11	Taurus	2:29
	12	20:28	13	Gemini	14:15
	15	22: 9	16	Cancer	0: 1
	18	2: 3	18	Leo	6:42
	20	8:27	20	Virgo	9:57
	22	9:11	22	Libra	10:32
	24	8:51	24	Scorpio	10: 8
	26	13:34	26	Sagittar	10:44
	28	12:50	28	Capricrn	14: 5
	30	0: 7	30	Aquarius	21:14
NOV	2	6:40	2	Pisces	7:50
	4	19:18	4	Aries	20:21
	7	8: 1	7	Taurus	8:54
	9	11: 2	9	Gemini	20:11
	12	4:58	12	Cancer	5:32
	14	10:49	14	Leo	12:34
	16	16:52	16	Virgo	17: 9
	18	19:21	18	Libra	19:30
	20	20:29	20	Scorpio	20:31
	22	5:45	22	Sagittar	21:35
	24	14:12	25	Capricrn	0:18
	26	13:23	27	Aquarius	6: 7
	29	13: 1	29	Pisces	15:34
DEC	1	10:26	2	Aries	3:43
	4	4:36	4	Taurus	16:21
	6	22:22	7	Gemini	3:25
	9	10: 1	9	Cancer	11:57
	11	4:55	11	Leo	18: 9
	13	12:41	13	Virgo	22:36
	15	23:36	16	Libra	1:53
	17	22: 1	18	Scorpio	4:28
	20	0:11	20	Sagittar	6:59
	22	6:21	22	Capricrn	10:21
	24	4:49	24	Aquarius	15:48
	26	13: 8	27	Pisces	0:19
	29	0:39	29	Aries	11:50

JAN	2	20:39	2 Virgo	21:50	JUL	2	9:56	2 Aries	14:48
	4	23: 1	5 Libra	0:45		4	19:54	5 Taurus	0: 6
	7	6: 3	7 Scorpio	7:17		7	1:51	7 Gemini	5:43
	9	4:17	9 Sagittar	17:14		9	6:48	9 Cancer	7:52
	12	4:15	12 Capricrn	5:27		11	4:25	11 Leo	7:54
	14	17:19	14 Aquarius	18:27		13	4:15	13 Virgo	7:44
	17	6:37	17 Pisces	7: 3		15	7:11	15 Libra	9:11
	19	16:15	19 Aries	18: 9		17	9:55	17 Scorpio	13:39
	22	1:42	22 Taurus	2:37		19	14:35	19 Sagittar	21:32
	23	18:53	24 Gemini	7:41		22	4:22	22 Capricrn	8:12
	26	8:43	26 Cancer	9:29		24	16:44	24 Aquarius	20:27
	28	8:26	28 Leo	9:11		27	5:41	27 Pisces	9:12
	30	7:51	30 Virgo	8:35		29	15:11	29 Aries	21:22
FEB	1	6:57	1 Libra	9:48	AUG	1	7:14	1 Taurus	7:38
	3	13:42	3 Scorpio	14:33		3	2:24	3 Gemini	14:44
	5	4:56	5 Sagittar	23:29		5	16: 2	5 Cancer	18:10
	8	10:36	8 Capricrn	11:34		7	16:47	7 Leo	18:38
	10	23:41	11 Aquarius	0:41		9	16:11	9 Virgo	17:50
	13	12: 2	13 Pisces	13: 3		11	15:42	11 Libra	17:52
	15	21:16	15 Aries	23:47		13	19:22	13 Scorpio	20:45
	18	7:30	18 Taurus	8:31		15	12:48	16 Sagittar	3:34
	20	9:23	20 Gemini	14:53		18	13: 6	18 Capricrn	14: 0
	22	18:14	22 Cancer	18:32		21	1:54	21 Aquarius	2:26
	24	19:32	24 Leo	19:47		23	15: 2	23 Pisces	15:11
	26	18:47	26 Virgo	19:50		26	0: 2	26 Aries	3: 9
	28	18:48	28 Libra	20:31		28	12:27	28 Taurus	13:39
MAR	2	22:33	2 Scorpio	23:51		30	18:17	30 Gemini	21:50
	5	0:34	5 Sagittar	7:16	SEP	1	22:44	2 Cancer	2:54
	7	16:53	7 Capricrn	18:30		4	0:59	4 Leo	4:48
	10	5:47	10 Aquarius	7:31		6	1: 0	6 Virgo	4:37
	12	18: 5	12 Pisces	19:48		8	2:37	8 Libra	4:14
	15	4:24	15 Aries	6: 1		10	2: 9	10 Scorpio	5:50
	17	12:34	17 Taurus	14: 5		12	3:25	12 Sagittar	11: 9
	19	17:46	19 Gemini	20:21		14	16:37	14 Capricrn	20:34
	21	23:31	22 Cancer	0:53		17	4:52	17 Aquarius	8:46
	24	1:42	24 Leo	3:44		19	17:49	19 Pisces	21:31
	26	4: 2	26 Virgo	5:19		22	6:37	22 Aries	9:11
	28	5:32	28 Libra	6:49		24	16: 3	24 Taurus	19:13
	30	8:37	30 Scorpio	9:57		26	23:58	27 Gemini	3:25
APR	31	11:53	1 Sagittar	16:20		29	8:43	29 Cancer	9:25
	4	0:59	4 Capricrn	2:30	OCT	1	10:34	1 Leo	12:55
	6	12: 3	6 Aquarius	15: 7		3	12: 7	3 Virgo	14:16
	9	1:58	9 Pisces	3:31		5	9:19	5 Libra	14:42
	11	12: 8	11 Aries	13:38		7	14: 9	7 Scorpio	16: 7
	13	19:32	13 Taurus	21: 0		8	0:31	9 Sagittar	20:21
	14	19: 9	16 Gemini	2:16		12	2:36	12 Capricrn	4:31
	18	4:48	18 Cancer	6:15		14	14:13	14 Aquarius	16: 1
	20	8:59	20 Leo	9:27		17	3: 7	17 Pisces	4:42
	22	10:42	22 Virgo	12:12		19	10:17	19 Aries	16:19
	24	13:31	24 Libra	15: 5		22	0:41	22 Taurus	1:48
	26	17:26	26 Scorpio	19: 5		23	4:22	24 Gemini	9:11
	28	16:28	29 Sagittar	1:29		26	14:39	26 Cancer	14:48
MAY	1	9: 3	1 Capricrn	11: 2		28	18:28	28 Leo	18:51
	3	18:34	3 Aquarius	23:10		30	21:10	30 Virgo	21:34
	6	9:34	6 Pisces	11:44	NOV	1	18:57	1 Libra	23:31
	8	21: 3	8 Aries	22:17		4	1:47	4 Scorpio	1:54
	11	5: 3	11 Taurus	5:37		5	23:51	6 Sagittar	6:10
	13	5:36	13 Gemini	10: 4		8	11:38	8 Capricrn	13:32
	15	11:48	15 Cancer	12:49		10	14:58	11 Aquarius	0:11
	17	13:48	17 Leo	15: 2		13	9:39	13 Pisces	12:42
	19	16: 9	19 Virgo	17:37		15	21:41	16 Aries	0:37
	21	18:46	21 Libra	21:12		18	5:54	18 Taurus	10: 7
	24	0:17	24 Scorpio	2:18		20	12:30	20 Gemini	16:46
	25	10:23	26 Sagittar	9:28		22	17:34	22 Cancer	21:11
	28	16:26	28 Capricrn	19: 8		23	23:57	25 Leo	0:20
	31	3:59	31 Aquarius	7: 0		26	23:45	27 Virgo	3: 3
JUN	2	16:27	2 Pisces	19:43		29	2:45	29 Libra	5:58
	5	4:56	5 Aries	7: 0	DEC	1	6:33	1 Scorpio	9:41
	7	11:48	7 Taurus	15: 6		2	4:59	3 Sagittar	14:57
	9	9:57	9 Gemini	19:38		5	20:42	5 Capricrn	22:29
	11	18:24	11 Cancer	21:33		6	20:29	8 Aquarius	8:40
	13	21:27	13 Leo	22:22		10	17:58	10 Pisces	20:54
	15	20:16	15 Virgo	23:39		13	6:35	13 Aries	9:17
	17	23: 0	18 Libra	2:37		15	17:10	15 Taurus	19:34
	20	4:57	20 Scorpio	8: 0		16	22:40	18 Gemini	2:24
	21	11:16	22 Sagittar	15:56		20	4:12	20 Cancer	6: 3
	24	21:44	25 Capricrn	2: 9		21	13:37	22 Leo	7:44
	27	9:33	27 Aquarius	14: 7		24	7:29	24 Virgo	9:32
	29	22:16	30 Pisces	2:53		26	9:51	26 Libra	11:19
						28	14: 5	28 Scorpio	15:27
						30	18:52	30 Sagittar	21:45

JAN

1	21:51	2	Aries	6:34
4	7:18	4	Taurus	11: 3
5	11:56	6	Gemini	12:49
8	7:55	8	Cancer	13: 2
10	8:11	10	Leo	13:22
12	10:13	12	Virgo	15:38
14	13:14	14	Libra	21:18
17	0:40	17	Scorpio	6:47
19	17:39	19	Sagittar	19: 1
22	1:39	22	Capricrn	7:52
24	17:33	24	Aquarius	19:26
26	23: 0	27	Pisces	4:50
29	5:49	29	Aries	11:59
31	11:44	31	Taurus	17: 4

FEB

2	11:35	2	Gemini	20:21
4	17:13	4	Cancer	22:19
6	18:44	6	Leo	23:51
8	20:58	9	Virgo	2:16
11	0:38	11	Libra	7: 3
13	9:14	13	Scorpio	15:17
15	20:22	16	Sagittar	2:46
18	14:51	18	Capricrn	15:37
20	21: 0	21	Aquarius	3:16
23	6: 9	23	Pisces	12:10
25	13:09	25	Aries	18:18
27	19:54	27	Taurus	22:33

MAR

2	1:25	2	Gemini	1:51
3	23:30	4	Cancer	4:49
6	2:31	6	Leo	7:51
8	6: 6	8	Virgo	11:28
10	11: 4	10	Libra	16:35
12	21:49	13	Scorpio	0:17
14	23:10	15	Sagittar	11: 4
17	17:43	17	Capricrn	23:48
20	10:55	20	Aquarius	11:54
22	15:33	22	Pisces	21: 2
24	21:03	25	Aries	2:38
27	0:43	27	Taurus	5:40
28	22:50	29	Gemini	7:45
31	9:32	31	Cancer	10:10

APR

2	6:34	2	Leo	13:37
4	14:56	4	Virgo	18:19
6	19: 1	7	Libra	0:27
9	2:52	9	Scorpio	8:34
9	22:52	11	Sagittar	19: 7
14	1:34	14	Capricrn	7:42
16	12:43	16	Aquarius	20:19
18	4: 3	19	Pisces	6:20
21	7: 0	21	Aries	12:24
23	9:51	23	Taurus	14:59
24	22:43	25	Gemini	15:49
27	11:31	27	Cancer	16:44
29	13:49	29	Leo	19:10

MAY

1	17:58	1	Virgo	23:46
4	6: 0	4	Libra	6:33
6	9: 1	6	Scorpio	15:25
8	0:46	9	Sagittar	2:17
11	17:16	11	Capricrn	14:50
13	17:16	14	Aquarius	3:45
16	8: 1	16	Pisces	14:47
18	17:31	18	Aries	22: 5
20	19:37	21	Taurus	1:23
21	5:26	23	Gemini	1:55
24	19:43	25	Cancer	1:39
26	18:37	27	Leo	2:28
29	2: 6	29	Virgo	5:44
31	4:52	31	Libra	12: 3

JUN

2	13:34	2	Scorpio	21:13
3	4:43	5	Sagittar	8:32
7	12:56	7	Capricrn	21:13
9	22:35	10	Aquarius	10: 9
12	13:32	12	Pisces	21:45
14	22:32	15	Aries	6:21
17	3:44	17	Taurus	11: 8
19	0:11	19	Gemini	12:35
21	11:53	21	Cancer	12:13
23	7:48	23	Leo	11:57
25	5:54	25	Virgo	13:37
27	10:10	27	Libra	18:31
29	18: 2	30	Scorpio	3: 2

JUL

30	20: 0	2	Sagittar	14:26
4	17:31	5	Capricrn	3:16
7	4:12	7	Aquarius	16: 4
9	17:58	10	Pisces	3:36
12	3:32	12	Aries	12:50
14	10: 9	14	Taurus	19: 1
16	11:25	16	Gemini	22: 4
18	19: 9	18	Cancer	22:47
20	18:57	20	Leo	22:36
22	14:44	22	Virgo	23:21
24	17:30	25	Libra	2:46
27	2: 9	27	Scorpio	9:59
28	3:15	29	Sagittar	20:48

AUG

1	7: 5	1	Capricrn	9:37
3	11: 0	3	Aquarius	22:18
6	0:20	6	Pisces	9:24
8	8: 4	8	Aries	18:21
10	16:49	11	Taurus	1: 1
13	2:33	13	Gemini	5:23
14	22:45	15	Cancer	7:41
16	23:58	17	Leo	8:41
18	2:46	19	Virgo	9:40
21	2:36	21	Libra	12:23
23	8:43	23	Scorpio	18:22
25	22:29	26	Sagittar	4:12
28	6:24	28	Capricrn	16:42
30	19:24	31	Aquarius	5:24

SEP

2	6:44	2	Pisces	16:12
4	13:52	5	Aries	0:25
7	4:56	7	Taurus	6:28
8	22: 0	9	Gemini	10:58
11	6:27	11	Cancer	14:19
13	9:14	13	Leo	16:47
15	13:52	15	Virgo	18:58
17	19:25	17	Libra	22: 4
19	19:38	20	Scorpio	3:33
22	10:46	22	Sagittar	12:31
24	16: 7	25	Capricrn	0:32
27	5:12	27	Aquarius	13:22
29	16:42	30	Pisces	0:19

OCT

1	22: 3	2	Aries	8: 7
4	6:34	4	Taurus	13:10
5	10:40	6	Gemini	16:40
8	13:31	8	Cancer	19:40
10	16:43	10	Leo	22:45
12	20:13	13	Virgo	2:10
14	21: 3	15	Libra	6:23
17	6:21	17	Scorpio	12:21
18	16:45	19	Sagittar	21: 1
22	5:36	22	Capricrn	8:39
24	18:20	24	Aquarius	21:37
27	3:38	27	Pisces	9:13
29	14:14	29	Aries	17:26
31	22: 1	31	Taurus	22: 4

NOV

2	5: 3	3	Gemini	0:23
4	21:49	5	Cancer	2: 0
7	0: 3	7	Leo	4:11
9	3:43	9	Virgo	7:41
11	4:32	11	Libra	12:46
13	16:28	13	Scorpio	19:43
15	21:23	16	Sagittar	4:52
18	13:59	18	Capricrn	16:22
21	3:57	21	Aquarius	5:21
23	16:30	23	Pisces	17:43
25	19:31	26	Aries	3: 8
28	8:20	28	Taurus	8:32
30	1:37	30	Gemini	10:37

DEC

2	8:31	2	Cancer	10:58
4	9: 4	4	Leo	11:27
6	11:10	6	Virgo	13:33
8	15:57	8	Libra	18:11
10	23:12	11	Scorpio	1:35
13	6:15	13	Sagittar	11:28
15	21: 0	15	Capricrn	23:16
18	10: 4	18	Aquarius	12:13
20	22:57	21	Pisces	0:57
23	10:34	23	Aries	11:35
25	17: 3	25	Taurus	18:38
27	12:47	27	Gemini	21:49
29	20:56	29	Cancer	22:13
31	20:34	31	Leo	21:34

JAN					
2	12:43	2	Sagittar	15:43	
4	14:41	5	Capricrn	1:42	
7	6:53	7	Aquarius	9:13	
9	12:38	9	Pisces	14:43	
11	16:52	11	Aries	18:44	
13	12:7	13	Taurus	21:46	
15	22:46	16	Gemini	0:18	
17	17:27	17	Cancer	3:8	
20	6:3	20	Leo	7:22	
22	12:49	22	Virgo	14:3	
24	22:38	24	Libra	23:46	
27	0:25	27	Scorpio	11:49	
29	23:23	30	Sagittar	0:12	
FEB 1	1:46	1	Capricrn	10:38	
3	17:26	3	Aquarius	17:56	
5	21:59	5	Pisces	22:22	
8	0:45	8	Aries	1:2	
9	17:38	10	Taurus	3:11	
12	5:43	12	Gemini	5:52	
14	1:27	14	Cancer	9:43	
16	15:10	16	Leo	15:11	
18	17:31	18	Virgo	22:35	
20	21:33	21	Libra	8:13	
23	9:1	23	Scorpio	19:55	
26	3:10	26	Sagittar	8:30	
28	9:26	28	Capricrn	19:47	
MAR 2	16:57	3	Aquarius	3:52	
4	23:15	5	Pisces	8:13	
7	1:16	7	Aries	9:49	
9	1:55	9	Taurus	10:23	
11	3:59	11	Gemini	11:43	
13	10:4	13	Cancer	15:6	
15	19:11	15	Leo	21:3	
17	19:30	18	Virgo	5:20	
20	15:23	20	Libra	15:31	
22	15:55	23	Scorpio	3:15	
25	15:43	25	Sagittar	15:52	
27	17:44	28	Capricrn	3:53	
30	12:57	30	Aquarius	13:16	
APR 1	18:19	1	Pisces	18:42	
3	20:0	3	Aries	20:26	
5	11:56	5	Taurus	20:5	
7	19:12	7	Gemini	19:48	
9	12:45	9	Cancer	21:34	
12	1:43	12	Leo	2:37	
14	9:52	14	Virgo	10:57	
16	20:22	16	Libra	21:39	
19	8:0	19	Scorpio	9:40	
21	20:37	21	Sagittar	22:16	
24	9:9	24	Capricrn	10:32	
26	19:5	26	Aquarius	20:58	
29	2:2	29	Pisces	3:57	
MAY 1	5:3	1	Aries	6:58	
2	22:21	3	Taurus	7:0	
5	3:57	5	Gemini	6:2	
6	21:10	7	Cancer	6:18	
9	7:3	9	Leo	9:41	
11	16:38	11	Virgo	16:56	
14	0:5	14	Libra	3:25	
16	4:0	16	Scorpio	15:38	
19	0:26	19	Sagittar	4:15	
21	4:39	21	Capricrn	16:21	
23	23:0	24	Aquarius	3:1	
26	7:7	26	Pisces	11:6	
28	5:39	28	Aries	15:45	
30	7:19	30	Taurus	17:11	
JUN 1	12:57	1	Gemini	16:49	
3	13:15	3	Cancer	16:39	
5	14:15	5	Leo	18:43	
7	19:27	8	Virgo	0:26	
10	4:28	10	Libra	9:56	
12	8:54	12	Scorpio	21:55	
15	4:34	15	Sagittar	10:32	
17	15:5	17	Capricrn	22:22	
20	2:37	20	Aquarius	8:37	
22	10:51	22	Pisces	16:45	
24	20:29	24	Aries	22:19	
26	21:51	27	Taurus	1:17	
29	0:45	29	Gemini	2:22	

JUL				
30	21:26	1	Cancer	2:58
2	22:50	3	Leo	4:48
5	3:1	5	Virgo	9:27
7	11:54	7	Libra	17:45
10	11:44	10	Scorpio	5:3
12	10:5	12	Sagittar	17:36
15	0:54	15	Capricrn	5:20
17	7:51	17	Aquarius	15:3
19	15:28	19	Pisces	22:26
22	2:20	22	Aries	3:44
24	6:41	24	Taurus	7:19
26	3:11	26	Gemini	9:42
27	23:5	28	Cancer	11:42
30	7:37	30	Leo	14:21
AUG 1	11:51	1	Virgo	18:55
3	8:55	4	Libra	2:25
5	21:42	6	Scorpio	12:59
8	17:26	9	Sagittar	1:23
10	22:0	11	Capricrn	13:21
13	15:36	13	Aquarius	22:57
16	4:23	16	Pisces	5:35
18	9:28	18	Aries	9:50
20	8:1	20	Taurus	12:44
22	14:16	22	Gemini	15:19
24	5:10	24	Cancer	18:17
26	15:39	26	Leo	22:11
28	20:52	29	Virgo	3:32
31	9:0	31	Libra	11:3
SEP 2	6:35	2	Scorpio	21:11
5	2:17	5	Sagittar	9:24
7	8:44	7	Capricrn	21:49
10	1:37	10	Aquarius	7:59
12	13:48	12	Pisces	14:35
14	12:31	14	Aries	17:56
16	8:7	16	Taurus	19:31
18	15:52	18	Gemini	21:0
20	19:48	20	Cancer	23:40
22	22:58	23	Leo	4:9
25	7:10	25	Virgo	9:39
27	13:29	27	Libra	18:41
29	16:13	30	Scorpio	4:53
OCT 2	11:56	2	Sagittar	17:0
4	17:13	5	Capricrn	5:50
7	13:56	7	Aquarius	17:2
9	20:43	10	Pisces	0:33
12	0:38	12	Aries	4:2
14	4:34	14	Taurus	4:44
16	1:45	16	Gemini	4:42
18	2:59	18	Cancer	5:53
20	6:45	20	Leo	9:35
22	14:25	22	Virgo	16:6
24	22:22	25	Libra	0:57
27	1:3	27	Scorpio	11:39
29	21:40	29	Sagittar	23:49
NOV 1	3:27	1	Capricrn	12:47
3	23:22	4	Aquarius	0:52
6	8:45	6	Pisces	9:53
8	13:50	8	Aries	14:39
10	10:19	10	Taurus	15:45
12	14:38	12	Gemini	15:0
14	10:29	14	Cancer	14:37
16	12:55	16	Leo	16:33
18	18:50	18	Virgo	21:54
21	4:10	21	Libra	6:34
23	16:16	23	Scorpio	17:37
25	20:22	26	Sagittar	6:1
28	10:28	28	Capricrn	18:53
DEC 30	23:4	1	Aquarius	7:10
3	23:22	3	Pisces	17:17
5	20:1	5	Aries	23:50
8	1:37	8	Taurus	2:32
9	21:54	10	Gemini	2:31
11	22:37	12	Cancer	1:41
14	0:36	14	Leo	2:9
16	0:15	16	Virgo	5:39
18	5:48	18	Libra	12:59
20	21:31	20	Scorpio	23:40
21	13:28	23	Sagittar	12:12
25	18:5	26	Capricrn	1:0
28	6:14	28	Aquarius	12:54
30	16:41	30	Pisces	23:2

Mon	D	Time	D	Sign	Time
JAN	1	9:54	1	Cancer	12:30
	3	15: 4	3	Leo	20:48
	5	20:22	6	Virgo	7:49
	8	14:34	8	Libra	20:39
	10	20: 2	11	Scorpio	8:56
	13	12:42	13	Sagittar	18:18
	15	23:30	15	Capricrn	23:52
	17	21:20	18	Aquarius	2:26
	19	19: 8	20	Pisces	3:34
	21	23:35	22	Aries	4:52
	23	17:28	24	Taurus	7:32
	26	6:16	26	Gemini	12:12
	28	12:44	28	Cancer	19: 3
	31	21:23	31	Leo	4: 9
FEB	2	5:50	2	Virgo	15:22
	4	20:31	5	Libra	4: 5
	7	0:53	7	Scorpio	16:47
	9	19:45	10	Sagittar	3:20
	12	2:55	12	Capricrn	10:13
	14	6:18	14	Aquarius	13:20
	16	8:52	16	Pisces	13:55
	18	6:33	18	Aries	13:43
	20	1:58	20	Taurus	14:36
	22	10:10	22	Gemini	17:59
	24	15:23	25	Cancer	0:35
	27	1: 0	27	Leo	10:11
	29	12:59	29	Virgo	21:54
MAR	3	1:40	3	Libra	10:41
	5	21:21	5	Scorpio	23:23
	8	2: 0	8	Sagittar	10:39
	10	7:57	10	Capricrn	19: 3
	12	16: 5	13	Aquarius	23:46
	14	23:41	15	Pisces	1:11
	16	18:57	17	Aries	0:42
	18	21: 6	19	Taurus	0:14
	20	21:43	21	Gemini	1:48
	23	1:45	23	Cancer	6:56
	25	6:49	25	Leo	15:59
	27	20:40	28	Virgo	3:53
	30	7:35	30	Libra	16:50
APR	1	21:21	2	Scorpio	5:22
	4	8:35	4	Sagittar	16:35
	6	18: 1	7	Capricrn	1:43
	8	23: 1	9	Aquarius	8: 0
	11	4:30	11	Pisces	11: 8
	13	8:46	13	Aries	11:41
	15	5:23	15	Taurus	11:11
	17	6: 1	17	Gemini	11:42
	19	14:39	19	Cancer	15:12
	21	12:19	21	Leo	22:53
	24	5:32	24	Virgo	10:13
	26	11:33	26	Libra	23:10
	29	9:11	29	Scorpio	11:36
MAY	1	21:14	1	Sagittar	22:22
	3	22:33	4	Capricrn	7:15
	6	3: 6	6	Aquarius	14: 4
	8	15:12	8	Pisces	18:34
	10	19:16	10	Aries	20:45
	12	8:39	12	Taurus	21:25
	14	14:35	14	Gemini	22: 8
	16	11: 2	17	Cancer	0:53
	19	4: 7	19	Leo	7:15
	21	4:11	21	Virgo	17:33
	23	16:18	24	Libra	6:12
	26	22:10	26	Scorpio	18:37
	28	15:35	29	Sagittar	5: 5
	31	11:57	31	Capricrn	13:15
JUN	2	6:36	2	Aquarius	19:30
	4	11:29	5	Pisces	0:11
	7	1:56	7	Aries	3:24
	9	2:18	9	Taurus	5:30
	10	18:48	11	Gemini	7:23
	13	3: 2	13	Cancer	
	15	2:15	15	Leo	16:23
	17	19:22	18	Virgo	1:48
	20	12:33	20	Libra	13:56
	22	14: 3	23	Scorpio	2:27
	25	2:52	25	Sagittar	13: 2
	27	7:33	27	Capricrn	20:47
	29	17:26	30	Aquarius	2: 4

Mon	D	Time	D	Sign	Time
JUL	1	15:51	2	Pisces	5:49
	4	2:37	4	Aries	8:47
	5	23:48	6	Taurus	11:31
	8	12:27	8	Gemini	14:34
	10	4:54	10	Cancer	18:45
	12	10:52	13	Leo	1: 3
	14	17:55	15	Virgo	10:12
	17	11:55	17	Libra	21:56
	20	5:51	20	Scorpio	10:34
	22	8:25	22	Sagittar	21:43
	24	17:38	25	Capricrn	5:45
	26	23:29	27	Aquarius	10:35
	29	3:10	29	Pisces	13:11
	31	7:19	31	Aries	14:54
AUG	2	11:46	2	Taurus	16:56
	4	10:29	4	Gemini	20:10
	6	15:34	7	Cancer	1:13
	8	22:48	9	Leo	8:24
	11		11	Virgo	17:55
	13	20:18	14	Libra	5:33
	16	5: 3	16	Scorpio	18:16
	18	22:20	19	Sagittar	6: 8
	21	12:36	21	Capricrn	15:12
	23	14:31	23	Aquarius	20:33
	25	19: 5	25	Pisces	22:44
	27	18:21	27	Aries	23:12
	29	8: 3	29	Taurus	23:42
SEP	31	21:32	1	Gemini	1:51
	3	2:36	3	Cancer	6:40
	5	10:38	5	Leo	14:23
	7	9: 6	8	Virgo	0:32
	10	9:38	10	Libra	12:23
	12	5:44	13	Scorpio	1: 7
	15	12: 0	15	Sagittar	13:29
	17	22:57	17	Capricrn	23:46
	20	6:16	20	Aquarius	6:31
	21	21:22	22	Pisces	9:28
	23	22:36	24	Aries	9:38
	26	0:12	26	Taurus	8:54
	27	23:19	28	Gemini	9:22
	30	3: 3	30	Cancer	12:47
OCT	2	10:14	2	Leo	19:58
	4	19:56	5	Virgo	6:20
	7	11:40	7	Libra	18:31
	9	14: 1	10	Scorpio	7:16
	12	13:37	12	Sagittar	19:38
	15	1:49	15	Capricrn	6:37
	17	11:16	17	Aquarius	14:54
	19	13:16	19	Pisces	19:32
	21	18:56	21	Aries	20:44
	23	7:28	23	Taurus	19:56
	25	18:46	25	Gemini	19:17
	27	15:15	27	Cancer	21: 1
	30	1:50	30	Leo	2:39
NOV	1	2: 7	1	Virgo	12:39
	3	14:21	4	Libra	0:32
	5	22:17	6	Scorpio	13:20
	8	16: 3	9	Sagittar	1:26
	10	22:11	11	Capricrn	11:40
	13	12:57	13	Aquarius	21:11
	15	19:50	16	Pisces	3:22
	18	1:21	18	Aries	6:22
	20	4:36	20	Taurus	6:52
	22	0:16	22	Gemini	6:28
	23	20: 2	24	Cancer	7:19
	26	4:52	26	Leo	11:24
	28	12:53	28	Virgo	19:38
DEC	1	0:30	1	Libra	7:14
	3	6:51	3	Scorpio	20: 1
	6	1:59	6	Sagittar	7:58
	8	6: 1	8	Capricrn	18:13
	10	21:31	11	Aquarius	2:37
	13	4:24	13	Pisces	9: 4
	15	9: 7	15	Aries	13:22
	17	8:17	17	Taurus	15:37
	19	13: 0	19	Gemini	16:40
	21	8: 0	21	Cancer	18: 4
	23	18: 1	23	Leo	21:34
	26	0:58	26	Virgo	4:33
	28	11:34	28	Libra	15: 6
	30	15:44	31	Scorpio	3:37

JAN				JUL			
1	23:22	2 Pisces	7: 9	1	6:35	1 Libra	19: 9
4	4:52	4 Aries	9:42	4	0:28	4 Scorpio	5:58
6	8:37	6 Taurus	15:18	5	13:49	6 Sagittar	12:56
8	5:10	8 Gemini	23:43	7	20:45	8 Capricrn	16: 8
10	12:57	11 Cancer	10:15	9	20: 3	10 Aquarius	17: 0
13	10:52	13 Leo	22:17	11	22:30	12 Pisces	17:23
15	15:26	16 Virgo	11:11	14	4: 8	14 Aries	18:58
18	20:49	18 Libra	23:41	16	11: 0	16 Taurus	22:44
20	13:52	21 Scorpio	9:52	18	20:57	19 Gemini	5: 0
23	0:38	23 Sagittar	16: 9	20	15: 1	21 Cancer	13:41
25	1:27	25 Capricrn	18:28	23	6: 0	24 Leo	0:31
27	16: 0	27 Aquarius	18:13	25	18: 9	26 Virgo	13: 2
29	5: 3	29 Pisces	17:26	28	21:14	29 Libra	2: 7
31	9: 6	31 Aries	18:12	31	2:44	31 Scorpio	13:47
FEB				AUG			
2	16:48	2 Taurus	22: 4	1	23:11	2 Sagittar	22: 6
4	12:12	5 Gemini	5:34	4	22:18	5 Capricrn	2:24
6	20:15	7 Cancer	16: 6	6	6:27	7 Aquarius	3:29
9	10: 1	10 Leo	4:26	8	9:36	9 Pisces	3: 6
12	7:59	12 Virgo	17:18	10	7:31	11 Aries	3:11
14	11:34	15 Libra	5:38	12	12: 3	13 Taurus	5:22
17	12:53	17 Scorpio	16:13	14	19: 3	15 Gemini	10:42
19	11:55	19 Sagittar	23:52	17	7:22	17 Cancer	19:18
21	19:59	22 Capricrn	4: 1	19	4:57	20 Leo	6:29
23	14:42	24 Aquarius	5:13	22	17:11	22 Virgo	19:25
26	2:43	26 Pisces	4:53	24	7:20	25 Libra	8:14
27	21:43	28 Aries	4:55	27	6:33	27 Scorpio	20:13
MAR				29	17:42	30 Sagittar	5:40
2	7: 0	2 Taurus	7:10	SEP			
4	12:30	4 Gemini	12:59	1	6: 6	1 Capricrn	11:34
6	3:49	6 Cancer	22:35	2	17:36	3 Aquarius	14: 0
9	9:41	9 Leo	10:48	5	6:10	5 Pisces	14: 4
11	5:17	11 Virgo	23:43	6	19:56	7 Aries	13:30
14	10:13	14 Libra	11:42	9	7:22	9 Taurus	15:10
16	20:12	16 Scorpio	21:50	11	11:24	11 Gemini	17:55
19	3:58	19 Sagittar	5:39	13	19:24	14 Cancer	1:28
20	18:20	21 Capricrn	10:57	16	10:14	16 Leo	12:26
23	12:14	23 Aquarius	13:53	18	20:56	19 Virgo	1:16
25	7:42	25 Pisces	15: 5	21	9:58	21 Libra	14:11
27	14:11	27 Aries	15:48	24	0:55	24 Scorpio	1:55
29	15:58	29 Taurus	17:37	26	10:29	26 Sagittar	11:36
31	20:27	31 Gemini	22: 9	28	18:26	28 Capricrn	18:41
APR				30	5:14	30 Aquarius	22:50
3	0:20	3 Cancer	6:24	OCT			
5	16:20	5 Leo	17:58	2	12:53	3 Pisces	0:24
7	11:28	8 Virgo	6:53	4	8:50	5 Aries	0:29
10	17:34	10 Libra	18:46	7	0:24	7 Taurus	0:45
13	3:23	13 Scorpio	4:16	8	11:10	9 Gemini	3: 8
15	10:42	15 Sagittar	11:19	11	9: 6	11 Cancer	9: 0
17	19:59	17 Capricrn	16:24	13	1:52	13 Leo	19:12
19	19:59	19 Aquarius	20: 3	15	14:51	16 Virgo	7:52
21	6:22	21 Pisces	22:42	18	4:14	18 Libra	20:45
23	8:33	24 Aries	0:52	21	2:24	21 Scorpio	8: 3
25	10:50	26 Taurus	3:28	23	2:49	23 Sagittar	17:10
27	13:14	28 Gemini	7:49	25	10:49	26 Capricrn	0:12
29	20:36	30 Cancer	15:12	28	1:19	28 Aquarius	5:17
MAY				29	20:41	30 Pisces	8:30
2	4:52	3 Leo	1:57	NOV			
4	21:20	5 Virgo	14:42	1	3:18	1 Aries	10:10
6	6:58	8 Libra	2:48	2	21:50	3 Taurus	11:17
10	10:41	10 Scorpio	12:11	5	2:43	5 Gemini	13:26
12	2: 2	12 Sagittar	18:25	7	7:33	7 Cancer	18:24
14	20:44	14 Capricrn	22:26	9	15:49	9 Leo	3:15
16	23:17	17 Aquarius	1:26	12	8:12	12 Virgo	15:21
18	23:58	19 Pisces	4:19	14	17:21	14 Libra	4:17
21	6:54	21 Aries	7:31	17	13:27	17 Scorpio	15:30
22	17:19	23 Taurus	11:21	19	19:49	19 Sagittar	23:57
25	13:32	25 Gemini	16:29	21	21:26	22 Capricrn	6: 2
27	4:11	27 Cancer	23:51	24	2:30	24 Aquarius	10:37
29	12:52	29 Leo	10: 9	26	9:37	26 Pisces	14:18
JUN				28	9:54	28 Aries	17:17
1	1: 7	1 Virgo	22:41	30	4:33	30 Taurus	19:55
3	15:31	4 Libra	11:12	DEC			
6	10: 3	6 Scorpio	21: 6	2	16: 0	2 Gemini	23: 3
8	21: 7	9 Sagittar	3:15	4	20:53	5 Cancer	4: 2
10	12: 7	11 Capricrn	6:24	7	4:48	7 Leo	12:10
12	16:10	13 Aquarius	8: 7	9	16:35	9 Virgo	23:33
14	22:41	15 Pisces	9:57	12	12:22	12 Libra	12:30
17	5: 2	17 Aries	12:53	14	7:57	15 Scorpio	0: 9
19	13:10	19 Taurus	17:19	17	2:26	17 Sagittar	8:37
21	17:42	21 Gemini	23:23	19	8:24	19 Capricrn	13:55
23	10:13	24 Cancer	7:25	21	14:48	21 Aquarius	17:13
26	15:53	26 Leo	17:48	23	9: 4	23 Pisces	19:51
28	10:34	29 Virgo	6:15	25	17:22	25 Aries	22:41
				27	11:33	28 Taurus	2: 8
				30	1:11	30 Gemini	6:33

Mon	Day	Time	Day	Sign	Time
JAN	1	14: 9	1	Libra	14:32
	3	19:43	3	Scorpio	20:36
	5	23: 0	5	Sagittar	23: 4
	7	22:43	7	Capricrn	22:55
	9	4: 1	9	Aquarius	22: 6
	11	22:17	11	Pisces	22:51
	13	23:58	14	Aries	3: 6
	16	10:22	16	Taurus	11:31
	18	21:37	18	Gemini	23: 7
	21	10: 1	21	Cancer	11:51
	22	21:29	24	Leo	0: 3
	26	8:31	26	Virgo	10:57
	28	18:13	28	Libra	20: 8
	31	0:14	31	Scorpio	3: 4
FEB	2	4:16	2	Sagittar	7:14
	4	5:44	4	Capricrn	8:51
	6	2:47	6	Aquarius	9: 5
	8	6: 7	8	Pisces	9:48
	10	6:20	10	Aries	12:57
	12	17:38	12	Taurus	19:51
	15	0:53	15	Gemini	6:25
	16	16:12	17	Cancer	18:56
	19	17:15	20	Leo	7:10
	22	11:12	22	Virgo	17:40
	24	18:52	25	Libra	2: 4
	27	1:48	27	Scorpio	8:29
MAR	1	6:17	1	Sagittar	13: 3
	3	9:45	3	Capricrn	15:59
	5	8:57	5	Aquarius	17:51
	7	13:51	7	Pisces	19:46
	9	21: 1	9	Aries	23: 9
	11	23:13	11	Taurus	5:19
	14	5:19	14	Gemini	14:49
	16	20:54	17	Cancer	2:50
	19	12:18	19	Leo	15:13
	21	21: 2	22	Virgo	1:50
	24	5:33	24	Libra	9:42
	26	11:27	26	Scorpio	15: 2
	28	11:44	28	Sagittar	18:38
	30	12:44	30	Capricrn	21:24
APR	1	22: 4	1	Aquarius	0: 6
	4	1:31	4	Pisces	3:21
	6	6:28	6	Aries	7:52
	8	13:29	8	Taurus	14:22
	10	11:33	10	Gemini	23:28
	12	22:32	13	Cancer	11: 0
	15	13:56	15	Leo	23:31
	18	6:38	18	Virgo	10:45
	20	2:46	20	Libra	18:54
	22	12:45	22	Scorpio	23:40
	24	21: 3	25	Sagittar	2: 1
	26	17: 0	27	Capricrn	3:28
	28	4:40	29	Aquarius	5:29
MAY	30	22: 0	1	Pisces	9: 0
	2	16:35	3	Aries	14:28
	5	10: 9	5	Taurus	21:53
	7	19:15	8	Gemini	7:19
	10	6:23	10	Cancer	18:42
	12	23: 1	13	Leo	7:17
	15	17:45	15	Virgo	19:16
	17	22:12	18	Libra	4:25
	20	5:51	20	Scorpio	9:40
	22	2:12	22	Sagittar	11:32
	24	2:41	24	Capricrn	11:42
	25	10:24	26	Aquarius	12:10
	28	5:19	28	Pisces	14:37
	30	4:32	30	Aries	19:53
JUN	1	18: 4	2	Taurus	3:51
	4	4: 7	4	Gemini	13:54
	6	17:31	7	Cancer	1:31
	8	20:21	9	Leo	14: 8
	12	0:19	12	Virgo	2:35
	14	8:41	14	Libra	12:56
	16	15:38	16	Scorpio	19:29
	18	15:38	18	Sagittar	22: 2
	20	20:31	20	Capricrn	21:53
	21	19:43	22	Aquarius	21: 8
	24	16:20	24	Pisces	21:57
	26	4: 3	27	Aries	1:54
	29	3:45	29	Taurus	9:22

Mon	Day	Time	Day	Sign	Time
JUL	1	15:11	1	Gemini	19:38
	4	2:36	4	Cancer	7:34
	5	17:25	6	Leo	20:14
	9	4:52	9	Virgo	8:45
	10	20:56	11	Libra	19:49
	14	1:14	14	Scorpio	3:48
	16	5:52	16	Sagittar	7:51
	18	7: 4	18	Capricrn	8:34
	20	3: 6	20	Aquarius	7:42
	22	6:39	22	Pisces	7:27
	23	21:41	24	Aries	9:46
	26	15: 4	26	Taurus	15:51
	27	17:30	29	Gemini	1:31
	31	8:28	31	Cancer	13:29
AUG	1	0:29	3	Leo	2:11
	4	9:50	5	Virgo	14:30
	8	1:21	8	Libra	1:30
	10	0:13	10	Scorpio	10:12
	12	7:12	12	Sagittar	15:44
	14	16:24	14	Capricrn	18: 4
	16	11:52	16	Aquarius	18:16
	18	11:23	18	Pisces	18: 5
	20	14:10	20	Aries	19:30
	22	23:10	23	Taurus	0: 6
	25	4:15	25	Gemini	8:32
	27	0:58	27	Cancer	20: 0
	30	6:16	30	Leo	8:40
SEP	1	10:11	1	Virgo	20:47
	4	6:53	4	Libra	7:16
	6	14:39	6	Scorpio	15:39
	8	19: 7	8	Sagittar	21:40
	10	14:54	11	Capricrn	1:20
	12	19:25	13	Aquarius	3: 9
	14	22:47	15	Pisces	4:10
	16	19: 2	17	Aries	5:51
	19	9: 8	19	Taurus	9:44
	21	13:33	21	Gemini	16:57
	23	16:31	24	Cancer	3:32
	26	15:55	26	Leo	16: 2
	28	0:32	29	Virgo	4:12
OCT	30	14:26	1	Libra	14:17
	2	20:47	3	Scorpio	21:49
	5	9:20	6	Sagittar	3: 7
	7	11:59	8	Capricrn	6:53
	9	21:54	10	Aquarius	9:43
	12	6:58	12	Pisces	12:13
	14	2:17	14	Aries	15: 7
	16	16:10	16	Taurus	19:23
	18	12:42	19	Gemini	2: 6
	21	7: 1	21	Cancer	11:53
	23	10:11	24	Leo	0: 5
	26	2:38	26	Virgo	12:33
	28	16:57	28	Libra	22:52
	30	7: 9	31	Scorpio	5:53
NOV	2	7:41	2	Sagittar	10: 4
	3	15:46	4	Capricrn	12:41
	5	18:15	6	Aquarius	15: 4
	7	21: 4	8	Pisces	18: 7
	9	23:53	10	Aries	22:12
	12	5:48	13	Taurus	3:36
	14	20: 1	15	Gemini	10:45
	16	20:59	17	Cancer	20:17
	20	2:57	20	Leo	8:10
	22	1:53	22	Virgo	20:58
	24	15:42	25	Libra	8: 8
	27	0:23	27	Scorpio	15:39
	28	22:57	29	Sagittar	19:24
DEC	1	6:44	1	Capricrn	20:45
	3	2:50	3	Aquarius	21:36
	5	14:32	5	Pisces	23:37
	7	21:12	8	Aries	3:40
	10	6:26	10	Taurus	9:51
	11	20:32	12	Gemini	17:55
	14	12:31	15	Cancer	3:50
	16	17:23	17	Leo	15:38
	19	23:59	20	Virgo	4:35
	21	19:19	22	Libra	16:41
	24	5: 9	25	Scorpio	1:33
	26	12:56	27	Sagittar	6: 8
	28	13:38	29	Capricrn	7:16
	30	20:29	31	Aquarius	6:54

Month	Date	Time	Day	Sign	Time
JAN	1	12:54	1	Gemini	19:43
	4	6:38	4	Cancer	7:13
	6	0:4	6	Leo	16:21
	8	7:33	8	Virgo	23:24
	10	13:19	11	Libra	4:48
	12	19:56	13	Scorpio	8:45
	15	2:42	15	Sagittar	11:19
	16	12:29	17	Capricrn	13:3
	19	14:12	19	Aquarius	15:13
	21	3:54	21	Pisces	19:31
	23	10:43	24	Aries	3:20
	25	15:50	26	Taurus	14:42
	28	18:54	29	Gemini	3:38
	31	12:6	31	Virgo	15:21
FEB	2	14:22	2	Leo	0:12
	4	15:51	5	Virgo	6:18
	7	7:43	7	Libra	10:37
	9	10:25	9	Scorpio	14:5
	11	4:13	11	Sagittar	17:12
	13	11:6	13	Capricrn	20:14
	15	11:15	15	Aquarius	23:46
	18	3:38	18	Pisces	4:45
	19	23:35	20	Aries	12:23
	21	19:39	23	Taurus	23:7
	24	23:18	25	Gemini	11:51
	27	15:0	28	Cancer	0:3
MAR	1	23:9	2	Leo	9:26
	4	6:13	4	Virgo	15:19
	6	10:22	6	Libra	18:35
	8	9:41	8	Scorpio	20:38
	10	15:35	10	Sagittar	22:42
	12	15:56	13	Capricrn	1:40
	14	23:44	15	Aquarius	6:1
	17	8:9	17	Pisces	12:6
	19	18:33	19	Aries	20:24
	21	18:59	22	Taurus	7:6
	23	15:50	24	Gemini	19:39
	26	16:48	27	Cancer	8:17
	29	16:53	29	Leo	18:41
APR	1	0:32	1	Virgo	1:26
	3	4:30	3	Libra	4:40
	4	9:42	5	Scorpio	5:40
	6	3:7	7	Sagittar	6:9
	8	12:35	9	Capricrn	7:41
	10	19:15	11	Aquarius	11:24
	13	5:11	13	Pisces	17:50
	15	8:29	16	Aries	2:53
	18	10:36	18	Taurus	14:3
	20	15:38	21	Gemini	2:38
	23	8:45	23	Cancer	15:26
	26	0:16	26	Leo	2:44
	27	9:38	28	Virgo	10:53
	29	14:43	30	Libra	15:13
MAY	1	17:11	2	Scorpio	16:24
	3	5:4	4	Sagittar	15:59
	5	16:41	6	Capricrn	15:55
	7	20:9	8	Aquarius	18:0
	10	4:53	10	Pisces	23:30
	12	16:39	13	Aries	8:30
	14	14:45	15	Taurus	20:5
	18	2:52	18	Gemini	8:51
	19	19:17	20	Cancer	21:36
	22	11:35	23	Leo	9:14
	25	1:34	25	Virgo	18:32
	26	22:1	28	Libra	0:29
	29	17:54	30	Scorpio	2:57
JUN	31	3:22	1	Sagittar	2:55
	2	22:21	3	Capricrn	2:8
	5	1:25	5	Aquarius	2:44
	6	19:25	7	Pisces	6:36
	9	10:5	9	Aries	14:35
	11	6:19	12	Taurus	1:57
	13	4:45	14	Gemini	14:50
	16	18:23	17	Cancer	3:29
	18	2:15	19	Leo	14:54
	21	3:48	22	Virgo	0:30
	23	22:28	24	Libra	7:36
	25	16:12	26	Scorpio	11:43
	27	22:19	28	Sagittar	13:3
	29	20:10	30	Capricrn	12:49

Month	Date	Time	Day	Sign	Time
JUL	2	5:22	2	Aquarius	12:57
	4	11:34	4	Pisces	15:32
	6	7:7	6	Aries	22:4
	9	3:10	9	Taurus	8:34
	11	12:32	11	Gemini	21:16
	13	19:0	14	Cancer	9:50
	16	19:46	16	Leo	20:52
	18	18:4	19	Virgo	5:59
	21	10:32	21	Libra	13:10
	23	8:50	23	Scorpio	18:14
	25	14:19	25	Sagittar	21:5
	27	21:0	27	Capricrn	22:16
	28	17:22	29	Aquarius	23:5
AUG	31	1:0	1	Pisces	1:24
	3	1:0	3	Aries	6:55
	5	10:55	5	Taurus	16:19
	7	7:32	8	Gemini	4:30
	10	13:31	10	Cancer	17:5
	12	1:20	13	Leo	3:57
	15	10:48	15	Virgo	12:26
	17	17:58	17	Libra	18:50
	19	23:26	19	Scorpio	23:36
	22		22	Sagittar	3:3
	23	20:58	24	Capricrn	5:31
	26	2:42	26	Aquarius	7:41
	28	6:46	28	Pisces	10:47
	30	14:36	30	Aries	16:12
SEP	1	11:2	2	Taurus	0:52
	3	22:39	4	Gemini	12:28
	6	11:53	7	Cancer	1:4
	8	8:3	9	Leo	12:14
	11	9:39	11	Virgo	20:35
	13	9:23	14	Libra	2:8
	15	20:33	16	Scorpio	5:46
	18	0:0	18	Sagittar	8:29
	20	6:19	20	Capricrn	11:5
	22	13:13	22	Aquarius	14:13
	24	10:41	24	Pisces	18:30
	25	23:20	27	Aries	0:41
	29	1:49	29	Taurus	9:22
OCT	1	13:15	1	Gemini	20:34
	3	9:18	4	Cancer	9:10
	6	1:30	6	Leo	20:58
	9	0:40	9	Virgo	5:59
	10	22:33	11	Libra	11:30
	13	10:7	13	Scorpio	14:12
	15	12:19	15	Sagittar	15:28
	17	13:24	17	Capricrn	16:51
	19	14:5	19	Aquarius	19:37
	21	21:32	22	Pisces	0:27
	24	5:30	24	Aries	7:35
	26	16:49	26	Taurus	16:54
	29	1:52	29	Gemini	4:9
	31	14:45	31	Cancer	16:41
NOV	2	9:41	2	Leo	5:4
	5	14:7	5	Virgo	15:17
	7	16:26	7	Libra	21:52
	10	0:25	10	Scorpio	0:43
	12	0:41	12	Sagittar	1:1
	14	0:37	14	Capricrn	0:51
	15	14:32	16	Aquarius	2:1
	17	21:53	18	Pisces	5:9
	20	9:21	20	Aries	13:14
	23	23:36	22	Taurus	23:10
	24	10:37	25	Gemini	10:49
	27	14:15	27	Cancer	23:21
	30	1:47	30	Leo	11:54
DEC	2	20:0	2	Virgo	23:9
	4	5:0	5	Libra	7:18
	6	11:55	7	Scorpio	11:34
	8	10:56	9	Sagittar	12:8
	10	17:33	11	Capricrn	11:27
	12	13:3	13	Aquarius	11:0
	15	1:3	15	Pisces	13:10
	17	10:38	17	Aries	19:12
	20	1:2	20	Taurus	4:55
	21	10:23	22	Gemini	16:52
	24	21:51	25	Cancer	5:30
	26	14:51	27	Leo	17:52
	29	12:46	30	Virgo	5:14

1976 RED LIGHTS, GREEN LIGHTS (Tables of the MOON)

Date	Time		Sign	Time
JAN 2	0:13	3	Aquarius	2:33
4	9:38	5	Pisces	11:36
6	19:18	7	Aries	23:22
9	12:40	10	Taurus	12:10
12	6:14	12	Gemini	23:02
14	6:55	15	Cancer	7:01
17	10:52	17	Leo	11:16
18	22:38	19	Virgo	13:26
21	14:13	21	Libra	15:11
23	16:32	23	Scorpio	17:49
25	20:14	25	Sagittar	21:52
27	6:35	28	Capricrn	3:25
30	8:10	30	Aquarius	10:35
FEB 31	22:48	1	Pisces	19:47
4	3:56	4	Aries	7:18
6	16:27	6	Taurus	20:14
9	4:16	9	Gemini	8:17
11	1:14	11	Cancer	16:59
13	18:24	13	Leo	21:33
15	16:44	15	Virgo	23:00
17	19:30	17	Libra	23:15
19	19:39	20	Scorpio	0:14
21	22:16	22	Sagittar	3:19
23	20:33	24	Capricrn	8:55
26	10:51	26	Aquarius	16:49
28	15:17	29	Pisces	2:42
MAR 2	7:34	2	Aries	14:23
4	20:11	5	Taurus	3:19
7	9:23	7	Gemini	15:56
9	19:02	10	Cancer	1:59
12	2:21	12	Leo	7:56
14	8:37	14	Virgo	9:59
16	8:14	16	Libra	9:45
18	9:11	18	Scorpio	9:18
20	10:29	20	Sagittar	10:34
22	13:13	22	Capricrn	14:49
24	21:40	24	Aquarius	22:20
26	1:07	27	Pisces	8:34
29	12:36	29	Aries	20:38
APR 1	1:31	1	Taurus	9:35
3	14:23	3	Gemini	22:16
6	3:54	6	Cancer	9:07
8	9:43	8	Leo	16:37
10	4:10	10	Virgo	20:17
12	14:57	12	Libra	20:55
14	14:26	14	Scorpio	20:15
16	14:22	16	Sagittar	20:16
18	20:53	18	Capricrn	22:44
20	22:24	21	Aquarius	4:48
22	23:21	23	Pisces	14:28
25	20:06	26	Aries	2:37
28	9:23	28	Taurus	15:38
MAY 30	22:14	1	Gemini	4:06
2	6:38	3	Cancer	14:54
5	18:21	5	Leo	23:10
7	5:18	8	Virgo	4:22
10	2:51	10	Libra	6:40
12	3:35	12	Scorpio	7:03
14	5:03	14	Sagittar	7:05
15	4:24	16	Capricrn	8:32
18	10:01	18	Aquarius	13:03
20	21:23	20	Pisces	21:27
23	6:35	23	Aries	9:08
25	20:03	25	Taurus	22:08
28	8:50	28	Gemini	10:23
30	11:22	30	Cancer	20:40
JUN 2	4:04	2	Leo	4:38
4	1:44	4	Virgo	10:22
6	6:34	6	Libra	14:00
7	18:41	8	Scorpio	15:59
10	13:14	10	Sagittar	17:02
12	4:16	12	Capricrn	18:46
14	2:30	14	Aquarius	22:32
16	21:51	17	Pisces	5:44
19	14:06	19	Aries	16:33
21	10:28	22	Taurus	5:22
24	2:19	24	Gemini	17:37
26	15:47	27	Cancer	3:30
28	19:34	29	Leo	10:40

Date	Time		Sign	Time
JUL 1	9:56	1	Virgo	15:47
3	16:33	3	Libra	19:35
5	21:28	5	Scorpio	22:34
7	13:55	8	Sagittar	1:06
8	20:49	10	Capricrn	3:50
12	1:33	12	Aquarius	7:54
14	4:26	14	Pisces	14:37
16	15:37	17	Aries	0:40
19	6:30	19	Taurus	13:12
22	0:21	22	Gemini	1:41
23	0:12	24	Cancer	11:40
26	12:17	26	Leo	18:19
28	17:09	28	Virgo	22:24
30	20:36	31	Libra	1:14
AUG 1	22:56	2	Scorpio	3:56
4	3:23	4	Sagittar	7:04
6	6:26	6	Capricrn	10:55
8	13:08	8	Aquarius	15:58
10	20:35	10	Pisces	23:01
13	6:50	13	Aries	8:50
15	5:56	15	Taurus	21:06
18	8:58	18	Gemini	9:55
20	16:18	20	Cancer	20:35
23	3:29	23	Leo	3:31
25	23:06	25	Virgo	7:04
26	20:50	27	Libra	8:42
28	3:06	29	Scorpio	10:06
31	9:41	31	Sagittar	12:29
SEP 1	7:44	2	Capricrn	16:30
3	12:13	4	Aquarius	22:21
5	19:10	7	Pisces	6:12
8	12:53	9	Aries	16:19
10	15:56	12	Taurus	4:31
13	23:52	14	Gemini	17:33
16	17:21	17	Cancer	5:07
19	6:46	19	Leo	13:11
21	7:10	21	Virgo	17:17
23	14:32	23	Libra	18:28
25	17:42	25	Scorpio	18:34
27	10:02	27	Sagittar	19:22
29	11:19	29	Capricrn	22:14
OCT 1	19:09	2	Aquarius	3:50
4	6:15	4	Pisces	12:10
6	14:05	6	Aries	22:50
8	4:56	9	Taurus	11:12
11	0:07	11	Gemini	0:15
13	17:35	14	Cancer	12:25
16	21:49	16	Leo	21:50
19	3:04	19	Virgo	3:25
21	4:48	21	Libra	5:27
23	5:10	23	Scorpio	5:18
25	3:32	25	Sagittar	4:49
26	23:41	27	Capricrn	5:56
29	7:48	29	Aquarius	10:06
31	16:54	31	Pisces	17:54
NOV 3	1:05	3	Aries	4:46
4	17:32	5	Taurus	17:24
8	1:19	8	Gemini	6:22
10	8:42	10	Cancer	18:29
12	22:39	13	Leo	4:37
15	7:39	15	Virgo	11:47
17	11:22	17	Libra	15:35
18	19:16	19	Scorpio	16:32
21	15:11	21	Sagittar	16:04
22	18:51	23	Capricrn	16:04
25	10:09	25	Aquarius	18:30
27	15:13	28	Pisces	0:48
30	4:04	30	Aries	11:02
DEC 2	11:46	2	Taurus	23:42
5	2:00	5	Gemini	12:39
6	22:18	8	Cancer	0:22
9	21:35	10	Leo	10:13
12	5:20	12	Virgo	17:56
14	10:48	14	Libra	23:14
16	17:34	17	Scorpio	2:02
18	14:46	19	Sagittar	2:55
21	2:09	21	Capricrn	3:12
22	15:34	23	Aquarius	4:49
25	0:07	25	Pisces	9:37
27	11:56	27	Aries	18:32
30	3:54	30	Taurus	6:44

Mon	Day	Time	Day	Sign	Time
JAN	31	16:50	1	Virgo	17:33
	3	13:37	3	Libra	19:22
	5	22:56	5	Scorpio	23:39
	8	4:25	8	Sagittar	6:40
	9	23:23	10	Capricrn	15:59
	12	10:20	13	Aquarius	3: 4
	15	5:46	15	Pisces	15:24
	17	22:25	18	Aries	4: 4
	20	15:15	20	Taurus	15:22
	22	5: 7	22	Gemini	23:23
	24	15:34	25	Cancer	3:21
	26	9: 4	27	Leo	4: 1
	29	0:51	29	Virgo	3:14
	30	9:24	31	Libra	3:14
FEB	1	21: 1	2	Scorpio	5:54
	4	0:10	4	Sagittar	12:11
	6	5: 1	6	Capricrn	21:43
	8	15:19	9	Aquarius	9:17
	11	5:18	11	Pisces	21:46
	13	18:37	14	Aries	10:23
	16	17: 3	16	Taurus	22:10
	18	21: 7	19	Gemini	7:35
	21	8:58	21	Cancer	13:19
	23	6: 1	23	Leo	15:14
	24	9:55	25	Virgo	14:38
	27	9: 4	27	Libra	13:39
MAR	1	12:24	1	Scorpio	14:34
	3	12:28	3	Sagittar	19: 6
	5	21:41	6	Capricrn	3:40
	8	10:11	8	Aquarius	15:10
	10	12:33	11	Pisces	3:50
	13	13:50	13	Aries	16:19
	16	2:54	16	Taurus	3:53
	18	13:40	18	Gemini	13:44
	20	20: 5	20	Cancer	20:49
	21	17:54	23	Leo	0:32
	24	2:29	25	Virgo	1:22
	25	23:25	27	Libra	0:52
	28	7: 9	29	Scorpio	1: 8
	30	13: 5	31	Sagittar	4:10
APR	2	3: 9	2	Capricrn	11: 9
	3	22: 9	4	Aquarius	21:46
	7	3: 5	7	Pisces	10:17
	9	12:15	9	Aries	22:45
	11	16:40	12	Taurus	9:54
	13	10:33	14	Gemini	19:15
	16	19:35	17	Cancer	2:28
	19	5:27	19	Leo	7:15
	20	2:45	21	Virgo	9:43
	22	7:33	23	Libra	10:42
	24	8:33	25	Scorpio	11:40
	26	11:35	27	Sagittar	14:20
	28	21:15	29	Capricrn	20: 9
MAY	2	5:32	2	Aquarius	5:34
	4	17:20	4	Pisces	17:35
	6	23:34	7	Aries	6: 3
	9	16:45	9	Taurus	17: 4
	11	11:56	12	Gemini	1:45
	14	7:15	14	Cancer	8: 8
	16	11:38	16	Leo	12:39
	18	14:39	18	Virgo	15:46
	20	17:19	20	Libra	18: 6
	22	19: 4	22	Scorpio	20:26
	23	23:49	24	Sagittar	23:52
	27	3:46	27	Capricrn	5:31
	29	12:11	29	Aquarius	14:10
JUN	31	23:20	1	Pisces	1:33
	3	7:28	3	Aries	14: 2
	6	0:27	6	Taurus	1:19
	7	11: 4	8	Gemini	9:50
	10	13: 2	10	Cancer	15:22
	12	16:25	12	Leo	18:46
	14	18:48	14	Virgo	21:11
	16	14:59	16	Libra	23:41
	19	0:24	19	Scorpio	3: 0
	20	12:38	21	Sagittar	7:35
	23	11: 1	23	Capricrn	13:57
	25	19:30	25	Aquarius	22:34
	28	6:21	28	Pisces	9:34
	30	2:51	30	Aries	22: 3

Mon	Day	Time	Day	Sign	Time
JUL	3	6:42	3	Taurus	9:55
	5	13:30	5	Gemini	18:59
	7	22:26	8	Cancer	0:24
	10	0: 9	10	Leo	2:51
	12	3:23	12	Virgo	3:56
	13	16:29	14	Libra	5:22
	16	5:36	16	Scorpio	8:24
	18	4:27	18	Sagittar	13:33
	20	17:51	20	Capricrn	20:46
	23	5:29	23	Aquarius	5:56
	25	14: 0	25	Pisces	16:59
	28	4:54	28	Aries	5:28
	30	15: 7	30	Taurus	17:54
AUG	1	18: 3	2	Gemini	4: 3
	4	8: 2	4	Cancer	10:18
	6	10:42	6	Leo	12:44
	8	11: 0	8	Virgo	12:54
	10	8:18	10	Libra	12:51
	12	12:42	12	Scorpio	14:31
	14	18:55	14	Sagittar	19: 0
	17	0:41	17	Capricrn	2:26
	19	10:31	19	Aquarius	12:10
	21	22: 3	21	Pisces	23:33
	24	6:55	24	Aries	12: 3
	26	23:39	27	Taurus	0:45
	29	8: 8	29	Gemini	11:54
	31	19:36	31	Cancer	19:36
SEP	2	22:44	2	Leo	23: 9
	4	23:15	4	Virgo	23:30
	6	21: 1	6	Libra	22:38
	8	21:26	8	Scorpio	22:46
	11	0:38	11	Sagittar	1:41
	13	0:36	13	Capricrn	8:12
	15	17:35	15	Aquarius	17:52
	17	20:22	18	Pisces	5:32
	20	11:51	20	Aries	18: 8
	22	22:27	23	Taurus	6:44
	25	11:19	25	Gemini	18:14
	27	22: 0	28	Cancer	3: 8
	29	21:53	30	Leo	8:21
OCT	2	8: 8	2	Virgo	10: 4
	4	3: 9	4	Libra	9:39
	6	3:42	6	Scorpio	9: 9
	8	11:41	8	Sagittar	10:36
	10	11:56	10	Capricrn	15:29
	12	4:36	13	Aquarius	0:10
	15	10:40	15	Pisces	11:41
	16	7:31	18	Aries	0:21
	20	5: 6	20	Taurus	12:44
	22	12:45	22	Gemini	23:52
	24	10:49	25	Cancer	8:58
	26	17:48	27	Leo	15:20
	28	21:57	29	Virgo	18:47
	31	6: 9	31	Libra	19:56
NOV	2	10:11	2	Scorpio	20: 8
	4	12:46	4	Sagittar	21:11
	6	19:50	7	Capricrn	0:46
	9	7:29	9	Aquarius	8: 0
	10	18:21	11	Pisces	18:42
	13	12: 1	14	Aries	7:18
	15	15:14	16	Taurus	19:38
	18	22:29	19	Gemini	6:15
	21	11:32	21	Cancer	14:37
	23	16:58	23	Leo	20:49
	26	0:58	26	Virgo	1: 5
	28	2:41	28	Libra	3:48
	30	3:28	30	Scorpio	5:37
DEC	30	13:46	2	Sagittar	7:34
	4	6:15	4	Capricrn	10:59
	6	16:30	6	Aquarius	17:13
	8	18:16	9	Pisces	2:52
	11	5:47	11	Aries	15: 7
	14	3:35	14	Taurus	3:40
	14	21:46	16	Gemini	14:13
	18	14:40	18	Cancer	21:50
	20	0:54	21	Leo	2:54
	22	13:58	23	Virgo	6:28
	24	17:42	25	Libra	9:28
	26	18:59	27	Scorpio	12:29
	29	9:27	29	Sagittar	15:54
	30	22:34	31	Capricrn	20:17

JAN	2	24: 0	3	Taurus	4:38
	4	6:59	5	Gemini	8: 0
	7	4:30	7	Cancer	8:29
	9	3:50	9	Leo	7:43
	11	7:17	11	Virgo	7:42
	13	9:38	13	Libra	10:22
	15	15:50	15	Scorpio	16:55
	17	22: 5	18	Sagittar	3:13
	20	13:57	20	Capricrn	15:48
	23	0:16	23	Aquarius	4:50
	25	14:37	25	Pisces	17: 1
	28	0:57	28	Aries	3:32
	30	11: 5	30	Taurus	11:42
FEB	1	14:29	1	Gemini	16:54
	3	16:22	3	Cancer	19: 6
	5	15:40	5	Leo	19:12
	7	15:56	7	Virgo	18:52
	9	16:57	9	Libra	20:11
	11	21:22	12	Scorpio	0:58
	14	1:50	14	Sagittar	10: 2
	18	10: 0	16	Capricrn	22:16
	19	6:33	19	Aquarius	11:21
	21	18:58	21	Pisces	23:16
	24	5:54	24	Aries	9:13
	26	15:28	26	Taurus	17:12
	28	20: 0	28	Gemini	23:11
MAR	3	2:32	3	Cancer	3: 0
	5	0:27	5	Leo	4:49
	7	5: 5	7	Virgo	5:34
	9	3:18	9	Libra	6:52
	11	6:56	11	Scorpio	10:40
	13	14: 7	13	Sagittar	18:20
	16	3:36	16	Capricrn	5:42
	18	13:45	18	Aquarius	18:39
	21	3: 2	21	Pisces	7:34
	23	12:52	23	Aries	16: 3
	25	20:17	25	Taurus	23:10
	27	11:21	28	Gemini	4:34
	30	6:19	30	Cancer	8:40
APR	1	5:35	1	Leo	11:41
	3	12: 4	3	Virgo	13:57
	5	14:42	5	Libra	16:23
	7	18:55	7	Scorpio	20:25
	9	22:23	10	Sagittar	3:28
	12	12:56	12	Capricrn	13:57
	14	18: 5	15	Aquarius	2:35
	17	14:32	17	Pisces	14:45
	19	23:58	20	Aries	0:21
	21	22:54	22	Taurus	6:54
	23	15:54	24	Gemini	11:11
	26	8:11	26	Cancer	14:18
	28	9: 0	28	Leo	17: 4
	30	11:44	30	Virgo	20: 1
MAY	2	19:46	2	Libra	23:40
	4	19:42	5	Scorpio	4:44
	6	13:21	7	Sagittar	12: 6
	9	11:58	9	Capricrn	22:16
	11	23:50	12	Aquarius	10:35
	14	12:17	14	Pisces	23: 8
	17	1:20	17	Aries	9:20
	19	6:17	19	Taurus	16:11
	21	0:15	21	Gemini	19:55
	23	12:23	23	Cancer	21:46
	25	13:41	25	Leo	23:13
	27	22:12	28	Virgo	1:26
	29	18:18	30	Libra	5:17
JUN	1	2:20	1	Scorpio	11:11
	3	12:58	3	Sagittar	19:22
	5	17:52	6	Capricrn	5:49
	8	17:40	8	Aquarius	18: 3
	10	18:21	11	Pisces	6:44
	13	1:46	13	Aries	17:53
	15	15: 9	16	Taurus	1:47
	17	13: 5	18	Gemini	6: 0
	20	4:56	20	Cancer	7:22
	22	23:58	22	Leo	7:30
	24	4:43	24	Virgo	8:12
	25	13:43	26	Libra	10:58
	28	5: 5	28	Scorpio	16:41

JUL	30	1:56	1	Sagittar	1:21
	2	23:43	3	Capricrn	12:20
	5	11:53	6	Aquarius	0:42
	8	0:40	8	Pisces	13:26
	10	1:13	11	Aries	1:11
	12	22:39	13	Taurus	10:22
	15	2:25	15	Gemini	15:55
	17	10:38	17	Cancer	17:57
	19	12: 7	19	Leo	17:44
	21	11: 4	21	Virgo	17:10
	22	21:30	23	Libra	18:19
	25	20:49	25	Scorpio	22:46
	27	6:40	28	Sagittar	7: 0
	30	6:12	30	Capricrn	18:11
AUG	1	18:46	2	Aquarius	6:47
	4	7:38	4	Pisces	19:27
	6	10:42	7	Aries	7:16
	9	6:23	9	Taurus	17:13
	11	17: 8	12	Gemini	0:16
	13	18:31	14	Cancer	3:49
	15	19:43	16	Leo	4:27
	17	19:44	18	Virgo	3:43
	19	3:43	20	Libra	3:45
	22	4:22	22	Scorpio	6:38
	23	13:16	24	Sagittar	13:35
	26	14:12	27	Capricrn	0:16
	29	2:53	29	Aquarius	12:53
SEP	31	15:50	1	Pisces	1:30
	3	2:59	3	Aries	12:59
	5	16:23	5	Taurus	22:51
	8	6:13	8	Gemini	6:37
	10	8:58	10	Cancer	11:40
	12	13:40	12	Leo	13:55
	14	7:38	14	Virgo	14:13
	16	2:46	16	Libra	14:17
	18	9:35	18	Scorpio	16:14
	20	16:53	20	Sagittar	21:47
	23	7: 9	23	Capricrn	7:22
	25	14: 0	25	Aquarius	19:39
	28	1:34	28	Pisces	8:15
	30	14:36	30	Aries	19:26
OCT	2	22:57	3	Taurus	4:40
	4	14:32	5	Gemini	12: 1
	7	12:40	7	Cancer	17:31
	9	16:37	9	Leo	21: 3
	11	18:50	11	Virgo	22:57
	13	5:27	14	Libra	0:11
	15	22:35	16	Scorpio	2:24
	17	10:59	18	Sagittar	7:15
	20	11:58	20	Capricrn	15:44
	23	1:54	23	Aquarius	3:21
	25	13:21	25	Pisces	15:57
	27	5:33	28	Aries	3:14
	30	9:33	30	Taurus	12: 1
NOV	31	22:32	1	Gemini	18:24
	3	21:13	3	Cancer	23: 2
	6	0:57	6	Leo	2:31
	8	3:59	8	Virgo	5:19
	9	13: 5	10	Libra	7:59
	12	10:20	12	Scorpio	11:24
	14	4:37	14	Sagittar	16:39
	17	0:10	17	Capricrn	0:42
	19	11:37	19	Aquarius	11:39
	21	22:40	22	Pisces	0:12
	23	13: 9	24	Aries	12: 0
	25	23:15	26	Taurus	21: 5
	28	17:16	29	Gemini	2:59
DEC	30	15:59	1	Cancer	6:22
	2	23:16	3	Leo	8:32
	5	3:54	5	Virgo	10:41
	7	9:28	7	Libra	13:43
	9	9:20	9	Scorpio	18:14
	11	1:38	11	Sagittar	0:35
	13	16:25	14	Capricrn	9: 4
	15	18:22	16	Aquarius	19:49
	17	1:39	19	Pisces	8:12
	21	19:44	21	Aries	20:36
	23	5: 8	24	Taurus	6:45
	25	13: 2	26	Gemini	16:16
	27	11: 1	28	Cancer	16:16
	30	2:35	30	Leo	17: 5

JAN

Day	Time	Day	Sign	Time
3	7:37	3	Capricrn	11:31
5	8:49	5	Aquarius	22:48
7	23: 2	8	Pisces	8: 3
10	12: 3	10	Aries	14:58
12	7:19	12	Taurus	19:25
14	12: 7	14	Gemini	21:42
16	11:18	16	Cancer	22:39
18	21:29	18	Leo	23:41
20	14:24	21	Virgo	2:24
23	7:14	23	Libra	8:17
25	5: 2	25	Scorpio	17:53
27	18: 7	28	Sagittar	6:11
30	4:57	30	Capricrn	18:55

FEB

Day	Time	Day	Sign	Time
1	23: 8	2	Aquarius	5:56
4	4: 0	4	Pisces	14:23
6	13:55	6	Aries	20:29
8	22: 7	9	Taurus	0:54
10	23:35	11	Gemini	4:11
12	20:41	13	Cancer	6:45
15	6:14	15	Leo	9:13
17	10: 8	17	Virgo	12:32
19	16:31	19	Libra	17:59
22	2: 3	22	Scorpio	2:36
24	2:27	24	Sagittar	14:15
26	22:25	27	Capricrn	3: 4

MAR

Day	Time	Day	Sign	Time
1	10:12	1	Aquarius	14:23
3	8:50	3	Pisces	22:32
6	0:54	6	Aries	3:38
7	17:57	8	Taurus	6:51
10	3:22	10	Gemini	9:31
12	3:27	12	Cancer	12:30
14	4:50	14	Leo	16: 8
16	6:44	16	Virgo	20:43
18	23:34	19	Libra	2:49
21	3:28	21	Scorpio	11:16
23	19:52	23	Sagittar	22:27
25	18:27	26	Capricrn	11:16
28	6:43	28	Aquarius	23:13
30	16:18	31	Pisces	7:56

APR

Day	Time	Day	Sign	Time
1	12:57	2	Aries	12:49
4	0:40	4	Taurus	14:59
5	21:54	6	Gemini	16:12
8	3:15	8	Cancer	18: 5
10	8:51	10	Leo	21:32
12	14:42	13	Virgo	2:47
15	6: 8	15	Libra	9:51
17	18:10	17	Scorpio	18:52
19	3:10	20	Sagittar	6: 2
21	23:38	22	Capricrn	18:50
24	12:18	25	Aquarius	7:22
27	2:27	27	Pisces	17:10
29	2:23	29	Aries	22:54

MAY

Day	Time	Day	Sign	Time
1	17:36	2	Taurus	1: 2
3	20:24	4	Gemini	1:16
6	1:24	6	Cancer	1:36
7	17:58	8	Leo	3:37
10	3:18	10	Virgo	8:13
11	22:50	12	Libra	15:31
14	5:46	15	Scorpio	1:10
17	4:59	17	Sagittar	12:42
19	6:28	20	Capricrn	1:31
21	17: 6	22	Aquarius	14:18
24	8:19	25	Pisces	1: 6
26	17:11	27	Aries	8:15
28	21:55	29	Taurus	11:28
30	12:55	31	Gemini	11:53

JUN

Day	Time	Day	Sign	Time
2	5:29	2	Cancer	11:21
3	18: 6	4	Leo	11:50
6	2:31	6	Virgo	14:52
8	3:39	8	Libra	21:16
10	18:11	11	Scorpio	6:52
13	8:40	13	Sagittar	18:43
16	1: 8	16	Capricrn	7:37
18	17:30	18	Aquarius	20:20
21	7: 2	21	Pisces	7:29
23	10: 9	23	Aries	15:49
25	18:45	25	Taurus	20:38
27	17: 3	27	Gemini	22:18
29	15:46	29	Cancer	22: 9

JUL

Day	Time	Day	Sign	Time
1	4:13	1	Leo	21:56
3	17:35	3	Virgo	23:31
5	22:31	6	Libra	4:24
8	7:24	8	Scorpio	13: 6
9	23:51	11	Sagittar	0:48
13	9: 5	13	Capricrn	13:46
15	11:57	16	Aquarius	2:15
18	9:53	18	Pisces	13: 8
20	19: 9	20	Aries	21:44
23	1:43	23	Taurus	3:41
24	21:47	25	Gemini	6:59
27	7: 9	27	Cancer	8:11
28	21:19	29	Leo	8:30
31	9:18	31	Virgo	9:35

AUG

Day	Time	Day	Sign	Time
2	1: 2	2	Libra	13:13
4	13:31	4	Scorpio	20:36
6	22:34	7	Sagittar	7:37
9	17:54	9	Capricrn	20:30
12	8:39	12	Aquarius	8:53
14	2:17	14	Pisces	19:15
16	22:39	17	Aries	3:16
19	2: 4	19	Taurus	9:14
21	10:23	21	Gemini	13:27
22	23:54	23	Cancer	16: 8
25	1:59	25	Leo	17:50
26	16:23	27	Virgo	19:34
28	5:13	29	Libra	22:53

SEP

Day	Time	Day	Sign	Time
31	12: 8	1	Scorpio	5:18
1	23: 2	3	Sagittar	15:25
5	9:39	6	Capricrn	4: 2
8	4:20	8	Aquarius	16:31
10	21: 8	11	Pisces	2:41
13	9: 0	13	Aries	9:57
15	0: 6	15	Taurus	15: 0
17	9: 4	17	Gemini	18:48
19	16:11	19	Cancer	22: 2
21	22:55	22	Leo	0:57
23	14:18	24	Virgo	3:59
25	3:35	26	Libra	8: 1
28	1:30	28	Scorpio	14:19
30	3:15	30	Sagittar	23:48

OCT

Day	Time	Day	Sign	Time
2	20:56	2	Capricrn	12: 3
5	16:29	6	Aquarius	0:49
8	9:21	8	Pisces	11:24
9	3:26	10	Aries	18:29
12	10:54	12	Taurus	22:37
13	23: 8	15	Gemini	1: 9
16	16:25	17	Cancer	3:29
18	22:33	19	Leo	6:25
21	6:19	21	Virgo	10:19
23	4: 0	23	Libra	15:29
25	11:14	25	Scorpio	22:28
28	0:35	28	Sagittar	7:58
30	19:25	30	Capricrn	19:58

NOV

Day	Time	Day	Sign	Time
2	6:56	2	Aquarius	8:59
4	18:40	5	Pisces	20:27
6	15: 2	7	Aries	4:20
9	3:43	9	Taurus	8:26
10	14:27	11	Gemini	10: 0
13	4:56	13	Cancer	10:47
15	5:48	15	Leo	12:20
17	8:24	17	Virgo	15:42
19	2:17	19	Libra	21:16
21	20:48	22	Scorpio	5: 7
23	15:32	24	Sagittar	15:11
26	18:52	27	Capricrn	3:13
28	8: 9	29	Aquarius	16:18

DEC

Day	Time	Day	Sign	Time
1	20:54	2	Pisces	4:33
4	8:45	4	Aries	13:51
6	17:38	7	Taurus	19: 9
8	20:55	8	Gemini	20:58
10	15:35	10	Cancer	20:52
12	15:59	12	Leo	20:45
14	18: 5	14	Virgo	22:21
16	17:13	17	Libra	2:54
19	8: 2	19	Scorpio	10:44
20	9:49	21	Sagittar	21:20
24	3:47	24	Capricrn	9:42
26	16:58	26	Aquarius	22:43
29	5:42	29	Pisces	11:10
30	3:36	31	Aries	21:35

JAN

1	11:17	2	Leo	8:22
4	2:40	4	Virgo	15:51
6	13:46	7	Libra	2:34
9	8:38	9	Scorpio	15: 4
12	2:49	12	Sagittar	2:58
14	7: 6	14	Capricrn	12:27
16	18:41	16	Aquarius	19: 4
18	23: 0	18	Pisces	23:29
21	2: 3	21	Aries	2:36
23	0:21	23	Taurus	5:18
25	7:35	25	Gemini	8:14
27	8:28	27	Cancer	12: 2
29	16:36	29	Leo	17:22

FEB

1	0: 8	1	Virgo	0:56
3	10:18	3	Libra	11: 7
5	22:59	5	Scorpio	23:18
8	10:55	8	Sagittar	11:38
10	3:46	10	Capricrn	21:51
13	4:13	13	Aquarius	4:37
15	7:50	15	Pisces	8:12
17	9:36	17	Aries	9:51
19	11: 3	19	Taurus	11:12
21	19:21	21	Gemini	13:36
22	20:33	23	Cancer	17:53
25	1:58	26	Leo	0:15
27	14: 0	28	Virgo	8:40

MAR

1	2:40	1	Libra	19: 1
3	23:46	4	Scorpio	7: 1
5	15: 5	6	Sagittar	19:37
8	7: 6	9	Capricrn	6:50
10	21:17	11	Aquarius	14:43
13	3: 6	13	Pisces	18:40
15	11:35	15	Aries	19:38
16	22:57	17	Taurus	19:28
19	19: 2	19	Gemini	20:13
21	0:49	21	Cancer	23:27
24	2: 0	24	Leo	5:47
26	14: 2	26	Virgo	14:48
28	12:37	29	Libra	1:42
30	12:54	31	Scorpio	13:49

APR

3	0:34	3	Sagittar	2:28
4	11:20	5	Capricrn	14:21
6	23:45	7	Aquarius	23:38
9	11: 7	10	Pisces	4:58
11	21: 8	12	Aries	6:33
13	20:32	14	Taurus	5:55
14	18:42	16	Gemini	5:17
18	6:44	18	Cancer	6:47
20	11:39	20	Leo	11:47
21	18:56	22	Virgo	20:25
25	7:13	25	Libra	7:35
27	1:50	27	Scorpio	19:56
30	7:57	30	Sagittar	8:31

MAY

2	19:50	2	Capricrn	20:29
5	5:53	5	Aquarius	6:36
7	10:20	7	Pisces	13:28
9	15:51	9	Aries	16:35
11	15:54	11	Taurus	16:48
13	15:10	13	Gemini	15:58
15	15:24	15	Cancer	16:17
17	18:39	17	Leo	19:38
20	1:17	20	Virgo	2:57
22	12:24	22	Libra	13:37
23	18:48	25	Scorpio	2: 1
27	13:16	27	Sagittar	14:34
30	0:55	30	Capricrn	2:13

JUN

1	10:59	1	Aquarius	12:16
3	17: 0	3	Pisces	19:53
5	23:18	6	Aries	0:28
7	9:39	8	Taurus	2:15
10	1:19	10	Gemini	2:25
12	2:43	12	Cancer	2:45
14	3:59	14	Leo	5:10
16	6:10	16	Virgo	11: 4
19	11:18	18	Libra	20:39
20	22:50	21	Scorpio	8:43
23	19:59	23	Sagittar	21:15
26	7:25	26	Capricrn	8:37
28	16:57	28	Aquarius	18: 3

JUL

30	6:46	1	Pisces	1:19
3	5:27	3	Aries	6:23
4	14:18	5	Taurus	9:25
7	10:18	7	Gemini	11: 5
9	11:46	9	Cancer	12:30
11	14:24	11	Leo	15: 6
12	23:30	13	Virgo	20:17
16	4:12	16	Libra	4:49
18	7:46	18	Scorpio	16:16
21	4:20	21	Sagittar	4:47
23	15:51	23	Capricrn	16:11
26	0:55	26	Aquarius	1: 8
28	6:56	28	Pisces	7:30
30	11: 1	30	Aries	11:51

AUG

1	13:53	1	Taurus	14:58
3	4:55	3	Gemini	17:34
5	20: 1	5	Cancer	20:18
6	22: 8	7	Leo	23:57
10	3:17	10	Virgo	5:23
12	11: 4	12	Libra	13:28
15	0:18	15	Scorpio	0:20
17	1:10	17	Sagittar	12:50
19	21:46	20	Capricrn	0:38
21	6:58	22	Aquarius	9:44
24	12:51	24	Pisces	15:29
26	16: 9	26	Aries	18:41
28	18:14	28	Taurus	20:43
30	8:14	30	Gemini	22:56

SEP

1	23:45	2	Cancer	2:12
3	23:37	4	Leo	6:54
6	10:54	6	Virgo	13:16
8	19:21	8	Libra	21:37
11	6: 9	11	Scorpio	8:16
13	1: 9	13	Sagittar	20:43
16	7:37	16	Capricrn	9: 8
18	10:50	18	Aquarius	19: 5
21	0:26	21	Pisces	1:10
23	3:22	23	Aries	3:45
25	4:23	25	Taurus	4:28
27	1: 5	27	Gemini	5:15
29	5:44	29	Cancer	7:39

OCT

30	15: 1	1	Leo	12:26
3	15:54	3	Virgo	19:31
5	10:30	6	Libra	4:35
8	12:33	8	Scorpio	15:28
8	23:47	11	Sagittar	3:53
12	21:33	13	Capricrn	16:45
15	12:55	16	Aquarius	3:52
18	1:55	18	Pisces	11:13
19	22:17	20	Aries	14:23
22	13:26	22	Taurus	14:38
24	1: 3	24	Gemini	14: 3
26	5:30	26	Cancer	14:45
28	13:17	28	Leo	18:15
30	6:15	31	Virgo	1: 0

NOV

1	14:40	1	Libra	10:28
4	6:27	4	Scorpio	21:47
6	1:22	7	Sagittar	10:17
9	14:45	9	Capricrn	23:12
12	6:18	12	Aquarius	11: 3
14	18:33	14	Pisces	19:57
16	15: 9	17	Aries	0:45
18	14: 9	19	Taurus	1:53
20	23: 7	21	Gemini	1: 5
22	21:13	23	Cancer	0:31
24	11:27	25	Leo	2:12
26	15:46	27	Virgo	7:25
29	15:30	29	Libra	16:16

DEC

1	10:56	2	Scorpio	3:43
4	9: 4	4	Sagittar	16:23
6	12:41	7	Capricrn	5: 7
9	11:45	9	Aquarius	16:54
12	1: 2	12	Pisces	2:33
13	22:21	14	Aries	9: 0
16	2:27	16	Taurus	12: 0
18	11:52	18	Gemini	12:25
20	9:46	20	Cancer	11:57
22	3: 0	22	Leo	12:35
24	8:28	24	Virgo	16: 3
26	18:19	26	Libra	23:22
28	19:32	29	Scorpio	10:11
30	21:36	31	Sagittar	22:52

January – June

Mon	Day	h:m	Day	Sign	h:m
JAN	1	0: 8	1	Pisces	4: 8
	3	6: 4	3	Aries	6:27
	5	7:20	5	Taurus	10: 1
	7	14:36	7	Gemini	15: 9
	9	21:34	9	Cancer	22: 9
	12	6:47	12	Leo	7:25
	14	7:53	14	Virgo	18:58
	17	7:10	17	Libra	7:54
	19	18: 9	19	Scorpio	20: 4
	22	4:31	22	Sagittar	5:16
	24	9:48	24	Capricrn	10:33
	26	11:51	26	Aquarius	12:37
	27	21:58	28	Pisces	13: 2
	30	12:46	30	Aries	13:37
FEB	1	7:51	1	Taurus	15:49
	3	19:32	3	Gemini	20:35
	6	2:56	6	Cancer	4: 7
	8	12:47	8	Leo	14: 7
	10	7:42	11	Virgo	1:58
	13	13:16	13	Libra	14:51
	15	20:24	16	Scorpio	3:22
	18	12:14	18	Sagittar	13:46
	20	18:59	20	Capricrn	20:37
	22	22: 6	22	Aquarius	23:44
	24	19:55	25	Pisces	0: 6
	26	21:47	26	Aries	23:30
	28	17:29	28	Taurus	23:55
MAR	3	0:57	3	Gemini	3: 2
	5	7:27	5	Cancer	9:48
	7	17:20	7	Leo	19:56
	10	5:29	10	Virgo	8:11
	12	18:11	12	Libra	21: 6
	13	22: 4	15	Scorpio	9:32
	17	17:22	17	Sagittar	20:24
	20	2:31	20	Capricrn	4:38
	22	6:35	22	Aquarius	9:29
	24	0:25	24	Pisces	11: 8
	26	7:55	26	Aries	10:46
	28	7:52	28	Taurus	10:16
	30	8:28	30	Gemini	11:44
APR	1	13:13	1	Cancer	16:51
	3	22: 5	4	Leo	2: 6
	5	19:33	6	Virgo	14:17
	8	22:53	9	Libra	3:17
	10	20:11	11	Scorpio	15:28
	13	21:39	14	Sagittar	2: 4
	16	6:18	16	Capricrn	10:39
	18	12:58	18	Aquarius	16:46
	20	17:59	20	Pisces	20: 0
	22	19:31	22	Aries	21: 9
	24	14:52	24	Taurus	21: 7
	26	17:42	26	Gemini	21:59
	28	21: 4	29	Cancer	1:44
MAY	1	6:59	1	Leo	9:35
	3	9:12	3	Virgo	21:49
	6	4:25	6	Libra	10: 0
	8	10:27	8	Scorpio	22: 4
	11	2:46	11	Sagittar	8: 8
	13	10:55	13	Capricrn	16:10
	15	20:15	15	Aquarius	22:20
	18	1:42	18	Pisces	2:40
	20	2:37	20	Aries	5:12
	20	21:19	22	Taurus	6:32
	24	3: 5	24	Gemini	8: 2
	26	6:12	26	Cancer	11:27
	28	13:18	28	Leo	18:17
	31	0:10	31	Virgo	4:49
JUN	2	13:24	2	Libra	17:27
	3	22: 5	5	Scorpio	5:37
	7	14:55	7	Sagittar	15:29
	9	17:19	9	Capricrn	22:46
	12	3:46	12	Aquarius	4: 3
	14	7: 7	14	Pisces	8: 2
	16	10:39	16	Aries	11: 6
	18	7:39	18	Taurus	13:39
	20	13:31	20	Gemini	16:24
	22	15:16	22	Cancer	20:31
	24	23:18	25	Leo	3:13
	27	8:36	27	Virgo	13: 7
	29	20:22	30	Libra	1:23

July – December

Mon	Day	h:m	Day	Sign	h:m
JUL	2	2: 0	2	Scorpio	13:47
	4	18:41	4	Sagittar	23:59
	7	2: 4	7	Capricrn	7: 4
	9	6:43	9	Aquarius	11:27
	11	8:59	11	Pisces	14:15
	13	12: 3	13	Aries	16:33
	15	5:47	15	Taurus	19:11
	17	18:16	17	Gemini	22:47
	19	23:21	20	Cancer	3:57
	22	9:16	22	Leo	11:17
	24	16:38	24	Virgo	21:10
	27	4:23	27	Libra	9:12
	29	17:47	29	Scorpio	21:51
AUG	1	4:30	1	Sagittar	8:50
	3	12:36	3	Capricrn	16:33
	5	17:11	5	Aquarius	20:47
	7	17:29	7	Pisces	22:35
	9	20:11	9	Aries	23:27
	11	4:47	12	Taurus	0:56
	14	0:54	14	Gemini	4:11
	16	6:32	16	Cancer	9:50
	18	14:40	18	Leo	17:58
	20	23:46	21	Virgo	4:55
	23	13:13	23	Libra	16:23
	24	19:42	26	Scorpio	5: 9
	28	14:13	28	Sagittar	16:57
	31	0:25	31	Capricrn	1:55
SEP	2	5: 7	2	Aquarius	7: 5
	4	7:23	4	Pisces	8:51
	6	7:40	6	Aries	8:44
	8	5:25	8	Taurus	8:38
	10	10: 9	10	Gemini	11:36
	12	13:48	12	Cancer	15:21
	14	22:10	14	Leo	23:38
	16	0: 6	17	Virgo	10:29
	19	21:37	19	Libra	22:48
	21	0:55	22	Scorpio	11:34
	24	22:58	24	Sagittar	23:44
	27	9:20	27	Capricrn	9:53
	29	16:17	29	Aquarius	16:39
OCT	30	20:36	1	Pisces	19:37
	3	19:36	3	Aries	19:41
	5	5:35	5	Taurus	18:42
	6	21: 5	7	Gemini	18:54
	9	17:17	9	Cancer	22:10
	11	9:36	12	Leo	5:31
	14	4:38	14	Virgo	16:10
	15	4: 9	17	Libra	4:48
	19	8: 0	19	Scorpio	17:31
	21	14: 9	22	Sagittar	5:32
	24	3:23	24	Capricrn	16: 6
	26	1:21	27	Aquarius	0:12
	28	21:30	29	Pisces	4:57
	30	20: 1	31	Aries	6:27
NOV	2	2:21	2	Taurus	5:56
	4	3:44	4	Gemini	5:28
	6	7: 3	6	Cancer	7:15
	7	11: 3	8	Leo	12:57
	9	20:52	10	Virgo	22:45
	12	13:52	13	Libra	11: 8
	14	20: 3	15	Scorpio	23:50
	18	1:46	18	Sagittar	11:30
	19	23:49	20	Capricrn	21:37
	22	5: 3	23	Aquarius	5:53
	25	3: 4	25	Pisces	11:48
	27	11:42	27	Aries	15: 4
	29	11:44	29	Taurus	16: 9
DEC	30	14: 7	1	Gemini	16:26
	3	14:53	3	Cancer	17:51
	4	23:30	5	Leo	22:17
	7	23:11	8	Virgo	6:41
	10	5:38	10	Libra	18:20
	12	12:14	13	Scorpio	7: 2
	15	4:12	15	Sagittar	18:38
	17	19: 3	18	Capricrn	4: 8
	20	4:36	20	Aquarius	11:33
	21	23:41	22	Pisces	17:10
	24	19: 1	24	Aries	21:10
	26	8:51	26	Taurus	23:46
	27	8: 9	29	Gemini	1:39
	30	14:32	31	Cancer	4: 2

```
JAN  2 11:30   2 Scorpio  12: 4     JUL  2 10: 1   2 Cancer   17:21
     4 16:33   4 Sagittar 16:34          5  1:21   5 Leo       4:26
     6 13:19   6 Capricrn 17:31          7 13:57   7 Virgo    17:12
     8 14: 3   8 Aquarius 16:48         10  2:47  10 Libra     6: 3
     9  6:39  10 Pisces   16:37         12 10:14  12 Scorpio  16:41
    12 14:14  12 Aries    18:48         14 20:27  14 Sagittar 23:26
    13 13:19  15 Taurus    0:21         16 21:11  17 Capricrn  2:20
    17  3:55  17 Gemini    9: 8         18 23:58  19 Aquarius  2:45
    19 14:48  19 Cancer   20:14         20 23:46  21 Pisces    2:37
    22  4:37  22 Leo       8:41         23  3:31  23 Aries     3:43
    23  2:26  24 Virgo    21:33         25  2:57  25 Taurus    7:19
    27  4: 8  27 Libra     9:43         27 10:29  27 Gemini   13:53
    28 14:29  29 Scorpio  19:35         29         29 Cancer   23:14
FEB 31 20:47   1 Sagittar  1:50     AUG  1  7:11   1 Leo      10:45
     2 23:34   3 Capricrn  4:22          3 20:33   3 Virgo    23:35
     4 23:39   5 Aquarius  4:20          6  8:46   6 Libra    12:33
     6 12:22   7 Pisces    3:38          8 22:14   8 Scorpio  23:57
     8 23:14   9 Aries     4:18         11  4:44  11 Sagittar  8: 8
    11  2:37  11 Taurus    8: 0         13 11:55  13 Capricrn 12:25
    13 13:59  13 Gemini   15:30         15 13:29  15 Aquarius 13:32
    15 19:55  16 Cancer    2:17         17 10: 5  17 Pisces   13: 2
    18  8:18  18 Leo      14:54         19  9:51  19 Aries    12:51
    20  6: 8  21 Virgo     3:42         21 11:19  21 Taurus   14:46
    23  8:52  23 Libra    15:30         23 16:43  23 Gemini   20: 4
    25 12:21  26 Scorpio   1:24         25 23:26  26 Cancer    4:59
    28  2:23  28 Sagittar  8:39         28 13: 2  28 Leo      16:39
MAR  2  7: 6   2 Capricrn 12:55         31  2: 1  31 Virgo     5:36
     4 11:35   4 Aquarius 14:35     SEP  2 14:57   2 Libra    18:26
     6 14:12   6 Pisces   14:49          5 14:59   5 Scorpio   5:55
     8 11:44   8 Aries    15:17          7 11:54   7 Sagittar 14:59
     9  3:43  10 Taurus   17:44          9 15:18   9 Capricrn 20:52
    12 16:32  12 Gemini   23:37         11 20:57  11 Aquarius 23:34
    15  1:39  15 Cancer    9:19         13 21:29  13 Pisces   23:58
    17 14:45  17 Leo      21:40         15 21:10  15 Aries    23:36
    18 19:22  20 Virgo    10:30         16 12:41  18 Taurus    0:21
    22 13:58  22 Libra    21:57         20  1:29  20 Gemini    4: 2
    24  7:38  25 Scorpio   7:11         22  9:43  22 Cancer   11:41
    27  6:32  27 Sagittar 14: 7         24 20:15  24 Leo      22:55
    29 11:36  29 Capricrn 19: 1         27  9:19  27 Virgo    11:54
    31 10:28  31 Aquarius 22: 9         29 22:10  30 Libra     0:34
APR  2 23: 5   3 Pisces    0: 1     OCT 30 18:35   2 Scorpio  11:36
     4 18:11   5 Aries     1:32          4 18:32   4 Sagittar 20:32
     6  4:10   7 Taurus    4: 2          7  1: 6   7 Capricrn  3:11
     9  0:48   9 Gemini    9: 2          9  5:50   9 Aquarius  7:26
    11  8:40  11 Cancer   17:34         11  8: 4  11 Pisces    9:31
    13 22:30  14 Leo       5:16         13  8:53  13 Aries    10:13
    16 15: 7  16 Virgo    18: 8         14 20:22  15 Taurus   11: 0
    18 20:18  19 Libra     5:36         17 12:31  17 Gemini   13:44
    19 16:47  21 Scorpio  14:16         19 19:12  19 Cancer   19:59
    23 11:39  23 Sagittar 20:15         22  5: 8  22 Leo       6:13
    25 15:59  26 Capricrn  0:27         24 18: 2  24 Virgo    18:58
    27 19:18  28 Aquarius  3:44         27  6:53  27 Libra     7:38
    29 17:47  30 Pisces    6:38         28  4:56  29 Scorpio  18:15
MAY  2  1: 0   2 Aries     9:33     NOV  1  2: 3   1 Sagittar  2:25
     4 12:11   4 Taurus   13: 5          3  6:19   3 Capricrn  8:33
     6 18: 2   6 Gemini   18:18          5 13: 7   5 Aquarius 13:11
    10  0:16   9 Cancer    2:17          7  0:40   7 Pisces   16:33
    11 12:56  11 Leo      13:22          9 17: 5   9 Aries    18:52
    14  1:36  14 Virgo     2:11         10 17:20  11 Taurus   20:51
    16 13:22  16 Libra    14: 3         13 22: 9  13 Gemini   23:49
    18 18:59  18 Scorpio  22:50         16  3:44  16 Cancer    5:24
    21  3:38  21 Sagittar  4:12         18 12:57  18 Leo      14:36
    23  3: 1  23 Capricrn  7:14         20 23:14  21 Virgo     2:50
    25  8:27  25 Aquarius  9:26         23 14:12  23 Libra    15:40
    27 10:53  27 Pisces   11:59         25 12:49  26 Scorpio   2:25
    29 14:14  29 Aries    15:27         28  8:54  28 Sagittar 10: 3
    31 18:16  31 Taurus   20: 4         30 14: 4  30 Capricrn 15: 6
JUN  3  0:40   3 Gemini    2:10     DEC  2 17:49   2 Aquarius 18:45
     5  3:52   5 Cancer   10:26          4 19:55   4 Pisces   21:56
     7 19:24   7 Leo      21:17          7  0:14   7 Aries     1: 4
    10  7:59  10 Virgo    10: 2          8  3:47   9 Taurus    4:25
    12 18:42  12 Libra    22:28         11  7:49  11 Gemini    8:34
    15  4:38  15 Scorpio   8: 2         13 13:42  13 Cancer   14:33
    17 11:37  17 Sagittar 13:40         15 22:38  15 Leo      23:22
    19 12:22  19 Capricrn 16: 5         18  2:30  18 Virgo    11: 5
    21 14:56  21 Aquarius 17: 1         20 23:21  21 Libra     0: 2
    23 16: 0  23 Pisces   18:12         22  2:45  23 Scorpio  11:28
    25 18:31  25 Aries    20:53         25 18:55  25 Sagittar 19:28
    27 18:37  28 Taurus    1:35         27 23:31  28 Capricrn  0: 2
    30  5:42  30 Gemini    8:25         30  1:55  30 Aquarius  2:24
```

1969 RED LIGHTS, GREEN LIGHTS (Tables of the MOON)

Mo	D	Time	D	Sign	Time
JAN	2	10:25	2	Cancer	15:53
	4	23:44	5	Leo	3:55
	7	10:46	7	Virgo	14:43
	9	19:53	9	Libra	23:33
	11	14: 1	12	Scorpio	5:33
	14	5:15	14	Sagittar	8:19
	16	0:43	16	Capricrn	8:40
	18	5:28	18	Aquarius	8:17
	20	6:27	20	Pisces	9:21
	22	10:42	22	Aries	13:44
	24	2:25	24	Taurus	22:13
	27	6:42	27	Gemini	9:54
	29	15:35	29	Cancer	22:37
FEB	1	8:55	1	Leo	10:25
	3	17:53	3	Virgo	20:41
	6	2:22	6	Libra	5: 1
	7	18:48	8	Scorpio	11:19
	10	13: 2	10	Sagittar	15:24
	12	8:30	12	Capricrn	17:29
	14	16:19	14	Aquarius	18:31
	16	17:50	16	Pisces	20: 4
	18	21:29	18	Aries	23:49
	20	15:45	21	Taurus	7: 2
	23	16:15	23	Gemini	17:42
	25	18:31	26	Cancer	6:12
	28	16:50	28	Leo	18:12
MAR	3	1:41	3	Virgo	4: 7
	5	9:14	5	Libra	11:34
	7	7:17	7	Scorpio	16:57
	9	18:34	9	Sagittar	20:48
	11	21:51	11	Capricrn	23:13
	13	23:55	14	Aquarius	2:10
	16	2:45	16	Pisces	5: 4
	18	7: 1	18	Aries	9:27
	20	10:16	20	Taurus	16:21
	22	23:25	23	Gemini	2:13
	25	6: 1	25	Cancer	14:19
	27	23:40	28	Leo	2:37
	30	10: 1	30	Virgo	12:54
APR	1	19:38	1	Libra	20: 4
	3	18:42	4	Scorpio	0:23
	6	1:42	6	Sagittar	2:58
	8	3:24	8	Capricrn	5: 5
	10	5:39	10	Aquarius	7:47
	12	8:37	12	Pisces	11:42
	14	14: 7	14	Aries	17:14
	16	21:36	17	Taurus	0:44
	19	6:45	19	Gemini	10:29
	21	20:13	21	Cancer	22:17
	24	9:27	24	Leo	10:51
	26	21:13	26	Virgo	21:57
	29	1:53	29	Libra	5:44
MAY	30	1: 9	1	Scorpio	9:50
	3	7:40	3	Sagittar	11:19
	5	6:25	5	Capricrn	11:57
	7	9:31	7	Aquarius	13:28
	9	12:50	9	Pisces	17: 4
	11	18:36	11	Aries	23: 9
	13	3:29	14	Taurus	7:29
	16	12:35	16	Gemini	17:42
	18	21:44	19	Cancer	5:31
	21	18:11	21	Leo	18:13
	24	0:37	24	Virgo	6: 7
	26	15: 0	26	Libra	15: 8
	28	8: 1	28	Scorpio	20: 6
	30	21:20	30	Sagittar	21:31
JUN	1	20:56	1	Capricrn	21: 7
	3	20:52	3	Aquarius	21: 4
	5	23: 4	5	Pisces	23:14
	8	4:23	8	Aries	4:37
	9	15:19	10	Taurus	13: 6
	12	23:35	12	Gemini	23:49
	15	11:41	15	Cancer	11:53
	18	0:26	18	Leo	0:36
	20	0:54	20	Virgo	12:54
	22	23: 2	22	Libra	23: 4
	23	17:15	25	Scorpio	5:32
	27	4:30	27	Sagittar	8: 0
	29	4:41	29	Capricrn	7:45

Mo	D	Time	D	Sign	Time
JUL	1	4: 4	1	Aquarius	6:50
	3	1:14	3	Pisces	7:27
	5	8:59	5	Aries	11:17
	7	17:22	7	Taurus	18:54
	10	4: 7	10	Gemini	5:32
	12	17: 1	12	Cancer	17:48
	15	6:25	15	Leo	6:30
	17	10:52	17	Virgo	18:43
	19	23:46	20	Libra	5:20
	22	12:10	22	Scorpio	13: 4
	24	10:26	24	Sagittar	17:11
	26	7:10	26	Capricrn	18:10
	28	11:14	28	Aquarius	17:35
	30	10:57	30	Pisces	17:31
AUG	1	16:56	1	Aries	19:55
	3	14: 1	4	Taurus	2: 2
	6	9: 2	6	Gemini	11:50
	8	10:52	8	Cancer	23:58
	11	4:28	11	Leo	12:39
	13	16:33	14	Virgo	0:33
	16	3: 7	16	Libra	10:51
	18	10:16	18	Scorpio	18:54
	20	20: 4	21	Sagittar	0:13
	23	2:28	23	Capricrn	2:49
	24	22:54	25	Aquarius	3:36
	26	21:38	27	Pisces	4: 4
	28	23:17	29	Aries	5:58
	30	12:35	31	Taurus	10:50
SEP	2	11:53	2	Gemini	19:24
	4	19:47	5	Cancer	6:58
	7	11:56	7	Leo	19:37
	9	23:57	10	Virgo	7:21
	12	10: 1	12	Libra	17: 2
	14	17:15	15	Scorpio	0:25
	16	23:22	17	Sagittar	5:43
	19	7:12	19	Capricrn	9:14
	21	8:30	21	Aquarius	11:32
	23	7:35	23	Pisces	13:23
	25	10: 4	25	Aries	15:56
	27	21:27	27	Taurus	20:29
	29	21:47	30	Gemini	4: 6
OCT	2	5:48	2	Cancer	14:53
	4	20:59	5	Leo	3:26
	7	9:15	7	Virgo	15:22
	9	19: 8	10	Libra	0:49
	11	9:40	12	Scorpio	7:19
	14	6:35	14	Sagittar	11:34
	16	12:20	16	Capricrn	14:36
	18	12:41	18	Aquarius	17:22
	20	15:50	20	Pisces	20:26
	22	19:43	23	Aries	0:18
	24	15:21	25	Taurus	5:33
	27	8:22	27	Gemini	13: 1
	29	16: 3	29	Cancer	23:13
NOV	1	10:43	1	Leo	11:35
	3	19:39	4	Virgo	0: 1
	6	6: 2	6	Libra	9:59
	8	11:26	8	Scorpio	16:18
	10	16:15	10	Sagittar	19:31
	12	15:49	12	Capricrn	21: 9
	14	19:54	14	Aquarius	22:53
	16	22:56	17	Pisces	1:53
	19	3:38	19	Aries	6:32
	21	4:19	21	Taurus	12:53
	23	18:13	23	Gemini	20:59
	26	1:23	26	Cancer	7:11
	28	16:48	28	Leo	19:23
DEC	1	5:52	1	Virgo	8:14
	3	17:13	3	Libra	19:17
	5	23:13	5	Scorpio	2:31
	8	4:12	8	Sagittar	5:43
	10	4:35	10	Capricrn	6:21
	12	5:15	12	Aquarius	6:28
	14	7:17	14	Pisces	7:57
	16	10:50	16	Aries	11:38
	18	11:55	18	Taurus	18:36
	21	2:35	21	Gemini	3:28
	23	8:57	23	Cancer	14: 9
	26	1:45	26	Leo	2:22
	28	14:54	28	Virgo	15:21
	31	3: 2	31	Libra	3:19

Mon	Day	Time	Day	Sign	Time
JAN	1	14:44	1	Aquarius	15:24
	3	12:46	3	Pisces	20:36
	6	4:13	6	Aries	5:46
	8	16:56	8	Taurus	18: 3
	11	5:18	11	Gemini	6:55
	13	16:19	13	Cancer	17:54
	16	0:37	16	Leo	2:10
	18	1:14	18	Virgo	8:11
	20	11:55	20	Libra	12:48
	22	7:14	22	Scorpio	16:28
	24	17:45	24	Sagittar	19:24
	26	20:15	26	Capricrn	21:57
	28	23:16	29	Aquarius	1: 6
	31	3:56	31	Pisces	6:16
FEB	2	12:24	2	Aries	14:40
	5	18: 7	5	Taurus	2:16
	7	12:31	7	Gemini	15: 9
	9	23:55	10	Cancer	2:35
	12	8:11	12	Leo	10:50
	14	11:24	14	Virgo	16: 3
	16	18:55	16	Libra	19:22
	18	20:46	18	Scorpio	22: 0
	20	21:50	21	Sagittar	0:48
	23	1: 3	23	Capricrn	4:12
	25	5:14	25	Aquarius	8:37
	27	14:36	27	Pisces	14:43
	29	19:12	29	Aries	23:15
MAR	3	9: 8	3	Taurus	10:28
	5	21:18	5	Gemini	23:17
	8	8:51	8	Cancer	11:22
	10	15:49	10	Leo	20:28
	12	22:45	13	Virgo	1:52
	14	23:55	15	Libra	4:24
	17	4:46	17	Scorpio	5:34
	19	4:39	19	Sagittar	6:54
	21	5: 3	21	Capricrn	9:35
	23	8:48	23	Aquarius	14:17
	25	18:11	25	Pisces	21:16
	28	0:12	28	Aries	6:32
	30	11: 7	30	Taurus	17:55
APR	1	23:37	2	Gemini	6:41
	4	12: 5	4	Cancer	19:13
	7	1: 9	7	Leo	5:29
	9	5:10	9	Virgo	12: 5
	11	8:40	11	Libra	15: 1
	13	9: 4	13	Scorpio	15:32
	15	9: 0	15	Sagittar	15:24
	17	12:18	17	Capricrn	16:23
	19	19:35	19	Aquarius	19:57
	22	0: 7	22	Pisces	2:46
	24	4:11	24	Aries	12:33
	26	16: 3	27	Taurus	0:23
	29	4:53	29	Gemini	13:12
MAY	1	22:30	2	Cancer	1:50
	4	7: 3	4	Leo	12:54
	6	20:38	6	Virgo	20:59
	8	17:30	9	Libra	1:21
	10	20:41	11	Scorpio	2:30
	12	20:23	13	Sagittar	1:54
	14	20: 5	15	Capricrn	1:31
	16	20:33	17	Aquarius	3:22
	19	5:45	19	Pisces	8:53
	21	8:43	21	Aries	18:15
	24	0:54	24	Taurus	6:16
	26	16:41	26	Gemini	19:13
	29	6:58	29	Cancer	7:43
	31	9:19	31	Leo	18:54
JUN	3	0:53	3	Virgo	3:53
	5	1:13	5	Libra	9:50
	7	10:44	7	Scorpio	12:31
	9	11:24	9	Sagittar	12:43
	11	11:12	11	Capricrn	12: 6
	13	4:42	13	Aquarius	12:47
	15	15:10	15	Pisces	16:42
	17	20:46	18	Aries	0:50
	20	11:26	20	Taurus	12:26
	22	15:43	22	Gemini	1:23
	25	4:23	25	Cancer	13:43
	27	15:33	28	Leo	0:31
	29	22:50	30	Virgo	9:26

Mon	Day	Time	Day	Sign	Time
JUL	2	8: 5	2	Libra	16:10
	4	11: 8	4	Scorpio	20:21
	6	14:55	6	Sagittar	22: 5
	8	16:16	8	Capricrn	22:24
	10	16: 2	10	Aquarius	23: 4
	12	17:19	13	Pisces	2: ,3
	15	8:25	15	Aries	8:52
	17	9:54	17	Taurus	19:31
	20	3: 3	20	Gemini	8:13
	22	12:54	22	Cancer	20:32
	24	23:47	25	Leo	6:55
	27	6:46	27	Virgo	15:10
	29	15:40	29	Libra	21:33
AUG	31	20:45	31	Scorpio	2:12
	3	2:21	3	Sagittar	5:11
	5	1:39	5	Capricrn	6:58
	7	3:26	7	Aquarius	8:38
	9	4: 1	9	Pisces	11:46
	11	12:31	11	Aries	17:53
	13	23:38	14	Taurus	3:36
	16	10:32	16	Gemini	15:52
	18	23:19	19	Cancer	4:16
	21	10:12	21	Leo	14:40
	23	13:50	23	Virgo	22:21
	26	0: 6	26	Libra	3:45
	27	23:23	28	Scorpio	7:39
	30	7:35	30	Sagittar	10:41
SEP	1	12:57	1	Capricrn	13:22
	3	13:38	3	Aquarius	16:20
	5	11:20	5	Pisces	20:28
	8	0:25	8	Aries	2:50
	10	1:33	10	Taurus	12: 6
	12	21:55	12	Gemini	23:55
	15	10:49	15	Cancer	12:26
	17	22: 8	17	Leo	23:26
	20	5:30	20	Virgo	7:16
	22	11:20	22	Libra	12: 0
	24	10:11	24	Scorpio	14:39
	26	16:18	26	Sagittar	16:31
	28	7:38	28	Capricrn	18:45
	30	12:47	30	Aquarius	22:11
OCT	2	17:43	3	Pisces	3:21
	5	0:42	5	Aries	10:36
	7	5:58	7	Taurus	20: 7
	9	21:24	10	Gemini	7:44
	12	12:27	12	Cancer	20:24
	14	22:23	15	Leo	8: 9
	17	8:16	17	Virgo	16:59
	19	19: 7	19	Libra	22: 6
	21	21:45	22	Scorpio	0: 6
	23	17:45	24	Sagittar	0:33
	25	18:57	26	Capricrn	1:14
	27	21:51	28	Aquarius	3:43
	30	0:49	30	Pisces	8:55
NOV	1	12: 0	1	Aries	16:51
	3	13:36	4	Taurus	3: 2
	6	11:30	6	Gemini	14:48
	9	3:18	9	Cancer	3:27
	11	14:17	11	Leo	15:45
	13	23:50	14	Virgo	1:55
	16	1:42	16	Libra	8:27
	17	18: 6	18	Scorpio	11: 7
	20	8: 2	20	Sagittar	11: 4
	22	2: 2	22	Capricrn	10:20
	24	5:11	24	Aquarius	11: 3
	26	11:58	26	Pisces	14:53
	28	16: 3	28	Aries	22:26
DEC	30	11:26	1	Taurus	8:58
	3	14:42	3	Gemini	21: 6
	5	23:35	6	Cancer	9:44
	8	19:22	8	Leo	22: 3
	11	3:23	11	Virgo	9: 0
	13	12: 1	13	Libra	17: 9
	15	19:27	15	Scorpio	21:32
	17	18:12	17	Sagittar	22:28
	19	18:19	19	Capricrn	21:33
	21	16:54	21	Aquarius	21: 0
	23	18:45	23	Pisces	23: 1
	26	0:33	26	Aries	5: 2
	28	13:25	28	Taurus	14:57
	30	22:38	31	Gemini	3:12

JAN	2 7:38	2	Libra	17: 4
	4 15:36	4	Scorpio	20:17
	6 14:39	7	Sagittar	0:28
	8 20: 3	9	Capricrn	5:54
	11 3:11	11	Aquarius	13: 6
	13 10:43	13	Pisces	22:45
	16 10:44	16	Aries	10:48
	18 22:55	18	Taurus	23:40
	21 9:18	21	Gemini	10:39
	23 10:14	23	Cancer	17:52
	25 19:12	25	Leo	21:21
	27 16:18	27	Virgo	22:37
	29 20:34	29	Libra	23:33
FEB	31 22:11	1	Scorpio	1:44
	3 1:45	3	Sagittar	5:56
	5 10:18	5	Capricrn	12:11
	7 17:54	7	Aquarius	20:17
	10 5:10	10	Pisces	6:19
	12 13:45	12	Aries	18:17
	14 23:45	15	Taurus	7:19
	16 16: 0	17	Gemini	19:16
	20 1:16	20	Cancer	3:48
	22 6: 9	22	Leo	8: 5
	24 0: 1	24	Virgo	9: 4
	26 7:41	26	Libra	8:45
	28 1:14	28	Scorpio	9:10
MAR	2 11:36	2	Sagittar	11:53
	4 4:26	4	Capricrn	17:36
	6 16: 4	7	Aquarius	2: 4
	9 1:27	9	Pisces	12:42
	11 13:56	12	Aries	0:53
	14 2:44	14	Taurus	13:54
	16 17:14	17	Gemini	2:19
	19 9:54	19	Cancer	12:10
	21 8:22	21	Leo	18: 4
	23 10:39	23	Virgo	20: 9
	25 11: 7	25	Libra	19:51
	27 10:25	27	Scorpio	19:11
	29 11: 1	29	Sagittar	20: 9
APR	31 23:49	1	Capricrn	0:11
	3 6: 8	3	Aquarius	7:49
	5 15:13	5	Pisces	18:29
	7 20:37	8	Aries	6:57
	10 13: 9	10	Taurus	19:57
	13 5:28	13	Gemini	8:15
	15 8:48	15	Cancer	18:37
	17 20:48	18	Leo	1:55
	20 4:45	20	Virgo	5:43
	22 0:13	22	Libra	6:42
	24 0:13	24	Scorpio	6:19
	26 0:31	26	Sagittar	6:27
	27 19: 8	28	Capricrn	8:54
	30 9:11	30	Aquarius	14:58
MAY	2 11:37	3	Pisces	0:48
	5 7:55	5	Aries	13:10
	7 21:36	8	Taurus	2:10
	10 10:22	10	Gemini	14: 9
	12 5:51	13	Cancer	0:11
	15 5:35	15	Leo	7:49
	17 5:18	17	Virgo	12:53
	19 14:33	19	Libra	15:31
	21 16: 4	21	Scorpio	16:30
	23 5:19	23	Sagittar	17: 6
	25 2:35	25	Capricrn	18:59
	27 10:28	27	Aquarius	23:44
	30 3:12	30	Pisces	8:19
JUN	1 11:37	1	Aries	20: 7
	4 3:41	4	Taurus	9: 5
	6 5:34	6	Gemini	20:53
	8 12: 4	9	Cancer	6:18
	10 23:22	11	Leo	13:19
	13 4:48	13	Virgo	18:24
	15 11:12	15	Libra	21:59
	17 17:28	18	Scorpio	0:26
	19 13:10	20	Sagittar	2:20
	21 12:43	22	Capricrn	4:47
	23 18:57	24	Aquarius	9:11
	26 1:34	26	Pisces	16:50
	28 11:42	29	Aries	3:53

JUL	1 3:44	1	Taurus	16:43
	3 20:37	4	Gemini	4:39
	6 10: 7	6	Cancer	13:48
	8 10:57	8	Leo	19:59
	10 16:59	11	Virgo	0: 8
	12 13:14	13	Libra	3:20
	15 2:29	15	Scorpio	6:18
	16 22:37	17	Sagittar	9:23
	19 12:39	19	Capricrn	13: 0
	21 14:40	21	Aquarius	18: 0
	23 9:40	24	Pisces	1:29
	25 19:31	26	Aries	12: 0
	27 17:45	29	Taurus	0:41
	30 20:59	31	Gemini	13: 1
AUG	2 7:39	2	Cancer	22:32
	4 16:43	4	Leo	4:27
	6 17:27	7	Virgo	7:36
	8 20:56	9	Libra	9:35
	10 14:22	11	Scorpio	11:45
	13 2:12	13	Sagittar	14:53
	15 6:30	15	Capricrn	19:19
	17 12:18	18	Aquarius	1:17
	20 2:27	20	Pisces	9:18
	22 6:13	22	Aries	19:48
	24 9:54	25	Taurus	8:22
	27 7:59	27	Gemini	21: 9
	29 19:25	30	Cancer	7:35
SEP	1 4: 2	1	Leo	14: 9
	3 9:59	3	Virgo	17: 8
	5 13:19	5	Libra	18: 4
	7 5:33	7	Scorpio	18:45
	9 20:26	9	Sagittar	20:40
	11 23: 4	12	Capricrn	0:43
	13 21: 3	14	Aquarius	5:59
	16 11:56	16	Pisces	15:53
	18 17: 0	19	Aries	2:47
	21 10:35	21	Taurus	15:21
	24 0: 6	24	Gemini	4:22
	26 12:35	26	Cancer	15:46
	28 20:55	28	Leo	23:42
OCT	1 3:15	1	Virgo	3:39
	3 21:44	3	Libra	4:35
	5 0:13	5	Scorpio	4:15
	7 1: 0	7	Sagittar	4:32
	9 4: 0	9	Capricrn	7: 0
	11 5:50	11	Aquarius	13: 0
	13 19:48	13	Pisces	21:38
	16 22: 0	16	Aries	8:58
	18 21:30	18	Taurus	21:42
	21 4:12	21	Gemini	10:38
	23 22: 5	23	Cancer	22:28
	26 2:16	26	Leo	7:41
	28 1:44	28	Virgo	13:20
	30 11:10	30	Libra	15:32
NOV	31 2:47	1	Scorpio	15:27
	3 10:56	3	Sagittar	14:52
	5 11:47	5	Capricrn	15:44
	7 16: 9	7	Aquarius	19:46
	9 15:51	9	Pisces	3:43
	12 10:53	12	Aries	14:59
	14 0: 6	14	Taurus	3:35
	17 13: 1	17	Gemini	16:41
	20 0:51	20	Cancer	4:13
	22 12:54	22	Leo	13:47
	24 10:39	24	Virgo	20:46
	26 22:20	27	Libra	0:49
	28 22:37	29	Scorpio	2:14
DEC	1 1:12	1	Sagittar	2:11
	3 0:21	3	Capricrn	2:25
	5 3:52	5	Aquarius	4:57
	7 1:38	7	Pisces	11:20
	9 19:33	9	Aries	21:44
	11 11:35	12	Taurus	10:00
	14 21:21	14	Gemini	23:18
	17 8:35	17	Cancer	10:31
	19 17:41	19	Leo	19:21
	22 1:27	22	Virgo	2:22
	24 6: 0	24	Libra	7:27
	25 15:10	26	Scorpio	10:37
	28 10:51	28	Sagittar	12:10
	30 11:53	30	Capricrn	13:11

JAN

Day	Time		Day	Sign	Time
1	7:11		1	Taurus	17:47
3	9: 7		4	Gemini	0: 7
5	22:20		6	Cancer	2:41
7	13:29		8	Leo	2:50
9	16: 1		10	Virgo	2:35
11	16:28		12	Libra	3:53
13	20: 0		14	Scorpio	8: 9
16	7:34		16	Sagittar	15:40
18	11: 6		19	Capricrn	1:45
20	21:11		21	Aquarius	13:27
23	15:21		24	Pisces	1:59
26	12:24		26	Aries	14:33
28	23:44		29	Taurus	1:43
30	19:15		31	Gemini	9:44

FEB

Day	Time		Day	Sign	Time
1	23:27		2	Cancer	13:42
4	1:40		4	Leo	14:14
6	0:52		6	Virgo	13:12
8	11:46		8	Libra	12:51
10	13:10		10	Scorpio	15:15
12	19:26		12	Sagittar	21:34
13	23:12		15	Capricrn	7:26
17	16: 2		17	Aquarius	19:26
19	16:16		20	Pisces	8: 6
22	18:53		22	Aries	20:31
25	7:48		25	Taurus	7:54
27	7: 5		27	Gemini	17: 3

MAR

Day	Time		Day	Sign	Time
1	19:56		1	Cancer	22:48
3	17:36		4	Leo	0:57
5	12:17		6	Virgo	0:37
7	21:48		7	Libra	23:49
9	11:32		10	Scorpio	0:47
11	15: 5		12	Sagittar	5:19
14	0:19		14	Capricrn	13:56
16	16:49		17	Aquarius	1:35
18	23:52		19	Pisces	14:19
21	12:50		22	Aries	2:34
24	0:40		24	Taurus	13:32
26	15:25		26	Gemini	22:42
28	19:49		29	Cancer	5:24
30	22:22		31	Leo	9:13

APR

Day	Time		Day	Sign	Time
2	3:28		2	Virgo	10:32
4	2:16		4	Libra	10:40
6	11:11		6	Scorpio	11:30
8	3:21		8	Sagittar	14:54
10	13:53		10	Capricrn	22: 2
13	1:32		13	Aquarius	8:43
15	18: 2		15	Pisces	21:14
18	3:16		18	Aries	9:28
20	14:50		20	Taurus	20: 1
22	19: 3		23	Gemini	4:27
25	7:26		25	Cancer	10:48
27	7:15		27	Leo	15:10
29	15:59		29	Virgo	17:50

MAY

Day	Time		Day	Sign	Time
1	18:20		1	Libra	19:32
3	20:50		3	Scorpio	21:24
5	18:17		6	Sagittar	0:53
8	2:20		8	Capricrn	7:13
10	10:19		10	Aquarius	16:52
12	11:19		13	Pisces	4:55
15	11:30		15	Aries	17:16
18	18:49		18	Taurus	3:50
20	9:43		20	Gemini	11:40
22	12:57		22	Cancer	17: 1
24	16:57		24	Leo	20:37
26	20:54		26	Virgo	23:23
28	22:12		29	Libra	2: 0
31	4: 2		31	Scorpio	5:12

JUN

Day	Time		Day	Sign	Time
2	6:51		2	Sagittar	9:39
4	13:31		4	Capricrn	16:11
6	22:50		7	Aquarius	1:21
8	17: 5		9	Pisces	12:57
11	23:22		12	Aries	1:27
13	21:49		14	Taurus	12:30
16	18:57		16	Gemini	20:27
18	23:50		19	Cancer	1: 6
21	2:24		21	Leo	3:29
22	22:12		23	Virgo	5: 8
25	5:29		25	Libra	7:23
26	17:59		27	Scorpio	11: 4
29	15:45		29	Sagittar	16:32

JUL

Day	Time		Day	Sign	Time
1	23: 8		1	Capricrn	23:52
4	8:33		4	Aquarius	9:15
6	14:30		6	Pisces	20:40
9	8:38		9	Aries	9:16
10	21:43		11	Taurus	21: 4
14	5:17		14	Gemini	5:52
16	10:11		16	Cancer	10:45
18	11:54		18	Leo	12:28
20	10:18		20	Virgo	12:47
22	12:58		22	Libra	13:39
23	18:29		24	Scorpio	16:32
26	21: 9		26	Sagittar	22: 5
29	5: 0		29	Capricrn	6: 5
31	14:46		31	Aquarius	16: 2

AUG

Day	Time		Day	Sign	Time
2	6:24		3	Pisces	3:36
5	14:34		5	Aries	16:15
7	9:26		8	Taurus	4:38
10	12:41		10	Gemini	14:39
12	18:42		12	Cancer	20:42
14	21:35		14	Leo	22:51
16	11:48		16	Virgo	22:35
18	19:43		18	Libra	22: 6
20	18:50		20	Scorpio	23:24
23	3: 2		23	Sagittar	3:51
25	8: 2		25	Capricrn	11:37
27	17:55		27	Aquarius	21:56
30	0:24		30	Pisces	9:49

SEP

Day	Time		Day	Sign	Time
1	17:38		1	Aries	22:28
4	3: 0		4	Taurus	11: 0
6	16:37		6	Gemini	21:53
9	0:13		9	Cancer	5:27
11	4:32		11	Leo	9: 2
12	17:22		13	Virgo	9:26
15	5:26		15	Libra	8:33
17	5:53		17	Scorpio	8:34
19	9: 6		19	Sagittar	11:22
21	14:25		21	Capricrn	17:53
24	2:46		24	Aquarius	3:48
26	20:20		26	Pisces	15:49
28	19:31		29	Aries	4:30

OCT

Day	Time		Day	Sign	Time
1	2:36		1	Taurus	16:47
3	18:25		4	Gemini	3:44
6	4:53		6	Cancer	12:13
8	8:33		8	Leo	17:25
10	17:26		10	Virgo	19:27
12	10:53		12	Libra	19:30
14	3:52		14	Scorpio	19:22
16	11:22		16	Sagittar	21: 0
18	16:34		18	Capricrn	1:56
21	5:35		21	Aquarius	10:41
23	13:17		23	Pisces	22:21
26	3:23		26	Aries	11: 4
26	17:58		28	Taurus	23: 6
30	21: 4		31	Gemini	9:28

NOV

Day	Time		Day	Sign	Time
2	5:36		2	Cancer	17:43
4	11:51		4	Leo	23:37
6	12:57		7	Virgo	3:10
8	17:47		9	Libra	4:55
9	11:52		11	Scorpio	5:54
13	7:20		13	Sagittar	7:36
15	0: 4		15	Capricrn	11:37
17	13: 5		17	Aquarius	19: 4
20	0:21		20	Pisces	5:53
22	5:52		22	Aries	18:32
23	3:35		25	Taurus	6:37
27	9:43		27	Gemini	16:31
29	19:43		29	Cancer	23:50

DEC

Day	Time		Day	Sign	Time
2	3:15		2	Leo	5: 2
3	20:10		4	Virgo	8:49
6	1:51		6	Libra	11:44
8	1:55		8	Scorpio	14:18
10	14:55		10	Sagittar	17:14
12	18:59		12	Capricrn	21:31
14	17:42		15	Aquarius	4:20
17	3:57		17	Pisces	14:18
19	21:41		19	Aries	2:40
21	6:25		21	Taurus	15: 8
24	14:39		25	Gemini	1:14
26	22: 2		27	Cancer	7:59
29	2:27		29	Leo	11:58
31	13:19		31	Virgo	14:34

JAN	1	7:43	1	Capricorn	20: 7	JUL	1	20:49	2 Virgo	17:12
	3	22: 9	4	Aquarius	9: 5		3	22: 8	4 Libra	19:43
	6	6:39	6	Pisces	21: 7		6	1:58	7 Scorpio	1:38
	8	23: 9	9	Aries	7: 9		8	10:24	9 Sagittar	10:54
	11	12:22	11	Taurus	14:11		10	22:43	11 Capricrn	22:29
	13	12:14	13	Gemini	17:49		13	17: 2	14 Aquarius	11: 8
	15	13:48	15	Cancer	18:35		16	3:38	16 Pisces	23:45
	17	13:41	17	Leo	17:58		19	3:55	19 Aries	11:13
	19	1:17	19	Virgo	17:55		21	17:54	21 Taurus	20:14
	21	16:31	21	Libra	20:28		23	22:16	24 Gemini	1:49
	22	19:41	24	Scorpio	3: 1		26	0:56	26 Cancer	3:54
	26	9:33	26	Sagittar	13:33		27	7:30	28 Leo	3:38
	28	22:23	29	Capricrn	2:22		30	2:32	30 Virgo	2:55
	31	11:17	31	Aquarius	15:18	AUG	1	15:12	1 Libra	3:55
FEB	2	7: 5	3	Pisces	2:56		2	19:23	3 Scorpio	8:21
	5	8:22	5	Aries	12:44		5	15:49	5 Sagittar	16:50
	6	22:18	7	Taurus	20:24		8	1:16	8 Capricrn	4:23
	9	20:38	10	Gemini	1:37		10	4: 8	10 Aquarius	17:10
	11	22:55	12	Cancer	4:14		12	20: 3	13 Pisces	5:38
	13	23: 7	14	Leo	4:55		15	7:18	15 Aries	16:57
	16	0:27	16	Virgo	5: 6		17	23:28	18 Taurus	2:28
	17	23: 4	18	Libra	6:45		20	3:51	20 Gemini	9:21
	20	8:54	20	Scorpio	11:46		22	11:40	22 Cancer	13: 5
	22	9:37	22	Sagittar	20:57		23	17:44	24 Leo	14: 2
	24	22: 5	25	Capricrn	9:18		26	8:37	26 Virgo	13:37
	27	7:18	27	Aquarius	22:15		29	3:18	28 Libra	13:53
MAR	1	14:16	2	Pisces	9:39		30	12:27	30 Scorpio	16:54
	4	1:35	4	Aries	18:45	SEP	1	6: 7	2 Sagittar	0: 0
	6	1:35	7	Taurus	1:50		4	7: 6	4 Capricrn	10:52
	8	15:43	9	Gemini	7:15		6	5:23	6 Aquarius	23:34
	10	17:53	11	Cancer	11: 3		9	9:29	9 Pisces	11:57
	13	0:27	13	Leo	13:23		11	21: 0	11 Aries	22:50
	15	2:10	15	Virgo	14:56		14	6:40	14 Taurus	7:57
	17	11:24	17	Libra	17: 4		16	2:27	16 Gemini	15: 7
	18	20:49	19	Scorpio	21:32		18	19:39	18 Cancer	20: 1
	21	21:10	22	Sagittar	5:37		20	18:35	20 Leo	22:36
	24	15:10	24	Capricrn	17: 7		22	10: 8	22 Virgo	23:30
	26	18:41	27	Aquarius	5:59		24	23:28	25 Libra	0:16
	29	7:36	29	Pisces	17:32		25	3:18	27 Scorpio	2:47
APR	31	17:46	1	Aries	2:19		29	1:56	29 Sagittar	8:42
	2	18:44	3	Taurus	8:29	OCT	30	16:45	1 Capricrn	18:29
	5	6:31	5	Gemini	12:55		3	16:54	4 Aquarius	6:49
	6	22:50	7	Cancer	16:25		6	11:56	6 Pisces	19:14
	9	14:39	9	Leo	19:24		9	4:49	9 Aries	5:54
	11	18:16	11	Virgo	22:15		11	9:57	11 Taurus	14:17
	13	22:23	14	Libra	1:39		13	0:17	13 Gemini	20:40
	16	0:59	16	Scorpio	6:42		15	11:20	16 Cancer	1:27
	18	12:49	18	Sagittar	14:32		17	19: 0	18 Leo	4:52
	19	17:38	21	Capricrn	1:24		20	1:17	20 Virgo	7:14
	22	15:57	23	Aquarius	14: 5		21	14:49	22 Libra	9:21
	25	4:21	26	Pisces	2: 3		23	11:35	24 Scorpio	12:32
	27	14:34	28	Aries	11:13		25	23:38	26 Sagittar	18: 9
	29	12:33	30	Taurus	17: 4		28	9:30	29 Capricrn	3: 5
MAY	2	1:33	2	Gemini	20:27		31	9:46	31 Aquarius	14:50
	4	1: 8	4	Cancer	22:39	NOV	2	21: 5	3 Pisces	3:23
	6	11:31	7	Leo	0:50		5	13:53	5 Aries	14:22
	8	19: 5	9	Virgo	3:48		7	13:13	7 Taurus	22:30
	11	4:17	11	Libra	8: 5		9	9:42	10 Gemini	3:55
	13	8:51	13	Scorpio	14:10		12	4:48	12 Cancer	7:30
	15	11:53	15	Sagittar	22:32		13	19:24	14 Leo	10:10
	17	5:13	18	Capricrn	9:20		16	1:54	16 Virgo	12:55
	20	21: 3	20	Aquarius	21:51		18	15:56	18 Libra	16:11
	22	10:50	23	Pisces	10:15		20	20: 0	20 Scorpio	20:37
	24	21:55	25	Aries	20:19		22	8:47	23 Sagittar	2:57
	27	4:37	28	Taurus	2:49		25	10: 9	25 Capricrn	11:46
	29	18:54	30	Gemini	5:59		27	5:53	27 Aquarius	23: 4
JUN	31	20: 7	1	Cancer	7: 6		30	8:50	30 Pisces	11:50
	2	12:33	3	Leo	7:47	DEC	2	20: 3	2 Aries	23:23
	5	7:23	5	Virgo	9:34		5	5:15	5 Taurus	8:31
	6	19:42	7	Libra	13:30		6	21:12	7 Gemini	13:28
	8	21:39	9	Scorpio	20: 4		9	11:43	9 Cancer	15:57
	11	13:27	12	Sagittar	5:10		11	2: 4	11 Leo	17: 9
	14	8:55	14	Capricrn	16:21		13	13:26	13 Virgo	18:36
	16	16:57	17	Aquarius	4:52		15	15:43	15 Libra	21:43
	19	13:33	19	Pisces	17:29		17	20: 2	18 Scorpio	2:41
	21	21:48	22	Aries	4:30		20	5:37	20 Sagittar	10: 2
	23	20:40	24	Taurus	12:17		22	11: 5	22 Capricrn	19:27
	26	14:16	26	Gemini	16:19		24	13:12	25 Aquarius	6:45
	28	17: 4	28	Cancer	17:20		27	9:14	27 Pisces	19:18
	30	16:33	30	Leo	16:59		29	21: 7	30 Aries	7:40

Month				Sign	
JAN	2	10:11	3	Virgo	2:48
	4	21:48	5	Libra	10:10
	7	12: 4	7	Scorpio	21: 4
	10	4:59	10	Sagittar	9:50
	12	10:49	12	Capricrn	22:14
	14	20:44	15	Aquarius	8:48
	17	2:33	17	Pisces	17: 4
	19	21: 6	19	Aries	23:11
	21	14:46	22	Taurus	3:24
	23	18:12	24	Gemini	6: 5
	25	20:32	26	Cancer	7:52
	27	13:02	28	Leo	9:45
	30	2: 4	30	Virgo	13: 9
FEB	31	21:16	1	Libra	19:26
	3	17:47	4	Scorpio	5:13
	6	6:26	6	Sagittar	17:36
	9	1:53	9	Capricrn	6:11
	10	17:16	11	Aquarius	16:40
	13	15:49	14	Pisces	0: 9
	15	7:54	16	Aries	5:10
	18	6:25	18	Taurus	8:10
	20	5:20	20	Gemini	11:48
	22	8:46	22	Cancer	14:50
	23	23:23	24	Leo	18:11
	26	17: 9	26	Virgo	22:30
	28	6:25	29	Libra	4:47
MAR	2	9: 4	2	Scorpio	13:54
	4	21:22	5	Sagittar	1:47
	7	10:48	7	Capricrn	14:36
	9	10:26	10	Aquarius	1:36
	12	6:43	12	Pisces	9: 6
	14	3:41	14	Aries	13:16
	16	14: 7	16	Taurus	15:31
	18	16:26	18	Gemini	17:26
	20	19:34	20	Cancer	20:12
	22	15:43	23	Leo	0:15
	24	21:52	25	Virgo	5:42
	27	9:48	27	Libra	12:48
	29	15:46	29	Scorpio	22: 4
APR	1	3:30	1	Sagittar	9:41
	3	18:29	3	Capricrn	22:37
	6	7:38	6	Aquarius	10:25
	8	17:15	8	Pisces	18:47
	10	1:12	10	Aries	23: 9
	12	12:38	13	Taurus	0:37
	14	4:12	15	Gemini	1: 6
	16	21:13	17	Cancer	2:24
	19	4:10	19	Leo	5:40
	20	11:47	21	Virgo	11:18
	22	20: 9	23	Libra	19: 9
	25	11: 4	26	Scorpio	5: 1
	27	14: 8	28	Sagittar	16:46
MAY	30	19:15	1	Capricrn	5:43
	3	11:58	3	Aquarius	18: 7
	6	1:34	6	Pisces	3:44
	8	8:26	8	Aries	9:16
	8	8:26	10	Taurus	11:10
	11	21: 2	12	Gemini	11: 2
	13	5:27	14	Cancer	10:54
	16	4:39	16	Leo	12:32
	18	12:43	18	Virgo	17: 3
	21	0:41	21	Libra	0:42
	21	11:35	23	Scorpio	10:58
	24	18:51	25	Sagittar	23: 4
	26	22:34	28	Capricrn	12: 1
	29	21:33	31	Aquarius	0:33
JUN	1	12:55	2	Pisces	11: 2
	4	2:18	4	Aries	18: 3
	5	20:25	6	Taurus	21:20
	8	19:35	8	Gemini	21:50
	10	4:23	10	Cancer	21:17
	12	15:55	12	Leo	21:35
	14	21:12	15	Virgo	0:28
	17	6:37	17	Libra	6:54
	19	14:33	19	Scorpio	16:50
	21	0:46	22	Sagittar	5: 4
	24	9:42	24	Capricrn	18: 2
	26	4:27	27	Aquarius	6:22
	29	4: 9	29	Pisces	16:57
JUL	1	10:55	2	Aries	0:53
	3	15:13	4	Taurus	5:43
	5	21:40	6	Gemini	7:43
	7	17: 1	8	Cancer	7:57
	9	15:11	10	Leo	8: 1
	11	17:29	12	Virgo	9:45
	13	23:24	14	Libra	14:42
	16	11:48	16	Scorpio	23:33
	19	4:26	19	Sagittar	11:29
	21	11:44	22	Capricrn	0:27
	23	20:24	24	Aquarius	12:31
	26	21: 4	26	Pisces	22:36
	29	4:30	29	Aries	6:26
	31	6:18	31	Taurus	12: 1
AUG	2	3:55	2	Gemini	15:29
	4	16:28	4	Cancer	17:13
	6	7:52	6	Leo	18:11
	8	9:38	8	Virgo	19:51
	10	13:28	10	Libra	23:52
	12	12: 9	13	Scorpio	7:32
	15	7:58	15	Sagittar	18:45
	17	21:26	18	Capricrn	7:39
	20	9:58	20	Aquarius	19:14
	22	20:20	23	Pisces	5:14
	25	4: 1	25	Aries	12:16
	26	19:58	27	Taurus	17:24
	29	13:54	29	Gemini	21:16
SEP	30	20:43	1	Cancer	0:14
	2	19:44	3	Leo	2:37
	4	22:22	5	Virgo	5:13
	7	7:43	7	Libra	9:20
	9	9:30	9	Scorpio	16:20
	11	22:44	12	Sagittar	2:48
	13	21:24	14	Capricrn	15:31
	16	20: 7	17	Aquarius	3:48
	19	13: 3	19	Pisces	13:23
	21	17:31	21	Aries	19:44
	23	23: 1	23	Taurus	23:47
	26	1:49	26	Gemini	2:47
	28	4:31	28	Cancer	5:40
	30	1:35	30	Leo	8:53
OCT	2	11: 9	2	Virgo	12:43
	4	9:40	4	Libra	17:45
	6	22:53	7	Scorpio	0:57
	9	8:41	9	Sagittar	11: 3
	11	20:55	11	Capricrn	23:32
	14	1:42	14	Aquarius	12:16
	16	19:50	16	Pisces	22:33
	18	18:56	19	Aries	8:25
	21	5:50	21	Taurus	8:25
	23	7:28	23	Gemini	10: 4
	25	8:57	25	Cancer	11:38
	27	5:49	27	Leo	14:14
	29	15:31	29	Virgo	18:26
NOV	31	11:14	1	Libra	0:25
	3	5:29	3	Scorpio	8:25
	5	18:20	5	Sagittar	18:44
	8	3:48	8	Capricrn	7: 6
	10	2:54	10	Aquarius	20: 9
	13	4:30	13	Pisces	7:29
	15	2: 5	15	Aries	15:11
	17	16:33	17	Taurus	18:57
	19	17:46	19	Gemini	19:59
	21	17:58	21	Cancer	20: 4
	23	18:21	23	Leo	20:59
	25	22: 2	26	Virgo	0: 3
	28	0:22	28	Libra	5:55
	30	14: 5	30	Scorpio	14:31
DEC	2	23:46	3	Sagittar	1:24
	5	12:30	5	Capricrn	13:54
	7	3:42	8	Aquarius	2:58
	10	14:15	10	Pisces	15: 0
	12	8: 6	13	Aries	0:13
	15	5:26	15	Taurus	5:33
	17	3: 0	17	Gemini	7:22
	19	2:42	19	Cancer	7: 3
	20	14:53	21	Leo	6:31
	22	18:18	23	Virgo	7:42
	24	21: 7	25	Libra	12: 5
	26	23: 6	27	Scorpio	20:12
	29	17:40	30	Sagittar	7:21

1963 RED LIGHTS, GREEN LIGHTS (Tables of the MOON)

JAN						JUL					
1	21:58		2	Aries	4:48	2	17: 3		3	Sagittar	8:12
3	21:57		4	Taurus	7:34	5	14:41		5	Capricrn	19: 3
6	9:46		6	Gemini	10:14	7	5:48		8	Aquarius	3:37
8	2:46		8	Cancer	13:42	9	19:46		10	Pisces	9:53
9	23: 9		10	Leo	19: 1	11	22:43		12	Aries	14:17
12	13:22		13	Virgo	3: 7	14	3:30		14	Taurus	17:15
15	2:32		15	Libra	14: 5	16	13:31		16	Gemini	19:28
17	20:35		18	Scorpio	2:36	18	13: 4		18	Cancer	21:45
20	13:56		20	Sagittar	14:21	20	20:43		21	Leo	1:15
22	4:47		22	Capricrn	23:24	22	15:13		23	Virgo	7: 7
24	19:26		25	Aquarius	5:14	25	14:11		25	Libra	16: 3
26	14: 8		27	Pisces	8:35	27	17:12		28	Scorpio	3:39
28	20:30		29	Aries	10:44	30	12:39		30	Sagittar	16: 8
31	2:32		31	Taurus	12:55	AUG 1	22:33		2	Capricrn	3:13
FEB 2	0: 8		2	Gemini	16: 3	3	15:58		5	Aquarius	11:26
4	18:35		4	Cancer	20:41	5	23:48		6	Pisces	16:46
6	13: 4		7	Leo	3: 6	7	15: 5		8	Aries	20: 7
8	14:52		9	Virgo	11:36	10	5:48		10	Taurus	22:38
11	14:44		11	Libra	22:19	12	8: 2		13	Gemini	1:16
14	8:20		14	Scorpio	10:39	14	13:11		15	Cancer	4:40
16	17:33		16	Sagittar	22:57	16	14:32		17	Leo	9:17
19	9: 0		19	Capricrn	9: 1	19	7:35		19	Virgo	15:41
20	21:24		21	Aquarius	15:24	21	14:45		22	Libra	0:26
22	19: 6		23	Pisces	18:18	24	9:33		24	Scorpio	11:39
25	5:38		25	Aries	19: 5	26	1:37		27	Sagittar	0:16
27	10: 8		27	Taurus	19:39	28	17: 2		29	Capricrn	11:58
MAR 1	16: 8		1	Gemini	21:39	31	5:54		31	Aquarius	20:38
3	12:32		4	Cancer	2: 8	SEP 2	14:30		3	Pisces	1:38
5	20: 2		6	Leo	9:15	4	0:11		5	Aries	3:53
8	16:57		8	Virgo	18:34	6	23: 9		7	Taurus	5: 3
10	17:53		11	Libra	5:35	8	10:34		9	Gemini	6:46
12	17: 9		13	Scorpio	17:52	11	8:58		11	Cancer	10: 8
15	21: 7		16	Sagittar	6:27	13	3:43		13	Leo	15:30
18	12: 8		18	Capricrn	17:35	14	23:35		15	Virgo	22:48
21	0:48		21	Aquarius	1:22	18	7:49		18	Libra	8: 0
22	14:16		23	Pisces	5: 5	19	17:51		20	Scorpio	19:11
25	2:22		25	Aries	5:38	23	6:53		23	Sagittar	7:50
26	23: 9		27	Taurus	4:57	25	4:16		25	Capricrn	20:16
29	3:28		29	Gemini	5:13	27	12:47		28	Aquarius	6: 4
31	6:37		31	Cancer	8:14	29	12:46		30	Pisces	11:47
APR 2	2:14		2	Leo	14:46	OCT 1	23:19		2	Aries	13:48
4	5:30		5	Virgo	0:21	3	20:43		4	Taurus	13:50
6	6: 2		7	Libra	11:50	6	4:47		6	Gemini	13:59
9	5:32		10	Scorpio	0:14	8	10:48		8	Cancer	16: 1
11	18:33		12	Sagittar	12:48	10	16:52		10	Leo	20:55
14	12:21		15	Capricrn	0:27	12	10:49		13	Virgo	4:35
17	2:53		17	Aquarius	9:35	14	23:30		15	Libra	14:25
19	12:45		19	Pisces	14:54	17	12:43		18	Scorpio	1:53
21	11:19		21	Aries	16:30	20	6:38		20	Sagittar	14:33
23	2:57		23	Taurus	15:51	23	1: 9		23	Capricrn	3:21
25	6:24		25	Gemini	15: 7	25	14: 9		25	Aquarius	14:21
27	2:59		27	Cancer	16:27	27	23: 9		27	Pisces	21:37
29	18:22		29	Leo	21:25	29	9:54		30	Aries	0:41
MAY 2	5:32		2	Virgo	6:13	NOV 31	3:23		1	Taurus	0:43
3	10:28		4	Libra	17:43	2	18:19		2	Gemini	23:49
6	15: 4		7	Scorpio	6:16	4	2:17		5	Cancer	0: 9
9	3:51		9	Sagittar	18:43	6	1:51		7	Leo	3:24
11	15:52		12	Capricrn	6:14	8	10:43		9	Virgo	10:14
14	13: 0		14	Aquarius	15:52	11	3:50		11	Libra	20: 8
16	17:44		16	Pisces	22:32	13	5:58		14	Scorpio	7:57
18	21: 9		19	Aries	1:48	16	6:51		16	Sagittar	20:40
20	15:56		21	Taurus	2:22	18	7:34		19	Capricrn	9:23
22	17: 2		23	Gemini	1:54	21	18:22		21	Aquarius	20:52
24	18:52		25	Cancer	2:29	23	15:49		24	Pisces	5:33
26	16:28		27	Leo	5:59	26	2:57		26	Aries	10:26
29	8:46		29	Virgo	13:22	29	9:19		28	Taurus	11:50
JUN 31	7:43		1	Libra	0: 9				30	Gemini	11:15
2	22:43		3	Scorpio	12:39	DEC 2	7: 0		2	Cancer	10:45
5	11:14		5	Sagittar	1: 1	3	13:20		4	Leo	12:20
7	22:40		8	Capricrn	12: 7	5	19:58		6	Virgo	17:27
10	16:29		10	Aquarius	21:22	8	0:15		9	Libra	2:22
13	0:56		13	Pisces	4:21	10	14:57		11	Scorpio	14: 5
14	20:54		15	Aries	8:47	13	3:57		14	Sagittar	2:54
17	3: 4		17	Taurus	10:55	16	2: 7		16	Capricrn	15:22
19	0:15		19	Gemini	11:44	18	13:55		19	Aquarius	2:29
21	11:46		21	Cancer	12:47	21	9:13		21	Pisces	11:29
22	15:33		23	Leo	15:44	23	17:34		23	Aries	17:41
25	8:28		25	Virgo	21:57	25	5:13		25	Taurus	20:58
27	7:27		27	Libra	7:41	27	6:54		27	Gemini	21:59
30	4:45		30	Scorpio	19:48	29	6:18		29	Cancer	22: 7
						31	6:23		31	Leo	23: 9

JAN			
3	6:17	3 Sagittar	6:24
4	2:6	5 Capricrn	10:24
7	11:37	7 Aquarius	12:0
8	9:23	9 Pisces	12:54
10	22:12	11 Aries	14:34
13	17:50	13 Taurus	18:2
15	23:22	15 Gemini	23:42
18	7:10	18 Cancer	7:40
20	14:46	20 Leo	17:50
23	5:1	23 Virgo	5:54
25	6:48	25 Libra	18:52
28	5:40	28 Scorpio	6:55
30	14:39	30 Sagittar	16:0

FEB			
1	19:46	1 Capricrn	21:10
2	19:51	3 Aquarius	22:57
5	21:19	5 Pisces	22:53
6	20:19	7 Aries	22:51
9	22:36	10 Taurus	0:35
12	3:2	12 Gemini	5:19
14	12:48	14 Cancer	13:20
15	15:28	17 Leo	0:4
19	9:15	19 Virgo	12:27
20	15:49	21 Libra	1:22
24	10:3	24 Scorpio	13:37
26	20:11	26 Sagittar	23:47

MAR			
1	3:6	1 Capricrn	6:39
2	17:5	3 Aquarius	9:52
5	6:50	5 Pisces	10:17
7	2:19	7 Aries	9:32
9	5:51	9 Taurus	9:40
11	11:51	11 Gemini	12:36
13	14:42	13 Cancer	19:26
15	19:28	16 Leo	5:56
18	15:17	18 Virgo	18:33
19	21:22	21 Libra	7:29
23	18:33	23 Scorpio	19:29
26	0:11	26 Sagittar	5:49
28	8:16	28 Capricrn	13:46
30	8:57	30 Aquarius	18:44

APR			
1	16:6	1 Pisces	20:43
3	0:1	3 Aries	20:42
5	15:13	5 Taurus	20:25
7	16:24	7 Gemini	22:0
9	21:4	10 Cancer	3:12
12	0:54	12 Leo	12:37
14	17:58	15 Virgo	0:57
17	10:20	17 Libra	13:54
20	0:34	20 Scorpio	1:37
22	4:44	22 Sagittar	11:27
24	12:48	24 Capricrn	19:20
26	21:58	27 Aquarius	1:8
28	22:37	29 Pisces	4:41

MAY			
30	23:45	1 Aries	6:13
3	0:59	3 Taurus	6:49
5	2:13	5 Gemini	8:17
7	6:0	7 Cancer	12:28
8	21:16	9 Leo	20:36
12	0:58	12 Virgo	8:12
14	6:53	14 Libra	21:3
17	1:49	17 Scorpio	8:43
19	14:32	19 Sagittar	18:3
21	22:35	21 Capricrn	1:9
23	23:55	24 Aquarius	6:31
26	7:2	26 Pisces	10:30
27	20:59	28 Aries	13:15
30	9:47	30 Taurus	15:17

JUN			
1	12:9	1 Gemini	17:41
3	16:15	3 Cancer	21:57
5	2:17	6 Leo	5:24
8	10:5	8 Virgo	16:13
10	12:45	11 Libra	4:51
13	11:3	13 Scorpio	16:45
15	23:17	16 Sagittar	2:4
18	3:38	18 Capricrn	8:30
19	12:27	20 Aquarius	12:49
22	11:38	22 Pisces	15:59
24	0:25	24 Aries	18:43
26	17:31	26 Taurus	21:35
28	21:10	29 Gemini	1:10

JUL			
1	2:21	1 Cancer	6:19
3	5:59	3 Leo	13:56
5	20:27	6 Virgo	0:23
8	11:51	8 Libra	12:48
11	0:7	11 Scorpio	1:6
13	8:1	13 Sagittar	11:1
15	14:56	15 Capricrn	17:32
17	11:41	17 Aquarius	21:8
19	20:58	19 Pisces	23:1
21	22:20	22 Aries	0:34
24	1:14	24 Taurus	2:57
26	5:23	26 Gemini	6:57
28	11:38	28 Cancer	13:1
30	1:6	30 Leo	21:21

AUG			
2	7:2	2 Virgo	7:58
4	10:51	4 Libra	20:18
7	8:36	7 Scorpio	8:56
9	19:47	9 Sagittar	19:49
11	14:30	12 Capricrn	3:18
12	22:24	14 Aquarius	7:8
16	1:33	16 Pisces	8:17
18	3:56	18 Aries	8:26
20	6:59	20 Taurus	9:20
22	10:27	22 Gemini	12:28
24	4:7	24 Cancer	18:34
26	19:51	27 Leo	3:30
28	20:55	29 Virgo	14:36

SEP			
30	12:52	1 Libra	3:1
3	8:58	3 Scorpio	15:47
4	15:4	6 Sagittar	3:26
7	6:45	8 Capricrn	12:20
9	18:10	10 Aquarius	17:27
11	19:7	12 Pisces	19:2
14	4:12	14 Aries	18:33
16	0:2	16 Taurus	18:1
18	11:7	18 Gemini	19:29
20	19:36	21 Cancer	0:26
23	8:49	23 Leo	9:7
25	3:55	25 Virgo	20:31
27	17:10	28 Libra	9:8
30	8:58	30 Scorpio	21:49

OCT			
2	24:0	3 Sagittar	9:40
4	15:26	5 Capricrn	19:35
7	22:31	8 Aquarius	2:22
9	20:17	10 Pisces	5:29
11	22:19	12 Aries	5:41
13	12:33	14 Taurus	4:44
15	23:22	16 Gemini	4:51
17	21:34	18 Cancer	8:5
20	10:42	20 Leo	15:31
23	0:47	23 Virgo	2:32
25	10:13	25 Libra	15:14
26	23:30	28 Scorpio	3:49
30	8:39	30 Sagittar	15:20

NOV			
1	14:38	2 Capricrn	1:18
4	6:38	4 Aquarius	9:3
6	3:16	6 Pisces	13:53
8	3:55	8 Aries	15:46
9	13:46	10 Taurus	15:45
12	0:21	12 Gemini	15:44
13	16:57	14 Cancer	17:49
16	11:55	16 Leo	23:40
19	2:10	19 Virgo	9:34
21	20:0	21 Libra	21:58
23	12:12	23 Scorpio	10:34
26	1:37	26 Sagittar	21:44
28	12:57	28 Capricrn	7:1

DEC			
30	9:19	1 Aquarius	14:26
3	5:19	3 Pisces	19:54
5	2:45	5 Aries	23:18
7	13:1	8 Taurus	1:0
9	14:50	10 Gemini	2:8
12	2:17	12 Cancer	4:22
13	5:37	14 Leo	9:21
16	6:43	16 Virgo	18:0
18	22:43	19 Libra	5:42
21	17:0	21 Scorpio	18:18
23	19:22	24 Sagittar	5:33
26	4:40	26 Capricrn	14:19
28	9:38	28 Aquarius	20:43
30	16:6	31 Pisces	1:21

```
JAN 31 15: 9   1 Cancer    0:22     JUL  1 17:38   2 Pisces    2:53
     2 16:11   3 Leo      12:54           4  1:11   4 Aries     5:12
     5 16:11   6 Virgo     1:49           6  5:32   6 Taurus   10: 2
     7 18:38   8 Libra    13:32           8 12:27   8 Gemini   17:28
    10 13:10  10 Scorpio  22: 9          10 15: 5  11 Cancer    3:13
    12 21:16  13 Sagittar  2:41          13  8:53  13 Leo      14:57
    14 19:37  15 Capricrn  3:42          15 15:49  16 Virgo     3:55
    16 21:30  17 Aquarius  2:56          18  9:53  18 Libra    16:39
    18 18:10  19 Pisces    2:32          20 23:14  21 Scorpio   3: 5
    20 14:40  21 Aries     4:27          23  3: 8  23 Sagittar  9:42
    23  0: 2  23 Taurus    9:52          25  3:35  25 Capricrn 12:29
    25  8:15  25 Gemini   18:50          27  6:18  27 Aquarius 12:42
    27 19:30  28 Cancer    6:22          29  4: 1  29 Pisces   12:13
    30 13:47  30 Leo      19: 6          31  6:39  31 Aries    12:56
FEB  1 20:11   2 Virgo     7:49     AUG  2 14:13   2 Taurus   16:19
     4  6:53   4 Libra    19:27           4 14:25   4 Gemini   23: 4
     6 17:39   7 Scorpio   4:51           6 23:52   6 Cancer    8:57
     9  0:42   9 Sagittar 11: 2           9 11:21   9 Leo      21: 0
    11  3:38  11 Capricrn 13:51          12  1:14  12 Virgo    10: 1
    13  5:38  13 Aquarius 14:15          14 22: 9  14 Libra    22:44
    15  8:11  15 Pisces   13:53          17  8:41  17 Scorpio   9:45
    17  6:26  17 Aries    14:41          19 16:18  19 Sagittar 17:44
    19 10: 0  19 Taurus   18:22          21 19:34  21 Capricrn 22: 8
    21 17:49  22 Gemini    1:52          23 21:30  23 Aquarius 23:26
    23 23:21  24 Cancer   12:49          25 17:36  25 Pisces   23: 3
    26 19: 7  27 Leo       1:35          27 20:20  27 Aries    22:49
MAR  1  6:31   1 Virgo    14:12          29 21:42  30 Taurus    0:37
     3 21:10   4 Libra     1:21     SEP  1  2:27   1 Gemini     5:53
     6  7:15   6 Scorpio  10:24           3 10:18   3 Cancer   15: 1
     8 14:51   8 Sagittar 17: 4           5 22:36   6 Leo       3: 1
    10 16:28  10 Capricrn 21:19           8 10:47   8 Virgo    16: 5
    12 22:46  12 Aquarius 23:29          10 23:44  11 Libra     4:34
    15 21:52  15 Pisces    0:27          13 10:55  13 Scorpio  15:23
    16 21:35  17 Aries     1:33          15 19:54  15 Sagittar 23:55
    19  2:45  19 Taurus    4:26          18  2: 8  18 Capricrn  5:42
    21  6:42  21 Gemini   10:33          20  4:18  20 Aquarius  8:44
    23 18:15  23 Cancer   20:23          22  6:57  22 Pisces    9:37
    25  5:45  26 Leo       8:49          24  5:22  24 Aries     9:40
    28 17: 8  28 Virgo    21:30          26  8:43  26 Taurus   10:32
    31  5:42  31 Libra     8:22          28 11:54  28 Gemini   14:32
APR  2 14:20   2 Scorpio  16:37          30 21: 5  30 Cancer   22:20
     4 20:36   4 Sagittar 22:34     OCT  3  4:37   3 Leo        9:44
     6 16:44   7 Capricrn  2:52           5 20:33   5 Virgo    22:46
     9  4:32   9 Aquarius  6: 2           8  6:26   8 Libra    11: 4
    10 18:47  11 Pisces    8:32          10 19:42  10 Scorpio  21:20
    13  9:44  13 Aries    10:56          13  3:59  13 Sagittar  5:21
    15 13:13  15 Taurus   14:17          15 10:15  15 Capricrn 11:24
    17 18:57  17 Gemini   19:55          17 14:32  17 Aquarius 15:38
    20  4:34  20 Cancer    4:50          19 17:24  19 Pisces   18:36
    22 15:57  22 Leo      16:43          21 17:16  21 Aries    19:36
    24 22:42  25 Virgo     5:31          23 20:37  23 Taurus   21: 7
    27 16: 5  27 Libra    16:35          26  0: 1  26 Gemini    0:25
    30  0: 3  30 Scorpio   0:27          28  6:47  28 Cancer    7: 3
MAY  2  5: 5   2 Sagittar  5:25          30 16:27  30 Leo      17:30
     3 18:31   4 Capricrn  8:40     NOV  2 14:47   2 Virgo      6:18
     6 11: 9   6 Aquarius 11:24           4  7:33   4 Libra    18:43
     8  5:34   8 Pisces   14:23           6 19:56   7 Scorpio   4:41
    10 17:41  10 Aries    17:56           9  5:50   9 Sagittar 11:51
    12 22: 9  12 Taurus   22:26          10  5:29  11 Capricrn 17: 0
    15  4:16  15 Gemini    4:35          13 20:57  13 Aquarius 21: 0
    16 21:29  17 Cancer   13:17          15 12:13  16 Pisces    0:19
    20  0:17  20 Leo       0:45          17 19:14  18 Aries     3:11
    21 21:10  22 Virgo    13:39          19 22:21  20 Taurus    6: 3
    25  0:39  25 Libra     1:18          22  9:44  22 Gemini    9:56
    27  8:52  27 Scorpio   9:35          23  3:50  24 Cancer   16:21
    29 13:24  29 Sagittar 14:11          26 18:15  27 Leo       2: 2
    31  4:14  31 Capricrn 16:21          29  9:27  29 Virgo    14:26
JUN  2 16:45   2 Aquarius 17:45     DEC  1 20: 9   2 Libra      3:20
     4 18:24   4 Pisces   19:51           4  7:20   4 Scorpio  13:30
     6 22: 3   6 Aries    23:24           6 15: 0   6 Sagittar 20:25
     9  3: 4   9 Taurus    4:38           8  3:17   9 Capricrn  0:31
    11  9:51  11 Gemini   11:41          10 22:49  11 Aquarius  3:12
    13  6:23  13 Cancer   20:50          12 14:24  13 Pisces    5:42
    16  5:48  16 Leo       8:16          15  5: 2  15 Aries     8:45
    18 15:22  18 Virgo    21:12          17  9:16  17 Taurus   12:39
    21  9: 2  21 Libra     9:32          19 14:45  19 Gemini   17:48
    23 15:48  23 Scorpio  18:51          22  0:42  22 Cancer    0:50
    25 21: 1  26 Sagittar  0: 6          24  8: 7  24 Leo      10:26
    28  1: 6  28 Capricrn  2: 0          26 16:36  26 Virgo    22:30
    29 23: 0  30 Aquarius  2:18          29 10:12  29 Libra    11:27
                                         31 22: 4  31 Scorpio  22:42
```

JAN	2	3:36	2 Pisces	9:19	JUL	1	3:46	1 Libra	8:47
	4	1:32	4 Aries	15:22		3	10:0	3 Scorpio	15:9
	6	14:18	7 Taurus	1:23		4	23:37	5 Sagittar	17:43
	8	18:6	9 Gemini	13:46		7	12:12	7 Capricrn	17:35
	11	23:4	12 Cancer	2:24		9	14:55	9 Aquarius	16:43
	13	23:51	14 Leo	14:0		11	10:55	11 Pisces	17:19
	16	8:46	17 Virgo	0:4		13	15:47	13 Aries	21:7
	19	4:47	19 Libra	8:15		15	20:34	16 Taurus	4:49
	21	8:27	21 Scorpio	14:0		18	6:59	18 Gemini	15:41
	22	23:53	23 Sagittar	17:3		20	18:28	21 Cancer	4:9
	25	14:54	25 Capricrn	18:0		23	3:6	23 Leo	16:46
	26	13:59	27 Aquarius	18:19		25	18:42	26 Virgo	4:32
	29	10:53	29 Pisces	19:57		28	8:24	28 Libra	14:34
FEB	31	15:42	1 Aries	0:40		30	11:57	30 Scorpio	21:55
	3	0:33	3 Taurus	9:17	AUG	2	1:57	2 Sagittar	2:5
	5	5:52	5 Gemini	20:59		3	18:5	4 Capricrn	3:26
	8	5:16	8 Cancer	9:38		5	18:1	6 Aquarius	3:21
	10	1:38	10 Leo	21:9		8	0:51	8 Pisces	3:42
	13	1:30	13 Virgo	6:35		10	5:5	10 Aries	6:22
	15	9:44	15 Libra	13:56		12	1:15	12 Taurus	12:36
	17	16:0	17 Scorpio	19:24		14	5:37	14 Gemini	22:30
	19	21:31	19 Sagittar	23:12		16	22:38	17 Cancer	10:43
	21	23:35	22 Capricrn	1:40		18	11:56	19 Leo	23:18
	23	14:20	24 Aquarius	3:33		22	9:16	22 Virgo	10:42
	26	5:1	26 Pisces	6:4		24	8:27	24 Libra	20:10
	28	10:6	28 Aries	10:38		26	16:14	27 Scorpio	3:24
MAR	29	19:53	1 Taurus	18:19		28	21:52	29 Sagittar	8:20
	3	20:8	4 Gemini	5:8		31	5:53	31 Capricrn	11:9
	6	6:3	6 Cancer	17:37	SEP	2	11:58	2 Aquarius	12:36
	8	14:33	8 Leo	5:26		4	4:58	4 Pisces	13:51
	11	3:24	11 Virgo	14:48		6	6:30	6 Aries	16:26
	13	8:26	13 Libra	21:20		8	11:58	8 Taurus	21:45
	16	1:36	16 Scorpio	1:38		11	2:39	11 Gemini	6:31
	18	0:16	18 Sagittar	4:38		13	9:51	13 Cancer	18:11
	20	6:41	20 Capricrn	7:15		15	16:17	16 Leo	6:47
	21	12:35	22 Aquarius	10:11		18	15:34	18 Virgo	18:7
	24	1:40	24 Pisces	14:2		21	2:56	21 Libra	2:59
	25	21:1	26 Aries	19:30		23	1:14	23 Scorpio	9:18
	28	20:48	29 Taurus	3:14		25	3:8	25 Sagittar	13:42
	31	10:46	31 Gemini	13:32		27	9:59	27 Capricrn	16:54
APR	2	8:7	3 Cancer	1:46		29	14:34	29 Aquarius	19:33
	5	3:31	5 Leo	14:1	OCT	1	16:9	1 Pisces	22:15
	6	23:37	8 Virgo	0:2		3	20:0	4 Aries	1:47
	9	16:51	10 Libra	6:36		6	1:38	6 Taurus	7:9
	11	20:28	12 Scorpio	10:2		8	4:48	8 Gemini	15:17
	14	7:52	14 Sagittar	11:38		10	21:32	11 Cancer	2:19
	16	6:52	16 Capricrn	13:1		12	17:26	13 Leo	14:55
	18	12:57	18 Aquarius	15:32		15	23:28	16 Virgo	2:41
	19	20:52	20 Pisces	19:56		18	9:13	18 Libra	11:33
	22	5:6	23 Aries	2:23		20	15:31	20 Scorpio	17:6
	24	13:8	25 Taurus	10:51		22	12:0	22 Sagittar	20:16
	26	23:43	27 Gemini	21:17		24	22:8	24 Capricrn	22:29
	29	23:51	30 Cancer	9:23		26	14:44	27 Aquarius	0:58
MAY	2	19:28	2 Leo	21:59		28	20:17	29 Pisces	4:27
	4	7:43	5 Virgo	8:59		30	21:11	31 Aries	9:12
	7	11:16	7 Libra	16:31	NOV	2	7:4	2 Taurus	15:28
	9	0:27	9 Scorpio	20:7		4	15:7	4 Gemini	23:45
	11	5:43	11 Sagittar	20:56		7	1:33	7 Cancer	10:26
	13	0:12	13 Capricrn	20:51		8	22:5	9 Leo	23:0
	15	13:1	15 Aquarius	21:52		12	3:39	12 Virgo	11:24
	17	20:24	18 Pisces	1:24		14	19:54	14 Libra	21:8
	20	6:30	20 Aries	7:56		16	19:26	17 Scorpio	2:54
	21	17:51	22 Taurus	17:0		18	23:47	19 Sagittar	5:17
	24	19:32	25 Gemini	3:55		20	23:10	21 Capricrn	6:2
	26	14:42	27 Cancer	16:7		22	12:21	23 Aquarius	7:5
	29	3:52	30 Leo	4:51		25	2:34	25 Pisces	9:50
JUN	1	11:49	1 Virgo	16:38		26	18:5	27 Aries	14:51
	2	6:4	3 Libra	1:32		28	10:29	29 Taurus	22:0
	5	11:27	6 Scorpio	6:20	DEC	1	22:56	2 Gemini	7:1
	7	11:50	8 Sagittar	7:31		4	9:32	4 Cancer	17:53
	10	6:46	10 Capricrn	6:48		7	4:46	7 Leo	6:21
	11	20:18	12 Aquarius	6:23		9	10:43	9 Virgo	19:14
	14	7:24	14 Pisces	8:18		11	9:39	11 Libra	6:11
	16	12:14	16 Aries	13:43		14	5:39	14 Scorpio	13:14
	18	20:25	18 Taurus	22:34		16	9:2	16 Sagittar	16:7
	20	22:37	21 Gemini	9:46		18	10:47	18 Capricrn	16:17
	23	18:40	23 Cancer	22:10		19	21:17	20 Aquarius	15:49
	26	7:19	26 Leo	10:52		22	9:28	22 Pisces	16:48
	28	18:13	28 Virgo	22:53		24	12:55	24 Aries	20:35
						27	2:58	27 Taurus	3:31
						29	4:10	29 Gemini	13:2

Date	Time		Sign	Time
JAN 1	14:34	1	Libra	15:22
3	18:21	3	Scorpio	18:42
5	17:34	5	Sagittar	20:56
7	15:57	7	Capricrn	22:50
9	18:7	10	Aquarius	1:52
12	0:7	12	Pisces	7:40
14	9:53	14	Aries	17:10
16	21:27	17	Taurus	5:33
19	15:57	19	Gemini	18:16
21	4:28	22	Cancer	4:47
24	8:19	24	Leo	12:14
26	14:1	26	Virgo	17:14
28	18:16	28	Libra	20:55
30	23:23	31	Scorpio	0:6
FEB 2	1:30	2	Sagittar	3:11
3	3:40	4	Capricrn	6:29
6	9:52	6	Aquarius	10:41
8	16:28	8	Pisces	16:51
9	14:30	11	Aries	1:55
13	0:47	13	Taurus	13:48
15	22:23	16	Gemini	2:40
18	12:7	18	Cancer	13:51
20	12:52	20	Leo	21:38
21	21:41	23	Virgo	2:6
23	23:53	25	Libra	4:29
26	2:40	27	Scorpio	6:15
MAR 28	18:40	1	Sagittar	8:33
3	5:25	3	Capricrn	12:6
4	11:9	5	Aquarius	17:17
6	17:1	8	Pisces	0:26
9	10:52	10	Aries	9:54
11	23:43	12	Taurus	21:37
14	21:26	15	Gemini	10:31
17	15:11	17	Cancer	22:28
20	5:53	20	Leo	7:23
21	17:49	22	Virgo	12:28
23	22:43	24	Libra	14:27
26	1:18	26	Scorpio	14:54
27	11:0	28	Sagittar	15:32
30	7:20	30	Capricrn	17:49
APR 31	16:27	1	Aquarius	22:42
3	23:37	4	Pisces	6:23
6	12:16	6	Aries	16:33
9	3:5	9	Taurus	4:32
11	8:57	11	Gemini	17:25
13	15:48	14	Cancer	5:48
16	7:33	16	Leo	15:55
18	18:56	18	Virgo	22:28
19	10:44	21	Libra	1:19
21	21:12	23	Scorpio	1:34
25	0:55	25	Sagittar	0:59
25	21:45	27	Capricrn	1:33
29	4:4	29	Aquarius	4:56
MAY 1	10:35	1	Pisces	11:59
3	20:18	3	Aries	22:19
5	23:51	6	Taurus	10:39
8	20:18	8	Gemini	23:35
11	7:6	11	Cancer	11:57
13	18:24	13	Leo	22:41
16	2:3	16	Virgo	6:38
18	6:22	18	Libra	11:7
20	0:54	20	Scorpio	12:25
22	6:39	22	Sagittar	11:51
23	7:51	24	Capricrn	11:24
26	7:17	26	Aquarius	13:10
28	11:10	28	Pisces	18:43
31	3:10	31	Aries	4:19
JUN 2	6:34	2	Taurus	16:37
5	1:35	5	Gemini	5:36
6	21:55	7	Cancer	17:44
9	17:41	10	Leo	4:19
12	2:10	12	Virgo	12:51
14	8:11	14	Libra	18:42
16	12:43	16	Scorpio	21:39
18	12:2	18	Sagittar	22:15
20	20:0	20	Capricrn	22:2
22	11:49	22	Aquarius	23:1
24	14:50	25	Pisces	3:10
27	7:37	27	Aries	11:28
29	7:10	29	Taurus	23:11

Date	Time		Sign	Time
JUL 2	1:0	2	Gemini	12:6
4	17:53	5	Cancer	0:4
6	19:37	7	Leo	10:8
9	5:28	9	Virgo	18:16
11	10:38	12	Libra	0:27
13	21:39	14	Scorpio	4:34
16	2:15	16	Sagittar	6:42
18	5:27	18	Capricrn	7:42
20	3:34	20	Aquarius	9:5
21	22:50	22	Pisces	12:41
24	5:4	24	Aries	19:54
26	8:33	27	Taurus	6:44
29	3:41	29	Gemini	19:24
AUG 31	4:48	1	Cancer	7:24
3	2:47	3	Leo	17:10
5	10:43	6	Virgo	0:30
7	16:58	8	Libra	5:57
10	10:59	10	Scorpio	10:0
12	0:59	12	Sagittar	12:59
13	23:49	14	Capricrn	15:19
16	6:21	16	Aquarius	17:54
18	12:51	18	Pisces	22:0
20	16:50	21	Aries	4:52
23	14:24	23	Taurus	14:59
25	15:16	26	Gemini	3:19
28	4:22	28	Cancer	15:34
30	18:2	31	Leo	1:34
SEP 1	23:18	2	Virgo	8:31
4	11:19	4	Libra	12:57
5	20:9	6	Scorpio	15:53
8	11:5	8	Sagittar	18:21
10	1:39	10	Capricrn	21:5
12	18:14	13	Aquarius	0:44
14	23:46	15	Pisces	5:54
17	7:31	17	Aries	13:17
19	1:46	19	Taurus	23:13
22	11:0	22	Gemini	11:16
24	23:46	24	Cancer	23:50
27	7:50	27	Leo	10:37
29	16:11	29	Virgo	18:5
OCT 1	21:1	1	Libra	22:9
3	9:0	3	Scorpio	23:54
5	8:18	6	Sagittar	0:55
7	23:35	8	Capricrn	2:39
9	16:28	10	Aquarius	6:13
12	0:35	12	Pisces	12:6
13	0:42	14	Aries	20:20
17	0:52	17	Taurus	6:40
18	23:17	19	Gemini	18:40
22	3:17	22	Cancer	7:23
24	2:6	24	Leo	19:4
26	18:17	27	Virgo	3:49
29	5:1	29	Libra	8:42
30	19:12	31	Scorpio	10:15
NOV 1	22:9	2	Sagittar	10:2
4	1:9	4	Capricrn	10:5
6	6:24	6	Aquarius	12:14
8	1:4	8	Pisces	17:36
10	1:5	11	Aries	2:10
12	19:11	13	Taurus	13:5
15	9:42	16	Gemini	1:17
17	19:49	18	Cancer	13:57
20	21:46	21	Leo	2:4
22	21:38	23	Virgo	12:8
25	18:5	25	Libra	18:42
27	6:40	27	Scorpio	21:22
29	16:42	29	Sagittar	21:12
DEC 1	9:0	1	Capricrn	20:11
3	12:50	3	Aquarius	20:35
5	20:34	6	Pisces	0:17
7	22:26	8	Aries	8:0
10	1:1	10	Taurus	18:56
13	6:35	13	Gemini	7:25
15	4:49	15	Cancer	20:1
16	16:48	18	Leo	7:58
20	14:36	20	Virgo	18:30
22	1:56	23	Libra	2:29
24	15:11	25	Scorpio	7:1
26	19:45	27	Sagittar	8:16
28	16:56	29	Capricrn	7:38
31	2:57	31	Aquarius	7:15

Month	Day	Time	Day	Sign	Time
JAN	1	8:43	2	Gemini	12:22
	4	16:42	4	Cancer	18:22
	6	20:11	6	Leo	21:22
	8	22:12	8	Virgo	22:59
	10	20: 7	11	Libra	0:52
	13	3:59	13	Scorpio	4: 3
	14	22:38	15	Sagittar	8:50
	16	23: 3	17	Capricrn	15:13
	19	22: 8	19	Aquarius	23:23
	21	17:16	22	Pisces	9:42
	24	6:55	24	Aries	22: 3
	26	23:46	27	Taurus	10:57
	28	21:19	29	Gemini	21:48
FEB	1	1:15	1	Cancer	4:41
	2	22:32	3	Leo	7:38
	4	20:57	5	Virgo	8:11
	6	21:20	7	Libra	8:24
	8	22:49	9	Scorpio	10: 3
	10	23:34	11	Sagittar	14:12
	13	10:11	13	Capricrn	20:56
	14	11:15	16	Aquarius	5:52
	18	15:39	18	Pisces	16:40
	20	17:17	21	Aries	5: 2
	23	13:13	23	Taurus	18: 5
	25	0:49	26	Gemini	5:53
	28	4:35	28	Cancer	14:17
MAR	1	23:32	2	Leo	18:27
	4	10:43	4	Virgo	19:15
	6	10:43	6	Libra	18:36
	8	10:36	8	Scorpio	18:35
	10	13:38	10	Sagittar	20:57
	12	17:55	13	Capricrn	2:37
	15	8:44	15	Aquarius	11:28
	17	13:34	17	Pisces	22:42
	20	9:50	20	Aries	11:17
	22	23:50	23	Taurus	0:16
	24	12:39	25	Gemini	12:20
	27	20:32	27	Cancer	21:53
	30	2: 5	30	Leo	3:46
APR	1	4:36	1	Virgo	6: 1
	2	23: 8	3	Libra	5:54
	5	2:55	5	Scorpio	5:17
	6	4:45	7	Sagittar	6: 7
	9	6: 6	9	Capricrn	10: 1
	11	16:44	11	Aquarius	17:42
	14	43:35	14	Pisces	4:39
	16	8:26	16	Aries	17:23
	19	6: 5	19	Taurus	6:17
	21	17:49	21	Gemini	18: 3
	24	3:31	24	Cancer	3:47
	26	2:59	26	Leo	10:44
	28	14:23	28	Virgo	14:41
	30	8:19	30	Libra	16: 7
MAY	2	15:55	2	Scorpio	16:15
	4	16:23	4	Sagittar	16:44
	6	18:59	6	Capricrn	19:21
	8	14:43	9	Aquarius	1:30
	11	11: 1	11	Pisces	11:27
	12	12:53	13	Aries	23:58
	16	12:24	16	Taurus	12:50
	18	23:50	19	Gemini	0:14
	21	9: 1	21	Cancer	9:23
	23	3:20	23	Leo	16:15
	25	20:43	25	Virgo	21: 0
	27	13:19	27	Libra	23:56
	30	1:20	30	Scorpio	1:34
JUN	1	2:42	1	Sagittar	2:54
	5	5:13	3	Capricrn	5:23
	5	8:48	5	Aquarius	10:34
	7	19:19	7	Pisces	19:24
	9	16:39	10	Aries	7:21
	12	5:10	12	Taurus	20:13
	14	2: 2	15	Gemini	7:31
	17	8: 0	17	Cancer	16: 4
	19	7:26	19	Leo	22: 4
	21	15:36	22	Virgo	2:22
	23	23:46	24	Libra	5:43
	25	18:42	26	Scorpio	8:31
	27	10:52	28	Sagittar	11:12
	30	0:37	30	Capricrn	14:33

Month	Day	Time	Day	Sign	Time
JUL	2	11:27	2	Aquarius	19:45
	4	12:51	5	Pisces	3:57
	6	20:50	7	Aries	15:18
	9	12:41	10	Taurus	4:10
	11	18: 3	12	Gemini	15:47
	14	16:29	15	Cancer	0:16
	17	0:47	17	Leo	5:31
	19	6:32	19	Virgo	8:42
	21	9:32	21	Libra	11:12
	23	8:31	23	Scorpio	13:58
	25	16: 9	25	Sagittar	17:26
	27	11: 3	27	Capricrn	21:53
	29	17: 6	30	Aquarius	3:53
AUG	1	1:25	1	Pisces	12:12
	3	2:11	3	Aries	23:15
	6	1:51	6	Taurus	12: 5
	8	5:25	9	Gemini	0:17
	11	1:20	11	Cancer	9:26
	13	9: 6	13	Leo	14:44
	15	10:55	15	Virgo	17: 7
	17	0:31	17	Libra	18:17
	19	14:36	19	Scorpio	19:50
	21	19:45	21	Sagittar	22:48
	24	2:50	24	Capricrn	3:39
	26	6:35	26	Aquarius	10:28
	28	16: 9	28	Pisces	19:25
	30	15:14	31	Aries	6:36
SEP	2	17:44	2	Taurus	19:24
	4	22:27	5	Gemini	8: 7
	7	13:51	7	Cancer	18:23
	9	18:28	10	Leo	0:42
	11	22:45	12	Virgo	3:20
	14	0:25	14	Libra	3:45
	15	10:56	16	Scorpio	3:50
	18	3:53	18	Sagittar	5:16
	20	3:18	20	Capricrn	9:13
	22	14:19	22	Aquarius	16: 4
	24	5:53	25	Pisces	1:34
	27	7: 3	27	Aries	13: 8
	29	5:54	30	Taurus	1:58
OCT	2	11:50	2	Gemini	14:51
	4	7:27	5	Cancer	2: 1
	6	2:13	7	Leo	9:51
	8	22:11	9	Virgo	13:50
	11	0: 8	11	Libra	14:44
	13	6:10	13	Scorpio	14:12
	14	15: 6	15	Sagittar	14: 9
	17	4:56	17	Capricrn	16:23
	19	14: 7	19	Aquarius	22: 4
	22	3:54	22	Pisces	7:20
	24	2:56	24	Aries	19:11
	27	20:23	27	Taurus	8: 8
	29	20:23	29	Gemini	20:50
NOV	31	17:46	1	Cancer	8: 9
	3	14: 1	3	Leo	17: 3
	5	18:40	5	Virgo	22:46
	7	20:14	8	Libra	1:17
	9	15:11	10	Scorpio	1:30
	11	17:55	12	Sagittar	1: 3
	13	15:49	14	Capricrn	1:55
	15	19:14	16	Aquarius	5:53
	18	8:33	18	Pisces	13:57
	20	21:34	21	Aries	1:29
	23	4:14	23	Taurus	14:31
	25	8:27	26	Gemini	3: 1
	28	5:12	28	Cancer	13:52
	30	2:44	30	Leo	22:41
DEC	2	22:16	2	Virgo	5:18
	5	3:14	5	Libra	9:31
	7	5:50	7	Scorpio	11:29
	8	18:57	9	Sagittar	12: 2
	11	7:54	11	Capricrn	12:47
	12	22:47	13	Aquarius	15:38
	15	17:36	15	Pisces	22:12
	18	4:27	18	Aries	8:46
	20	18:19	20	Taurus	21:38
	23	18:38	23	Gemini	10: 9
	25	18: 9	25	Cancer	20:33
	27	15:59	28	Leo	4:34
	30	9:24	30	Virgo	10:41

Mo	D	Time	D	Sign	Time
JAN	2	12: 4	2	Aquarius	17:25
	4	8:36	5	Pisces	6: 5
	7	6:58	7	Aries	18:23
	9	21:29	10	Taurus	4:27
	11	19:30	12	Gemini	10:44
	13	22:42	14	Cancer	13: 6
	16	6:22	16	Leo	12:51
	18	11:57	18	Virgo	12: 4
	19	6:51	20	Libra	12:55
	22	16:46	22	Scorpio	17: 3
	25	0:28	25	Sagittar	0:52
	27	11: 1	27	Capricrn	11:33
	29	4:24	29	Aquarius	23:42
FEB	1	11:35	1	Pisces	12:21
	3	19:39	4	Aries	0:42
	6	10:40	6	Taurus	11:38
	8	18:35	8	Gemini	19:35
	10	22:38	10	Cancer	23:39
	11	13:51	13	Leo	0:19
	14	22:11	14	Virgo	23:17
	15	20: 3	16	Libra	22:50
	18	23:42	18	Scorpio	1: 6
	21	7: 5	21	Sagittar	7:23
	23	16:37	23	Capricrn	17:27
	26	4:19	26	Aquarius	5:43
	28	16:18	28	Pisces	18:25
MAR	3	4:17	3	Aries	6:31
	5	15: 5	5	Taurus	17:21
	7	23:48	8	Gemini	2: 4
	10	5:32	10	Cancer	7:45
	12	6:16	12	Leo	10:20
	14	8:10	14	Virgo	10:20
	16	8:26	16	Libra	9:59
	18	8:47	18	Scorpio	11:15
	20	15:28	20	Sagittar	15:54
	22	21:33	23	Capricrn	0:35
	25	11: 4	25	Aquarius	12: 8
	27	21:40	28	Pisces	1: 0
	30	3:38	30	Aries	12:55
APR	1	19:51	1	Taurus	23:11
	4	4:14	4	Gemini	7:31
	6	10:25	6	Cancer	13:38
	8	7:38	8	Leo	17:25
	10	16: 9	10	Virgo	19:13
	12	10: 2	12	Libra	20: 9
	14	18:31	14	Scorpio	21:46
	16	22:15	17	Sagittar	1:43
	19	7:10	19	Capricrn	9: 8
	21	5:56	21	Aquarius	19:54
	24	4:19	24	Pisces	8:23
	26	10:10	26	Aries	20:51
	29	2:25	29	Taurus	6:18
MAY	1	10: 3	1	Gemini	13:47
	3	18:10	3	Cancer	19: 9
	5	9:26	5	Leo	22:54
	7	22: 8	8	Virgo	1:37
	9	20:30	10	Libra	3:58
	12	3:15	12	Scorpio	6:49
	14	7:32	14	Sagittar	11:14
	16	14:21	16	Capricrn	18:14
	18	23:45	19	Aquarius	4:13
	21	12:13	21	Pisces	16:21
	23	12:22	24	Aries	4:34
	26	10:55	26	Taurus	14:44
	28	18:14	28	Gemini	21:47
	30	22:44	31	Cancer	2: 6
JUN	1	13:32	2	Leo	4:46
	4	3:46	4	Virgo	7: 0
	6	8:38	6	Libra	9:46
	8	10:25	8	Scorpio	13:41
	10	15:51	10	Sagittar	19:10
	12	23:14	13	Capricrn	2:37
	15	4:38	15	Aquarius	12:24
	18	0:12	18	Pisces	0:15
	20	11:28	20	Aries	12:46
	22	23:29	22	Taurus	23:59
	25	4:19	25	Gemini	7: 7
	27	10:49	27	Cancer	11: 1
	29	12:18	29	Leo	12:31

Mo	D	Time	D	Sign	Time
JUL	1	13:10	1	Virgo	13:24
	3	6:21	3	Libra	15:16
	5	18:53	5	Scorpio	19:10
	7	23: 0	8	Sagittar	1:21
	10	9:16	10	Capricrn	9:35
	12	19:23	12	Aquarius	19:43
	15	7:12	15	Pisces	7:33
	17	13:26	17	Aries	20:15
	20	7:40	20	Taurus	7:58
	22	15:44	22	Gemini	16:34
	24	20:52	24	Cancer	21: 6
	26	22: 6	26	Leo	22:17
	28	21:51	28	Virgo	22: 0
	30	20:16	30	Libra	22:20
AUG	2	0:55	2	Scorpio	1: 1
	4	5:54	4	Sagittar	6:48
	6	15:14	6	Capricrn	15:24
	7	21:19	9	Aquarius	2: 2
	11	13:32	11	Pisces	14: 2
	13	10:46	14	Aries	2:46
	14	14:51	16	Taurus	15: 1
	19	0:51	19	Gemini	0:52
	21	2:58	21	Cancer	6:49
	22	23:46	23	Leo	8:52
	23	22:55	25	Virgo	8:26
	27	0: 8	27	Libra	7:42
	27	22:54	29	Scorpio	8:46
	31	3:18	31	Sagittar	13: 7
SEP	2	8:34	2	Capricrn	21: 6
	4	15:35	5	Aquarius	7:50
	7	3: 4	7	Pisces	20: 4
	9	13:43	10	Aries	8:45
	12	17:21	12	Taurus	20:58
	14	19:53	15	Gemini	7:27
	17	6:50	17	Cancer	14:50
	19	13:32	19	Leo	18:31
	20	11:22	21	Virgo	19:12
	23	18: 6	23	Libra	18:33
	24	11: 3	25	Scorpio	18:41
	26	20:54	27	Sagittar	21:28
	29	7: 5	29	Capricrn	4: 0
OCT	1	23:37	2	Aquarius	14: 4
	4	13:33	5	Pisces	2:18
	7	8:45	7	Aries	14:57
	8	21:45	10	Taurus	2:48
	11	0:27	12	Gemini	13: 1
	14	3:33	14	Cancer	20:55
	16	13:44	17	Leo	2: 0
	18	20:28	19	Virgo	4:24
	19	22:45	21	Libra	5: 4
	23	4:44	23	Scorpio	5:31
	24	0:15	25	Sagittar	7:34
	26	21: 1	27	Capricrn	12:41
	29	7:57	29	Aquarius	21:33
NOV	31	22:40	1	Pisces	9:19
	3	17: 3	3	Aries	22: 0
	6	13:13	6	Taurus	9:38
	8	9:26	8	Gemini	19: 9
	10	7:42	11	Cancer	2:24
	12	14:23	13	Leo	7:37
	14	22: 0	15	Virgo	11: 7
	17	4:22	17	Libra	13:26
	19	1: 5	19	Scorpio	15:18
	21	16:20	21	Sagittar	17:52
	23	8:42	23	Capricrn	22:30
	25	16:27	26	Aquarius	6:16
	28	5:53	28	Pisces	17:16
DEC	1	2:18	1	Aries	5:57
	3	12:32	3	Taurus	17:48
	6	2: 9	6	Gemini	3: 1
	8	0:20	8	Cancer	9:16
	10	5:23	10	Leo	13:24
	12	9:11	12	Virgo	16:29
	14	9:14	14	Libra	19:23
	16	16:25	16	Scorpio	22:36
	18	21:30	19	Sagittar	2:31
	21	6:12	21	Capricrn	7:47
	23	10:26	23	Aquarius	15:19
	25	21:15	26	Pisces	1:41
	27	15:47	28	Aries	14:13
	30	23:34	31	Taurus	2:38

JAN					JUL				
1	15:46	1	Virgo	17:31	2	20:51	2	Taurus	22:26
3	20:18	3	Libra	21:44	5	1:37	5	Gemini	2:26
6	2:43	6	Scorpio	6: 0	7	3: 9	7	Cancer	3:20
8	16:48	8	Sagittar	17:33	8	23: 0	9	Leo	2:42
11	2:55	11	Capricrn	6:34	10	22:45	11	Virgo	2:35
13	18:51	13	Aquarius	19:20	12	22:43	13	Libra	4:55
16	3:17	16	Pisces	6:48	15	6:35	15	Scorpio	10:57
18	11:18	18	Aries	16:18	17	15: 8	17	Sagittar	20:38
20	22:59	20	Taurus	23:12	20	3:59	20	Capricrn	8:41
23	2:16	23	Gemini	3: 6	22	16:48	22	Aquarius	21:29
25	3:11	25	Cancer	4:20	25	5:17	25	Pisces	9:51
25	20:29	27	Leo	4: 7	27	13:28	27	Aries	20:54
29	2:23	29	Virgo	4:18	30	1:32	30	Taurus	5:41
31	6:42	31	Libra	6:56	AUG 1	7:11	1	Gemini	11:16
FEB 2	13:29	2	Scorpio	13:33	2	12:39	3	Cancer	13:33
4	23:33	4	Sagittar	0:13	5	10: 3	5	Leo	13:27
7	8:27	7	Capricrn	13: 9	7	9:27	7	Virgo	12:50
10	0:47	10	Aquarius	1:52	9	7:33	9	Libra	13:51
12	8: 1	12	Pisces	12:52	11	14:40	11	Scorpio	18:21
14	21:21	14	Aries	21:49	13	23:12	14	Sagittar	3: 0
17	3:21	17	Taurus	4:49	16	11: 1	16	Capricrn	14:48
19	9:22	19	Gemini	9:51	18	23:45	19	Aquarius	3:38
21	8:16	21	Cancer	12:50	21	12:38	21	Pisces	15:48
23	12:29	23	Leo	14:11	23	20:16	24	Aries	2:30
25	11:28	25	Virgo	15: 5	26	8:31	26	Taurus	11:24
27	16: 2	27	Libra	17:21	28	15:23	28	Gemini	18: 0
29	20:28	29	Scorpio	22:45	30	19:30	30	Cancer	21:52
MAR 3	5:35	3	Sagittar	8:10	SEP 1	20:40	1	Leo	23:14
5	15:16	5	Capricrn	20:33	3	21:19	3	Virgo	23:21
8	6:27	8	Aquarius	9:20	5	19:48	6	Libra	0: 5
10	18:13	10	Pisces	20:12	8	2:58	8	Scorpio	3:27
13	1:37	13	Aries	4:27	10	8:44	10	Sagittar	10:46
15	10:25	15	Taurus	10:32	12	19:47	12	Capricrn	21:46
17	12:23	17	Gemini	15:12	15	8: 3	15	Aquarius	10:28
19	18:31	19	Cancer	18:48	17	20:55	17	Pisces	22:34
21	21:10	21	Leo	21:31	20	5:24	20	Aries	8:48
23	23:27	23	Virgo	23:53	22	15:45	22	Taurus	17: 1
26	0: 0	26	Libra	3: 0	24	22:18	24	Gemini	23:25
28	7:39	28	Scorpio	8:19	27	3: 2	27	Cancer	4: 0
30	13:30	30	Sagittar	16:56	29	5:36	29	Leo	6:49
APR 2	3:39	2	Capricrn	4:38	OCT 1	7:40	1	Virgo	8:25
4	16:18	4	Aquarius	17:25	3	8:53	3	Libra	10: 2
7	3:26	7	Pisces	4:38	5	12:44	5	Scorpio	13:19
9	9:33	9	Aries	12:47	7	19:16	7	Sagittar	19:46
11	16:46	11	Taurus	18: 4	10	5:22	10	Capricrn	5:48
13	20:17	13	Gemini	21:31	12	17:40	12	Aquarius	18:10
15	22:48	16	Cancer	0:15	15	6:12	15	Pisces	6:25
18	1:28	18	Leo	3: 1	16	23:26	17	Aries	16:36
20	4:37	20	Virgo	6:17	20	0: 7	20	Taurus	0: 8
22	7:41	22	Libra	10:37	21	15:17	22	Gemini	5:29
24	14:44	24	Scorpio	16:45	23	20:15	24	Cancer	9:24
26	22:23	27	Sagittar	1:26	26	0:47	26	Leo	12:27
29	10:17	29	Capricrn	12:45	28	6:29	28	Virgo	15:10
MAY 1	22:51	2	Aquarius	1:28	30	13:24	30	Libra	18:10
4	10:37	4	Pisces	13:16	NOV 31	6: 5	1	Scorpio	22:25
6	20:32	6	Aries	22: 6	3	18:29	4	Sagittar	4:57
9	1:11	9	Taurus	3:24	6	4:13	6	Capricrn	14:24
11	3:59	11	Gemini	6: 1	8	16:41	9	Aquarius	2:20
13	4:46	13	Cancer	7:21	10	15:10	11	Pisces	14:51
15	8:43	15	Leo	8:52	13	18: 1	14	Aries	1:37
17	11:15	17	Virgo	11:40	15	10:44	16	Taurus	9:13
19	15:42	19	Libra	16:27	18	12:45	18	Gemini	13:45
21	21:51	21	Scorpio	23:29	20	11:30	20	Cancer	16:18
24	7:18	24	Sagittar	8:47	22	13:54	22	Leo	18:10
26	16:25	26	Capricrn	20:12	24	18:58	24	Virgo	20:32
29	7:45	29	Aquarius	8:52	26	20:47	27	Libra	0:11
31	18:35	31	Pisces	21:10	28	1:19	29	Scorpio	5:35
JUN 3	6:28	3	Aries	7: 5	DEC 1	10:28	1	Sagittar	12:59
5	12:59	5	Taurus	13:22	3	20:35	3	Capricrn	22:36
7	15:58	7	Gemini	16:10	6	10:14	6	Aquarius	10:17
9	13:18	9	Cancer	16:42	7	17:52	8	Pisces	22:57
11	13:27	11	Leo	16:45	11	10:17	11	Aries	10:37
13	14:24	13	Virgo	18: 4	13	2:50	13	Taurus	19:16
15	17:51	15	Libra	21:59	15	15:15	16	Gemini	0: 7
18	0:50	18	Scorpio	5: 3	17	19: 7	18	Cancer	1:52
20	9:49	20	Sagittar	14:56	19	3:31	20	Leo	2:11
22	22: 8	22	Capricrn	2:43	20	15: 9	22	Virgo	2:56
25	10:46	25	Aquarius	15:26	23	15: 4	24	Libra	5:39
28	0:29	28	Pisces	3:55	26	0:15	26	Scorpio	11: 9
30	8:44	30	Aries	14:43	28	11:44	28	Sagittar	19:20
					29	19:20	31	Capricrn	5:37

JAN	31	20:26	1	Aries	1:57			
	3	2: 6	3	Taurus	5:25			
	5	5:40	5	Gemini	7: 5			
	7	4:54	7	Cancer	8: 1			
	9	6:32	9	Leo	9:42			
	11	10:24	11	Virgo	13:43			
	13	19:22	13	Libra	21:15			
	16	4:37	16	Scorpio	8:15			
	18	16:36	18	Sagittar	21: 2			
	21	5:39	21	Capricrn	9:10			
	23	15:39	23	Aquarius	18:59			
	25	23: 1	26	Pisces	2:11			
	27	22:53	28	Aries	7:20			
	30	8: 6	30	Taurus	11: 6			
FEB	1	12:37	1	Gemini	14: 3			
	3	16: 1	3	Cancer	16:37			
	5	16:27	5	Leo	19:29			
	7	20:34	7	Virgo	23:43			
	9	20:33	10	Libra	6:34			
	12	13: 1	12	Scorpio	16:39			
	14	20: 8	15	Sagittar	5: 7			
	17	13:54	17	Capricrn	17:35			
	20	0: 1	20	Aquarius	3:34			
	22	6:47	22	Pisces	10:10			
	24	4: 9	24	Aries	14: 6			
	26	13:28	26	Taurus	16:47			
	28	11:21	28	Gemini	19:24			
MAR	2	19:10	2	Cancer	22:40			
	4	23:11	5	Leo	2:49			
	7	4:21	7	Virgo	8: 9			
	9	3:48	9	Libra	15:20			
	11	20:45	12	Scorpio	1: 5			
	14	4:17	14	Sagittar	13:14			
	16	23:51	17	Capricrn	2: 2			
	19	8:57	19	Aquarius	12:47			
	21	15:28	21	Pisces	19:45			
	23	12:29	23	Aries	23:10			
	25	20:25	26	Taurus	0:32			
	27	20:35	28	Gemini	1:42			
	30	3:25	30	Cancer	4: 6			
APR	1	3:36	1	Leo	8:21			
	3	9:30	3	Virgo	14:31			
	5	19:44	5	Libra	22:34			
	8	3: 0	8	Scorpio	8:38			
	10	20:33	10	Sagittar	20:42			
	13	3:36	13	Capricrn	9:41			
	15	15:22	15	Aquarius	21:20			
	18	0:26	18	Pisces	5:29			
	20	0: 9	20	Aries	9:30			
	22	5:17	22	Taurus	10:30			
	24	9:59	24	Gemini	10:24			
	26	5:37	26	Cancer	11: 9			
	28	8:13	28	Leo	14: 9			
	30	13:36	30	Virgo	19:58			
MAY	2	17: 0	3	Libra	4:26			
	5	7:57	5	Scorpio	15: 4			
	7	15:44	8	Sagittar	3:19			
	10	8:45	10	Capricrn	16:19			
	12	21: 1	13	Aquarius	4:29			
	15	6:45	15	Pisces	13:54			
	17	12: 8	17	Aries	19:21			
	19	14:49	19	Taurus	21:12			
	21	14:33	21	Gemini	20:57			
	23	18: 9	23	Cancer	20:33			
	25	16:13	25	Leo	21:53			
	27	20:43	28	Virgo	2:16			
	30	6:18	30	Libra	10: 8			
JUN	1	18:14	1	Scorpio	20:54			
	4	6: 2	4	Sagittar	9:24			
	6	19:32	6	Capricrn	22:21			
	9	9: 7	9	Aquarius	10:30			
	11	16:44	11	Pisces	20:32			
	13	19:53	14	Aries	3:24			
	15	23:58	16	Taurus	6:50			
	18	1:13	18	Gemini	7:37			
	20	4:12	20	Cancer	7:15			
	22	1:25	22	Leo	7:37			
	24	2:38	24	Virgo	10:26			
	26	10:19	26	Libra	16:56			
	28	20:22	29	Scorpio	3: 5			

JUL	1	8:59	1	Sagittar	15:34
	3	19:20	4	Capricrn	4:30
	6	10:31	6	Aquarius	16:19
	8	17:33	9	Pisces	2: 9
	11	4:46	11	Aries	9:33
	13	14:18	13	Taurus	14:21
	15	12:47	15	Gemini	16:43
	17	10:13	17	Cancer	17:30
	19	14:34	19	Leo	18: 4
	21	12:31	21	Virgo	20: 7
	23	21:50	24	Libra	1:16
	26	6:56	26	Scorpio	10:19
	28	19:12	28	Sagittar	22:24
	31	2:53	31	Capricrn	11:19
AUG	2	20:23	2	Aquarius	22:52
	5	0:33	5	Pisces	8: 4
	7	13:13	7	Aries	15: 0
	9	18:34	9	Taurus	20: 3
	11	22:20	11	Gemini	23:34
	14	0: 9	14	Cancer	1:51
	16	2:46	16	Leo	3:34
	17	23:50	18	Virgo	5:58
	20	10: 8	20	Libra	10:34
	22	18:25	22	Scorpio	18:38
	25	4:34	25	Sagittar	6: 4
	27	12:17	27	Capricrn	18:57
	29	23:11	30	Aquarius	6:36
SEP	1	9:35	1	Pisces	15:23
	2	20:43	3	Aries	21:24
	5	20:27	6	Taurus	1:37
	7	23:59	8	Gemini	4:59
	10	3: 9	10	Cancer	8: 1
	12	5:12	12	Leo	11: 2
	14	9:49	14	Virgo	14:34
	16	14:20	16	Libra	19:35
	18	22:22	19	Scorpio	2:39
	21	9:26	21	Sagittar	14:12
	23	22: 2	24	Capricrn	3: 1
	26	9:44	26	Aquarius	15: 8
	28	20:58	29	Pisces	0:15
OCT	30	15:27	1	Aries	5:47
	3	6:18	3	Taurus	8:52
	5	7:24	5	Gemini	11: 0
	7	9:50	7	Cancer	13:23
	9	12:23	9	Leo	16:42
	11	18:25	11	Virgo	21:12
	13	8:40	13	Libra	3:14
	16	7:46	16	Scorpio	11:24
	18	18:27	18	Sagittar	22: 8
	21	7:12	21	Capricrn	10:52
	23	23: 5	23	Aquarius	23:33
	26	6:26	26	Pisces	9:38
	28	0:45	28	Aries	15:47
	30	13:36	30	Taurus	18:30
NOV	1	16:47	1	Gemini	19:23
	3	17:45	3	Cancer	20:12
	5	21:59	5	Leo	22:20
	8	2: 3	8	Virgo	2:37
	10	20:13	10	Libra	9:16
	12	17:21	12	Scorpio	18:13
	15	4:55	15	Sagittar	5:17
	17	15:50	17	Capricrn	17:59
	20	5: 2	20	Aquarius	6:59
	22	17:29	22	Pisces	18:11
	24	18:59	25	Aries	1:48
	27	4:13	27	Taurus	5:27
	29	3:58	29	Gemini	6:11
DEC	1	4:48	1	Cancer	5:47
	3	5:13	3	Leo	6: 8
	5	7:59	5	Virgo	8:50
	7	7:48	7	Libra	14:49
	9	23:18	9	Scorpio	24: 0
	12	8:43	12	Sagittar	11:34
	14	23:56	15	Capricrn	0:24
	17	13: 0	17	Aquarius	13: 0
	20	0:50	20	Pisces	1: 2
	22	9:40	22	Aries	10: 6
	24	12:56	24	Taurus	15:34
	26	15: 3	26	Gemini	17:34
	28	14:49	28	Cancer	17:18
	30	14:37	30	Leo	16:36

JAN				
1	6:29	1	Sagittar	16:40
3	17:17	4	Capricrn	0:46
5	23: 3	6	Aquarius	6:10
8	2:51	8	Pisces	9:43
9	21:31	10	Aries	12:27
12	8:23	12	Taurus	15:10
14	8:59	14	Gemini	18:30
16	15:59	16	Cancer	23: 1
19	2:37	19	Leo	5:25
21	6:37	21	Virgo	14:14
23	6:39	24	Libra	1:30
26	6: 7	26	Scorpio	14: 4
28	14:18	29	Sagittar	1:43
31	3:12	31	Capricrn	10:27

FEB				
2	8:50	2	Aquarius	15:38
4	13:11	4	Pisces	18: 8
6	16:23	6	Aries	19:15
8	14: 9	8	Taurus	20:47
10	13:40	10	Gemini	23:55
12	23:59	13	Cancer	5:10
15	5: 1	15	Leo	12:36
17	19:18	17	Virgo	22: 1
19	12:27	20	Libra	9:15
22	13:23	22	Scorpio	21:44
24	21: 5	25	Sagittar	10: 1
27	12: 4	27	Capricrn	19:58

MAR				
1	18:43	2	Aquarius	2: 7
3	21:33	4	Pisces	4:33
5	17:38	6	Aries	4:40
7	21:32	8	Taurus	4:33
10	3:40	10	Gemini	6: 6
12	2:39	12	Cancer	10:38
14	9:47	14	Leo	18:17
16	19:27	17	Virgo	4:22
19	12:43	19	Libra	15:58
21	19: 1	22	Scorpio	4:26
24	2:44	24	Sagittar	16:56
26	18:42	27	Capricrn	3:56
29	2:55	29	Aquarius	11:38
31	7: 6	31	Pisces	15:17

APR				
2	9:13	2	Aries	15:41
4	9:38	4	Taurus	14:43
6	2:50	6	Gemini	14:40
8	14:46	8	Cancer	17:29
10	16:15	11	Leo	0: 6
12	23:45	13	Virgo	10: 3
15	6:43	15	Libra	21:58
18	5:49	18	Scorpio	10:33
20	8: 3	20	Sagittar	22:55
22	23:27	23	Capricrn	10:12
25	11:15	25	Aquarius	19: 3
27	22:17	28	Pisces	0:22
29	18: 5	30	Aries	2: 9

MAY				
1	18:30	2	Taurus	1:43
3	13:13	4	Gemini	1: 7
5	20: 5	6	Cancer	2:30
7	20:45	8	Leo	7:29
10	10:47	10	Virgo	16:23
12	23:19	13	Libra	4: 4
15	13: 1	15	Scorpio	16:42
17	21:47	18	Sagittar	4:54
20	14:20	20	Capricrn	15:49
22	13:10	23	Aquarius	0:49
24	20: 1	25	Pisces	7: 9
27	0:52	27	Aries	10:32
29	8:17	29	Taurus	11:34
30	23:57	31	Gemini	11:41

JUN				
2	2: 4	2	Cancer	12:46
4	5: 7	4	Leo	16:35
6	11:46	7	Virgo	0: 7
8	17:22	9	Libra	10:59
11	10:14	11	Scorpio	23:30
13	3:12	14	Sagittar	11:38
16	12: 6	16	Capricrn	22: 6
18	18: 9	19	Aquarius	6:26
21	11:50	21	Pisces	12:37
23	2:57	23	Aries	16:44
25	8: 2	25	Taurus	19: 9
27	9:28	27	Gemini	20:42
29	11:20	29	Cancer	22:36

JUL				
1	14:30	2	Leo	2:17
4	8:22	4	Virgo	8:56
6	16:58	6	Libra	18:54
9	3:47	9	Scorpio	7: 4
11	15:22	11	Sagittar	19:19
14	0:26	14	Capricrn	5:40
16	1:11	16	Aquarius	13:20
18	12:21	18	Pisces	18:33
20	17:48	20	Aries	22: 8
23	0:14	23	Taurus	0:53
24	17:13	25	Gemini	3:31
26	23:11	27	Cancer	6:41
29	0:45	29	Leo	11:11
31	9:40	31	Virgo	17:50

AUG				
2	18:52	3	Libra	3:14
5	6:52	5	Scorpio	15: 3
8	1:26	8	Sagittar	3:33
10	7:43	10	Capricrn	14:21
12	12:51	12	Aquarius	21:55
14	21:51	15	Pisces	2:17
17	1: 8	17	Aries	4:38
19	3:49	19	Taurus	6:26
21	4:51	21	Gemini	8:56
23	12:33	23	Cancer	12:50
25	10:34	25	Leo	18:23
27	16:20	28	Virgo	1:44
30	3:16	30	Libra	11:12

SEP				
1	14:51	1	Scorpio	22:49
4	3:47	4	Sagittar	11:33
6	23: 9	6	Capricrn	23:10
9	0:57	9	Aquarius	7:31
11	4:11	11	Pisces	11:55
13	7:49	13	Aries	13:23
15	8:21	15	Taurus	13:45
17	9:29	17	Gemini	14:55
19	11:11	19	Cancer	18:13
21	21: 1	22	Leo	0: 4
24	0:13	24	Virgo	8:11
26	12:27	26	Libra	18:11
29	0: 8	29	Scorpio	5:52

OCT				
1	13: 3	1	Sagittar	18:42
3	23:16	4	Capricrn	7: 5
6	11:50	6	Aquarius	16:46
8	15:42	8	Pisces	22:17
10	20:23	10	Aries	23:59
12	20:22	12	Taurus	23:32
14	20:16	14	Gemini	23:10
16	18:38	17	Cancer	0:50
19	4:21	19	Leo	5:41
21	13:14	21	Virgo	13:45
23	22:14	23	Libra	0:12
26	10:32	26	Scorpio	12:11
29	0:40	29	Sagittar	0:59
31	6:47	31	Capricrn	13:37

NOV				
2	23:39	3	Aquarius	0:22
5	6:48	5	Pisces	7:35
7	10:22	7	Aries	10:43
9	10:34	9	Taurus	10:49
11	9:40	11	Gemini	9:51
13	4:39	13	Cancer	10: 0
15	12:57	15	Leo	13: 3
17	13:56	17	Virgo	19:53
20	5:54	20	Libra	6: 3
22	18: 0	22	Scorpio	18:13
25	6:41	25	Sagittar	7: 2
27	13:45	27	Capricrn	19:24
30	5:40	30	Aquarius	6:20

DEC				
2	12:18	2	Pisces	14:39
4	18:37	4	Aries	19:36
6	20:15	6	Taurus	21:23
8	19:57	8	Gemini	21:17
10	17: 9	10	Cancer	21: 7
12	20:52	12	Leo	22:49
14	23:37	15	Virgo	3:54
17	9:51	17	Libra	12:52
19	21: 8	20	Scorpio	0:44
22	9:28	22	Sagittar	13:35
24	21:29	25	Capricrn	1:41
27	8: 3	27	Aquarius	12: 1
29	16:26	29	Pisces	20:10

JAN				
1	13:54	1	Leo	21:18
4	6:58	4	Virgo	9:41
5	19:22	6	Libra	22:37
9	3:19	9	Scorpio	9:44
11	4:13	11	Sagittar	17:15
13	15:39	13	Capricrn	20:55
15	17: 1	15	Aquarius	21:58
17	17:18	17	Pisces	22: 7
19	22:27	19	Aries	23: 9
21	21:19	22	Taurus	2:21
24	3:20	24	Gemini	8:21
26	11:45	26	Cancer	17: 7
28	22:38	29	Leo	4: 6
31	11: 4	31	Virgo	16:36
FEB 2	21:37	3	Libra	5:32
5	12: 3	5	Scorpio	17:21
7	11:46	8	Sagittar	2:21
10	2:52	10	Capricrn	7:32
12	4:51	12	Aquarius	9:17
14	4:36	14	Pisces	8:58
15	8:36	16	Aries	8:31
18	8:52	18	Taurus	9:51
19	23:46	20	Gemini	14:27
22	17: 1	22	Cancer	22:48
25	3:58	25	Leo	10: 6
27	16:28	27	Virgo	22:51
MAR 2	11: 2	2	Libra	11:41
4	16:55	4	Scorpio	23:31
6	17:13	7	Sagittar	9:20
9	12:31	9	Capricrn	16:10
11	17:49	11	Aquarius	19:38
13	19:47	13	Pisces	20:17
15	11: 5	15	Aries	19:39
16	18:38	17	Taurus	19:45
19	20:45	19	Gemini	22:35
21	21:19	22	Cancer	5:30
24	7:17	24	Leo	16:15
26	19:35	27	Virgo	5: 4
28	23:16	29	Libra	17:52
APR 1	4:40	1	Scorpio	5:20
2	23:26	3	Sagittar	14:59
5	18: 9	5	Capricrn	22:29
7	21:19	8	Aquarius	3:28
9	21:59	10	Pisces	5:50
11	21:27	12	Aries	6:19
13	20:49	14	Taurus	6:32
16	5:49	16	Gemini	8:27
18	10:21	18	Cancer	13:53
20	14:51	20	Leo	23:27
23	4:11	23	Virgo	11:53
25	18:15	25	Libra	0:41
27	22: 7	28	Scorpio	11:52
30	20:21	30	Sagittar	20:53
MAY 2	14:30	3	Capricrn	3:55
5	7:27	5	Aquarius	9:13
7	11:56	7	Pisces	12:47
8	18:43	9	Aries	14:49
11	3: 4	11	Taurus	16:12
13	5: 6	13	Gemini	18:27
15	8:27	15	Cancer	23:17
18	1:37	18	Leo	7:47
20	18:21	20	Virgo	19:31
22	3:52	23	Libra	8:16
25	3:59	25	Scorpio	19:33
27	11:20	28	Sagittar	4: 9
30	1:49	30	Capricrn	10:17
JUN 1	9:23	1	Aquarius	14:46
3	15:50	3	Pisces	18:12
5	19:14	5	Aries	21: 2
7	16:20	7	Taurus	23:42
9	11:43	10	Gemini	3: 3
12	5:58	12	Cancer	8:18
13	23:39	14	Leo	16:28
16	18: 8	17	Virgo	3:37
19	12: 1	19	Libra	16:17
21	17:22	21	Scorpio	3:58
24	8:38	24	Sagittar	12:48
26	3:29	26	Capricrn	18:29
28	6:49	28	Aquarius	21:52

JUL				
30	12:19	1	Pisces	0: 9
2	18:19	3	Aries	2:24
4	15: 7	5	Taurus	5:24
7	9:39	7	Gemini	9:43
9	0:50	9	Cancer	15:55
11	7:29	12	Leo	0:28
13	19:21	14	Virgo	11:29
16	11: 7	17	Libra	0: 4
19	4:48	19	Scorpio	12:17
21	19:36	21	Sagittar	21:59
23	14:22	24	Capricrn	4: 7
26	3: 6	26	Aquarius	7: 3
27	19:39	28	Pisces	8: 7
30	7:20	30	Aries	8:56
AUG 1	7:48	1	Taurus	10:57
3	10:55	3	Gemini	15:11
5	8:12	5	Cancer	22: 0
8	3:33	8	Leo	7:16
10	4: 3	10	Virgo	18:34
12	12:12	13	Libra	7: 9
15	5:28	15	Scorpio	19:44
17	20: 8	18	Sagittar	6:30
20	8:34	20	Capricrn	13:53
22	6:16	22	Aquarius	17:29
24	7: 7	24	Pisces	18:12
26	11: 3	26	Aries	17:46
28	15:25	28	Taurus	18:10
30	20:48	30	Gemini	21: 7
SEP 1	16:49	2	Cancer	3:30
4	2:19	4	Leo	13: 5
6	14:25	7	Virgo	0:48
9	2: 9	9	Libra	13:28
11	22:31	12	Scorpio	2: 6
14	13:18	14	Sagittar	13:32
16	14:35	16	Capricrn	22:21
18	20:42	19	Aquarius	3:30
20	23: 6	21	Pisces	5: 7
23	4:16	23	Aries	4:31
24	22:31	25	Taurus	3:45
26	19:11	27	Gemini	5: 1
29	4:50	29	Cancer	9:57
OCT 1	13:59	1	Leo	18:54
4	5:17	4	Virgo	6:41
6	12: 5	6	Libra	19:28
9	4:42	9	Scorpio	7:57
11	8:34	11	Sagittar	19:20
14	2:56	14	Capricrn	4:52
16	10:15	16	Aquarius	11:35
18	14: 7	18	Pisces	14:56
20	9:47	20	Aries	15:27
22	12:56	22	Taurus	14:47
24	6:34	24	Gemini	15: 4
26	11:47	26	Cancer	18:24
28	23: 8	29	Leo	1:55
31	12:59	31	Virgo	13: 5
NOV 2	17:32	3	Libra	1:51
5	5:42	5	Scorpio	14:12
7	23:58	8	Sagittar	1: 7
10	6:51	10	Capricrn	10:19
12	8:45	12	Aquarius	17:31
14	13:39	14	Pisces	22:18
16	15:57	17	Aries	0:36
18	17:12	19	Taurus	1:15
20	23:13	21	Gemini	1:55
22	19:55	23	Cancer	4:32
25	1:21	25	Leo	10:41
27	10:55	27	Virgo	20:41
29	19:25	30	Libra	9: 6
DEC 2		2	Scorpio	21:31
5	7:14	5	Sagittar	8: 9
7	7:57	7	Capricrn	16:33
9	21:17	9	Aquarius	23: 0
11	19:53	12	Pisces	3:47
13	17:58	14	Aries	7: 7
16	5: 5	16	Taurus	9:23
18	2:55	18	Gemini	11:28
20	11:44	20	Cancer	14:40
22	12:30	22	Leo	20:23
24	21: 7	25	Virgo	5:24
27	12: 1	27	Libra	17:11
30	4: 1	30	Scorpio	5:43

Mo	Day	Time	Day	Sign	Time
JAN	31	22:33	1	Pisces	2:11
	2	9:33	3	Aries	5:42
	4	22:59	5	Taurus	12:44
	7	5:16	7	Gemini	22:43
	10	2:47	10	Cancer	10:35
	12	16:13	12	Leo	23:20
	15	7:31	15	Virgo	12: 1
	17	16:34	17	Libra	23:20
	20	6: 9	20	Scorpio	7:45
	21	20:38	22	Sagittar	12:22
	24	7: 4	24	Capricrn	13:39
	26	0: 4	26	Aquarius	13: 7
	27	23:27	28	Pisces	12:46
	30	4:16	30	Aries	14:33
FEB	1	15:47	1	Taurus	19:51
	3	10:29	3	Gemini	4:55
	5	23:56	6	Cancer	16:44
	8	12:38	9	Leo	5:36
	11	1:16	11	Virgo	18: 2
	13	10:31	14	Libra	5: 1
	16	7:24	16	Scorpio	13:45
	18	18: 2	18	Sagittar	19:43
	20	8:37	20	Capricrn	22:50
	22	10: 2	22	Aquarius	23:49
	24	10:15	25	Pisces	0: 1
	25	22:59	27	Aries	1:12
	28	13:46	29	Taurus	5: 2
MAR	1	17:22	2	Gemini	12:37
	4	11:33	4	Cancer	23:41
	7	11:39	7	Leo	12:31
	9	7:15	10	Virgo	0:52
	11	18:14	12	Libra	11:17
	14	14:53	14	Scorpio	19:21
	18	18:23	17	Sagittar	1:16
	19	2:40	19	Capricrn	5:20
	20	16:42	21	Aquarius	7:55
	23	18:58	23	Pisces	9:39
	24	16:17	25	Aries	11:34
	27	1:20	27	Taurus	15: 6
	29	1:49	29	Gemini	21:36
APR	31	18:18	1	Cancer	7:39
	3	7:42	3	Leo	20:10
	5	21:40	6	Virgo	8:41
	8	15:53	8	Libra	18:56
	10	18:22	11	Scorpio	2:14
	12	12:15	13	Sagittar	7: 8
	15	5: 6	15	Capricrn	10:42
	17	9: 8	17	Aquarius	13:44
	19	15:52	19	Pisces	15:41
	20	16:53	21	Aries	19:57
	23	22: 9	24	Taurus	0:15
	25	10:35	26	Gemini	6:41
	28	16: 0	28	Cancer	16: 6
MAY	30	19:20	1	Leo	4:13
	3	15: 8	3	Virgo	16:58
	4	21:24	6	Libra	3:39
	7	18:39	8	Scorpio	10:49
	9	20:16	10	Sagittar	14:51
	12	12:13	12	Capricrn	17: 9
	14	8:18	14	Aquarius	19:15
	16	14:40	16	Pisces	22: 6
	18	22:25	19	Aries	2: 7
	20	12:23	21	Taurus	7:30
	23	1:29	23	Gemini	14:38
	25	3:15	26	Cancer	0: 6
	28	11: 9	28	Leo	12: 0
	30	21:56	31	Virgo	0:57
JUN	1	1:23	2	Libra	12:26
	4	0:58	4	Scorpio	20:20
	6	6:20	7	Sagittar	0:21
	8	8:32	9	Capricrn	1:47
	10	8:38	11	Aquarius	2:27
	12	22:17	13	Pisces	4: 1
	14	20:28	15	Aries	7:29
	17	5:50	17	Taurus	13:11
	19	1:31	19	Gemini	21: 4
	21	10:53	22	Cancer	7: 4
	23	20:45	24	Leo	19: 3
	26	11:19	27	Virgo	8: 7
	29	18: 9	29	Libra	20:19

Mo	Day	Time	Day	Sign	Time
JUL	1	10:40	2	Scorpio	5:26
	3	17:11	4	Sagittar	10:27
	5	19:51	6	Capricrn	12: 3
	7	18:35	8	Aquarius	11:55
	9	20: 3	10	Pisces	11:59
	12	4:38	12	Aries	13:56
	14	14:12	14	Taurus	18:46
	16	15:13	17	Gemini	2:38
	18	22:27	19	Cancer	13: 5
	21	23:31	22	Leo	1:21
	24	6: 3	24	Virgo	14:25
	26	2:24	27	Libra	2:54
	29	7:42	29	Scorpio	13: 5
	31	14:25	31	Sagittar	19:38
AUG	2	16:45	2	Capricrn	22:28
	4	5:37	4	Aquarius	22:42
	6	15:32	6	Pisces	22: 5
	8	5: 1	8	Aries	22:34
	10	11:24	11	Taurus	1:46
	12	16:32	13	Gemini	8:37
	15	3:32	15	Cancer	18:53
	17	19:36	18	Leo	7:19
	20	15:21	20	Virgo	20:23
	23	3:15	23	Libra	8:42
	25	2:56	25	Scorpio	19:11
	27	11:38	28	Sagittar	2:54
	29	22: 0	30	Capricrn	7:24
SEP	1	4:46	1	Aquarius	9: 3
	2	21:44	3	Pisces	9: 0
	4	18:23	5	Aries	8:57
	7	10:38	7	Taurus	10:48
	9	1:29	9	Gemini	16: 6
	11	9:53	12	Cancer	1:24
	13	19:19	14	Leo	13:39
	16	10:52	17	Virgo	2:42
	19	7:22	19	Libra	14:42
	21	10: 6	22	Scorpio	0:44
	23	18:37	24	Sagittar	8:33
	26	11:24	26	Capricrn	14: 6
	28	1:57	28	Aquarius	17:25
	30	6:44	30	Pisces	18:53
OCT	2	8:20	2	Aries	19:34
	4	12: 1	4	Taurus	21: 6
	6	12:14	7	Gemini	1:15
	9	5:12	9	Cancer	9:16
	11	11:19	11	Leo	20:50
	13	19:20	14	Virgo	9:51
	16	7:33	16	Libra	21:45
	18	22:43	19	Scorpio	7:10
	21	12:42	21	Sagittar	14:12
	23	7:12	23	Capricrn	19:29
	25	9:26	25	Aquarius	23:28
	27	16: 2	28	Pisces	2:23
	29	23:36	30	Aries	4:35
NOV	31	19:21	1	Taurus	6:59
	2	22:56	3	Gemini	11: 2
	5	5:20	5	Cancer	18:13
	7	13:36	8	Leo	4:57
	10	3:59	10	Virgo	17:47
	12	23: 5	13	Libra	5:58
	15	14:49	15	Scorpio	15:19
	17	15:59	17	Sagittar	21:34
	19	14: 5	20	Capricrn	1:41
	22	4:35	22	Aquarius	4:52
	23	20:27	24	Pisces	7:55
	25	14:47	26	Aries	11:10
	28	3:34	28	Taurus	15:19
	30	7:50	30	Gemini	19:53
DEC	2	15:42	3	Cancer	3: 9
	5	1:47	5	Leo	13:23
	7	14:31	8	Virgo	1:58
	10	14:10	10	Libra	14:36
	12	14:53	13	Scorpio	0:39
	14	18:57	15	Sagittar	7: 0
	17	2:13	17	Capricrn	10:18
	19	4:22	19	Aquarius	12: 3
	21	13:10	21	Pisces	13:46
	22	18:36	23	Aries	16:30
	25	13:30	25	Taurus	20:46
	27	22:38	28	Gemini	2:48
	30	10:12	30	Cancer	10:54

JAN	2	3:38	2	Scorpio 15:58
	4	10:39	4	Sagittar 17:39
	6	0:49	6	Capricrn 17:32
	8	0:36	8	Aquarius 17:36
	10	3:10	10	Pisces 19:56
	12	10: 8	13	Aries 2: 6
	15	0:27	15	Taurus 12:11
	17	18:11	18	Gemini 0:36
	20	9:44	20	Cancer 13: 6
	22	3:47	23	Leo 0:12
	24	16:35	25	Virgo 0:12
	26	6: 8	27	Libra 16:46
	29	17:28	29	Scorpio 22: 4
FEB	31	6:28	1	Sagittar 1:17
	2	9:38	3	Capricrn 2:53
	4	16:20	5	Aquarius 4: 4
	6	12:32	7	Pisces 6:29
	9	10:57	9	Aries 11:43
	11	4:21	11	Taurus 20:34
	13	20:56	14	Gemini 8:19
	15	15: 7	16	Cancer 20:52
	18	16:56	19	Leo 8: 1
	20	20:45	21	Virgo 16:43
	23	20:34	23	Libra 23: 1
	25	19:22	26	Scorpio 3:31
	28	5:57	28	Sagittar 6:50
MAR	1	15:10	2	Capricrn 9:30
	3	17:41	4	Aquarius 12:11
	5	20:44	6	Pisces 15:46
	8	21: 5	8	Aries 21:16
	10	8:27	11	Taurus 5:33
	13	15:40	13	Gemini 16:36
	16	3:46	16	Cancer 5: 6
	18	15: 4	18	Leo 16:45
	21	0:47	21	Virgo 1:39
	23	5:13	23	Libra 7:21
	24	15:18	25	Scorpio 10:36
	27	10: 6	27	Sagittar 12:41
	29	11:58	29	Capricrn 14:51
	31	14:48	31	Aquarius 18: 3
APR	2	12:15	2	Pisces 22:45
	5	1:11	5	Aries 5:16
	7	9:34	7	Taurus 13:53
	9	19:36	10	Gemini 0:41
	12	8:48	12	Cancer 13: 5
	15	0:31	15	Leo 1:18
	17	4:17	17	Virgo 11: 8
	19	16:28	19	Libra 17:14
	20	23:42	21	Scorpio 19:55
	23	15: 8	23	Sagittar 20:40
	25	15:32	25	Capricrn 21:20
	27	17:19	27	Aquarius 23:33
	29	6:10	30	Pisces 4:13
MAY	2	4:13	2	Aries 11:27
	4	18:33	4	Taurus 20:47
	6	23:48	7	Gemini 7:51
	9	17: 4	9	Cancer 20:13
	12	6:38	12	Leo 8:50
	14	19:33	14	Virgo 19:44
	16	21: 2	17	Libra 3: 6
	18	9:27	19	Scorpio 6:24
	21	6:18	21	Sagittar 6:44
	22	23: 5	23	Capricrn 6: 7
	24	23:21	25	Aquarius 6:42
	26	12:24	27	Pisces 10: 5
	29	8:33	29	Aries 16:54
JUN	31	12:33	1	Taurus 2:34
	3	5:32	3	Gemini 14: 3
	5	17:36	6	Cancer 2:32
	8	12:11	8	Leo 15:12
	10	4:10	11	Virgo 2:47
	13	3:41	13	Libra 11:31
	15	4:51	15	Scorpio 16:17
	17	10:49	17	Sagittar 17:27
	19	12:36	19	Capricrn 16:38
	21	9:39	21	Aquarius 16: 4
	23	16: 5	23	Pisces 17:49
	25	16:12	25	Aries 23:14
	28	0:25	28	Taurus 8:18
	30	12:40	30	Gemini 19:52

JUL	3	7:33	3	Cancer 8:28
	5	14:24	5	Leo 21: 1
	7	9:46	8	Virgo 8:36
	10	12:30	10	Libra 18: 5
	12	4:57	13	Scorpio 0:19
	14	22:40	15	Sagittar 3: 3
	16	23:15	17	Capricrn 3:15
	18	22:56	19	Aquarius 2:42
	20	11:10	21	Pisces 3: 9
	23	6:40	23	Aries 7:22
	25	9:35	25	Taurus 15: 7
	27	22:53	28	Gemini 2: 8
	30	11:53	30	Cancer 14:43
AUG	2	0:49	2	Leo 3: 8
	3	17:12	4	Virgo 14:19
	6	22:18	6	Libra 23:35
	8	19:11	9	Scorpio 6:24
	11	10: 7	11	Sagittar 10:31
	13	12:17	13	Capricrn 12:19
	15	9:42	15	Aquarius 12:53
	17	3: 0	17	Pisces 13:53
	18	19:49	19	Aries 16:59
	21	19:34	21	Taurus 23:27
	23	13:26	24	Gemini 9:28
	26	1:19	26	Cancer 21:45
	28	9:29	29	Leo 10:10
	31	1:44	31	Virgo 21: 0
SEP	1	21:44	3	Libra 5:32
	4	18:18	5	Scorpio 16:12
	6	23:21	7	Sagittar 16:12
	9	2:48	9	Capricrn 19: 7
	11	1:24	11	Aquarius 21:12
	13	7:17	13	Pisces 23:22
	15	12:39	16	Aries 2:48
	17	15:23	18	Taurus 8:42
	20	11:20	20	Gemini 17:47
	23	4:14	23	Cancer 5:35
	24	19:10	25	Leo 18: 8
	27	20:34	28	Virgo 5: 6
	30	5:21	30	Libra 13: 9
OCT	2	15:52	2	Scorpio 18:24
	4	21:42	4	Sagittar 21:49
	6	9:20	7	Capricrn 0:30
	8	8:47	9	Aquarius 3:19
	10	15:25	11	Pisces 6:47
	12	7: 4	13	Aries 11:20
	15	2:58	15	Taurus 17:37
	17	9:29	18	Gemini 2:22
	20	5:44	20	Cancer 13:43
	22	23:56	23	Leo 2:25
	24	21: 5	25	Virgo 14: 2
	26	23:27	27	Libra 22:26
	29	12:22	30	Scorpio 3:10
NOV	31	15:17	1	Sagittar 5:20
	2	19:54	3	Capricrn 6:40
	5	1: 7	5	Aquarius 8:43
	7	10:23	7	Pisces 12:23
	9	17:49	9	Aries 17:53
	11	9:19	12	Taurus 1: 8
	13	22:43	14	Gemini 10:16
	16	12:31	16	Cancer 21:28
	19	4:15	19	Leo 10:12
	21	20: 2	21	Virgo 22:36
	23	16:13	24	Libra 8: 9
	26	3:59	26	Scorpio 13:32
	28	1:34	28	Sagittar 15:20
	30	13:42	30	Capricrn 15:23
DEC	2	5:10	2	Aquarius 15:45
	4	11:18	4	Pisces 18: 8
	5	17: 2	6	Aries 23:18
	8	15: 2	9	Taurus 7: 5
	11	0:18	11	Gemini 16:54
	14	11:10	14	Cancer 4:23
	15	23:23	16	Leo 17: 5
	18	22:13	19	Virgo 5:52
	21	14:38	21	Libra 16:41
	23	8:24	23	Scorpio 23:39
	25	12: 7	26	Sagittar 2:27
	27	13: 0	28	Capricrn 2:24
	29	18: 2	30	Aquarius 1:36

```
JAN  2 10:56    3 Cancer    6:57      JUL 30  7:37    1 Aquarius   9:20
     4 18:49    5 Leo      13:58           2 14: 4    3 Pisces    13:52
     6 22:52    7 Virgo    19: 6           4 17: 0    5 Aries     22:25
     9  4:46    9 Libra    23: 9           7  7:38    8 Taurus    10:14
    11 10:32   12 Scorpio   2:28           9 20:50   10 Gemini    23: 2
    13 17:24   14 Sagittar  5:17          12 10:25   13 Cancer    10:34
    15 13:44   16 Capricrn  8: 7          15 15:47   15 Leo       19:53
    18  8: 0   18 Aquarius 12: 7          17 16: 6   18 Virgo      3: 6
    19 19:24   20 Pisces   18:42          20  3: 4   20 Libra      8:34
    22 11:30   23 Aries     4:38          22 11:57   22 Scorpio   12:27
    24 19:38   25 Taurus   17: 8          23 17:39   24 Sagittar  14:56
    27  7: 9   28 Gemini    5:43          26  1:39   26 Capricrn  16:40
    29 18:10   30 Cancer   15:50          28  5:38   28 Aquarius  18:56
                                          30 16:12   30 Pisces    23:19
FEB  1  2: 5    1 Leo      22:34
     3  4:49    6 Virgo     2:37      AUG  1  6:54    2 Aries      7: 3
     5 14:12    6 Libra     5:19           4 10:40    4 Taurus    18: 6
     7 19:41    8 Scorpio   7:51           6  6: 0    7 Gemini     6:44
    10  2: 8   10 Sagittar 10:52           9 17:19    9 Cancer    18:27
    12  2:12   12 Capricrn 14:45          11 16:28   12 Leo        3:37
    13 21:55   14 Aquarius 19:58          13 16:49   14 Virgo     10: 1
    16 22:53   17 Pisces    3:11          15 19:40   16 Libra     14:31
    18 12:18   19 Aries    13: 1          18  9: 4   18 Scorpio   17:49
    21  1:59   22 Taurus    1:12          20 15:36   20 Sagittar  20:36
    23 16: 6   24 Gemini   14: 3          22 22: 4   22 Capricrn  23:23
    26  5:12   27 Cancer    1: 3          24 23:45   25 Aquarius   2:53
                                          26 11: 2   27 Pisces     8: 2
MAR 28  8:48    1 Leo       8:31          28 21:39   29 Aries     15:45
     2 23: 8    3 Virgo    12:25
     4 15:28    5 Libra    14: 1      SEP 31  3:26    1 Taurus      2:19
     7 14: 2    7 Scorpio  14:56           2 20:48    3 Gemini     14:46
     9  3:39    9 Sagittar 16:33           5 16:10    6 Cancer      2:54
    11  7:27   11 Capricrn 20: 7           7 20:51    8 Leo        12:34
    13 11:56   14 Aquarius  1:53           9 23:47   10 Virgo      18:55
    15 22: 9   16 Pisces   10: 0          12 19:43   13 Libra      22:28
    18 15:20   18 Aries    20:21          14  5:57   15 Scorpio     0:27
    20 22: 9   21 Taurus    8:32          17  1:51   17 Sagittar    2:13
    23 17:51   23 Gemini   21:28          19  4: 4   19 Capricrn    4:49
    26  1:23   26 Cancer    9:17          21  4:50   21 Aquarius    9: 0
    28 17:53   28 Leo      18: 5          23 13:32   23 Pisces     15:10
    30 17:48   30 Virgo    23: 1          25 11:47   25 Aries      23:32
                                          28  7:33   28 Taurus     10: 8
APR  1 21:58    2 Libra     0:41          30 19:25   30 Gemini     22:27
     3 21: 1    4 Scorpio   0:36
     5 23:38    6 Sagittar  0:37      OCT  1  8:48    3 Cancer     11: 0
     8  1: 5    8 Capricrn  2:30           5 12:16    5 Leo        21:40
     9 23:30   10 Aquarius  7:25           8  1:23    8 Virgo       4:54
    12 14:39   12 Pisces   15:38          10  1:10   10 Libra       8:29
    14 15:18   15 Aries     2:32          12  6: 7   12 Scorpio     9:31
    17  8:26   17 Taurus   15: 0          14  6: 7   14 Sagittar    9:44
    19 14:18   20 Gemini    3:55          16  7: 5   16 Capricrn   10:55
    22  1:54   22 Cancer   16: 2          18  8:29   18 Aquarius   14:27
    24 14: 9   25 Leo       1:58          20 16:27   20 Pisces     20:53
    27  0:35   27 Virgo     8:30          23  0:26   23 Aries       5:59
    29  5:53   29 Libra    11:26          25 12:15   25 Taurus     17: 3
                                          28  0:43   28 Gemini      5:23
MAY 30 13: 0    1 Scorpio  11:38          30 13:58   30 Cancer     18: 4
     2  6:56    3 Sagittar 10:51
     5 10:29    5 Capricrn 11: 8      NOV  2  2:11    2 Leo         5:38
     7  9: 0    7 Aquarius 14:22           4 11:55    4 Virgo      14:21
     9 14:14    9 Pisces   21:34           6 16:58    6 Libra      19:11
    11 22:19   12 Aries     8:19           8 17:16    8 Scorpio    20:29
    13 16:11   14 Taurus   20:59          10 18:17   10 Sagittar   19:52
    17  0:55   17 Gemini    9:53          12 18:17   12 Capricrn   19:26
    19  8:53   19 Cancer   21:51          14 20:31   14 Aquarius   21:15
    21 20:29   22 Leo       8: 7          16 23:56   17 Pisces      2:39
    23 21:49   24 Virgo    15:51          19 11: 0   19 Aries      11:40
    26 11:50   26 Libra    20:27          21 21: 0   21 Taurus     23: 8
    28 14:50   28 Scorpio  22: 1          24 10: 0   24 Gemini     11:39
    30 15:30   30 Sagittar 21:44          26 23: 7   27 Cancer      0:14
                                          28 13:46   29 Leo        12: 2
JUN  1 16: 1    1 Capricrn 21:27
     3 18:38    3 Aquarius 23:18      DEC  1 12: 5    1 Virgo      21:54
     5 13:22    6 Pisces    4:57           4  1:58    4 Libra       4:29
     8 12:24    8 Aries    14:44           5 19: 1    6 Scorpio     7:20
    10  4:19   11 Taurus    3:13           7 22: 9    8 Sagittar    7:17
    13 13:38   13 Gemini   16: 5           9 20: 5   10 Capricrn    6:16
    15 15:53   16 Cancer    3:45          12  2:21   12 Aquarius    6:34
    17 15:46   18 Leo      13:38          14  8:46   14 Pisces     10:11
    20 19:29   20 Virgo    21:32          16  5:57   16 Aries      17:59
    22 17:28   23 Libra     3:10          18 22: 0   19 Taurus      5:10
    24  7:33   25 Scorpio   6:19          20 20:53   21 Gemini     17:50
    27  7: 9   27 Sagittar  7:26          23  9:29   24 Cancer      6:18
    28 19:30   29 Capricrn  7:49          25 20:46   26 Leo        17:46
                                          28  7:44   29 Virgo       3:42
                                          30 16:35   31 Libra      11:20
```

JAN 31	20:17	1 Aquarius	2: 8	JUL 2	12:29	2 Libra	13:22
3	8:53	3 Pisces	12:59	4	15: 3	4 Scorpio	16:22
6	0:34	6 Aries	1:41	6	18: 0	6 Sagittar	19:45
8	9:36	8 Taurus	14: 3	8	20:17	9 Capricrn	0: 3
10	4: 2	10 Gemini	23:31	11	3:17	11 Aquarius	6: 9
13	4:33	13 Cancer	4:57	13	1:39	13 Pisces	15: 2
14	22: 0	15 Leo	7: 8	15	22:20	16 Aries	2:43
17	3:42	17 Virgo	7:52	18	10:34	18 Taurus	15:36
19	7:14	19 Libra	9: 3	20	22:48	21 Gemini	2:58
21	7:17	21 Scorpio	12: 0	23	3: 8	23 Cancer	10:52
22	22:59	23 Sagittar	17: 9	25	9:32	25 Leo	15:19
25	19: 0	26 Capricrn	0:22	26	17:56	27 Virgo	17:36
27	9:28	28 Aquarius	9:27	29	12:50	29 Libra	19:20
30	14:26	30 Pisces	20:27	31	14:39	31 Scorpio	21:44
FEB 2	2:49	2 Aries	9: 5	AUG 2	17:41	3 Sagittar	1:25
4	17:51	4 Taurus	21:57	4	14:45	5 Capricrn	6:36
7	1:37	7 Gemini	8:41	7	4:20	7 Aquarius	13:34
9	12:16	9 Cancer	15:23	8	20: 6	9 Pisces	22:46
11	0:56	11 Leo	18: 1	11	23:17	12 Aries	10:20
13	12:50	13 Virgo	18: 6	14	11:36	14 Taurus	23:18
15	17:48	15 Libra	17:44	17	3:23	17 Gemini	11:23
17	16:43	17 Scorpio	18:53	19	18:36	19 Cancer	20:15
19	7:36	19 Sagittar	22:50	21	14: 8	22 Leo	1: 8
21	23:24	22 Capricrn	5:51	23	4:59	24 Virgo	2:56
24	0:32	24 Aquarius	15:26	25	21:23	26 Libra	3:24
29	19:56	27 Pisces	2:54	27	17:21	28 Scorpio	4:20
MAR 1	8:31	1 Aries	15:36	29	21:58	30 Sagittar	7: 1
3	21:30	4 Taurus	4:33	SEP 31	12:31	1 Capricrn	12: 5
6	5: 0	6 Gemini	16: 6	3	15:22	3 Aquarius	19:37
8	18: 2	9 Cancer	0:22	5	7:44	6 Pisces	5:26
10	20:23	11 Leo	4:34	8	2:10	8 Aries	17:13
13	2:26	13 Virgo	5:24	10	20:57	11 Taurus	6:12
14	23:15	15 Libra	4:40	13	3:34	13 Gemini	18:47
16	22:53	17 Scorpio	4:26	15	14:29	16 Cancer	4:52
19	3:26	19 Sagittar	6:31	18	2: 1	18 Leo	11: 5
21	11:27	21 Capricrn	12: 5	19	19:28	20 Virgo	13:34
23	15:55	23 Aquarius	21:11	22	12:21	22 Libra	13:42
26	2:12	26 Pisces	8:50	24	1:11	24 Scorpio	13:21
28	17:46	28 Aries	21:42	26	1:46	26 Sagittar	14:21
31	7:20	31 Taurus	10:30	27	20:16	28 Capricrn	18: 7
APR 2	19:40	2 Gemini	22: 3	OCT 30	11:15	1 Aquarius	1:14
5	6:59	5 Cancer	7:10	2	17:53	3 Pisces	11:20
7	11:55	7 Leo	13: 0	5	11:58	5 Aries	23:28
9	15: 5	9 Virgo	15:32	7	22: 3	8 Taurus	12:27
11	15:36	11 Libra	15:48	10	11:12	11 Gemini	1: 3
13	14:48	13 Scorpio	15:28	12	19:59	13 Cancer	11:51
15	15:37	15 Sagittar	16:24	15	7:45	15 Leo	19:35
17	19:20	17 Capricrn	20:16	17	14:32	17 Virgo	23:43
20	3:20	20 Aquarius	4: 0	19	14:55	20 Libra	0:48
22	13:53	22 Pisces	15: 8	21	21:23	22 Scorpio	0:19
24	23: 9	25 Aries	4: 1	23	21:13	24 Sagittar	0: 8
27	15:20	27 Taurus	16:41	26	1:13	26 Capricrn	2:11
30	2:28	30 Gemini	3:48	27	22: 7	28 Aquarius	7:50
MAY 2	11:27	2 Cancer	12:44	30	2:27	30 Pisces	17:22
4	20:48	4 Leo	19:12	NOV 1	20: 7	2 Aries	5:35
6	22: 5	6 Virgo	23:12	4	15: 9	4 Taurus	18:37
8	22:13	9 Libra	1: 7	6	23: 1	7 Gemini	6:55
11	0:55	11 Scorpio	1:54	8	18:42	9 Cancer	17:35
13	2: 1	13 Sagittar	2:57	10	20: 1	12 Leo	2: 1
15	5: 3	15 Capricrn	5:57	13	15:48	14 Virgo	7:43
17	4:45	17 Aquarius	12:19	16	6:22	16 Libra	10:36
19	21:40	19 Pisces	22:26	18	7:45	18 Scorpio	11:19
22	8:51	22 Aries	11: 2	20	8:15	20 Sagittar	11:16
24	23:18	24 Taurus	23:42	21	16:46	22 Capricrn	12:20
27	10:16	27 Gemini	10:27	24	14:21	24 Aquarius	16:25
29	17:26	29 Cancer	18:39	26	1:59	27 Pisces	0:36
JUN 31	12:28	1 Leo	0:36	29	11:48	29 Aries	12:18
3	4:12	3 Virgo	4:54	DEC 1	17: 3	2 Taurus	1:22
5	7:29	5 Libra	7:58	4	10:17	4 Gemini	13:29
7	10:10	7 Scorpio	10:14	6	7:58	6 Cancer	23:32
9	11:44	9 Sagittar	12:24	8	17:27	9 Leo	7:28
10	21:46	11 Capricrn	15:40	11	13:31	11 Virgo	13:32
12	13:34	13 Aquarius	21:27	13	8:20	13 Libra	17:45
15	19:35	16 Pisces	6:39	15	8:41	15 Scorpio	20:14
18	12:30	18 Aries	18:45	17	15:41	17 Sagittar	21:32
21	6:36	21 Taurus	7:31	19	18:56	19 Capricrn	23: 0
22	20:51	23 Gemini	18:20	21	23:22	22 Aquarius	2:25
24	22:24	26 Cancer	2: 2	23	10:46	24 Pisces	9:20
28	6:55	28 Leo	7: 1	26	4:20	26 Aries	20: 5
29	9:41	30 Virgo	10:27	29	0:42	29 Taurus	8:58
				31	19:45	31 Gemini	21:13

JAN

Day	Time	Day	Sign	Time
2	2:55	2	Libra	14:10
4	7:42	4	Scorpio	19:51
6	12:41	7	Sagittar	4:41
9	2: 9	9	Capricrn	15:41
11	19: 1	12	Aquarius	3:54
14	7:10	14	Pisces	16:36
16	20: 3	17	Aries	4:44
19	11:33	19	Taurus	14:43
21	4:41	21	Gemini	21: 2
23	11:27	23	Cancer	23:24
24	20:12	25	Leo	23: 0
27	10:16	27	Virgo	21:56
29	16: 9	29	Libra	22:29

FEB

Day	Time	Day	Sign	Time
1	0: 1	1	Scorpio	2:28
2	14:56	3	Sagittar	10:26
5	6:16	5	Capricrn	21:30
8	0:52	8	Aquarius	9:59
10	8:28	10	Pisces	22:37
12	21:32	13	Aries	10:38
15	18:37	15	Taurus	21: 8
18	1:55	18	Gemini	4:56
20	3:59	20	Cancer	9: 9
21	6: 5	22	Leo	10: 7
24	3:11	24	Virgo	9:23
26	1:37	26	Libra	9: 5
28	3:53	28	Scorpio	11:24

MAR

Day	Time	Day	Sign	Time
1	4:58	1	Sagittar	17:42
3	20:25	4	Capricrn	3:51
6	12: 3	6	Aquarius	16:15
8	22:31	9	Pisces	4:54
11	10:51	11	Aries	16:33
13	21:36	14	Taurus	2:41
16	7: 6	16	Gemini	10:46
18	12:28	18	Cancer	16:14
19	14:10	20	Leo	18:58
22	16:37	22	Virgo	19:43
24	17: 8	24	Libra	20: 2
26	19: 1	26	Scorpio	21:50
28	13:23	29	Sagittar	2:47
31	8:49	31	Capricrn	11:34

APR

Day	Time	Day	Sign	Time
2	19:42	2	Aquarius	23:19
5	9:30	5	Pisces	11:56
7	21:14	7	Aries	23:29
10	6:55	10	Taurus	8:59
11	20:31	12	Gemini	16:20
14	19:51	14	Cancer	21:42
16	19:42	17	Leo	1:16
19	1:43	19	Virgo	3:31
21	3:26	21	Libra	5:17
23	5:51	23	Scorpio	7:49
24	21:55	25	Sagittar	12:32
27	17:53	27	Capricrn	20:22
28	17:29	30	Aquarius	7:16

MAY

Day	Time	Day	Sign	Time
2	16:40	2	Pisces	19:44
5	4:18	5	Aries	7:29
7	13:25	7	Taurus	16:48
9	17: 5	9	Gemini	23:20
11	23:58	12	Cancer	3:39
13	18:38	14	Leo	6:39
16	7:31	16	Virgo	9:15
18	7:32	18	Libra	12: 7
20	10:53	20	Scorpio	15:56
21	21:38	22	Sagittar	21:22
24	22:46	25	Capricrn	5: 8
26	1: 5	27	Aquarius	15:31
29	19:54	30	Pisces	3:46

JUN

Day	Time	Day	Sign	Time
1	7:37	1	Aries	15:55
3	17:18	4	Taurus	1:44
5	10:26	6	Gemini	8: 7
8	4:20	8	Cancer	11:29
9	4:50	10	Leo	13:12
12	8: 9	12	Virgo	14:49
14	10:55	14	Libra	17:34
16	15:24	16	Scorpio	22: 4
18	8:11	19	Sagittar	4:29
21	6:14	21	Capricrn	12:51
22	20:45	23	Aquarius	23:16
26	4:58	26	Pisces	11:24
28	23:43	28	Aries	23:56

JUL

Day	Time	Day	Sign	Time
1	8:43	1	Taurus	10:40
3	3:34	3	Gemini	17:48
5	18:17	5	Cancer	21: 7
7	13: 1	7	Leo	21:53
9	20:35	9	Virgo	22: 4
11	19:42	11	Libra	23:31
13	23:39	14	Scorpio	3:28
16	9:17	16	Sagittar	10:11
18	15:34	18	Capricrn	19:14
21	2:31	21	Aquarius	6: 3
23	14:56	23	Pisces	18:13
26	3:57	26	Aries	6:58
28	15:55	28	Taurus	18:34
30	16:40	31	Gemini	3: 2

AUG

Day	Time	Day	Sign	Time
2	6:36	2	Cancer	7:21
3	1: 5	4	Leo	8:14
6	6: 3	6	Virgo	7:33
8	6: 6	8	Libra	7:30
10	8:37	10	Scorpio	9:57
12	7: 5	12	Sagittar	15:49
14	23:46	15	Capricrn	0:52
16	12:55	17	Aquarius	12: 3
19	23:39	20	Pisces	0:23
22	12:33	22	Aries	13: 6
25	0:42	25	Taurus	1: 4
27	5:22	27	Gemini	10:40
29	16:31	29	Cancer	16:34
31	15:34	31	Leo	18:42

SEP

Day	Time	Day	Sign	Time
2	17:28	2	Virgo	18:21
4	11: 9	4	Libra	17:36
6	16: 1	6	Scorpio	18:34
8	20:36	8	Sagittar	22:52
11	5: 5	11	Capricrn	6:57
12	22: 7	13	Aquarius	17:59
16	5:44	16	Pisces	6:27
18	9:43	18	Aries	19: 2
20	17:29	21	Taurus	6:46
22	13:41	23	Gemini	16:40
25	21:28	25	Cancer	23:46
27	3:36	28	Leo	3:35
29	16:21	30	Virgo	4:41

OCT

Day	Time	Day	Sign	Time
1	16:14	2	Libra	4:30
4	0:21	4	Scorpio	4:59
6	7:31	6	Sagittar	7:55
8	1:45	8	Capricrn	14:31
10	15:25	11	Aquarius	0:43
13	7:23	13	Pisces	13: 4
15	23:50	16	Aries	1:37
18	9:59	18	Taurus	12:54
19	20:27	20	Gemini	22:15
23	4:48	23	Cancer	5:22
24	19:16	25	Leo	10:10
27	6:43	27	Virgo	12:54
29	8:50	29	Libra	14:16
31	10:39	31	Scorpio	15:32

NOV

Day	Time	Day	Sign	Time
1	19: 7	2	Sagittar	18:11
4	19:47	4	Capricrn	23:40
7	0:59	7	Aquarius	8:42
9	19:49	9	Pisces	20:34
12	7:56	12	Aries	9:13
14	20:16	14	Taurus	20:24
16	18:32	17	Gemini	5: 2
19	10:48	19	Cancer	11:12
21	14: 8	21	Leo	15:33
23	18:11	23	Virgo	18:49
25	20:48	25	Libra	21:33
27	23:25	28	Scorpio	0:19
29	14:34	30	Sagittar	3:52

DEC

Day	Time	Day	Sign	Time
2	8: 1	2	Capricrn	9:17
3	12:20	4	Aquarius	17:32
7	2:59	7	Pisces	4:46
9	15:29	9	Aries	17:30
12	3: 1	12	Taurus	5: 9
13	23:14	14	Gemini	13:45
16	16:47	16	Cancer	19: 1
18	18:52	18	Leo	22: 3
20	22:37	21	Virgo	0:19
23	0:20	23	Libra	3: 0
25	3:46	25	Scorpio	6:39
26	23:17	27	Sagittar	11:29
29	14:23	29	Capricrn	17:47

JAN	1	22: 3	2 Taurus 1: 6		JUL	1	22:53	2 Capricrn 13: 3
	4	1:23	4 Gemini 3:26			4	19: 7	5 Aquarius 1:50
	5	9:41	6 Cancer 3:28			7	11:25	7 Pisces 14: 3
	7	13:23	8 Leo 2:53			9	14:24	10 Aries 0:35
	9	14:11	10 Virgo 3:45			11	20:32	12 Taurus 8:12
	11	17:54	12 Libra 7:54			13	22:45	14 Gemini 12:17
	14	2:56	14 Scorpio 16:16			16	3:18	16 Cancer 13:15
	16	19:39	17 Sagittar 4: 3			18	4:16	18 Leo 12:35
	18	17:24	19 Capricrn 17:11			20	2:37	20 Virgo 12:19
	22	0:13	22 Aquarius 5:37			22	12:35	22 Libra 14:34
	24	4:49	24 Pisces 16:23			24	9:55	24 Scorpio 20:41
	26	14:37	27 Aries 1:11			26	15: 8	27 Sagittar 6:41
	28	15:45	29 Taurus 7:46			29	7:47	29 Capricrn 19: 2
	31	3:12	31 Gemini 11:52		AUG	1	5:51	1 Aquarius 7:50
FEB	2	6:51	2 Cancer 13:39			3	9:18	3 Pisces 19:49
	4	6:36	4 Leo 14: 2			5	20:20	6 Aries 6:20
	6	9:53	6 Virgo 14:42			8	8:20	8 Taurus 14:44
	8	10:21	8 Libra 17:40			10	0:21	10 Gemini 20:18
	10	7: 2	11 Scorpio 0:28			12	21:46	12 Cancer 22:50
	13	3:45	13 Sagittar 11:16			14	5:30	14 Leo 23: 7
	15	16:22	16 Capricrn 0:12			16	15:13	16 Virgo 22:49
	18	6: 1	18 Aquarius 12:39			18	16:13	19 Libra 0: 4
	20	16:55	20 Pisces 22:58			20	23:26	21 Scorpio 4:45
	23	1:25	23 Aries 6:58			23	12:41	23 Sagittar 13:35
	25	2:27	25 Taurus 13: 8			26	0:44	26 Capricrn 1:31
	27	12:58	27 Gemini 17:47			27	18:45	28 Aquarius 14:19
MAR	1	17: 1	1 Cancer 20:59			30	17:37	31 Pisces 2: 4
	3	20:25	3 Leo 23: 0		SEP	2	4: 0	2 Aries 12: 3
	5	20:31	6 Virgo 0:47			4	12:30	4 Taurus 20:11
	7	23:30	8 Libra 3:51			6	11:18	7 Gemini 2:19
	9	11:29	10 Scorpio 9:51			8	23:18	9 Cancer 6:13
	12	14:45	12 Sagittar 19:34			11	6:22	11 Leo 8: 3
	14	18:28	15 Capricrn 8: 1			13	2:22	13 Virgo 8:51
	17	15:42	17 Aquarius 20:36			15	3:39	15 Libra 10:16
	20	2:14	20 Pisces 6:58			17	7:11	17 Scorpio 14:11
	22	9:48	22 Aries 14:23			19	13:45	19 Sagittar 21:50
	24	5:42	24 Taurus 19:29			22	5:42	22 Capricrn 8:58
	26	18:41	26 Gemini 23:16			24	13:54	24 Aquarius 21:38
	28	22:26	29 Cancer 2:26			27	1:52	27 Pisces 9:25
	31	0:31	31 Leo 5:22			29	18:59	29 Aries 18:59
APR	2	3:24	2 Virgo 8:31		OCT	1	19:19	2 Taurus 2:16
	4	7:11	4 Libra 12:40			4	0:47	4 Gemini 7:44
	5	21:42	6 Scorpio 18:57			6	5:13	6 Cancer 11:47
	8	23:41	9 Sagittar 4:13			8	9:25	8 Leo 14:42
	11	15:40	11 Capricrn 16: 9			10	12:24	10 Virgo 16:57
	13	22:45	14 Aquarius 4:52			12	15:36	12 Libra 19:32
	16	8: 0	16 Pisces 15:48			14	16:51	14 Scorpio 23:46
	18	15:42	18 Aries 23:26			17	4:12	17 Sagittar 6:53
	20	8:58	21 Taurus 3:56			19	9:24	19 Capricrn 17:17
	23	2:25	23 Gemini 6:28			22	4:51	22 Aquarius 5:39
	24	14:22	25 Cancer 8:23			24	9:48	24 Pisces 17:46
	27	1:58	27 Leo 10:44			26	19:51	27 Aries 3:31
	29	4:50	29 Virgo 14:15			29	2:55	29 Taurus 10:17
MAY	1	9:11	1 Libra 19:24			31	0:25	31 Gemini 14:36
	4	1:59	4 Scorpio 2:36		NOV	2	10:24	2 Cancer 17:32
	5	23:58	6 Sagittar 12:10			4	15:56	4 Leo 20: 4
	8	4:10	8 Capricrn 23:55			6	15:31	6 Virgo 22:55
	10	22:47	11 Aquarius 12:41			8	19: 2	9 Libra 2:43
	13	13: 8	14 Pisces 0:21			10	23:59	11 Scorpio 8:12
	15	22:22	16 Aries 8:57			13	1:26	13 Sagittar 15:34
	18	10:27	18 Taurus 13:52			15	16:31	16 Capricrn 1:37
	20	13:44	20 Gemini 15:52			18	3:33	18 Aquarius 13:45
	22	1:16	22 Cancer 16:27			20	21:44	21 Pisces 2:34
	24	3:17	24 Leo 17:18			23	3:33	23 Aries 12:54
	26	4:48	26 Virgo 19:50			25	16:13	25 Taurus 20: 6
	28	8:37	29 Libra 0:54			27	21:42	27 Gemini 23:56
	31	0: 9	31 Scorpio 8:43			30	0:40	30 Cancer 1:31
JUN	2	0: 5	2 Sagittar 18:54		DEC	1	12: 1	2 Leo 2:30
	4	13:29	5 Capricrn 6:52			3	19:27	4 Virgo 4:24
	7	3: 0	7 Aquarius 19:38			6	4:44	6 Libra 8:14
	9	22:15	10 Pisces 7:47			8	4:19	8 Scorpio 14:25
	12	14:38	12 Aries 17:34			10	8:48	10 Sagittar 22:50
	14	10:38	14 Taurus 23:46			12	22: 1	13 Capricrn 9:14
	16	8:48	17 Gemini 2:22			14	20:22	15 Aquarius 21:16
	18	21:26	19 Cancer 2:33			18	0:21	18 Pisces 9:59
	20	14:40	21 Leo 2: 7			20	17:44	20 Aries 21:37
	22	16:59	23 Virgo 3: 1			23	2:20	23 Taurus 6:12
	24	23: 0	25 Libra 6:52			24	21:39	25 Gemini 10:48
	27	7:37	27 Scorpio 14:17			27	1:55	27 Cancer 12: 3
	29	23: 6	30 Sagittar 0:46			28	8:37	29 Leo 11:42
						31	1:18	31 Virgo 11:47

JAN	2	2:16	2 Capricrn 12:11	JUL	2	1:32	2 Virgo 20:45
	4	15:54	4 Aquarius 21:38		4	20:24	5 Libra 3:21
	6	22: 3	7 Pisces 4:47		7	6:57	7 Scorpio 13:42
	9	9:27	9 Aries 9:56		9	20: 6	10 Sagittar 2:21
	11	6:27	11 Taurus 13:26		12	12: 4	12 Capricrn 15: 6
	13	5: 3	13 Gemini 15:43		14	21:36	15 Aquarius 2:17
	15	11:19	15 Cancer 17:33		16	15:57	17 Pisces 11:16
	17	14:47	17 Leo 20: 4		19	14:45	19 Aries 17:59
	19	18:32	19 Virgo 0:41		21	19:59	21 Taurus 22:36
	22	6:58	22 Libra 8:32		23	23:15	24 Gemini 1:19
	24	13:23	24 Scorpio 19:40		25	11:28	26 Cancer 2:44
	27	1: 4	27 Sagittar 8:28		28	2:47	28 Leo 3:57
	29	14:39	29 Capricrn 20:18		29	13:59	30 Virgo 6:33
FEB	1	0:12	1 Aquarius 5:24	AUG	1	11:49	1 Libra 12: 5
	3	6:43	3 Pisces 11:33		3	3:30	3 Scorpio 21:23
	4	21:43	5 Aries 15:38		6	5:23	6 Sagittar 9:37
	7	14:16	7 Taurus 18:47		8	21:34	8 Capricrn 22:24
	9	7:53	9 Gemini 21:46		10	17:41	11 Aquarius 9:24
	11	20:28	12 Cancer 0:59		13	3:21	13 Pisces 17:41
	14	0:14	14 Leo 4:51		15	7:39	15 Aries 23:37
	16	5:14	16 Virgo 10: 3		17	17:58	18 Taurus 4: 0
	17	20:31	18 Libra 17:36		20	1:17	20 Gemini 7:23
	20	22:33	21 Scorpio 4: 5		22	7:46	22 Cancer 10: 7
	22	17:26	23 Sagittar 16:41		24	2:26	24 Leo 12:38
	25	23: 9	26 Capricrn 5: 2		26	6: 4	26 Virgo 15:54
	28	8:50	28 Aquarius 14:35		28	5:40	28 Libra 21:15
MAR	2	14:49	2 Pisces 20:25		30	20:22	31 Scorpio 5:50
	4	7:39	4 Aries 23:24	SEP	2	13:11	2 Sagittar 17:31
	6	19:22	7 Taurus 1: 9		5	2:38	5 Capricrn 6:24
	8	20:57	9 Gemini 3:12		7	10:54	7 Aquarius 17:42
	11	5: 6	11 Cancer 6:29		9	20:11	10 Pisces 1:46
	13	4: 8	13 Leo 11:15		11	16:21	12 Aries 6:49
	15	9:51	15 Virgo 17:33		14	6:18	14 Taurus 10: 4
	17	19:11	18 Libra 1:41		16	1:58	16 Gemini 12:46
	20	2:52	20 Scorpio 12: 5		18	13:21	18 Cancer 15:25
	22	0:52	23 Sagittar 0:31		20	17:35	20 Leo 19:13
	25	2:52	25 Capricrn 13:18		22	22:45	22 Virgo 23:38
	27	22:24	27 Aquarius 23:51		24	14:41	25 Libra 5:40
	29	20:19	30 Pisces 6:27		26	22:28	27 Scorpio 14:12
APR	31	0:36	1 Aries 9:17		29	4:43	30 Sagittar 1:33
	3	6:25	3 Taurus 9:57	OCT	1	21:48	2 Capricrn 14:30
	5	7:34	5 Gemini 10:25		4	16:53	5 Aquarius 2:28
	7	8:31	7 Cancer 12:21		7	9:50	7 Pisces 11: 9
	9	12:24	9 Leo 16:38		9	10: 8	9 Aries 16: 5
	11	9:48	11 Virgo 23:20		11	4:49	11 Taurus 18:21
	14	5:52	14 Libra 8:14		13	17:39	13 Gemini 19:37
	16	13:46	16 Scorpio 19: 4		15	7:27	15 Cancer 21:23
	19	4:19	19 Sagittar 7:30		17	13:28	18 Leo 0:35
	21	3: 9	21 Capricrn 20:29		19	22:17	20 Virgo 5:36
	23	18:24	24 Aquarius 7:57		21	20:53	22 Libra 12:34
	26	9: 7	26 Pisces 15:55		24	5:17	24 Scorpio 21:41
	28	18:21	28 Aries 19:46		27	1:26	27 Sagittar 9: 3
	30	5: 4	30 Taurus 20:31		29	4:26	29 Capricrn 22: 0
MAY	2	3:32	2 Gemini 20: 4	NOV	1	2:32	1 Aquarius 10:37
	4	3:56	4 Cancer 20:23		3	16:24	3 Pisces 20:32
	6	8:45	6 Leo 23: 5		6	1:36	6 Aries 2:28
	8	20:45	9 Virgo 4:57		7	14:13	8 Taurus 4:49
	10	19: 5	11 Libra 13:54		10	3:48	10 Gemini 5: 8
	13	6: 6	14 Scorpio 1: 1		11	14:43	12 Cancer 5:16
	16	2:53	16 Sagittar 13:46		14	1:55	14 Leo 6:53
	18	12:58	19 Capricrn 2:42		16	3:39	16 Virgo 11: 5
	21	14:21	21 Aquarius 14:32		18	9:40	18 Libra 18:13
	23	23:14	23 Pisces 23:39		20	9:46	21 Scorpio 3:58
	26	0:53	26 Aries 5: 5		23	8:54	23 Sagittar 15:44
	27	17:45	28 Taurus 7: 4		25	9:16	25 Capricrn 4:40
	29	18:20	30 Gemini 6:55		28	1:26	28 Aquarius 17:30
JUN	31	13: 4	1 Cancer 6:29	DEC	30	11:29	1 Pisces 4:30
	2	19: 5	3 Leo 7:40		2	20:35	3 Aries 12: 6
	4	20:35	5 Virgo 11:57		5	0: 6	5 Taurus 15:49
	7	9:14	7 Libra 19:57		7	6:58	7 Gemini 16:30
	9	19:17	10 Scorpio 7: 5		9	6: 8	9 Cancer 15:50
	12	10:50	12 Sagittar 19:51		11	12:59	11 Leo 15:47
	15	2:43	15 Capricrn 8:40		13	13: 4	13 Virgo 18: 9
	17	19:20	17 Aquarius 20:16		15	21:58	16 Libra 0: 8
	20	5:35	20 Pisces 5:43		18	0:53	18 Scorpio 9:43
	22	2:56	22 Aries 12:20		20	0:57	20 Sagittar 21:49
	24	7:43	24 Taurus 15:56		22	13: 8	23 Capricrn 10:51
	26	14:31	26 Gemini 17: 8		25	7:59	25 Aquarius 23:30
	27	23: 4	28 Cancer 17:11		27	22:42	28 Pisces 10:44
	30	10:48	30 Leo 17:48		30	11: 6	30 Aries 19:31

JAN

2	11:59	2	Virgo	16:49
5	3:45	5	Libra	4:44
7	5:28	7	Scorpio	17:13
9	23:8	10	Sagittar	3:56
12	8:13	12	Capricrn	11:28
14	11:39	14	Aquarius	15:57
15	8:9	16	Pisces	18:28
18	17:30	18	Aries	20:21
19	13:35	20	Taurus	22:48
22	21:53	23	Gemini	2:35
25	3:4	25	Cancer	8:5
27	10:9	27	Leo	15:33
28	9:5	30	Virgo	1:9

FEB

1	10:57	1	Libra	12:46
3	20:41	4	Scorpio	1:23
6	6:9	6	Sagittar	12:58
8	14:46	8	Capricrn	21:30
10	21:37	11	Aquarius	2:13
12	17:34	13	Pisces	3:53
14	21:22	15	Aries	4:13
17	1:52	17	Taurus	5:5
18	23:55	19	Gemini	8:1
21	6:33	21	Cancer	13:43
23	12:7	23	Leo	21:59
25	14:59	25	Virgo	8:14
28	8:25	28	Libra	19:57

MAR

2	22:31	3	Scorpio	8:33
5	8:6	5	Sagittar	20:45
8	3:23	8	Capricrn	6:38
10	11:50	10	Aquarius	12:40
11	22:0	12	Pisces	14:50
13	3:51	14	Aries	14:33
16	2:43	16	Taurus	13:55
18	10:51	18	Gemini	15:5
20	19:12	20	Cancer	19:32
22	11:11	23	Leo	3:32
24	23:19	25	Virgo	14:11
27	7:47	28	Libra	2:15
30	8:34	30	Scorpio	14:50

APR

1	7:35	2	Sagittar	3:8
4	9:48	4	Capricrn	13:52
6	16:45	6	Aquarius	21:29
9	0:7	9	Pisces	1:11
10	8:34	11	Aries	1:38
12	20:10	13	Taurus	0:40
14	6:35	15	Gemini	0:31
16	21:7	17	Cancer	3:14
19	7:47	19	Leo	9:52
21	4:17	21	Virgo	20:4
23	18:5	24	Libra	8:15
25	23:50	26	Scorpio	20:53
29	3:15	29	Sagittar	8:56

MAY

1	18:2	1	Capricrn	19:40
3	6:30	4	Aquarius	4:6
5	15:22	6	Pisces	9:21
7	15:4	8	Aries	11:25
10	0:17	10	Taurus	11:25
11	20:22	12	Gemini	11:12
14	8:19	14	Cancer	12:51
16	9:3	16	Leo	17:57
18	22:13	19	Virgo	2:56
20	13:45	21	Libra	14:43
23	11:0	24	Scorpio	3:21
25	14:50	26	Sagittar	15:12
28	15:40	29	Capricrn	1:25
31	3:13	31	Aquarius	9:35

JUN

2	12:16	2	Pisces	15:26
3	22:47	4	Aries	18:51
6	14:27	6	Taurus	20:24
8	2:20	8	Gemini	21:15
10	22:20	10	Cancer	23:2
12	7:17	13	Leo	3:20
14	22:41	15	Virgo	11:8
17	18:55	17	Libra	22:7
20	7:48	20	Scorpio	10:36
22	1:57	22	Sagittar	22:28
24	13:3	25	Capricrn	8:15
26	21:43	27	Aquarius	15:37
29	5:58	29	Pisces	20:52

JUL

1	18:53	2	Aries	0:30
3	1:41	4	Taurus	3:5
6	2:38	6	Gemini	5:20
7	17:43	8	Cancer	8:11
9	22:13	10	Leo	12:44
12	5:23	12	Virgo	19:58
14	18:24	15	Libra	6:13
17	7:1	17	Scorpio	18:29
20	2:7	20	Sagittar	6:36
22	9:12	22	Capricrn	16:29
24	12:45	24	Aquarius	23:17
26	10:14	27	Pisces	3:27
28	21:28	29	Aries	6:8
31	0:7	31	Taurus	8:29

AUG

2	3:51	2	Gemini	11:23
4	8:21	4	Cancer	15:23
6	14:21	6	Leo	20:53
8	3:16	9	Virgo	4:24
11	9:1	11	Libra	14:21
13	6:30	14	Scorpio	2:25
16	11:28	16	Sagittar	14:56
18	23:8	19	Capricrn	1:31
21	7:8	21	Aquarius	8:33
23	12:3	23	Pisces	12:5
25	3:10	25	Aries	13:30
27	8:24	27	Taurus	14:34
29	14:56	29	Gemini	16:47
31	13:11	31	Cancer	21:0

SEP

2	11:23	3	Leo	3:20
5	8:46	5	Virgo	11:37
7	5:40	7	Libra	21:49
9	17:41	10	Scorpio	9:48
12	6:55	12	Sagittar	22:38
14	17:39	15	Capricrn	10:12
17	7:31	17	Aquarius	18:20
19	11:47	19	Pisces	22:19
21	20:46	21	Aries	23:11
23	21:23	23	Taurus	22:54
25	18:15	25	Gemini	23:32
27	4:54	28	Cancer	2:39
29	21:2	30	Leo	8:47

OCT

1	17:29	2	Virgo	17:34
4	16:15	5	Libra	4:17
7	4:24	7	Scorpio	16:24
9	17:30	10	Sagittar	5:18
12	9:7	12	Capricrn	17:33
14	16:49	15	Aquarius	3:7
16	20:42	17	Pisces	8:34
19	1:26	19	Aries	10:9
21	5:32	21	Taurus	9:30
23	0:23	23	Gemini	8:50
24	12:31	25	Cancer	10:11
27	5:41	27	Leo	14:55
29	7:44	29	Virgo	23:12

NOV

1	3:34	1	Libra	10:8
3	17:36	3	Scorpio	22:39
6	8:6	6	Sagittar	11:18
8	14:24	8	Capricrn	23:36
11	9:45	11	Aquarius	9:59
12	23:55	13	Pisces	17:5
15	11:48	15	Aries	20:25
17	12:32	17	Taurus	20:48
19	15:13	19	Gemini	20:3
21	4:38	21	Cancer	20:14
23	13:49	23	Leo	23:12
25	16:39	26	Virgo	6:0
28	5:21	28	Libra	16:19

DEC

30	17:18	1	Scorpio	4:43
3	10:26	3	Sagittar	17:30
5	11:29	6	Capricrn	5:24
8	4:6	8	Aquarius	15:35
10	8:18	10	Pisces	23:21
12	17:27	13	Aries	4:16
14	19:58	15	Taurus	6:30
16	20:33	17	Gemini	7:3
19	2:18	19	Cancer	7:28
22	20:12	21	Leo	9:31
23	3:12	23	Virgo	14:44
25	12:35	25	Libra	23:45
28	10:37	28	Scorpio	11:43
30	21:49	31	Sagittar	0:33

JAN

1	21:59	2	Aries	0:34
3	22:28	4	Taurus	4:59
6	4:39	6	Gemini	11:45
8	13:5	8	Cancer	20:48
10	10:10	11	Leo	7:58
13	11:39	13	Virgo	20:39
15	22:47	16	Libra	9:29
18	15:32	18	Scorpio	20:28
21	3:52	21	Sagittar	3:54
22	22:26	23	Capricrn	7:27
23	20:20	25	Aquarius	8:10
27	6:6	27	Pisces	7:48
28	16:10	29	Aries	8:15
31	0:4	31	Taurus	11:7

FEB

2	5:0	2	Gemini	17:18
4	13:8	5	Cancer	2:40
6	23:40	7	Leo	14:20
9	11:42	10	Virgo	3:8
11	19:14	12	Libra	15:55
14	17:48	15	Scorpio	3:24
17	7:42	17	Sagittar	12:15
19	23:55	19	Capricrn	17:33
21	9:27	21	Aquarius	19:27
23	4:21	23	Pisces	19:9
25	2:10	25	Aries	18:31
27	6:7	27	Taurus	19:36

MAR

29	16:45	1	Gemini	0:6
2	12:59	3	Cancer	8:38
4	11:48	5	Leo	20:20
7	13:15	8	Virgo	9:19
10	4:29	10	Libra	21:55
12	23:15	13	Scorpio	9:12
15	15:6	15	Sagittar	18:31
17	20:5	18	Capricrn	1:14
20	3:58	20	Aquarius	4:55
22	0:57	22	Pisces	5:59
24	4:11	24	Aries	5:42
26	4:11	26	Taurus	6:1
27	11:15	28	Gemini	8:59
29	23:41	30	Cancer	15:59

APR

1	20:17	2	Leo	2:54
3	22:15	4	Virgo	15:49
6	19:16	7	Libra	4:22
8	23:16	9	Scorpio	15:12
13	23:44	12	Sagittar	0:3
13	19:39	14	Capricrn	6:56
16	4:59	16	Aquarius	11:46
18	11:40	18	Pisces	14:28
20	3:50	20	Aries	15:36
22	4:56	22	Taurus	16:29
23	21:8	24	Gemini	18:59
26	12:37	27	Cancer	0:49
28	19:52	29	Leo	10:36

MAY

1	14:50	1	Virgo	23:5
4	0:1	4	Libra	11:40
6	11:39	6	Scorpio	22:18
8	15:51	9	Sagittar	6:27
11	3:37	11	Capricrn	12:33
13	7:59	13	Aquarius	17:10
15	12:56	15	Pisces	20:35
17	18:26	17	Aries	23:4
19	22:43	20	Taurus	1:16
22	4:1	22	Gemini	4:27
24	3:42	24	Cancer	10:4
26	12:16	26	Leo	19:5
29	6:47	29	Virgo	6:59
31	14:32	31	Libra	19:38

JUN

3	2:16	3	Scorpio	6:32
4	21:58	5	Sagittar	14:28
7	16:51	7	Capricrn	19:41
9	18:42	9	Aquarius	23:12
12	0:9	12	Pisces	1:59
14	3:19	14	Aries	4:41
16	6:58	16	Taurus	7:52
17	23:44	18	Gemini	12:11
20	17:0	20	Cancer	18:28
20	21:13	23	Leo	3:26
25	6:55	25	Virgo	14:58
26	12:9	28	Libra	3:40
30	5:29	30	Scorpio	15:11

JUL

2	15:19	2	Sagittar	23:39
4	21:35	5	Capricrn	4:42
6	15:24	7	Aquarius	7:14
9	5:46	9	Pisces	8:39
10	21:22	11	Aries	10:19
13	8:55	13	Taurus	13:17
15	14:41	15	Gemini	18:12
17	22:18	18	Cancer	1:22
20	5:43	20	Leo	10:51
22	21:7	22	Virgo	22:25
23	22:19	25	Libra	11:8
27	19:59	27	Scorpio	23:17
29	3:59	30	Sagittar	8:50

AUG

31	17:25	1	Capricrn	14:43
2	13:20	3	Aquarius	17:11
5	7:14	5	Pisces	17:35
6	19:0	7	Aries	17:44
9	17:38	9	Taurus	19:20
11	3:27	11	Gemini	23:09
13	13:27	14	Cancer	7:4
16	0:53	16	Leo	17:8
18	20:25	19	Virgo	5:1
21	7:46	21	Libra	17:45
22	19:44	24	Scorpio	6:13
26	13:53	26	Sagittar	16:52
29	0:12	29	Capricrn	0:13
30	19:21	31	Aquarius	3:45

SEP

1	1:3	2	Pisces	4:15
3	8:3	4	Aries	3:27
5	0:8	6	Taurus	3:29
7	3:21	8	Gemini	6:14
9	12:3	10	Cancer	12:47
12	1:32	12	Leo	22:51
14	1:1	15	Virgo	11:1
17	12:38	17	Libra	23:48
19	14:54	20	Scorpio	12:11
22	22:52	22	Sagittar	23:17
25	0:36	25	Capricrn	7:56
27	11:32	27	Aquarius	13:10
28	23:5	29	Pisces	14:58

OCT

1	3:53	1	Aries	14:30
3	2:39	3	Taurus	13:46
4	14:3	5	Gemini	15:0
7	12:34	7	Cancer	19:57
10	0:26	10	Leo	5:4
12	15:55	12	Virgo	17:5
14	9:15	15	Libra	5:56
17	5:35	17	Scorpio	18:4
19	22:14	20	Sagittar	4:50
22	11:52	22	Capricrn	13:49
24	0:24	24	Aquarius	20:19
25	18:17	26	Pisces	23:54
28	8:12	29	Aries	0:54
29	9:37	31	Taurus	0:45

NOV

1	9:37	2	Gemini	1:29
3	12:45	4	Cancer	5:5
5	23:40	6	Leo	12:44
8	18:51	8	Virgo	23:59
13	23:38	11	Libra	12:45
13	18:43	14	Scorpio	0:48
15	22:30	16	Sagittar	11:2
18	6:34	18	Capricrn	19:20
20	23:10	21	Aquarius	1:47
23	3:12	23	Pisces	6:19
25	8:35	25	Aries	8:57
27	0:38	27	Taurus	10:23
29	2:53	29	Gemini	11:55

DEC

1	15:16	1	Cancer	15:17
3	12:44	3	Leo	21:53
4	22:2	6	Virgo	8:4
8	14:10	8	Libra	20:29
10	9:12	11	Scorpio	8:42
13	11:29	13	Sagittar	18:51
15	19:42	16	Capricrn	2:22
18	1:37	18	Aquarius	7:44
20	8:52	20	Pisces	11:40
22	9:19	22	Aries	14:43
24	15:50	24	Taurus	17:25
26	15:24	26	Gemini	20:26
28	19:43	29	Cancer	0:44
31	2:14	31	Leo	7:19

JAN	1	4: 8	1 Scorpio 9:40	JUL	1	16: 1	1 Cancer 17:14
	3	1:28	3 Sagittar 12:34		4	4:29	4 Leo 5:40
	4	11: 8	5 Capricrn 12:35		6	16:59	6 Virgo 18:45
	7	9:41	7 Aquarius 11:42		9	5:45	9 Libra 6:45
	8	14:40	9 Pisces 12: 3		10	21:32	11 Scorpio 15:41
	10	22:16	11 Aries 15:21		13	19:53	13 Sagittar 20:37
	13	7:49	13 Taurus 22:22		15	21:29	15 Capricrn 22: 7
	15	22:37	16 Gemini 8:39		17	21:12	17 Aquarius 21:46
	18	8:33	18 Cancer 20:54		19	7:24	19 Pisces 21:31
	20	11:22	21 Leo 9:44		21	22:40	21 Aries 23: 8
	23	17:38	23 Virgo 22: 3		23	12:55	24 Taurus 3:53
	26	8: 9	26 Libra 8:47		26	11:43	26 Gemini 12: 4
	28	15:31	28 Scorpio 16:51		28	22:49	28 Cancer 23: 4
	30	18: 7	30 Sagittar 21:34		31	.11:36	31 Leo 11:43
FEB	31	15:56	1 Capricrn 23:16	AUG	2	14:52	3 Virgo 0:46
	3	15:31	3 Aquarius 23:11		4	23: 0	5 Libra 12:52
	4	23:29	5 Pisces 23: 8		7	9:56	7 Scorpio 22:40
	7	16:48	8 Aries 1: 1		9	14: 3	10 Sagittar 5: 9
	9	22:56	10 Taurus 6:17		11	21:40	12 Capricrn 8:10
	12	10:19	12 Gemini 15:25		13	23:18	14 Aquarius 8:37
	14	17:38	15 Cancer 3:25		16	0:48	16 Pisces 8: 7
	16	18:21	17 Leo 16:19		18	2:59	18 Aries 8:33
	18	3:52	20 Virgo 4:20		20	5:12	20 Taurus 11:40
	22	6:55	22 Libra 14:30		22	17:12	22 Gemini 18:35
	24	5:38	24 Scorpio 22:25		25	0:48	25 Cancer 5: 7
	26	15: 3	27 Sagittar 3:59		26	17:45	27 Leo 17:50
MAR	28	4:14	1 Capricrn 7:19		29	20:59	30 Virgo 6:47
	3	2:19	3 Aquarius 8:57	SEP	1	9:21	1 Libra 18:34
	4	18: 7	5 Pisces 9:54		3	19:47	4 Scorpio 4:21
	7	10:18	7 Aries 11:41		5	7:19	6 Sagittar 11:39
	9	11: 4	9 Taurus 15:54		8	8:56	8 Capricrn 16:14
	11	4: 7	11 Gemini 23:39		9	19:37	10 Aquarius 18:19
	13	19:30	14 Cancer 10:51		12	12:17	12 Pisces 18:47
	16	13:45	16 Leo 23:41		14	12:43	14 Aries 19: 9
	19	5:12	19 Virgo 11:43		16	14:39	16 Taurus 21:15
	20	18:31	21 Libra 21:21		18	17:22	19 Gemini 2:42
	23	1:50	24 Scorpio 4:23		21	7: 7	21 Cancer 12:11
	26	1:25	26 Sagittar 9:24		21	22: 0	24 Leo 0:34
	27	9:54	28 Capricrn 13: 5		26	6:23	26 Virgo 13:31
	29	15:44	30 Aquarius 15:57		28	18:40	29 Libra 0:57
APR	31	21:28	1 Pisces 18:27	OCT	1	3:39	1 Scorpio 10: 5
	2	21:20	3 Aries 21:18		3	7:29	3 Sagittar 17: 3
	5	9:33	6 Taurus 1:38		5	16:17	5 Capricrn 22:11
	7	19: 2	8 Gemini 8:42		7	18:59	8 Aquarius 1:40
	10	12: 2	10 Cancer 19: 3		9	22:50	10 Pisces 3:45
	13	0:52	13 Leo 7:40		11	23:38	12 Aries 5:12
	15	19:58	15 Virgo 19:59		14	1:41	14 Taurus 7:26
	18	5:39	18 Libra 5:41		15	21:43	16 Gemini 11: 3
	20	11:11	20 Scorpio 12: 4		18	13:49	18 Cancer 20:28
	22	15:44	22 Sagittar 15:56		21	1:42	21 Leo 8:13
	24	18:23	24 Capricrn 18:40		23	20:15	23 Virgo 21:10
	26	21: 0	26 Aquarius 21:21		26	1:37	26 Libra 8:38
	28	21:22	29 Pisces 0:36		28	10:27	28 Scorpio 17:15
MAY	1	4: 8	1 Aries 4:40		30	14: 4	30 Sagittar 23:15
	2	15:37	3 Taurus 9:57	NOV	1	20:57	2 Capricrn 3:37
	5	16:32	5 Gemini 17:16		3	21:55	4 Aquarius 7:10
	8	2:26	8 Cancer 3:17		6	3:24	6 Pisces 10:16
	10	14:42	10 Leo 15:39		8	11: 5	8 Aries 13:11
	12	9:53	13 Virgo 4:22		10	9:11	10 Taurus 16:33
	15	13:43	15 Libra 14:45		12	13:28	12 Gemini 21:32
	17	5:58	17 Scorpio 21:20		14	21:14	15 Cancer 5:25
	19	23:34	20 Sagittar 0:33		17	13:15	17 Leo 16:28
	22	0:59	22 Capricrn 2: 0		19	22:43	20 Virgo 5:22
	24	2:20	24 Aquarius 3:23		22	16:20	22 Libra 17:19
	25	3:13	26 Pisces 5:58		24	19:40	25 Scorpio 2: 9
	28	9: 5	28 Aries 10:17		27	1:41	27 Sagittar 7:35
	30	4:45	30 Taurus 16:25		29	5:11	29 Capricrn 10:43
JUN	1	23:10	2 Gemini 0:30	DEC	30	23:23	1 Aquarius 13: 1
	4	9:21	4 Cancer 10:46		3	10:19	3 Pisces 15:36
	6	21:45	6 Leo 23: 3		5	12:19	5 Aries 19: 0
	9	7:23	9 Virgo 12: 3		7	23:13	7 Taurus 23:30
	11	21:59	11 Libra 23:22		10	0: 7	10 Gemini 5:33
	14	0:42	14 Scorpio 6:59		12	8: 9	12 Cancer 13:47
	16	9:25	16 Sagittar 10:36		13	4:20	15 Leo 0:37
	18	10:22	18 Capricrn 11:30		17	7:21	17 Virgo 13:23
	20	10:26	20 Aquarius 11:34		19	20: 4	19 Libra 1:56
	21	17:39	22 Pisces 12:36		22	11:17	22 Scorpio 12: 5
	24	14:42	24 Aries 15:53		24	12:18	24 Sagittar 17:44
	26	20:17	26 Taurus 21:52		26	15: 7	26 Capricrn 20:24
	29	5:46	29 Gemini 6:27		28	12:15	28 Aquarius 21:21
					30	16:42	30 Pisces 22:17

JAN				
1	16:27	1	Cancer	16:42
4	3:19	4	Leo	3:33
6	7:38	6	Virgo	12:43
8	19:34	8	Libra	19:49
10	23:37	10	Scorpio	0:25
13	2:16	13	Sagittar	2:32
15	2:50	15	Capricrn	3: 7
17	3:34	17	Aquarius	3:53
19	0:33	19	Pisces	6:43
21	12:42	21	Aries	13: 8
23	5:10	23	Taurus	23:19
26	11: 8	26	Gemini	11:44
28	23:24	29	Cancer	0: 4
31	9:55	31	Leo	10:37
FEB				
2	13: 4	2	Virgo	18:58
5	0:30	5	Libra	1:18
8	19:38	7	Scorpio	5:56
9	8:13	9	Sagittar	9: 7
11	10:22	11	Capricrn	11:19
13	12:26	13	Aquarius	13:28
15	10:35	15	Pisces	16:51
17	21:28	17	Aries	22:47
18	22: 0	20	Taurus	7:58
22	18: 7	22	Gemini	19:48
25	6:29	25	Cancer	8:16
27	17:17	27	Leo	19: 6
MAR				
L	21:17	2	Virgo	3: 6
4	6:32	4	Libra	8:23
5	13:58	6	Scorpio	11:50
8	12:29	8	Sagittar	14:28
10	15: 3	10	Capricrn	17: 9
12	18:16	12	Aquarius	20:31
14	20:12	14	Pisces	1: 9
17	5: 3	17	Aries	7:41
19	10:45	19	Taurus	16:39
22	0:53	22	Gemini	4: 0
24	13:17	24	Cancer	16:33
27	0:47	27	Leo	4: 5
29	8: 9	29	Virgo	12:37
31	14:30	31	Libra	17:37
APR				
2	13:59	2	Scorpio	19:55
4	19:41	4	Sagittar	21: 5
6	19:23	6	Capricrn	22:42
8	22:32	9	Aquarius	1:57
11	3:58	11	Pisces	7:20
13	13:13	13	Aries	14:49
15	14:34	16	Taurus	0:18
18	8:37	18	Gemini	11:37
20	19:28	21	Cancer	0:10
23	9:56	23	Leo	12:22
25	21:38	25	Virgo	22: 3
28	2: 9	28	Libra	3:50
29	15:15	30	Scorpio	6: 0
MAY				
4	4:52	2	Sagittar	6: 3
4	2:36	4	Capricrn	6: 5
6	7:23	6	Aquarius	7:56
8	12:40	8	Pisces	12:44
10	20: 3	10	Aries	20:32
12	18:15	13	Taurus	6:37
15	12:43	15	Gemini	18:15
18	1:11	18	Cancer	6:49
20	17:27	20	Leo	19:21
22	22:13	23	Virgo	6: 8
25	8:18	25	Libra	13:22
27	11:22	27	Scorpio	16:32
29	12: 7	29	Sagittar	16:39
31	13: 5	31	Capricrn	15:44
JUN				
2	11:14	2	Aquarius	16: 0
4	16:57	4	Pisces	19:14
7	0:44	7	Aries	2:11
9	11:51	9	Taurus	12:16
11	21:22	12	Gemini	0:12
14	6:58	14	Cancer	12:50
16	19:32	17	Leo	1:20
19	7:29	19	Virgo	12:34
21	20:45	21	Libra	21: 5
23	3:38	24	Scorpio	1:51
25	23:29	26	Sagittar	3: 9
27	22: 6	28	Capricrn	2:30
29	21:32	30	Aquarius	2: 1

JUL				
1	8:50	2	Pisces	3:46
4	4: 9	4	Aries	9:11
6	3:18	6	Taurus	18:23
9	0:49	9	Gemini	6:10
11	15:35	11	Cancer	18:52
14	2: 1	14	Leo	7: 8
16	1:26	16	Virgo	18: 9
18	22:27	19	Libra	3: 2
23	5:13	21	Scorpio	9: 2
23	11:58	23	Sagittar	11:59
25	8:54	25	Capricrn	12:38
27	8:57	27	Aquarius	12:37
29	10:46	29	Pisces	13:49
31	14: 1	31	Aries	17:55
AUG				
1	15:19	3	Taurus	1:48
5	8:48	5	Gemini	12:55
7	21:31	8	Cancer	1:31
10	9:53	10	Leo	13:40
12	23:52	13	Virgo	0: 9
15	5:17	15	Libra	8:31
17	3:16	17	Scorpio	14:38
19	15:50	19	Sagittar	18:35
21	18:13	21	Capricrn	20:47
23	19:41	23	Aquarius	22: 7
24	17:18	25	Pisces	23:56
28	1:17	28	Aries	3:39
29	10:53	30	Taurus	10:29
SEP				
1	18:21	1	Gemini	20:41
4	6:49	4	Cancer	9: 1
6	19:17	6	Leo	21:16
9	4: 9	9	Virgo	7:31
11	13:36	11	Libra	15: 5
13	2:33	13	Scorpio	20:19
15	22:51	15	Sagittar	23:58
18	1:50	18	Capricrn	2:48
20	4:37	20	Aquarius	5:27
21	21:50	22	Pisces	8:34
24	12:21	24	Aries	12:57
26	11:39	26	Taurus	19:35
29	4:46	29	Gemini	5: 5
OCT				
1	16:55	1	Cancer	17: 3
4	3: 4	4	Leo	5:36
6	2: 4	6	Virgo	16:14
8	11:29	8	Libra	23:33
10	16:42	11	Scorpio	3:47
12	19:43	13	Sagittar	6:11
14	16:41	15	Capricrn	8:14
17	0:57	17	Aquarius	11: 1
19	6:46	19	Pisces	15: 5
21	10:35	21	Aries	20:37
23	17:46	24	Taurus	3:52
26	3: 4	26	Gemini	13:19
28	19:25	29	Cancer	1: 0
31	11:51	31	Leo	13:49
NOV				
2	11:38	3	Virgo	1:19
5	0:34	5	Libra	9:22
7	5:20	7	Scorpio	13:27
9	7: 2	9	Sagittar	14:47
10	8: 7	11	Capricrn	15:18
13	8:50	13	Aquarius	16:49
15	6:57	15	Pisces	20:28
17	17:42	18	Aries	2:31
20	1:25	20	Taurus	10:38
22	20:25	22	Gemini	20:35
23	15:43	25	Cancer	8:17
27	10:44	27	Leo	21:10
29	11: 2	30	Virgo	9:30
DEC				
2	8:57	2	Libra	18:56
4	14:35	5	Scorpio	0: 7
6	16:22	7	Sagittar	1:34
8	11: 5	9	Capricrn	1: 7
10	19:26	11	Aquarius	0:57
12	23:41	13	Pisces	2:56
15	7:35	15	Aries	8: 5
17	6: 7	17	Taurus	16:16
19	13: 7	20	Gemini	2:46
20	17:44	22	Cancer	14:46
24	12:22	25	Leo	3:36
25	18:10	27	Virgo	16:11
29	13:15	30	Libra	2:45

JAN 1	16:35	1 Pisces	20:35	JUL 1	10:30	1 Libra	11:17
4	6:51	4 Aries	7:35	2	6:12	3 Scorpio	14:34
6	0:30	6 Taurus	20:29	5	14:19	5 Sagittar	16:14
9	3:53	9 Gemini	8:27	7	9:25	7 Capricrn	17:21
11	13:12	11 Cancer	17:34	9	17:55	9 Aquarius	19:36
13	19:29	13 Leo	23:40	11	23: 5	12 Pisces	0:42
15	14:25	16 Virgo	3:46	14	8: 2	14 Aries	9:35
18	2:59	18 Libra	7: 0	16	8: 8	16 Taurus	21:30
20	10: 2	20 Scorpio	10: 4	19	8:58	19 Gemini	10:10
22	9: 5	22 Sagittar	13:17	21	12:27	21 Cancer	21:15
24	12:42	24 Capricrn	17: 1	24	5: 1	24 Leo	5:48
26	17:34	26 Aquarius	22: 6	26	11:27	26 Virgo	12: 4
28	14:47	28 Pisces	5:34	28	16:12	28 Libra	16:41
31	10:53	31 Aries	16: 2	29	23:24	30 Scorpio	20: 9
FEB 3	3:22	3 Taurus	4:41	AUG 1	22:35	1 Sagittar	22:50
5	13:52	5 Gemini	17:10	3	18:11	3 Capricrn	1:17
7	21:51	8 Cancer	2:58	6	4:28	6 Aquarius	4:32
10	4:15	10 Leo	9: 8	8	5:25	8 Pisces	9:51
12	5:46	12 Virgo	12:22	10	13:47	10 Aries	18:13
14	10: 6	14 Libra	14: 8	12	8:20	13 Taurus	5:32
16	14:18	16 Scorpio	15:53	15	14: 1	15 Gemini	18:10
18	18: 8	18 Sagittar	18:37	17	22:24	18 Cancer	5:38
20	17:34	20 Capricrn	22:54	20	13:13	20 Leo	14:16
22	23:24	23 Aquarius	5: 2	22	18:34	22 Virgo	19:53
24	23: 6	25 Pisces	13:19	24	20:28	24 Libra	23:22
27	17:34	27 Aries	23:55	26	13:49	27 Scorpio	1:49
MAR 2	11:12	2 Taurus	12:24	29	1:32	29 Sagittar	4:13
4	18:31	5 Gemini	1:12	31	1:35	31 Capricrn	7:18
7	11:43	7 Cancer	12: 4	SEP 2	8:58	2 Aquarius	11:39
9	13: 9	9 Leo	19:19	4	15: 8	4 Pisces	17:52
11	20:59	11 Virgo	22:52	6	23:39	7 Aries	2:29
13	18: 6	13 Libra	23:52	9	0:56	9 Taurus	13:32
15	23:41	16 Scorpio	0: 3	11	23:10	12 Gemini	2: 6
17	19:52	18 Sagittar	1: 8	14	12:40	14 Cancer	14: 9
20	2:52	20 Capricrn	4:25	16	20:51	16 Leo	23:36
22	3:32	22 Aquarius	10:34	19	2:51	19 Virgo	5:29
24	6:38	24 Pisces	19:30	21	5:43	21 Libra	8:18
26	22:48	27 Aries	6:40	22	22:29	23 Scorpio	9:39
29	13:44	29 Taurus	19:14	25	7:43	25 Sagittar	10:25
APR 1	6:24	1 Gemini	8: 7	27	10:52	27 Capricrn	12:45
3	11:39	3 Cancer	19:44	29	14: 7	29 Aquarius	17:17
5	20:43	6 Leo	4:26	OCT 1	20:51	2 Pisces	0:18
7	23: 4	8 Virgo	9:21	4	5:51	4 Aries	9:38
10	5:45	10 Libra	10:55	6	3:45	6 Taurus	20:52
11	21:15	12 Scorpio	10:32	9	9:10	9 Gemini	9:23
14	3: 4	14 Sagittar	10: 8	11	18:17	11 Cancer	21:53
16	4:32	16 Capricrn	11:39	14	8: 1	14 Leo	8:29
18	13: 3	18 Aquarius	16:31	16	15: 3	16 Virgo	15:36
20	14:48	21 Pisces	1: 7	18	18:16	18 Libra	18:55
23	3:19	23 Aries	12:35	20	14:20	20 Scorpio	19:26
25	11:19	26 Taurus	1:23	22	18:11	22 Sagittar	19: 1
28	4:41	28 Gemini	14:11	24	17:25	24 Capricrn	19:40
MAY 30	16:35	1 Cancer	1:56	26	21:53	26 Aquarius	23: 3
3	2:50	3 Leo	11:34	29	4:27	29 Pisces	5:51
5	10: 7	5 Virgo	18: 6	31	14: 0	31 Aries	15:38
7	13:55	7 Libra	21:12	NOV 2	20:58	3 Taurus	3:19
9	14:28	9 Scorpio	21:34	5	13:51	5 Gemini	15:53
11	16:15	11 Sagittar	20:50	8	2:34	8 Cancer	4:26
13	18:21	13 Capricrn	21: 4	10	14: 9	10 Leo	15:49
15	19:48	16 Aquarius	0:15	12	22: 9	13 Virgo	0:29
18	3:48	18 Pisces	7:34	15	4: 7	15 Libra	5:22
20	17: 6	20 Aries	18:34	16	13:18	17 Scorpio	6:40
22	7:32	23 Taurus	7:27	19	4:53	19 Sagittar	5:54
25	19:50	25 Gemini	20:10	21	4:14	21 Capricrn	5:12
28	3: 8	28 Leo	7:37	23	5:50	23 Aquarius	6:54
30	11:28	30 Leo	17:15	25	8:45	25 Pisces	12: 9
JUN 1	19:21	2 Virgo	0:39	27	20:33	27 Aries	21:27
4	0:30	4 Libra	5:17	29	21:54	30 Taurus	9:19
6	3:32	6 Scorpio	7:14	DEC 2	21:40	2 Gemini	22: 0
8	3:18	8 Sagittar	7:24	5	9:42	5 Cancer	10:22
9	23:17	10 Capricrn	7:32	7	21: 9	7 Leo	21:48
12	5:39	12 Aquarius	9:41	10	2:38	10 Virgo	7:13
14	11:25	14 Pisces	15:34	12	13:21	12 Libra	13:46
16	21:21	17 Aries	1:31	14	3: 8	14 Scorpio	16:52
19	9:21	19 Taurus	14: 3	16	16:52	16 Sagittar	17:10
21	23: 5	22 Gemini	2:45	18	16:10	18 Capricrn	16:27
24	4:36	24 Cancer	13:51	20	16:38	20 Aquarius	16:54
26	19:57	26 Leo	22:55	22	15:24	22 Pisces	20:33
29	3:24	29 Virgo	6: 3	25	4: 9	25 Aries	21:27
				27	0:59	27 Taurus	15:43
				30	4:13	30 Gemini	4:27

Month	Day	Time	Day	Sign	Time
JAN	1	7:38	1	Libra	10:44
	3	6:41	3	Scorpio	14:36
	5	12:4	5	Sagittar	20:13
	7	19:4	8	Capricrn	3:30
	10	3:56	10	Aquarius	12:42
	12	13:18	13	Pisces	0:3
	15	3:38	15	Aries	12:56
	17	23:50	18	Taurus	1:16
	20	9:0	20	Gemini	10:32
	22	7:37	22	Cancer	15:35
	24	15:3	24	Leo	17:11
	26	9:32	26	Virgo	17:12
	28	9:56	28	Libra	17:43
	30	12:25	30	Scorpio	20:18
FEB	1	16:51	2	Sagittar	1:36
	4	1:21	4	Capricrn	9:27
	6	11:18	6	Aquarius	19:22
	8	23:4	9	Pisces	6:59
	11	18:41	11	Aries	19:50
	14	4:41	14	Taurus	8:36
	16	12:56	16	Gemini	19:10
	19	0:24	19	Cancer	1:47
	20	23:29	21	Leo	4:19
	22	23:50	23	Virgo	4:12
	24	19:1	25	Libra	3:29
	27	0:14	27	Scorpio	4:14
	29	3:23	29	Sagittar	7:55
MAR	2	13:34	2	Capricrn	15:3
	4	21:45	5	Aquarius	1:8
	7	10:13	7	Pisces	13:8
	10	0:25	10	Aries	2:1
	12	12:57	12	Taurus	14:45
	14	17:27	15	Gemini	1:53
	17	9:20	17	Cancer	9:57
	19	14:6	19	Leo	14:15
	21	2:53	21	Virgo	15:21
	23	5:13	23	Libra	14:48
	25	18:27	25	Scorpio	14:34
	27	10:27	27	Sagittar	16:31
	29	10:32	29	Capricrn	22:0
APR	1	6:34	1	Aquarius	7:14
	3	16:56	3	Pisces	19:11
	5	19:4	6	Aries	8:10
	8	2:28	8	Taurus	20:39
	10	18:50	11	Gemini	7:33
	13	8:7	13	Cancer	16:4
	15	18:51	15	Leo	21:44
	17	20:44	18	Virgo	0:35
	19	14:30	20	Libra	1:23
	21	16:12	22	Scorpio	1:33
	23	15:23	24	Sagittar	2:48
	25	22:17	26	Capricrn	6:50
	28	6:33	28	Aquarius	14:39
MAY	30	18:38	1	Pisces	1:56
	3	9:23	3	Aries	14:52
	6	2:9	6	Taurus	3:13
	7	23:59	8	Gemini	13:34
	10	19:14	10	Cancer	21:34
	13	2:4	13	Leo	3:23
	15	6:53	15	Virgo	7:18
	17	9:27	17	Libra	9:41
	19	22:12	19	Scorpio	11:12
	21	12:50	21	Sagittar	13:0
	23	3:53	23	Capricrn	16:35
	25	9:45	25	Aquarius	23:19
	27	19:28	28	Pisces	9:39
	30	8:4	30	Aries	22:19
JUN	1	23:21	2	Taurus	10:44
	4	8:4	4	Gemini	20:50
	6	14:54	7	Cancer	4:2
	8	21:43	9	Leo	9:1
	11	1:48	11	Virgo	12:41
	13	5:8	13	Libra	15:44
	15	8:30	15	Scorpio	18:32
	17	11:16	17	Sagittar	21:34
	19	23:2	20	Capricrn	1:45
	21	23:56	22	Aquarius	8:15
	24	6:46	24	Pisces	17:56
	26	21:47	27	Aries	6:13
	29	13:58	29	Taurus	18:53
JUL	2	3:43	2	Gemini	5:16
	3	23:37	4	Cancer	12:11
	6	7:27	6	Leo	16:13
	8	16:33	8	Virgo	18:45
	10	17:43	10	Libra	21:7
	12	19:43	13	Scorpio	0:7
	14	19:42	15	Sagittar	4:5
	17	3:35	17	Capricrn	9:18
	19	9:56	19	Aquarius	16:22
	21	20:5	22	Pisces	1:58
	24	9:26	24	Aries	14:2
	26	23:4	27	Taurus	2:56
	29	5:44	29	Gemini	14:4
	31	21:23	31	Cancer	21:32
AUG	2	18:15	3	Leo	1:20
	4	20:3	5	Virgo	2:51
	6	21:21	7	Libra	3:50
	9	1:35	9	Scorpio	5:46
	11	8:51	11	Sagittar	9:29
	13	7:55	13	Capricrn	15:15
	15	15:37	15	Aquarius	23:7
	18	7:29	18	Pisces	9:10
	20	13:19	20	Aries	21:14
	22	5:45	23	Taurus	10:17
	25	14:38	25	Gemini	22:13
	28	1:53	28	Cancer	6:54
	30	4:58	30	Leo	11:32
SEP	1	6:43	1	Virgo	12:57
	3	6:46	3	Libra	13:17
	5	7:53	5	Scorpio	13:17
	7	13:41	7	Sagittar	15:36
	9	11:33	9	Capricrn	20:46
	11	21:25	12	Aquarius	4:52
	14	7:39	14	Pisces	15:26
	16	19:42	16	Aries	3:43
	19	22:50	19	Taurus	16:46
	22	3:1	22	Gemini	5:6
	24	6:26	24	Cancer	14:58
	26	13:57	26	Leo	21:9
	28	16:52	28	Virgo	23:42
	30	18:53	30	Libra	23:47
OCT	2	21:50	2	Scorpio	23:12
	4	23:14	4	Sagittar	23:54
	6	20:16	7	Capricrn	3:29
	9	3:10	9	Aquarius	10:44
	11	12:21	11	Pisces	21:18
	14	2:5	14	Aries	9:59
	16	8:15	16	Taurus	22:49
	19	3:46	19	Gemini	11:0
	21	17:51	21	Cancer	21:18
	23	22:33	24	Leo	4:51
	26	2:22	26	Virgo	9:10
	28	6:5	28	Libra	10:37
	30	11:20	30	Scorpio	10:25
NOV	1	9:44	1	Sagittar	10:21
	3	6:56	3	Capricrn	12:23
	5	12:18	5	Aquarius	18:3
	7	17:20	8	Pisces	3:46
	10	10:9	10	Aries	16:13
	12	18:40	13	Taurus	5:13
	15	11:24	15	Gemini	17:1
	17	23:28	18	Cancer	2:53
	20	10:18	20	Leo	10:39
	22	7:7	22	Virgo	16:11
	24	14:58	24	Libra	19:25
	25	2:30	26	Scorpio	20:45
	28	17:7	28	Sagittar	21:19
	30	18:33	30	Capricrn	22:50
DEC	2	22:41	2	Aquarius	3:13
	4	23:25	5	Pisces	11:35
	7	18:29	7	Aries	23:27
	9	10:31	10	Taurus	12:28
	12	19:28	13	Gemini	0:8
	15	4:55	15	Cancer	9:20
	17	12:3	17	Leo	16:17
	19	19:23	19	Virgo	21:35
	21	21:38	22	Libra	1:37
	23	13:16	24	Scorpio	4:30
	26	2:46	26	Sagittar	6:37
	28	5:55	28	Capricrn	8:58
	30	9:3	30	Aquarius	13:9

JAN

2	18:47	2	Gemini	21:20
4	11:38	4	Cancer	22:20
6	11: 3	6	Leo	21:32
8	13:23	8	Virgo	21: 8
10	19:48	10	Libra	23:11
12	13:11	13	Scorpio	4:54
15	2:34	15	Sagittar	14:10
17	12: 6	18	Capricrn	1:44
20	13:27	20	Aquarius	14:15
22	18:41	23	Pisces	2:51
25	9:53	25	Aries	14:42
27	8:35	28	Taurus	0:29
29	23: 9	30	Gemini	6:51

FEB

1	0:14	1	Cancer	9:22
2	22: 1	3	Leo	9: 6
5	6:10	5	Virgo	8: 3
6	20:42	7	Libra	8:30
9	12:18	9	Scorpio	12:22
11	20:14	11	Sagittar	20:24
13	20: 8	14	Capricrn	7:42
16	19:59	16	Aquarius	20:22
19	8:28	19	Pisces	8:52
21	19:50	21	Aries	20:23
24	5:42	24	Taurus	6:19
26	13:19	26	Gemini	13:48
28	5: 3	28	Cancer	18: 7

MAR

2	18:48	2	Leo	19:30
4	3:43	4	Virgo	19:17
6	18:37	6	Libra	19:26
8	21: 5	8	Scorpio	22: 0
11	3:20	11	Sagittar	4:23
13	5:32	13	Capricrn	14:36
16	1:46	16	Aquarius	3: 2
18	12:23	18	Pisces	15:32
21	2:28	21	Aries	2:41
23	10:41	23	Taurus	11:59
25	17:58	25	Gemini	19:15
27	16:51	28	Cancer	0:20
30	2: 1	30	Leo	3:15

APR

31	11:36	1	Virgo	4:39
3	4:34	3	Libra	5:49
5	7: 2	5	Scorpio	8:22
7	12:22	7	Sagittar	13:48
9	9:22	9	Capricrn	22:47
12	9: 0	12	Aquarius	10:34
14	10:10	14	Pisces	23: 5
17	8:44	17	Aries	10:14
19	17:32	19	Taurus	18:57
21	23:55	22	Gemini	1:17
24	2:39	24	Cancer	5:44
26	7:40	26	Leo	8:55
27	23:46	28	Virgo	11:27
30	12:50	30	Libra	14: 2

MAY

2	16:24	2	Scorpio	17:36
4	21:57	4	Sagittar	23:11
7	5:54	7	Capricrn	7:34
9	17:58	9	Aquarius	18:41
11	23:28	12	Pisces	7: 9
14	17:36	14	Aries	18:41
17	2:30	17	Taurus	3:28
19	8:15	19	Gemini	9: 7
21	5:20	21	Cancer	12:23
23	13:51	23	Leo	14:34
25	10:35	25	Virgo	16:51
27	19:29	27	Libra	20: 6
30	0:14	30	Scorpio	0:48

JUN

1	6:45	1	Sagittar	7:15
3	10:32	3	Capricrn	15:50
6	2:20	6	Aquarius	2:41
8	10:31	8	Pisces	15: 5
11	3: 2	11	Aries	3:11
13	12:41	13	Taurus	12:43
15	2: 4	15	Gemini	18:33
17	18:48	17	Cancer	21: 7
19	19:59	19	Leo	21:58
21	22:20	21	Virgo	22:57
23	9:33	24	Libra	1:31
26	5: 9	26	Scorpio	6:25
28	7:55	28	Sagittar	13:39
30	22:12	30	Capricrn	22:54

JUL

3	9:32	3	Aquarius	9:54
5	22:15	5	Pisces	22:17
8	9: 4	8	Aries	10:50
9	19:49	10	Taurus	21:27
12	12:27	13	Gemini	4:21
14	16:24	14	Cancer	7:16
16	21: 3	17	Leo	7:31
18	17:14	19	Virgo	7: 8
21	4: 1	21	Libra	8:11
23	11:34	23	Scorpio	12: 4
25	17: 8	25	Sagittar	19:10
27	17:35	27	Capricrn	4:51
30	11:31	30	Aquarius	16:15

AUG

1	15: 0	2	Pisces	4:42
4	10: 8	4	Aries	17:23
6	20:44	7	Taurus	4:48
9	4:42	9	Gemini	13: 6
11	3:25	11	Cancer	17:21
13	9:42	13	Leo	18:10
15	4:37	15	Virgo	17:19
17	7:44	17	Libra	17: 4
19	11:44	19	Scorpio	19:20
21	21:21	22	Sagittar	1:14
24	3:58	24	Capricrn	10:34
26	10: 2	26	Aquarius	22: 9
28	18:28	29	Pisces	10:43
31	11:48	31	Aries	23:15

SEP

3	0:12	3	Taurus	10:49
5	14:55	5	Gemini	20: 2
7	13: 9	8	Cancer	1:52
9	21:22	10	Leo	4:12
11	15:19	12	Virgo	4: 9
13	22:32	14	Libra	3:39
16	0:19	16	Scorpio	4:44
18	5:29	18	Sagittar	9: 2
20	10:35	20	Capricrn	17:11
23	4:17	23	Aquarius	4:24
25	16:34	25	Pisces	17: 0
27	16:18	28	Aries	5:22
30	15:24	30	Taurus	16:29

OCT

2	13:44	3	Gemini	1:38
5	6:42	5	Cancer	8:20
7	10:24	7	Leo	12:10
9	11:49	9	Virgo	13:46
11	4:30	11	Libra	14:16
13	14:14	13	Scorpio	15:18
15	8:16	15	Sagittar	18:36
17	21:52	18	Capricrn	1:22
20	7:35	20	Aquarius	11:40
22	21:11	23	Pisces	0: 5
25	1:19	25	Aries	12:28
27	18: 4	27	Taurus	23: 9
30	7:29	30	Gemini	7:31

NOV

1	10:50	1	Cancer	13:42
3	17:24	3	Leo	18: 2
5	18: 0	5	Virgo	20:57
7	22: 0	7	Libra	23: 3
9	19: 6	10	Scorpio	1:14
12	3:13	12	Sagittar	4:42
14	8:58	14	Capricrn	10:42
16	18: 1	16	Aquarius	20: 0
19	7:34	19	Pisces	8: 0
21	18:22	21	Aries	20:36
23	22:38	24	Taurus	7:23
26	13: 7	26	Gemini	15: 9
28	18:17	28	Cancer	20:12
30	21:46	30	Leo	23:34

DEC

2	17:54	3	Virgo	2:23
5	3:46	5	Libra	5:23
6	23:59	7	Scorpio	8:57
9	12:11	9	Sagittar	13:28
11	18:40	11	Capricrn	19:51
14	3:45	14	Aquarius	4:29
16	5:15	16	Pisces	16:14
19	4:48	19	Aries	5: 3
21	14:15	21	Taurus	16:32
23	21:27	23	Gemini	0:37
25	21:25	26	Cancer	5: 3
27	23:42	28	Leo	7: 5
29	23:16	30	Virgo	8:29

Mo	Day	Time	Day	Sign	Time
JAN	3	8:15	3	Aquarius	9:31
	4	4:52	5	Pisces	20: 7
	8	3:42	8	Aries	4:29
	10	9: 0	10	Taurus	10: 6
	12	12:37	12	Gemini	12:50
	13	23: 0	14	Cancer	13:22
	16	11:40	16	Leo	13:10
	17	4:48	18	Virgo	14:13
	20	16:37	20	Libra	18:27
	23	1:58	23	Scorpio	2:55
	25	12:34	25	Sagittar	14:52
	28	0: 8	28	Capricrn	3:58
	30	13:34	30	Aquarius	16: 0
FEB	31	13:35	2	Pisces	1:59
	4	7:27	4	Aries	9:55
	6	13:31	6	Taurus	15:59
	8	17:41	8	Gemini	20: 8
	10	10: 4	10	Cancer	22:26
	12	21: 5	12	Leo	23:34
	14	21:54	15	Virgo	0:57
	17	1:38	17	Libra	4:28
	19	8:30	19	Scorpio	11:37
	21	19:10	21	Sagittar	22:34
	24	0:31	24	Capricrn	11:28
	26	20: 6	26	Aquarius	23:36
MAR	28	17:20	1	Pisces	9:14
	3	12:57	3	Aries	16:17
	5	18:12	5	Taurus	21:30
	7	22:16	8	Gemini	1:33
	10	2: 1	10	Cancer	4:46
	12	7:22	12	Leo	7:23
	13	15:55	14	Virgo	10: 6
	16	10:35	16	Libra	14: 8
	18	17: 4	18	Scorpio	20:54
	21	2:56	21	Sagittar	7: 1
	23	1:52	23	Capricrn	19:32
	26	3:47	26	Aquarius	7:56
	28	7:21	28	Pisces	17:52
	30	20:47	31	Aries	0:34
APR	2	1: 4	2	Taurus	4:43
	4	3:57	4	Gemini	7:34
	6	0: 8	6	Cancer	10: 8
	8	9:24	8	Leo	13: 5
	10	7:56	10	Virgo	16:51
	12	18:10	12	Libra	22: 2
	15	1:19	15	Scorpio	5:21
	17	11: 6	17	Sagittar	15:20
	20	2:12	20	Capricrn	3:32
	22	14:34	22	Aquarius	16:11
	25	1: 1	25	Pisces	2:54
	27	6:24	27	Aries	10: 9
	29	10:45	29	Taurus	14: 2
MAY	1	13: 4	1	Gemini	15:45
	3	14:38	3	Cancer	16:51
	5	15:18	5	Leo	18:42
	7	20:55	7	Virgo	22:17
	10	0:29	10	Libra	4: 6
	12	11:52	12	Scorpio	12:16
	14	18:54	14	Sagittar	22:41
	16	15:13	17	Capricrn	10:51
	19	19:55	19	Aquarius	23:38
	22	5:24	22	Pisces	11: 9
	24	16:23	24	Aries	19:36
	26	21:22	27	Taurus	0:17
	28	23: 9	29	Gemini	1:52
	30	18: 7	31	Cancer	1:53
JUN	1	23:32	2	Leo	2: 9
	4	0:54	4	Virgo	4:21
	6	8:45	6	Libra	9:36
	8	15:12	8	Scorpio	18: 1
	11	2: 9	11	Sagittar	4:57
	12	23:47	13	Capricrn	17:21
	16	3:31	16	Aquarius	6: 8
	18	11:15	18	Pisces	18: 3
	21	1:52	21	Aries	3:40
	23	7:52	23	Taurus	9:50
	25	10:40	25	Gemini	12:25
	26	18:20	27	Cancer	12:28
	29	10:14	29	Leo	11:46

Mo	Day	Time	Day	Sign	Time
JUL	30	15:28	1	Virgo	12:24
	3	14:37	3	Libra	16: 9
	5	22:18	5	Scorpio	23:49
	8	9:18	8	Sagittar	10:46
	10	14:51	10	Capricrn	23:22
	13	10:55	13	Aquarius	12: 6
	14	23:49	15	Pisces	23:56
	18	9:11	18	Aries	10: 3
	20	16:49	20	Taurus	17:31
	22	21:41	22	Gemini	21:43
	24	18:43	24	Cancer	22:55
	26	22: 6	26	Leo	22:17
	28	3: 2	28	Virgo	22:17
	31	0:24	31	Libra	0:35
AUG	2	6:45	2	Scorpio	6:50
	4	15:47	4	Sagittar	17: 2
	7	3:40	7	Capricrn	5:34
	8	21:18	9	Aquarius	18:15
	12	2:43	12	Pisces	5:45
	13	20: 2	14	Aries	15:35
	16	19:29	16	Taurus	23:26
	19	0:36	19	Gemini	4:51
	21	3:23	21	Cancer	7:40
	22	16:26	23	Leo	8:27
	25	3:27	25	Virgo	8:43
	26	17:55	27	Libra	10:26
	29	8:31	29	Scorpio	15:26
SEP	31	16:29	1	Sagittar	0:28
	3	12: 7	3	Capricrn	12:30
	5	22:57	6	Aquarius	1:11
	8	10:49	8	Pisces	12:29
	10	4:13	10	Aries	21:41
	12	18:54	13	Taurus	4:54
	15	0:17	15	Gemini	10:23
	17	4: 0	17	Cancer	14:10
	19	9:26	19	Leo	16:26
	21	7:32	21	Virgo	18: 1
	23	5:25	23	Libra	20:19
	25	12:56	26	Scorpio	0:57
	27	21:38	28	Sagittar	9: 2
	30	18:55	30	Capricrn	20:21
OCT	2	18:33	3	Aquarius	8:58
	5	10:16	5	Pisces	20:27
	7	22:53	8	Aries	5:23
	9	22:24	10	Taurus	11:43
	12	15: 5	12	Gemini	16:11
	14	7:46	14	Cancer	19:31
	16	17:19	16	Leo	22:20
	18	16: 0	19	Virgo	1: 9
	21	0: 2	21	Libra	4:43
	23	8:43	23	Scorpio	10: 0
	25	3:34	25	Sagittar	17:54
	27	14:48	28	Capricrn	4:39
	30	1:53	30	Aquarius	17: 9
NOV	1	14:43	2	Pisces	5: 9
	4	7:13	4	Aries	14:35
	6	8:14	6	Taurus	20:41
	8	12:23	9	Gemini	0: 4
	10	14:47	11	Cancer	2: 0
	12	15:50	13	Leo	3:50
	14	19:37	15	Virgo	6:38
	17	9:18	17	Libra	11: 3
	19	6:20	19	Scorpio	17:26
	22	0: 5	22	Sagittar	1:57
	24	1:41	24	Capricrn	12:38
	26	12: 8	27	Aquarius	0:59
	29	8:54	29	Pisces	13:30
DEC	2	22:28	2	Aries	0: 3
	4	6:35	4	Taurus	7: 1
	6	3:42	6	Gemini	10:19
	8	8:49	8	Cancer	11: 8
	10	9:42	10	Leo	11:18
	12	7:31	12	Virgo	12:38
	14	4:37	14	Libra	16:27
	16	18:53	16	Scorpio	23:13
	19	4:48	19	Sagittar	8:31
	21	18: 7	21	Capricrn	19:39
	23	18:31	24	Aquarius	7:59
	26	19:34	26	Pisces	20:41
	28	23:17	29	Aries	8:15
	30	14:54	31	Taurus	16:48

JAN 31	20:45	1 Virgo	1:46	JUL 2	20:52	3 Taurus 0:35
3	6:56	3 Libra	10:55	4	22:46	5 Gemini 2:16
5	22:30	5 Scorpio	22:58	6	5:11	7 Cancer 2:54
8	7:25	8 Sagittar	11:43	9	0:37	9 Leo 3:59
10	1:12	10 Capricrn	22:54	10	15:0	11 Virgo 7:16
13	8:16	13 Aquarius	7:25	13	10:28	13 Libra 14:4
13	17:43	15 Pisces	13:29	15	20:55	16 Scorpio 0:36
17	13:46	17 Aries	17:49	18	9:44	18 Sagittar 13:20
19	20:2	19 Taurus	21:7	19	23:36	21 Capricrn 1:51
21	19:47	21 Gemini	23:54	23	9:12	23 Aquarius 12:20
23	6:30	24 Cancer	2:38	25	10:5	25 Pisces 20:21
26	1:44	26 Leo	6:8	27	23:35	28 Aries 2:16
27	1:33	28 Virgo	11:31	30	4:2	30 Taurus 6:32
30	14:45	30 Libra	19:49	AUG 1	7:9	1 Gemini 9:30
FEB 2	1:46	2 Scorpio	7:11	3	8:50	3 Cancer 11:34
4	14:27	4 Sagittar	19:59	5	11:27	5 Leo 13:36
6	13:27	7 Capricrn	7:34	7	15:57	7 Virgo 16:54
10	10:49	9 Aquarius	16:0	9	20:49	9 Libra 22:59
11	7:35	11 Pisces	21:10	12	6:27	12 Scorpio 8:37
14	0:11	14 Aries	0:12	14	18:53	14 Sagittar 20:59
15	21:36	16 Taurus	2:35	16	20:40	17 Capricrn 9:38
18	3:50	18 Gemini	5:22	19	18:22	19 Aquarius 20:5
19	19:38	20 Cancer	9:4	22	0:47	22 Pisces 3:29
22	8:22	22 Leo	13:51	24	7:1	24 Aries 8:24
24	9:3	24 Virgo	20:5	26	10:41	26 Taurus 11:57
26	22:23	27 Libra	4:27	30	17:23	28 Gemini 15:2
MAR 1	9:0	1 Scorpio	15:23			30 Cancer 18:4
3	21:48	3 Sagittar	4:8	SEP 1	20:46	1 Leo 21:21
6	12:42	6 Capricrn	16:23	2	20:52	4 Virgo 1:35
9	1:3	9 Aquarius	1:36	6	6:53	6 Libra 7:48
11	5:49	11 Pisces	6:50	8	16:7	8 Scorpio 17:0
13	3:30	13 Aries	9:0	11	4:10	11 Sagittar 4:59
15	4:25	15 Taurus	9:54	13	2:49	13 Capricrn 17:52
17	5:40	17 Gemini	11:19	16	4:16	16 Aquarius 4:51
19	11:46	19 Cancer	14:25	17	21:43	18 Pisces 12:19
21	14:4	21 Leo	19:36	20	16:8	20 Aries 16:31
22	9:6	24 Virgo	2:44	22	18:30	22 Taurus 18:50
26	5:6	26 Libra	11:47	24	20:30	24 Gemini 20:46
28	15:55	28 Scorpio	22:51	26	19:23	26 Cancer 23:25
31	5:36	31 Sagittar	11:33	29	3:4	29 Leo 3:14
APR 2	19:4	3 Capricrn	0:17	OCT 30	2:9	1 Virgo 8:29
6	6:17	5 Aquarius	10:39	3	15:27	3 Libra 15:32
8	17:2	7 Pisces	17:0	6	0:53	6 Scorpio 0:55
9	16:34	9 Aries	19:29	7	15:50	8 Sagittar 12:44
11	14:5	11 Taurus	19:40	10	4:52	11 Capricrn 1:47
13	17:28	13 Gemini	19:35	12	21:10	13 Aquarius 13:38
15	19:22	15 Cancer	21:3	15	6:27	15 Pisces 22:4
17	23:45	18 Leo	1:12	17	22:55	18 Aries 2:33
20	7:56	20 Virgo	8:16	19	21:40	20 Taurus 4:10
22	17:18	22 Libra	17:51	22	4:15	22 Gemini 4:40
24	22:38	25 Scorpio	5:21	24	5:8	24 Cancer 5:47
27	11:35	27 Sagittar	18:5	26	7:49	26 Leo 8:43
29	13:26	30 Capricrn	6:57	27	5:47	28 Virgo 14:2
MAY 2	12:27	2 Aquarius	18:9	30	20:20	30 Libra 21:47
4	14:35	5 Pisces	1:57	NOV 1	17:22	2 Scorpio 7:49
7	1:7	7 Aries	5:48	4	17:44	4 Sagittar 19:46
9	2:9	9 Taurus	6:32	7	6:34	7 Capricrn 8:50
11	1:39	11 Gemini	5:56	9	18:54	9 Aquarius 21:19
12	13:14	13 Cancer	6:0	12	5:46	12 Pisces 7:8
15	8:14	15 Leo	8:27	14	10:37	14 Aries 13:0
17	12:42	17 Virgo	14:19	16	4:17	16 Taurus 15:12
19	20:29	19 Libra	23:35	18	12:49	18 Gemini 15:10
22	5:45	22 Scorpio	11:18	20	12:20	20 Cancer 14:47
24	18:27	25 Sagittar	0:10	22	15:49	22 Leo 15:55
27	11:28	27 Capricrn	12:54	23	17:39	24 Virgo 19:56
29	18:24	30 Aquarius	0:13	27	3:20	27 Libra 3:22
JUN 1	5:7	1 Pisces	8:58	29	13:41	29 Scorpio 13:46
3	9:21	3 Aries	14:22	DEC 2	1:56	2 Sagittar 2:6
5	11:56	5 Taurus	16:36	4	11:47	4 Capricrn 15:8
7	12:17	7 Gemini	16:46	7	3:23	7 Aquarius 3:40
8	20:43	9 Cancer	16:32	8	19:32	9 Pisces 14:22
11	13:10	11 Leo	17:45	11	21:32	11 Aries 21:55
13	21:58	13 Virgo	22:1	14	1:25	14 Taurus 1:50
16	1:5	16 Libra	6:8	16	2:15	16 Gemini 2:43
18	12:22	18 Scorpio	17:31	17	23:49	18 Cancer 2:3
21	1:21	21 Sagittar	6:26	20	1:47	20 Leo 1:49
22	15:34	23 Capricrn	18:58	22	3:46	22 Virgo 3:57
26	1:19	26 Aquarius	5:54	24	9:4	24 Libra 9:53
28	3:19	28 Pisces	14:37	26	18:47	26 Scorpio 19:45
30	19:50	30 Aries	20:51	29	7:6	29 Sagittar 8:12
				31	19:33	31 Capricrn 21:17

Month	Day	Time	Day	Sign	Time
JAN	2	19:24	3	Taurus	1:11
	5	2:11	5	Gemini	5: 4
	6	23:45	7	Cancer	10:29
	9	11:23	9	Leo	18: 2
	12	0: 6	12	Virgo	4: 5
	14	8:50	14	Libra	16:11
	16	21:16	17	Scorpio	4:39
	19	11:51	19	Sagittar	15:12
	21	6:26	22	Capricrn	22:19
	23	19:34	24	Aquarius	2: 3
	25	22:20	26	Pisces	3:35
	28	3:45	28	Aries	4:36
	29	23:54	30	Gemini	6:38
FEB	1	3:33	1	Gemini	10:39
	2	18:58	3	Cancer	16:58
	5	17:34	6	Leo	1:26
	7	13:48	8	Virgo	11:48
	10	15:16	10	Libra	23:46
	13	3:48	13	Scorpio	12:25
	15	15:46	15	Sagittar	23:56
	18	5:27	18	Capricrn	8:22
	20	10:32	20	Aquarius	12:47
	21	23:21	22	Pisces	13:56
	24	6:30	24	Aries	13:35
	26	6:30	26	Taurus	13:51
	28	8:40	28	Gemini	16:30
MAR	1	7:43	1	Cancer	22:26
	3	22:28	4	Leo	7:21
	6	3:28	6	Virgo	18:18
	8	21: 3	9	Libra	6:26
	11	14: 4	11	Scorpio	19: 4
	13	22: 6	14	Sagittar	7: 6
	16	14:32	16	Capricrn	16:52
	18	19:28	18	Aquarius	22:52
	20	14:49	21	Pisces	0:59
	22	17: 2	23	Aries	1:30
	24	16: 2	24	Taurus	23:38
	26	16:29	27	Gemini	0:31
	28	23:38	29	Cancer	4:52
	31	11: 1	31	Leo	13: 4
APR	2	12:49	3	Virgo	0: 8
	5	2:44	5	Libra	12:31
	7	15:20	8	Scorpio	1: 5
	10	11:44	10	Sagittar	13: 3
	12	13:13	12	Capricrn	23:23
	14	22: 8	15	Aquarius	6:49
	17	5:40	17	Pisces	10:38
	19	3:40	19	Aries	11:21
	21	3: 4	21	Taurus	10:37
	23	2:49	23	Gemini	10:38
	25	3: 7	25	Cancer	13:23
	27	11: 7	27	Leo	20: 4
	30	4:44	30	Virgo	6:22
MAY	2	9:10	2	Libra	18:43
	5	6:52	5	Scorpio	7:17
	7	10:37	7	Sagittar	18:54
	9	15:54	10	Capricrn	4:57
	12	11:38	12	Aquarius	12:48
	14	6:12	14	Pisces	17:53
	16	12:46	16	Aries	20:14
	18	13:34	18	Taurus	20:48
	20	20:35	20	Gemini	21:12
	22	9:32	22	Cancer	23:20
	24	20:59	25	Leo	4:42
	27	7:36	27	Virgo	13:48
	29	16:57	30	Libra	1:39
JUN	1	5:38	1	Scorpio	14:12
	3	17:24	3	Sagittar	1:37
	5	19:44	6	Capricrn	11: 3
	8	10:52	8	Aquarius	18:18
	10	5:17	10	Pisces	23:27
	12	20: 1	13	Aries	2:47
	14	22:16	15	Taurus	4:49
	17	0: 0	17	Gemini	6:30
	19	5:15	19	Cancer	9: 9
	21	7:14	21	Leo	14: 6
	23	19:32	23	Virgo	22:16
	26	2: 2	26	Libra	9:24
	28	14:36	28	Scorpio	21:53

Month	Day	Time	Day	Sign	Time
JUL	1	2:31	1	Sagittar	9:27
	3	4:37	3	Capricrn	18:34
	5	18:52	6	Aquarius	0:57
	8	2:56	8	Pisces	5:11
	10	2:35	10	Aries	8:10
	12	5:17	12	Taurus	10:46
	14	8:12	14	Gemini	13:39
	16	4:13	16	Cancer	17:28
	18	17:23	18	Leo	22:58
	20	3:16	21	Virgo	6:54
	23	11:40	23	Libra	17:31
	26	0: 6	26	Scorpio	5:54
	28	12:24	28	Sagittar	17:56
	30	12:19	31	Capricrn	3:24
AUG	2	4:44	2	Aquarius	9:26
	4	0:35	4	Pisces	12:36
	6	10: 7	6	Aries	14:22
	8	14:14	8	Taurus	16:12
	10	18:31	10	Gemini	19:12
	12	8:24	12	Cancer	23:52
	15	2: 1	15	Leo	6:20
	17	3:21	17	Virgo	14:45
	19	20:53	20	Libra	1:17
	22	11:58	22	Scorpio	13:36
	24	21:58	25	Sagittar	2:10
	27	12: 1	27	Capricrn	12:35
	29	15:43	29	Aquarius	19:13
	30	21:19	31	Pisces	22: 6
SEP	2	19:40	2	Aries	22:43
	4	20: 3	4	Taurus	23: 4
	6	21:50	7	Gemini	0:55
	8	10:28	9	Cancer	5:16
	11	9: 0	11	Leo	12:13
	13	5: 8	13	Virgo	21:20
	16	4:57	16	Libra	8:13
	18	17:18	18	Scorpio	20:32
	21	6:16	21	Sagittar	9:25
	23	17:23	23	Capricrn	20:53
	26	2:13	26	Aquarius	4:53
	28	7:44	28	Pisces	8:40
	30	6:54	30	Aries	9:10
OCT	2	6:12	2	Taurus	8:25
	4	6:21	4	Gemini	8:37
	6	16:20	6	Cancer	11:29
	8	15:16	8	Leo	17:45
	10	6:57	11	Virgo	3: 2
	13	11:44	13	Libra	14:19
	16	0:11	16	Scorpio	2:47
	18	13: 4	18	Sagittar	15:38
	20	22:24	21	Capricrn	3:38
	23	12:54	23	Aquarius	13: 0
	25	4:55	25	Pisces	18:28
	27	18:10	27	Aries	20:10
	29	17:38	29	Taurus	19:34
	31	16:51	31	Gemini	18:49
NOV	2	9:27	2	Cancer	20: 0
	4	22:22	5	Leo	0:37
	6	22:36	7	Virgo	9: 0
	9	17:43	9	Libra	20:15
	12	6:17	12	Scorpio	8:52
	14	18:58	14	Sagittar	21:34
	17	2:50	17	Capricrn	9:21
	19	16:41	19	Aquarius	19:11
	22	1:19	22	Pisces	2: 4
	24	3:20	24	Aries	5:37
	26	4:18	26	Taurus	6:29
	28	3:57	28	Gemini	6:12
	30	5:54	30	Cancer	6:40
DEC	2	7:19	2	Leo	9:43
	3	22: 4	4	Virgo	16:31
	6	23:53	7	Libra	2:56
	9	13:11	9	Scorpio	15:28
	12	0:54	12	Sagittar	4: 7
	13	23:25	14	Capricrn	15:26
	16	21:32	17	Aquarius	0:43
	19	2:23	19	Pisces	7:44
	21	11:30	21	Aries	12:27
	23	12: 5	23	Taurus	15: 6
	25	13:23	25	Gemini	16:25
	27	9: 0	27	Cancer	17:37
	29	16:53	29	Leo	20:14

January – June

	Date	Time	Date	Sign	Time
JAN	1	20:15	2	Sagittar	4:27
	4	2:39	4	Capricrn	6:44
	6	3: 4	6	Aquarius	7: 4
	8	3:14	8	Pisces	7:18
	10	0:46	10	Aries	9: 3
	12	11:42	12	Taurus	13:25
	14	13:55	14	Gemini	20:43
	17	1:49	17	Cancer	6:38
	19	15:49	19	Leo	18:27
	22	2:27	22	Virgo	7:20
	24	9:32	24	Libra	20: 0
	27	2:34	27	Scorpio	6:46
	29	10:44	29	Sagittar	14:11
	31	16:21	31	Capricrn	17:48
FEB	2	14:58	2	Aquarius	18:26
	4	15:54	4	Pisces	17:47
	6	8:54	6	Aries	17:49
	8	19: 9	8	Taurus	20:22
	11	1:48	11	Gemini	2:36
	13	12: 9	13	Cancer	12:24
	15	20:56	15	Leo	0:35
	18	11:17	18	Virgo	13:33
	20	14:32	21	Libra	2: 3
	23	10: 6	23	Scorpio	13: 4
	25	21:23	25	Sagittar	21:41
	28	0:45	28	Capricrn	3: 5
MAR	2	3:13	2	Aquarius	5:17
	4	3:22	4	Pisces	5:13
	5	19:13	6	Aries	4:41
	8		8	Taurus	5:43
	9	23:22	10	Gemini	10:11
	12	17:20	12	Cancer	18:52
	15	5:27	15	Leo	6:48
	17	18:13	17	Virgo	19:52
	20	5:32	20	Libra	8: 8
	22	18:12	22	Scorpio	18:45
	24	16: 0	25	Sagittar	3:24
	27	9:45	27	Capricrn	9:49
	29	3:16	29	Aquarius	13:42
	31	3:14	31	Pisces	15:15
APR	2	5:38	2	Aries	15:32
	4	6: 9	4	Taurus	16:18
	6	12:58	6	Gemini	19:35
	8	3: 2	9	Cancer	2:49
	11	1:30	11	Leo	13:52
	13	20:51	14	Virgo	2:47
	16	2:49	16	Libra	15: 1
	18	21:50	19	Scorpio	1:10
	20	21:50	21	Sagittar	9: 6
	23	11:21	23	Capricrn	15:14
	25	9:11	25	Aquarius	19:44
	27	5:54	27	Pisces	22:40
	29	14:26	30	Aries	0:27
MAY	1	16: 5	2	Taurus	2:10
	3	18:57	4	Gemini	5:26
	5	23: 1	6	Cancer	11:50
	8	10: 7	8	Leo	21:55
	11	9:11	11	Virgo	10:26
	13	11: 1	13	Libra	22:48
	15	21:47	16	Scorpio	8:55
	18	9:57	18	Sagittar	16:13
	20	2:49	20	Capricrn	21:21
	22	15:17	23	Aquarius	1: 9
	24	20:19	25	Pisces	4:14
	27	3: 4	27	Aries	6:59
	29	9:25	29	Taurus	9:59
	31	4:19	31	Gemini	14:11
JUN	1	11:20	2	Cancer	20:44
	5	0:25	5	Leo	6:20
	6	12:35	7	Virgo	18:26
	9	20:13	10	Libra	7: 0
	12	7:24	12	Scorpio	17:36
	14	15:27	15	Sagittar	0:57
	16	20:20	17	Capricrn	5:21
	18	23:17	19	Aquarius	7:56
	21	9:19	21	Pisces	9:56
	23	9:47	23	Aries	12:21
	25	11:21	25	Taurus	15:54
	27	12:11	27	Gemini	21: 7
	29	20:20	30	Cancer	4:27

July – December

	Date	Time	Date	Sign	Time
JUL	2	4:45	2	Leo	14:13
	4	20:39	4	Virgo	2: 9
	7	6:36	7	Libra	14:53
	9	20:31	10	Scorpio	2:15
	12	2: 8	12	Sagittar	10:28
	14	1:20	14	Capricrn	15: 3
	16	9:37	16	Aquarius	16:54
	18	7:56	18	Pisces	17:31
	20	13:24	20	Aries	18:33
	22	19:42	22	Taurus	21:21
	24	19: 1	25	Gemini	2:42
	27	8:17	27	Cancer	10:44
	29	12:59	29	Leo	21: 4
AUG	31	0:53	1	Virgo	9: 7
	3	13:54	3	Libra	21:55
	6	2:16	6	Scorpio	9:57
	8	12:16	8	Sagittar	19:25
	10	10:41	11	Capricrn	1:10
	12	21:18	13	Aquarius	3:22
	14	21:17	15	Pisces	3:19
	16	21: 8	17	Aries	2:55
	18	22: 8	19	Taurus	4: 8
	21	3:18	21	Gemini	8:26
	23	15:26	23	Cancer	16:17
	25	20:14	26	Leo	3: 1
	27	12:59	28	Virgo	15:21
	30	21:28	31	Libra	4: 8
SEP	2	9:56	2	Scorpio	16:22
	4	20:44	5	Sagittar	2:49
	6	8:47	7	Capricrn	10: 8
	9	8:34	9	Aquarius	13:44
	11	8:46	11	Pisces	14:15
	13	10: 4	13	Aries	13:21
	15	8:19	15	Taurus	13:10
	17	10:39	17	Gemini	15:48
	19	14:23	19	Cancer	22:27
	22	5:25	22	Leo	8:50
	24	14:42	24	Virgo	21:19
	27	4:26	27	Libra	10: 6
	29	16:36	29	Scorpio	22: 6
OCT	2	3:24	2	Sagittar	8:41
	3	13:40	4	Capricrn	17: 3
	6	17:41	6	Aquarius	22:21
	8	13:41	9	Pisces	0:27
	10	20: 8	11	Aries	0:20
	12	23:34	12	Taurus	23:54
	14	20:50	15	Gemini	1:18
	16	22: 9	17	Cancer	6:21
	19	10:28	19	Leo	15:36
	21	22:54	22	Virgo	3:45
	24	11:18	24	Libra	16:32
	27	1:47	27	Scorpio	4:15
	29	9:52	29	Sagittar	14:18
	31	7:17	31	Capricrn	22:31
NOV	3	2:19	3	Aquarius	4:38
	5	6:56	5	Pisces	8:21
	7	9:17	7	Aries	9:54
	9	8:53	9	Taurus	10:29
	11	7:29	11	Gemini	11:52
	13	15:53	13	Cancer	15:57
	15	18:45	15	Leo	23:51
	18	0:36	18	Virgo	11:10
	20	18:53	20	Libra	23:52
	23	6:17	23	Scorpio	11:36
	25	15:59	25	Sagittar	21: 9
	27	5:22	28	Capricrn	4:29
	30	5: 5	30	Aquarius	10: 0
DEC	2	1:41	2	Pisces	14: 3
	4	13:28	4	Aries	16:53
	6	18:31	6	Taurus	19: 4
	8	16:39	8	Gemini	21:37
	10	3:11	11	Cancer	1:54
	13	3:28	13	Leo	9: 7
	15	10:22	15	Virgo	19:33
	18	7:54	18	Libra	7:59
	20	15:47	20	Scorpio	20: 3
	22	23:48	23	Sagittar	5:45
	24	12:41	25	Capricrn	12:28
	27	11:11	27	Aquarius	16:46
	29	9:21	29	Pisces	19:42
	31	16:38	31	Aries	22:16

```
JAN  2  1:38    2 Leo      13:56      JUL  2 14: 2    3 Aries     0:39
     4 13:10    5 Virgo     2: 9           5  2:24    5 Taurus     6:48
     7  0:36    7 Libra    12:21           7 11: 7    7 Gemini    15:56
     9  8: 6    9 Scorpio  19:11           9 22:10   10 Cancer     3:21
    11 11:53   11 Sagittar 22:18          12  4:14   12 Leo       16: 8
    13 12:25   13 Capricrn 22:37          15  4: 8   15 Virgo      5: 7
    15 13:37   15 Aquarius 21:56          17  5:37   17 Libra     16:48
    17 11:44   17 Pisces   22:18          19 19:48   20 Scorpio    1:31
    20  0:10   20 Aries     1:28          22  4:12   22 Sagittar   6:28
    21 20:27   22 Taurus    8:27          24  2:37   24 Capricrn   8: 4
    24  5:54   24 Gemini   18:54          25 23: 6   26 Aquarius   7:44
    26 18:40   27 Cancer    7:24          28  1:31   28 Pisces     7:20
    29  7:39   29 Leo      20:12          29 23:43   30 Aries      8:46
FEB  1  3:17    1 Virgo     8: 1      AUG  1  6:20    1 Taurus    13:25
     3  5: 7    3 Libra    18: 0           3 13:56    3 Gemini    21:49
     5 23: 8    6 Scorpio   1:32           6  0:40    6 Cancer     9:13
     7 18:27    8 Sagittar  6:15           8 19:36    8 Leo       22: 8
     9 22:42   10 Capricrn  8:24          11  1:40   11 Virgo     10:59
    11 23:35   12 Aquarius  8:57          13 12:47   13 Libra     22:33
    14  0:44   14 Pisces    9:28          16  4:32   16 Scorpio    7:51
    15 23:41   16 Aries    11:39          18  5:35   18 Sagittar  14:12
    18 15:48   18 Taurus   17: 7          20 12: 4   20 Capricrn  17:27
    20 12:27   21 Gemini    2:17          22 10:39   22 Aquarius  18:19
    23  3:24   23 Cancer   14:23          24 16:54   24 Pisces    18: 8
    25 16:30   26 Leo       3:14          26 14:33   26 Aries     18:44
    28  4:39   28 Virgo    14:46          28 19:57   28 Taurus    21:55
MAR  2 10:27    3 Libra     0: 2          30 20:15   31 Gemini     4:56
     4 22: 0    5 Scorpio   6:59      SEP  2  3:10    2 Cancer    15:41
     7  2: 4    7 Sagittar 11:59           4 19:24    5 Leo        4:32
     9  8:45    9 Capricrn 15:22           7  7:49    7 Virgo     17:17
    11 13:59   11 Aquarius 17:36          10  3:16   10 Libra      4:23
    13 11:49   13 Pisces   19:26          12  5:13   12 Scorpio   13: 3
    15 12: 9   15 Aries    22: 0          14 12:21   14 Sagittar  20: 4
    17 18:55   18 Taurus    2:46          16 15:48   17 Capricrn   0:36
    20  9: 5   20 Gemini   10:52          18 20: 5   19 Aquarius   3: 7
    22 13:57   22 Cancer   22:13          20 21:18   21 Pisces     4:14
    25  3: 1   25 Leo      11: 3          23  4:19   23 Aries      5:13
    27 15:16   27 Virgo    22:46          25  1:55   25 Taurus     7:47
    29 17:46   30 Libra     7:37          27  5:27   27 Gemini    13:33
APR  1  7:17    1 Scorpio  13:36          29 21:22   29 Cancer    23:15
     3 13:19    3 Sagittar 17:37      OCT  2  7:53    2 Leo       11:45
     5 19:54    5 Capricrn 20:45           4 21:49    5 Virgo      0:31
     7 18:15    7 Aquarius 23:43           7  3:38    7 Libra     11:21
     9 21:35   10 Pisces    2:52           9 18:58    9 Scorpio   19:32
    11 22:47   12 Aries     6:40          11 18:44   12 Sagittar   1:32
    14  6:48   14 Taurus   11:56          14  5:37   14 Capricrn   6: 4
    16 12: 2   16 Gemini   19:42          16  9: 6   16 Aquarius   9:32
    19  3:12   19 Cancer    6:27          18 11:36   18 Pisces    12:10
    21 17:47   21 Leo      19:10          20  7:52   20 Aries     14:29
    24  2:51   24 Virgo     7:20          22 16:42   22 Taurus    17:35
    26  2:48   26 Libra    16:33          24 15:48   24 Gemini    22:58
    28 18:38   28 Scorpio  22: 7          27  6:24   27 Cancer     7:46
MAY 30 19:58    1 Sagittar  1: 2          29 18: 5   29 Leo       19:43
     2 23:57    3 Capricrn  2:54      NOV  1  6:47    1 Virgo      8:36
     5  2:50    5 Aquarius  5: 6           3 12: 7    3 Libra     19:41
     7  5:47    7 Pisces    8:26           6  1:34    6 Scorpio    3:33
     9  0:17    9 Aries    13: 9           8  1:42    8 Sagittar   8:33
    11 17: 2   11 Taurus   19:24          10  9:48   10 Capricrn  11:57
    13 23: 8   14 Gemini    3:38          12 12:35   12 Aquarius  14:52
    16 12:14   16 Cancer   14:18          15 14:31   14 Pisces    17:57
    19  1: 5   19 Leo       2:55          16 14:32   16 Aries     21:26
    21 15:20   21 Virgo    15:36          18 23: 0   19 Taurus     1:47
    23 12:28   24 Libra     1:43          21  5:32   21 Gemini     7:47
    26  6:56   26 Scorpio   7:52          23  5: 3   23 Cancer    16:25
    28  7:19   28 Sagittar 10:29          26  0:15   26 Leo        3:54
    30 10:40   30 Capricrn 11:12          28 13: 2   28 Virgo     16:52
JUN  1 11:32    1 Aquarius 11:55      DEC 30 20:32    1 Libra      4:39
     3 13:53    3 Pisces   14: 7           3  9:25    3 Scorpio   13: 6
     5  6:30    6 Aries    18:32           5 16:19    5 Sagittar  17:53
     7 21:55    8 Taurus    1:17           7 17: 4    7 Capricrn  20: 9
    10  6:43   10 Gemini    9:53           9 20:17    9 Aquarius  21:34
    12 17:35   12 Cancer   21:14          11 19:46   11 Pisces    23:31
    14 20:34   15 Leo       9:53          13 22:10   14 Aries      2:51
    17 19: 4   17 Virgo    22:52          16  3:47   16 Taurus     7:57
    20  6:37   20 Libra     9:59          18  6:42   18 Gemini    14:58
    22 13:54   22 Scorpio  17:25          20 20:54   21 Cancer     0:11
    24 17:28   24 Sagittar 21:25          23  6:46   23 Leo       11:38
    26 18: 6   26 Capricrn 21:25          25 19:34   26 Virgo      0:32
    28 11:30   28 Aquarius 21: 2          28  3:48   28 Libra     12:59
    30 18: 0   30 Pisces   21:38          30 18: 4   30 Scorpio   22:42
```

JAN				JUL			
2	2:13	2 Aries	15:14	2	9:34	2 Scorpio	10:57
4	15:52	5 Taurus	2:37	4	10:23	4 Sagittar	12:32
7	1:42	7 Gemini	15:20	6	11:54	6 Capricrn	12:16
9	15:31	10 Cancer	3:17	8	7:30	8 Aquarius	12: 5
12	0:31	12 Leo	13:27	10	9:13	10 Pisces	14: 2
14	2:20	14 Virgo	21:42	12	6:30	12 Aries	19:31
16	21:31	17 Libra	4: 3	14	23:29	15 Taurus	4:49
19	6:16	19 Scorpio	8:25	17	4:56	17 Gemini	16:45
20	23:16	21 Sagittar	10:55	20	0: 3	20 Cancer	5:25
23	0:40	23 Capricrn	12:18	22	16: 3	22 Leo	17:19
25	6:43	25 Aquarius	13:57	24	22:36	25 Virgo	3:36
26	23:41	27 Pisces	17:31	26	23:23	27 Libra	11:45
29	10:23	30 Aries	0:21	29	12:50	29 Scorpio	17:22
FEB 31	18:45	1 Taurus	10:40	31	9:25	31 Sagittar	20:27
3	13:16	3 Gemini	23: 5	AUG 2	17:29	2 Capricrn	21:41
5	19:18	6 Cancer	11:14	4	18: 9	4 Aquarius	22:22
8	5:41	8 Leo	21:17	6	19:48	7 Pisces	0:11
10	17:01	11 Virgo	4:43	8	17:14	9 Aries	4:41
12	19:29	13 Libra	9:59	11	7:43	11 Taurus	12:45
15	7:14	15 Scorpio	13:47	13	12:33	13 Gemini	23:58
17	14: 9	17 Sagittar	16:43	16	7:11	16 Cancer	12:33
19	3:31	19 Capricrn	19:23	18	19: 6	19 Leo	0:23
21	8: 3	21 Aquarius	22:29	21	5:48	21 Virgo	10: 8
23	10:34	24 Pisces	2:56	23	10:46	23 Libra	17:30
25	17:56	26 Aries	9:42	25	22:22	25 Scorpio	22:45
28	12: 4	28 Taurus	19:20	27	21:36	28 Sagittar	2:21
MAR 3	6:51	3 Gemini	7:18	30	0:56	30 Capricrn	4:52
5	2: 5	5 Cancer	19:43	SEP 1	3:48	1 Aquarius	7: 0
7	13:47	8 Leo	6:18	3	4:39	3 Pisces	9:44
9	22:14	10 Virgo	13:42	5	12:28	5 Aries	14:15
12	3:13	12 Libra	18: 3	7	15:45	7 Taurus	21:35
14	6:34	14 Scorpio	20:28	9	20:45	10 Gemini	8: 1
16	14:57	16 Sagittar	22:19	12	13:54	12 Cancer	20:25
18	21: 5	19 Capricrn	0:47	15	7:49	15 Leo	8:31
20	14:39	21 Aquarius	4:39	17	11:53	17 Virgo	18:14
22	20: 0	23 Pisces	10:16	19	18:21	20 Libra	0:52
25	13: 4	25 Aries	17:50	21	22:58	22 Scorpio	5: 0
27	12:39	28 Taurus	3:32	23	10:56	24 Sagittar	7:49
30	8:30	30 Gemini	15:14	26	4:10	26 Capricrn	10:23
APR 1	18:54	2 Cancer	3:50	28	7: 1	28 Aquarius	13:27
4	5: 7	4 Leo	15:17	30	10:44	30 Pisces	17:27
6	10:39	6 Virgo	23:33	OCT 2	14: 4	2 Aries	22:51
8	19:29	9 Libra	4: 1	5	1:55	5 Taurus	6:18
10	18:27	11 Scorpio	5:32	7	13:38	7 Gemini	16:18
13	0:34	13 Sagittar	5:52	9	19:59	10 Cancer	4:30
15	3:41	15 Capricrn	6:54	12	8:26	12 Leo	17: 2
17	9:42	17 Aquarius	10: 3	14	19: 4	15 Virgo	3:25
19	14:11	19 Pisces	15:54	17	0:49	17 Libra	10: 8
21	7:40	22 Aries	0:14	19	5:47	19 Scorpio	13:28
23	22:36	24 Taurus	10:31	21	6:19	21 Sagittar	14:54
26	24:56	26 Gemini	22:18	23	15:53	23 Capricrn	16:14
28	23:16	29 Cancer	10:58	25	10:32	25 Aquarius	18:49
MAY 1	11:56	1 Leo	23: 7	27	19:11	27 Pisces	23:18
3	22:23	4 Virgo	8:41	29	20: 3	30 Aries	5:41
5	23:25	6 Libra	14:17	NOV 1	4:11	1 Taurus	13:53
8	11: 1	8 Scorpio	16: 7	3	13:42	4 Gemini	0: 2
10	6:19	10 Sagittar	15:43	6	11:41	6 Cancer	12: 5
12	7: 9	12 Capricrn	15:15	8	14:18	9 Leo	0:58
14	15:49	14 Aquarius	16:46	11	1:46	11 Virgo	12:24
16	12:51	16 Pisces	21:34	13	12:21	13 Libra	20:13
19	1:10	19 Aries	5:46	15	19:28	15 Scorpio	23:52
21	7:20	21 Taurus	16:27	17	20:56	18 Sagittar	0:35
23	21: 3	23 Gemini	4:32	19	15:10	20 Capricrn	0:50
26	8:24	26 Cancer	17:12	22	0: 6	22 Aquarius	1:21
28	21: 7	29 Leo	5:34	23	18:28	24 Pisces	4:50
31	8:14	31 Virgo	16: 6	26	1:10	26 Aries	11:13
JUN 2	9:48	2 Libra	23:15	28	9:33	28 Taurus	20: 3
4	19:56	5 Scorpio	2:25	DEC 30	21:35	1 Gemini	6:45
6	13:54	7 Sagittar	2:32	3	6:26	3 Cancer	18:53
8	19:39	9 Capricrn	1:33	5	20:30	6 Leo	7:49
10	19:39	11 Aquarius	1:41	8	11: 5	8 Virgo	20: 0
12	22:30	13 Pisces	4:50	11	2:53	11 Libra	5:19
14	23:26	16 Aries	11:51	13	0:42	13 Scorpio	10:27
17	15:25	18 Taurus	22:12	15	2:37	15 Sagittar	11:49
19	18:54	20 Gemini	10:26	17	2:53	17 Capricrn	11: 8
22	14:02	22 Cancer	23: 7	19	1:20	19 Aquarius	10:37
25	6:49	25 Leo	11:17	21	10:48	21 Pisces	12:15
27	16: 3	27 Virgo	22: 1	23	10:33	23 Aries	17:16
29	23:19	30 Libra	6:11	25	22:21	26 Taurus	1:43
				28	0:50	28 Gemini	12:48
				30	18:57	31 Cancer	1: 7

JAN	2	2: 1	2	Scorpio	12:24	JUL	2	10:52	3 Cancer 0: 7
	4	5:18	4	Sagittar	15:16		4	19:40	5 Leo 8:19
	6	4:59	6	Capricrn	18:37		7	2:23	7 Virgo 14:33
	8	14: 4	8	Aquarius	23:44		9	4:33	9 Libra 19:13
	11	0:31	11	Pisces	7:50		11	11:38	11 Scorpio 22:28
	13	17:15	13	Aries	19: 8		13	14:41	14 Sagittar 0:38
	16	5:11	16	Taurus	8: 3		16	1:32	16 Capricrn 2:36
	18	19: 7	18	Gemini	19:48		17	21: 7	18 Aquarius 5:45
	20	9:52	21	Cancer	4:23		20	9:34	20 Pisces 11:34
	23	3:22	23	Leo	9:40		22	20:25	22 Aries 20:52
	24	18:57	25	Virgo	12:47		25	7:28	25 Taurus 8:55
	27	9:53	27	Libra	15: 8		27	15:12	27 Gemini 21:27
	29	12:51	29	Scorpio	17:43		30	3:10	30 Cancer 8: 8
	31	16:35	31	Sagittar	21: 7	AUG	1	3:54	1 Leo 15:57
FEB	2	5: 7	3	Capricrn	1:39		3	20: 6	3 Virgo 21:15
	5	3:57	5	Aquarius	7:49		5	11:45	6 Libra 0:56
	6	16:56	7	Pisces	16:15		8	2:40	8 Scorpio 3:50
	10	0:12	10	Aries	3:18		10	6: 9	10 Sagittar 6:32
	12	13:32	12	Taurus	16: 5		12	7:27	12 Capricrn 9:39
	15	2:32	15	Gemini	4:28		14	13:46	14 Aquarius 13:54
	17	9:25	17	Cancer	14: 3		16	11:41	16 Pisces 20:14
	19	19: 1	19	Leo	19:49		19	4:35	19 Aries 5:18
	21	18:41	21	Virgo	22:25		21	15:53	21 Taurus 16:56
	23	23:21	23	Libra	23:22		24	4:13	24 Gemini 5:34
	25	8:18	26	Scorpio	0:20		26	3:25	26 Cancer 16:50
	27	10: 1	28	Sagittar	2:39		28	23:22	29 Leo 1: 3
MAR	29	13:28	1	Capricrn	7: 7		30	17:51	31 Virgo 5:59
	3	0:55	3	Aquarius	14: 0	SEP	2	6:38	2 Libra 8:32
	5	15:31	5	Pisces	23:16		4	8: 4	4 Scorpio 10: 6
	8	4: 9	8	Aries	10:36		6	9:46	6 Sagittar 12: 0
	10	3: 8	10	Taurus	23:20		8	13:14	8 Capricrn 15:12
	12	20: 4	13	Gemini	12: 3		10	17:35	10 Aquarius 20:16
	15	12:41	15	Cancer	22:46		12	13:43	13 Pisces 3:31
	18	1: 1	18	Leo	5:56		15	9:49	15 Aries 13: 1
	19	13:26	20	Virgo	9:19		17	21: 9	18 Taurus 0:34
	21	18:16	22	Libra	9:57		20	12:53	20 Gemini 13:14
	23	20: 4	24	Scorpio	9:35		23	0:47	23 Cancer 1:14
	25	23:27	26	Sagittar	10: 7		25	8: 7	25 Leo 10:32
	28	4:50	28	Capricrn	13: 8		27	2:23	27 Virgo 16: 7
	30	14: 8	30	Aquarius	19:31		29	15:18	29 Libra 18:23
APR	1	22:39	2	Pisces	5: 5	OCT	1	15:43	1 Scorpio 18:44
	4	16:10	4	Aries	16:53		3	15:59	3 Sagittar 19: 3
	6	15:30	7	Taurus	5:44		5	18:11	5 Capricrn 21: 0
	8	22:14	9	Gemini	18:27		7	22:22	8 Aquarius 1:44
	11	13: 3	12	Cancer	5:47		9	22: 2	10 Pisces 9:27
	14	3:16	14	Leo	14:22		12	16: 3	12 Aries 19:36
	16	13: 4	16	Virgo	19:22		15	3:52	15 Taurus 7:24
	18	4:46	18	Libra	21: 0		17	16:37	17 Gemini 20: 3
	20	4:51	20	Scorpio	20:34		20	1:21	20 Cancer 8:26
	22	4: 6	22	Sagittar	19:57		22	17:14	22 Leo 18:57
	24	4:47	24	Capricrn	21:15		24	9:58	25 Virgo 2: 3
	26	8:32	27	Aquarius	2: 5		27	2:58	27 Libra 5:16
	28	22:36	29	Pisces	10:56		29	3:27	29 Scorpio 5:31
MAY	1	14:42	1	Aries	22:47		31	2:45	31 Sagittar 4:40
	4	8:23	4	Taurus	11:46	NOV	1	18:53	2 Capricrn 4:55
	6	4:37	7	Gemini	0:20		4	6:19	4 Aquarius 8: 6
	9	6:56	9	Cancer	11:35		6	7:59	6 Pisces 15: 7
	11	19:54	11	Leo	20:47		8	23:56	9 Aries 1:25
	13	22:43	14	Virgo	3:14		11	12:22	11 Taurus 13:34
	15	21:54	16	Libra	6:33		14	1:12	14 Gemini 2:14
	17	17:31	18	Scorpio	7:15		15	18:54	16 Cancer 14:32
	20	5: 9	20	Sagittar	6:48		19	1:27	19 Leo 1:36
	21	17:28	22	Capricrn	7:13		21	7:58	21 Virgo 10: 9
	23	19:58	24	Aquarius	10:31		23	3:36	23 Libra 15: 8
	26	2:25	26	Pisces	17:58		25	13:50	25 Scorpio 16:38
	28	10:13	29	Aries	5: 9		27	5:23	27 Sagittar 15:59
	31	1:53	31	Taurus	18: 5		29	0:41	29 Capricrn 15:16
JUN	2	11:52	3	Gemini	6:33	DEC	1	5:13	1 Aquarius 16:47
	5	2:20	5	Cancer	17:21		3	3:22	3 Pisces 22: 8
	7	11:54	8	Leo	2:15		5	18: 5	6 Aries 7:35
	9	19:28	10	Virgo	9: 7		8	5:41	8 Taurus 19:42
	12	0:53	12	Libra	13:42		10	18:21	11 Gemini 8:26
	14	6:22	14	Scorpio	16: 0		13	5: 0	13 Cancer 20:28
	16	9:51	16	Sagittar	16:46		15	17:48	16 Leo 7:13
	18	12:38	18	Capricrn	17:31		18	9:22	18 Virgo 16: 9
	20	18:11	20	Aquarius	20:12		20	21:37	20 Libra 22:32
	22	13: 8	23	Pisces	2:26		22	13:50	23 Scorpio 1:53
	24	19: 9	25	Aries	12:34		24	15:22	25 Sagittar 2:43
	27	10:53	28	Taurus	1: 8		26	15:23	27 Capricrn 2:31
	30	6:27	30	Gemini	13:35		28	15:56	29 Aquarius 3:23
							30	12:35	31 Pisces 7:16

Month	Date	Time	Date	Sign	Time
JAN	1	8:46	1	Gemini	11:35
	2	14:23	3	Cancer	15:21
	5	0:12	5	Leo	16:32
	6	15:43	7	Virgo	17:6
	9	1:46	9	Libra	18:49
	11	5:9	11	Scorpio	22:41
	13	15:1	14	Sagittar	4:51
	15	2:40	16	Capricrn	13:2
	18	18:36	18	Aquarius	23:4
	20	0:34	21	Pisces	10:55
	23	2:37	23	Aries	23:55
	25	15:18	26	Taurus	12:10
	28	1:40	28	Gemini	21:19
	30	14:7	31	Cancer	2:10
FEB	1	10:14	2	Leo	3:25
	3	22:46	4	Virgo	2:57
	6	2:12	6	Libra	2:55
	7	20:30	8	Scorpio	5:5
	10	7:16	10	Sagittar	10:22
	12	4:19	12	Capricrn	18:39
	14	7:46	15	Aquarius	5:15
	17	13:11	17	Pisces	17:24
	20	4:38	20	Aries	6:21
	22	16:14	22	Taurus	18:54
	25	1:57	25	Gemini	5:13
	27	0:47	27	Cancer	11:47
MAR	1	10:44	1	Leo	14:25
	2	12:6	3	Virgo	14:21
	5	12:53	5	Libra	13:33
	7	9:49	7	Scorpio	14:3
	9	12:58	9	Sagittar	17:30
	11	5:15	12	Capricrn	0:39
	14	6:20	14	Aquarius	11:1
	15	15:20	16	Pisces	23:27
	19	8:34	19	Aries	12:24
	21	21:40	22	Taurus	0:45
	24	9:8	24	Gemini	11:19
	26	7:24	26	Cancer	19:5
	28	23:2	28	Leo	23:29
	30	23:25	31	Virgo	0:58
APR	1	12:50	2	Libra	0:50
	3	12:48	4	Scorpio	0:51
	5	14:20	6	Sagittar	2:52
	7	7:52	8	Capricrn	8:21
	9	3:39	10	Aquarius	17:40
	12	12:55	13	Pisces	5:49
	15	4:37	15	Aries	18:48
	18	1:0	18	Taurus	6:51
	20	3:50	20	Gemini	16:56
	22	17:23	23	Cancer	0:43
	25	4:10	25	Leo	6:1
	26	10:23	27	Virgo	9:10
	28	23:35	29	Libra	10:35
MAY	1	0:28	1	Scorpio	11:26
	3	1:54	3	Sagittar	13:14
	4	18:22	5	Capricrn	17:36
	7	12:42	8	Aquarius	1:37
	9	12:48	10	Pisces	13:2
	12	12:10	13	Aries	1:57
	15	0:27	15	Taurus	13:55
	17	15:23	17	Gemini	23:27
	20	4:26	20	Cancer	6:26
	21	23:14	22	Leo	11:28
	23	23:41	24	Virgo	15:7
	26	5:52	26	Libra	17:51
	28	8:38	28	Scorpio	20:8
	30	12:59	30	Sagittar	22:48
JUN	1	18:55	2	Capricrn	3:8
	3	20:17	4	Aquarius	10:23
	6	16:53	6	Pisces	21:1
	9	2:30	9	Aries	9:44
	11	6:33	11	Taurus	21:55
	14	5:44	14	Gemini	7:22
	16	3:2	16	Cancer	13:38
	18	6:49	18	Leo	17:37
	20	17:53	20	Virgo	20:33
	22	14:13	22	Libra	23:23
	24	20:8	25	Scorpio	2:35
	26	22:40	27	Sagittar	6:27
	28	16:2	29	Capricrn	11:35

Month	Date	Time	Date	Sign	Time
JUL	1	12:23	1	Aquarius	18:57
	3	14:37	4	Pisces	5:10
	5	12:50	6	Aries	17:40
	9	5:11	9	Taurus	6:14
	11	13:51	11	Gemini	16:14
	13	3:36	13	Cancer	22:31
	16	1:13	16	Leo	1:42
	17	9:48	18	Virgo	3:22
	19	22:54	20	Libra	5:6
	22	5:16	22	Scorpio	7:57
	24	3:6	24	Sagittar	12:19
	26	12:1	26	Capricrn	18:23
	28	22:1	29	Aquarius	2:25
	30	15:49	31	Pisces	12:46
AUG	3	0:54	3	Aries	1:10
	4	19:54	5	Taurus	14:5
	7	7:48	8	Gemini	1:2
	9	12:58	10	Cancer	8:11
	11	20:45	12	Leo	11:31
	13	20:27	14	Virgo	12:25
	15	22:38	16	Libra	12:45
	18	4:37	18	Scorpio	14:11
	20	11:37	20	Sagittar	17:47
	22	21:48	22	Capricrn	23:59
	24	16:17	25	Aquarius	8:38
	26	21:38	27	Pisces	19:28
	29	14:49	30	Aries	7:57
SEP	1	3:58	1	Taurus	20:59
	3	16:23	4	Gemini	8:44
	6	3:35	6	Cancer	17:15
	8	11:45	9	Leo	21:48
	10	15:53	11	Virgo	23:9
	12	9:46	13	Libra	22:43
	14	19:56	14	Scorpio	22:41
	16	16:21	16	Sagittar	0:40
	19	2:24	19	Capricrn	5:48
	21	9:21	21	Aquarius	14:18
	23	1:48	24	Pisces	1:29
	25	21:54	26	Aries	14:10
	28	10:58	29	Taurus	3:7
OCT	1	2:25	1	Gemini	15:4
	3	21:47	4	Cancer	0:38
	5	16:54	6	Leo	6:50
	7	19:26	8	Virgo	9:35
	9	21:20	10	Libra	9:50
	12	4:23	12	Scorpio	9:17
	13	20:55	14	Sagittar	9:51
	15	22:32	16	Capricrn	13:58
	18	9:20	18	Aquarius	20:39
	21	4:34	21	Pisces	7:33
	23	10:0	23	Aries	20:21
	25	17:24	26	Taurus	9:12
	30	11:46	28	Gemini	20:48
			31	Cancer	6:27
NOV	2	0:55	2	Leo	13:40
	4	11:16	4	Virgo	18:8
	6	18:9	6	Libra	20:3
	8	7:44	8	Scorpio	20:21
	10	7:50	10	Sagittar	20:39
	12	8:15	12	Capricrn	22:52
	14	14:3	15	Aquarius	4:40
	17	2:14	17	Pisces	14:33
	19	20:5	20	Aries	2:33
	22	0:9	22	Taurus	16:0
	24	12:8	25	Gemini	3:12
	27	1:15	27	Cancer	2:10
	29	4:28	29	Leo	19:6
DEC	1	12:56	2	Virgo	0:17
	3	19:41	4	Libra	3:45
	6	0:36	6	Scorpio	5:44
	7	18:56	8	Sagittar	7:4
	9	20:48	10	Capricrn	9:18
	11	23:12	12	Aquarius	14:10
	14	8:30	14	Pisces	22:51
	16	22:43	17	Aries	10:50
	19	17:25	19	Taurus	23:46
	22	2:0	22	Gemini	11:0
	24	9:24	24	Cancer	19:22
	26	13:5	27	Leo	1:17
	28	15:54	29	Virgo	5:41
	30	22:23	31	Libra	9:18

JAN

1	16:30	1	Aquarius	18:30
2	10:11	4	Pisces	7: 5
5	20:11	6	Aries	18:28
8	5:53	9	Taurus	2:59
10	13:50	11	Gemini	7:35
11	21: 9	13	Cancer	8:35
14	22:21	15	Leo	7:37
15	19:51	17	Virgo	6:57
19	6: 5	19	Libra	8:44
21	8:12	21	Scorpio	14:25
23	23:54	23	Sagittar	23:56
25	15:55	26	Capricrn	11:53
28	12: 5	28	Aquarius	0:35
29	19: 8	31	Pisces	12:59

FEB

2	18:20	3	Aries	0:23
5	7:44	5	Taurus	9:49
7	4:30	7	Gemini	16: 9
9	2:43	9	Cancer	18:56
11	13: 6	11	Leo	19: 1
13	11:24	13	Virgo	18:14
14	22:49	15	Libra	18:50
17	19:57	17	Scorpio	22:45
19	7:27	20	Sagittar	6:49
21	4:43	22	Capricrn	18:13
24	6: 0	25	Aquarius	6:57
26	14: 3	27	Pisces	19:13

MAR

1	6: 2	2	Aries	6: 9
3	21:56	4	Taurus	15:19
6	12:43	6	Gemini	22:16
9	0: 3	9	Cancer	2:35
11	0:32	11	Leo	4:26
12	23:31	13	Virgo	4:54
14	18:59	15	Libra	5:43
16	11: 6	17	Scorpio	8:46
19	11:56	19	Sagittar	15:24
21	4: 8	22	Capricrn	1:40
24	3: 3	24	Aquarius	14: 5
28	22:44	27	Pisces	2:24
28	12:44	29	Aries	13: 0
31	8: 9	31	Taurus	21:24

APR

2	5:12	3	Gemini	3:43
5	6:22	5	Cancer	8:11
6	21:59	7	Leo	11: 9
9	8:35	9	Virgo	13:11
10	21:15	11	Libra	15:17
13	5:49	13	Scorpio	18:45
15	11:37	16	Sagittar	0:50
18	5: 7	18	Capricrn	10: 8
20	15:37	20	Aquarius	21:59
22	16:34	23	Pisces	10:24
25	10:52	25	Aries	21:10
27	6:19	28	Taurus	5: 9
30	10:14	30	Gemini	10:26

MAY

1	16:33	2	Cancer	13:54
3	19:45	4	Leo	16:32
5	23:28	6	Virgo	19:11
8	3:15	8	Libra	22:30
10	8: 7	11	Scorpio	3: 7
12	17:30	13	Sagittar	9:39
14	23:55	15	Capricrn	18:40
18	5:14	18	Aquarius	6: 4
20	16:22	20	Pisces	18:34
23	0:52	23	Aries	5:56
25	1:49	25	Taurus	14:16
27	10:11	27	Gemini	19: 7
29	15:54	29	Cancer	21:26
31	19:55	31	Leo	22:45

JUN

3	0:29	3	Virgo	0:37
4	19:14	5	Libra	4: 4
7	1:15	7	Scorpio	9:30
9	9:20	9	Sagittar	16:56
11	19:36	12	Capricrn	2:21
14	13: 7	14	Aquarius	13:39
16	21:33	17	Pisces	2:12
19	10:52	19	Aries	14:15
21	23:15	21	Taurus	23:36
23	9:18	24	Gemini	5: 1
26	6:43	26	Cancer	6:58
27	13:11	28	Leo	7: 6
29	15:17	30	Virgo	7:29

JUL

2	0: 6	2	Libra	9:47
4	13:39	4	Scorpio	14:56
6	12: 5	6	Sagittar	22:50
8	19:26	9	Capricrn	8:50
11	16:22	11	Aquarius	20:23
14	8:43	14	Pisces	8:58
16	10: 4	16	Aries	21:26
18	23:29	19	Taurus	7:55
21	11: 2	21	Gemini	14:40
22	17: 6	23	Cancer	17:23
25	0:43	25	Leo	17:19
26	17:28	27	Virgo	16:34
29	0: 7	29	Libra	17:18
31	9:54	31	Scorpio	21: 5

AUG

3	1: 2	3	Sagittar	4:25
5	3:51	5	Capricrn	14:35
7	21:40	8	Aquarius	2:27
9	14:20	10	Pisces	15: 3
12	7:21	13	Aries	3:32
14	21:50	15	Taurus	14:38
17	11:31	17	Gemini	22:46
19	20:28	20	Cancer	3: 2
21	19:50	22	Leo	3:58
23	22:43	24	Virgo	3:14
26	1:57	26	Libra	2:58
28	4:53	28	Scorpio	5:11
29	17:17	30	Sagittar	11: 5

SEP

1	9: 0	1	Capricrn	20:36
4	2: 9	4	Aquarius	8:28
6	20:28	6	Pisces	21: 7
8	14:24	9	Aries	9:22
11	1:56	11	Taurus	20:18
13	11:31	14	Gemini	5: 1
15	21:13	16	Cancer	10:43
18	4:17	18	Leo	13:19
19	12:15	20	Virgo	13:46
22	11:42	22	Libra	13:44
23	23:35	24	Scorpio	15: 8
26	8:31	26	Sagittar	19:35
28	13:34	29	Capricrn	3:49

OCT

30	23:18	1	Aquarius	15:10
3	15:47	3	Pisces	3:48
6	8: 5	6	Aries	15:52
8	14:39	8	Taurus	2:15
11	9:40	11	Gemini	10:30
12	20:34	13	Cancer	16:30
15	16:13	15	Leo	20:20
17	11:28	17	Virgo	22:22
19	23:13	19	Libra	23:44
21	21:48	22	Scorpio	1:33
23	13:21	24	Sagittar	5:24
26	1:11	26	Capricrn	12:27
28	20:22	28	Aquarius	22:54
29	23:59	31	Pisces	11:23

NOV

2	5:25	2	Aries	23:35
4	16:13	5	Taurus	9:38
7	0:21	7	Gemini	16:59
8	14:45	9	Cancer	22: 5
11	5:10	12	Leo	1:46
13	19:39	14	Virgo	4:42
16	4:43	16	Libra	7:27
17	18:45	18	Scorpio	10:37
20	10:21	20	Sagittar	15: 1
23	13:39	23	Capricrn	21:42
25	4: 0	25	Aquarius	7:23
27	13:16	27	Pisces	19:33
29	23:19	30	Aries	8: 7

DEC

2	5:15	2	Taurus	18:32
4	14: 5	5	Gemini	1:32
6	5:19	7	Cancer	5:32
8	19:16	9	Leo	7:53
10	20:54	11	Virgo	10: 4
12	23:26	13	Libra	13: 5
15	4: 5	15	Scorpio	17:20
17	9: 9	17	Sagittar	22:55
20	1:24	20	Capricrn	6:12
22	3: 9	22	Aquarius	15:44
24	16:28	25	Pisces	3:36
27	7:44	27	Aries	16:30
29	12:26	30	Taurus	3:52

JAN

Date	Time		Day	Sign	Time
1	11:41		1	Libra	20: 8
4	0:28		4	Scorpio	6:10
6	12:49		6	Sagittar	18:50
8	20:55		9	Capricrn	7:51
11	0:28		11	Aquarius	19:33
13	20: 8		14	Pisces	5:22
16	5: 5		16	Aries	13: 7
18	15:15		18	Taurus	18:37
20	1: 9		20	Gemini	21:44
22	16:32		22	Cancer	22:52
24	7:12		24	Leo	23:17
26	18:54		27	Virgo	0:48
28	23:23		29	Libra	5:19
31	8: 0		31	Scorpio	13:57

FEB

Date	Time		Day	Sign	Time
2	11:15		3	Sagittar	1:59
5	9:47		5	Capricrn	15: 1
7	0:27		8	Aquarius	2:35
10	7:42		10	Pisces	11:43
12	15:10		12	Aries	18:41
14	20:56		15	Taurus	0: 2
17	0:23		17	Gemini	4:21
19	4:21		19	Cancer	6:45
20	11:56		21	Leo	8:41
23	10:47		23	Virgo	10:59
25	13:30		25	Libra	15:15
27	22:27		27	Scorpio	22:54

MAR

Date	Time		Day	Sign	Time
2	9:27		3	Sagittar	10: 3
4	22:10		4	Capricrn	22:55
7	9:33		7	Aquarius	10:45
9	19:15		9	Pisces	19:44
12	1:36		12	Aries	1:52
14	5:59		14	Taurus	6: 5
16	8:15		16	Gemini	9:24
18	11:11		18	Cancer	12:24
20	14:37		20	Leo	15:28
22	17:40		22	Virgo	19: 5
23	23:32		25	Libra	0:12
27	6: 5		27	Scorpio	7:50
29	16:30		29	Sagittar	18:26

APR

Date	Time		Day	Sign	Time
1	4:59		1	Capricrn	7: 3
3	18:56		3	Aquarius	19:18
6	2:49		6	Pisces	4:52
8	10:31		8	Aries	10:58
10	12:18		10	Taurus	14:17
12	14:13		12	Gemini	16:13
14	16: 1		14	Cancer	18: 5
16	14: 9		16	Leo	20:51
18	22:49		19	Virgo	1: 6
20	9:27		21	Libra	7:14
23	13: 1		23	Scorpio	15:35
25	23:34		26	Sagittar	2:16
28	11:56		28	Capricrn	14:43

MAY

Date	Time		Day	Sign	Time
30	15:24		1	Aquarius	3:19
3	12:37		3	Pisces	13:51
5	20:48		5	Aries	20:51
8	0: 6		8	Taurus	0:18
9	23: 6		10	Gemini	1:22
12	1:15		12	Cancer	1:45
13	15:25		14	Leo	3: 3
16	5:39		16	Virgo	6:34
18	11:41		18	Libra	12:53
20	20:23		20	Scorpio	21:54
23	6:21		23	Sagittar	9: 4
25	19:23		25	Capricrn	21:35
28	3: 7		28	Aquarius	10:18
30	19: 7		30	Pisces	21:38

JUN

Date	Time		Day	Sign	Time
2	3: 8		2	Aries	5:58
4	8:29		4	Taurus	10:35
6	10: 1		6	Gemini	11:57
8	9:44		8	Cancer	11:35
10	10:39		10	Leo	11:25
12	11:26		12	Virgo	13:20
14	14: 9		14	Libra	18:39
17	1:33		17	Scorpio	3:33
19	13: 6		19	Sagittar	15: 3
22	1:53		22	Capricrn	3:45
23	15: 9		24	Aquarius	16:24
27	2:25		27	Pisces	3:59
29	6:46		29	Aries	13:42

JUL

Date	Time		Day	Sign	Time
1	18:20		1	Taurus	19:32
3	21:44		3	Gemini	22:14
5	21:27		5	Cancer	22:21
7	21:18		7	Leo	21:37
9	21:24		9	Virgo	22:10
11	18: 5		12	Libra	1:54
14	9: 7		14	Scorpio	9:45
16	20:30		16	Sagittar	21: 0
19	9:27		19	Capricrn	9:48
21	19:21		21	Aquarius	22:20
23	23:40		24	Pisces	9:39
26	15:15		26	Aries	19:13
28	16:48		29	Taurus	2:25
30	10:53		31	Gemini	6:43

AUG

Date	Time		Day	Sign	Time
2	2:39		2	Cancer	8:16
3	13:56		4	Leo	8:11
5	23: 8		6	Virgo	8:23
8	0:58		8	Libra	10:56
10	13:45		10	Scorpio	17:22
12	16: 5		13	Sagittar	3:45
15	7:51		15	Capricrn	16:21
17	23:52		18	Aquarius	4:50
20	9:43		20	Pisces	15:46
22	13:24		23	Aries	0:47
24	20:53		25	Taurus	7:55
27	5:34		27	Gemini	13: 3
29	14:34		29	Cancer	16:47
30	23:40		31	Leo	17:27

SEP

Date	Time		Day	Sign	Time
2	8:27		2	Virgo	2:52
4	10:27		4	Libra	20:51
6	15:15		7	Scorpio	2:21
8	14:45		9	Sagittar	11:39
11	11:41		11	Capricrn	23:45
13	17: 2		14	Aquarius	12:17
16	11:52		16	Pisces	23: 7
18	23:16		19	Aries	7:31
21	4: 4		21	Taurus	13:26
23	14: 2		23	Gemini	18:45
25	12:31		25	Cancer	21:52
27	14:23		28	Leo	0:28
29	19:14		30	Virgo	2:52

OCT

Date	Time		Day	Sign	Time
1	21:10		2	Libra	6:10
4	9: 1		4	Scorpio	11:40
6	0:16		6	Sagittar	20:19
8	22:13		9	Capricrn	7:50
10	23:28		11	Aquarius	20:26
13	23: 3		14	Pisces	7:40
16	8:12		16	Aries	16: 2
18	14:19		18	Taurus	21:29
20	7:18		21	Gemini	0:55
23	2: 2		23	Cancer	3:24
24	12:24		25	Leo	5:55
27	3:15		27	Virgo	9: 9
29	7:55		29	Libra	12:40
31	14:26		31	Scorpio	20: 2

NOV

Date	Time		Day	Sign	Time
2	8:49		3	Sagittar	4:47
5	15:25		5	Capricrn	15:57
7	13:58		8	Aquarius	4:33
10	12:24		10	Pisces	16:31
12	22:18		13	Aries	1:43
15	4:31		15	Taurus	7:19
17	8:28		17	Gemini	9:53
19	8:58		19	Cancer	10:53
21	9:40		21	Leo	10:53
23	13:16		23	Virgo	14:32
25	18:30		25	Libra	19:23
28	2:14		28	Scorpio	2:40
29	17:45		30	Sagittar	12: 8

DEC

Date	Time		Day	Sign	Time
1	11: 0		2	Capricrn	23:26
5	6:51		5	Aquarius	11:58
7	4:13		8	Pisces	0:28
10	0:10		10	Aries	10:57
12	15: 6		12	Taurus	17:50
14	2:40		14	Gemini	20:49
16	11:38		16	Cancer	21: 5
18	3: 8		18	Leo	20:35
20	18:45		20	Virgo	21: 5
22	16: 5		23	Libra	1: 3
25	2: 2		25	Scorpio	8:12
27	0:19		27	Sagittar	18:12
30	3:22		30	Capricrn	5:56

JAN	1	21:27	1 Taurus 23:15		JUL	1	23:50	2 Capricrn 5:24
	4	0:57	4 Gemini 1:20			3	13:43	4 Aquarius 15:32
	6	3:9	6 Cancer 3:28			6	18:29	6 Pisces 23:23
	8	6:38	8 Leo 6:53			8	7:18	9 Aries 5:4
	10	10:38	10 Virgo 12:54			11	4:30	11 Taurus 8:49
	12	22:17	12 Libra 22:18			13	6:53	13 Gemini 11:0
	15	7:46	15 Scorpio 10:27			15	8:22	15 Cancer 12:20
	17	21:17	17 Sagittar 23:7			17	12:29	17 Leo 14:6
	20	8:54	20 Capricrn 9:50			19	13:50	19 Virgo 17:53
	22	17:20	22 Aquarius 17:28			21	22:55	22 Libra 1:2
	24	19:44	24 Pisces 22:25			24	7:32	24 Scorpio 11:48
	26	21:21	27 Aries 1:48			26	20:26	27 Sagittar 0:35
	29	1:54	29 Taurus 4:43			29	8:56	29 Capricrn 12:47
	31	4:52	31 Gemini 7:47			31	11:54	31 Aquarius 22:33
FEB	2	8:31	2 Cancer 11:22		AUG	3	2:32	3 Pisces 5:35
	3	14:24	5 Leo 15:53			5	6:9	5 Aries 10:33
	6	18:41	6 Virgo 22:10			7	11:31	7 Taurus 14:19
	8	6:20	9 Libra 7:4			9	14:45	9 Gemini 17:22
	11	14:37	11 Scorpio 18:42			11	17:34	11 Cancer 20:4
	14	3:19	14 Sagittar 7:32			13	1:44	13 Leo 22:57
	16	14:44	16 Capricrn 18:54			16	0:48	16 Virgo 3:8
	18	18:7	19 Aquarius 2:47			17	10:57	18 Libra 9:53
	21	3:13	21 Pisces 7:6			20	17:41	20 Scorpio 19:57
	23	2:43	23 Aries 9:9			23	8:22	23 Sagittar 8:29
	25	6:58	25 Taurus 10:42			25	19:6	25 Capricrn 20:59
	27	12:9	27 Gemini 13:8			27	11:5	28 Aquarius 6:57
			29 Cancer 17:5			30	12:8	30 Pisces 13:31
MAR	1	19:53	2 Leo 22:38		SEP	1	9:59	1 Aries 17:27
	5	0:56	5 Virgo 5:52			3	19:4	3 Taurus 20:7
	6	17:19	7 Libra 15:5			5	21:48	5 Gemini 22:43
	9	20:57	10 Scorpio 2:31			8	1:3	8 Cancer 1:52
	12	9:39	12 Sagittar 15:25			9	9:3	10 Leo 5:50
	14	23:27	15 Capricrn 3:34			12	10:28	12 Virgo 11:2
	17	5:55	17 Aquarius 12:31			14	1:28	14 Libra 18:13
	19	12:19	19 Pisces 17:20			17	3:47	17 Scorpio 4:5
	21	1:8	21 Aries 18:54			19	16:16	19 Sagittar 16:23
	23	14:8	23 Taurus 19:6			22	2:58	22 Capricrn 5:16
	25	14:43	25 Gemini 19:54			24	8:43	24 Aquarius 16:2
	27	17:12	27 Cancer 22:42			26	21:21	26 Pisces 23:2
	29	1:2	30 Leo 4:5			28	23:32	29 Aries 2:31
APR	1	5:43	1 Virgo 11:54		OCT	1	2:35	1 Taurus 4:0
	3	1:24	3 Libra 21:47			2	9:58	3 Gemini 5:10
	6	7:28	6 Scorpio 9:28			4	4:56	5 Cancer 7:21
	8	15:26	8 Sagittar 22:20			6	14:54	7 Leo 11:18
	11	10:38	11 Capricrn 10:57			8	14:5	9 Virgo 17:14
	13	8:9	13 Aquarius 21:7			11	3:17	12 Libra 1:15
	15	21:15	16 Pisces 3:20			13	15:57	14 Scorpio 11:29
	17	11:17	18 Aries 5:40			16	5:4	16 Sagittar 23:45
	20	5:25	20 Taurus 5:36			19	3:44	19 Capricrn 12:51
	23	23:29	22 Gemini 5:9			21	21:6	22 Aquarius 0:34
	24	0:17	24 Cancer 6:14			23	6:54	23 Pisces 8:50
	26	5:51	26 Leo 10:12			25	17:17	26 Aries 13:5
	28	10:42	28 Virgo 17:29			28	8:6	28 Taurus 14:16
MAY	30	4:39	1 Libra 3:36			30	19:38	30 Gemini 14:11
	3	9:8	3 Scorpio 15:38		NOV	1	4:44	1 Cancer 14:41
	5	21:12	6 Sagittar 4:33			3	6:44	3 Leo 17:14
	8	9:55	8 Capricrn 17:9			5	13:5	5 Virgo 22:42
	11	2:19	11 Aquarius 3:58			7	8:48	8 Libra 7:5
	13	5:6	13 Pisces 11:35			10	16:17	10 Scorpio 17:53
	15	13:50	15 Aries 15:30			12	9:36	13 Sagittar 6:21
	17	10:42	17 Taurus 16:26			15	15:26	15 Capricrn 19:26
	19	13:14	19 Gemini 15:56			17	22:27	18 Aquarius 7:40
	21	11:11	21 Cancer 15:58			20	13:36	20 Pisces 17:20
	23	14:1	23 Leo 18:17			22	4:0	22 Aries 23:14
	25	20:28	26 Virgo 0:7			24	7:55	25 Taurus 1:31
	28	8:2	28 Libra 9:37			26	12:38	27 Gemini 1:24
	30	19:50	30 Scorpio 21:40			28	8:30	29 Cancer 0:44
JUN	2	3:40	2 Sagittar 10:38		DEC	30		1 Leo 1:29
	4	16:14	4 Capricrn 23:0			2	12:1	3 Virgo 5:17
	6	6:17	7 Aquarius 9:41			4	20:26	5 Libra 12:53
	9	11:50	9 Pisces 17:55			7	12:56	7 Scorpio 23:46
	11	6:1	11 Aries 23:14			10	8:18	10 Sagittar 12:30
	13	20:26	14 Taurus 1:46			12	8:2	13 Capricrn 1:30
	15	21:16	16 Gemini 2:24			14	13:20	15 Aquarius 13:36
	17	21:29	18 Cancer 2:35			17	15:11	17 Pisces 23:49
	19	20:4	20 Leo 4:3			20	7:12	20 Aries 7:16
	22	4:40	22 Virgo 8:27			22	9:58	22 Taurus 11:25
	23	14:30	24 Libra 16:43			23	16:39	24 Gemini 12:40
	26	22:20	26 Scorpio 4:17			26	8:32	26 Cancer 12:17
	29	11:23	29 Sagittar 17:14			27	16:6	28 Leo 12:7
						30	7:39	30 Virgo 14:13

Month	Day	Time	Day	Sign	Time
JAN	2	17: 2	2	Capricrn	22:52
	4	19:18	5	Aquarius	2:10
	6	24: 0	7	Pisces	4: 6
	9	5:26	9	Aries	6: 0
	11	6:13	11	Taurus	8:56
	13	11:33	13	Gemini	13:31
	15	18:53	15	Cancer	19:59
	17	22:27	18	Leo	4:31
	20	7:50	20	Virgo	15:10
	22	23:55	23	Libra	3:27
	25	8:17	25	Scorpio	15:54
	27	20:41	28	Sagittar	2:21
	30	3:30	30	Capricrn	9:12
FEB	1	7:11	1	Aquarius	12:22
	3	6:36	3	Pisces	13: 7
	5	8:34	5	Aries	13:20
	7	7:50	7	Taurus	14:51
	9	17:26	9	Gemini	18:55
	11	20:56	12	Cancer	1:51
	14	6:19	14	Leo	11:12
	16	16:53	16	Virgo	22:16
	19	7:43	19	Libra	10:31
	21	13:57	21	Scorpio	23: 9
	24	6:42	24	Sagittar	10:35
	26	15:33	26	Capricrn	18:56
	28	20:18	28	Aquarius	23:14
MAR	2	16:25	3	Pisces	0: 6
	4	20:55	4	Aries	23:19
	6	15: 9	6	Taurus	23: 7
	8	23:15	9	Gemini	1:29
	11	18:51	11	Cancer	7:30
	13	14:51	13	Leo	16:52
	15	18: 1	16	Virgo	4:23
	18	15:18	18	Libra	16:49
	21	0:37	21	Scorpio	5:21
	23	16:13	23	Sagittar	17: 7
	26	2: 4	26	Capricrn	2:39
	28	8:19	28	Aquarius	8:40
	30	2: 0	30	Pisces	10:53
APR	31	19:49	1	Aries	10:31
		0:52	3	Taurus	9:36
	5	1:10	5	Gemini	10:25
	7	4:40	7	Cancer	14:42
	9	5:35	9	Leo	23: 0
	12	4:39	12	Virgo	10:19
	14	20:17	14	Libra	22:54
	17	3:36	17	Scorpio	11:20
	19	11:33	19	Sagittar	22:49
	21	21:41	22	Capricrn	8:36
	24	1:49	24	Aquarius	15:43
	26	9:52	26	Pisces	19:38
	28	9:44	28	Aries	20:44
	30	11:16	30	Taurus	20:29
MAY	2	11:22	2	Gemini	20:53
	4	18:19	4	Cancer	23:52
	6	20:59	7	Leo	6:39
	9	10:20	9	Virgo	17: 3
	12	5: 7	12	Libra	5:27
	14	6:17	14	Scorpio	17:52
	16	22:38	17	Sagittar	4:58
	19	8:53	19	Capricrn	14:11
	21	20:53	21	Aquarius	21:16
	23	16: 8	24	Pisces	2: 2
	26	1:48	26	Aries	4:38
	27	20:35	28	Taurus	5:51
	30	5:18	30	Gemini	7: 2
JUN	1	8:35	1	Cancer	9:50
	3	14:43	3	Leo	15:38
	5	14: 4	6	Virgo	0:56
	7	7:49	8	Libra	12:50
	10	14:19	11	Scorpio	1:16
	13	1:46	13	Sagittar	12:16
	15	10:55	15	Capricrn	20:52
	17	8:23	18	Aquarius	3: 5
	20	3:41	20	Pisces	7:25
	22	1:35	22	Aries	10:29
	24	7:31	24	Taurus	12:54
	26	12:58	26	Gemini	15:26
	28	10:13	28	Cancer	19: 4

Month	Day	Time	Day	Sign	Time
JUL	29	22: 2	1	Leo	0:49
	3	0:52	3	Virgo	9:27
	4	15:33	5	Libra	20:48
	7	23:38	8	Scorpio	9:17
	10	11:26	10	Sagittar	20:37
	12	20:34	13	Capricrn	5: 7
	15	9:19	15	Aquarius	10:31
	17	6: 7	17	Pisces	13:43
	19	10:22	19	Aries	15:58
	21	14:44	21	Taurus	18:24
	23	20:10	23	Gemini	21:46
	25	19: 0	26	Cancer	2:31
	27	18:35	28	Leo	9: 1
	30	9:53	30	Virgo	17:42
AUG	1	12:41	1	Libra	4:44
	4	9:25	4	Scorpio	17:16
	6	21:46	7	Sagittar	5:14
	9	7:32	9	Capricrn	14:23
	11	18:58	11	Aquarius	19:46
	13	16:14	13	Pisces	22: 5
	15	14: 6	15	Aries	22:58
	17	16:34	18	Taurus	0:12
	19	21:24	20	Gemini	3: 9
	22	4:54	22	Cancer	8:19
	24	5:47	24	Leo	15:39
	26	19: 0	27	Virgo	0:56
	28	23:16	29	Libra	12: 3
SEP	31	18:46	1	Scorpio	0:36
	3	7:37	3	Sagittar	13:10
	5	18:23	5	Capricrn	23:29
	8	3: 3	8	Aquarius	5:50
	10	4: 7	10	Pisces	8:16
	12	8: 4	12	Aries	8:18
	14	4:12	14	Taurus	8: 3
	16	8:21	16	Gemini	9:29
	18	12: 6	18	Cancer	13:50
	20	18:50	20	Leo	21:13
	23	2:56	23	Virgo	7: 2
	25	14:41	25	Libra	18:30
	28	3:10	28	Scorpio	7: 6
	30	16:10	30	Sagittar	19:54
OCT	3	7:21	3	Capricrn	7:13
	5	9:24	5	Aquarius	15: 7
	7	16: 6	7	Pisces	18:51
	9	13:25	9	Aries	19:15
	11	15:52	11	Taurus	18:18
	13	15:47	13	Gemini	18:12
	15	18:20	15	Cancer	20:50
	17	18:33	18	Leo	3: 7
	20	10: 7	20	Virgo	12:43
	22	14:17	23	Libra	0:28
	25	12:28	25	Scorpio	13: 9
	27	23:28	28	Sagittar	1:48
	30	11:12	30	Capricrn	13:23
NOV	1	13:27	1	Aquarius	22:27
	4	2: 9	4	Pisces	3:56
	6	5:49	6	Aries	5:54
	8	4: 5	8	Taurus	5:37
	10	4:50	10	Gemini	5: 4
	12	5:56	12	Cancer	6:16
	14	10:23	14	Leo	10:49
	16	17:31	16	Virgo	19:14
	19	6: 1	19	Libra	6:41
	21	17:44	21	Scorpio	19:26
	24	7: 5	24	Sagittar	7:54
	26	18:10	26	Capricrn	19: 1
	29	3:26	29	Aquarius	4: 7
DEC	1	9:11	1	Pisces	10:37
	3	13:31	3	Aries	14:20
	5	14:28	5	Taurus	15:47
	7	15:22	7	Gemini	16:11
	9	16:21	9	Cancer	17:11
	11	19:38	11	Leo	20:32
	14	1:49	14	Virgo	3:25
	16	12:57	16	Libra	13:55
	19	0:43	19	Scorpio	2:32
	21	14: 6	21	Sagittar	14:59
	24	0:50	24	Capricrn	1:38
	26	9:12	26	Aquarius	9:55
	28	14:44	28	Pisces	16: 0
	30	19:46	30	Aries	20:19

JAN				JUL			
3	0: 7	3 Virgo	11:26	1	19:17	1 Aries	20:14
5	23:43	5 Libra	23:44	3	18:10	3 Taurus	23:59
8	1:14	8 Scorpio	9:20	6	4:56	6 Gemini	5:57
10	6:14	10 Sagittar	15: 2	8	13:12	8 Cancer	14:17
12	9:46	12 Capricrn	17: 9	10	23:43	11 Leo	0:51
14	7:33	14 Aquarius	17: 7	13	5: 7	13 Virgo	13: 8
16	10:26	16 Pisces	16:48	16	0:39	16 Libra	1:52
18	14:17	18 Aries	18: 3	18	4:37	18 Scorpio	13: 8
20	14:58	20 Taurus	22:16	20	20: 0	20 Sagittar	21:11
22	21:29	22 Gemini	5:55	23	0:19	23 Capricrn	1:28
25	6:28	25 Cancer	16:30	25	1:39	25 Aquarius	2:48
27	18:33	28 Leo	4:52	26	21:49	27 Pisces	2:46
30	7:47	30 Virgo	17:49	29	1:56	29 Aries	3:13
				31	4:38	31 Taurus	5:47
FEB				AUG			
1	20:36	2 Libra	6:11	2	9:49	2 Gemini	11:25
4	10:19	4 Scorpio	16:39	4	18:21	4 Cancer	20: 8
6	15:51	7 Sagittar	0: 2	7	5:15	7 Leo	7:13
8	16:57	9 Capricrn	3:50	9	7:53	9 Virgo	19:39
10	21:38	11 Aquarius	4:38	12	6:12	12 Libra	8:27
12	21:10	13 Pisces	3:57	14	11:26	14 Scorpio	20:18
14	20:55	15 Aries	3:48	17	3:20	17 Sagittar	5:40
17	3:48	17 Taurus	6: 9	19	9: 7	19 Capricrn	11:24
19	4:41	19 Gemini	12:22	21	11:16	21 Aquarius	13:31
21	10:49	21 Cancer	22:28	23	12:38	23 Pisces	13:14
24	2:51	24 Leo	11: 0	25	10: 5	25 Aries	12:30
26	15:57	26 Virgo	24: 0	27	4:49	27 Taurus	13:25
MAR				29	14:39	29 Gemini	17:39
1	4:15	1 Libra	12: 4	SEP			
3	8:50	3 Scorpio	22:28	31	22:26	1 Cancer	1:49
5	23:28	6 Sagittar	6:40	3	9:20	3 Leo	13: 1
8	3:17	8 Capricrn	12: 7	5	15:55	6 Virgo	1:41
10	8:11	10 Aquarius	14:40	8	10:17	8 Libra	14:23
12	8:45	12 Pisces	15: 4	11	0:38	11 Scorpio	2:16
14	8:29	14 Aries	14:52	13	8: 8	13 Sagittar	12:22
16	7:49	16 Taurus	16: 7	15	5:28	15 Capricrn	19:37
18	15:48	18 Gemini	20:42	17	19:22	17 Aquarius	23:23
21	5:12	21 Cancer	5:31	19	17:14	20 Pisces	0: 7
23	9: 8	23 Leo	17:36	21	20:19	21 Aries	23:59
25	22: 0	26 Virgo	6:37	23	16:24	23 Taurus	23:12
28	10:45	28 Libra	18:27	25	21: 5	26 Gemini	1:51
30	18: 8	31 Scorpio	4:17	28	3:15	28 Cancer	8:35
APR				30	13:21	30 Leo	19:11
2	6: 3	2 Sagittar	12: 8	OCT			
4	15:47	4 Capricrn	18: 5	2	23:53	2 Virgo	7:49
6	16:14	6 Aquarius	22: 1	5	20:24	5 Libra	20:29
8	16: 7	9 Pisces	0: 4	8	2:28	8 Scorpio	7:59
10	19:52	11 Aries	1: 3	10	11:37	10 Sagittar	17:54
12	13:21	13 Taurus	2:31	12	19:36	13 Capricrn	1:47
15	1: 6	15 Gemini	6:21	15	1: 3	15 Aquarius	7: 3
17	8:30	17 Cancer	13:55	17	3:40	17 Pisces	9:30
19	23:23	20 Leo	1: 7	19	4:10	19 Aries	9:56
22	2:35	22 Virgo	13:59	21	5:15	21 Taurus	10: 1
24	21: 3	25 Libra	1:52	23	6: 2	23 Gemini	11:50
27	2:21	27 Scorpio	11:19	25	10:58	25 Cancer	17: 8
29	14:18	29 Sagittar	18:19	27	21:40	28 Leo	2:31
MAY				30	12:25	30 Virgo	14:43
1	21:14	1 Capricrn	23:33	NOV			
4	0: 2	4 Aquarius	3:32	1	20: 0	2 Libra	3:23
5	21:20	6 Pisces	6:32	4	8:25	4 Scorpio	14:38
8	5:49	8 Aries	8:55	6	18: 2	6 Sagittar	23:52
10	3: 7	10 Taurus	11:34	9	1:29	9 Capricrn	7:11
12	12:48	12 Gemini	15:46	11	8:12	11 Aquarius	12:42
14	19:53	14 Cancer	22:53	13	12:28	13 Pisces	16:22
17	6:22	17 Leo	9:20	15	15: 4	15 Aries	18:28
19	17:49	19 Virgo	21:54	17	14:52	17 Taurus	19:54
22	7:28	22 Libra	10: 4	19	19:31	19 Gemini	22:10
24	12:51	24 Scorpio	19:42	21	21:26	22 Cancer	2:55
27	0:10	27 Sagittar	2:14	24	9:13	24 Leo	11:10
29	4:31	29 Capricrn	6:24	26	21: 9	26 Virgo	22:36
31	7:33	31 Aquarius	9: 7	29	10:24	29 Libra	11:14
JUN				DEC			
2	11:11	2 Pisces	11:53	1	16:48	1 Scorpio	22:40
4	13:10	4 Aries	14:46	4	1:57	4 Sagittar	7:32
6	13:16	6 Taurus	18:29	6	8:30	6 Capricrn	13:53
8	22:12	8 Gemini	23:43	8	11:17	8 Aquarius	18:22
11	5:45	11 Cancer	7:15	10	17: 4	10 Pisces	21:44
13	16: 1	13 Leo	17:29	12	23: 5	13 Aries	0:33
16	0: 4	16 Virgo	5:49	14	23:55	15 Taurus	3:23
18	16:59	18 Libra	18:19	17	1:37	17 Gemini	7: 0
21	2:44	21 Scorpio	4:40	19	6:41	19 Cancer	12:20
23	10:30	23 Sagittar	11:35	21	11:57	21 Leo	20:17
25	14:18	25 Capricrn	15:18	24	0:43	24 Virgo	7: 3
27	16: 4	27 Aquarius	17: 1	26	10:50	26 Libra	19:31
29	13: 6	29 Pisces	18:13	29	1: 6	29 Scorpio	7:29
				31	10:44	31 Sagittar	16:50

Date	Time	Date	Sign	Time
JAN 1	2:10	1	Aries	2:57
3	7:19	3	Taurus	11:31
5	7: 8	5	Gemini	22:53
8	5:12	8	Cancer	11:33
10	2:48	11	Leo	0:14
13	10:38	13	Virgo	11:55
15	11:50	15	Libra	21:33
17	23:33	18	Scorpio	4:12
20	7: 8	20	Sagittar	7:34
21	19: 8	22	Capricrn	8:23
23	19:18	24	Aquarius	8: 9
25	21:41	26	Pisces	8:46
27	17: 1	28	Aries	12: 0
30	11:47	30	Taurus	18:58
FEB 1	13:40	2	Gemini	5:33
4	17:15	4	Cancer	18:11
7	6:38	7	Leo	6:50
9	0:58	9	Virgo	18: 1
11	8: 1	12	Libra	3: 6
14	0:37	14	Scorpio	9:55
16	9:42	16	Sagittar	14:28
18	16:14	18	Capricrn	17: 2
20	2:30	20	Aquarius	18:21
22	10: 7	22	Pisces	19:37
24	6: 6	24	Aries	22:22
26	15:48	27	Taurus	4:24
MAR 1	6:45	1	Gemini	13:26
3	7:16	4	Cancer	1:38
5	20:24	6	Leo	14:23
8	7: 1	9	Virgo	1:24
11	0:41	11	Libra	9:44
12	22:37	13	Scorpio	15:38
15	10:19	15	Sagittar	19:52
17	17:22	17	Capricrn	23: 7
19	23:57	20	Aquarius	1:51
22	2:27	22	Pisces	4:34
23	23: 4	24	Aries	8: 4
25	23:52	26	Taurus	13:35
28	7:24	28	Gemini	22: 8
31	7:24	31	Cancer	9:43
APR 2	18:30	2	Leo	22:33
4	14:24	5	Virgo	9:55
7	5: 6	7	Libra	18: 5
9	7:29	9	Scorpio	23: 4
11	14:30	12	Sagittar	2: 5
13	17:11	14	Capricrn	4:32
16	7: 2	16	Aquarius	7:23
18	8:16	18	Pisces	11: 3
20	4:20	20	Aries	15:45
22	13:40	22	Taurus	22: 0
24	18:36	25	Gemini	6:33
27	5:31	27	Cancer	17:46
29	18:26	30	Leo	6:37
MAY 2	9:11	2	Virgo	18:38
4	21:33	5	Libra	3:26
7	5:24	7	Scorpio	8:22
9	1:14	9	Sagittar	10:28
11	3:27	11	Capricrn	11:30
13	8:22	13	Aquarius	13:24
15	13:55	15	Pisces	16:24
17	14:39	17	Aries	21:35
19	14:32	20	Taurus	4:42
22	3:53	22	Gemini	13:50
24	14:58	25	Cancer	1: 8
27	3:47	27	Leo	13:59
29	6:35	30	Virgo	2:35
JUN 1	3:21	1	Libra	12:31
3	5:52	3	Scorpio	18:22
5	17:50	5	Sagittar	20:34
7	18: 8	7	Capricrn	20:45
9	13:16	9	Aquarius	20:54
11	6:14	11	Pisces	22:40
13	18:46	14	Aries	3: 3
15	23:34	16	Taurus	10:16
18	10:59	18	Gemini	19:57
21	6:17	21	Cancer	7:37
23	17: 5	23	Leo	20:31
25	14:24	26	Virgo	9:22
28	11:34	28	Libra	20:15

Date	Time	Date	Sign	Time
JUL 30	21:40	1	Scorpio	3:33
3	6:13	3	Sagittar	6:55
5	0:12	5	Capricrn	7:24
6	23:38	7	Aquarius	6:49
8	16:23	9	Pisces	7: 6
11	1:57	11	Aries	9:53
12	23:40	13	Taurus	16: 5
15	16:36	16	Gemini	1:38
18	4:10	18	Cancer	13:33
20	21:40	21	Leo	2:32
23	8:12	23	Virgo	15:18
25	17:35	26	Libra	2:30
27	19:31	28	Scorpio	10:57
30	7:35	30	Sagittar	15:56
AUG 1	9:47	1	Capricrn	17:47
3	9:49	3	Aquarius	17:41
5	9:48	5	Pisces	17:23
7	10:15	7	Aries	18:46
9	19:54	9	Taurus	23:24
12	7:14	12	Gemini	7:57
14	9: 1	14	Cancer	19:39
16	21:48	17	Leo	8:41
19	13:15	19	Virgo	21:13
21	21:26	21	Libra	8: 6
24	3: 3	24	Scorpio	16:45
26	12:48	26	Sagittar	22:50
29	0: 3	29	Capricrn	2:19
30	18:12	31	Aquarius	3:41
SEP 1	22:33	2	Pisces	4: 3
3	19: 7	4	Aries	5: 2
6	2:28	6	Taurus	8:28
8	11:20	8	Gemini	15:39
11	2:21	11	Cancer	2:35
13	8:56	13	Leo	15:30
15	14:50	16	Virgo	3:57
18	4:13	18	Libra	14:18
20	10:30	20	Scorpio	22:18
23	3:33	23	Sagittar	4:17
25	4:37	25	Capricrn	8:37
27	10: 0	27	Aquarius	11:29
29	3: 9	29	Pisces	13:19
OCT 1	3:18	1	Aries	15: 6
3	7:50	3	Taurus	18:20
5	16:50	6	Gemini	0:35
7	22:52	8	Cancer	10:33
10	21:30	10	Leo	23: 9
13	0:12	13	Virgo	11:44
15	7:32	15	Libra	21:58
17	18:59	18	Scorpio	5:13
20	0:23	20	Sagittar	10:12
22	11:28	22	Capricrn	13:58
24	3:49	24	Aquarius	17:13
26	10:54	26	Pisces	20:15
30	17:57	28	Aries	23:24
		31	Taurus	3:29
NOV 1	23:46	2	Gemini	9:44
4	13:58	4	Cancer	19: 6
6	22:18	7	Leo	7:16
9	14:49	9	Virgo	20: 7
11	14:59	12	Libra	6:52
14	4:40	14	Scorpio	14: 6
16	9:16	16	Sagittar	18:13
18	11:54	18	Capricrn	20:38
20	19:24	20	Aquarius	22:48
22	16:44	23	Pisces	1:38
24	18:36	25	Aries	5:32
27	2:44	27	Taurus	10:46
29	8: 7	29	Gemini	17:51
DEC 1	21:51	2	Cancer	3:19
4	13: 6	4	Leo	15:13
6	18:13	7	Virgo	4:14
9	3:46	9	Libra	15:53
11	14:30	12	Scorpio	0: 4
13	19:32	14	Sagittar	4:24
15	21:21	16	Capricrn	5:59
17	23:36	18	Aquarius	6:36
20	4: 9	20	Pisces	7:52
22	5: 5	22	Aries	10:57
24	11:12	24	Taurus	16:25
26	22:55	27	Gemini	0:19
28	23:40	29	Cancer	10:27
31	20: 1	31	Leo	22:27

JAN

Date	Time		Sign	Time
1	7:26	1	Scorpio	10:23
3	10: 1	3	Sagittar	11:48
4	20: 2	5	Capricrn	12:22
7	10:21	7	Aquarius	13:54
9	6: 6	9	Pisces	18:14
11	16:21	12	Aries	2:23
14	0: 0	14	Taurus	13:49
16	22:47	16	Gemini	2:49
18	17:37	19	Cancer	14: 6
20	19: 6	21	Leo	23:34
23	11:38	24	Virgo	6:49
25	10: 5	26	Libra	12:14
27	21:52	28	Scorpio	16: 9
30	0:52	30	Sagittar	18:53

FEB

Date	Time		Sign	Time
1	3: 3	1	Capricrn	21: 3
3	3: 0	3	Aquarius	23:43
5	8:52	5	Pisces	4:12
7	23:46	8	Aries	11:37
10	13:17	10	Taurus	22: 9
13	8:33	13	Gemini	10:35
13	13:57	15	Cancer	22:34
17	6:21	18	Leo	8: 9
19	20:40	20	Virgo	14:46
22	4: 7	22	Libra	18:57
24	9:37	24	Scorpio	21:47
26	4:58	27	Sagittar	0:16
28	19: 6	29	Capricrn	3:13

MAR

Date	Time		Sign	Time
1	15: 7	2	Aquarius	7:11
4	10:16	4	Pisces	12:45
5	22:40	6	Aries	20:26
9	6: 2	9	Taurus	6:36
10	22:46	11	Gemini	18:44
13	16:51	14	Cancer	7: 8
16	9: 0	16	Leo	17:32
18	5:22	19	Virgo	0:27
21	2: 9	21	Libra	4: 0
24	12:24	23	Scorpio	5:28
24	11:30	25	Sagittar	6:29
26	15:16	27	Capricrn	8:37
28	22:42	29	Aquarius	12:47
31	19:13	31	Pisces	19:13

APR

Date	Time		Sign	Time
2	22:58	3	Aries	3:46
3	13:48	5	Taurus	14:12
7	5:10	8	Gemini	2:13
10	14:15	10	Cancer	14:53
13	1:17	13	Leo	2:15
15	9: 8	15	Virgo	10:22
17	7: 6	17	Libra	14:27
19	14:11	19	Scorpio	15:24
21	12: 7	21	Sagittar	15: 4
23	13:25	23	Capricrn	15:33
25	15:57	25	Aquarius	18:30
27	21:38	28	Pisces	0:39
29	23:21	30	Aries	9:39

MAY

Date	Time		Sign	Time
2	16:41	2	Taurus	20:37
4	13:30	5	Gemini	8:48
7	16:47	7	Cancer	21:31
10	4:33	10	Leo	9:30
13	13:59	12	Virgo	18:57
14	13: 8	15	Libra	0:29
16	21:26	17	Scorpio	2:11
18	21:53	19	Sagittar	1:34
20	19:44	21	Capricrn	0:49
23	20:31	23	Aquarius	2: 5
25	0:38	25	Pisces	6:50
26	22:16	27	Aries	15:16
29	19: 6	30	Taurus	2:23

JUN

Date	Time		Sign	Time
31	21: 7	1	Gemini	14:48
3	19:38	4	Cancer	3:27
6	7:38	6	Leo	15:29
8	17:59	9	Virgo	1:41
11	3:59	11	Libra	8:41
13	5: 1	13	Scorpio	11:57
15	6:49	15	Sagittar	12:49
17	7:17	17	Capricrn	11:29
19	4:39	19	Aquarius	11:42
21	14:43	21	Pisces	14:52
23	5: 7	23	Aries	21:56
25	23:46	26	Taurus	8:28
28	3:41	28	Gemini	20:52

JUL

Date	Time		Sign	Time
1	0:39	1	Cancer	9:28
3	12:35	3	Leo	21:11
5	22:59	6	Virgo	7:16
7	23:22	8	Libra	14:55
10	12:17	10	Scorpio	19:37
12	18:39	12	Sagittar	21:32
14	15: 7	14	Capricrn	21:49
16	15:28	16	Aquarius	22:11
18	17:31	19	Pisces	0:31
21	2:34	21	Aries	6:12
23	7:58	23	Taurus	15:37
25	10:49	26	Gemini	3:37
28	8:59	28	Cancer	16:12
31	20:41	31	Leo	3:38

AUG

Date	Time		Sign	Time
2	6:37	2	Virgo	13: 5
4	3:54	4	Libra	20:20
6	19:53	7	Scorpio	1:24
8	13: 4	9	Sagittar	4:32
11	1:33	11	Capricrn	6:21
13	3:17	13	Aquarius	7:52
15	5:59	15	Pisces	10:29
16	23:24	17	Aries	15:32
19	19:31	19	Taurus	23:54
22	9:11	22	Gemini	11:15
24	23:38	24	Cancer	23:48
27	8: 5	27	Leo	11:19
29	17:52	29	Virgo	20:19

SEP

Date	Time		Sign	Time
31	20:30	1	Libra	2:38
3	5: 7	3	Scorpio	6:55
5	15: 7	5	Sagittar	10: 0
7	11:36	7	Capricrn	12:41
9	14:49	9	Aquarius	15:33
13	18:54	11	Pisces	19:17
13	7: 0	14	Aries	0:42
16	0:16	16	Taurus	8:39
18	10:18	18	Gemini	19:24
21	3:35	21	Cancer	7:55
23	22:21	23	Leo	19:53
25	20:35	26	Virgo	5: 7
27	15:26	28	Libra	10:54
30	6:51	30	Scorpio	14: 0

OCT

Date	Time		Sign	Time
2	9:15	2	Sagittar	15:54
4	12:18	4	Capricrn	18: 3
6	20:23	6	Aquarius	21:20
8	20:56	9	Pisces	2: 7
10	11:24	11	Aries	8:31
13	13:24	13	Taurus	16:50
16	1: 9	16	Gemini	3:23
18	15: 4	18	Cancer	15:48
20	22:55	21	Leo	4:22
23	14:22	23	Virgo	14:33
25	3:14	25	Libra	20:49
27	10:49	27	Scorpio	23:27
29	16:36	30	Sagittar	0: 3

NOV

Date	Time		Sign	Time
31	21:19	1	Capricrn	0:39
2	6:16	3	Aquarius	2:53
4	18: 7	5	Pisces	7:35
6	22:38	7	Aries	14:40
9	9:20	9	Taurus	23:44
12	10:21	12	Gemini	10:35
14	7:52	14	Cancer	22:57
17	0:31	17	Leo	11:51
19	17:39	19	Virgo	23:11
22	6:18	22	Libra	6:52
24	3:31	24	Scorpio	10:18
25	22:53	26	Sagittar	10:38
28	2:45	28	Capricrn	9:58
29	15:44	30	Aquarius	10:26

DEC

Date	Time		Sign	Time
2	12:33	2	Pisces	13:39
4	14:24	4	Aries	20:11
7	0:35	7	Taurus	5:34
9	4:50	9	Gemini	16:53
12	2:30	12	Cancer	5:21
14	12:16	14	Leo	18:13
17	5:39	17	Virgo	6: 7
19	10:12	19	Libra	15:15
21	19:56	21	Scorpio	20:26
23	9:37	23	Sagittar	21:56
25	9:18	25	Capricrn	21:19
27	1:33	27	Aquarius	20:41
29	9: 5	29	Pisces	22: 6

JAN			
1	10:22	2 Cancer	5:40
4	8:58	5 Leo	10:34
5	20:16	6 Virgo	14: 0
8	0:17	8 Libra	16:59
10	2:37	10 Scorpio	20: 5
12	12:19	12 Sagittar	23:34
14	19:24	15 Capricrn	3:56
17	4:23	17 Aquarius	10: 6
18	23:41	19 Pisces	18:58
21	2:43	22 Aries	6:37
23	23:26	24 Taurus	19:34
26	5:53	27 Gemini	7: 8
28	23:38	29 Cancer	15:19
31	2:56	31 Leo	19:57

FEB			
2	15:34	2 Virgo	22:12
4	20:43	4 Libra	23:39
7	1:19	7 Scorpio	1:37
9	3:42	9 Sagittar	4:59
10	17:58	11 Capricrn	10: 8
13	17: 7	13 Aquarius	17:19
15	19: 7	16 Pisces	2:44
17	15:20	18 Aries	14:20
20	10:26	21 Taurus	3:15
22	17: 9	23 Gemini	15:31
25	16:34	26 Cancer	0:58
28	1: 9	28 Leo	6:31

MAR			
2	6:40	2 Virgo	8:42
4	5:23	6 Libra	9: 1
5	16: 1	6 Scorpio	9:16
7	22:20	8 Sagittar	11: 5
10	8:12	10 Capricrn	15:34
12	5:23	12 Aquarius	23: 2
14	11:13	15 Pisces	9: 8
17	12:51	17 Aries	21: 6
19	10: 2	20 Taurus	10: 0
21	23:33	22 Gemini	22:33
24	16:12	25 Cancer	9: 6
27	4:24	27 Leo	16:14
29	14:31	29 Virgo	19:37
31	2:33	31 Libra	20: 7

APR			
1	23:17	2 Scorpio	19:26
4	6:19	4 Sagittar	19:34
5	23:45	6 Capricrn	22:19
8	19:27	9 Aquarius	4:49
11	8:24	11 Pisces	14:51
14	0:13	14 Aries	3: 9
16	6:29	16 Taurus	16: 7
18	9: 3	19 Gemini	4:33
21	2:55	21 Cancer	15:28
23	17:40	23 Leo	23:51
25	14:16	26 Virgo	4:56
27	23:16	28 Libra	6:49
29	7:27	30 Scorpio	6:33

MAY			
1	8:30	2 Sagittar	5:59
3	8:48	4 Capricrn	7:15
5	12: 1	6 Aquarius	12: 5
7	18:18	8 Pisces	21: 7
10	10:25	11 Aries	9:13
13	1:21	13 Taurus	22:15
15	22:39	16 Gemini	10:27
18	14: 2	18 Cancer	21: 3
21	4:44	21 Leo	5:41
23	2:49	23 Virgo	11:54
25	9:20	25 Scorpio	15:26
27	13: 2	27 Scorpio	16:35
29	20:19	29 Sagittar	16:38
30	20:37	31 Capricrn	17:27

JUN			
1	22:54	2 Aquarius	21: 4
4	2:41	5 Pisces	4:43
6	18:56	7 Aries	16: 3
9	3: 4	10 Taurus	4:57
12	9:40	12 Gemini	17: 3
14	12:42	15 Cancer	3:10
16	12: 9	17 Leo	11:12
19	12:23	19 Virgo	17:23
21	20:46	21 Libra	21:44
23	1:19	24 Scorpio	0:21
25	5:21	26 Sagittar	1:47
27	6:39	28 Capricrn	3:20
29	12: 8	30 Aquarius	6:44

JUL			
1	18:19	2 Pisces	13:28
4	9:52	4 Aries	23:51
7	8: 0	7 Taurus	12:25
9	16:30	10 Gemini	0:37
11	10:36	12 Cancer	10:34
14	16:17	14 Leo	17:54
16	0:11	16 Virgo	23:10
18	18:41	19 Libra	3: 6
21	1:32	21 Scorpio	6: 8
23	7:46	23 Sagittar	8:43
24	13:51	25 Capricrn	11:33
26	22:58	27 Aquarius	15:42
28	23: 4	29 Pisces	22:23

AUG			
1	1:51	1 Aries	8:11
3	4:28	3 Taurus	20:22
6	3:53	6 Gemini	8:48
7	19:42	8 Cancer	19: 8
10	2:15	11 Leo	2:19
12	11:17	13 Virgo	6:44
14	10:52	15 Libra	9:27
17	0: 2	17 Scorpio	11:38
19	6: 7	19 Sagittar	14:12
21	13:23	21 Capricrn	17:49
23	13: 8	23 Aquarius	23: 3
26	1:57	26 Pisces	6:25
28		28 Aries	16:15
31	3: 2	31 Taurus	4:12

SEP			
1	18: 1	2 Gemini	16:51
4	6: 9	4 Cancer	3:59
6	14:29	7 Leo	11:54
8	21:19	9 Virgo	16:17
10	21: 5	11 Libra	18: 3
13	1: 2	13 Scorpio	18:47
15	8: 5	15 Sagittar	20: 6
17	15:41	17 Capricrn	23:14
20	2:31	20 Aquarius	4:53
21	18: 0	22 Pisces	13: 3
23	22: 2	24 Aries	23:24
26	16:20	27 Taurus	11:23
29	2:58	30 Gemini	0: 6

OCT			
1	18:32	2 Cancer	12: 1
4	20:50	4 Leo	21:15
6	12:19	7 Virgo	2:41
9	2:46	9 Libra	4:36
10	19:47	11 Scorpio	4:25
12	22:47	13 Sagittar	4: 9
15	2:23	15 Capricrn	5:43
17	9:35	17 Aquarius	10:30
19	9: 2	19 Pisces	18:43
21	14:45	22 Aries	5:35
24	5:26	24 Taurus	17:48
26	17:36	27 Gemini	6:29
29	7:42	29 Cancer	18:39

NOV			
1	1:43	1 Leo	5: 0
3	3:36	3 Virgo	12: 7
5	9:33	5 Libra	15:24
7	8:38	7 Scorpio	15:38
9	9:17	9 Sagittar	14:37
11	8: 9	11 Capricrn	14:37
13	13:17	13 Aquarius	17:40
15	21: 8	16 Pisces	0:47
18	8:36	18 Aries	11:25
20	18: 1	20 Taurus	23:53
23	11:59	23 Gemini	12:32
25	19:49	26 Cancer	0:28
28	7: 2	28 Leo	11: 2
30	15:58	30 Virgo	19: 3

DEC			
2	3:20	3 Libra	0:25
3	23:59	5 Scorpio	2:15
6	10:43	7 Sagittar	1:57
8	23:55	9 Capricrn	1:31
11	1:47	11 Aquarius	3:10
13	7:29	13 Pisces	8:35
15	2:38	15 Aries	18: 8
18	6: 2	18 Taurus	6:22
20	3:33	20 Gemini	19: 3
22	11:17	23 Cancer	6:40
25	14:59	25 Leo	16:40
27	6:30	28 Virgo	0:51
30	1:12	30 Libra	6:52

Month	Day	Time	Day	Sign	Time
JAN	1	13: 1	2	Pisces	14:44
	4	2: 7	5	Aries	3:42
	6	23:47	7	Taurus	14:59
	9	16:26	9	Gemini	22:27
	11	5:50	12	Cancer	1:47
	13	14:36	14	Leo	2:21
	15	7:34	16	Virgo	2:13
	17	22:26	18	Libra	3:21
	20	6: 0	20	Scorpio	7: 2
	22	8:25	22	Sagittar	13:33
	24	3:44	24	Capricrn	22:29
	26	11: 8	27	Aquarius	9:17
	29	16:15	29	Pisces	21:34
FEB	31	15:17	1	Aries	10:36
	3	0:41	3	Taurus	22:41
	5	19:18	6	Gemini	7:42
	7	17:23	8	Cancer	12:30
	10	6:43	10	Leo	13:40
	12	8:38	12	Virgo	12:58
	14	9: 2	14	Libra	12:35
	16	12:21	16	Scorpio	14:23
	18	18:18	18	Sagittar	19:32
	20	6:39	21	Capricrn	4: 5
	22	15:54	23	Aquarius	15:12
	25	3:42	26	Pisces	3:45
	27	4:29	28	Aries	16:42
MAR	2	4:29	3	Taurus	4:52
	4	18:10	5	Gemini	14:49
	7	7:44	7	Cancer	21:19
	9	16:21	10	Leo	0:10
	11	12:47	12	Virgo	0:23
	13	11:43	13	Libra	23:44
	15	19:28	16	Scorpio	0:13
	18	3:16	18	Sagittar	3:33
	20	8:43	20	Capricrn	10:41
	21	17: 6	22	Aquarius	21:18
	24	4:23	25	Pisces	9:56
	26	18:58	27	Aries	22:50
	29	15: 0	30	Taurus	10:38
APR	1	0:11	1	Gemini	20:29
	3	21:38	4	Cancer	3:46
	6	7:29	6	Leo	8:13
	9	18:12	8	Virgo	10: 9
	9	19:58	10	Libra	10:36
	11	21:12	12	Scorpio	11: 7
	13	8:57	14	Sagittar	13:25
	16	11: 3	16	Capricrn	19: 2
	19	0:54	19	Aquarius	4:28
	21	10: 9	21	Pisces	16:44
	23	17:37	24	Aries	5:38
	26	6:15	26	Taurus	17: 8
	28	21:22	29	Gemini	2:20
MAY	1	0: 8	1	Cancer	9:12
	2	22:53	3	Leo	14: 5
	5	11:16	5	Virgo	17:19
	7	11:31	7	Libra	19:22
	9	13: 9	9	Scorpio	21: 1
	11	6: 6	11	Sagittar	23:32
	13	19:32	14	Capricrn	4:25
	16	2: 0	16	Aquarius	12:46
	18	18:17	19	Pisces	0:21
	21	12:31	21	Aries	13:13
	23	20:23	24	Taurus	0:46
	25	2:32	26	Gemini	9:29
	28	12:12	28	Cancer	15:27
	29	21:22	30	Leo	19:34
JUN	1	8:43	1	Virgo	22:48
	3	10:40	4	Libra	1:44
	5	12:12	6	Scorpio	4:42
	7	6:38	8	Sagittar	8:18
	9	18: 1	10	Capricrn	13:30
	12	4:23	12	Aquarius	21:25
	15	4:35	15	Pisces	8:25
	17	16:21	17	Aries	21:13
	20	5:25	20	Taurus	9: 9
	21	12:14	22	Gemini	18: 2
	24	11:40	24	Cancer	23:27
	25	22:45	27	Leo	2:28
	28	15:35	29	Virgo	4:37

Month	Day	Time	Day	Sign	Time
JUL	30	17:48	1	Libra	7: 5
	2	21:29	3	Scorpio	10:30
	4	17:35	5	Sagittar	15: 5
	7	11: 0	7	Capricrn	21:12
	9	3: 7	10	Aquarius	5:27
	12	13:32	12	Pisces	16:16
	14	11: 5	15	Aries	5: 0
	17	5:11	17	Taurus	17:28
	19	20:20	20	Gemini	3:10
	21	6:33	22	Cancer	8:56
	23	8:48	24	Leo	11:27
	25	12:15	26	Virgo	12:22
	28	1:44	28	Libra	13:27
	30	12:16	30	Scorpio	15:59
AUG	1	1:56	1	Sagittar	20:35
	3	13: 6	3	Capricrn	3:22
	6	3: 5	6	Aquarius	12:19
	7	18:53	8	Pisces	23:23
	10	5:26	11	Aries	12: 6
	13	18:52	14	Taurus	0:57
	16	20:46	16	Gemini	11:43
	18	9: 7	18	Cancer	18:40
	19	22:41	20	Leo	21:45
	22	20:34	22	Virgo	22:16
	24	6: 9	24	Libra	22: 5
	26	8: 1	26	Scorpio	23: 2
	28	14: 4	29	Sagittar	2:26
	31	3: 8	31	Capricrn	8:54
SEP	2	8:15	2	Aquarius	18:12
	5	1: 2	5	Pisces	5:42
	7	11:55	7	Aries	18:29
	10	3:42	10	Taurus	7:24
	11	19:54	12	Gemini	18:51
	14	10:41	15	Cancer	3:13
	16	20: 8	17	Leo	7:48
	18	20: 2	19	Virgo	9: 8
	21	4:38	21	Libra	8:44
	23	0:57	23	Scorpio	8:27
	24	12:46	25	Sagittar	10:11
	27	12:31	27	Capricrn	15:16
	29	23:17	30	Aquarius	0: 3
OCT	2	0:53	2	Pisces	11:41
	4	15: 1	5	Aries	0:36
	7	11:30	7	Taurus	13:20
	9	23:25	10	Gemini	0:44
	12	3:56	12	Cancer	9:52
	14	11:19	14	Leo	16: 2
	16	15:24	16	Virgo	19: 4
	18	6: 0	18	Libra	19:43
	20	17:19	20	Scorpio	19:26
	22	10:38	22	Sagittar	20: 6
	24	22:50	24	Capricrn	23:34
	27	2: 7	27	Aquarius	7: 0
	28	18:11	29	Pisces	18: 7
NOV	30	16:42	1	Aries	7: 4
	3	3:19	3	Taurus	19:40
	5	7:28	6	Gemini	6:34
	8	14:27	8	Cancer	15:23
	9	22:10	10	Leo	22: 6
	12	7:52	13	Virgo	2:37
	14	14:51	15	Libra	5: 1
	16	10:47	17	Scorpio	5:59
	19	0: 6	19	Sagittar	6:53
	20	13:15	21	Capricrn	9:32
	23	1:11	23	Aquarius	15:32
	25	18:49	26	Pisces	1:40
	26	23:24	28	Aries	14:21
DEC	30	10:45	1	Taurus	3: 0
	3	8:59	3	Gemini	13:34
	5	13:32	5	Cancer	21:34
	7	20: 4	8	Leo	3:33
	10	6:32	10	Virgo	8: 9
	12	2:46	12	Libra	11:40
	14	7: 1	14	Scorpio	14:14
	16	7:15	16	Sagittar	16:28
	18	12:20	18	Capricrn	19:35
	20	15:58	21	Aquarius	1: 8
	23	1:33	23	Pisces	10:14
	25	15: 1	26	Aries	22:23
	27	13:19	28	Taurus	11:13
	30	19:27	30	Gemini	22: 3

JAN	2 13:23	2 Scorpio	17:27		
	5 3:43	5 Sagittar	3:58		
	7 5:39	7 Capricrn	16:10		
	9 18:16	10 Aquarius	4:50		
	11 6:59	12 Pisces	17:11		
	14 17:58	15 Aries	4:15		
	17 7:8	17 Taurus	12:40		
	19 15:48	19 Gemini	17:24		
	21 9:51	21 Cancer	18:36		
	23 9:8	23 Leo	17:45		
	24 13:29	25 Virgo	17:4		
	27 9:7	27 Libra	18:47		
	29 0:53	30 Scorpio	0:25		
FEB	1 6:58	1 Sagittar	10:4		
	3 16:10	3 Capricrn	22:14		
	5 23:49	6 Aquarius	10:59		
	8 0:37	8 Pisces	23:4		
	11 7:1	11 Aries	9:52		
	13 7:43	13 Taurus	18:45		
	15 18:53	16 Gemini	0:55		
	18 2:9	18 Cancer	3:58		
	19 17:24	20 Leo	4:34		
	21 9:59	22 Virgo	4:21		
	23 17:15	24 Libra	5:21		
	25 19:55	26 Scorpio	9:28		
	28 3:1	28 Sagittar	17:37		
MAR	2 22:16	2 Capricrn	5:3		
	5 15:9	5 Aquarius	17:46		
	7 3:2	8 Pisces	5:44		
	9 23:55	10 Aries	15:58		
	12 6:26	13 Taurus	0:15		
	14 19:14	15 Gemini	6:29		
	17 3:49	17 Cancer	10:36		
	19 10:0	19 Leo	12:52		
	21 9:27	21 Virgo	14:8		
	23 0:7	23 Libra	15:50		
	24 10:47	25 Scorpio	19:34		
	27 8:21	28 Sagittar	2:34		
	29 17:23	30 Capricrn	12:58		
APR	1 5:0	2 Aquarius	1:22		
	3 3:14	4 Pisces	13:28		
	6 3:39	6 Aries	23:31		
	8 9:5	9 Taurus	7:0		
	11 4:53	11 Gemini	12:16		
	13 14:46	13 Cancer	15:59		
	15 10:11	15 Leo	18:48		
	17 16:28	17 Virgo	21:21		
	19 5:15	20 Libra	0:25		
	20 19:22	22 Scorpio	4:54		
	23 19:39	24 Sagittar	11:45		
	26 20:27	26 Capricrn	21:28		
	29 5:58	29 Aquarius	9:26		
MAY	1 15:35	1 Pisces	21:47		
	5 5:47	4 Aries	8:14		
	6 6:39	6 Taurus	15:32		
	7 23:25	8 Gemini	19:51		
	10 12:30	10 Cancer	22:19		
	12 14:7	13 Leo	0:17		
	15 1:32	15 Virgo	2:52		
	16 22:53	17 Libra	6:47		
	19 2:8	19 Scorpio	12:22		
	20 21:22	21 Sagittar	19:53		
	23 21:3	24 Capricrn	5:35		
	26 10:28	26 Aquarius	17:17		
	29 1:25	29 Pisces	5:51		
	30 17:48	31 Aries	17:5		
JUN	2 4:29	3 Taurus	1:4		
	4 9:4	5 Gemini	5:17		
	6 17:28	7 Cancer	6:47		
	8 12:19	9 Leo	7:19		
	10 23:51	11 Virgo	8:41		
	13 5:32	13 Libra	12:10		
	15 14:9	15 Scorpio	18:11		
	17 4:51	18 Sagittar	2:28		
	20 9:41	20 Capricrn	12:39		
	22 5:27	23 Aquarius	0:24		
	24 10:33	25 Pisces	13:4		
	27 6:34	28 Aries	1:3		
	29 15:42	30 Taurus	10:14		

JUL	2 5:17	2 Gemini	15:23		
	4 0:2	4 Cancer	16:56		
	6 13:57	6 Leo	16:34		
	7 12:13	8 Virgo	16:26		
	10 1:30	10 Libra	18:28		
	12 4:16	12 Scorpio	23:43		
	14 16:6	15 Sagittar	8:5		
	17 0:9	17 Capricrn	18:43		
	20 0:8	20 Aquarius	6:44		
	21 10:3	22 Pisces	19:24		
	24 19:12	25 Aries	7:42		
	27 9:16	27 Taurus	17:58		
	29 19:19	30 Gemini	0:37		
AUG	31 18:33	1 Cancer	3:18		
	3 2:50	3 Leo	3:11		
	5 1:20	5 Virgo	2:18		
	6 22:58	7 Libra	2:52		
	8 4:21	9 Scorpio	6:33		
	11 0:50	11 Sagittar	14:0		
	13 11:17	14 Capricrn	0:30		
	15 23:47	16 Aquarius	12:42		
	18 15:28	19 Pisces	1:20		
	21 1:55	21 Aries	13:30		
	23 4:34	24 Taurus	0:7		
	25 22:26	26 Gemini	7:58		
	28 3:50	28 Cancer	12:18		
	30 10:44	30 Leo	13:31		
SEP	31 18:23	1 Virgo	13:7		
	3 6:11	3 Libra	13:5		
	4 23:41	5 Scorpio	15:24		
	7 17:1	7 Sagittar	21:21		
	10 0:14	10 Capricrn	6:58		
	12 13:10	12 Aquarius	19:1		
	15 2:4	15 Pisces	7:39		
	17 15:57	17 Aries	19:29		
	19 14:33	20 Taurus	5:41		
	22 12:20	22 Gemini	13:42		
	24 18:39	24 Cancer	19:6		
	26 19:44	26 Leo	21:58		
	28 21:27	28 Virgo	23:2		
	30 22:19	30 Libra	23:41		
OCT	2 0:58	3 Scorpio	1:37		
	5 5:49	5 Sagittar	6:22		
	7 14:44	7 Capricrn	14:45		
	8 21:4	10 Aquarius	2:13		
	11 14:1	12 Pisces	14:51		
	14 11:25	15 Aries	2:34		
	16 23:0	17 Taurus	12:8		
	19 17:5	19 Gemini	19:21		
	21 20:54	22 Cancer	0:32		
	23 13:17	24 Leo	4:8		
	25 6:51	26 Virgo	6:40		
	27 22:47	28 Libra	8:49		
	29 11:29	30 Scorpio	11:34		
NOV	1 10:21	1 Sagittar	16:8		
	3 20:19	3 Capricrn	23:38		
	6 9:59	6 Aquarius	10:18		
	8 8:56	8 Pisces	22:51		
	10 10:3	11 Aries	10:52		
	13 20:14	13 Taurus	20:20		
	15 13:39	16 Gemini	2:41		
	17 6:35	18 Cancer	6:41		
	20 5:4	20 Leo	9:32		
	22 11:41	22 Virgo	12:17		
	23 10:0	24 Libra	15:32		
	25 19:7	26 Scorpio	19:38		
	28 6:39	29 Sagittar	1:3		
DEC	30 6:13	1 Capricrn	8:32		
	3 14:23	3 Aquarius	18:42		
	6 2:42	6 Pisces	7:3		
	7 13:19	8 Aries	19:37		
	10 11:46	11 Taurus	5:46		
	12 10:54	13 Gemini	12:8		
	15 4:1	15 Cancer	15:12		
	17 7:43	17 Leo	16:35		
	19 13:15	19 Virgo	18:2		
	21 19:54	21 Libra	20:52		
	24 0:51	24 Scorpio	1:33		
	25 5:41	26 Sagittar	8:2		
	28 8:17	28 Capricrn	16:17		
	30 1:6	31 Aquarius	2:32		

JAN				JUL			
2	20:40	2 Gemini	22:13	2	20:43	3 Aquarius	2:31
4	20:57	4 Cancer	22:19	5	9:42	5 Pisces	13:37
6	4:43	6 Leo	22:30	8	18:43	7 Aries	22:38
8	23:35	9 Virgo	0:46	10	4:22	10 Taurus	4:46
10	10:17	11 Libra	6:48	11	17:4	12 Gemini	7:40
13	16:3	13 Scorpio	16:57	13	16:54	14 Cancer	8:3
16	5:3	16 Sagittar	5:44	16	2:8	16 Leo	7:32
18	18:9	18 Capricrn	18:34	17	17:52	18 Virgo	8:12
21	5:27	21 Aquarius	5:40	20	7:6	20 Libra	12:3
23	8:17	23 Pisces	14:34	22	19:20	22 Scorpio	20:3
25	15:54	25 Aries	21:32	24	16:58	25 Sagittar	7:31
28	0:6	28 Taurus	2:43	27	6:47	27 Capricrn	20:22
29	2:38	30 Gemini	6:6	28	16:39	30 Aquarius	8:37
FEB 31	4:45	1 Cancer	7:54	AUG 1	8:27	1 Pisces	19:18
2	0:42	3 Leo	9:6	4	3:26	4 Aries	4:10
4	8:42	5 Virgo	11:18	6	9:36	6 Taurus	10:56
6	4:32	7 Libra	16:19	8	14:18	8 Gemini	15:15
9	9:47	10 Scorpio	1:14	10	13:57	10 Cancer	17:11
12	7:58	12 Sagittar	13:21	11	18:23	12 Leo	17:41
14	15:28	15 Capricrn	2:14	14	13:55	14 Virgo	18:27
16	22:38	17 Aquarius	13:20	16	0:35	16 Libra	21:28
19	21:35	19 Pisces	21:39	19	0:50	19 Scorpio	4:12
22	1:13	22 Aries	3:37	21	12:16	21 Sagittar	14:45
22	22:22	24 Taurus	8:6	24	1:59	24 Capricrn	3:22
25	21:32	26 Gemini	11:42	26	3:35	26 Aquarius	15:36
28	6:56	28 Cancer	14:41	28	17:22	29 Pisces	1:55
MAR 1	15:0	1 Leo	17:23	31	4:39	31 Aries	10:3
3	10:35	3 Virgo	20:41	SEP 1	8:30	2 Taurus	16:20
4	21:13	6 Libra	1:53	4	19:30	4 Gemini	20:58
7	7:41	8 Scorpio	10:10	5	22:16	7 Cancer	0:4
10	0:20	10 Sagittar	21:35	8	1:16	9 Leo	2:2
13	19:58	13 Capricrn	10:25	9	22:53	11 Virgo	3:55
15	11:26	15 Aquarius	21:58	12	18:57	13 Libra	7:11
18	5:29	18 Pisces	6:25	14	5:42	15 Scorpio	13:19
20	10:56	20 Aries	11:43	17	11:41	17 Sagittar	22:58
21	3:13	22 Taurus	14:58	20	4:55	20 Capricrn	11:9
24	10:22	24 Gemini	17:26	22	22:46	22 Aquarius	23:33
26	10:22	26 Cancer	20:2	24	22:28	25 Pisces	9:58
28	11:24	28 Leo	23:21	26	18:28	27 Aries	17:35
29	14:42	31 Virgo	3:48	29	6:37	29 Taurus	22:49
APR 1	18:49	2 Libra	9:59	OCT 1	5:48	2 Gemini	2:32
3	10:53	5 Scorpio	18:34	4	2:14	4 Cancer	5:29
6	16:26	7 Sagittar	5:42	5	12:37	6 Leo	8:14
9	11:58	9 Capricrn	18:25	7	22:17	8 Virgo	11:23
11	20:32	12 Aquarius	6:32	10	5:7	10 Libra	15:44
14	4:52	14 Pisces	15:50	12	14:15	12 Scorpio	22:14
16	19:54	16 Aries	21:29	14	11:2	15 Sagittar	7:31
18	21:43	19 Taurus	0:8	17	18:6	17 Capricrn	19:17
19	14:32	21 Gemini	1:15	20	0:29	20 Aquarius	7:53
21	20:49	23 Cancer	2:22	22	17:1	22 Pisces	18:57
25	3:58	25 Leo	4:49	24	17:46	25 Aries	2:53
27	3:7	27 Virgo	9:21	26	3:11	27 Taurus	7:34
27	22:35	29 Libra	16:19	29	8:36	29 Gemini	10:0
MAY 1	19:55	2 Scorpio	1:37	30	21:3	31 Cancer	11:35
3	1:47	4 Sagittar	12:59	NOV 1	23:11	2 Leo	13:37
6	17:43	7 Capricrn	1:39	3	12:55	4 Virgo	17:3
9	3:33	9 Aquarius	14:9	6	7:39	6 Libra	22:23
11	13:10	12 Pisces	0:32	8	8:24	9 Scorpio	5:49
13	18:19	14 Aries	7:24	11	14:5	11 Sagittar	15:27
15	22:52	16 Taurus	10:36	13	17:13	14 Capricrn	3:3
18	6:25	18 Gemini	11:13	16	3:8	16 Aquarius	15:45
19	22:35	20 Cancer	11:1	18	20:13	19 Pisces	3:40
22	5:22	22 Leo	11:49	21	10:37	21 Aries	12:46
24	0:35	24 Virgo	15:11	23	12:43	23 Taurus	18:2
26	11:29	26 Libra	21:50	25	17:43	25 Gemini	20:0
28	14:35	29 Scorpio	7:33	27	9:50	27 Cancer	20:12
30	8:26	31 Sagittar	19:21	29	10:12	29 Leo	20:33
JUN 2	14:21	3 Capricrn	8:5	DEC 1	3:15	1 Virgo	22:45
3	3:17	5 Aquarius	20:38	3	16:47	4 Libra	3:50
7	15:16	8 Pisces	7:43	5	20:41	6 Scorpio	11:51
9	18:58	10 Aries	15:58	8	15:33	8 Sagittar	22:10
12	7:0	12 Taurus	20:35	10	22:27	11 Capricrn	9:59
13	21:25	14 Gemini	21:57	13	11:14	13 Aquarius	22:39
16	13:41	16 Cancer	21:27	15	22:26	16 Pisces	11:3
18	10:0	18 Leo	21:2	18	14:40	18 Aries	21:30
20	21:22	20 Virgo	22:45	21	2:31	21 Taurus	4:22
23	0:53	23 Libra	4:6	22	22:27	23 Gemini	7:15
25	10:57	25 Scorpio	13:19	24	22:53	25 Cancer	7:13
26	23:30	28 Sagittar	1:15	26	21:59	27 Leo	6:16
30	6:30	30 Capricrn	14:6	29	0:22	29 Virgo	6:37
				31	9:57	31 Libra	10:7

Month	Day	Time	Day	Sign	Time
JAN	1	7:51	1	Capricrn	12: 2
	3	3:38	3	Aquarius	19:16
	5	20: 7	6	Pisces	0:19
	7	23:39	8	Aries	4: 1
	10	2:35	10	Taurus	7: 2
	12	5:10	12	Gemini	9:49
	14	8: 1	14	Cancer	12:56
	16	8:44	16	Leo	17:16
	18	18: 6	18	Virgo	23:57
	19	16: 0	21	Libra	9:43
	23	15:54	23	Scorpio	22: 0
	26	8:51	26	Sagittar	10:35
	28	14:23	28	Capricrn	20:54
	30	16:22	31	Aquarius	3:44
FEB	2	6: 8	2	Pisces	7:38
	2	19:30	4	Aries	10: 2
	6	7:24	6	Taurus	12:22
	8	10:39	8	Gemini	15:31
	10	15: 1	10	Cancer	19:46
	11	17: 0	13	Leo	1:18
	15	3:58	15	Virgo	8:32
	16	17: 7	17	Libra	18: 4
	20	1:42	20	Scorpio	6: 4
	22	14:54	22	Sagittar	18:57
	25	2:33	25	Capricrn	6: 8
	27	2:56	27	Aquarius	13:36
MAR	1	14:33	1	Pisces	17:15
	3	14:28	3	Aries	18:28
	5	16:59	5	Taurus	19:14
	7	19: 2	7	Gemini	21:10
	9	23: 8	10	Cancer	1: 9
	11	12:51	12	Leo	7:19
	14	13:44	14	Virgo	15:26
	16	15:41	17	Libra	1:29
	19	12: 9	19	Scorpio	13:25
	22	1:23	22	Sagittar	2:24
	24	13:42	24	Capricrn	14:25
	26	7:42	26	Aquarius	23:12
	29	3:31	29	Pisces	3:46
	29	16:26	31	Aries	4:58
APR	1	15:38	2	Taurus	4:40
	3	15:27	4	Gemini	4:56
	5	19:16	6	Cancer	7:23
	8	3: 9	8	Leo	12:48
	10	14:32	10	Virgo	21: 7
	12	21:17	13	Libra	7:43
	15	8:25	15	Scorpio	19:54
	17	15:21	18	Sagittar	8:52
	20	20:38	20	Capricrn	21:14
	21	18: 9	23	Aquarius	7: 9
	24	22: 6	25	Pisces	13:17
	26	7:41	27	Aries	15:40
	29	1:58	29	Taurus	15:36
MAY	1	1:21	1	Gemini	15: 0
	3	1:39	3	Cancer	15:51
	4	20:38	5	Leo	19:38
	7	15:44	8	Virgo	3: 1
	10	7:52	10	Libra	13:32
	12	16:45	13	Scorpio	1:58
	15	1: 1	15	Sagittar	14:54
	17	10:53	18	Capricrn	3: 7
	20	10:14	20	Aquarius	13:24
	22	15:59	22	Pisces	20:45
	24	23: 3	25	Aries	0:47
	26	13:34	27	Taurus	2: 3
	28	13:48	29	Gemini	1:53
	30	13:55	31	Cancer	2: 5
JUN	2	3:18	2	Leo	4:26
	3	21: 1	4	Virgo	10:19
	6	16:10	6	Libra	19:58
	8	18:21	9	Scorpio	8:16
	11	7:42	11	Sagittar	21:12
	13	22:44	14	Capricrn	9: 5
	15	23: 5	16	Aquarius	18:59
	18	20:12	19	Pisces	2:32
	21	1: 2	21	Aries	7:38
	23	1: 2	23	Taurus	10:29
	25	2:47	25	Gemini	11:42
	27	3:51	27	Cancer	12:28
	29	6:21	29	Leo	14:24

Month	Day	Time	Day	Sign	Time
JUL	1	10:19	1	Virgo	19: 6
	3	21:14	4	Libra	3:35
	6	12:59	6	Scorpio	15:19
	8	19:56	9	Sagittar	4:13
	11	8:27	11	Capricrn	15:57
	13	17: 3	14	Aquarius	1:14
	16	2:10	16	Pisces	8: 6
	18	7:15	18	Aries	13: 6
	20	11:58	20	Taurus	16:43
	22	17:22	22	Gemini	19:20
	24	17:34	24	Cancer	21:25
	26	21:33	27	Leo	0: 0
	29	1:42	29	Virgo	4:28
	31	11:18	31	Libra	12: 6
AUG	2	21: 0	2	Scorpio	23: 8
	5	10: 9	5	Sagittar	11:58
	7	22:45	7	Capricrn	23:52
	9	22:22	9	Aquarius	8:57
	12	5: 6	12	Pisces	14:59
	14	12: 4	14	Aries	18:59
	16	14:48	16	Taurus	22: 5
	19	0:54	19	Gemini	1: 3
	21	3:57	21	Cancer	4:14
	23	3:12	23	Leo	8: 0
	25	12:31	25	Virgo	13: 8
	27	14:39	27	Libra	20:41
	30	6:12	30	Scorpio	7:15
SEP	1	18:41	1	Sagittar	19:58
	4	6:55	4	Capricrn	8:21
	6	5:23	6	Aquarius	19:30
	8	23:14	8	Pisces	23:46
	10	11:30	11	Aries	2:48
	13	2:50	13	Taurus	4:36
	15	4:41	15	Gemini	6:35
	17	7:34	17	Cancer	9:39
	19	5:42	19	Leo	14: 8
	21	17:45	21	Virgo	20:15
	23	22:40	24	Libra	4:34
	26	11:59	26	Scorpio	15: 0
	29	0:22	29	Sagittar	3:37
OCT	1	13: 8	1	Capricrn	16:29
	2	17:30	4	Aquarius	3: 3
	6	6:35	6	Pisces	9:44
	8	5:16	8	Aries	12:45
	10	10:30	10	Taurus	13:33
	12	10:51	12	Gemini	13:59
	14	12:19	14	Cancer	15:39
	16	5: 5	16	Leo	19:32
	18	22:10	19	Virgo	1:59
	20	7:11	21	Libra	10:51
	23	20:39	23	Scorpio	21:53
	26	6: 7	26	Sagittar	10:31
	28	19:10	28	Capricrn	23:35
	31	4:14	31	Aquarius	11: 8
NOV	2	15:19	2	Pisces	19:18
	4	16:53	4	Aries	23:31
	6	20:58	7	Taurus	0:31
	8	23:34	9	Gemini	0: 4
	10	20:27	11	Cancer	0: 3
	12	8:43	13	Leo	2:14
	15	3:38	15	Virgo	7:41
	17	4:29	17	Libra	16:32
	19	23:38	20	Scorpio	3:59
	22	15:20	22	Sagittar	16:48
	25	1:31	25	Capricrn	5:46
	27	14:27	27	Aquarius	17:38
	29	23:17	30	Pisces	3: 3
DEC	2	1:40	2	Aries	9: 3
	4	8:24	4	Taurus	11:34
	6	8:38	6	Gemini	11:36
	8	9:37	8	Cancer	10:55
	9	5:16	10	Leo	11:28
	12	12: 2	12	Virgo	15: 7
	14	6: 2	14	Libra	22:48
	17	6:50	17	Scorpio	10: 1
	19	19:56	19	Sagittar	22:59
	22	10:55	22	Capricrn	11:49
	23	20:57	24	Aquarius	23:20
	27	6:37	27	Pisces	8: 6
	29	2:52	29	Aries	16: 6
	31	18:42	31	Taurus	20:29

JAN	1	2:25	1 Virgo 18:24	**JUL**	2	16:43	2 Taurus 20:44
	4	2:57	4 Libra 6:57		4	19:26	5 Gemini 0:4
	6	8:48	6 Scorpio 18:50		7	2:15	7 Cancer 4:42
	9	2:55	9 Sagittar 3:58		8	8:22	8 Leo 11:21
	11	4:4	11 Capricrn 9:27		11	19:56	11 Virgo 20:33
	12	22:36	13 Aquarius 11:56		13	12:40	14 Libra 8:9
	15	9:41	15 Pisces 12:54		16	14:38	16 Scorpio 20:41
	17	8:9	17 Aries 14:4		19	1:51	19 Sagittar 7:49
	19	14:38	19 Taurus 16:49		21	10:2	21 Capricrn 15:46
	21	19:6	21 Gemini 21:52		22	18:18	23 Aquarius 20:20
	24	1:56	24 Cancer 5:17		25	17:22	25 Pisces 22:32
	24	23:22	26 Leo 14:45		26	7:59	27 Aries 23:59
	28	19:59	29 Virgo 1:59		29	20:16	30 Taurus 2:7
	30	8:58	31 Libra 14:26	**AUG**	31	23:36	1 Gemini 5:48
FEB	2	16:36	2 Scorpio 2:52		3	4:48	3 Cancer 11:22
	5	1:1	5 Sagittar 13:15		5	5:10	5 Leo 18:49
	7	8:12	7 Capricrn 19:57		7	20:53	8 Virgo 4:17
	9	21:37	9 Aquarius 22:46		9	18:3	10 Libra 15:46
	11	12:48	11 Pisces 22:57		12	23:11	13 Scorpio 4:27
	12	4:44	13 Aries 22:31		15	8:22	15 Sagittar 16:23
	15	17:14	15 Taurus 23:31		17	17:35	18 Capricrn 1:17
	18	0:57	18 Gemini 3:30		19	7:33	20 Aquarius 6:11
	19	23:42	20 Cancer 10:51		22	5:2	22 Pisces 7:48
	20	17:37	22 Leo 20:53		23	9:42	24 Aries 7:56
	24	21:17	25 Virgo 8:33		26	1:9	26 Taurus 8:35
	27	19:50	27 Libra 21:1		28	3:22	28 Gemini 11:20
MAR	2	22:49	2 Scorpio 9:32		30	8:17	30 Cancer 16:50
	4	16:38	4 Sagittar 20:48	**SEP**	31	11:46	2 Leo 0:53
	6	23:42	7 Capricrn 5:5		4	1:24	4 Virgo 10:56
	9	3:4	9 Aquarius 9:23		5	11:23	6 Libra 22:35
	11	2:31	11 Pisces 10:12		9	3:38	9 Scorpio 11:19
	13	1:4	13 Aries 9:15		11	23:13	11 Sagittar 23:51
	15	1:21	15 Taurus 8:48		14	0:9	14 Capricrn 10:2
	17	3:37	17 Gemini 10:58		16	3:0	16 Aquarius 16:15
	19	13:30	19 Cancer 16:58		18	9:41	18 Pisces 18:27
	21	9:57	22 Leo 2:37		20	13:1	20 Aries 18:7
	24	6:8	24 Virgo 14:31		22	8:41	22 Taurus 17:27
	26	6:16	27 Libra 3:7		24	10:29	24 Gemini 18:31
	29	7:38	29 Scorpio 15:28		26	12:41	26 Cancer 22:45
APR	31	19:22	1 Sagittar 2:47		29	3:31	29 Leo 6:25
	3	8:9	3 Capricrn 11:59	**OCT**	1	5:25	1 Virgo 16:46
	4	18:26	5 Aquarius 17:56		3	22:30	4 Libra 4:44
	7	14:38	7 Pisces 20:22		6	6:43	6 Scorpio 17:28
	8	21:38	9 Aries 20:19		8	19:56	9 Sagittar 6:5
	11	14:11	11 Taurus 19:40		11	7:50	11 Capricrn 17:7
	13	15:9	13 Gemini 20:37		13	5:0	14 Aquarius 0:54
	15	19:13	15 Cancer 0:57		15	21:21	16 Pisces 4:42
	18	4:7	18 Leo 9:19		17	5:49	18 Aries 5:14
	20	20:39	20 Virgo 20:46		20	2:50	20 Taurus 4:20
	22	2:56	23 Libra 9:25		21	21:53	22 Gemini 4:10
	25	15:56	25 Scorpio 21:37		24	0:14	24 Cancer 6:40
	28	3:6	28 Sagittar 8:31		26	2:55	26 Leo 12:54
	30	12:28	30 Capricrn 17:33		28	18:41	28 Virgo 22:42
MAY	2	16:23	2 Aquarius 0:13		30	17:5	31 Libra 10:45
	4	23:43	5 Pisces 4:8	**NOV**	2	17:27	2 Scorpio 23:32
	6	4:53	7 Aries 5:41		5	6:12	5 Sagittar 11:52
	9	2:1	9 Taurus 6:5		7	17:37	7 Capricrn 22:50
	11	2:58	11 Gemini 7:6		9	5:23	10 Aquarius 7:26
	13	6:12	13 Cancer 10:31		12	8:38	12 Pisces 12:52
	15	5:24	15 Leo 17:31		14	0:4	14 Aries 15:12
	17	23:16	18 Virgo 4:1		16	11:51	16 Taurus 15:27
	20	13:51	20 Libra 16:26		18	11:50	18 Gemini 15:20
	23	0:1	23 Scorpio 4:38		20	13:14	20 Cancer 16:47
	25	10:43	25 Sagittar 15:9		22	20:57	22 Leo 21:23
	27	19:14	27 Capricrn 23:28		25	2:3	25 Virgo 5:51
	29	20:56	30 Aquarius 5:38		27	8:11	27 Libra 17:25
JUN	1	6:5	1 Pisces 9:54		30	3:10	30 Scorpio 6:13
	2	22:12	3 Aries 12:37	**DEC**	2	14:47	2 Sagittar 18:21
	5	10:42	5 Taurus 14:30		5	3:18	5 Capricrn 4:41
	7	12:44	7 Gemini 16:36		6	17:11	7 Aquarius 12:52
	9	16:11	9 Cancer 20:14		9	15:43	9 Pisces 18:48
	11	16:49	12 Leo 2:36		11	10:42	11 Aries 22:33
	14	7:35	14 Virgo 12:11		13	21:41	14 Taurus 0:36
	16	17:48	17 Libra 0:10		15	22:54	16 Gemini 1:49
	19	7:44	19 Scorpio 12:30		18	0:32	18 Cancer 3:35
	21	21:24	21 Sagittar 23:5		20	7:19	20 Leo 7:25
	24	3:30	24 Capricrn 6:51		22	14:27	22 Virgo 14:33
	26	5:44	26 Aquarius 12:1		24	4:9	25 Libra 1:10
	28	13:56	28 Pisces 15:27		27	9:42	27 Scorpio 13:49
	30	13:16	30 Aries 18:5		29	21:52	30 Sagittar 2:4

JAN					
1	22:10	2	Taurus	1: 4
4	6:15	4	Gemini	9:39
6	12:25	6	Cancer	20:35
9	8:47	9	Leo	9: 3
11	14:22	11	Virgo	22: 2
14	7:16	14	Libra	10: 4
16	14:24	16	Scorpio	19:32
18	23:32	19	Sagittar	1:18
20	22:39	21	Capricrn	3:29
22	22:59	23	Aquarius	3:19
24	22:39	25	Pisces	2:41
26	21:33	27	Aries	3:34
29	3:55	29	Taurus	7:35
31	7:52	31	Gemini	15:26

FEB					
2	23:40	3	Cancer	2:31
5	13: 6	5	Leo	15:16
8	2:45	8	Virgo	4: 9
10	6:48	10	Libra	16: 4
12	21:32	13	Scorpio	2: 6
15	7:37	15	Sagittar	9:23
17	10:23	17	Capricrn	13:24
19	6: 4	19	Aquarius	14:32
20	22:55	21	Pisces	14: 6
23	5: 7	23	Aries	14: 0
25	6:40	25	Taurus	16:19
27	11:55	27	Gemini	22:35

MAR					
2	2:50	2	Cancer	8:52
4	9:32	4	Leo	21:36
5	5:58	7	Virgo	10:29
9	10: 4	9	Libra	22: 1
11	20: 0	12	Scorpio	7:41
14	3:58	14	Sagittar	15:18
16	12:33	16	Capricrn	20:39
18	19:37	18	Aquarius	23:33
20	11:22	21	Pisces	0:31
22	19:58	23	Aries	0:54
24	15:52	25	Taurus	2:35
27	4: 5	27	Gemini	7:28
29	1:24	29	Cancer	16:28

APR					
31	15:49	1	Leo	4:39
3	2:22	3	Virgo	17:33
5	16:44	6	Libra	4:54
8	11: 0	8	Scorpio	13:55
10	9:46	10	Sagittar	20:50
12	13:34	13	Capricrn	2: 8
14	20:12	15	Aquarius	5:57
17	2:36	17	Pisces	8:25
19	0:31	19	Aries	10:10
21	11:49	21	Taurus	12:31
23	6:59	23	Gemini	17: 5
25	12:12	26	Cancer	1: 7
28	6:36	28	Leo	12:32

MAY					
30	22:18	1	Virgo	1:19
3	11:29	3	Libra	12:52
5	12:35	5	Scorpio	21:39
8	2:24	8	Sagittar	3:44
10	20:54	10	Capricrn	8: 0
12	7:34	12	Aquarius	11:18
14	10:29	14	Pisces	14:11
16	10: 9	16	Aries	17: 4
18	13:53	18	Taurus	20:38
21	0:47	21	Gemini	1:53
22	21:50	23	Cancer	9:49
25	14:13	25	Leo	20:42
27	20:37	28	Virgo	9:21
30	15:53	30	Libra	21:20

JUN					
2	1:55	2	Scorpio	6:35
4	8:29	4	Sagittar	12:28
6	9: 1	6	Capricrn	15:45
8	14:44	8	Aquarius	17:46
10	14:36	10	Pisces	19:42
12	20:11	12	Aries	22:31
15	0:50	15	Taurus	2:49
17	7:28	17	Gemini	9: 2
19	13: 2	19	Cancer	17:34
22	3:53	22	Leo	4:27
24	14:40	24	Virgo	17: 0
27	4:15	27	Libra	5:26
29	4: 7	29	Scorpio	15:37

JUL					
1	16:59	1	Sagittar	22:14
3	14: 8	4	Capricrn	1:25
4	21:40	6	Aquarius	2:25
7	15:44	8	Pisces	2:53
9	6:58	10	Aries	4:25
11	19:54	12	Taurus	8:13
14	1:41	14	Gemini	14:48
16	10:10	16	Cancer	24: 0
19	3: 0	19	Leo	11:17
21	14:54	21	Virgo	23:52
24	7:19	24	Libra	12:33
26	22: 4	26	Scorpio	23:41
28	17:52	29	Sagittar	7:39
31	4:28	31	Capricrn	11:48

AUG					
31	19:45	2	Aquarius	12:50
3	24: 0	4	Pisces	12:20
5	2:29	6	Aries	12:19
8	0:56	8	Taurus	14:37
10	5:35	10	Gemini	20:24
12	13:48	13	Cancer	5:40
14	23: 0	15	Leo	17:19
17	18:21	18	Virgo	6: 2
20	14: 1	20	Libra	18:42
23	5:16	23	Scorpio	6:16
25	13:24	25	Sagittar	15:28
27	5:58	27	Capricrn	21:15
29	8:55	29	Aquarius	23:28
31	9:12	31	Pisces	23:11

SEP					
2	12:28	2	Aries	22:20
4	14:55	4	Taurus	23: 6
6	21: 2	7	Gemini	3:19
8	17:59	9	Cancer	11:40
11	22:34	11	Leo	23:13
14	6:33	14	Virgo	12: 2
16	20: 0	17	Libra	0:33
18	17:14	19	Scorpio	11:55
21	18: 5	21	Sagittar	21:32
23	12:48	24	Capricrn	4:37
25	15:37	26	Aquarius	8:34
27	17:54	28	Pisces	9:39
29	16:59	30	Aries	9:16

OCT					
1	17:22	2	Taurus	9:25
3	22:48	4	Gemini	12:30
6	9:23	6	Cancer	19: 6
9	2:40	9	Leo	5:50
11	17:59	11	Virgo	18:32
12	17:23	14	Libra	7:15
16	2:41	16	Scorpio	17:54
18	11:13	19	Sagittar	3: 1
21	5:14	21	Capricrn	10:14
23	14:38	23	Aquarius	15:17
25	10:40	25	Pisces	18: 3
26	22:26	27	Aries	19: 9
29	16:35	29	Taurus	19:59
31	20:56	31	Gemini	22:26

NOV					
2	19: 1	3	Cancer	4: 9
4	1:17	5	Leo	13:42
7	5:20	7	Virgo	1:56
9	19:17	10	Libra	14:27
12	5:37	12	Scorpio	1:13
15	8: 0	15	Sagittar	9:36
16	21:53	17	Capricrn	15:55
19	14:57	19	Aquarius	20:38
21	22:29	22	Pisces	0: 4
23	5:31	24	Aries	2:36
25	12:15	26	Taurus	4:56
27	18:41	28	Gemini	8:13
29	22:14	30	Cancer	13:48

DEC					
2	17: 6	2	Leo	22:32
5	9:10	5	Virgo	10: 7
6	21: 2	7	Libra	22:42
9	15:21	9	Scorpio	9:53
12	0:47	12	Sagittar	18:11
14	9:17	14	Capricrn	23:35
16	12:24	17	Aquarius	3: 0
18	23:40	19	Pisces	5:31
21	6: 7	21	Aries	8: 7
22	19:51	23	Taurus	11:26
25	6:46	25	Gemini	16: 3
27	14:21	27	Cancer	22:29
30	0:20	30	Leo	7:15

Month	Day	Time	Day	Sign	Time
JAN	2	7:25	2	Sagittar	7:44
	4	7: 2	4	Capricrn	7:26
	6	1:51	6	Aquarius	6:58
	8	7:27	8	Pisces	8:22
	10	1:31	10	Aries	13: 7
	12	19:33	12	Taurus	21:43
	15	6:11	15	Gemini	9:18
	17	17:56	17	Cancer	22: 7
	20	8:29	20	Leo	10:33
	22	15: 8	22	Virgo	21:33
	24	23:27	25	Libra	6:26
	27	4:24	27	Scorpio	12:43
	29	11:28	29	Sagittar	16:18
	31	13:44	31	Capricrn	17:43
FEB	2	14:52	2	Aquarius	18: 9
	4	6:36	4	Pisces	19:16
	6	20:42	6	Aries	22:45
	8	12:19	9	Taurus	5:50
	11	16:14	11	Gemini	16:30
	13	16:19	14	Cancer	5:13
	16	1:47	16	Leo	17:39
	19	2:28	19	Virgo	4: 9
	21	22:59	21	Libra	12:14
	22	18:24	23	Scorpio	18: 9
	24	23:31	25	Sagittar	22:20
	27	3: 8	28	Capricrn	1:13
MAR	29	8:38	1	Aquarius	3:18
	2	15: 7	3	Pisces	5:27
	4	3:58	5	Aries	8:56
	7	9:42	7	Taurus	15: 8
	9	10: 1	10	Gemini	0:46
	12	5:15	12	Cancer	13: 4
	14	12:55	15	Leo	1:41
	16	12:53	17	Virgo	12:13
	19	19:37	19	Libra	19:38
	22	0:24	22	Scorpio	0:27
	24	3:43	24	Sagittar	3:48
	25	10:50	26	Capricrn	6:44
	28	9:38	28	Aquarius	9:47
	30		30	Pisces	13:18
APR	1	17:37	1	Aries	17:49
	3	23:58	4	Taurus	0:11
	6	9: 5	6	Gemini	9:19
	7	22:38	8	Cancer	21:11
	9	9:45	11	Leo	10: 1
	13	7:42	13	Virgo	21: 7
	16	4:27	16	Libra	4:41
	18	8:36	18	Scorpio	8:48
	20	10:42	20	Sagittar	10:53
	21	18:44	22	Capricrn	12:34
	24	14:59	24	Aquarius	15: 7
	26	3:31	26	Pisces	19: 5
	29	0:19	29	Aries	0:35
MAY	1	7:47	1	Taurus	7:49
	2	20:51	3	Gemini	17:12
	5	8:44	6	Cancer	4:53
	7	21:48	8	Leo	17:52
	10	14: 4	11	Virgo	5:45
	12	23:21	13	Libra	14:15
	15	8:28	15	Scorpio	18:42
	17	14:11	17	Sagittar	20:10
	19	13:44	19	Capricrn	20:30
	21	10:12	21	Aquarius	21:34
	23	20:37	24	Pisces	0:35
	25	10:39	26	Aries	6: 1
	28	13:43	28	Taurus	13:54
	30	3:44	30	Gemini	23:54
JUN	2	2:51	2	Cancer	11:46
	4	16:51	5	Leo	0:47
	7	6:31	7	Virgo	13:15
	9	3:16	9	Libra	22:59
	12	0:23	12	Scorpio	4:40
	13	13:50	14	Sagittar	6:40
	16	3:50	16	Capricrn	6:33
	18	4: 6	18	Aquarius	6:17
	20	6: 0	20	Pisces	7:40
	21	14:39	22	Aries	11:55
	24	19: 2	24	Taurus	19:26
	26	8:39	27	Gemini	5:43
	28	20: 9	29	Cancer	17:55

Month	Day	Time	Day	Sign	Time
JUL	1	7:46	2	Leo	6:57
	4	0:26	4	Virgo	19:33
	6	18:39	7	Libra	6: 6
	9	9:24	9	Scorpio	13:16
	11	4:58	11	Sagittar	16:44
	13	8: 5	13	Capricrn	17:21
	15	9:29	15	Aquarius	16:46
	16	22:32	17	Pisces	16:55
	19	15:52	19	Aries	19:33
	21	23:33	22	Taurus	1:46
	24	3:34	24	Gemini	11:36
	26	0:16	26	Cancer	23:53
	28	21: 2	29	Leo	12:56
AUG	31	1:37	1	Virgo	1:18
	2	22: 5	3	Libra	11:54
	5	7:21	5	Scorpio	19:56
	7	17: 9	7	Sagittar	0:57
	10	3: 0	10	Capricrn	3: 8
	11	17:45	12	Aquarius	3:28
	13	12: 0	14	Pisces	3:30
	15	19:36	16	Aries	5: 2
	18	0:10	18	Taurus	9:45
	20	12:53	20	Gemini	18:27
	23	5:50	23	Cancer	6:21
	25	10:19	25	Leo	19:24
	27	15:47	28	Virgo	7:30
	30	10: 7	30	Libra	17:34
SEP	1	18:43	2	Scorpio	1:25
	4	1: 5	4	Sagittar	7: 6
	6	8: 2	6	Capricrn	10:44
	8	12:24	8	Aquarius	12:39
	9	10:50	10	Pisces	13:42
	12	10:59	12	Aries	15:18
	14	14:57	14	Taurus	19: 9
	16	22:31	17	Gemini	2:38
	19	5:35	19	Cancer	13:45
	21	23:56	22	Leo	2:41
	23	20:10	24	Virgo	14:47
	26	21:55	27	Libra	0:22
	29	5:20	29	Scorpio	7:21
OCT	1	10:47	1	Sagittar	12:28
	3	7:43	3	Capricrn	16:23
	5	18:21	5	Aquarius	19:28
	7	21:59	7	Pisces	22: 0
	9	23:59	9	Aries	0:41
	12	4:15	12	Taurus	4:45
	14	11:20	14	Gemini	11:38
	16	7:16	16	Cancer	21:58
	19	6:31	19	Leo	10:40
	21	22:49	21	Virgo	23: 4
	23	9:11	23	Libra	8:46
	25	13:44	26	Scorpio	15: 9
	28	7:36	28	Sagittar	19: 7
	30	21: 2	30	Capricrn	22: 1
NOV	1	23:23	2	Aquarius	0:50
	4	2:59	4	Pisces	4: 5
	5	11:50	5	Aries	8: 0
	8	10: 7	8	Taurus	13: 7
	9	20:18	10	Gemini	20:19
	13	1:55	13	Cancer	6:19
	15	13:39	15	Leo	18:45
	18	1:59	18	Virgo	7:33
	20	14:10	20	Libra	18: 3
	22	19: 5	23	Scorpio	0:48
	24	4:47	25	Sagittar	4:12
	27	4:10	27	Capricrn	5:45
	29	2:30	29	Aquarius	7: 6
DEC	1	9: 3	1	Pisces	9:30
	2	10:35	3	Aries	13:35
	5	11:59	5	Taurus	19:35
	8	3:39	8	Gemini	3:41
	10	7:54	10	Cancer	14: 0
	13	1:46	13	Leo	2:18
	15	6:10	15	Virgo	15:19
	18	1:46	18	Libra	2:50
	20	9:37	20	Scorpio	10:53
	22	13:33	22	Sagittar	14:58
	24	8:46	24	Capricrn	16: 7
	26	14:10	26	Aquarius	16: 5
	28	9:20	28	Pisces	16:42
	30	16:58	30	Aries	19:25

Date			Sign	
JAN 3	1:20	3	Leo	2:12
5	5:13	5	Virgo	9:28
7	13:52	7	Libra	14:53
9	17:20	9	Scorpio	18:25
11	19:16	11	Sagittar	20:25
13	16:57	13	Capricrn	21:52
15	22:53	16	Aquarius	0:17
17	23:19	18	Pisces	5:15
20	12:31	20	Aries	13:42
22	23:10	23	Taurus	1:13
25	11:37	25	Gemini	13:48
27	21:53	28	Cancer	1: 8
30	7:40	30	Leo	9:55
FEB 1	15:10	1	Virgo	16:10
3	18:14	3	Libra	20:33
5	22:34	5	Scorpio	23:48
8	0: 6	8	Sagittar	2:33
9	21:57	10	Capricrn	5:25
12	6:25	12	Aquarius	9: 9
14	6:29	14	Pisces	14:40
16	19:33	16	Aries	22:46
19	8:54	19	Taurus	9:37
21	18:28	21	Gemini	22: 5
24	8:26	24	Cancer	9:57
26	15:40	26	Leo	19:11
MAR 28	16:57	1	Virgo	1: 4
3	0:55	3	Libra	4:15
5	3:28	5	Scorpio	6: 5
7	4:54	7	Sagittar	7:59
9	10:52	9	Capricrn	10:59
11	11:53	11	Aquarius	15:41
13	14: 8	13	Pisces	22:17
16	2:42	16	Aries	6:55
18	16:23	18	Taurus	17:38
21	4:58	21	Gemini	5:58
23	7:40	23	Cancer	18:22
26	0:17	26	Leo	4:38
28	4:31	28	Virgo	11:13
30	10:19	30	Libra	14:10
APR 1	14:46	1	Scorpio	14:49
3	11:17	3	Sagittar	15: 5
5	11:12	5	Capricrn	16:47
7	16:51	7	Aquarius	21: 3
9	22:32	10	Pisces	4: 8
12	8:58	12	Aries	13:32
14	19:58	15	Taurus	0:38
17	8:14	17	Gemini	12:57
19	23:13	20	Cancer	1:37
22	8:26	22	Leo	12:54
24	17:44	24	Virgo	20:53
27	0:46	27	Libra	0:47
28	23:16	29	Scorpio	1:24
MAY 30	21: 7	1	Sagittar	0:37
2	23: 6	3	Capricrn	0:39
4	23:36	5	Aquarius	3:23
7	8:46	7	Pisces	9:41
9	18:43	9	Aries	19:10
12	2:34	12	Taurus	6:41
14	15: 6	14	Gemini	19: 9
16	18:53	17	Cancer	7:48
19	15:47	19	Leo	19:32
21	22:58	22	Virgo	4:47
24	7:19	24	Libra	10:16
26	9:12	26	Scorpio	12: 2
28	8:47	28	Sagittar	11:27
30	2:12	30	Capricrn	10:39
JUN 1	9: 7	1	Aquarius	11:49
2	14:45	3	Pisces	16:32
5	22:15	6	Aries	1: 7
8	9:42	8	Taurus	12:31
10	22:25	11	Gemini	1: 7
13	6:33	13	Cancer	13:38
15	22:54	16	Leo	1:12
18	2:59	18	Virgo	10:53
20	15:50	20	Libra	17:39
22	19:28	22	Scorpio	21: 3
24	20:21	24	Sagittar	21:45
26	17:41	26	Capricrn	21:22
28	20:41	28	Aquarius	21:55

Date			Sign	
JUL 30	18:21	1	Pisces	1:14
3	7:16	3	Aries	8:24
5	18: 1	5	Taurus	19: 2
8	6:40	8	Gemini	7:30
10	16:43	10	Cancer	19:57
13	6:39	13	Leo	7: 6
14	11:15	15	Virgo	16:22
17	23:15	17	Libra	23:21
19	21: 9	20	Scorpio	3:51
22	3:38	22	Sagittar	6: 6
24	4:35	24	Capricrn	7: 4
26	5:35	26	Aquarius	8:10
27	8:44	28	Pisces	11: 4
30	13:58	30	Aries	17: 6
AUG 1	20:56	2	Taurus	2:40
4	10:52	4	Gemini	14:43
6	23: 6	7	Cancer	3:11
9	9:53	9	Leo	14: 8
11	13:11	11	Virgo	22:42
14	0:25	14	Libra	4:56
16	5:45	16	Scorpio	9:17
18	9:44	18	Sagittar	12:19
20	9:26	20	Capricrn	14:38
22	11:27	22	Aquarius	17: 3
24	11:51	24	Pisces	20:35
26	19:27	27	Aries	2:21
28	2:50	29	Taurus	11: 8
31	13:57	31	Gemini	22:39
SEP 3	4:10	3	Cancer	11:12
5	12:51	5	Leo	22:25
6	22:21	8	Virgo	6:42
10	2:23	10	Libra	12: 0
11	13:10	12	Scorpio	15:15
14	7:29	14	Sagittar	17:11
16	9:34	16	Capricrn	20:20
18	17:26	18	Aquarius	23:50
20	13:11	21	Pisces	4:32
23	9:53	23	Aries	10:56
25	14:10	25	Taurus	19:35
27	19:19	28	Gemini	6:42
30	2:51	30	Cancer	19:21
OCT 3	1:58	3	Leo	7:13
4	14:10	5	Virgo	16: 5
7	5:36	7	Libra	21: 9
9	10:21	9	Scorpio	23:20
11	8:55	12	Sagittar	0:21
13	22: 8	14	Capricrn	1:56
15	13:51	16	Aquarius	5:10
17	22:52	18	Pisces	10:38
19	22:49	20	Aries	17:57
23	0:15	23	Taurus	3: 8
24	17: 5	25	Gemini	14:15
27	12:17	28	Cancer	2:53
29	22:28	30	Leo	15:27
NOV 1	9: 7	2	Virgo	1:31
3	20:51	4	Libra	7:29
5	23:26	6	Scorpio	9:37
8	8:50	8	Sagittar	9:36
10	6:52	10	Capricrn	9:34
11	16:11	12	Aquarius	11:23
13	23: 3	14	Pisces	16: 5
16	10:27	16	Aries	23:40
18	14:19	19	Taurus	9:29
21	17:36	21	Gemini	20:57
23	17:31	24	Cancer	9:34
26	6: 8	26	Leo	22:23
29	2:40	29	Virgo	9:33
DEC 1	14:33	1	Libra	17: 9
3	12:46	3	Scorpio	20:33
5	14:19	5	Sagittar	20:47
7	14:16	7	Capricrn	19:53
9	3: 6	9	Aquarius	20: 1
11	18:29	11	Pisces	22:57
13	11:38	14	Aries	5:30
16	12: 5	16	Taurus	15:15
19	0:39	19	Gemini	3: 3
21	14: 3	21	Cancer	15:45
23	20:57	24	Leo	4:24
26	15:10	26	Virgo	15:51
28	9:18	29	Libra	0:42
31	5:37	31	Scorpio	5:56

JAN			
3	9:43	3 Aries	9:58
5	22:23	5 Taurus	22:43
8	3:45	8 Gemini	9:13
10	15:44	10 Cancer	16:12
12	16:38	12 Leo	20:13
14	22: 6	14 Virgo	22:40
17	0:15	17 Libra	0:53
19	3: 2	19 Scorpio	3:44
21	7:32	21 Sagittar	7:40
23	12: 6	23 Capricrn	12:59
25	13:53	25 Aquarius	20:13
28	4:48	28 Pisces	5:54
30	16:44	30 Aries	17:57

FEB			
2	5:37	2 Taurus	6:55
4	11:16	4 Gemini	18:20
7	1: 0	7 Cancer	2:16
9	0: 5	9 Leo	6:27
11	6:47	11 Virgo	8: 0
13	7:22	13 Libra	8:37
15	8:36	15 Scorpio	9:55
17	11:57	17 Sagittar	13: 4
19	17: 7	19 Capricrn	18:38
21	18:57	22 Aquarius	2:41
24	11:18	24 Pisces	13: 1
26	23:22	27 Aries	1: 9

MAR			
1	12:18	1 Taurus	14: 8
3	17:50	3 Gemini	2:15
6	9:53	6 Cancer	11:34
8	9:33	8 Leo	17: 3
10	17:32	10 Virgo	19: 2
12	17:29	12 Libra	18:57
14	17:10	14 Scorpio	18:40
16	12:32	16 Sagittar	20: 1
18	22:43	19 Capricrn	0:23
21	8: 0	21 Aquarius	8:15
23	17:13	23 Pisces	19: 1
26	5:40	26 Aries	7:30
28	18:39	28 Taurus	20:27
30	23:39	31 Gemini	8:42

APR			
2	17:22	2 Cancer	18:59
4	20:58	5 Leo	2: 6
7	4:15	7 Virgo	5:37
9	4:56	9 Libra	6:12
11	4:13	11 Scorpio	5:27
12	21:58	13 Sagittar	5:23
15	6:42	15 Capricrn	7:59
17	7:52	17 Aquarius	14:31
19	23:32	20 Pisces	0:53
22	12:12	22 Aries	13:30
25	1:15	25 Taurus	2:28
27	10:14	27 Gemini	14:29
29	23:50	30 Cancer	0:50

MAY			
2	0:51	2 Leo	8:53
4	13:16	4 Virgo	14: 2
6	15:33	6 Libra	16:14
8	15:45	8 Scorpio	16:20
10	9:14	10 Sagittar	16: 4
12	17: 0	12 Capricrn	17:30
14	14:51	14 Aquarius	22:29
17	7:16	17 Pisces	7:40
19	19:36	19 Aries	19:54
22	8:40	22 Taurus	8:52
24	12:51	24 Gemini	20:37
26	15: 3	27 Cancer	6:28
29	7:20	29 Leo	14:22
31	11:21	31 Virgo	20:13

JUN			
2	23: 0	2 Libra	23:51
4	19:32	5 Scorpio	1:30
6	20:22	7 Sagittar	2:12
8	14:46	9 Capricrn	3:40
11	1:34	11 Aquarius	7:47
13	1:18	13 Pisces	15:44
15	20:30	16 Aries	3:12
18	11:56	18 Taurus	16: 1
20	21:44	21 Gemini	3:44
23	10: 6	23 Cancer	13: 7
25	14:49	25 Leo	20:14
27	14:10	28 Virgo	1:35
30	3:23	30 Libra	5:33

JUL			
2	6:47	2 Scorpio	8:20
4	8:53	4 Sagittar	10:26
6	3:43	6 Capricrn	12:54
8	13:43	8 Aquarius	17:11
10	15:22	11 Pisces	0:33
13	6:32	13 Aries	11:14
15	19:14	15 Taurus	23:49
18	7:31	18 Gemini	11:47
20	14:24	20 Cancer	21:12
23	2:38	23 Leo	3:43
25	2:40	25 Virgo	8: 0
27	7:59	27 Libra	11: 5
29	10:47	29 Scorpio	13:45
31	13:44	31 Sagittar	16:36

AUG			
2	16:30	2 Capricrn	20:14
4	22:42	5 Aquarius	1:27
7	5:54	7 Pisces	9: 4
9	17: 5	9 Aries	19:25
12	5:26	12 Taurus	7:46
14	17:47	14 Gemini	20: 7
17	4:55	17 Cancer	6:11
19	11: 5	19 Leo	12:52
21	16: 3	21 Virgo	16:30
23	18:10	23 Libra	18:19
25	18:24	25 Scorpio	19:44
27	20:45	27 Sagittar	22: 0
29	9:12	30 Capricrn	1:58

SEP			
1	6:58	1 Aquarius	8: 4
3	8:15	3 Pisces	16:26
6	2: 6	6 Aries	3: 0
8	14:29	8 Taurus	15:15
11	3:16	11 Gemini	3:54
12	17:48	13 Cancer	14:56
15	22:12	15 Leo	22:41
17	13:12	18 Virgo	2:42
20	3:44	20 Libra	3:52
22	3:49	22 Scorpio	3:53
23	4:59	24 Sagittar	4:36
26	3:42	26 Capricrn	7:34
28	22:12	28 Aquarius	13:36
30	18:38	30 Pisces	22:33

OCT			
2	22:14	3 Aries	9:38
4	10:39	5 Taurus	21:58
7	7:59	8 Gemini	10:40
9	17:57	10 Cancer	22:26
12	9:33	13 Leo	7:36
14	20:49	15 Virgo	13: 2
16	17:58	17 Libra	14:50
19	6:33	19 Scorpio	14:21
20	22:46	21 Sagittar	13:40
23	13:46	23 Capricrn	14:55
25	6:28	25 Aquarius	19:40
27	14:41	28 Pisces	4:14
30	0:31	30 Aries	15:35

NOV			
31	18:18	2 Taurus	4: 8
4	6:24	4 Gemini	16:44
5	20: 8	7 Cancer	4:33
9	11:58	9 Leo	14:37
10	23:37	11 Virgo	21:42
13	8:38	14 Libra	1:10
15	1: 2	16 Scorpio	1:36
17	16: 2	18 Sagittar	0:42
19	0:34	20 Capricrn	0:42
22	1:49	22 Aquarius	3:42
23	7:55	24 Pisces	10:53
25	11:27	26 Aries	21:44
28	6:38	29 Taurus	10:22

DEC			
1	2:21	1 Gemini	22:54
3	8:56	4 Cancer	10:19
6	19:29	6 Leo	20:13
9	3:47	9 Virgo	4: 3
11	8:36	11 Libra	9: 9
13	10:35	13 Scorpio	11:23
15	11:39	15 Sagittar	11:40
17	10:27	17 Capricrn	11:46
19	13:37	19 Aquarius	13:46
21	18:54	21 Pisces	19:25
24	4:38	24 Aries	5: 3
26	16:46	26 Taurus	17:19
29	5:13	29 Gemini	5:53
31	13:11	31 Cancer	17: 2

Date	Aspect	Date	Ingress	
JAN	1	9:14	1	Scorpio	9:50
	3	12:49	3	Sagittar	17: 2
	5	23:43	6	Capricrn	2:10
	8	8:15	8	Aquarius	13: 7
	10	22:52	11	Pisces	1:39
	13	11:46	13	Aries	14:36
	15	22:59	16	Taurus	1:46
	18	4:42	18	Gemini	9: 7
	20	9:43	20	Cancer	12:14
	22	8: 0	22	Leo	12:26
	24	9:16	24	Virgo	11:48
	26	9:44	26	Libra	12:26
	28	12:55	28	Scorpio	15:50
	30	17:13	30	Sagittar	22:30
FEB	2	6:31	2	Capricrn	7:59
	4	13:50	4	Aquarius	19:25
	7	4:25	7	Pisces	8: 3
	9	17:19	9	Aries	21: 0
	12	5:11	12	Taurus	8:47
	14	12:55	14	Gemini	17:38
	16	19:17	16	Cancer	22:29
	18	23:20	18	Leo	23:47
	20	20: 8	20	Virgo	23: 8
	22	19:31	22	Libra	22:37
	24	20:53	25	Scorpio	0:11
	27	1:28	27	Sagittar	5:11
MAR	1	10: 3	1	Capricrn	13:52
	3	22: 1	4	Aquarius	1:22
	6	13:58	6	Pisces	14:10
	9	0: 5	9	Aries	2:57
	11	10:41	11	Taurus	14:35
	13	22: 0	14	Gemini	0: 0
	16	2:50	16	Cancer	6:21
	18	8:50	18	Leo	9:28
	20	9:16	20	Virgo	10: 8
	22	9:19	22	Libra	9:55
	24	7:21	24	Scorpio	10:37
	26	8:41	26	Sagittar	14: 0
	28	19: 0	28	Capricrn	21: 9
	30	18:21	31	Aquarius	7:53
APR	2	16:46	2	Pisces	20:39
	5	5:34	5	Aries	9:22
	7	16:54	7	Taurus	20:32
	10	4:41	10	Gemini	5:31
	12	11:33	12	Cancer	12: 9
	14	5:39	14	Leo	16:31
	16	15:57	16	Virgo	18:53
	18	17:12	18	Libra	20: 3
	20	18:24	20	Scorpio	21:14
	22	12:29	22	Sagittar	0: 3
	25	2:53	25	Capricrn	5:56
	27	2:30	27	Aquarius	15:33
	30	0:43	30	Pisces	3:54
MAY	2	13:35	2	Aries	16:39
	5	0:57	5	Taurus	3:35
	7	10:53	7	Gemini	11:50
	9	15:14	9	Cancer	17:43
	11	20:52	11	Leo	21:58
	13	22:56	14	Virgo	1:10
	16	1:36	16	Libra	3:44
	18	4:10	18	Scorpio	6:15
	20	7:18	20	Sagittar	9:38
	22	13: 8	22	Capricrn	15:13
	24	18:54	25	Aquarius	0: 0
	27	9:42	27	Pisces	11:47
	29	22:39	30	Aries	0:36
JUN	1	10: 0	1	Taurus	11:46
	3	9: 5	3	Gemini	19:43
	5	23:16	6	Cancer	0:41
	7	18:11	8	Leo	3:52
	10	5:19	10	Virgo	6:31
	12	8:20	12	Libra	9:27
	14	11:57	14	Scorpio	13: 1
	16	7:54	16	Sagittar	17:31
	18	22:46	18	Capricrn	23:41
	20	22:10	21	Aquarius	8:21
	23	18:59	23	Pisces	19:45
	26	7:59	26	Aries	8:38
	28	19:52	28	Taurus	20:23

Date	Aspect	Date	Ingress	
JUL	30	19:46	1	Gemini	4:47
	3	9:14	3	Cancer	9:30
	5	6:41	5	Leo	11:40
	7	12:55	7	Virgo	13: 1
	9	14:59	9	Libra	15: 0
	11	10:32	11	Scorpio	18:26
	13	15:35	13	Sagittar	23:37
	15	5:55	16	Capricrn	6:39
	18	7:29	18	Aquarius	15:48
	20	15: 8	21	Pisces	3:12
	23	7:45	23	Aries	16: 7
	25	20:32	26	Taurus	4:30
	28	12:50	28	Gemini	13:58
	30	6:43	30	Cancer	19:23
AUG	1	15:16	1	Leo	21:25
	3	17:47	3	Virgo	21:44
	5	22: 6	5	Libra	22:13
	7	18:19	8	Scorpio	0:22
	9	22:50	10	Sagittar	5: 3
	11	14:29	12	Capricrn	12:25
	14	15:41	14	Aquarius	22:10
	16	20:27	17	Pisces	9:52
	19	16:24	19	Aries	22:47
	22	8:46	22	Taurus	11:30
	24	16:24	24	Gemini	22: 3
	27	7:31	27	Cancer	4:54
	29	3:15	29	Leo	7:55
	30	18:56	31	Virgo	8:16
SEP	2	3:28	2	Libra	7:47
	4	7:58	4	Scorpio	8:21
	6	6:59	6	Sagittar	11:32
	8	10:25	8	Capricrn	18: 7
	10	23: 5	11	Aquarius	3:56
	13	13:32	13	Pisces	15:58
	16	0:10	16	Aries	4:56
	18	13: 0	18	Taurus	17:34
	21	0:17	21	Gemini	4:35
	23	12:30	23	Cancer	12:45
	25	13:49	25	Leo	17:27
	26	23:46	27	Virgo	19: 2
	29	15:32	29	Libra	18:47
OCT	1	15:16	1	Scorpio	18:31
	3	16:45	3	Sagittar	20: 8
	5	16:59	6	Capricrn	1:10
	8	22: 5	8	Aquarius	10: 9
	13	7:22	10	Pisces	22: 7
	15	19:51	13	Aries	11: 9
	18	6:44	15	Taurus	23:31
	20	17:35	18	Gemini	10:13
	22	22:53	20	Cancer	18:45
	24	15:47	22	Leo	0:45
	27	2:26	25	Virgo	4: 7
	29	2:40	27	Libra	5:18
	31	3:34	29	Scorpio	5:30
			31	Sagittar	6:29
NOV	1	11:49	2	Capricrn	10: 8
	4	14:21	4	Aquarius	17:44
	6	8:54	7	Pisces	5: 2
	9	14:24	9	Aries	18: 2
	12	2:44	12	Taurus	6:17
	14	12:58	14	Gemini	16:24
	15	23: 8	17	Cancer	0:17
	19	3: 1	19	Leo	6:18
	21	7:56	21	Virgo	10:40
	23	11:44	23	Libra	13:30
	25	12: 2	25	Scorpio	15:13
	27	13:38	27	Sagittar	17:19
	28	18:53	29	Capricrn	20:12
DEC	1	22:55	2	Aquarius	2:42
	4	2:22	4	Pisces	13: 1
	6	22: 5	7	Aries	1:46
	9	9:55	9	Taurus	14:12
	11	21: 3	12	Gemini	0: 9
	13	15: 0	14	Cancer	7:12
	16	8: 8	16	Leo	12: 9
	18	8:53	18	Virgo	16: 0
	20	16:16	20	Libra	19:19
	22	18:11	22	Scorpio	22:21
	24	21:11	25	Sagittar	1:28
	26	17:25	27	Capricrn	5:36
	29	7: 9	29	Aquarius	12: 1
	31	21:29	31	Pisces	21:38

JAN	1 14:40	1	Gemini	17:29
	3 13:49	3	Cancer	17:25
	5 13:58	5	Leo	16:17
	7 12:30	7	Virgo	16:23
	9 17:30	9	Libra	19:42
	12 1:0	12	Scorpio	3:7
	14 12:2	14	Sagittar	13:57
	16 21:20	17	Capricrn	2:28
	19 13:47	19	Aquarius	15:.7
	21 22:0	22	Pisces	3:6
	24 12:58	24	Aries	13:41
	26 21:26	26	Taurus	21:52
	29 2:31	29	Gemini	2:42
	30 23:48	31	Cancer	4:15
FEB	1 15:1	2	Leo	3:47
	3 22:52	4	Virgo	3:23
	6 2:38	6	Libra	5:13
	8 5:35	8	Scorpio	10:53
	10 4:13	10	Sagittar	20:36
	13 2:57	13	Capricrn	8:52
	15 4:32	15	Aquarius	21:34
	18 5:44	18	Pisces	9:13
	20 13:36	20	Aries	19:17
	23 2:11	23	Taurus	3:26
	24 18:0	25	Gemini	9:15
	27 7:27	27	Cancer	12:30
	28 23:33	29	Leo	13:43
MAR	2 9:18	2	Virgo	14:14
	4 10:45	4	Libra	15:54
	6 14:55	6	Scorpio	20:25
	8 15:55	9	Sagittar	4:44
	11 14:23	11	Capricrn	16:12
	13 13:59	14	Aquarius	4:50
	16 10:30	16	Pisces	16:28
	18 22:9	19	Aries	1:59
	21 3:46	21	Taurus	9:16
	22 22:50	23	Gemini	14:37
	25 13:19	25	Cancer	18:22
	27 12:51	27	Leo	20:54
	29 18:17	29	Virgo	22:58
APR	31 21:27	1	Libra	1:40
	3 5:20	3	Scorpio	6:16
	4 20:47	5	Sagittar	13:48
	7 23:9	8	Capricrn	0:24
	10 9:37	10	Aquarius	12:48
	12 19:4	13	Pisces	0:42
	15 4:57	15	Aries	10:15
	17 11:52	17	Taurus	16:51
	19 5:43	19	Gemini	21:3
	21 19:16	21	Cancer	23:53
	23 11:25	24	Leo	2:22
	26 0:43	26	Virgo	5:18
	28 4:37	28	Libra	9:15
	30 10:4	30	Scorpio	14:48
MAY	2 7:16	2	Sagittar	22:30
	5 4:4	5	Capricrn	8:42
	7 5:49	7	Aquarius	20:50
	10 4:18	10	Pisces	9:8
	12 14:50	12	Aries	19:20
	14 22:25	15	Taurus	2:4
	16 22:14	17	Gemini	5:33
	19 3:24	19	Cancer	7:4
	21 8:7	21	Leo	8:18
	23 7:0	23	Virgo	10:41
	25 12:2	25	Libra	15:0
	27 20:56	27	Scorpio	21:27
	29 2:30	30	Sagittar	5:54
JUN	1 12:26	1	Capricrn	16:17
	3 23:33	4	Aquarius	4:19
	6 13:14	6	Pisces	16:55
	9 0:38	9	Aries	4:3
	11 8:42	11	Taurus	11:47
	13 11:.1	13	Gemini	15:33
	15 13:49	15	Cancer	16:24
	17 12:43	17	Leo	16:16
	19 14:38	19	Virgo	17:9
	21 17:58	21	Libra	20:38
	24 0:44	24	Scorpio	2:58
	26 9:41	26	Sagittar	11:58
	28 20:15	28	Capricrn	22:50

JUL	1 9:42	1	Aquarius	10:58
	3 22:57	3	Pisces	23:40
	6 11:21	6	Aries	11:30
	8 18:36	8	Taurus	20:33
	10 18:56	11	Gemini	1:34
	13 1:22	13	Cancer	2:55
	14 17:12	15	Leo	2:16
	17 1:47	17	Virgo	1:49
	19 3:2	19	Libra	3:37
	21 7:26	21	Scorpio	8:52
	23 12:11	23	Sagittar	17:34
	26 4:24	26	Capricrn	4:41
	28 4:47	28	Aquarius	17:1
	31 4:30	31	Pisces	5:40
AUG	2 16:37	2	Aries	17:40
	5 2:42	5	Taurus	3:37
	7 0:5	7	Gemini	10:10
	9 12:17	9	Cancer	12:57
	11 4:13	11	Leo	13:0
	13 11:42	13	Virgo	12:14
	15 12:18	15	Libra	12:48
	17 15:59	17	Scorpio	16:28
	19 16:56	19	Sagittar	23:59
	22 10:18	22	Capricrn	10:43
	24 12:46	24	Aquarius	23:7
	27 11:23	27	Pisces	11:40
	29 23:8	29	Aries	23:21
SEP	1 9:10	1	Taurus	9:20
	3 11:1	3	Gemini	16:45
	5 21:2	5	Cancer	21:6
	7 22:35	7	Leo	22:43
	9 21:14	9	Virgo	22:51
	11 23:1	11	Libra	23:18
	14 1:31	14	Scorpio	1:54
	16 7:29	16	Sagittar	7:59
	18 7:55	18	Capricrn	17:43
	21 5:10	21	Aquarius	5:52
	23 0:13	23	Pisces	18:25
	26 4:57	26	Aries	5:45
	28 14:16	28	Taurus	15:4
	30 21:23	30	Gemini	22:12
OCT	2 8:44	3	Cancer	3:9
	5 5:23	5	Leo	6:11
	6 19:22	7	Virgo	7:55
	9 8:37	9	Libra	9:25
	11 11:15	11	Scorpio	12:5
	13 16:26	13	Sagittar	17:18
	15 23:7	16	Capricrn	1:56
	18 12:36	18	Aquarius	13:31
	21 2:7	21	Pisces	2:8
	23 13:26	23	Aries	13:29
	25 22:10	25	Taurus	22:15
	28 3:47	28	Gemini	4:22
	30 8:36	30	Cancer	8:36
NOV	1 11:20	1	Leo	11:46
	3 14:20	3	Virgo	14:34
	5 17:15	5	Libra	17:32
	7 21:5	7	Scorpio	21:17
	10 2:37	10	Sagittar	2:44
	12 10:18	12	Capricrn	10:48
	14 13:39	14	Aquarius	21:45
	17 9:44	17	Pisces	10:24
	19 21:33	19	Aries	22:17
	22 6:28	22	Taurus	7:13
	24 5:27	24	Gemini	12:41
	26 14:48	26	Cancer	15:37
	28 15:35	28	Leo	17:34
	30 19:54	30	Virgo	19:55
DEC	2 23:8	2	Libra	23:26
	5 3:13	5	Scorpio	4:22
	7 9:50	7	Sagittar	10:48
	9 17:46	9	Capricrn	19:10
	12 4:5	12	Aquarius	5:51
	14 16:45	14	Pisces	18:26
	17 5:15	17	Aries	7:0
	19 15:13	19	Taurus	16:57
	21 20:9	21	Gemini	22:51
	23 23:32	23	Cancer	1:11
	25 22:49	26	Leo	1:43
	28 0:39	28	Virgo	2:27
	30 3:29	30	Libra	4:56

JAN						
2	8:27	2 Aquarius	9: 2	JUL 2	10:30	2 Libra	13:59
4	17:17	4 Pisces	17:50	4	19:33	4 Scorpio	23:27
6	18:24	7 Aries	0:33	7	11: 0	7 Sagittar	11:39
9	4:34	9 Taurus	5: 1	9	20:18	10 Capricrn	0:32
10	22:58	11 Gemini	7:17	12	9:39	12 Aquarius	12:34
13	7:45	13 Cancer	8: 3	14	22: 7	14 Pisces	23: 4
15	8:35	15 Leo	8:50	17	4: 1	17 Aries	7:35
17	11:21	17 Virgo	11:31	19	10:16	19 Taurus	13:34
19	14:51	19 Libra	17:47	21	12:44	21 Gemini	16:42
21	20:44	22 Scorpio	4: 6	23	14:38	23 Cancer	17:30
24	8:14	24 Sagittar	16:54	25	12:56	25 Leo	17:24
26	22:23	27 Capricrn	5:30	27	15:35	27 Virgo	18:26
29	8:24	29 Aquarius	15:57	29	19:32	29 Libra	22:32
31	17:34	31 Pisces	23:55	AUG 1	3:36	1 Scorpio	6:44
FEB 2	23:24	3 Aries	5:57	3	11:59	3 Sagittar	18:21
5	4:25	5 Taurus	10:36	6	4: 5	6 Capricrn	7:10
7	8:12	7 Gemini	14: 3	8	12:27	8 Aquarius	19: 2
9	9:53	9 Cancer	16:28	11	2:17	11 Pisces	5: 1
11	15: 9	11 Leo	18:33	13	10:28	13 Aries	13: 2
13	14:45	13 Virgo	21:39	15	16:47	15 Taurus	19:12
15	21:53	16 Libra	3:22	17	20:46	17 Gemini	23:24
18	9:59	18 Scorpio	12:39	19	23:58	20 Cancer	1:43
20	19:22	21 Sagittar	0:53	22	1:43	22 Leo	2:54
23	5:29	23 Capricrn	13:38	24	4:14	24 Virgo	4:26
25	20: 7	26 Aquarius	0:18	26	7: 9	26 Libra	8: 6
28	0:27	28 Pisces	7:51	28	13: 1	28 Scorpio	15:16
MAR 2	8:55	2 Aries	12:49	30	23:42	31 Sagittar	2: 1
4	15:42	4 Taurus	16:21	SEP 2	12:20	2 Capricrn	14:37
6	15:54	6 Gemini	19:23	5	2: 6	5 Aquarius	2:35
8	15:24	8 Cancer	22:24	7	10:14	7 Pisces	12:17
10	22:33	11 Leo	1:45	9	17:35	9 Aries	19:31
12	22:49	13 Virgo	6: 4	11	22:58	12 Taurus	0:49
15	9:13	15 Libra	12:19	13	21:14	14 Gemini	4:47
17	18:15	17 Scorpio	21:21	16	6: 3	16 Cancer	7:48
20	6: 5	20 Sagittar	9: 5	18	2:47	18 Leo	10:18
22	18:57	22 Capricrn	21:54	20	11:22	20 Virgo	13: 5
25	6:39	25 Aquarius	9:13	22	15:34	22 Libra	17:21
27	9:52	27 Pisces	17:14	24	22:24	25 Scorpio	0:17
29	9:50	29 Aries	21:52	27	1:20	27 Sagittar	10:21
APR 31	22:22	1 Taurus	0:14	29	20:38	29 Capricrn	22:39
3	0: 3	3 Gemini	1:49	OCT 2	1:49	2 Aquarius	10:56
5	3: 9	5 Cancer	3:53	4	19: 7	4 Pisces	21: 0
7	5:34	7 Leo	7:15	7	2: 9	7 Aries	3:56
9	5:16	9 Virgo	12:23	9	6:29	9 Taurus	8:13
11	17:58	11 Libra	19:36	11	3:14	11 Gemini	10:56
14	3:30	14 Scorpio	5: 7	13	11:29	13 Cancer	13:12
16	15:11	16 Sagittar	16:46	15	8:57	15 Leo	15:54
19	1:15	19 Capricrn	5:34	17	17:51	17 Virgo	19:42
21	16: 9	21 Aquarius	17:33	19	23: 7	20 Libra	1: 5
23	19:43	24 Pisces	2:41	22	6:34	22 Scorpio	8:36
26	6:53	26 Aries	8: 3	24	9:49	24 Sagittar	18:34
28	9: 8	28 Taurus	10:13	27	4:20	27 Capricrn	6:37
30	9:36	30 Gemini	10:39	29	10:28	29 Aquarius	19:14
MAY 2	5:12	2 Cancer	11: 6	NOV 1	3:56	1 Pisces	6:12
4	12: 3	4 Leo	13: 9	3	11:39	3 Aries	13:50
6	11:27	6 Virgo	17:50	5	15:49	5 Taurus	17:54
9	0:12	9 Libra	1:26	7	17:43	7 Gemini	19:29
11	10:17	11 Scorpio	11:36	9	18: 5	9 Cancer	20:11
13	22:10	13 Sagittar	23:33	11	20:47	11 Leo	21:39
16	5:32	16 Capricrn	12:21	13	22:44	14 Virgo	1: 6
18	23:13	19 Aquarius	0:40	16	4:31	16 Libra	7: 4
21	9:23	21 Pisces	10:53	18	12:45	18 Scorpio	15:28
23	16:17	23 Aries	17:41	20	20:49	21 Sagittar	1:54
25	19:26	25 Taurus	20:48	23	10:54	23 Capricrn	13:55
27	19:50	27 Gemini	21:12	25	20: 9	26 Aquarius	2:40
29	15:46	29 Cancer	20:37	28	11:25	28 Pisces	14:32
31	19:30	31 Leo	21: 3	30	23: 5	30 Aries	23:36
JUN 2	19: 1	3 Virgo	0:14	DEC 3	1:52	3 Taurus	4:43
5	5: 9	5 Libra	7: 7	5	4:26	5 Gemini	6:18
7	15:11	7 Scorpio	17:21	7	3:10	7 Cancer	5:55
10	3:16	10 Sagittar	5:37	9	5:21	9 Leo	5:39
12	12:55	12 Capricrn	18:28	11	4:20	11 Virgo	7:27
15	4: 8	15 Aquarius	6:44	13	9:10	13 Libra	12:36
17	12:24	17 Pisces	17:27	15	17:27	15 Scorpio	21: 9
19	22:53	20 Aries	1:32	18	3:10	18 Sagittar	8: 8
22	5:11	22 Taurus	6:14	20	16:20	20 Capricrn	20:47
24	5:11	24 Gemini	7:46	23	4:35	23 Aquarius	9: 6
26	3:32	26 Cancer	7:20	25	17: 6	25 Pisces	21:18
28	4: 7	28 Leo	6:54	28	6:14	28 Aries	7:36
30	4:37	30 Virgo	8:35	30	11:16	30 Taurus	14:31

Month	Date:Time	Date Sign	Time		Month	Date:Time	Date Sign	Time
JAN	2 8: 2	2 Libra	12:37		JUL	1 13:14	1 Taurus	18:48
	4 16:15	5 Scorpio	1:19			3 10:21	3 Gemini	20:38
	7 6:33	7 Sagittar	13:20			5 17:47	5 Cancer	22: 9
	9 18:32	9 Capricrn	22:40			7 13:47	7 Leo	0:44
	11 17:36	12 Aquarius	4:53			10 0:14	10 Virgo	5:54
	14 8: 5	14 Pisces	8:51			12 8:44	12 Libra	14:41
	16 3:52	16 Aries	11:46			14 20:30	15 Scorpio	2:35
	18 10:20	18 Taurus	14:38			17 2:34	17 Sagittar	15:26
	20 17:39	20 Gemini	17:58			19 21: 4	20 Capricrn	2:41
	22 21:53	22 Cancer	22: 3			22 8:37	22 Aquarius	11: 6
	24 12:47	25 Leo	3:24			24 15:36	24 Pisces	16:57
	27 1:44	27 Virgo	10:52			26 16:23	26 Aries	21: 8
	29 11:27	29 Libra	21: 5			28 19:49	29 Taurus	0:27
FEB	1 7:32	1 Scorpio	9:33			30 20:45	31 Gemini	3:20
	3 18: 0	3 Sagittar	22: 5		AUG	2 1:56	2 Cancer	6:11
	6 1:59	6 Capricrn	8: 4			4 20:44	4 Leo	9:40
	8 8:15	8 Aquarius	14:14			6 10:20	6 Virgo	14:58
	10 8:51	10 Pisces	17:13			8 18:22	8 Libra	23:13
	12 15:33	12 Aries	18:41			11 5:35	11 Scorpio	10:34
	14 19:25	14 Taurus	20:20			13 9: 2	13 Sagittar	23:27
	16 18:32	16 Gemini	23:19			16 6:26	16 Capricrn	11: 5
	19 3:22	19 Cancer	4: 3			18 18:28	18 Aquarius	19:31
	20 22:19	21 Leo	10:29			20 20:39	21 Pisces	0:40
	23 8:57	23 Virgo	18:41			22 23:50	23 Aries	3:42
	25 18:51	26 Libra	4:59			25 2:13	25 Taurus	6: 2
	28 6:50	28 Scorpio	17:16			26 18:46	27 Gemini	8:44
MAR	2 17:44	3 Sagittar	6:10			29 8:23	29 Cancer	12:14
	5 7:18	5 Capricrn	17:12			31 2: 5	31 Leo	16:49
	7 17:13	8 Aquarius	0:23		SEP	2 18:57	2 Virgo	22:57
	9 23: 9	10 Pisces	3:33			3 3:14	5 Libra	7:22
	12 1:59	12 Aries	4:10			7 14:12	7 Scorpio	18:29
	13 19:56	14 Taurus	4:15			10 0:28	10 Sagittar	7:22
	15 20:13	16 Gemini	5:39			12 15:30	12 Capricrn	19:39
	18 3:37	18 Cancer	9:31			14 20:19	15 Aquarius	4:53
	20 14:24	20 Leo	16: 4			17 6:37	17 Pisces	10:12
	22 15: 5	23 Virgo	0:57			19 9:44	19 Aries	12:30
	25 1:37	25 Libra	11:46			21 10: 8	21 Taurus	13:29
	27 13:47	28 Scorpio	0: 7			23 14:15	23 Gemini	14:49
	30 3:29	30 Sagittar	13: 6			25 14: 5	25 Cancer	17:37
APR	1 19:28	2 Capricrn	0:56			27 6:59	27 Leo	22:26
	4 0:16	4 Aquarius	9:32			30 1:33	30 Virgo	5:22
	5 5:31	6 Pisces	14: 1		OCT	2 10:30	2 Libra	14:29
	8 7: 7	8 Aries	15: 5			4 21:37	5 Scorpio	1:45
	10 7:15	10 Taurus	14:32			7 7:34	7 Sagittar	14:37
	12 6:29	12 Gemini	14:27			9 23:26	10 Capricrn	3:26
	14 9:31	14 Cancer	16:34			12 1:15	12 Aquarius	13:51
	16 14:56	16 Leo	21:56			14 16:42	14 Pisces	20:23
	19 3: 4	19 Virgo	6:35			16 19:38	16 Aries	23: 6
	21 8: 8	21 Libra	17:44			18 20: 8	18 Taurus	23:27
	24 0:28	24 Scorpio	6:19			20 9:47	20 Gemini	23:18
	26 9:33	26 Sagittar	19:14			22 22: 8	23 Cancer	0:26
	29 3:54	29 Capricrn	7:12			24 21:21	25 Leo	4: 8
MAY	1 13:10	1 Aquarius	16:46			27 6:47	27 Virgo	10:54
	3 19:58	3 Pisces	22:51			29 16: 8	29 Libra	20:30
	5 23:29	6 Aries	1:24		NOV	1 3:40	1 Scorpio	8:12
	7 23:45	8 Taurus	1:33			3 4:14	3 Sagittar	21: 6
	9 17:24	10 Gemini	1: 3			6 9:48	6 Capricrn	10: 1
	12 0:47	12 Cancer	1:50			8 20: 8	8 Aquarius	21:19
	14 4:52	14 Leo	5:32			11 5:14	11 Pisces	5:26
	16 12:48	16 Virgo	12:58			13 5:38	13 Aries	9:43
	18 17:32	18 Libra	23:46			15 6:52	15 Taurus	10:47
	21 3:45	21 Scorpio	12:27			17 4:54	17 Gemini	10:12
	23 15:13	24 Sagittar	1:17			19 5:50	19 Cancer	9:53
	26 4:46	26 Capricrn	12:57			21 8:37	21 Leo	11:45
	28 12:57	28 Aquarius	22:33			23 16:49	23 Virgo	17: 8
	30 22:15	31 Pisces	5:31			25 21:10	26 Libra	2:17
JUN	2 9:24	2 Aries	9:38			28 8:49	28 Scorpio	14:13
	4 4:52	4 Taurus	11:19		DEC	30 12:26	1 Sagittar	3:15
	6 10:14	6 Gemini	11:40			3 10:24	3 Capricrn	15:57
	8 5:56	8 Cancer	12:16			5 13:32	6 Aquarius	3:17
	10 14: 5	10 Leo	14:52			8 11:31	8 Pisces	12:20
	12 13:53	12 Virgo	20:52			10 13:17	10 Aries	18:22
	15 1:40	15 Libra	6:42			12 16:22	12 Taurus	21:14
	17 17:20	17 Scorpio	19: 8			14 15:10	14 Gemini	21:39
	19 20:24	20 Sagittar	7:57			16 21: 6	16 Cancer	21:12
	22 12:23	22 Capricrn	19:14			18 21:37	18 Leo	21:48
	24 17:13	25 Aquarius	4:15			21 1: 7	21 Virgo	1:25
	27 5:36	27 Pisces	10:59			23 3: 8	23 Libra	9:10
	29 15:23	29 Aries	15:44			25 20: 5	25 Scorpio	20:36
						27 22:57	28 Sagittar	9:41
						30 21:38	30 Capricrn	22:14

Date	Time		Sign	Time		Date	Time		Sign	Time
JAN 2	15:54	3	Gemini	0:54	JUL 2	9:22	2	Capricrn	17: 4
4	22: 0	5	Cancer	8:25		4	8:23	4	Aquarius	21:14
7	14:43	7	Leo	18: 1		6	16:39	6	Pisces	23:41
9	18:16	10	Virgo	5:34		8	18:47	9	Aries	1:45
12	9: 8	12	Libra	18:11		10	23:47	11	Taurus	4:29
15	4: 5	15	Scorpio	6: 2		13	2:32	13	Gemini	8:30
17	8:49	17	Sagittar	15: 2		15	9:46	15	Cancer	14: 7
19	10:12	19	Capricrn	20: 9		17	19: 3	17	Leo	21:42
21	2: 0	21	Aquarius	22: 0		19	23:51	19	Virgo	7:32
23	12:48	23	Pisces	22: 9		22	17:54	22	Libra	19:26
25	13: 0	25	Aries	22:36		25	0:21	25	Scorpio	8: 1
27	17:29	28	Taurus	1: 2		27	15: 9	27	Sagittar	19: 0
30	1:43	30	Gemini	6:22		29	19:51	30	Capricrn	2:32
FEB 1	11:37	1	Cancer	14:32	AUG 31	18:54	1	Aquarius	6:22
3	11:12	4	Leo	0:50		3	1:47	3	Pisces	7:42
6	7:20	6	Virgo	12:35		5	2:30	5	Aries	8:22
8	12:55	9	Libra	1:10		7	4: 4	7	Taurus	10: 5
11	1:23	11	Scorpio	13:30		8	20:54	9	Gemini	13:55
13	12:47	13	Sagittar	23:48		11	13:42	11	Cancer	20: 8
16	0:41	16	Capricrn	6:28		13	15:29	13	Leo	4:29
17	15:26	18	Aquarius	9: 8		16	7:58	16	Virgo	14:42
20	4:54	20	Pisces	9: 0		18	19:46	19	Libra	2:36
22	6:11	22	Aries	8: 8		21	10:46	21	Scorpio	15:24
23	22:32	24	Taurus	8:44		23	6:16	24	Sagittar	3:17
25	20:35	26	Gemini	12:33		26	5:59	26	Capricrn	12: 2
28	8:58	28	Cancer	20: 8		28	7:13	28	Aquarius	16:37
MAR 2	10:40	3	Leo	6:41		30	12:33	30	Pisces	17:45
5	6:19	5	Virgo	18:48	SEP 1	12:12	1	Aries	17:19
7	18:52	8	Libra	7:23		3	12:12	3	Taurus	17:27
10	7:17	10	Scorpio	19:40		5	6:20	5	Gemini	19:55
12	19:45	13	Sagittar	6:37		7	19:45	8	Cancer	1:35
15	10: 6	15	Capricrn	14:46		9	20:57	10	Leo	10:12
17	12:54	17	Aquarius	19: 9		12	14:40	12	Virgo	20:54
19	10:16	19	Pisces	20: 8		15	2:41	15	Libra	9: 0
21	9:38	21	Aries	19:17		17	15:29	17	Scorpio	21:49
23	8:56	23	Taurus	18:50		20	3:15	20	Sagittar	10:11
25	13: 5	25	Gemini	20:55		22	18:31	22	Capricrn	20:13
28	0: 7	28	Cancer	2:55		24	19:58	25	Aquarius	2:22
29	22:23	30	Leo	12:44		26	23:36	27	Pisces	4:32
APR 1	12:33	2	Virgo	0:51		29	3: 8	29	Aries	4: 7
4	7:20	4	Libra	13:31	OCT 30	23:21	1	Taurus	3:14
6	21:38	7	Scorpio	1:33		3	1:17	3	Gemini	4: 4
9	11:49	9	Sagittar	12:17		5	5:35	5	Cancer	8:10
11	9:51	11	Capricrn	20:57		7	14:11	7	Leo	15:58
13	14:30	14	Aquarius	2:44		9	20:49	10	Virgo	2:42
15	21:36	16	Pisces	5:26		12	8:39	12	Libra	15: 1
17	20:26	18	Aries	5:51		14	21:23	15	Scorpio	3:46
20	4:51	20	Taurus	5:43		17	7:38	17	Sagittar	16: 2
21	16: 6	22	Gemini	7: 2		19	20:30	20	Capricrn	2:37
24	1: 6	24	Cancer	11:35		22	7: 3	22	Aquarius	10:13
26	2:51	26	Leo	20: 2		24	8:43	24	Pisces	14: 9
28	20: 2	29	Virgo	7:33		26	9:49	26	Aries	15: 2
MAY 1	8:42	1	Libra	20:11		28	9:16	28	Taurus	14:27
3	20:56	4	Scorpio	8: 4		30	7:26	30	Gemini	14:27
6	1: 5	6	Sagittar	18:16	NOV 1	11:11	1	Cancer	16:57
8	16:12	9	Capricrn	2:26		3	15:58	3	Leo	23:10
10	19:26	11	Aquarius	8:26		6	6:18	6	Virgo	9: 4
13	4:46	13	Pisces	12:14		8	15: 6	8	Libra	21:19
15	11:37	15	Aries	14:13		11	3: 6	11	Scorpio	10: 4
17	6:35	17	Taurus	15:24		13	18: 5	13	Sagittar	21:58
19	13:42	19	Gemini	17:13		16	5:37	16	Capricrn	8: 9
21	16:29	21	Cancer	21:15		18	14:51	18	Aquarius	16: 5
23	11:12	24	Leo	4:36		20	17:29	20	Pisces	21:20
26	6:26	26	Virgo	15:14		22	17:59	23	Aries	0: 2
28	21:12	29	Libra	3:39		24	19: 0	25	Taurus	0:57
31	10:42	31	Scorpio	15:37		26	10:19	27	Gemini	1:31
JUN 2	7:31	3	Sagittar	1:32		28	21: 4	29	Cancer	3:26
5	4:18	5	Capricrn	8:54	DEC 30	23:56	1	Leo	8:17
6	21:15	7	Aquarius	14: 4		3	9:24	3	Virgo	16:50
9	16:37	9	Pisces	17:40		5	20:39	6	Libra	4:30
11	12:17	11	Aries	20:22		8	9:20	8	Scorpio	17:17
13	14:49	13	Taurus	22:50		10	7:53	11	Sagittar	5: 1
15	8:57	16	Gemini	1:53		13	7:27	13	Capricrn	16:33
17	23:28	18	Cancer	6:28		15	2:40	15	Aquarius	21:39
19	21:32	20	Leo	13:32		17	19:36	18	Pisces	2:48
22	14:33	22	Virgo	23:29		20	2:18	20	Aries	6:25
25	2:33	25	Libra	11:36		22	8:46	22	Taurus	8:57
27	15: 4	27	Scorpio	23:52		23	18:23	24	Gemini	11: 1
29	23: 4	30	Sagittar	10: 3		26	6:26	26	Cancer	13:46
						28	0:57	28	Leo	18:17
						30	17:31	31	Virgo	1:49

JAN	31	12:49	1 Sagittar	1:28		JUL	2	17:11	3 Virgo	3:58
	2	16:51	3 Capricrn	2:25			5	13: 0	5 Libra	16:20
	4	18:50	5 Aquarius	1:58			8	2:18	8 Scorpio	2:23
	6	15:19	7 Pisces	2: 3			9	9:12	10 Sagittar	8:49
	9	1:49	9 Aries	4:24			13	3:14	12 Capricrn	11:40
	10	21:48	11 Taurus	10: 5			13	21:48	14 Aquarius	12: 7
	13	5: 5	13 Gemini	19:10			16	3:56	16 Pisces	11:58
	15	18:52	16 Cancer	6:45			18	4:56	18 Aries	13: 2
	18	13:37	18 Leo	19:33			20	12: 2	20 Taurus	16:46
	20	18:33	21 Virgo	8:23			22	23:12	22 Gemini	23:48
	23	7:31	23 Libra	20: 3			25	0:15	25 Cancer	9:44
	25	16:21	26 Scorpio	5:17			26	16: 8	27 Leo	21:38
	28	0:46	28 Sagittar	11: 8			30	0:47	30 Virgo	10:24
	30	4: 9	30 Capricrn	13:33		AUG	1	13:32	1 Libra	22:56
FEB	1	4:48	1 Aquarius	13:32			4	0:55	4 Scorpio	9:53
	3	7:57	3 Pisces	12:50			6	14:14	6 Sagittar	17:47
	5	5: 3	5 Aries	13:31			8	14:14	8 Capricrn	21:57
	7	4:48	7 Taurus	17:24			10	0: 3	10 Aquarius	22:53
	9	16:29	10 Gemini	1:23			12	15: 5	12 Pisces	22: 9
	12	8:29	12 Cancer	12:48			14	14:36	14 Aries	21:49
	14	17:29	15 Leo	1:47			16	16:17	16 Taurus	23:55
	17	9: 5	17 Virgo	14:28			18	23:32	19 Gemini	5:48
	19	18:58	20 Libra	1:48			21	13:30	21 Cancer	15:26
	22	10:18	22 Scorpio	11:14			22	23:42	24 Leo	3:32
	24	12:59	24 Sagittar	18:15			26	8:56	26 Virgo	16:23
	26	12:54	26 Capricrn	22:29			28	20:11	29 Libra	4:47
	28	20: 8	29 Aquarius	0: 4			31	10:56	31 Scorpio	15:56
MAR	1	12:35	2 Pisces	0: 5		SEP	2	21: 5	3 Sagittar	0:52
	3	21:10	4 Aries	0:20			5	3:59	5 Capricrn	6:40
	5	17:30	6 Taurus	2:50			7	7:58	7 Aquarius	9: 6
	8	6:34	8 Gemini	9:13			9	1:42	9 Pisces	9: 4
	10	17:27	10 Cancer	19:39			11	2:12	11 Aries	8:22
	13	6:52	13 Leo	8:28			13	22:32	13 Taurus	9:11
	15	6:40	15 Virgo	21: 9			15	13:52	15 Gemini	13:27
	18	7:46	18 Libra	8: 4			17	3: 7	17 Cancer	21:57
	20	3:24	20 Scorpio	16:52			20	14: 9	20 Leo	9:42
	22	4:13	22 Sagittar	23:45			22	2:31	22 Virgo	22:35
	24	16:17	25 Capricrn	4:48			25	19: 8	25 Libra	10:46
	26	19: 3	27 Aquarius	7:57			27	19: 8	27 Scorpio	21:31
	28	23:24	29 Pisces	9:33			29	17:51	30 Sagittar	6:28
	31	2:53	31 Aries	10:41		OCT	2	5:46	2 Capricrn	13:12
APR	2	0:54	2 Taurus	13: 4			4	10:58	4 Aquarius	17:16
	4	16: 1	4 Gemini	18:26			6	15:59	6 Pisces	18:50
	6	13:53	7 Cancer	3:43			8	17:27	8 Aries	19: 1
	9	4:32	9 Leo	15:58			10	12:48	10 Taurus	19:43
	11	14:36	12 Virgo	4:41			12	0:28	12 Gemini	22:55
	14	2: 6	14 Libra	15:33			14	22: 1	15 Cancer	6: 0
	16	16:55	16 Scorpio	23:44			17	3:35	17 Leo	16:51
	18	6:22	19 Sagittar	5:41			19	21:38	20 Virgo	5:33
	20	22:14	21 Capricrn	10:10			22	9:14	22 Libra	17:43
	22	15:18	23 Aquarius	13:40			24	19:46	25 Scorpio	3:59
	25	4:57	25 Pisces	16:25			26	19:36	27 Sagittar	12:12
	27	7:31	27 Aries	18:57			29	10:47	29 Capricrn	18:34
	29	12:19	29 Taurus	22:16			31	17:38	31 Aquarius	23:12
MAY	1	3:59	2 Gemini	3:44		NOV	2	0:44	3 Pisces	2:10
	4	10: 4	4 Cancer	12:23			4	20:38	5 Aries	3:58
	5	21:32	7 Leo	0: 1			7	2: 9	7 Taurus	5:43
	8	23:32	9 Virgo	12:46			8	10:31	9 Gemini	9: 0
	11	14:33	12 Libra	0: 0			11	15: 8	11 Cancer	15:18
	13	21:50	14 Scorpio	8:12			13	9:29	14 Leo	1: 7
	16	4:32	16 Sagittar	13:26			16	4: 4	16 Virgo	13:23
	18	12:14	18 Capricrn	16:44			18	17:47	19 Libra	1:44
	20	18: 2	20 Aquarius	19:15			21	6:42	21 Scorpio	12: 4
	22	11:12	22 Pisces	21:49			22	19:33	23 Sagittar	19:39
	24	14:21	25 Aries	1: 3			25	19:17	26 Capricrn	0:55
	26	20:23	27 Taurus	5:30			28	4: 6	28 Aquarius	4:40
	28	11:42	29 Gemini	11:48			29	23:27	30 Pisces	7:39
	31	8:54	31 Cancer	20:37		DEC	2	6:35	2 Aries	10:26
JUN	2	10:22	3 Leo	7:59			4	5:10	4 Taurus	13:37
	5	8:38	5 Virgo	20:42			5	18:32	6 Gemini	18: 1
	7	20:58	8 Libra	8:34			8	15:16	9 Cancer	0:33
	10	6:41	10 Scorpio	17:30			10	7:38	11 Leo	9:52
	12	8:32	12 Sagittar	22:52			13	11:21	13 Virgo	21:38
	14	15:55	15 Capricrn	1:25			15	23:51	16 Libra	10:12
	16	13:10	17 Aquarius	2:35			18	14: 3	18 Scorpio	21:12
	18	23:18	19 Pisces	3:51			21	1: 2	21 Sagittar	5: 2
	21	5:26	21 Aries	6:27			23	0:33	23 Capricrn	9:38
	23	1:15	23 Taurus	11: 9			24	17:56	25 Aquarius	12: 1
	25	2:40	25 Gemini	18:16			27	4:45	27 Pisces	13:38
	27	17:10	28 Cancer	3:44			29	6:40	29 Aries	15:48
	30	5: 2	30 Leo	15:14			31	9:54	31 Taurus	19:24

JAN	31	1: 4	1	Leo	14:29	JUL	1	16:35	1 Aries 21:)
	3	15:44	4	Virgo	1:19		3	16:55	4 Taurus 4:5
	8	7:45	6	Libra	9:41		6	10:36	6 Gemini 15:4
	8	1:35	8	Scorpio	14:55		8	23: 6	9 Cancer 4:)
	9	22:14	10	Sagittar	17: 7		11	12: 8	11 Leo 17:)
	12	4:58	12	Capricrn	17:21		13	17:23	14 Virgo 5:2
	14	5:57	14	Aquarius	17:20		16	10:41	16 Libra 15:3
	16	5:43	16	Pisces	18:55		18	13:11	18 Scorpio 22:3
	18	19:18	18	Aries	23:42		20	21:46	21 Sagittar 2:)
	20	17: 5	21	Taurus	8:21		22	22:48	23 Capricrn 3:
	23	10:58	23	Gemini	20: 4		24	22:26	25 Aquarius 2:4
	25	6:46	26	Cancer	8:56		26	17:30	27 Pisces 3:
	28	11:49	28	Leo	21: 0		29	2:52	29 Aries 5:3
	31	1:13	31	Virgo	7:12		31	6:55	31 Taurus 11:5
FEB	2	12: 4	2	Libra	15:10	AUG	2	16:49	2 Gemini 21:5
	4	17:32	4	Scorpio	20:55		5	4: 7	5 Cancer 10:2
	6	5:44	7	Sagittar	0:34		7	18:33	7 Leo 23:2
	8	15:25	9	Capricrn	2:35		10	0:17	10 Virgo 11:)
	10	2:12	11	Aquarius	3:51		12	18:37	12 Libra 21:
	12	17:43	13	Pisces	5:41		15	3: 6	15 Scorpio 4:3
	14	19:10	15	Aries	9:38		17	8:56	17 Sagittar 9:3
	17	12:37	17	Taurus	16:58		19	5:45	19 Capricrn 12:
	18	22:48	20	Gemini	3:46		21	6:36	21 Aquarius 13:
	21	23:47	22	Cancer	16:31		23	12:15	23 Pisces 13:3
	24	11:18	25	Leo	4:41		25	8:18	25 Aries 15:2
	26	22:52	27	Virgo	14:29		27	17:18	27 Taurus 20:2
MAR	1	18: 8	1	Libra	21:31		30	0:26	30 Gemini 5:1
	3	20:36	4	Scorpio	2:26	SEP	1	7:50	1 Cancer 17:2
	6	4:48	6	Sagittar	6: 4		3	20:28	3 Leo 6:2
	7	19: 3	8	Capricrn	9: 4		6	7:38	6 Virgo 17:5
	9	15:22	10	Aquarius	11:50		8	17:18	9 Libra 3:
	12	0:47	12	Pisces	14:56		11	0:35	11 Scorpio 10:
	14	18:37	14	Aries	19:20		13	5:41	13 Sagittar 15:
	16	10:52	17	Taurus	2:10		15	17: 3	15 Capricrn 18:4
	19	7:19	19	Gemini	12:10		17	11:20	17 Aquarius 21:1
	21	13:18	22	Cancer	0:36		19	14:24	19 Pisces 23:
	23	20:39	24	Leo	13: 7		22	0:59	22 Aries 1:2
	26	17:37	26	Virgo	23:11		24	5:54	24 Taurus 5:5
	29	2:37	29	Libra	5:46		26	1:14	26 Gemini 13:4
	31	8:23	31	Scorpio	9:33		28	14:41	29 Cancer 1:
APR	1	20: 6	2	Sagittar	11:59	OCT	1	1:46	1 Leo 14:
	4	0:42	4	Capricrn	14:24		3	22:14	4 Virgo 1:4
	6	2: 9	6	Aquarius	17:35		6	2:50	6 Libra 10:4
	8	7:38	8	Pisces	21:47		8	11:29	8 Scorpio 16:3
	13	13:49	11	Aries	3:16		10	17:57	10 Sagittar 20:4
	12	19:35	13	Taurus	10:36		12	16:26	13 Capricrn 0:
	15	14:25	15	Gemini	20:24		15	0:31	15 Aquarius 3:1
	18	8:20	18	Cancer	8:34		16	21:20	17 Pisces 6:2
	20	20:38	20	Leo	21:25		19	0:46	19 Aries 9:5
	22	17: 9	23	Virgo	8:17		21	9:17	21 Taurus 15:
	25	11: 1	25	Libra	15:22		23	9:21	23 Gemini 22:3
	27	5:41	27	Scorpio	18:47		25	22:43	26 Cancer 9:2
	29	9:31	29	Sagittar	20: 2		28	17: 5	28 Leo 22:1
MAY	1	10:44	1	Capricrn	20:59		31	8:18	31 Virgo 10:2
	3	12:52	3	Aquarius	23: 7	NOV	2	18:56	2 Libra 19:4
	5	18:13	5	Pisces	3:12		4	15:49	5 Scorpio 1:2
	7	23: 1	8	Aries	9:20		7	2:19	7 Sagittar 4:2
	10	3: 8	10	Taurus	17:29		8	21:11	9 Capricrn 6:2
	12	17:25	13	Gemini	3:41		11	0:55	11 Aquarius 8:3
	15	5:42	15	Cancer	15:50		13	6:13	13 Pisces 11:5
	17	20:16	18	Leo	4:52		15	2:26	15 Aries 16:2
	20	13:27	20	Virgo	16:37		17	12: 9	17 Taurus 22:3
	22	22:58	23	Libra	0:54		20	0: 1	20 Gemini 6:4
	24	16:47	25	Scorpio	5: 3		22	8: 7	22 Cancer 17:2
	26	23:29	27	Sagittar	6: 5		24	11: 6	25 Leo 6:
	28	23:34	29	Capricrn	5:54		27	16:48	27 Virgo 18:5
	31	0: 7	31	Aquarius	6:26		29	21: 3	30 Libra 5:
JUN	1	20:58	2	Pisces	9:10	DEC	2	9:36	2 Scorpio 11:3
	4	8:13	4	Aries	14:46		3	23: 2	4 Sagittar 14:2
	6	9:53	6	Taurus	23:12		6	5:36	6 Capricrn 15:1
	9	3:18	9	Gemini	9:55		8	9:44	8 Aquarius 15:5
	11	15:46	11	Cancer	22:16		10	16:39	10 Pisces 17:4
	14	5:40	14	Leo	11:21		12	10:58	12 Aries 21:4
	16	12: 3	16	Virgo	23:35		14	16:58	15 Taurus 4:2
	19	3:41	19	Libra	9: 5		16	20:47	17 Gemini 13:2
	21	12:58	21	Scorpio	14:43		19	17:55	20 Cancer 0:3
	23	12:12	23	Sagittar	16:42		21	23:31	22 Leo 13:
	25	12:12	25	Capricrn	16:30		24	13:14	25 Virgo 2:
	27	11:44	27	Aquarius	16: 0		27	1: 5	27 Libra 13:2
	29	6:23	29	Pisces	17: 7		29	17:24	29 Scorpio 21:2

Month	Day	Time	Day	Sign	Time
JAN	1	16: 2	1	Aries	16:16
	4	3:41	4	Taurus	4:33
	6	16:36	6	Gemini	16:58
	8	17:50	9	Cancer	3:38
	11	5:46	11	Leo	11:57
	13	12: 5	13	Virgo	18:11
	15	16:46	15	Libra	22:48
	17	20:49	18	Scorpio	2: 8
	20	3:13	20	Sagittar	4:36
	21	15:53	22	Capricrn	6:59
	24	7:33	24	Aquarius	10:26
	26	9:47	26	Pisces	16:13
	28	18:24	29	Aries	1: 6
	31	5:34	31	Taurus	12:45
FEB	2	22: 9	3	Gemini	1:17
	4	18:38	5	Cancer	12:21
	7	14:58	7	Leo	20:32
	9	20:46	10	Virgo	1:50
	12	0:27	12	Libra	5: 7
	13	22: 1	14	Scorpio	7:34
	16	6: 0	16	Sagittar	10: 8
	18	11:40	18	Capricrn	13:32
	20	14:37	20	Aquarius	18:17
	22	21:29	23	Pisces	0:52
	25	6:43	25	Aries	9:45
	27	2:26	27	Taurus	20:58
MAR	2	7:30	2	Gemini	9:31
	4	7:29	4	Cancer	21:19
	7	5:33	7	Leo	6:16
	9	11:27	9	Virgo	11:34
	11	7:10	11	Libra	13:53
	13	9:58	13	Scorpio	14:48
	15	5:38	15	Sagittar	16: 1
	17	11:57	17	Capricrn	18:54
	19	21: 8	20	Aquarius	0: 6
	21	14:18	22	Pisces	7:38
	23	23:16	24	Aries	17:10
	26	10: 5	27	Taurus	4:27
	27	22:45	29	Gemini	16:58
APR	1	11:21	1	Cancer	5:20
	3	4:52	3	Leo	15:31
	5	17:31	5	Virgo	21:53
	7	9:27	8	Libra	0:25
	9	10: 6	10	Scorpio	0:29
	11	4:32	12	Sagittar	0: 8
	13	13: 9	14	Capricrn	1:23
	15	20:37	16	Aquarius	5:39
	18	8:12	18	Pisces	13:10
	20	12: 0	20	Aries	23:15
	22	17: 8	23	Taurus	10:56
	25	19:23	25	Gemini	23:28
	27	18:21	28	Cancer	12: 2
	30	20: 5	30	Leo	23: 9
MAY	2	15:14	3	Virgo	7: 3
	4	20:19	5	Libra	10:53
	6	21:41	7	Scorpio	11:23
	8	14: 9	9	Sagittar	10:24
	11	0:54	11	Capricrn	10:12
	13	8:15	13	Aquarius	12:45
	15	7: 3	15	Pisces	19: 6
	17	21: 1	18	Aries	4:54
	20	0:20	20	Taurus	16:49
	21	21: 4	23	Gemini	5:27
	25	15: 9	25	Cancer	17:54
	27	11:45	28	Leo	5:14
	30	8: 3	30	Virgo	14:11
JUN	1	7:26	1	Libra	19:38
	3	12:34	3	Scorpio	21:35
	4	21: 1	5	Sagittar	21:15
	7	16:15	7	Capricrn	20:40
	8	22:25	9	Aquarius	21:55
	11	14: 5	12	Pisces	2:40
	14	9:40	14	Aries	11:20
	16	12:55	16	Taurus	22:55
	19	8:20	19	Gemini	11:35
	21	23: 6	21	Cancer	23:51
	23	9:49	24	Leo	10:49
	26	5:49	26	Virgo	19:50
	28	20:23	29	Libra	2:13

Month	Day	Time	Day	Sign	Time
JUL	30	18:40	1	Scorpio	5:43
	2	6:32	3	Sagittar	6:53
	4	22: 3	5	Capricrn	7: 6
	6	9:25	7	Aquarius	8:11
	9	3:34	9	Pisces	11:52
	11	11:17	11	Aries	19:12
	1	1:15	14	Taurus	5:55
	16	3:37	16	Gemini	18:25
	19	1:39	19	Cancer	6:37
	21	12:59	21	Leo	17: 9
	23	22:47	24	Virgo	1:29
	26	6: 6	26	Libra	7:38
	28	10:53	28	Scorpio	11:46
	30	7:41	30	Sagittar	14:17
AUG	1	8:55	1	Capricrn	15:58
	3	2:40	3	Aquarius	17:57
	5	11:11	5	Pisces	21:36
	7	21:16	8	Aries	4: 7
	10	0:57	10	Taurus	13:55
	12	4: 4	13	Gemini	2: 3
	15	1:22	15	Cancer	14:23
	16	16:11	18	Leo	0:50
	20	1:27	20	Virgo	8:31
	22	2:27	22	Libra	13:40
	24	6:16	24	Scorpio	17:10
	26	6:10	26	Sagittar	19:55
	28	11:51	28	Capricrn	22:39
	30	11: 0	31	Aquarius	1:56
SEP	1	19:33	2	Pisces	6:28
	4	1:23	4	Aries	13: 4
	6	20:45	6	Taurus	22:21
	9	5:53	9	Gemini	10: 5
	11	21:52	11	Cancer	22:40
	13	14: 0	14	Leo	9:37
	16	6: 0	16	Virgo	17:18
	18	12:33	18	Libra	21:39
	20	13:33	20	Scorpio	23:53
	23	0: 0	23	Sagittar	1:35
	24	17:27	25	Capricrn	4: 2
	26	12:18	27	Aquarius	7:58
	29		29	Pisces	13:34
OCT	1	9:16	1	Aries	20:56
	3	18:13	3	Taurus	6:20
	6	13: 8	6	Gemini	17:52
	8	20:37	9	Cancer	6:38
	11	17:42	11	Leo	18:27
	13	15:30	14	Virgo	3: 2
	15	20:50	16	Libra	7:34
	17	22:45	18	Scorpio	9: 0
	19	22:56	20	Sagittar	9:14
	22	6:51	22	Capricrn	10:14
	24	6:58	24	Aquarius	13:24
	26	7:29	26	Pisces	19:11
	29	1:59	29	Aries	3:18
	31	0:39	31	Taurus	13:18
NOV	1	14: 7	3	Gemini	0:56
	5	0:27	5	Cancer	13:43
	6	16:51	8	Leo	2:13
	9	23:44	10	Virgo	12:10
	12	6:28	12	Libra	18: 0
	14	9: 4	14	Scorpio	19:54
	16	8:36	16	Sagittar	19:29
	18	8:12	18	Capricrn	18:58
	20	16: 3	20	Aquarius	20:23
	23	0:39	23	Pisces	0:59
	25	19:51	25	Aries	8:53
	27	5:42	27	Taurus	19:17
	28	19:27	30	Gemini	7:16
DEC	2	5:50	2	Cancer	20: 1
	4	16:45	5	Leo	8:37
	7	18:44	7	Virgo	19:30
	10	1:38	10	Libra	3: 0
	12	0:56	12	Scorpio	6:31
	13	1:52	14	Sagittar	6:55
	16	4:46	16	Capricrn	6: 2
	18	5:21	18	Aquarius	6: 3
	20	7:50	20	Pisces	8:48
	22	15: 4	22	Aries	15:17
	24	10:39	25	Taurus	1:15
	26	0: 4	27	Gemini	13:23
	29	10:58	30	Cancer	2:11

```
JAN  1 22:32    2 Sagittar 10: 8      JUL  1  7:45    1 Cancer   23:17
     4  8:28    4 Capricrn 15:20           3 23:46    4 Leo       5:27
     6 15:50    6 Aquarius 22:43           6  6:10    6 Virgo     9:53
     9  4:17    9 Pisces    8:57           8  9:18    8 Libra    13:16
    11  1:32   11 Aries    21:29          10  2:15   10 Scorpio  16: 4
    13 20:11   14 Taurus   10:11          12 16:12   12 Sagittar 18:46
    16,12:22   16 Gemini   20:25          14  8:12   14 Capricrn 22:12
    18 13: 0   19 Cancer    2:56          17  2:13   17 Aquarius  3:29
    20 17:25   21 Leo       6:13          19 11: 4   19 Pisces   11:36
    22 19:39   23 Virgo     7:46          21 19:16   21 Aries    22:39
    24 16:34   25 Libra     9: 9          24  3: 8   24 Taurus   11:16
    26 23:56   27 Scorpio  11:35          26 22: 9   26 Gemini   23: 1
    29  6:14   29 Sagittar 15:44          28 17:29   29 Cancer    8: 0
    31 16:53   31 Capricrn 21:51          30 18:20   31 Leo      13:47

FEB  2 18:53    3 Aquarius  6: 8      AUG  2  9:54    2 Virgo    17: 9
     5  5:41    5 Pisces   16:39           4 16:18    4 Libra    19:20
     8  1:37    8 Aries     5: 3           6  8:37    6 Scorpio  21:28
    10  8:27   10 Taurus   18: 0           8 12:28    8 Sagittar  0:24
    12 16:36   13 Gemini    5:17          10 15:20   11 Capricrn  4:45
    15  6: 3   15 Cancer   13: 5          13  2:25   13 Aquarius 11: 0
    17 11: 6   17 Leo      17: 0          15 13: 3   15 Pisces   19:34
    19 13: 2   19 Virgo    18: 5          18  2:27   18 Aries     6:30
    21  1:37   21 Libra    18: 3          20 18:27   20 Taurus   19: 2
    23 14:46   23 Scorpio  18:42          23  6:22   23 Gemini    7:18
    25 14:33   25 Sagittar 21:31          25 15:58   25 Cancer   17:12
    28  0:27   28 Capricrn  3:19          27 12:40   27 Leo      23:31
                                          30  0:55   30 Virgo     2:32

MAR  2 10: 0    2 Aquarius 12: 5      SEP  1  2: 7    1 Libra     3:32
     4 22: 2    4 Pisces   23:12           3  2: 6    3 Scorpio   4:12
     6 17:48    7 Aries    11:46           5  3:38    5 Sagittar  6: 4
     9 17:28   10 Taurus    0:42           7  7:23    7 Capricrn 10:13
    12  6: 7   12 Gemini   12:35           8 13:41    9 Aquarius 17: 2
    14 17:51   14 Cancer   21:48          11 22:37   12 Pisces    2:20
    16 19:37   17 Leo       3:19          13 23: 4   14 Aries    13:35
    19  1:12   19 Virgo     5:18          16 21:33   17 Taurus    2: 5
    21  4:55   21 Libra     5: 3          19  9:52   19 Gemini   14:40
    23  1: 5   23 Scorpio   4:26          21 22:13   22 Cancer    1:37
    25  2:16   25 Sagittar  5:25          23  5:12   24 Leo       9:17
    27  6:42   27 Capricrn  9:07          26 11:45   26 Virgo    13: 7
    29  8:37   29 Aquarius 17:47          28  3: 3   28 Libra    13:54
                                          30  8:37   30 Scorpio  13:22

APR  1  3:28    1 Pisces    5: 3      OCT  2  8:31    2 Sagittar 13:35
     3  7:55    3 Aries    17:52           4 12: 6    4 Capricrn 16:20
     5  5:25    6 Taurus    6:44           5 12:54    6 Aquarius 22:36
     8 17:45    8 Gemini   18:35           8  1:32    9 Pisces    8: 9
    11  4: 6   11 Cancer    4:28          11  5: 8   11 Aries    19:49
    13  1:34   13 Leo      11:30          14  1:15   14 Taurus    8:25
    15  6: 9   15 Virgo    15:13          16 13:43   16 Gemini   20:59
    17  6: 9   17 Libra    16: 4          19  2: 1   19 Cancer    8:29
    19 13:38   19 Scorpio  15:30          21 17:27   21 Leo      17:33
    21  4: 7   21 Sagittar 15:28          23 22:48   23 Virgo    23: 3
    23  1: 0   23 Capricrn 18: 3          25 12:49   26 Libra     0:55
    25  9:34   26 Aquarius  0:41          27 18:28   28 Scorpio   0:24
    27 17:52   28 Pisces   11:15          29 17:32   29 Sagittar 23:33

MAY 30  4:43    1 Aries     0: 3      NOV  1 18:14    1 Capricrn  0:37
     3  8:26    3 Taurus   12:52           2 15:44    3 Aquarius  5:19
     5  2:29    6 Gemini    0:21           5  7:13    5 Pisces   14: 6
     8  4:48    8 Cancer   10: 1           7 10:28    8 Aries     1:48
    10 16:47   10 Leo      17:34          10  7: 1   10 Taurus   14:32
    12 20:52   12 Virgo    22:40          12 19:35   13 Gemini    2:54
    14 13:44   15 Libra     1:12          15  7:10   15 Cancer   14:14
    16 23: 9   17 Scorpio   1:50          17 23:33   17 Leo      23:50
    18 21:36   19 Sagittar  2: 5          20  1:34   20 Virgo     6:47
    21  1: 9   21 Capricrn  3:56          22  9:31   22 Libra    10:29
    23  6:44   23 Aquarius  9:12          24  6: 1   24 Scorpio  11:19
    25 16:57   25 Pisces   18:34          26  5:41   26 Sagittar 10:47
    27 12:15   28 Aries     6:53          28 18:57   28 Capricrn 11: 3
    30  1:17   30 Taurus   19:41          29 18:11   30 Aquarius 14:11

JUN  1 10:54    2 Gemini    6:55      DEC  2 15:54    2 Pisces   21:26
     3 23: 3    4 Cancer   15:57           5  8:18    5 Aries     8:24
     6 16:27    6 Leo      22:59           7 15:47    7 Taurus   21: 6
     8 13: 6    9 Virgo     4:17          10  8: 3   10 Gemini    9:25
    10 18: 2   11 Libra     7:53          12 15:48   12 Cancer   20:14
    12 19:25   13 Scorpio  10: 1          15  2:59   15 Leo       5:19
    14 23:35   15 Sagittar 11:29          17  9:47   17 Virgo    12:30
    17  5:51   17 Capricrn 13:46          19 14:25   19 Libra    17:25
    19  7:15   19 Aquarius 18:33          21 18:48   21 Scorpio  20: 1
    21 20:19   22 Pisces    2:57          23 18:39   23 Sagittar 21: 0
    24  4: 0   24 Aries    14:33          25 19:47   25 Capricrn 21:53
    26 10: 8   27 Taurus    3:16          27 20:11   28 Aquarius  0:32
    29  6:31   29 Gemini   14:37          30  4:51   30 Pisces    6:30
```

JAN						JUL					
2	6: 1	2	Cancer	11:25		2	1:50	2	Pisces	6:58	
4	9:56	4	Leo	11:18		4	14:35	4	Aries	19:55	
6	6:22	6	Virgo	11:22		7	2:11	7	Taurus	7:29	
8	8:20	8	Libra	13:25		8	21: 7	9	Gemini	15:32	
10	13:11	10	Scorpio	18:19		11	15:54	11	Cancer	19:41	
12	15:38	13	Sagittar	2: 3		13	17:55	13	Leo	21:10	
15	6:55	15	Capricrn	11:57		15	18:55	15	Virgo	21:48	
17	15:47	17	Aquarius	23:32		17	18:45	17	Libra	23:14	
20	7:38	20	Pisces	12:18		20	0:13	20	Scorpio	2:34	
22	20:49	23	Aries	1:10		22	6:19	22	Sagittar	8:10	
25	8:16	25	Taurus	12: 9		24	14:15	24	Capricrn	16: 1	
27	6: 1	27	Gemini	19:26		27	0:30	27	Aquarius	2: 1	
29	21:33	29	Cancer	22:32		29	12:51	29	Pisces	13:58	
31	12:10	31	Leo	22:38							
FEB						**AUG**					
2	19:12	2	Virgo	21:45		31	19:46	1	Aries	2:59	
4	19:32	4	Libra	22: 1		3	14:45	3	Taurus	15:13	
6	22:38	7	Scorpio	1: 8		5	12:56	6	Gemini	0:30	
8	22:47	9	Sagittar	7:49		8	5:42	8	Cancer	5:44	
11	15:17	11	Capricrn	17:41		10	2:12	10	Leo	7:30	
14	2:23	14	Aquarius	5:36		12	5:20	12	Virgo	7:25	
16	16:24	16	Pisces	18:27		14	6:31	14	Libra	7:25	
19	5:20	19	Aries	7:10		16	2:36	16	Scorpio	9:12	
21	16:55	21	Taurus	18:31		18	4:27	18	Sagittar	13:50	
24	3: 4	24	Gemini	3: 5		20	16:14	20	Capricrn	21:37	
26	6:53	26	Cancer	8: 0		23	1:14	23	Aquarius	8: 2	
28	8:56	28	Leo	9:36		25	12:10	25	Pisces	20:16	
						28	1: 6	28	Aries	9:17	
MAR						30	13:42	30	Taurus	21:44	
1	8:24	1	Virgo	9:16		**SEP**					
3	8: 5	3	Libra	8:53		1	20:57	2	Gemini	7:59	
5	9:40	5	Scorpio	10:24		4	14:28	4	Cancer	14:46	
6	13:29	7	Sagittar	15:18		6	17:24	6	Leo	17:53	
9	23:26	10	Capricrn	0: 3		8	17:39	8	Virgo	18:18	
11	17: 4	12	Aquarius	11:47		10	14:46	10	Libra	17:44	
15	0:16	15	Pisces	0:43		12	16:57	12	Scorpio	18: 5	
17	12:51	17	Aries	13:13		14	11:27	14	Sagittar	21: 5	
19	23:52	20	Taurus	0: 9		17	1:46	17	Capricrn	3:45	
22	2: 1	22	Gemini	8:52		19	11:25	19	Aquarius	13:55	
24	14:45	24	Cancer	14:55		21	23:16	22	Pisces	2:20	
26	3:42	26	Leo	18:16		24	7:27	24	Aries	15:20	
28	19:25	28	Virgo	19:31		26	23:30	27	Taurus	3:33	
30	19:49	30	Libra	19:54		29	11:30	29	Gemini	13:59	
APR						**OCT**					
1	20:59	1	Scorpio	21: 4		1	17: 7	1	Cancer	21:50	
3	4:14	3	Sagittar	0:41		3	21:44	3	Leo	2:38	
6	7:52	6	Capricrn	7:57		5	23:30	6	Virgo	4:36	
8	6:54	8	Aquarius	18:49		8	2:20	8	Libra	4:45	
11	7:30	11	Pisces	7:38		9	23: 1	10	Scorpio	4:43	
13	19:54	13	Aries	20: 4		11	4:15	12	Sagittar	6:25	
16	6:19	16	Taurus	6:31		14	5:18	14	Capricrn	11:31	
17	19: 7	18	Gemini	14:31		16	11:49	16	Aquarius	20:39	
20	20: 5	20	Cancer	20:22		19	2:16	19	Pisces	8:50	
22	10:27	23	Leo	0:27		21	15:30	21	Aries	21:51	
25	2:48	25	Virgo	3:10		24	3:45	24	Taurus	9:44	
27	4:39	27	Libra	5: 5		25	14:24	26	Gemini	19:38	
29	6:36	29	Scorpio	7: 6		28	22:12	29	Cancer	3:24	
						30	21:45	31	Leo	9: 4	
MAY						**NOV**					
1	4:12	1	Sagittar	10:36		2	8:11	2	Virgo	12:40	
3	16:13	3	Capricrn	16:58		4	10:15	4	Libra	14:27	
5	22:47	6	Aquarius	2:50		6	11:19	6	Scorpio	15:20	
8	14:13	8	Pisces	15:17		8	4:59	8	Sagittar	16:54	
11	2:40	11	Aries	3:51		10	16:56	10	Capricrn	20:56	
13	12:56	13	Taurus	14:12		13	0: 6	13	Aquarius	4:47	
15	18:28	15	Gemini	21:30		15	12:10	15	Pisces	16:14	
18	0:58	18	Cancer	2:21		18	3:55	18	Aries	5:14	
20	3:35	20	Leo	5:50		20	13:41	20	Taurus	17: 6	
22	7:14	22	Virgo	8:49		21	22:40	23	Gemini	2:25	
24	10: 5	24	Libra	11:48		25	6:37	25	Cancer	9:17	
26	13:15	26	Scorpio	15: 8		26	22:23	27	Leo	14:26	
28	11:39	28	Sagittar	19:29		29	16:19	29	Virgo	18:27	
30	23:34	31	Capricrn	1:53		**DEC**					
JUN						1	19:40	1	Libra	21:33	
1	18:22	2	Aquarius	11:13		3	22:27	3	Scorpio	0: 1	
4	20:20	4	Pisces	23:15		5	10:18	6	Sagittar	2:38	
7	8:37	7	Aries	12: 2		8	5:27	8	Capricrn	6:46	
9	19:43	9	Taurus	22:50		10	6:49	10	Aquarius	13:53	
12	1:24	12	Gemini	6: 6		12	23:36	13	Pisces	0:30	
14	7: 5	14	Cancer	10:10		15	12:42	15	Aries	13:19	
16	2:27	16	Leo	12:26		18	1:15	18	Taurus	1:33	
18	11: 6	18	Virgo	14:26		19	11: 8	20	Gemini	10:57	
20	15:10	20	Libra	17:11		22	0:20	22	Cancer	17: 8	
22	17:23	22	Scorpio	21: 9		24	4:33	24	Leo	21: 4	
24	9:34	25	Sagittar	2:31		26	7:50	27	Virgo	0: 1	
27	5:22	27	Capricrn	9:39		28	10:38	29	Libra	2:56	
29	11:35	29	Aquarius	19: 7		30	17:43	31	Scorpio	6:12	

JAN					
2	16:37	3	Pisces		7:12
5	14: 2	5	Aries		17:14
7	21:38	8	Taurus		0: 9
10	1:23	10	Gemini		3:19
11	16:39	12	Cancer		3:28
14	1:21	14	Leo		2:27
15	15:42	16	Virgo		2:32
18	5:26	18	Libra		5:47
20	11:49	20	Scorpio		13:14
22	10:29	23	Sagittar		0:15
25	0:27	25	Capricrn		12:55
26	16: 1	28	Aquarius		1:27
30	2:57	30	Pisces		12:55
FEB					
1	11:50	1	Aries		22:52
3	23:27	4	Taurus		6:36
6	5:38	6	Gemini		11:27
8	8:43	8	Cancer		13:25
9	14:54	10	Leo		13:33
12	10:35	12	Virgo		13:41
14	6:52	14	Libra		15:53
16	20: 8	16	Scorpio		21:43
19	6:58	19	Sagittar		7:29
21	9:39	21	Capricrn		19:46
23	21:51	24	Aquarius		8:20
26	10: 5	26	Pisces		19:31
MAR					
28	19:46	1	Aries		4:45
3	3:27	3	Taurus		12: 0
4	17:28	5	Gemini		17:16
7	12:47	7	Cancer		20:34
9	1:26	9	Leo		22:23
11	16:17	11	Virgo		23:47
13	18:35	14	Libra		2:18
15	23:18	16	Scorpio		7:26
18	9:28	18	Sagittar		16: 1
21	2: 8	21	Capricrn		3:33
23	13:51	23	Aquarius		16: 6
25	18:54	26	Pisces		3:24
28	4: 6	28	Aries		12:13
30	10:04	30	Taurus		18:29
APR					
1	22:35	1	Gemini		22:50
3	18:36	4	Cancer		2: 0
5	1:51	6	Leo		4:39
7	23:59	8	Virgo		7:27
10	3:30	10	Libra		11:11
12	8:43	12	Scorpio		16:45
14	16:43	15	Sagittar		0:56
17	3:46	17	Capricrn		11:49
20	0:11	20	Aquarius		0:15
22	3: 4	22	Pisces		12: 1
24	19: 3	24	Aries		21: 7
26	18:47	27	Taurus		2:55
29	3: 1	29	Gemini		6: 7
MAY					
1	4:33	1	Cancer		8: 2
3	6:10	3	Leo		10: 2
5	4:47	5	Virgo		13: 8
7	13:22	7	Libra		17:52
9	15:47	10	Scorpio		0:26
12	4:12	12	Sagittar		9: 2
14	14:58	14	Capricrn		19:46
17	3:35	17	Aquarius		8: 5
19	15:18	19	Pisces		20:21
22	6:20	22	Aries		6:22
24	3: 5	24	Taurus		12:40
26	14: 0	26	Gemini		15:27
28	15:25	28	Cancer		16:10
30	16:41	30	Leo		16:42
JUN					
1	8:57	1	Virgo		18:45
3	12:51	3	Libra		23:18
5	23:59	6	Scorpio		6:28
8	14:40	8	Sagittar		15:46
10	14:36	11	Capricrn		2:47
12	22:28	13	Aquarius		15: 6
15	14:57	16	Pisces		3:42
18	6:44	18	Aries		14:43
20	19: 9	20	Taurus		22:17
22	13:21	23	Gemini		1:46
24	15:33	25	Cancer		2:12
26	14:13	27	Leo		1:35
28	14:47	29	Virgo		2: 4

JUL					
30	17: 9	1	Libra		5:19
3	3:17	3	Scorpio		11:58
5	17:27	5	Sagittar		21:31
8	0:38	8	Capricrn		8:56
10	7:47	10	Aquarius		21:21
12	19: 4	13	Pisces		9:59
15	8:28	15	Aries		21:36
17	19:24	18	Taurus		6:28
20	5: 7	20	Gemini		11:26
22	1:51	22	Cancer		12:47
24	8:13	24	Leo		12: 6
26	1: 0	26	Virgo		11:33
28	1:19	28	Libra		13:13
30	10:52	30	Scorpio		18:27
AUG					
1	13:20	2	Sagittar		3:21
4	12:17	4	Capricrn		14:49
6	16:20	7	Aquarius		3:21
9	15:29	9	Pisces		15:50
11	22:27	12	Aries		3:23
13	21:22	14	Taurus		12:52
16	18:32	16	Gemini		19:15
18	12:54	18	Cancer		22:12
20	8:32	20	Leo		22:37
22	19:51	22	Virgo		22:12
24	12:25	24	Libra		23: 0
26	11:59	27	Scorpio		2:46
28	15:47	29	Sagittar		10:33
31	4:34	31	Capricrn		21:14
SEP					
2	12:41	3	Aquarius		9:45
5	5:23	5	Pisces		22: 7
8	7:28	8	Aries		9:12
10	2:42	10	Taurus		18:22
12	19:29	13	Gemini		1:11
14	21:56	15	Cancer		5:27
17	1:18	17	Leo		7:30
19	4:34	19	Virgo		8:20
21	8: 3	21	Libra		9:28
22	22:21	23	Scorpio		12:33
24	23:40	25	Sagittar		18:53
27	12:52	28	Capricrn		4:45
29	15:43	30	Aquarius		16:59
OCT					
2	13:29	3	Pisces		5:24
5	0:57	5	Aries		16:11
7	10: 7	8	Taurus		0:34
9	5: 4	10	Gemini		6:41
11	21:45	12	Cancer		11: 0
13	19:57	14	Leo		14: 3
16	3:47	16	Virgo		16:24
18	6:14	18	Libra		18:49
20	15:30	20	Scorpio		22:23
22	7:49	23	Sagittar		4:15
24	23:55	25	Capricrn		13:14
27	7:37	28	Aquarius		0:58
30	7:43	30	Pisces		13:35
NOV					
1	22:46	2	Aries		0:36
3	20:19	4	Taurus		8:36
6	10:41	6	Gemini		13:39
8	5:49	8	Cancer		16:50
9	20:14	10	Leo		19:24
12	11:32	12	Virgo		22:16
14	15:12	15	Libra		1:55
16	19:55	17	Scorpio		6:41
19	5:10	19	Sagittar		13: 6
21	10:39	21	Capricrn		21:50
23	3:23	24	Aquarius		9: 9
26	10:43	26	Pisces		21:55
28	23:10	29	Aries		9:42
DEC					
1	8:38	1	Taurus		18:14
3	11: 1	3	Gemini		22:56
5	18: 8	6	Cancer		0:55
7	23: 3	8	Leo		1:58
9	22:20	10	Virgo		3:47
12	7:12	12	Libra		7:21
14	4:49	14	Scorpio		12:55
15	17:26	16	Sagittar		20:19
18	21:27	19	Capricrn		5:34
20	13:11	21	Aquarius		16:48
23	21:40	24	Pisces		5:35
26	10:42	26	Aries		18: 8
28	21:15	29	Taurus		3:57
31	5:46	31	Gemini		9:33

Mo	Day	Time	Day	Sign	Time
JAN	3	7:0	3	Scorpio	7:30
	5	13:42	5	Sagittar	20:36
	8	8:1	8	Capricrn	8:47
	10	7:39	10	Aquarius	18:48
	13	1:45	13	Pisces	2:40
	15	7:44	15	Aries	8:44
	17	12:2	17	Taurus	13:6
	19	13:26	19	Gemini	15:49
	21	16:11	21	Cancer	17:21
	23	13:23	23	Leo	18:56
	25	20:50	25	Virgo	22:16
	28	3:20	28	Libra	4:57
	30		30	Scorpio	15:28
FEB	2	2:4	2	Sagittar	4:17
	4	14:38	4	Capricrn	16:38
	6	11:13	7	Aquarius	2:27
	9	7:32	9	Pisces	9:29
	11	12:33	11	Aries	14:30
	13	16:27	13	Taurus	18:26
	15	14:56	15	Gemini	21:43
	17	22:34	18	Cancer	0:37
	19	16:17	20	Leo	3:37
	22	5:32	22	Virgo	7:44
	24	11:55	24	Libra	14:18
	26	21:32	27	Scorpio	0:5
MAR	1	0:51	1	Sagittar	12:27
	3	22:26	4	Capricrn	1:4
	6	1:43	6	Aquarius	11:22
	8	15:54	8	Pisces	18:16
	10	20:5	10	Aries	22:21
	12	22:42	13	Taurus	0:55
	14	21:37	15	Gemini	3:13
	17	3:49	17	Cancer	6:4
	19	5:54	19	Leo	9:54
	21	12:52	21	Virgo	15:12
	23	20:7	23	Libra	22:31
	26	5:51	26	Scorpio	8:20
	28	13:17	28	Sagittar	20:24
	31	6:16	31	Capricrn	9:12
APR	2	14:8	2	Aquarius	20:20
	5	2:0	5	Pisces	4:3
	7	6:18	7	Aries	8:11
	9	8:4	9	Taurus	9:50
	11	6:4	11	Gemini	10:37
	13	10:22	13	Cancer	12:3
	15	10:44	15	Leo	15:18
	17	19:16	17	Virgo	20:57
	20	3:24	20	Libra	5:5
	22	13:51	22	Scorpio	15:28
	24	22:52	25	Sagittar	3:36
	27	15:1	27	Capricrn	16:26
	29	23:51	30	Aquarius	4:16
MAY	2	12:12	2	Pisces	13:16
	4	17:37	4	Aries	18:30
	6	19:38	6	Taurus	20:23
	8	17:54	8	Gemini	20:21
	9	19:43	10	Cancer	20:15
	12	18:9	12	Leo	21:54
	15	2:13	15	Virgo	2:36
	17	10:26	17	Libra	10:42
	19	21:26	19	Scorpio	21:33
	22	5:11	22	Sagittar	9:58
	24	12:9	24	Capricrn	22:47
	27	5:55	27	Aquarius	10:50
	29	8:57	29	Pisces	20:50
JUN	31	22:55	1	Aries	3:35
	3	5:20	3	Taurus	6:46
	5	4:35	5	Gemini	7:10
	6	13:52	7	Cancer	6:26
	9	1:45	9	Leo	6:39
	10	15:7	11	Virgo	9:44
	13	10:41	13	Libra	16:45
	15	20:43	16	Scorpio	3:22
	18	8:54	18	Sagittar	15:58
	21	2:17	21	Capricrn	4:46
	23	9:7	23	Aquarius	16:37
	25	16:43	26	Pisces	2:50
	28	8:43	28	Aries	10:39
	30	12:7	30	Taurus	15:26

Mo	Day	Time	Day	Sign	Time
JUL	2	10:7	2	Gemini	17:14
	4	12:41	4	Cancer	17:7
	6	9:24	6	Leo	16:54
	8	14:43	8	Virgo	18:43
	10	21:33	11	Libra	0:16
	12	23:48	13	Scorpio	9:56
	15	11:29	15	Sagittar	22:17
	18	7:47	18	Capricrn	11:4
	20	16:45	20	Aquarius	22:38
	23	2:20	23	Pisces	8:24
	25	15:59	25	Aries	16:15
	27	11:3	27	Taurus	21:57
	29	14:35	30	Gemini	1:16
AUG	31	9:4	1	Cancer	2:34
	2	16:20	3	Leo	3:6
	4	10:48	5	Virgo	4:43
	6	20:47	7	Libra	9:14
	9	4:2	9	Scorpio	17:43
	11	14:50	12	Sagittar	5:26
	14	4:19	14	Capricrn	18:10
	16	22:59	17	Aquarius	5:38
	19	6:3	19	Pisces	14:51
	21	7:48	21	Aries	21:57
	23	13:47	24	Taurus	3:20
	25	20:34	26	Gemini	7:13
	27	16:24	28	Cancer	9:50
	30	6:5	30	Leo	11:45
SEP	31	20:37	1	Virgo	14:12
	3	17:42	3	Libra	18:42
	5	10:21	6	Scorpio	2:25
	8	0:24	8	Sagittar	13:25
	10	19:51	11	Capricrn	2:1
	12	20:42	13	Aquarius	13:44
	15	3:34	15	Pisces	22:53
	17	18:23	18	Aries	5:14
	19	18:40	20	Taurus	9:31
	22	10:2	22	Gemini	12:24
	24	9:19	24	Cancer	15:23
	26	15:52	26	Leo	18:16
	28	4:3	28	Virgo	21:58
OCT	30	11:33	1	Libra	3:19
	2	18:29	3	Scorpio	11:7
	5	17:14	5	Sagittar	21:40
	7	14:35	8	Capricrn	10:6
	10	5:6	10	Aquarius	22:19
	12	19:49	13	Pisces	8:7
	14	23:23	15	Aries	14:30
	17	14:50	17	Taurus	17:56
	19	15:32	19	Gemini	19:40
	21	19:5	21	Cancer	21:10
	23	22:58	23	Leo	23:39
	25	14:53	26	Virgo	3:53
	27	19:30	28	Libra	10:14
	30	16:52	30	Scorpio	18:46
NOV	2	14:5	2	Sagittar	5:26
	4	1:34	4	Capricrn	17:44
	6	20:23	7	Aquarius	6:22
	9	14:33	9	Pisces	17:16
	11	11:56	12	Aries	0:44
	13	16:43	14	Taurus	4:24
	15	18:23	16	Gemini	5:19
	17	13:4	18	Cancer	5:14
	20	0:43	20	Leo	6:5
	22	7:47	22	Virgo	9:24
	24	4:29	24	Libra	15:49
	26	13:35	27	Scorpio	1:1
	29	10:11	29	Sagittar	12:11
DEC	1	6:14	2	Capricrn	0:33
	4	2:46	4	Aquarius	13:16
	6	7:16	7	Pisces	1:1
	9	1:20	9	Aries	10:3
	11	7:30	11	Taurus	15:11
	13	11:42	13	Gemini	16:38
	15	12:37	15	Cancer	15:55
	17	13:20	17	Leo	15:12
	19	10:16	19	Virgo	16:40
	21	20:0	21	Libra	21:46
	24	0:34	24	Scorpio	6:39
	26	12:26	26	Sagittar	18:9
	28	15:13	29	Capricrn	6:44
	31	14:46	31	Aquarius	19:20

JAN			
31	12:33	1 Gemini	19:54
3	19: 8	3 Cancer	23:36
5	0:13	6 Leo	4:59
8	8:27	8 Virgo	13: 4
10	20:25	11 Libra	0: 7
13	10:16	13 Scorpio	12:52
15	14:30	16 Sagittar	0:43
18	9: 6	18 Capricrn	9:30
20	14:36	20 Aquarius	14:47
22	12:37	22 Pisces	17:41
24	14:37	24 Aries	19:44
26	16:58	26 Taurus	22:16
27	22:42	29 Gemini	1:54
31	1: 7	1 Cancer	6:49
FEB			
1	19:33	2 Leo	13:12
4	15:16	4 Virgo	21:33
7	2:11	7 Libra	8:18
9	14: 6	9 Scorpio	20:56
11	18:12	12 Sagittar	9:26
14	12:46	14 Capricrn	19:10
16	20:12	17 Aquarius	0:50
19	2:45	19 Pisces	3: 6
22	22: 5	21 Aries	3:44
22	22:53	23 Taurus	4:41
24	17:21	25 Gemini	7:21
27	5:59	27 Cancer	12:20
MAR			
1	3:45	1 Leo	19:30
4	2:57	4 Virgo	4:37
6	8:31	6 Libra	15:37
8	23: 3	9 Scorpio	4:11
11	10:25	11 Sagittar	17: 4
13	21: 9	14 Capricrn	3:56
16	1:42	16 Aquarius	10:56
18	8: 3	18 Pisces	13:52
20	12:53	20 Aries	14: 6
22	8: 6	22 Taurus	13:41
24	4:23	24 Gemini	14:37
26	12: 7	26 Cancer	18:14
28	23:10	29 Leo	1: 0
31	3:51	31 Virgo	10:29
APR			
2	15:11	2 Libra	21:57
5	3:51	5 Scorpio	10:37
7	9:36	7 Sagittar	23:31
10	4:42	10 Capricrn	11: 2
12	11:22	12 Aquarius	19:27
14	18:35	14 Pisces	23:56
16	20: 5	17 Aries	1: 6
18	21:37	19 Taurus	0:33
20	15:33	21 Gemini	0:18
22	21: 3	23 Cancer	2:11
24	6:50	25 Leo	7:28
27	10:45	27 Virgo	16:20
29	22:15	30 Libra	3:54
MAY			
2	12:35	2 Scorpio	16:43
5	1:31	5 Sagittar	5:27
7	14:35	7 Capricrn	16:54
9	7:33	10 Aquarius	1:58
12	3:38	12 Pisces	7:55
14	6:47	14 Aries	10:43
16	7:34	16 Taurus	11:16
18	5:37	18 Gemini	11: 7
20	8:24	20 Cancer	12: 3
21	15: 0	22 Leo	15:47
24	19:25	24 Virgo	23:18
26	13:48	27 Libra	10:18
29	19:20	29 Scorpio	23: 7
JUN			
31	6:28	1 Sagittar	11:44
3	19:28	3 Capricrn	22:43
5	3:44	6 Aquarius	7:30
8	11:13	8 Pisces	13:55
12	15:35	10 Aries	18: 1
12	17:56	12 Taurus	20:10
13	23:28	14 Gemini	21:10
16	20:22	16 Cancer	22:22
18	9:40	19 Leo	1:23
21	6: 5	21 Virgo	7:40
23	15:48	23 Libra	17:42
26	4:29	26 Scorpio	6:14
28	10:38	28 Sagittar	18:51

JUL			
1	4:14	1 Capricrn	5:31
3	9:28	3 Aquarius	13:34
5	18:29	5 Pisces	19:22
7	22:52	7 Aries	23:36
10	2: 9	10 Taurus	2:45
12	3:34	12 Gemini	5:10
14	7:11	14 Cancer	7:31
15	22:10	16 Leo	10:54
18	16:38	18 Virgo	16:43
20	20:48	21 Libra	1:55
23	13:58	23 Scorpio	14: 0
25	16:42	26 Sagittar	2:45
28	10:22	28 Capricrn	13:33
29	22:23	30 Aquarius	21: 9
AUG			
1	5:36	2 Pisces	1:59
3	14:23	4 Aries	5:16
5	21:43	6 Taurus	8: 7
8	6: 4	8 Gemini	11: 8
9	18:39	10 Cancer	14:37
11	20:41	12 Leo	19: 3
14	8:27	14 Virgo	1:17
16	18:25	17 Libra	10:14
19	13:33	19 Scorpio	21:58
22	7:59	22 Sagittar	10:53
24	17:42	24 Capricrn	22:18
27	0:40	27 Aquarius	6:13
29	7:54	29 Pisces	10:36
30	17:53	31 Aries	12:44
SEP			
1	19:29	2 Taurus	14:17
3	18:23	4 Gemini	16:32
6	4:58	6 Cancer	20:10
8	17:41	9 Leo	1:26
10	17:30	11 Virgo	8:33
12	21:18	13 Libra	17:52
16	2:10	16 Scorpio	5:31
18	7:43	18 Sagittar	18:33
21	1:33	21 Capricrn	6:44
23	15:33	23 Aquarius	15:45
25	6:38	25 Pisces	22:29
27	3:58	27 Aries	22:29
29	19:51	29 Taurus	22:47
OCT			
1	8:13	1 Gemini	23:28
3	19:45	4 Cancer	1:54
5	19:45	6 Leo	6:52
8	6: 2	8 Virgo	14:28
10	19:52	11 Libra	0:26
13	13:22	13 Scorpio	12:19
14	19:52	16 Sagittar	1: 3
18	2: 1	18 Capricrn	14: 1
20	17:58	21 Aquarius	0:18
23	5:12	23 Pisces	6:46
24	17:34	25 Aries	9:26
26	15:13	27 Taurus	9:34
28	15:49	29 Gemini	9: 1
30	18:38	31 Cancer	9:42
NOV			
1	12:13	2 Leo	13: 9
4	13: 9	4 Virgo	20: 6
7	4:54	7 Libra	6:15
8	19: 5	9 Scorpio	18:30
11	7:34	11 Sagittar	7:32
14	5: 3	14 Capricrn	20: 9
16	18:59	17 Aquarius	7: 4
19	8:24	19 Pisces	15: 4
21	17:22	21 Aries	19:31
23	20:26	23 Taurus	20:52
25	3:15	25 Gemini	20:24
27	0:45	27 Cancer	20: 2
29	11: 1	29 Leo	21:43
DEC			
1	12:11	2 Virgo	3: 2
4	10: 6	4 Libra	12:24
5	23:51	6 Scorpio	0:38
8	9:22	9 Sagittar	13:32
11	2:53	12 Capricrn	2: 3
13	11:52	14 Aquarius	13:22
16	9:39	16 Pisces	21:12
18	20:35	19 Aries	3: 9
21	4: 5	21 Taurus	6:23
22	18:28	23 Gemini	7:22
25	4:18	25 Cancer	7:23
27	0:31	27 Leo	8:18
29	11:52	29 Virgo	12: 4
31	19:36	31 Libra	19:56

ABOUT THE AUTHOR

Debbi Kempton Smith grew up in New York, Tel Aviv, Rome, Florence, Madrid, Barcelona, Paris, Geneva, London, New York, Nuremberg, New York, London, Oxford, Los Angeles, and London. Her clients include psychiatrists, psychoanalysts, corporations, financial analysts and human beings. She is an active member of Mensa, and is fond of iguanas. She currently resides in New York and London, and wishes she resided in New Orleans.

The Edgar Cayce story is one of the most compelling in inspirational literature. Over the course of forty years, "The Sleeping Prophet" would close his eyes, enter an altered state of consciousness, and then speak to the very heart and spirit of mankind on subjects such as health, healing, dreams, meditation, and reincarnation. His more than 14,000 readings are preserved at the Association for Research and Enlightenment.

EXPLORE THE SPIRITUAL
WORLD WITH SHIRLEY MacLAINE

Titles by Shirley MacLaine

- ☐ 27557 DANCING IN THE LIGHT $4.95
- ☐ 27370 OUT ON A LIMB $4.95
- ☐ 27438 "DON'T FALL OFF
  THE MOUNTAIN" $4.95
- ☐ 26173 YOU CAN GET THERE
  FROM HERE $4.95
- ☐ 27299 IT'S ALL IN THE PLAYING $4.95
- ☐ 28331 GOING WITHIN $5.95

- ☐ 45220 GOING WITHIN: Meditations $14.95
  For Stress Reduction and Relaxation
  An audio companion to the bestselling
  book on which, Shirley McLaine guides
  the listener through chakra and
  sound meditations. 180 Mins.

Look for them at your bookstore or use this page to order: